CONSOLIDATED
ONTARIO
FAMILY LAW
STATUTES
AND
REGULATIONS
2003

Ken Murphy, B.A. (Hons.), LL.B.

D1319550

THOMSON
CARSWELL

Canadian Cataloguing in Publication Data

The National Library of Canada has catalogued this publication as follows:

Consolidated Ontario family law statutes and regulations

Annual.
1995-
ISSN 1202-4244
ISBN 0-459-24384-7 (2003 edition)

I. Carswell Company

KEO213.C8 1995-   343.71301'5'0263   C95-300142-3
KF505.ZB3C66

One Corporate Plaza
2075 Kennedy Road
Toronto, Ontario
M1T 3V4

Customer Relations
Toronto 1-416-609-3800
Elsewhere in Canada/U.S. 1-800-387-5164
Fax 1-416-298-5082
World Wide Web: http://www.carswell.com
E-mail: orders@carswell.com

INTRODUCTION

The *Consolidated Ontario Family Law Statutes and Regulations 2003* is an annual publication designed to consolidate the Ontario statutes and regulations most relevant to the practice of family law in that province.

This edition includes the new *Interjurisdictional Support Orders Act*, S.O. 2002, c. 13, which is scheduled to come into force March 31, 2003, and will repeal the *Reciprocal Enforcement of Support Orders Act*. Also included are corresponding regulations under the new Act. Notwithstanding the repeal of the *Reciprocal Enforcement of Support Orders Act*, the Act will continue in force in respect of proceedings commenced under them before the new Act comes into force.

We have also included additional regulations under the *Children's Law Reform Act*, the *Divorce Act*, the *Family Law Act*, the *Family Orders and Agreements Enforcement Assistance Act*, the *Family Responsibility and Support Arrears Enforcement Act*, the *Marriage Act*, and the *Succession Law Reform Act*.

The federal legislation in this edition is current to March 25, 2003, up to and including the Canada Gazette volume 137:2. The provincial legislation is current to March 15, 2003, up to and including the Ontario Gazette volume 136:11.

SUMMARY TABLE OF CONTENTS

Summary Table of Contents

TABLE OF CONTENTS

vii

Table of Contents

PART V — ADMINISTRATION OF ESTATES
Procedure at Meetings

Claims Provable

Scheme of Distribution

PART VI — BANKRUPTS
Discharge of Bankrupts

CANADA EVIDENCE ACT

PART I — APPLICATION
Witnesses

Oaths and Solemn Affirmations

CHANGE OF NAME ACT

ELECTION BY SPOUSE

CHANGE OF NAME OF PERSON OVER SIXTEEN

CHANGE OF CHILD'S NAME

PROCEDURE

DUTY OF REGISTRAR GENERAL

SUBSTITUTION OF NEW NAME

REVOCATION OF CHANGE OF NAME

Table of Contents

Table of Contents

Children's Aid Societies

Agreements with Other Governments

Revocation and Take-Over Powers

Offences

PART II — VOLUNTARY ACCESS TO SERVICES

Consents

Temporary Care Agreements

Special Needs Agreements

Expiry and Termination of Agreements

Review by Residential Placement Advisory Committee

PART III — CHILD PROTECTION

Legal Representation

Parties and Notice

Commencing Child Protection Proceedings

Special Cases of Apprehension of Children

Table of Contents

Power of Entry and Other Provisions for Special Cases of Apprehension

Table of Contents

Table of Contents

Corporal Punishment

Office of Child and Family Service Advocacy

Rights of Children in Care

Complaint and Review Procedures

PART VI — EXTRAORDINARY MEASURES

Secure Treatment Programs

Commitment to Secure Treatment

Extension of Period of Commitment

Release by Administrator

Review of Commitment

Emergency Admission

Police Assistance

Secure Isolation

Review Teams

[Proposed] Intrusive Procedures

Table of Contents

Table of Contents

Table of Contents

[Proposed] General

Table of Contents

REG. 70 — GENERAL
SCHEDULE — [FORMS]

REG. 71 — REGISTER

SCHEDULE [FORMS]

O. REG. 206/00 — PROCEDURES, PRACTICES AND STANDARDS OF SERVICE FOR CHILD PROTECTION CASES

Table of Contents

CHILDREN'S LAW REFORM ACT

PART I — EQUAL STATUS OF CHILDREN

PART II — ESTABLISHMENT OF PARENTAGE

PART III — CUSTODY, ACCESS AND GUARDIANSHIP INTERPRETATION

Custody and Access

Custody and Access — Orders

Custody and Access — Assistance to Court

Custody and Access — Enforcement

Table of Contents

Table of Contents

72 — FORMS

SCHEDULE [FORMS]

CREDITORS' RELIEF ACT

CRIMINAL CODE

DIVORCE ACT
Short Title

Interpretation

Jurisdiction

Table of Contents

Table of Contents

Table of Contents

Table of Contents

COMMENCEMENT AND SHORT TITLE

EVIDENCE ACT

655/00 — FAMILY CASE MANAGEMENT RULES FOR THE SUPERIOR COURT OF JUSTICE IN TORONTO

FAMILY LAW ACT

PART I — FAMILY PROPERTY

PART II — MATRIMONIAL HOME

Table of Contents

Table of Contents

PART VI — AMENDMENTS TO THE COMMON LAW

Table of Contents

Variation of Orders for the Support of a Child

Income

Income Information

Coming into Force

SCHEDULE I

Child Support Table for Ontario

Notes:

SCHEDULE II

Comparison of Household Standards of Living Test

SCHEDULE III

Adjustments to Income

O. REG. 114/99 — FAMILY LAW RULES (SUPERIOR COURT OF JUSTICE AND ONTARIO COURT OF JUSTICE)

Table of Contents

FAMILY ORDERS AND AGREEMENTS ENFORCEMENT ASSISTANCE ACT

Table of Contents

Regulations

PART II — GARNISHMENT OF FEDERAL MONEYS TO SATISFY SUPPORT ORDERS AND SUPPORT PROVISIONS

Interpretation

Garnishment of Her Majesty

Garnishee Summons

Garnishee Summons of Continuing Effect

Service of Documents

Administrative Procedures

Response to Garnishee Summons

Discharge of Liability

Notice to Judgment Debtor

Delay of Payments

Table of Contents

Table of Contents

Offence

No Liability

Regulations

PART IV — RELEASE AUTHORIZATION AND CONFIDENTIALITY

Release Authorization

Prohibition, Offence and Punishment

CAN. REG. 87-315 — RELEASE OF INFORMATION FOR FAMILY ORDERS AND AGREEMENTS ENFORCEMENT REGULATIONS

CAN. REG. 97-180 — DENIAL OF LICENCES FOR FAMILY ORDERS AND AGREEMENTS ENFORCEMENT REGULATIONS

Interpretation

Application for Licence Denial

Request to Terminate an Application

Documentation

Coming Into Force

Table of Contents

FAMILY RESPONSIBILITY AND SUPPORT ARREARS ENFORCEMENT ACT, 1996

Table of Contents

Table of Contents

O. REG. 176/98 — COST OF LIVING ADJUSTMENTS — METHODS OF CALCULATION

O. REG. 167/97 — FAMILY RESPONSIBILITY AND SUPPORT ARREARS ENFORCEMENT REGULATION
General
Termination of Support Obligation

Support Deduction Orders

Income Sources

Suspension Orders

Suspension of Drivers' Licences

Financial Statement and Proof of Income

Service and Delivery of Documents

Application of Payments

Consumer Reporting Information

Repeal and Commencement

Table of Contents

O. REG. 160/00 — FEES CHARGED BY DIRECTOR

GARNISHMENT, ATTACHMENT AND PENSION DIVERSION ACT

PART I — GARNISHMENT AND ATTACHMENT PROCEEDINGS

Interpretation

Garnishment of Her Majesty

DIVISION I — DEPARTMENTS AND CERTAIN CROWN CORPORATIONS

DIVISION II — CROWN CORPORATIONS NOT COVERED BY DIVISION I

DIVISION III — CANADIAN FORCES

DIVISION IV — SENATE, HOUSE OF COMMONS AND LIBRARY OF PARLIAMENT

DIVISION V — GENERAL

Table of Contents

Table of Contents

INTERCOUNTRY ADOPTION ACT, 1998

SCHEDULE
Convention on Protection of Children and Co-operation in Respect of Intercountry Adoption

O. REG. 200/99 — GENERAL REGULATION

Table of Contents

Table of Contents

REG. 738 — GENERAL

SCHEDULE [FORMS]

MARRIAGE (PROHIBITED DEGREES) ACT

PARENTAL RESPONSIBILITY ACT, 2000

Table of Contents

INTERJURISDICTIONAL SUPPORT ORDERS ACT, 2002

PART I — GENERAL

PART II — NEW ORDERS

Claimant in Ontario

Claimant Outside Ontario

PART III — REGISTRATION AND ENFORCEMENT OF ORDERS MADE OUTSIDE ONTARIO

PART IV — VARIATION OF ORDERS

Table of Contents

Table of Contents

O. REG. 140/94 — RECIPROCATING STATES [REVOKED]
Reciprocating States

REG. 194 — RULES OF CIVIL PROCEDURE
COMMENCEMENT OF PROCEEDINGS

PARTICULAR PROCEEDINGS

SUCCESSION LAW REFORM ACT

PART I — TESTATE SUCCESSION
General

Table of Contents

Conflict of Laws

International Wills

PART II — INTESTATE SUCCESSION

PART III — DESIGNATION OF BENEFICIARIES OF INTEREST IN FUNDS OR PLANS

Table of Contents

BANKRUPTCY AND INSOLVENCY ACT

An Act respecting Bankruptcy and Insolvency

R.S.C. 1985, c. B-3, as am. R.S.C. 1985, c. 27 (1st Supp.), s. 203; R.S.C. 1985, c. 31 (1st Supp.), ss. 3, 28, 69-77; R.S.C. 1985, c. 3 (2nd Supp.), s. 28; R.S.C. 1985, c. 27 (2nd Supp.), s. 10 (Sched., item 2); S.C. 1990, c. 17, s. 3; 1991, c. 46, s. 584; 1992, c. 1, ss. 12-20, 143 (Sched. VI, item 2), 145, 161; 1992, c. 27, ss. 1-90; 1993, c. 28, s. 78 (Sched. III, items 6, 7) [Amended 1999, c. 3, s. 12 (Sched., item 3).]; 1993, c. 34, s. 10; 1994, c. 26, ss. 6-9, 46; 1995, c. 1, s. 62(1)(a); 1996, c. 6, s. 167(1)(b), (2); 1996, c. 23, s. 168; 1997, c. 12, ss. 1-119; 1998, c. 19, s. 250; 1998, c. 21, s. 103; 1998, c. 30, s. 14(a); 1999, c. 3, s. 15; 1999, c. 28, ss. 146, 147; 1999, c. 31, ss. 17-26; 2000, c. 12, ss. 8-21; 2000, c. 30, ss. 143-148; 2001, c. 4, ss. 25-33, 177 [ss. 28, 33(1): (Fr.).]; 2001, c. 9, ss. 572-574; 2002, c. 7, ss. 83-85 [Not in force at date of publication.]; 2002, c. 8, s. 182(1)(b) [Not in force at date of publication.].

[Note: only sections 2(1), 3, 4, 38, 40, 41, 62(2), 66.28(2), 67(1), 68, 69.3, 69.4, 69.41, 70, 71(2), 72(1), 81, 91, 95, 96, 97(3),100, 109(6), (7), 113(3), 121, 136, 137, 170(7), 172, 178, 181 are reproduced here.]

. . . . .

INTERPRETATION

2. (1) Definitions — In this Act

"affidavit" includes statutory declaration and solemn affirmation; *("affidavit")*

"assignment" means an assignment filed with the official receiver; *("cession")*

"bank" means

(a) every bank and every authorized foreign bank within the meaning of section 2 of the *Bank Act*,

(b) every other member of the Canadian Payments Association established by the *Canadian Payments Act*, and

(c) every local cooperative credit society, as defined in subsection 2(1) of the Act referred to in paragraph (b), that is a member of a central cooperative credit society, as defined in that subsection, that is a member of that Association; *("banque")*

"bankrupt" means a person who has made an assignment or against whom a receiving order has been made or the legal status of that person; *("failli")*

"bankruptcy" means the state of being bankrupt or the fact of becoming bankrupt; *("faillite")*

"child" [Repealed 2000, c. 12, s. 8(1).]

1

"claim provable in bankruptcy," "provable claim" or **"claim provable"** includes any claim or liability provable in proceedings under this Act by a creditor; *("réclamation prouvable en matière de faillite" ou "réclamation prouvable")*

"common-law partner", in relation to an individual, means a person who is cohabiting with the individual in a conjugal relationship, having so cohabited for a period of at least one year; *("conjoint de fait")*

"common-law partnership" means the relationship between two persons who are common-law partners of each other; *("union de fait")*

"corporation" includes any company or legal person incorporated by or under an Act of Parliament or of any province, and any incorporated company, wherever incorporated, that is authorized to carry on business in Canada or that has an office or property in Canada, but does not include banks, authorized foreign banks within the meaning of section 2 of the *Bank Act*, insurance companies, trust companies, loan companies or railway companies; *("personne morale")*

"court", except in paragraphs 178(1)(a) and (a.1) and sections 204.1 to 204.3 and subject to subsection 243(1), means the court having jurisdiction in bankruptcy or a judge thereof, and includes a registrar when exercising the powers of the court conferred on a registrar under this Act; *("tribunal")*

"creditor" means a person having a claim, unsecured, preferred by virtue of priority under section 136 or secured, provable as a claim under this Act; *("créancier")*

"date of the initial bankruptcy event", in respect of a person, means the earliest of the date of filing of or making of

(a) an assignment by or in respect of the person,

(b) a proposal by or in respect of the person,

(c) a notice of intention by the person,

(d) the first petition for a receiving order against the person, in any case

(i) referred to in paragraph 50.4(8)(a) or 57(a) or subsection 61(2), or

(ii) where a notice of intention to make a proposal has been filed under section 50.4 or a proposal has been filed under section 62 in respect of the person and the person files an assignment before the court has approved the proposal, or

(e) the petition in respect of which a receiving order is made, in the case of a petition other than one referred to in paragraph (d); *("ouverture de la faillite")*

"debtor" includes an insolvent person and any person who, at the time an act of bankruptcy was committed by him, resided or carried on business in Canada and, where the context requires, includes a bankrupt; *("débiteur")*

"General Rules" means the General Rules referred to in section 209; *("Règles générales")*

"insolvent person" means a person who is not bankrupt and who resides, carries on business or has property in Canada, whose liabilities to creditors provable as claims under this Act amount to one thousand dollars, and

(a) who is for any reason unable to meet his obligations as they generally become due,

(b) who has ceased paying his current obligations in the ordinary course of business as they generally become due, or

(c) the aggregate of whose property is not, at a fair valuation, sufficient, or, if disposed of at a fairly conducted sale under legal process, would not be sufficient to enable payment of all his obligations, due and accruing due; *("personne insolvable")*

"locality of a debtor" means the principal place

(a) where the debtor has carried on business during the year immediately preceding his bankruptcy,

(b) where the debtor has resided during the year immediately preceding his bankruptcy, or

(c) in cases not coming within paragraph (a) or (b), where the greater portion of the property of the debtor is situated;

("localité d'un débiteur")

"Minister" means the Minister of Industry; *("ministre")*

"official receiver" means an officer appointed under subsection 12(2); *("séquestre officiel")*

"person" includes a partnership, an unincorporated association, a corporation, a cooperative society or an organization, the successors of a partnership, association, corporation, society or organization, and the heirs, executors, liquidators of the succession, administrators or other legal representative of a person, according to the law of that part of Canada to which the context extends; *("personne")*

"prescribed"

(a) in the case of the form of a document that is by this Act to be prescribed and the information to be given therein, means prescribed by directive issued by the Superintendent under paragraph 5(4)(e), and

(b) in any other case, means prescribed by the General Rules; *("prescrit")*

"property" includes money, goods, things in action, land and every description of property, whether real or personal, legal or equitable, and whether situated in Canada or elsewhere, and includes obligations, easements and every description of estate, interest and profit, present or future, vested or contingent, in, arising out of or incident to property; *("biens")*

"proposal" means

(a) in any provision of Division I of Part III, a proposal made under that Division, and

(b) in any other provision, a proposal made under Division I of Part III or a consumer proposal made under Division II of Part III

and includes a proposal or consumer proposal, as the case may be, for a composition, for an extension of time or for a scheme or arrangement; *("proposition concordataire" ou "proposition")*

"public utility" includes a person or body who supplies fuel, water or electricity, or supplies telecommunications, garbage collection, pollution control or postal services; *("entreprise de service public")*

"resolution" or **"ordinary resolution"** means a resolution carried in the manner provided by section 115; *("résolution" ou "résolution ordinaire")*

"secured creditor" means a person holding a mortgage, hypothec, pledge, charge or lien on or against the property of the debtor or any part of that property as security for a debt due or accruing due to the person from the debtor, or a person whose claim is based on, or secured by, a negotiable instrument held as collateral security and on which the debtor is only indirectly or secondarily liable, and includes

> (a) a person who has a right of retention or a prior claim constituting a real right, within the meaning of the *Civil Code of Québec* or any other statute of the Province of Quebec, on or against the property of the debtor or any part of that property, or
>
> (b) any of
>
> > (i) the vendor of any property sold to the debtor under a conditional or instalment sale,
> >
> > (ii) the purchaser of any property from the debtor subject to a right of redemption, or
> >
> > (iii) the trustee of a trust constituted by the debtor to secure the performance of an obligation,
>
> if the exercise of the person's rights is subject to the provisions of Book Six of the *Civil Code of Québec* entitled *Prior Claims and Hypothecs* that deal with the exercise of hypothecary rights; *("créancier garanti")*

Editor's Note: S.C. 2001, c. 4, s. 25 replaced the definition of "secured creditor". S.C. 2001, c. 4, s. 177(1) provides as follows:

> *(1) The definition of "secured creditor" in subsection 2(1) of the* Bankruptcy and Insolvency Act, *as enacted by section 25 of this Act [i.e. 2001, c. 4], applies only to bankruptcies or proposals in respect of which proceedings are commenced after the coming into force of that section, but nothing in this subsection shall be construed as changing the status of any person who was a secured creditor in respect of a bankruptcy or a proposal in respect of which proceedings were commenced before the coming into force of that section.*

*Immediately before the replacement, the definition of **"secured creditor"** read as follows:*

> *"secured creditor" means a person holding a mortgage, hypothec, pledge, charge, lien or privilege on or against the property of the debtor or any part thereof as security for a debt due or accruing due to him from the debtor, or a person whose claim is based on, or secured by, a negotiable instrument held as collateral security and on which the debtor is only indirectly or secondarily liable.*

"settlement" includes a contract, covenant, transfer, gift and designation of beneficiary in an insurance contract, to the extent that the contract, covenant, transfer, gift or designation is gratuitous or made for merely nominal consideration; *("disposition")*

"sheriff" includes bailiff and any officer charged with the execution of a writ or other process under this Act or any other Act or proceeding with respect to any property of a debtor; *("huissier-exécutant")*

"special resolution" means a resolution decided by a majority in number and three-fourths in value of the creditors with proven claims present, personally or by proxy, at a meeting of creditors and voting on the resolution; *("résolution spéciale")*

"Superintendent" means the Superintendent of Bankruptcy appointed under subsection 5(1); *("surintendant")*

"Superintendent of Financial Institutions" means the Superintendent of Financial Institutions appointed under subsection 5(1) of the *Office of the Superintendent of Financial Institutions Act*; *("surintendant des institutions financières")*

"trustee" or **"licensed trustee"** means a person who is licensed or appointed under this Act. *("syndic" ou "syndic autorisé")*

. . . . .

R.S.C. 1985, c. 31 (1st Supp.), s. 69; 1992, c. 27, s. 3; 1995, c. 1, s. 62(1)(a); 1997, c. 12, s. 1; 1999, c. 28, s. 146; 1999, c. 31, s. 17; 2000, c. 12, s. 8; 2001, c. 4, s. 25; 2001, c. 9, s. 572

Note:

S.C. 2000, c. 12, s. 8, amended s. 2(1) by repealing the definition of "child", and adding definitions of "common law partner" and "common law partnership". Pursuant to S.C. 2000, c. 12, s. 21, the amendments apply only to bankruptcies, proposals and receiverships commenced after the coming into force of S.C. 2000, c. 12, s. 21 on July 31, 2000. Prior to its repeal, the definition of "child" read as follows:

"child" includes a child born out of marriage;

. . . . .

3. (1) Reviewable transaction — For the purposes of this Act, a person who has entered into a transaction with another person otherwise than at arm's length shall be deemed to have entered into a reviewable transaction.

(2) Question of fact — It is a question of fact whether persons not related to one another within the meaning of section 4 were at a particular time dealing with each other at arm's length.

(3) Presumption — Persons related to each other within the meaning of section 4 shall be deemed not to deal with each other at arm's length while so related.

4. (1) Definitions — In this section

"related group" means a group of persons each member of which is related to every other member of the group;

"unrelated group" means a group of persons that is not a related group.

(2) Definition of "related persons" — For the purposes of this Act, persons are related to each other and are **"related persons"** if they are

(a) individuals connected by blood relationship, marriage, common-law partnership or adoption;

(b) a corporation and

(i) a person who controls the corporation, if it is controlled by one person,

(ii) a person who is a member of a related group that controls the corporation, or

(iii) any person connected in the manner set out in paragraph (a) to a person described in subparagraph (i) or (ii); or

(c) two corporations

(i) controlled by the same person or group of persons,

(ii) each of which is controlled by one person and the person who controls one of the corporations is related to the person who controls the other corporation,

(iii) one of which is controlled by one person and that person is related to any member of a related group that controls the other corporation,

(iv) one of which is controlled by one person and that person is related to each member of an unrelated group that controls the other corporation,

5

(v) one of which is controlled by a related group a member of which is related to each member of an unrelated group that controls the other corporation, or

(vi) one of which is controlled by an unrelated group each member of which is related to at least one member of an unrelated group that controls the other corporation.

(3) Relationships — For the purposes of this section,

(a) where two corporations are related to the same corporation within the meaning of subsection (2), they shall be deemed to be related to each other;

(b) where a related group is in a position to control a corporation, it shall be deemed to be a related group that controls the corporation whether or not it is part of a larger group by whom the corporation is in fact controlled;

(c) a person who has a right under a contract, in equity or otherwise, either immediately or in the future and either absolutely or contingently, to, or to acquire, shares in a corporation, or to control the voting rights of shares in a corporation, shall, except where the contract provides that the right is not exercisable until the death of an individual designated therein, be deemed to have the same position in relation to the control of the corporation as if he owned the shares;

(d) where a person owns shares in two or more corporations, he shall, as shareholder of one of the corporations, be deemed to be related to himself as shareholder of each of the other corporations;

(e) persons are connected by blood relationship if one is the child or other descendant of the other or one is the brother or sister of the other;

(f) persons are connected by marriage if one is married to the other or to a person who is connected by blood relationship or adoption to the other;

(f.1) persons are connected by common-law partnership if one is in a common-law partnership with the other or with a person who is connected by blood relationship or adoption to the other; and

(g) persons are connected by adoption if one has been adopted, either legally or in fact, as the child of the other or as the child of a person who is connected by blood relationship, otherwise than as a brother or a sister to the other.

2000, c. 12, s. 9

Note:

S.C. 2000, c. 12, s. 9, amended s. 4 by replacing paragraphs 4(2)(a) and 4(3)(f), and by adding paragraph 4(3)(f.1). Pursuant to S.C. 2000, c. 12, s. 21, the amendments apply only to bankruptcies, proposals and receiverships commenced after the coming into force of S.C. 2000, c. 12, s. 21 on July 31, 2000. Prior to the amendments, paragraphs 4(2)(a) and 4(3)(f) read respectively as follows:

4. (2)

(a) individuals connected by blood relationship, marriage or adoption;

(3)

(f) persons are connected by marriage if one is married to the other or to a person who is connected by blood relationship to the other; and;

. . . . .

PART I — ADMINISTRATIVE OFFICIALS

. . . . .

Corporations as Trustees

. . . . .

Duties and Powers of Trustees

. . . . .

38. (1) Proceeding by creditor when trustee refuses to act — Where a creditor requests the trustee to take any proceeding that in his opinion would be for the benefit of the estate of a bankrupt and the trustee refuses or neglects to take the proceeding, the creditor may obtain from the court an order authorizing him to take the proceeding in his own name and at his own expense and risk, on notice being given the other creditors of the contemplated proceeding, and on such other terms and conditions as the court may direct.

(2) Transfer to creditor — On an order under subsection (1) being made, the trustee shall assign and transfer to the creditor all his right, title and interest in the chose in action or subject-matter of the proceeding, including any document in support thereof.

(3) Benefits belong to creditor — Any benefit derived from a proceeding taken pursuant to subsection (1), to the extent of his claim and the costs, belongs exclusively to the creditor instituting the proceeding, and the surplus, if any, belongs to the estate.

(4) Trustee may institute proceeding — Where, before an order is made under subsection (1), the trustee, with the permission of the inspectors, signifies to the court his readiness to institute the proceeding for the benefit of the creditors, the order shall fix the time within which he shall do so, and in that case the benefit derived from the proceeding, if instituted within the time so fixed, belongs to the estate.

. . . . .

Discharge of Trustee

40. (1) Disposal of unrealizable property — With the permission of the inspectors, any property of a bankrupt found incapable of realization shall be returned to the bankrupt prior to the trustee's application for discharge.

(2) Final disposition of property — Where a trustee is unable to dispose of any property as provided in this section, the court may make such order as it may consider necessary.

41. (1) Application to court — When a trustee has completed the duties required of him with respect to the administration of the property of a bankrupt, he shall apply to the court for a discharge.

(2) Discharge of trustee — The court may discharge a trustee with respect to any estate on full administration thereof or, for sufficient cause, before full administration.

(3) When another trustee has been appointed — A trustee when replaced by another trustee is entitled to be discharged if he has accounted to the satisfaction of the inspectors and the court for all property that came to his hands, and a period of three months has elapsed after the date of the replacement without any undisposed of claim or objection having been made by the bankrupt or any creditor.

(4) When estate deemed fully administered — When a trustee's accounts have been approved by the inspectors and taxed by the court and all objections, applications and appeals have been settled or disposed of and all dividends have been paid, the estate is deemed to have been fully administered.

(5) Objections to be filed with court and trustee — Any interested person desiring to object to the discharge of a trustee shall, at least five days prior to the date of the hearing, file notice of objection with the registrar of the court setting out the reasons for the objection and serve a copy of the notice on the trustee.

(6) Court may grant discharge — The court shall consider the objection filed under subsection (5) and may grant or withhold a discharge accordingly or give such directions as it may deem proper in the circumstances.

(7) Fraud or breach of trust — Nothing in or done under authority of this section relieves or discharges or shall be deemed to relieve or discharge a trustee from the results of any fraud.

(8) Effect of discharge of trustee — The discharge of a trustee discharges him from all liability

> (a) in respect of any act done or default made by him in the administration of the property of the bankrupt, and

> (b) in relation to his conduct as trustee,

but any discharge may be revoked by the court on proof that it was obtained by fraud or by suppression or concealment of any material fact.

(8.1) Investigation not precluded — Nothing in subsection (8) shall be construed to prevent an investigation or a proceeding in respect of a trustee under subsection 14.01(1).

(9) Security released — The discharge of a trustee under this section operates as a release of the security provided pursuant to subsection 16(1).

(10) Trustee remains — Notwithstanding his discharge, the trustee remains the trustee of the estate for the performance of such duties as may be incidental to the full administration of the estate.

(11) Appointment of trustee by court to complete administration — The court, on being satisfied that there are assets that have not been realized or distributed, may, on the application of any interested person, appoint a trustee to complete the administration of the estate of the bankrupt, and the trustee shall be governed by the provisions of this Act, in so far as they are applicable.

1997, c. 12, s. 25, 62(2), 66.28(2)

PART III — PROPOSALS

SECTION I — GENERAL SCHEME FOR PROPOSALS

. . . . . .

62. (2) On whom approval binding — A proposal accepted by the creditors and approved by the court is binding on creditors in respect of

(a) all unsecured claims, and

(b) the secured claims in respect of which the proposal was made and that were in classes in which the secured creditors voted for the acceptance of the proposal by a majority in number and two thirds in value of the secured creditors present, personally or by proxy, at the meeting and voting on the resolution to accept the proposal,

but does not release the insolvent person from the debts and liabilities referred to in section 178, unless the creditor assents thereto.

1992, c. 27, s. 26; 1997, c. 12, s. 39

. . . . .

SECTION II — CONSUMER PROPOSALS

. . . . .

66.28 (1) Time for determining claims — The time with respect to which the claims of creditors shall be determined is the time of the filing of the consumer proposal.

(2) On whom approval binding — A consumer proposal accepted, or deemed accepted, by the creditors and approved, or deemed approved, by the court is binding on creditors in respect of

(a) all unsecured claims, and

(b) secured claims for which proofs of claim have been filed in the manner provided for in sections 124 to 134,

but does not release the consumer debtor from the debts and liabilities referred to in section 178, unless the creditor assents thereto.

(3) Certain persons not released — The acceptance of a consumer proposal by a creditor does not release any person who would not be released under this Act by the discharge of the consumer debtor.

1992, c. 27, s. 32(1)

PART IV — PROPERTY OF THE BANKRUPT

67. (1) Property of bankrupt — The property of a bankrupt divisible among his creditors shall not comprise

(a) property held by the bankrupt in trust for any other person,

(b) any property that as against the bankrupt is exempt from execution or seizure under any laws applicable in the province within which the property is situated and within which the bankrupt resides, or

(b.1) such goods and services tax credit payments and prescribed payments relating to the essential needs of an individual as are made in prescribed circumstances and are not property referred to in paragraph (a) or (b),

but it shall comprise

(c) all property wherever situated of the bankrupt at the date of his bankruptcy or that may be acquired by or devolve on him before his discharge, and

(d) such powers in or over or in respect of the property as might have been exercised by the bankrupt for his own benefit.

Note:

S.C. 1997, c. 12, s. 59(2), provides as follows:

(2) Application — Subsection (1) [S.C. 1997, c. 12, s. 59(1), which re-enacted s. 67(1)(b) and enacted s. 67(1)(b.1)] applies to bankruptcies in respect of which proceedings are commenced after that subsection came into force [on September 30, 1997].

. . . . .

1992, c. 27, s. 33; 1996, c. 23, s. 168; 1997, c. 12, s. 59; 1998, c. 19, s. 250

68. (1) Directives re standard of living factors — The Superintendent shall, by directive, establish in respect of the provinces or one or more bankruptcy districts or parts of bankruptcy districts, the standards for determining the portion of the total income of an individual bankrupt that exceeds that which is necessary to enable the bankrupt to maintain a reasonable standard of living.

(2) Interpretation — For the purposes of this section,

(a) **"total income"** referred to in subsection (1) includes, notwithstanding paragraphs 67(1)(b) and (b.1), all revenues of a bankrupt of whatever nature or source; and

(b) a requirement that a bankrupt pay an amount to the estate of the bankrupt is enforceable against all property of the bankrupt, other than property referred to in paragraphs 67(1)(b) and (b.1).

(3) Trustee to fix amount to be paid — The trustee shall

(a) having regard to the applicable standards established under subsection (1), and to the personal and family situation of the bankrupt, fix the amount that the bankrupt is required to pay to the estate of the bankrupt;

(b) inform the official receiver in writing of the amount fixed under paragraph (a); and

(c) take reasonable measures to ensure that the bankrupt complies with the requirement to pay.

(4) Modification by trustee — The trustee may, at any time, amend an amount fixed under subsection (3) to take into account

(a) material changes that have occurred in the personal or family situation of the bankrupt; or

(b) a recommendation made by the official receiver under subsection (5).

(5) Official receiver recommendation — Where the official receiver determines that the amount required to be paid by the bankrupt under subsection (3) or (4) is substantially not in accordance with the applicable standards established under subsection (1), the official receiver shall recommend to the trustee and to the bankrupt an amount required to be paid that the official receiver determines is in accordance with the applicable standards.

(6) Trustee may request mediation — Where the trustee and the bankrupt are not in agreement with the amount that the bankrupt is required to pay under subsection (3) or (4), the trustee shall, forthwith, in the prescribed form, send to the official receiver a request that the matter be determined by mediation and send a copy of the request to the bankrupt.

(7) Creditor may request mediation — On the request in writing of a creditor made within thirty days after the date of bankruptcy or an amendment referred to in subsection (4), the trustee shall, within the five days following the thirty day period, send to the official receiver a request in the prescribed form that the matter of the amount the bankrupt is required to pay under subsection (3) or (4) be determined by mediation and send a copy of the request to the bankrupt and the creditor.

(8) Mediation procedure — A mediation shall be in accordance with prescribed procedures.

(9) File — Documents contained in a file on the mediation of a matter under this section form part of the records referred to in subsection 11.1(2).

(10) Court determination — Where

(a) the trustee has not implemented a recommendation made by the official receiver under subsection (5),

(b) the issue submitted to mediation requested under subsection (6) or (7) is not thereby resolved, or

(c) the bankrupt fails to comply with the requirement to pay as determined under this section,

the trustee may, or on the request of the inspectors, any of the creditors or the official receiver shall, apply to the court for the hearing of the matter, and the court may, on the hearing, in accordance with the standards established under subsection (1) and having regard to the personal and family situation of the bankrupt, by order, fix the amount that the bankrupt is required to pay to the estate of the bankrupt.

(11) Fixing fair and reasonable remuneration in the case of related persons — The court may fix an amount that is fair and reasonable

(a) as salary, wages or other remuneration for the services being performed by a bankrupt for a person employing the bankrupt, or

(b) as payment for or commission in respect of any services being performed by a bankrupt for a person,

where the person is related to the bankrupt, and the court may, by order, determine the part of the salary, wages or other remuneration, or the part of the payment or commission, that shall be paid to the trustee on the basis of the amount so fixed by the court, unless it appears to the court that the services have been performed for the benefit of the bankrupt and are not of any substantial benefit to the person for whom they were performed.

(12) Modification of order — On the application of any interested person, the court may, at any time, amend an order made under this section to take into account material changes that have occurred in the personal or family situation of the bankrupt.

(13) Default by other person — An order of the court made under this section may be served on a person from whom the bankrupt is entitled to receive money and, in such case,

(a) the order binds the person to pay to the estate of the bankrupt the amount fixed by the order; and

(b) if the person fails to comply with the terms of the order, the court may, on the application of the trustee, order the person to pay the trustee the amount of money that the estate of the bankrupt would have received had the person complied with the terms of the order.

(14) Application is a proceeding — For the purposes of section 38, an application referred to in subsection (10) is deemed to be a proceeding for the benefit of the estate.

Note:

S.C. 1997, c. 12, s. 60(2), provides as follows:

(2) **Application** — Subsection (1) [S.C. 1997, c. 12, s. 60(1), which re-enacted s. 68] applies to bankruptcies in respect of which proceedings are commenced after that subsection comes into force [April 30, 1998].

1992, c. 27, s. 34; 1997, c. 12, s. 60(1)

. . . . .

Stay of Proceedings

. . . . .

69.3 (1) Stays of proceedings — bankruptcies — Subject to subsection (2) and sections 69.4 and 69.5, on the bankruptcy of any debtor, no creditor has any remedy against the debtor or the debtor's property, or shall commence or continue any action, execution or other proceedings, for the recovery of a claim provable in bankruptcy, until the trustee has been discharged.

(2) Secured creditors — Subject to sections 79 and 127 to 135 and subsection 248(1), the bankruptcy of a debtor does not prevent a secured creditor from realizing or otherwise dealing with his security in the same manner as he would have been entitled to realize or deal with it if this section had not been passed, unless the court otherwise orders, but in so ordering the court shall not postpone the right of the secured creditor to realize or otherwise deal with his security, except as follows:

(a) in the case of a security for a debt that is due at the date the bankrupt became bankrupt or that becomes due not later than six months thereafter, that right shall not be postponed for more than six months from that date; and

(b) in the case of a security for a debt that does not become due until more than six months after the date the bankrupt became bankrupt, that right shall not be postponed for more than six months from that date, unless all instalments of interest that are more than six months in arrears are paid and all other defaults of more than six months standing are cured, and then only so long as no instalment of interest remains in arrears or defaults remain uncured for more than six months, but, in any event, not beyond the date at which the debt secured by the security becomes payable under the instrument or law creating the security.

1992, c. 27, s. 36(1)

. . . . .

69.4 Court may declare that stays, etc., cease — A creditor who is affected by the operation of sections 69 to 69.31 or any other person affected by the operation of section 69.31 may apply to the court for a declaration that those sections no longer operate in respect of that creditor or person, and the court may make such a declaration, subject to any qualifications that the court considers proper, if it is satisfied

(a) that the creditor or person is likely to be materially prejudiced by the continued operation of those sections; or

(b) that it is equitable on other grounds to make such a declaration.

Note:

S.C. 1997, c. 12, s. 65(2), provides as follows:

(2) Subsection (1) [S.C. 1997, c. 12, s. 65(1), which added ss. 69.31 and 69.41 and re-enacted s. 69.4] applies to bankruptcies or proposals in respect of which proceedings are commenced after that subsection comes into force [September 30, 1997].

1992, c. 27, s. 36(1); 1997, c. 12, s. 65(1)

69.41 (1) Non-application of certain provisions — Sections 69 to 69.31 do not apply in respect of a claim referred to in subsection 121(4).

(2) No remedy, etc. — Notwithstanding subsection (1), no creditor with a claim referred to in subsection 121(4) has any remedy, or shall commence or continue any action, execution or other proceeding, against

(a) property of a bankrupt that has vested in the trustee; or

(b) amounts that are payable to the estate of the bankrupt under section 68.

Note:

S.C. 1997, c. 12, s. 65(2), provides as follows:

(2) Application — Subsection (1) [S.C. 1997, c. 12, s. 65(1), which added ss. 69.31 and 69.41 and re-enacted s. 69.4] applies to bankruptcies or proposals in respect of which proceedings are commenced after that subsection comes into force [September 30, 1997].

1997, c. 12, s. 65(1)

. . . . .

General Provisions

70. (1) Precedence of receiving orders and assignments — Every receiving order and every assignment made in pursuance of this Act takes precedence over all judicial or other attachments, garnishments, certificates having the effect of judgments, judgments, certificates of judgment, judgments operating as hypothecs, executions or other process against the property of a bankrupt, except those that have been completely executed by payment to the creditor or his agent, and except the rights of a secured creditor.

(2) Costs — Notwithstanding subsection (1), one solicitor's bill of costs, including sheriff's fees and land registration fees, shall be payable to the creditor who has first attached by way of garnishment or lodged with the sheriff an attachment, execution or other process against the property of the bankrupt.

(3) [Repealed 1992, c. 27, s. 37.]

1992, c. 27, s. 37

71.

. . . . .

(2) Vesting of property in trustee — On a receiving order being made or an assignment being filed with an official receiver, a bankrupt ceases to have any capacity to dispose of or otherwise deal with his property, which shall, subject to this Act and to the rights of secured creditors, forthwith pass to and vest in the trustee named in the receiving order or assignment, and in any case of change of trustee the property shall pass from trustee to trustee without any conveyance, assignment or transfer.

1997, c. 12, s. 67

72. (1) Application of other substantive law — The provisions of this Act shall not be deemed to abrogate or supersede the substantive provisions of any other law or statute relating to property and civil rights that are not in conflict with this Act, and the trustee is entitled to avail himself of all rights and remedies provided by that law or statute as supplementary to and in addition to the rights and remedies provided by this Act.

. . . . .

81. (1) Persons claiming property in possession of bankrupt — Where a person claims any property, or interest therein, in the possession of a bankrupt at the time of the bankruptcy, he shall file with the trustee a proof of claim verified by affidavit giving the grounds on which the claim is based and sufficient particulars to enable the property to be identified.

(2) How claim disposed of — The trustee with whom a proof of claim is filed under subsection (1) shall within fifteen days thereafter or within fifteen days after the first meeting of creditors, whichever is the later, either admit the claim and deliver possession of the property to the claimant or give notice in writing to the claimant that the claim is disputed with his reasons therefor, and, unless the claimant appeals therefrom to the court within fifteen days after the mailing of the notice of dispute, he shall be deemed to have abandoned or relinquished all his right to or interest in the property to the trustee who thereupon may sell or dispose of the property free of any lien, right, title or interest of the claimant.

(3) Onus on claimant — The onus of establishing a claim to or in property under this section is on the claimant.

(4) Require proof of claim — The trustee may give notice in writing to any person to prove his claim to or in property under this section, and, unless that person files with the trustee a proof of claim in the prescribed form within fifteen days after the mailing of the notice, the trustee may thereupon with the leave of the court sell or dispose of the property free of any lien, right, title or interest of that person.

(5) No other proceeding to be instituted — No proceedings shall be instituted to establish a claim to, or to recover any right or interest in, any property in the possession of a bankrupt at the time of the bankruptcy, except as provided in this section.

(6) Rights of others not extended — Nothing in this section shall be construed as extending the rights of any person other than the trustee.

. . . . .

Settlements and Preferences

91. (1) Certain settlements void — Any settlement of property made within the period beginning on the day that is one year before the date of the initial bankruptcy event in respect of the settlor and ending on the date that the settlor became bankrupt, both dates included, is void against the trustee.

(2) If bankrupt within five years — Any settlement of property made within the period beginning on the day that is five years before the date of the initial bankruptcy event in respect of the settlor and ending on the date that the settlor became bankrupt, both dates included, is void against the trustee if the trustee can prove that the settlor was, at the time of making the settlement, unable to pay all the settlor's debts without the aid of the property comprised in the settlement or that the interest of the settlor in the property did not pass on the execution thereof.

(3) Non-application of section — This section does not extend to any settlement made in favour of a purchaser or incumbrancer in good faith and for valuable consideration.

Note:

S.C. 2000, c. 12, s. 11, amended s. 91 by replacing s. 91(3). Pursuant to S.C. 2000, c. 12, s. 21, the amendment applies only to bankruptcies, proposals and receiverships commenced after the coming into force of S.C. 2000, c. 12, s. 21, on July 31, 2000. Prior to the amendment, s. 91(3) read as follows:

> 91. *(3) Non-application of section — This section does not extend to any settlement made*
>
> > *(a) before and in consideration of marriage;*
> >
> > *(b) in favour of a purchaser or incumbrancer in good faith and for valuable consideration; or*
> >
> > *(c) on or for the spouse or children of the settlor of property that has accrued to the settlor after marriage in right of the settlor's spouse or children.*
> >
> > R.S.C. 1985, c. 31 (1st Supp.), s. 70; 1997, c. 12, s. 75; 2000, c. 12, s. 11

. . . . .

95. (1) Avoidance of preference in certain cases — Every conveyance or transfer of property or charge thereon made, every payment made, every obligation incurred and every judicial proceeding taken or suffered by any insolvent person in favour of any creditor or of any person in trust for any creditor with a view to giving that creditor a preference over the other creditors is, where it is made, incurred, taken or suffered within the period beginning on the day that is three months before the date of the initial bankruptcy event and ending on the date the insolvent person became bankrupt, both dates included, deemed fraudulent and void as against the trustee in the bankruptcy.

(2) When view to prefer presumed — Where any conveyance, transfer, charge, payment, obligation or judicial proceeding mentioned in subsection (1) has the effect of giving any creditor a preference over other creditors, or over any one or more of them, it shall be presumed, in the absence of evidence to the contrary, to have been made, incurred, taken, paid or suffered with a view to giving the creditor a preference over other creditors, whether or not it was made voluntarily or under pressure and evidence of pressure shall not be admissible to support the transaction.

(2.1) Exception — Subsection (2) does not apply in respect of a margin deposit made by a clearing member with a clearing house.

(3) Definitions — In this section,

"clearing house" means a body that acts as an intermediary for its clearing members in effecting securities transactions; *("chambre de compensation")*

"clearing member" means a person engaged in the business of effecting securities transactions who uses a clearing house as intermediary; *("membre")*

"creditor" includes a surety or guarantor for the debt due to the creditor; *("creéancier")*

"margin deposit" means a payment, deposit or transfer to a clearing house under the rules of the clearing house to assure the performance of the obligations of a clearing member in connection with security transactions, including, without limiting the generality of the foregoing, transactions respecting futures, options or other derivatives or to fulfil any of those obligations. *("dépôt de couverture")*

1997, c. 12, s. 78(1), (2)

96. Extended period — Where the conveyance, transfer, charge, payment, obligation or judicial proceeding mentioned in section 95 is in favour of a person related to the insolvent person, the period referred to in subsection 95(1) shall be one year instead of three months.

1997, c. 12, s. 79

97.

. . . . .

(3) Law of set-off to apply — The law of set-off applies to all claims made against the estate of the bankrupt and also to all actions instituted by the trustee for the recovery of debts due to the bankrupt in the same manner and to the same extent as if the bankrupt were plaintiff or defendant, as the case may be, except in so far as any claim for set-off is affected by the provisions of this Act respecting frauds or fraudulent preferences.

1992, c. 27, s. 41; 1997, c. 12, s. 80

. . . . .

100. (1) Examination of consideration in a reviewable transaction — Where a bankrupt sold, purchased, leased, hired, supplied or received property or services in a reviewable transaction within the period beginning on the day that is one year before the date of the initial bankruptcy event and ending on the date of the bankruptcy, both dates included, the court may, on the application of the trustee, inquire into whether the bankrupt gave or received, as the case may be, fair market value in consideration for the property or services concerned in the transaction.

(2) Judgment for difference — Where the court in proceedings under this section finds that the consideration given or received by the bankrupt in the reviewable transaction was conspicuously greater or less than the fair market value of the property or services concerned in the transaction, the court may give judgment to the trustee against the other party to the transaction, against any other person being privy to the transaction with the bankrupt or against all those persons for the difference between the actual consideration given or received by the bankrupt and the fair market value, as determined by the court, of the property or services concerned in the transaction.

(3) Establishing values — In making an application under this section, the trustee shall state what in his opinion was the fair market value of the property or services concerned in the transaction and what in his opinion was the value of the actual consideration given or received by the bankrupt in the transaction, and the values on which the court makes any finding pursuant to this section shall be the values so stated by the trustee unless other values are proven.

1997, c. 12, s. 81

. . . . .

PART V — ADMINISTRATION OF ESTATES

. . . . .

Procedure at Meetings

. . . . .

109.

. . . . .

(6) Creditor not dealing at arm's length — Except as otherwise provided by this Act, a creditor is not entitled to vote at any meeting of creditors if the creditor did not, at all times within the period beginning on the day that is one year before the date of the initial bankruptcy event in respect of the debtor and ending on the date of the bankruptcy, both dates included, deal with the debtor at arm's length.

(7) Exception — A creditor who is not entitled to vote at a meeting of creditors by virtue of subsection (6) may with leave of the court vote at the meeting of creditors when all the creditors who have dealt with the debtor at arm's length do not together represent at least twenty per cent in value of the claims against the debtor.

1992, c. 27, s. 46; 1997, c. 12, s. 86

. . . . .

113.

. . . . .

(3) Persons not entitled to vote — The following persons are not entitled to vote on the appointment of a trustee or inspectors:

(a) the father, mother, child, sister, brother, uncle or aunt, by blood, adoption, marriage or common-law partnership, or the spouse or common-law partner, of the bankrupt;

(b) where the bankrupt is a corporation, any officer, director, or employee thereof; and

(c) where the bankrupt is a corporation, any wholly owned subsidiary corporation or any officer, director or employee thereof.

R.S.C. 1985, c. 31 (1st Supp.), s. 73; 2000, c. 12, s. 13

Note:

S.C. 2000, c. 12, s. 13, amended s. 113 by replacing paragraph 113(3)(a). Pursuant to S.C. 2000, c. 12, s. 21, the amendment applies only to bankruptcies, proposals and receiverships commenced after the coming into force of S.C. 2000, c. 12, s. 21, on July 31, 2000. Prior to the amendment, paragraph 113(3)(a) read as follows:

113. (3)

(a) the father, mother, child, sister, brother, uncle or aunt by blood or marriage, or spouse of the bankrupt;

. . . . .

Claims Provable

121. (1) Claims provable — All debts and liabilities, present or future, to which the bankrupt is subject on the day on which the bankrupt becomes bankrupt or to which the bankrupt may become subject before the bankrupt's discharge by reason of any obligation incurred before the day on which the bankrupt becomes bankrupt shall be deemed to be claims provable in proceedings under this Act.

(2) Contingent and unliquidated claims — The determination whether a contingent or unliquidated claim is a provable claim and the valuation of such a claim shall be made in accordance with section 135.

(3) Debts payable at a future time — A creditor may prove a debt not payable at the date of the bankruptcy and may receive dividends equally with the other creditors, deducting only thereout a rebate of interest at the rate of five per cent per annum computed from the declaration of a dividend to the time when the debt would have become payable according to the terms on which it was contracted.

(4) Family support claims — A claim in respect of a debt or liability referred to in paragraph 178(1)(b) or (c) payable under an order or agreement made before the date of the initial bankruptcy event in respect of the bankrupt and at a time when the spouse, former spouse, former common-law partner or child was living apart from the bankrupt, whether the order or agreement provides for periodic amounts or lump sum amounts, is a claim provable under this Act.

1992, c. 27, s. 50; 1997, c. 12, s. 87(1), (2); 2000, c. 12, s. 14

Note:

S.C. 2000, c. 12, s. 14, amended s. 121 by replacing s. 121 (4). Pursuant to S.C. 2000, c. 12, s. 21, the amendment applies only to bankruptcies, proposals and receiverships commenced after the coming into force of S.C. 2000, c. 12, s. 21, on July 31, 2000. Prior to the amendment, s. 121(4) read as follows:

> *121.(4) Family support claims — A claim in respect of a debt or liability referred to in paragraph 178(1)(b) or (c) payable under an order or agreement made before the date of the initial bankruptcy event in respect of the bankrupt and at a time when the spouse or child was living apart from the bankrupt, whether the order or agreement provides for periodic amounts or lump sum amounts, is a claim provable under this Act.*

. . . . .

Scheme of Distribution

136. (1) Priority of claims — Subject to the rights of secured creditors, the proceeds realized from the property of a bankrupt shall be applied in priority of payment as follows:

(a) in the case of a deceased bankrupt, the reasonable funeral and testamentary expenses incurred by the legal personal representative of the deceased bankrupt;

(b) the costs of administration, in the following order,

(i) the expenses and fees of any person acting under a direction made under paragraph 14.03(1)(a),

(ii) the expenses and fees of the trustee, and

(iii) legal costs;

(c) the levy payable under section 147;

(d) wages, salaries, commissions or compensation of any clerk, servant, travelling salesman, labourer or workman for services rendered during the six months immediately preceding the bankruptcy to the extent of two thousand dollars in each case, together with, in the case of a travelling salesman, disbursements properly incurred by that salesman in and about the bankrupt's business, to the extent of an additional one thousand dollars in each case, during the same period, and for the purposes of this paragraph commissions payable when goods are shipped, delivered or paid for, if shipped, delivered or paid for within the six month period, shall be deemed to have been earned therein;

(d.1) claims in respect of debts or liabilities referred to in paragraph 178(1)(b) or (c), if provable by virtue of subsection 121(4), for periodic amounts accrued in the year before the date of the bankruptcy that are payable, plus any lump sum amount that is payable;

(e) municipal taxes assessed or levied against the bankrupt, within the two years immediately preceding the bankruptcy, that do not constitute a secured claim against the real property or immovables of the bankrupt, but not exceeding the value of the interest of the bankrupt in the property in respect of which the taxes were imposed as declared by the trustee;

Editor's Note: S.C. 2001, c. 4, s. 31 replaced paragraph 136(1)(e). S.C. 2001, c. 4, s. 177(2) provides that:

(2) Paragraph 136(1)(e) of the Bankruptcy and Insolvency Act, as enacted by section 31 of this Act [i.e. 2001, c. 4], applies only to bankruptcies or proposals in respect of which proceedings are commenced after the coming into force of that section, but nothing in this subsection shall be construed as changing the status of any person who was a secured creditor in respect of a bankruptcy or a proposal in respect of which proceedings were commenced before the coming into force of that section.

Immediately before the replacement, the wording in the section dealing with priority of claims of municipal taxes read as follows:

(e) municipal taxes assessed or levied against the bankrupt, within the two years immediately preceding his bankruptcy, and that do not constitute a preferential lien or charge against the real property of the bankrupt, but not exceeding the value of the interest of the bankrupt in the property in respect of which the taxes were imposed as declared by the trustee;

(f) the landlord for arrears of rent for a period of three months immediately preceding the bankruptcy and accelerated rent for a period not exceeding three months following the bankruptcy if entitled thereto under the lease, but the total amount so payable shall not exceed the realization from the property on the premises under lease, and any payment made on account of accelerated rent shall be credited against the amount payable by the trustee for occupation rent;

(g) the fees and costs referred to in subsection 70(2) but only to the extent of the realization from the property exigible thereunder;

(h) in the case of a bankrupt who became bankrupt before the prescribed date, all indebtedness of the bankrupt under any Act respecting workers' compensation, under any Act respecting unemployment insurance or under any provision of the *Income Tax Act* creating an obligation to pay to Her Majesty amounts that have been deducted or withheld, rateably;

(i) claims resulting from injuries to employees of the bankrupt in respect of which the provisions of any Act respecting workers' compensation do not apply, but only to the extent of moneys received from persons guaranteeing the bankrupt against damages resulting from those injuries; and

(j) in the case of a bankrupt who became bankrupt before the prescribed date, claims of the Crown not mentioned in paragraphs (a) to (i), in right of Canada or any province, rateably notwithstanding any statutory preference to the contrary.

(2) Payment as funds available — Subject to the retention of such sums as may be necessary for the costs of administration or otherwise, payment in accordance with subsection (1) shall be made as soon as funds are available for the purpose.

(3) Balance of claim — A creditor whose rights are restricted by this section is entitled to rank as an unsecured creditor for any balance of claim due him.

1992, c. 1, s. 143; 1992, c. 27, s. 54; 1997, c. 12, s. 90(1), (2); 2001, c. 4, s. 31

137. (1) Postponement of claims from reviewable transactions — A creditor who entered into a reviewable transaction with a debtor at any time prior to the bankruptcy of the debtor is not entitled to claim a dividend in respect of a claim arising out of that transaction until all claims of the other creditors have been satisfied unless the transaction was in the opinion of the trustee or of the court a proper transaction.

(2) Claim of present or former spouse or common-law partner — A spouse or common-law partner, or former spouse or common-law partner, of a bankrupt is not entitled to claim a dividend in respect of wages, salary, commission or compensation for work done or services rendered in connection with the trade or business of the bankrupt until all claims of the other creditors have been satisfied.

2000, c. 12, s. 15

Note:

S.C. 2000, c. 12, s. 15, amended s. 137 by replacing s. 137 (2). Pursuant to S.C. 2000, c. 12, s. 21, the amendment applies only to bankruptcies, proposals and receiverships commenced after the coming into force of S.C. 2000, c. 12, s. 21, on July 31, 2000. Prior to the amendment, s. 137(2) read as follows:

> *137. (2) Claim of spouse — A spouse or former spouse of a bankrupt is not entitled to claim a dividend in respect of wages, salary, commission or compensation for work done or services rendered in connection with the trade or business of the bankrupt until all claims of the other creditors have been satisfied.*

· · · · ·

PART VI — BANKRUPTS

· · · · ·

Discharge of Bankrupts

· · · · ·

170.

· · · · ·

(7) Right of creditors to oppose — A creditor who intends to oppose the discharge of a bankrupt on grounds other than those mentioned in the trustee's report shall give notice of the intended opposition, stating the grounds thereof to the trustee and to the bankrupt at or before the time appointed for the hearing of the application for discharge.

1997, c. 12, s. 100

· · · · ·

172. (1) Court may grant or refuse discharge — On the hearing of an application of a bankrupt for a discharge, the court may either grant or refuse an absolute order of discharge or suspend the operation of the order for a specified time, or grant an order of discharge subject to any terms or conditions with respect to any earnings or income that may afterwards become due to the bankrupt or with respect to his after-acquired property.

(2) Powers of court to refuse or suspend discharge or grant conditional discharge — The court shall on proof of any of the facts mentioned in section 173

   (a) refuse the discharge of a bankrupt;

   (b) suspend the discharge for such period as the court thinks proper; or

   (c) require the bankrupt, as a condition of his discharge, to perform such acts, pay such moneys, consent to such judgments or comply with such other terms as the court may direct.

(3) Court may modify after year — Where at any time after the expiration of one year after the date of any order made under this section the bankrupt satisfies the court that there is no reasonable probability of his being in a position to comply with the terms of the order, the court may modify the terms of the order or of any substituted order, in such manner and on such conditions as it may think fit.

(4) Power to suspend — The powers of suspending and of attaching conditions to the discharge of a bankrupt may be exercised concurrently.

. . . . .

178. (1) Debts not released by order of discharge — An order of discharge does not release the bankrupt from

   (a) any fine, penalty, restitution order or other order similar in nature to a fine, penalty or restitution order, imposed by a court in respect of an offence, or any debt arising out of a recognizance or bail;

   (a.1) any award of damages by a court in civil proceedings in respect of

      (i) bodily harm intentionally inflicted, or sexual assault, or

      (ii) wrongful death resulting therefrom;

   (b) any debt or liability for alimony;

   (c) any debt or liability under a support, maintenance or affiliation order, or under an agreement for maintenance and support of a spouse, former spouse, former common-law partner or child living apart from the bankrupt;

   (d) any debt or liability arising out of fraud, embezzlement, misappropriation or defalcation while acting in a fiduciary capacity or, in the Province of Quebec, as a trustee or administrator of the property of others;

Note:

S.C. 2001, c. 4, s. 32 replaced paragraph 178(1)(d). S.C.2001, c. 4, s. 177(3) provides that:

> (3) Paragraph 178(1)(d) of the Bankruptcy and Insolvency Act, as enacted by section 32 of this Act [i.e. 2001, c. 4], applies only to bankruptcies in respect of which proceedings are commenced after the coming into force of that section.

Immediately before the replacement, the wording in the section dealing with debts not released by order of discharge read as follows:

(d) any debt or liability arising out of fraud, embezzlement, misappropriation or defalcation while acting in a fiduciary capacity;

(e) any debt or liability for obtaining property by false pretences or fraudulent misrepresentation;

(f) liability for the dividend that a creditor would have been entitled to receive on any provable claim not disclosed to the trustee, unless the creditor had notice or knowledge of the bankruptcy and failed to take reasonable action to prove his claim;

(g) any debt or obligation in respect of a loan made under the *Canada Student Loans Act*, the *Canada Student Financial Assistance Act* or any enactment of a province that provides for loans or guarantees of loans to students where the date of bankruptcy of the bankrupt occurred

(i) before the date on which the bankrupt ceased to be a full- or part-time student, as the case may be, under the applicable Act or enactment, or

(ii) within ten years after the date on which the bankrupt ceased to be a full- or part-time student; or

(h) any debt for interest owed in relation to an amount referred to in any of paragraphs (a) to (g).

(1.1) Court may order non-application of subsection (1) — At any time after ten years after a bankrupt who has a debt referred to in paragraph (1)(g) ceases to be a full- or part-time student, as the case may be, under the applicable Act or enactment, the court may, on application, order that subsection (1) does not apply to the debt if the court is satisfied that

(a) the bankrupt has acted in good faith in connection with the bankrupt's liabilities under the loan; and

(b) the bankrupt has and will continue to experience financial difficulty to such an extent that the bankrupt will be unable to pay the liabilities under the loan.

(2) Claims released — Subject to subsection (1), an order of discharge releases the bankrupt from all claims provable in bankruptcy.

Note:

S.C. 2000, c. 12, s. 18, amended s. 178 by replacing paragraph 178(1)(c). Pursuant to S.C. 2000, c. 12, s. 21, the amendment applies only to bankruptcies, proposals and receiverships commenced after the coming into force of S.C. 2000, c. 12, s. 21, on July 31, 2000. Prior to the amendment, paragraph 178(1)(c) read as follows:

178. (1)

(c) any debt or liability under a support, maintenance or affiliation order or under an agreement for maintenance and support of a spouse or child living apart from the bankrupt;

Note:

S.C. 1998, c. 21, ss. 103(3)–(4), provide as follows:

(3) Application — Subsection (1) [which replaced s. 178(1)(g)(ii)], applies to debts and obligations regardless of whether they were incurred before or after this section comes into force [June 18, 1998].

(4) **Application** — Subsections (1) [which replaced s. 178(1)(g)(ii)] and (2) [which replaced that portion of s. 178(1.1) before paragraph (a)] apply only in respect of bankruptcies and proposals in respect of which proceedings are commenced after this section comes into force [June 18, 1998].

Note:

S.C. 1997, c. 12, s. 105(4), provides as follows:

(4) **Application** — Subsection (1) [which added s. 178(1)(a.1)], (2) [which added s. 178(1)(g) and (h)] or (3) [which added s. 178(1.1)] applies to bankruptcies or proposals in respect of which proceedings are commenced after that subsection comes into force [September 30, 1997].

R.S.C. 1985, c. 3 (2nd Supp.), s. 28; 1992, c. 27, s. 64; 1997, c. 12, s. 105(1)–(3); 1998, c. 21, s. 103; 2000, c. 12, s. 18; 2001, c. 4, s. 32

. . . . .

181. (1) Power of court to annul bankruptcy — Where, in the opinion of the court, a receiving order ought not to have been made or an assignment ought not to have been filed, the court may by order annul the bankruptcy.

(2) Effect of annulment of bankruptcy — Where an order is made under subsection (1), all sales, dispositions of property, payments duly made and acts done theretofore by the trustee or other person acting under his authority, or by the court, are valid, but the property of the bankrupt shall vest in such person as the court may appoint, or, in default of any appointment, revert to the bankrupt for all the estate or interest of the trustee therein on such terms and subject to such conditions, if any, as the court may order.

. . . . .

CANADA EVIDENCE ACT

An Act respecting Witnesses and Evidence

R.S.C. 1985, c. C-5, as am. R.S.C. 1985, c. 27 (1st Supp.), s. 203; R.S.C. 1985, c. 19 (3rd Supp.), ss. 17, 18; S.C. 1992, c. 1, s. 142 (Sched. V, item 9), 144 (Sched. VII, item 5) (Fr.); 1992, c. 47, s. 66; 1993, c. 28, s. 78 (Sched. III, item 8); 1993, c. 34, s. 15; 1994, c. 44, ss. 85–93; 1995, c. 28, s. 47; 1997, c. 18, ss. 116–118; 1998, c. 9, s. 1; 1999, c. 18, ss. 89–91; 1999, c. 28, ss. 149, 150; 2000, c. 5, ss. 52–57; 2001, c. 41, ss. 43, 44 (Sched. 2), 124, 140, 141(1), (3)–(7) [ss. 140, 141(4)–(7) conditions not yet satisfied.]; 2002, c. 1, s. 166; 2002, c. 7, s. 96; 2002, c. 8, ss. 118, 119, 183(1)(b) [Not in force at date of publication.] [s. 119 repealed 2001, c. 41, s. 141(3)(a).].

[Note: only sections 4(1)–(6) and 16(1)–(5) are reproduced here.]

. . . . .

PART I — APPLICATION

. . . . .

Witnesses

. . . . .

4. (1) Accused and spouse — Every person charged with an offence, and, except as otherwise provided in this section, the wife or husband, as the case may be, of the person so charged, is a competent witness for the defence whether the person so charged is charged solely or jointly with any other person.

(2) Accused and spouse — The wife or husband of a person charge with an offence under subsection 136(1) of the *Youth Criminal Justice Act* or with an offence under any of sections 151, 152, 153, 155 or 159, subsection 160(2) or (3), or sections 170 to 173, 179, 212, 215, 218, 271 to 273, 280 to 283, 291 to 294 or 329 of the *Criminal Code*, or an attempt to commit any such offence, is a competent and compellable witness for the prosecution without the consent of the person charged.

(3) Communications during marriage — No husband is compellable to disclose any communication made to him by his wife during their marriage, and no wife is compellable to disclose any communication made to her by her husband during their marriage.

(4) Offences against young persons — The wife or husband of a person charged with an offence against any of ections 220, 221, 235, 236, 237, 239, 240, 266, 267, 268 or 269 of the *Criminal Code* where the complainant or victim is under the age of fourteen years is a competent and compellable witness for the prosecution without the consent of the person charged.

(5) Saving — Nothing in this section affects a case where the wife or husband of a person charged with an offence may at common law be called as a witness without the consent of that person.

(6) Failure to testify — The failure of the person charged, or of the wife or husband of that person, to testify shall not be made the subject of comment by the judge or by counsel for the prosecution.

R.S.C. 1985, c. 19 (3rd Supp.), s. 17; 2002, c. 1, s. 166

. . . . .

Oaths and Solemn Affirmations

. . . . .

16. (1) Witness whose capacity is in question — Where a proposed witness is a person under fourteen years of age or a person whose mental capacity is challenged, the court shall, before permitting the person to give evidence, conduct an inquiry to determine

    (a) whether the person understands the nature of an oath or a solemn affirmation; and

    (b) whether the person is able to communicate the evidence.

(2) Testimony under oath or solemn affirmation — A person referred to in subsection (1) who understands the nature of an oath or a solemn affirmation and is able to communicate the evidence shall testify under oath or solemn affirmation.

(3) Testimony on promise to tell truth — A person referred to in subsection (1) who does not understand the nature of an oath or a solemn affirmation but is able to communicate the evidence may, notwithstanding any provision of any Act requiring an oath or a solemn affirmation, testify on promising to tell the truth.

(4) Inability to testify — A person referred to in subsection (1) who neither understands the nature of an oath or a solemn affirmation nor is able to communicate the evidence shall not testify.

(5) Burden as to capacity of witness — A party who challenges the mental capacity of a proposed witness of fourteen years of age or more has the burden of satisfying the court that there is an issue as to the capacity of the proposed witness to testify under an oath or a solemn affirmation.

R.S.C. 1985, c. 19 (3rd Supp.), s. 18; 1994, c. 44, s. 89

. . . . .

CHANGE OF NAME ACT

R.S.O. 1990, c. C.7, as am. S.O. 1994, c. 27, s. 75; 1997, c. 17, ss. 1–5; 1998, c. 18, Sched. E, ss. 46–49; 1999, c. 6, s. 4; 2000, c. 26, Sched. B, s. 5 [s. 5(2) not in force at date of publication.].

1. Definitions — In this Act,

"change" means any change by way of alteration, substitution, addition or abandonment;

"child" means a person under the age of eighteen years;

"court" means the Ontario Court of Justice. ("tribunal")

"file" means file in the office of the Registrar General;

"joint declaration" means the declaration referred to in subsection 3(6);

"prescribed" means prescribed by the regulations made under this Act;

"Registrar General" means the Registrar General under the *Vital Statistics Act*;

"spouse" has the same meaning as in section 1 of the *Family Law Act*.

2000, c. 26, Sched. B, s. 5(1)

2. (1) Person's name — For all purposes of Ontario law,

(a) a person whose birth is registered in Ontario is entitled to be recognized by the name appearing on the person's birth certificate or change of name certificate, unless clause (c) applies;

(b) a person whose birth is not registered in Ontario is entitled to be recognized by,

(i) the name appearing on the person's change of name certificate, if the person's name has been changed under this Act or a predecessor of it, or

(ii) in all other cases, the name recognized in law in the last place with which the person had a real and substantial connection before residing in Ontario,

unless clause (c) applies; and

(c) a person who adopted a name on marriage before the 1st day of April, 1987 is entitled to be recognized by that name unless the person subsequently changed that name under this Act or a predecessor of it.

(2) Saving — Nothing in this Act shall be deemed to affect a change of name effected under a right that existed at law before the 26th day of June, 1939.

(3) Surname and forename — A person's name may not be changed under this Act so as to include no surname or so as to include no forename.

ELECTION BY SPOUSE

3. (1) Election by spouse to change surname — A spouse may, at any time while married, elect in the prescribed manner,

    (a) to change his or her surname to,

        (i) the surname that the other spouse had immediately before their marriage,

        (ii) a surname consisting of the surnames that both spouses had immediately before their marriage, hyphenated or combined; or

    (b) to resume the surname that the spouse had immediately before the marriage.

(2) Resuming name when marriage dissolved — Within ninety days after a marriage is dissolved by divorce, annulment or death, the former spouse may elect in the prescribed manner to resume the surname that the spouse had immediately before the marriage.

Proposed Amendment — 3(2)

(2) Resuming name when marriage dissolved — At any time after a marriage is dissolved by divorce, annulment or death, the former spouse may elect in the prescribed manner to resume the surname that the spouse had immediately before the marriage.
2000, c. 26, Sched. B, s. 5(2) [Not in force at date of publication.]

(3) Procedure — A person who wishes to elect under subsection (1) or (2) shall pay the required fee and provide the prescribed documents, accompanied by all birth certificates and change of name certificates that are in the person's possession.

(3.1) Police records check — A person who wishes to elect under subsection (1) or (2) shall provide the Registrar General with a police records check, as described in subsections 6(9) and (10), if the person would be required to submit it if making an application under subsection 4(1) or 5(1).

(4) Certificate — On receiving the fee and documents, the Registrar General shall,

    (a) if the person's birth was registered in Ontario, register the change of name, note it on the birth registration and issue a change of name certificate and a new birth certificate to the person; and

    (b) if the person's birth was not registered in Ontario, register the change of name and issue a change of name certificate to the person.

(5) Application — This section applies to spouses whether married before or after the 1st day of April, 1987.

(6) Joint declaration of conjugal relationship — Subsection (1) applies with necessary modifications to two persons of the opposite sex or the same sex who file a joint declaration in the prescribed form acknowledging that they live together in a conjugal relationship outside marriage.

(7) Revocation of joint declaration — Subsection (2) applies with necessary modifications to two persons who have filed a joint declaration if one of them files a declaration, in the prescribed form, stating that the relationship has ended.

(8) No notice required — A person who elects to change his or her surname under this section need not notify the other spouse or other person.
1997, c. 17, s. 1; 1998, c. 18, Sched. E, s. 46; 1999, c. 6, s. 4

CHANGE OF NAME OF PERSON OVER SIXTEEN

4. (1) Application for change of name — A person at least sixteen years of age who has been ordinarily resident in Ontario for at least one year immediately before making the application may apply to the Registrar General in accordance with section 6 to change his or her forename or surname or both.

(2) Notice to spouse, etc. — An applicant who is a spouse or has filed a joint declaration that has not been revoked shall give the other spouse or other person notice of the application.

(3) Consent required where applicant under 18 — An application by a child requires the written consent of every person who has lawful custody of the child.

(4) Application to dispense with consent — If the required consent cannot be obtained or is refused, the child may apply to the court for an order dispensing with the consent.

(5) How application determined — The court shall determine an application under subsection (4) in accordance with the best interests of the child.

CHANGE OF CHILD'S NAME

5. (1) Application to change child's name — A person with lawful custody of,

(a) a child whose birth was registered in Ontario and who is ordinarily resident there; or

(b) a child who has been ordinarily resident in Ontario for at least one year immediately before the application is made,

may apply to the Registrar General in accordance with section 6 to change the child's forename or surname or both, unless a court order or separation agreement prohibits the change.

(2) Consents required — The application under subsection (1) requires the written consent of,

(a) any other person with lawful custody of the child;

(b) any person whose consent is necessary in accordance with a court order or separation agreement; and

(c) the child, if the child is twelve years of age or older.

(3) Where child lacks capacity — Clause (2)(c) does not apply if a legally qualified medical practitioner states in writing, not more than one year before the application is made, that in his or her opinion the child does not have capacity to consent.

(4) Application to dispense with consent — If the required consent cannot be obtained or is refused, the person seeking to change the child's name may apply to the court for an order dispensing with that consent.

(5) How application determined — The court shall determine an application under subsection (4) in accordance with the best interests of the child.

(6) Notice to persons with access — The applicant under subsection (1) shall give notice of the application to every person who is lawfully entitled to access to the child.

(7) Notice to spouse, etc. — An applicant who proposes to change the child's surname to the surname of the applicant's spouse or of a person with whom the applicant has filed a joint declaration that has not been revoked shall give the spouse or other person notice of the application.

PROCEDURE

6. (1) Definition — In this section, **"application"** means an application made under subsection 4(1) or 5(1). ("demande")

(2) Contents of application — An application shall be in the prescribed form and shall state, by way of statutory declaration, in respect of the person to whose name the application relates,

    (a) the person's date and place of birth;

    (b) if the person is married, the full name, before marriage, of the person's spouse and the date and place of the marriage;

    (c) if the person has filed a joint declaration that has not been revoked, the full name of the other person who made the joint declaration, its date and the place where it was made;

    (d) the full names, and all former names, if known, of the person's father and mother;

    (e) the length of the person's residence in Ontario, and the person's current address;

    (f) in the case of an application under subsection 5(1),

        (i) that the applicant has lawful custody of the child,

        (ii) that no court order or separation agreement prohibits the change of name that is sought,

        (iii) whether a court order or separation agreement provides that the child's name shall not be changed without a person's consent and, if so, particulars of the order or agreement;

    (g) particulars of every criminal offence of which the person has been convicted, except an offence in respect of which a pardon has been granted under the *Criminal Records Act* (Canada);

    (g.1) particulars of every criminal offence of which the person has been found guilty and has been discharged, except an offence in respect of which the *Criminal Records Act* (Canada) requires that the record be purged;

    (h) particulars of every criminal offence of which the person has been found guilty under the *Young Offenders Act* (Canada), except an offence in respect of which that Act requires that the record be destroyed;

    (h.1) particulars of every outstanding law enforcement order against the person, including a warrant, prohibition order, restraining order, driver's licence suspension, probation order and parole order, of which he or she is aware;

    (h.2) particulars of every pending criminal charge against the person, including every pending criminal charge against the person under the *Young Offenders Act* (Canada), of which he or she is aware.

    (i) particulars of every unsatisfied order for payment of money, unsatisfied execution and pending court proceeding, other than a proceeding referred to in clause (h. 2), against the person of which he or she is aware;

(j) particulars of every,

    (i) lien against or security interest in the person's personal property, and

    (ii) financing statement that is registered under the *Personal Property Security Act* and names the person as debtor,

of which he or she is aware;

(k) whether the person is an undischarged bankrupt and, if so, particulars of the bankruptcy;

(l) particulars of any change of name made before the current application;

(m) the proposed name;

(n) the reasons for the change of name;

(o) that every consent required for the application has been given or has been dispensed with by the court;

(p) that every person entitled to notice of the application has been given notice;

(q) that the application is not made for an improper purpose; and

(r) any other information that is prescribed.

(3) Accompanying statement — An application shall be accompanied by a statement in the prescribed form, made by a member of a prescribed class or, if no member of a prescribed class is available, any other person.

(4) Idem — If the author of the statement is a member of a prescribed class, it shall set out that the person to whose name the application relates is known to the author and has, to the author's knowledge, resided in Ontario for at least one year immediately before the making of the application or, if the person is less than one year old, since birth.

(5) Idem — If the author of the statement is a person who is not a member of a prescribed class, it shall set out that the person to whose name the application relates has been known to the author for at least five years or, if the person is less than five years old, since birth, and has, to the author's knowledge, resided in Ontario for at least one year immediately before the making of the application or, if the person is less than one year old, since birth.

(6) Evidence of consent, etc. — If a person's consent to an application is required, the applicant shall provide with the application that person's written consent or a certified copy of the order dispensing with that person's consent.

(7) Notice of application — If anyone is entitled to notice of an application, the applicant shall,

    (a) at least 30 days before filing the application, send notice and a copy of the application by registered or certified mail to the last known address of the person entitled to notice; or

    (b) obtain an acknowledgment of notice, signed by the person entitled to notice, and provide it with the application to the Registrar General.

(8) Old certificates to be surrendered — An application shall be accompanied by all birth certificates and change of name certificates of the person to whose name the application relates that are in the applicant's possession.

(9) Police records check — An application shall be accompanied by a police records check that is prepared and certified by an employee of an Ontario police force if the application discloses particulars described in clause (2)(g), (g.1), (h), (h.1) or (h.2).

31

(10) Same — The police records check shall contain the particulars of,

(a) every criminal offence of which the person to whose name the application relates has been convicted, except an offence in respect of which a pardon has been granted under the *Criminal Records Act* (Canada);

(b) every criminal offence of which the person to whose name the application relates has been found guilty and has been discharged, except an offence in respect of which the *Criminal Records Act* (Canada) requires that the record be purged;

(c) every criminal offence of which the person to whose name the application relates has been found guilty under the *Young Offenders Act* (Canada), except an offence in respect of which that Act requires that the record be destroyed;

(d) every outstanding law enforcement order against the person to whose name the application relates, including a warrant, prohibition order, restraining order, driver's licence suspension, probation order and parole order;

(e) every pending criminal charge, including every pending criminal charge under the *Young Offenders Act* (Canada), against the person to whose name the application relates.

(11) Disclosure of personal information — An employee of a police force shall disclose personal information about an individual for the purpose of preparing a police records check that complies with subsection (10).

(12) Exception — Subsection (9) does not apply in respect of a change of name that has been certified as described in subsection 8(2) by the Attorney General or a person authorized by the Attorney General.

1994, c. 27, s. 75; 1997, c. 17, s. 2

Duty of Registrar General

7. (1) Certificate — When an applicant under subsection 4(1) or 5(1) complies with the requirements of this Act and pays the required fee,

(a) if the birth of the person to whose name the application relates was registered in Ontario, the Registrar General shall register the change of name, note it on the birth registration and issue a change of name certificate and a new birth certificate to the person;

(b) if the person's birth was not registered in Ontario, the Registrar General shall register the change of name and issue a change of name certificate to the person,

unless the Registrar General believes on reasonable grounds that the applicant seeks the change of name for an improper purpose.

(2) Refusal of application — If the Registrar General believes on reasonable grounds that an applicant seeks the change of name for an improper purpose, the Registrar General shall,

(a) refuse the application; and

(b) advise the applicant and any person who was entitled to notice of the application,

(i) that it was refused, and

(ii) that the applicant has the right to make an application under subsection (3).

(3) Application to court — The applicant whose application is refused may, on notice to the Registrar General, apply to the court for an order granting the application.

(4) Registrar General's reasons for refusal — The Registrar General may file with the court his or her reasons for refusing the application and the court may take them into account if it is satisfied that the applicant has had notice of the reasons and an opportunity to respond to them.

(5) Power of court — If the court is satisfied that the applicant does not seek the change of name for an improper purpose, the court shall, by order, grant the application.

(6) Duty of Registrar General — On receiving a certified copy of the order, the Registrar General shall,

> (a) if the birth of the person to whose name the application relates was registered in Ontario, register the change of name, note it on the birth registration and issue a change of name certificate and a new birth certificate to the person;

> (b) if the person's birth was not registered in Ontario, register the change of name and issue a change of name certificate to the person.

1998, c. 18, Sched. E, s. 47

7.1 (1) Check with Ministry of the Solicitor General — Despite any other Act, before registering a change of name requested under section 3 or registering or refusing a change of name requested under section 4 or 5, the Registrar General shall ask the Ministry of the Solicitor General if the Ministry has any information about the person to whose name the election or application relates that would be included in a police records check as described in subsection 6(10) and the Ministry shall so advise the Registrar General.

(2) Personal information — For the purpose of subsection (1), the Registrar General shall disclose to the Ministry of the Solicitor General the person's name and other personal information that will assist the Ministry in identifying the person and the Ministry of the Solicitor General and Registrar General shall collect personal information from each other, and subsection 39(2) of the *Freedom of Information and Protection of Privacy Act* does not apply to any such collection of personal information.

(3) No name change consideration until police records check provided — Subsections 3(4), 7(1) and 7(2) do not apply if a police records check has not been provided as required by subsection 3(3.1) or 6(9), as the case may be, and the Ministry of the Solicitor General has advised the Registrar General that it has information about the person that would be included in a police records check, until the person electing or applying for a change of name provides the required police records check.

(4) Exception — This section does not apply in respect of a change of name that has been certified as described in subsection 8(2) by the Attorney General or a person authorized by the Attorney General.

(5) Same — This section does not apply if the person to whose name the application relates is younger than a "young person" as defined in the *Young Offenders Act* (Canada).

1997, c. 17, s. 3

8. (1) Publication, registration and notice — On registering a change of name made under this Act, the Registrar General shall,

> (a) promptly cause a notice of the change of name to be published in *The Ontario Gazette*;

> (b) enter the change of name in the change of name index maintained under section 2 of the *Vital Statistics Act*; and

(b.1) cause notice of the change of name, together with a copy of the police records check that was provided by the person electing or applying for a change of name, to be given to the Ministry of the Solicitor General if the Registrar General was advised under section 7.1 that the Ministry of the Solicitor General has information about the person whose name has been changed that would be included in a police records check.

1997, c. 17, s. 4

(c) in the case of a change of name made on an application under subsection 4(1) or 5(1), cause notice of the change to be given,

    (i) to the sheriff of the appropriate area, if the application discloses an unsatisfied order for payment of money or unsatisfied execution against the property of the person whose name has been changed,

    (ii) to the Registrar of Personal Property Security, if the application discloses that a financing statement registered under the *Personal Property Security Act* names the person as debtor,

    (iii) to the Registrar in Bankruptcy, if the application discloses that the person is an undischarged bankrupt, and

    (iv) to the clerk or registrar of the appropriate court, if the application discloses a pending court proceeding against the person other than a proceeding referred to in clause 4(2)(h.1).

(1.1) Ministry of the Solicitor General, access to records — Despite any other Act,

(a) the Registrar General may, on request from the Ministry of the Solicitor General, provide the Ministry with any information from records in the Registrar General's possession or control that may be relevant in determining whether there has been a change of name of a person and, if there has been a change of name of the person, any information from such records regarding or relevant to the change of name;

(b) the Registrar General may give the Ministry of the Solicitor General access to any or all the records in the Registrar General's possession or control in order to allow the Ministry to search for and obtain the information described in clause (a).

(1.2) Further notice by Ministry of the Solicitor General — On receiving notice under clause (1)(b.1) or receiving or obtaining information under subsection (1.1), the Ministry of the Solicitor General may, despite any other Act, cause the information or notice of the change of name, together with any information in the police records check, to be given to the Ministry of Correctional Services, the Ministry of Transportation, any police force or any other ministry, agency or institution that, in the opinion of the Ministry, should know about the change of name for law enforcement or corrections purposes.

(1.3) Personal information — Where a disclosure is made under subsection (1.1) or (1.2), the Registrar General and the Ministry of the Solicitor General shall disclose personal information about an individual and the Ministry of the Solicitor General and any ministry, agency or institution that receives information under subsection (1.2) shall collect such information and subsections 39(2) of the *Freedom of Information and Protection of Privacy Act* and 29(2) of the *Municipal Freedom of Information and Protection of Privacy Act* do not apply to the collection of personal information under clause (1)(b.1) or subsection (1.1) or (1.2).

(1.4) Incidental information not to be disclosed — The Ministry of the Solicitor General shall not, under subsection (1.2), give any information that it has obtained under clause (1.1)(b), other than information that may be relevant in determining whether there has been a change of name of a person or, if there has been a change of name of the person, any information regarding or relevant to the change of name.

(2) Where change of name to be kept confidential — Despite subsection (1), if the Attorney General or a person authorized by the Attorney General certifies that a change of name is intended to prevent significant harm to the person to whose name the application relates, and certifies that he or she has reviewed a police records check as described in subsection 6(10) in respect of that person

(a) the application shall be sealed and filed in the office of the Registrar General;

(b) no notice of the change of name shall be published in *The Ontario Gazette* and no notice of the application or of the change of name shall be given to the Ministry of the Solicitor General or any person;

(c) if the person's birth was registered in Ontario, the original registration shall be withdrawn from the registration files and sealed in a separate file, and a new birth registration showing the new name shall be made; and

(d) the change of name shall not be entered in the change of name index or noted under section 31 of the *Vital Statistics Act*.

(3) Same — Subsection (1.1) does not apply in respect of a change of name that has been certified as described in subsection (2) by the Attorney General or a person authorized by the Attorney General.

1997, c. 17, s. 4

SUBSTITUTION OF NEW NAME

9. Substitution of new name in documents — A person whose name has been changed under this Act is entitled to have the change of name noted on any public or private record or document that mentions the person's name, on payment of any applicable fee prescribed by law and on producing satisfactory proof of identity and the change of name certificate or new birth certificate.

REVOCATION OF CHANGE OF NAME

10. (1) Application to revoke change of name — A person who has reason to believe that a change of name has been obtained under this Act or a predecessor of it by fraud or misrepresentation or for an improper purpose may apply to the court for an order revoking the change of name.

(2) Affidavit giving reasons — The application shall be accompanied by the applicant's affidavit setting out the reasons for believing that the change of name was obtained by fraud or misrepresentation or for an improper purpose.

(3) Service of applications — Notice of the application shall be served on such persons as the court directs.

(4) Revocation of change of name — If the court is satisfied that the change of name was obtained by fraud or misrepresentation or for an improper purpose, the court may by order revoke it in whole or in part.

(5) Clerk to send copy of order to Registrar General — The clerk of the court shall send a certified copy of the order to the Registrar General.

(6) Surrender of certificate on revocation; notice — On receiving a copy of the order, the Registrar General,

    (a) may require the person to whom a birth certificate or change of name certificate has been issued in connection with the change of name to surrender it immediately;

    (b) shall promptly cause a notice of the revocation to be published in *The Ontario Gazette*; and

    (b.1) shall cause notice of the revocation to be given to the Ministry of the Solicitor General if the Ministry was given notice of the change of name under clause 8(1)(b.1); and

    (c) shall cause notice of the revocation to be given to any persons who were given notice of the change of name under clause 8(1)(c) (notice to sheriff, etc.).

(7) Further notice — On receiving notice under clause (6)(b.1), the Ministry of the Solicitor General shall give notice of the revocation to every ministry, police force, agency or institution to whom the Ministry had previously given notice under subsection 8(1.2) and subsections 39(2) of the *Freedom of Information and Protection of Privacy Act* and 29(2) of the *Municipal Freedom of Information and Protection of Privacy Act* do not apply to the collection of personal information under clause (6)(b.1) or this subsection.

1997, c. 17, s. 5

APPEALS

11. (1) Appeal to Superior Court of Justice — An appeal from an order under subsection 4(4) or 5(4) (dispensing with consent) may be made to the Superior Court of Justice by the applicant or the person whose consent is dispensed with.

(2) Idem — An appeal from an order under subsection 7(5) (review of Registrar General's refusal of application) may be made to the Superior Court of Justice by the applicant or the Registrar General.

(3) Idem — An appeal from an order under subsection 10(4) (revocation of change of name) may be made to the Superior Court of Justice by,

    (a) the applicant;

    (b) the Registrar General; or

    (c) the person to whose change of name the order relates.

2000, c. 26, Sched. B, s. 5(3)

OFFENCES

12. (1) Obtaining change of name by fraud, etc. — A person who obtains a change of name under this Act by fraud or misrepresentation is guilty of an offence and on conviction is liable to a fine of not more than $2,000.

(2) Use of name obtained by fraud, etc. — A person who uses a name in respect of which he or she was convicted under subsection (1) is guilty of an offence and on conviction is liable to a fine of not more than $2,000.

(3) Use of name after refusal or revocation — A person who uses a name,

    (a) that he or she sought to adopt in an application that was refused under section 7; or

(b) that was the subject of an order under subsection 10(4) (revocation of change of name),

knowing that the change of name was refused or revoked, as the case may be, is guilty of an offence and on conviction is liable to a fine of not more than $2,000.

(4) Failure to surrender certificate on revocation — A person who knowingly fails to comply with a requirement of the Registrar General under clause 10(6)(a) (surrender of certificate upon revocation of change) is guilty of an offence and on conviction is liable to a fine of not more than $2,000.

(5) Use of superseded certificate — A person who, after his or her name is changed under this Act, knowingly uses a birth certificate or change of name certificate that was issued in Ontario and shows a former name of the person is guilty of an offence and on conviction is liable to a fine of not more than $2,000.

(6) Limitation one year — No proceeding shall be commenced in respect of an offence under this Act more than one year after the Deputy Registrar General appointed under the *Vital Statistics Act* becomes aware of the facts on which the proceeding is based.

(7) Evidence — A statement as to the time when the Deputy Registrar General became aware of the facts on which the proceeding is based, purporting to be certified by the Deputy Registrar General, is, without proof of that person's office or signature, evidence of the facts stated in it.

12.1 Power of Registrar General — The Registrar General may by order set and collect fees for,

(a) elections under subsection 3(1) made at the time of marriage or at the time of filing a joint declaration;

(b) elections under subsection 3(2) and elections under subsection 3(1) made after the time of marriage or after the time of filing a joint declaration;

(c) applications under subsectins 4(1) and 5(1);

(d) any other services that the Registrar General provides under this Act,

1998, c. 18, Sched. E, s. 48

REGULATIONS

13. Regulations — The Lieutenant Governor in Council may make regulations,

(a) prescribing the manner in which elections are to be made under subsections 3(1) and (2) (election by spouse, etc., to change surname);

(b) [Repealed 1998, c. 18, Sched. E, s. 49.]

(c) [Repealed 1998, c. 18, Sched. E, s. 49.]

(d) prescribing the documents to be provided where elections are made under subsections 3(1) and (2);

(e) [Repealed 1998, c. 18, Sched. E, s. 49.]

(f) prescribing forms;

(g) prescribing classes of persons for the purpose of subsection 6(3) (accompanying statement).

1998, c. 18, Sched. E, s. 49

ONT. REG. 68 — GENERAL

made under the *Change of Name Act*

R.R.O. 1990, Reg. 68, as am. O. Reg. 326/91; 41/00.

1. (1) Election by spouse, etc. — An election under subsection 3(1) of the Act (election by spouse, etc., to change surname) shall be made by filing Form 1 with the Registrar General and providing the applicable prescribed document, if any.

(2) An election under subsection 3(2) of the Act (resuming name when marriage dissolved, etc.) shall be made by filing Form 2 with the Registrar General and providing the applicable prescribed document, if any.

(3) The prescribed documents for the purpose of elections under subsections 3(1) and (2) of the Act are:

    1 A certificate of the spouses' marriage, issued by the proper authority of the jurisdiction where the marriage was solemnized.

    2 A certificate of the death of one of the spouses, issued by the proper authority of the jurisdiction where the death occurred.

    3 A certificate of the spouses' divorce or of the annulment of their marriage, issued by the proper authority of the jurisdiction where the divorce or annulment was granted.

(4) If all or part of a prescribed document is written in a language other than English or French, a translation into English or French, together with the translator's written declaration, shall be provided with the prescribed document.

(5) The translator's declaration shall state that,

    (a) the translator understands both English or French and the language of the original;

    (b) the translator is of the opinion that the translation is complete and correct.

(6) The joint declaration referred to in subsection 3(6) of the Act (conjugal relationship) shall be in Form 3.

(7) The declaration referred to in subsection 3(7) of the Act (revocation of joint declaration) shall be in Form 4.

2. (1) Change of name of person over sixteen — An application under subsection 4(1) of the Act (change of name) shall be in Form 5.

(2) A notice of application given under subsection 4(2) of the Act (notice to spouse, etc.) may be in Form 6.

(3) The written consent referred to in subsection 4(3) of the Act (consent to application of person under eighteen) may be in Form 7.

3. (1) Change of child's name — An application under subsection 5(1) of the Act (change of child's name) shall be in Form 5.

(2) The written consent referred to in subsection 5(2) of the Act (consent of persons with custody, etc.) may be in Form 7.

(3) A notice of application given under subsection 5(6) of the Act (notice to persons with access) may be in Form 6.

(4) A notice of application given under subsection 5(7) of the Act (notice to spouse, etc.) may be in Form 6.

4. (1) Accompanying Statement — The statement referred to in subsection 6(3) of the Act (accompanying statement) shall be in Form 8.

(2) The following classes of persons are prescribed for the purpose of subsection 6(3) of the Act:

1. Provincial judges appointed under the *Courts of Justice Act*.

2. Justices of the peace appointed under the *Justices of the Peace Act*.

3. Chiefs of Indian bands that are located in Ontario.

4. Persons authorized under the *Marriage Act* to solemnize marriages.

5. Legally qualified medical practitioners.

6. Members of The Law Society of Upper Canada.

7. Heads of municipal councils in Ontario.

8. Clerks of municipalities in Ontario.

9. Principals of elementary and secondary schools, as defined in the *Education Act*.

10. Managers or signing officers of Ontario branches of banks listed in Schedule I or II of the *Bank Act* (Canada), loan corporations, trust corporations, credit unions and caisses populaires.

5. Fees — The following fees are payable under the Act:

1.	For an election under subsection 3(1) of the Act made at the time of marriage or at the time of filing a joint declaration	no fee
2.	For an election under subsection 3(1) of the Act made after the time of marriage or after the time of filing a joint declaration	$25
3.	For an election under subsection 3(2) of the Act	25
4.	For an application under subsection 4(1) of the Act	137
5.	For an application under subsection 5(1) of the Act, except as described in paragraph 6	137
6.	For an application under subsection 5(1) of the Act that is made simultaneously with an application under subsection 4(1) of the Act by the same applicant	21

(O. Reg. 326/91)

Schedule [Forms]

Form 1 — Change of Name Act

Election to Change Surname

A. — While Married

I, ...(forename(s)) (surname immediately before marriage), of

.... (city, town or village) was married to

....(forename(s)) (surname immediately before marriage)

on .... (date) at ....(city, town or village and province, state or country where marriage took place)

We are still married to each other.

I elect to change my surname to . . . .

I have attached a marriage cerificate issued by the vital statistics office of the province, state or country where the marriage took place.

I have completed Part C of this form.

I have attached all my birth certificates and change of name certificates that are in my possession.

.... (date)

.... (signature of person making election)

(For Office Use)

Marriage Registration Number..

B. — While Living in Conjugal Relationship Outside Marriage

I, ...(forename(s)) (surname immediately before filing declaration), of

....(city, town or village) began living in a conjugal

relationship outside marriage with.................................. (forename(s)) (surname immediately before filing declaration)

on ....(date). We still live together.

I elect to change my surname to . . . .

I have attached a joint declaration (Form 3) signed by myself and . . . . . . (forename(s)) (present surname)

I have completed Part C of this form.

I have attached all my birth certificates and change of name certificates that are in my possession.

.... (date)

.... (signature of person making election)

Form 1   Ont. Reg. 68 — General

C. — Details About Myself

Present forename(s) and surname ....

Proposed surname ....

Date of birth ....

Place of birth ....

Birth registration number (if known) ....

Father's forename(s) and surname..

Mother's forename(s) and surname at her birth ....

....

FOR OFFICE USE

CHANGE OF NAME REGISTRATION NUMBER ....

REGISTRATION   DATE..................................   DEPUTY   REGISTRAR
GENERAL..................................

O. Reg. 64/87, Form 1.

Form 2 — Change of Name Act

Election to Resume Former Surname

A. — When Marriage Ends

I, ...forename(s)) (present surname), of

....(city, town or village) was married to

....(forename(s) and surname of former spouse)

The marriage was dissolved on the ....(date) by

❑ divorce

❑ annulment

❑ death

I elect to resume the following surname: .... (surname immediately before marriage)

I have attached one of the following:

❑ original or certified copy of certificate of divorce

❑ original or certified copy of certificate of annulment of marriage

❑ death certificate issued by the vital statistics office of the province, state or country where the death took place

I have completed Part C of this form.

I have attached all my birth certificates and change of name certificates that are in my possession.

....date

.... (signature of person making election)

(For Office Use)

Death Registration Number..................................

Divorce Registration Number ....

B. — When Conjugal Relationship Outside Marriage Ends

I, ...(forename(s)) (present surname), of

....(city, town or village) filed a joint declaration

of conjugal relationship with .... (forename(s) and surname of former spouse)

on .... (date)

The relationship has ended.

I elect to resume the following surname: .... (surname immediately before filing declaration)

I have attached my declaration (Form 4) stating that the relationship has ended.

I have completed Part C of this form.

I have attached all my birth certificates and change of name certificates that are in my possession.

.... (date)

.... (signature of person making election)

C. — Details About Myself

Present forename(s) and surname . . . .

Proposed surname . . . .

Date of birth . . . .

Place of birth . . . .

Birth registration number (if known) . . . .

Father's forename(s) and surname . . . .

Mother's forename(s) and surname at her birth . . . .

FOR OFFICE USE

CHANGE OF NAME REGISTRATION NUMBER . . . .

REGISTRATION   DATE   ....DEPUTY   REGISTRAR GENERAL....................................

O. Reg. 64/87, Form 2.

Form 3 — Change of Name Act

Joint Declaration of Conjugal Relationship

We, ... (forename(s)   and   surname)   and

.... (forename(s)   and   surname)   of

.... (city, town or village) declare that we began living together in a conjugal relationship outside marriage on .... (date) and that we still live together.

. . . . (date)

.... (signature)

.... (signature)

O. Reg. 41/00, s. 1

Form 4 — Change of Name Act

Declaration that Conjugal Relationship has Ended

I, ...(forename(s) and present surname) of
.... (city, town or village) filed a joint declaration of
conjugal relationship with .... (forename(s) and surname of other person who made declaration of conjugal relationship) on ....
(date) I declare that the relationship has ended.

..............................(date) .... (signature of person making this declaration)

O. Reg. 41/00, s. 1

Form 5 — Change of Name Act

Application for Change of Name

Part A

I, ...   (present   forename(s)   and   surname)   of
....   (current   address)
.... apply to change

❏ my own name

❏ my own name and the name(s) of my child(ren)

❏ the name(s) of my child(ren)

.... (perforated)

Change of Name Registration

(*For Office Use* Registration Number

Give the following information about every person whose name you are applying to change:

PRESENT NAME .... (forename(s)) (surname)

PROPOSED NAME .... (forename(s)) (surname)

Date of birth .... Place of birth .... (city, town or village and province, state or country)

Sex ....

Birth registration number (if known) . . . .

Father's forename(s) and surname . . . .

Former name(s), if any . . . .

Mother's forename(s) and surname . . . .

Former name(s), if any . . . .

(*For Office Use*)

This application is complete. ❏

The required documents have been submitted. ❏

..................................(date of registration)

.... (signature of Deputy Registrar General)

Part B

You must complete a *separate set* of Part B for each person whose name is being changed. Give complete answers. If there is not enough space, add extra pages.

OTHER INFORMATION ABOUT .... (person's present name)

Name at birth .... (forename(s)) (surname)

1. What is your marital status?

❑married ❑divorced ❑widowed ❑never married

If you are married, what was your spouse's name before marriage?

.... (forename(s)) (surname)

Date and place of marriage ....

Have you filed a joint declaration of conjugal relationship with another person?

❑yes ❑no

If yes, has it been revoked?

❑yes ❑no

If the declaration has not been revoked, what is the other person's name?

.... (forename(s)) (surname)

Date and place declaration filed ....

2. What are the reasons for the change of name? Give a full explanation.

....

3. How long have you lived in Ontario? ....

Current address ....

4. Have you ever been convicted of a criminal offence?

❑yes ❑no

(If the only offence of which you have ever been convicted has been pardoned under the *Criminal Records Act* (Canada), answer "No".)

If yes, give full details

....

Have you ever been convicted of a criminal offence under the *Young Offenders Act* (Canada)?

❑yes ❑no

(If the record of the offence is required to be destroyed under the *Y.O.A.* (Canada), answer "No".)

If yes, give full details

....

5. Are there any unsatisfied orders for payment of money, any unsatisfied executions or any pending court proceedings against you?

❑yes ❑none that I am aware of

If yes, give full details

....

6. Are there any liens or security interests against your personal property?

❑yes ❑none that I am aware of

If yes, give full details

. . . .

7. Have any financing statements naming you as debtor been registered under the *Personal Property Security Act*?

❑yes ❑none that I am aware of

If yes, give full details

. . . .

8. Are you an undischarged bankrupt?

❑yes ❑no

If yes, give full details

. . . .

9. Have you ever changed your name before?

❑yes ❑no

(This includes a woman's adoption of her husband's surname by custom.)

If yes, give full details, including your full names before and after the change

. . . .

10. Have you ever applied for a change of name and been refused?

❑yes ❑no

If yes, give full details

. . . .

Application for Change of Name

Part C

I declare that:

1. (Cross out if application does not relate to a child's name)

I have lawful custody of the child(ren) named in this application and no court order or separation agreement prohibits the change of name.

(Cross out parts that are not applicable.) (A court order made by .... (judge's name) on.................................. (date))

(A separation agreement made by .... (name of one party) and ....(name of other party) on .... (date)) provides that the name of .... (child's present name) shall not be changed without the consent of .... (name of person whose consent is required)

2. The following persons are entitled to notice of this application: (see instructions)

. . . .

I have given notice to each of them, and I have attached *one* of the following in respect of each of them:

A.❑ An acknowledgment of notice, signed by the person.

B.❏ Evidence that I sent notice and a copy of this application to the person, by registered mail or certified mail, at least thirty days before making the application.

3. The consent of the following persons to this application is required: (see instructions)

. . . .

I have attached *one* of the following in respect of each of them.

A.❏ A consent, signed by the person.

B.❏ A certified copy of a court order dispensing with the person's consent.

4. I have also attached to this application the following:

A. All birth certificates and change of name certificates of every person whose name is to be changed by the application that are in my possession.

B. A guarantor's statement. (See instructions)

5. This application is not made for an improper purpose.

6. The information I have provided in this application is true and complete.

I make this solemn declaration conscientiously believing it to be true and knowing it is of the same force and effect as if made under oath.

Declared before me at the ....

of .... in the ....

.... of ....

on the .... day of ...., 19..........

.... (signature of declarant)

.... Commissioner for taking affidavits

O. Reg. 64/87, Form 5.

Form 6 — Change of Name Act

Notice of Application

This gives notice to .... (name of person entitled to notice) of .... (address) that an application will be made under the *Change of Name Act* to change the name of .... (present forename(s) and surname) to .... (proposed forename(s) and surname)

I have enclosed a copy of the application with this notice.

.... (applicant's name)

.... (date)

.... (applicant's signature)

.... (applicant's address)

.... (perforated)

Acknowledgment of Notice

I, ... (forename(s)) (surname) of .... (address) acknowledge that I have received notice and a copy of the application described above.

I am the .... (state relationship) of the person to whose name the application relates.

.... (date)

.... (signature)

Note: When you sign this acknowledgment, you are *not* indicating that you agree or disagree with the application. You are only acknowledging that you have received a copy of the application.

The Registrar General may proceed with the application if satisfied that you were in fact given notice, whether you sign the acknowledgment or not.

Declared before me at the ....

of .... in the ....

.... of ....

on the .... day of ...., 19..........

.... (signature of declarant)

.... Commissioner for taking affidavits

O. Reg. 64/87, Form 6.

Form 7 — Change of Name Act

Consent to Application to Change Child's Name

This consent relates to an application to change the name of .... (present forename(s) and surname) a child who was born on .... (date) at .... (place of birth) to .... (proposed forename(s) and surname)

I, ... (name of person consenting) of .... (address) state that:

❏ I share lawful custody of the child with .... (name)

❏ a court order or separation agreement provides that the child's name shall not be changed without my consent.

❏ I am the child.

I consent to the application.

..........(date)

.... (signature)

Note: Each person whose consent is necessary should complete a separate copy of this form.

O. Reg. 64/87, Form 7.

Form 8 — Change of Name Act

Statement of Guarantor

Part A

Note: The following persons may act as guarantors under Part A:

      Provincial court judges

      Justices of the peace

      Chiefs of Indian bands

Persons authorized to perform marriages

Medical doctors

Lawyers

Heads of municipal councils

Municipal clerks

Elementary and secondary school principals

Managers and signing officers of branches of banks, loan corporations, trust corporations, credit unions and caisses populaires

Guarantors who are not described in this list must complete Part B of this form.

The guarantor must know that each person whose name is to be changed has lived in Ontario for at least one year (or since birth).

I, ...   (forename(s)   and   surname)   of
.... (address) .... (occupation)
state that I know the following person(s) and know that (he) (she) (they) (has) (have) lived in
Ontario since ....(date)

(List present name of each person whose name is to be changed.)

(If a person whose name is to be changed is less than one year old, add the following:

I state that I know the following person(s) and know that (he) (she) (they) (has) (have) lived in Ontario since birth.)

(List present name of each person aged less than one year.)

...................................(date)

.... (guarantor's signature)

Part B

Note: The guarantor who uses Part B must have known each person whose name is to be changed *for at least five years* (or since birth, if the person is less than five years old).

The guarantor must know that each person whose name is to be changed has lived in Ontario for at least one year (or since birth).

I, ... (forename(s) and surname) of .... (address) state
that I have known the following person(s) since .... (date) and know that
(he) (she) (they) (has) (have) lived in Ontario since .... (date)

(List present name of each person whose name is to be changed.)

(If a person whose name is to be changed is less than five but more than one year old, add the following:

I state that I have known the following person(s) since birth and know that (he) (she) (they) (has) (have) lived in Ontario since .... (date))

(List present name of each person who is less than five but more than one year old.)

(If a person whose name is to be changed is less than one year old, add the following:

I state that I have known the following person(s) and know that (he) (she) (they) (has) (have) lived in Ontario since birth.)

(List present name of each person who is less than one year old.)

.... (date)

.... (guarantor's signature)

O. Reg. 64/87, Form 8.

TABLE OF CONCORDANCE

Child and Family Services Act, 1984 S.O. 1984, c. 55	Child and Family Services Act R.S.O. 1990, c. C-11	Child and Family Services Act, 1984 S.O. 1984, c. 55	Child and Family Services Act R.S.O. 1990, c. C-11
1,2	1,2	60	64
3(1)	3(1)	61	65
3(2)	3(2)	62	66
4–23	4–23	63(1)	67(1)
24(1,2)	24(1,2)	63(2)	67(2)
24(3)	24(3)	64	68
24(4)	24(4)	65(1)	69(1)
25-33	25-33	65(2,3)	69(2,3)
34(1–6)	34(1–6)	65(4)	69(4)
34(7)	—	65(5–8)	69(5–8)
34(8–11)	34(7–10)	66	70
35–39	35–39	67	71
40(1)	40(1)	68	72
40(2)	40(2)	69	73
40(2a)	40(3)	70	74
40(3)	40(4)	71	75
40(4)	40(5)	72	76
40(5)	40(6)	73	77
40(6)	40(7)	74(1)	78(1)
40(7–9)	40(8–10)	74(2)	78(2)
40(10–13)	40(11–14)	74(3–7)	78(3–7)
40(14–17)	—	75(1–4)	79(1–4)
40a	41	75(5,6)	79(5,6)
40b	42	75(7)	79(7)
40c	43	76	80
40d	44	77	81
41	45	78	82
42(1)	46(1)	79	83
42(2)	46(2)	80	84
43(1)	47(1)	81	85
43(2,3)	47(2,3)	82	86
44	48	83(1)	87(1)
45	49	83(2)	87(2)

CFSA

Child and Family Services Act, 1984 S.O. 1984, c. 55	Child and Family Services Act R.S.O. 1990, c. C-11	Child and Family Services Act, 1984 S.O. 1984, c. 55	Child and Family Services Act R.S.O. 1990, c. C-11
46	50	—	—
47	51	95	99
48	52	96	100
49	53	97	101
50	54	98	102
51	55	99	103
52	56	100	104
53	57	101	105
54	58	102	106
55	59	103	107
56	60	104	108
57	61	105	109
58	62		
59	63		
106	110	158f	170
107	111	158g	171
—	—	158h	172
130(1)	136(1)	158i	173
130(2,3)	136(2,3)	158j	174
131(1–3)	137(1–3)	159	175
131(4)	137(4)	160(1–3)	176(1–3)
131(5–13)	137(5–13)	160(4)	176(4)
132	138	160(5)	176(5)
133	139	161(1)	177(1)
134	140	161(2)	177(2)
135	141	162	178
136	142	163(1)	179(1)
137	143	163(2)	179(2)
138	144	164	180
139	145	165	181
140(1)	146(1)	166	182
140(2–5)	146(2–5)	166a	183
141	147	167	184
142	148	168	185
143	149	169	186
144	150	170	187
145	151	171	188
146(1)	152(1)	172	189
146(2)	152(2)	173	190

Child and Family Services Act, 1984 S.O. 1984, c. 55	Child and Family Services Act R.S.O. 1990, c. C-11	Child and Family Services Act, 1984 S.O. 1984, c. 55	Child and Family Services Act R.S.O. 1990, c. C-11
146(3,4)	152(3,4)	174	191
147	153	—	—
148	154	191	208
149	155	192	209
150(1–3)	156(1–3)	193	210
150(4–6)	156(5–6)	194	211
151	157	195	212
152(1)	158(1)	196	213
152(2)	158(2)	197	214
152(3)	158(3)	198	215
152(4–6)	158(4–6)	199	216
153	159	—	—
154(1)	160(1)	201	218
154(2)	160(2)	—	—
155	161	203(1)	220(1)
156(1)	162(1)	203(2)	220(2)
156(2,3)	162(2,3)	204	221
157	163	—	—
158	164	206	223
158a	165		
158b	166		
158c	167		
158d	168		
158e	169		

CFSA

CHILD AND FAMILY SERVICES ACT

R.S.O. 1990, c. C.11 [ss. 130, 131, 132(4), (5), 178, 179(1), (2)(a)–(c), (e)–(g), 180–182, 184–191 not in force at date of publication.], as am. S.O. 1992, c. 32, s. 3; 1993, c. 27, Sched.; 1994, c. 27, s. 43(2); 1996, c. 2, s. 62; 1999, c. 2 [ss. 2(3), 11, 23(2), 27, 28, 30(2), (3), (5), 31, 33(2) not in force at date of publication.]; 1999, c. 6, s. 6; 1999, c. 12, Sched. E, s. 1 (Fr.); 1999, c. 12, Sched. G, s. 16; 2001, c. 13, s. 5; 2002, c. 17, Sched. F, s. 1; 2002, c. 18, Sched. D, s. 1.

1. (1) Paramount purpose — The paramount purpose of this Act is to promote the best interests, protection and well being of children.

(2) Other purposes — The additional purposes of this Act, so long as they are consistent with the best interests, protection and well being of children, are:

1. To recognize that while parents may need help in caring for their children, that help should give support to the autonomy and integrity of the family unit and, wherever possible, be provided on the basis of mutual consent.

2. To recognize that the least disruptive course of action that is available and is appropriate in a particular case to help a child should be considered.

3. To recognize that children's services should be provided in a manner that,

    i. respects children's needs for continuity of care and for stable family relationships, and

    ii. takes into account physical and mental developmental differences among children.

4. To recognize that, wherever possible, services to children and their families should be provided in a manner that respects cultural, religious and regional differences.

5. To recognize that Indian and native people should be entitled to provide, wherever possible, their own child and family services, and that all services to Indian and native children and families should be provided in a manner that recognizes their culture, heritage and traditions and the concept of the extended family.

1999, c. 2, s. 1

Transitional Provision

Pursuant to 1999, c. 2, s. 37(5), section 1 of the Child and Family Services Act, *as it read on the day before the March 31, 2000 proclamation of 1999, c. 2, s. 1, continues to apply to any proceeding under Part III, including a status review proceeding, commenced before that date.*

On the day before the proclamation, s. 1 read as follows:

1. Declaration of principles — The purposes of this Act are,

(a) as a paramount objective, to promote the best interests, protection and well-being of children;

(b) to recognize that while parents often need help in caring for their children, that help should give support to the autonomy and integrity of the family unit and, wherever possible, be provided on the basis of mutual consent;

(c) to recognize that the least restrictive or disruptive course of action that is available and is appropriate in a particular case to help a child or family should be followed;

(d) to recognize that children's services should be provided in a manner that,

> *(i) respects children's needs for continuity of care and for stable family relationships, and*

> *(ii) takes into account physical and mental developmental differences among children;*

(e) to recognize that, wherever possible, services to children and their families should be provided in a manner that respects cultural, religious and regional differences; and

(f) to recognize that Indian and native people should be entitled to provide, wherever possible, their own child and family services, and that all services to Indian and native children and families should be provided in a manner that recognizes their culture, heritage and traditions and the concept of the extended family.

2. (1) French language services — Service providers shall, where appropriate, make services to children and their families available in the French language.

(2) Duties of service providers — Service providers shall ensure,

(a) that children and their parents have an opportunity where appropriate to be heard and represented when decisions affecting their interests are made and to be heard when they have concerns about the services they are receiving; and

(b) that decisions affecting the interests and rights of children and their parents are made according to clear, consistent criteria and are subject to procedural safeguards.

Interpretation

3. (1) Definitions — In this Act,

"agency" means a corporation; *("agence")*

"approved agency" means an agency that is approved under subsection 8(1) of Part I (Flexible Services); *("agence agréé")*

"approved service" means a service provided,

(a) under subsection 7(1) of Part I or with the support of a grant or contribution made under subsection 7(2) of that Part,

(b) by an approved agency, or

(c) under the authority of a licence; *("service agréé")*

"band" has the same meaning as in the *Indian Act* (Canada); *("bande")*

"Board" means the Child and Family Services Review Board continued under Part IX (Licensing); *("Commission")*

"child" means a person under the age of eighteen years; *("enfant")*

"child development service" means a service for a child with a developmental disability or physical disability, for the family of a child with a developmental disability or physical disability, or for the child and the family; *("service de développement de l'enfant")*

"child treatment service" means a service for a child with a mental or psychiatric disorder, for the family of a child with a mental or psychiatric disorder, or for the child and the family; *("service de traitement de l'enfant")*

"child welfare service" means,

    (a) a residential or non-residential service, including a prevention service,

    (b) a service provided under Part III (Child Protection),

    (c) a service provided under Part VII (Adoption), or

    (d) individual or family counselling; *("service de bien-être de l'enfance")*

"community support service" means a support service or prevention service provided in the community for children and their families; *("service communautaire d'appoint")*

"court" means the Ontario Court of Justice or the Family Court of the Superior Court of Justice; *("tribunal")*

"developmental disability" means a condition of mental impairment present or occurring in a person's formative years that is associated with limitations in adaptive behaviour; *("déficience intellectuelle")*

"developmental handicap" [Repealed 2001, c. 13, s. 5(2).]

"Director" means a Director appointed under subsection 5(1) of Part I (Flexible Services); *("directeur")*

"foster care" means the provision of residential care to a child, by and in the home of a person who,

    (a) receives compensation for caring for the child, except under the *Ontario Works Act, 1997*, the *Ontario Disability Support Program Act, 1997* or the *Family Benefits Act*, and

    (b) is not the child's parent or a person with whom the child has been placed for adoption under Part VII,

and "foster home" and "foster parent" have corresponding meanings; *("soins fournis par une famille d'accueil", "famille d'accueil", "père de famille d'accueil", "mère de famille d'accueil")*

Proposed Amendment — "foster care"

"foster care" means the provision of residential care to a child, by and in the home of a person who,

    (a) receives compensation for caring for the child, except under the *Ontario Works Act, 1997* or the *Ontario Disability Support Program Act, 1997*, and

    (b) is not the child's parent or a person with whom the child has been placed for adoption under Part VII,

and "foster home" and "foster parent" have corresponding meanings; *("soins fournis par une famille d'accueil", "famille d'accueil", "père de famille d'accueil", "mère de famille d'accueil")*

1999, c. 2, s. 2(3) [Not in force at date of publication.]

"Indian" has the same meaning as in the *Indian Act* (Canada); *("Indien")*

"licence" means a licence issued under Part IX (Licensing), and "licensed" and "licensee" have corresponding meanings; *("permis", "autorisé en vertu d'un permis", "titulaire de permis")*

"local director" means a local director appointed under section 16 of Part I (Flexible Services); *("directeur local")*

"Minister" means the Minister of Community and Social Services; *("ministre")*

"municipality" does not include a lower-tier municipality that is situated within a regional municipality; *("municipalité")*

"native community" means a community designated by the Minister under section 209 of Part X (Indian and Native Child and Family Services; *("communauté autochtone")*

"native person" means a person who is a member of a native community but is not a member of a band, and "native child" has a corresponding meaning; *("autochtone", "enfant autochtone")*

"order" includes a refusal to make an order; *("arrêté, order et ordonnance")*

"prescribed" means prescribed by the regulations; *("prescrit")*

"program supervisor" means a program supervisor appointed under subsection 5(2) of Part I (Flexible Services); *("superviseur de programme")*

"regulations" means the regulations made under this Act; *("règlements")*

"residential service" means boarding, lodging and associated supervisory, sheltered or group care provided for a child away from the home of the child's parent, and "residential care" and "residential placement" have corresponding meanings; *("service en établissement", "soins en établissement", "placement en établissement")*

"service" means

    (a) a child development service,

    (b) a child treatment service,

    (c) a child welfare service,

    (d) a community support service, or

    (e) a young offenders service; *("service")*

"service provider" means,

    (a) the Minister,

    (b) an approved agency,

    (c) a society,

    (d) a licensee, or

    (e) a person who provides an approved service or provides a service purchased by the Minister or an approved agency,

but does not include a foster parent; *("fournisseur de services")*

"society" means an approved agency designated as a children's aid society under subsection 15(2) of Part I (Flexible Services); *("société")*

"Tribunal" means the Licence Appeal Tribunal; *("Tribunal")*

"young offenders service" means a service provided under Part IV (Young Offenders) or under a program established under that Part. *("service aux jeunes contrevenants").*

(2) Idem: "parent" — In this Act, a reference to a child's parent shall be deemed to be a reference to,

    (a) both parents, where both have custody of the child;

    (b) one parent, where that parent has lawful custody of the child or the other parent is unavailable or unable to act as the context requires; or

    (c) another individual, where that individual has lawful custody of the child,

except where this Act provides otherwise.
1999, c. 2, s. 2(1), (2); 1999, c. 12, Sched. G, s. 16(1); 2001, c. 13, s. 5(1)–(3); 2002, c. 17, Sched. F, s. 1

Consents and Participation in Agreements

4. (1) Definitions — In this section,

"capacity" means the capacity to understand and appreciate the nature of a consent or agreement and the consequences of giving, withholding or revoking the consent or making, not making or terminating the agreement; *("jouit de toutes ses facultés mentales")* and

"nearest relative", when used in reference to a person who is less than 16 years old, means the person with lawful custody of him or her, and when used in reference to a person who is 16 years old or more, means the person who would be authorized to give or refuse consent to a treatment on his or her behalf under the *Health Care Consent Act, 1996* if he or she were incapable with respect to the treatment under that Act. *("parent le plus proche")*

(2) Elements of valid consent or agreement, etc. — A person's consent or revocation of a consent or participation in or termination of an agreement under this Act is valid if, at the time the consent is given or revoked or the agreement is made or terminated, the person,

    (a) has capacity;

    (b) is reasonably informed as to the nature and consequences of the consent or agreement, and of alternatives to it;

    (c) gives or revokes the consent or executes the agreement or notice of termination voluntarily, without coercion or undue influence; and

    (d) has had a reasonable opportunity to obtain independent advice.

(3) Where person lacks capacity — A person's nearest relative may give or revoke a consent or participate in or terminate an agreement on the person's behalf if it has been determined on the basis of an assessment, not more than one year before the nearest relative acts on the person's behalf, that the person does not have capacity.

(4) Exception — Subsection (3) does not apply to a consent under section 137 (consents to adoption) of Part VII (Adoption) or to a parent's consent referred to in clause 37(2)(l) (child in need of protection) of Part III (Child Protection).

(5) Consent, etc., of minor — A person's consent or revocation of a consent or participation in or termination of an agreement under this Act is not invalid by reason only that the person is less than eighteen years old.

1992, c. 32, s. 3; 1996, c. 2, s. 62

PART I — FLEXIBLE SERVICES

Directors and Program Supervisors

5. (1) Appointment of Director — The Minister may appoint any person as a Director to perform any or all of the duties and functions and exercise any or all of the powers of a Director under this Act and the regulations.

(2) Appointment of program supervisor — The Minister may appoint any person as a program supervisor to perform any or all of the duties and functions and exercise any or all of the powers of a program supervisor under this Act and the regulations.

(3) Limitations, etc., on appointments — The Minister may set out in an appointment made under this section any conditions or limitations to which it is subject.

(4) Remuneration and expenses — The remuneration and expenses of a person appointed under this section who is not a public servant under the *Public Service Act* shall be fixed by the Minister and shall be paid out of legislative appropriations.

(5) Reports and information — A service provider shall,

(a) make the prescribed reports and furnish the prescribed information to the Minister, in the prescribed form and at the prescribed intervals; and

(b) make a report to the Minister whenever the Minister requests it, in the form and containing the information specified by the Minister.

6. (1) Powers of program supervisor — For the purpose of ensuring compliance with this Act and the regulations a program supervisor may, at all reasonable times, upon producing proper identification, enter premises where an approved service is provided, inspect the facilities, the service provided, the books of account and the records relating to the service, and make copies of those books and records or remove them from the premises to copy them as may be reasonably required.

(2) Offence — No person shall hinder, obstruct or attempt to hinder or obstruct a program supervisor in the performance of the program supervisor's duties or knowingly give false information about an approved service to a program supervisor.

(3) Idem — No service provider or person in charge of premises where an approved service is provided shall refuse to give a program supervisor access to the books and records referred to in subsection (1) or refuse to give a program supervisor information about the approved service that the program supervisor reasonably requires.

(4) Regulations re exercise of power of entry — A program supervisor shall exercise the power of entry set out in subsection (1) in accordance with the regulations.

Approvals and Funding

7. (1) Provision of services directly or by purchase — The Minister may,

(a) provide services and establish, operate and maintain facilities for the provision of services; and

(b) make agreements with persons, municipalities and agencies for the provision of services,

and may make payments for those services and facilities out of legislative appropriations.

(2) Grants and contributions for services, consultation, etc. — The Minister may make grants and contributions, out of legislative appropriations, to any person, organization or municipality for consultation, research and evaluation with respect to services and for the provision of services.

8. (1) Approval of agencies — Where the Minister is satisfied that an agency is, with financial assistance under this Part and the regulations, financially capable of establishing, maintaining and operating a service and that its affairs are carried on under competent management in good faith, the Minister may approve the agency to provide that service.

(2) Funding for establishment of services — Where the Minister intends to approve an agency to provide a service under subsection (1), the Minister may enter into an agreement with the agency for the establishment of the service.

(3) Financial assistance, etc. — Where the Minister approves an agency to provide a service under subsection (1), the Minister may give the agency financial and other assistance, in accordance with the regulations.

(4) Effective date — The Minister's approval under subsection (1) shall be deemed to have retroactive effect if the Minister so specifies.

9. (1) Approval of premises for provision of services — Where the Minister is satisfied that premises are suitable for providing a service, the Minister may approve all or any part of the premises for the provision of the service by an approved agency and may give the agency financial and other assistance in accordance with the regulations, for the maintenance and operation of the premises and the provision of the service.

(2) Approval may relate to all or part of building, etc. — The Minister's approval under subsection (1) may specify a building, a group of buildings, part of a building or a location in a building as the approved premises.

(3) Effective date — The Minister's approval of premises under subsection (1) shall be deemed to have retroactive effect if the Minister so specifies, but it shall not be deemed to take effect on a day before the Minister's approval of the agency concerned becomes effective under section 8.

10. (1) Terms and conditions — The Minister may impose terms and conditions on an approval given under subsection 8(1) or 9(1) and, upon reasonable written notice to the approved agency, may vary, remove or amend the terms and conditions or impose new terms and conditions.

(2) Duty of Director — A Director shall review any objections from an approved agency which has received notice under subsection (1).

(3) Transfer of assets — An approved agency shall not transfer or assign any of its assets acquired with financial assistance from the Province of Ontario, except in accordance with the regulations.

(4) Services to persons over eighteen — The Minister may,

    (a) provide services under clause 7(1)(a);

    (b) make agreements for the provision of services under clause 7(1)(b);

    (c) make grants and contributions for the provision of services under subsection 7(2);

    (d) approve agencies for the provision of services under subsection 8(1);

    (e) approve premises for the provision of services under subsection 9(1),

to persons who are not children, and to their families, as if those persons were children.

11. Co-ordinating or advisory groups — The Minister may make agreements with persons, organizations or municipalities for the establishment, support and operation of co-ordinating or advisory groups or committees, may make payments for the purpose out of legislative appropriations and may give other assistance for the purpose.

12. Security for payment of funds — The Minister may, as a condition of making a payment under this Part or the regulations, require the recipient of the funds to secure them by way of mortgage, lien, registration of agreement or in such other manner as the Minister determines.

13. (1) By-laws of approved agency — An approved agency shall file a certified copy of its by-laws and of any amendment to them with the Minister forthwith after they are made.

(2) Idem — The by-laws of an approved agency shall contain the prescribed provisions.

(3) Band or native community representatives — An approved agency that provides services to Indian or native children and families shall have the prescribed number of band or native community representatives on its board of directors, appointed in the prescribed manner and for the prescribed terms.

(4) Employee may not sit on board — An employee of an approved agency shall not be a member of the agency's board of directors.

14. Placements must comply with Act and regulations — No approved agency shall place a child in a residential placement except in accordance with this Act and the regulations.

Children's Aid Societies

15. (1) Definition — In this section, **"prescribed"** means prescribed in a regulation made by the Minister under subsection 214(4) of Part XI (Regulations). *("prescrit")*

(2) Designation of children's aid society — The Minister may designate an approved agency as a children's aid society for a specified territorial jurisdiction and for any or all of the functions set out in subsection (3), may impose terms and conditions on a designation and may vary, remove or amend the terms and conditions or impose new terms and conditions or impose new terms and conditions at any time, and may at any time amend a designation to provide that the society is no longer designated for a particular function set out in subsection (3) or to alter the society's territorial jurisdiction.

(3) Functions of society — The functions of a children's aid society are to,

(a) investigate allegations or evidence that children who are under the age of sixteen years or are in the society's care or under its supervision may be in need of protection;

(b) protect, where necessary, children who are under the age of sixteen years or are in the society's care or under its supervision;

(c) provide guidance, counselling and other services to families for protecting children or for the prevention of circumstances requiring the protection of children;

(d) provide care for children assigned or committed to its care under this Act;

(e) supervise children assigned to its supervision under this Act;

(f) place children for adoption under Part VII; and

(g) perform any other duties given to it by this or any other Act.

(4) Prescribed standards, etc. — A society shall,

(a) provide the prescribed standard of services in its performance of its functions; and

(b) follow the prescribed procedures and practices.

(5) [Repealed 2002, c. 18, Sched. D, s. 1.]

(6) Protection from personal liability — No action shall be instituted against an officer or employee of a society for an act done in good faith in the execution or intended execution of the person's duty or for an alleged neglect or default in the execution in good faith of the person's duty.

2002, c. 18, Sched. D, s. 1

16. Appointment of local director — Every society shall appoint a local director with the prescribed qualifications, powers and duties.

17. (1) Duties of Director with respect to societies — A Director,

(a) shall advise and supervise societies;

(b) shall inspect or direct and supervise the inspection of the operation and records of societies;

(c) shall exercise the powers and duties of a society in any area in which no society is functioning;

(d) shall inspect or direct and supervise the inspection of places in which children in the care of societies are placed; and

(e) shall ensure that societies provide the standard of services and follow the procedures and practices required by subsection 15(4).

(2) Director may designate places of safety — A Director may designate a place as a place of safety, and may designate a class of places as places of safety, for the purposes of Part III (Child Protection).

18. [Repealed 1999, c. 2, s. 3.]

19. (1) [Repealed 1999, c. 2, s. 4(1).]

(2) Payments by Minister — The Minister shall pay to every society out of legislative appropriations an amount determined in accordance with the regulations.

(3) [Repealed 1999, c. 2, s. 4(1).]

(4) How society's estimates determined — A society's estimated expenditures shall be determined and shall be approved by the Minister in accordance with the regulations.

(5) [Repealed 1999, c. 2, s. 4(1).]

(6) Manner of payment — An amount payable to a society under subsection (2), including advances on expenditures before they are incurred, shall be paid at the times and in the manner determined by the Minister.

1999, c. 2, s. 4

20. (1) Power to make levies — [Repealed 1999, c. 2, s. 5.]

(2) Society deemed to be a local board — A society shall be deemed to be a local board of each municipality in which it has jurisdiction for the purposes of the *Ontario Municipal Employees Retirement System Act* and the *Municipal Conflict of Interest Act*.

20.1 Directives to societies — A Director may issue directives to one or more societies, including directives respecting their provision of services under this Act.

1999, c. 2, s. 6

Agreements with Other Governments

21. Minister may make agreements with other governments — The Minister may, with the approval of the Lieutenant Governor in Council, make agreements on behalf of the Government of Ontario with the Crown in right of Canada and with the Crown in right of any other province of Canada respecting services under this Act or the care or protection of children.

Revocation and Take-Over Powers

22. (1) Powers of Minister — Where the Minister believes on reasonable grounds that,

(a) an approved agency is not providing services in accordance with this Act or the regulations or in accordance with any term or condition imposed on the approval under subsection 8(1) or 9(1) or, in the case of a society, on the designation under subsection 15(2);

(b) a director, officer or employee of an approved agency has contravened or knowingly permitted any person under his or her control and direction to contravene any provision of this Act or the regulations or any term or condition imposed on the approval under subsection 8(1) or 9(1) or, in the case of a society, on the designation under subsection 15(2);

(c) approval of the agency under subsection 8(1) or of the premises under subsection 9(1) would be refused if it were being applied for in the first instance; or

(d) in the case of a society, the society,

(i) is not able to or fails to perform any or all of its functions under section 15,

(ii) fails to perform any or all of its functions in any part of its territorial jurisdiction, or

(iii) fails to follow a directive issued under section 20.1.

the Minister may,

(e) revoke or suspend the approval; or

(f) in the case of a society,

(i) revoke or suspend the designation under subsection 15(2),

(ii) remove any or all of the members of the board of directors and appoint others in their place, or

(iii) operate and manage the society in the place of the board of directors.

(2) Notice of proposal — Where the Minister proposes to act under clause 1(e) or (f), the Minister shall serve notice of the proposal and written reasons for it on the approved agency, unless the agency has requested that the Minister so act or has consented to the Minister's proposal.

(3) Request for hearing — A notice under subsection (2) shall inform the agency that it is entitled to a hearing under this section if the agency mails or delivers to the Minister, within sixty days after the notice under subsection (2) is served, a written request for a hearing.

(4) Where agency does not request hearing — Where the agency does not require a hearing under subsection (3), the Minister may carry out the proposal stated in the Minister's notice under subsection (2) without a hearing.

(5) Hearing — Where the agency requires a hearing under subsection (3),

(a) if the Minister proposes to act under clause (1)(e) only, the Minister; and

(b) in all other cases, the Lieutenant Governor in Council,

shall appoint one or more persons not employed by the Ministry to hear the matter and recommend whether the Minister should carry out the proposal.

(6) Procedure — Sections 17, 18, 19 and 20 of the *Statutory Powers Procedure Act* do not apply to a hearing under this section.

(7) Report to Minister — The person or persons appointed under subsection (5) shall hold a hearing and make a report to the Minister setting out,

(a) recommendations as to the carrying out of the proposal; and

(b) the findings of fact, any information or knowledge used in making the recommendations and any conclusions of law arrived at that are relevant to the recommendations,

and shall provide a copy of the report to the agency.

(8) Minister's decision — After considering a report made under this section, the Minister may carry out the proposal and shall give notice of the Minister's decision to the agency with reasons.

(9) Provisional suspension — Despite subsection (2), the Minister, by notice to the agency and without a hearing, may provisionally exercise any of the powers set out in clauses (1)(e) and (f) where it is necessary to do so, in the Minister's opinion, to avert an immediate threat to the public interest or to a person's health, safety or welfare and the

CFSA

Minister so states in the notice, with reasons, and thereafter the Minister shall cause a hearing to be held and subsections (3) to (8) apply with necessary modifications.

1999, c. 2, s. 7

23. (1) Minister's order to cease activity — Where the Minister is of the opinion, upon reasonable grounds, that an activity carried on, or the manner of carrying on an activity, in the course of the provision of an approved service is causing or is likely to cause harm to a person's health, safety or welfare, the Minister may by order require the service provider to suspend or cease the activity and may take such other action as the Minister deems to be in the best interests of the persons receiving the approved service.

(2) Notice of proposal — Where the Minister proposes to make an order requiring the suspension or cessation of an activity under subsection (1), the Minister shall serve notice of the proposal and written reasons for it on the service provider, and subsections 22(3) to (8), except clause (5)(b), apply with necessary modifications.

(3) Where order may be made immediately — Despite subsection (2), the Minister, by notice to the service provider and without a hearing, may require that the service provider immediately suspend or cease the activity where the continuation of the activity is, in the Minister's opinion, an immediate threat to the public interest or to a person's health, safety or welfare and the Minister so states in the notice, with reasons, and thereafter the Minister shall cause a hearing to be held and subsections 22(3) to (8), except clause (5)(b), apply with necessary modifications.

24. (1) Minister has powers of board — Where the Minister operates and manages a society under subclause 22(1)(f)(iii), the Minister has all the powers of its board of directors.

(2) Idem — Without restricting the generality of subsection (1), where the Minister operates and manages a society under subclause 22(1)(f)(iii), the Minister may,

    (a) carry on the society's business;

    (b) enter into contracts on the society's behalf;

    (c) arrange for bank accounts to be opened in the society's name, and authorize persons to sign cheques and other documents on the society's behalf;

    (d) appoint or dismiss employees of the society; and

    (e) make by-laws.

(3) Occupation and operation of premises — Without restricting the generality of subsection (1), where the Minister operates and manages a society under subclause 22(1)(f)(iii), the Minister may,

    (a) despite sections 25 and 41 of the *Expropriations Act*, immediately occupy and operate, or arrange for the occupation and operation by a person or organization designated by the Minister, of any premises occupied or used by the society for the provision of approved services; or

    (b) apply without notice to the Superior Court of Justice for an order directing the sheriff to assist the Minister as may be necessary in occupying the premises.

(4) Maximum period — The Minister shall not occupy and operate premises under subsection (3) for a period exceeding one year without the society's consent, but the Lieutenant Governor in Council may extend the period from time to time.

1999, c. 2, s. 35

Offences

25. Offence — A person who knowingly,

(a) fails to furnish a report required by the Minister under subsection 5(5);

(b) contravenes subsection 6(2) or (3) (obstructing program supervisor, etc.); or

(c) furnishes false information in an application under this Part or in a report or return required under this Part or the regulations,

and a director, officer or employee of a corporation who authorizes, permits or concurs in such a contravention or furnishing by the corporation, is guilty of an offence and is liable upon conviction to a fine of not more than $2,000.

PART II — VOLUNTARY ACCESS TO SERVICES

26. Definitions — In this Part,

"advisory committee" means a Residential Placement Advisory Committee established under subsection 34(2); *("comité consultatif")*

"institution" means,

(a) a children's residence, other than a maternity home, operated by the Minister or under the authority of a licence issued under Part IX (Licensing) with the capacity of providing residential services to ten or more children at a time, or

(b) premises designated by a Director under subsection 34(5); *("foyer")*

"record", when used in reference to a person, has the same meaning as in Part VIII (Confidentiality of and Access to Records; *("dossier")*

"special need" means a need that is related to or caused by a developmental disability or a behavioural, emotional, physical, mental or other disability. *("besoin particulier")*

2001, c. 13, s. 5(4)

Consents

27. (1) Consent to service: person over sixteen — A service provider may provide a service to a person who is sixteen years of age or older only with the person's consent, except where the court orders under this Act that the service be provided to the person.

(2) Consent to residential service: child under sixteen — A service provider may provide a residential service to a child who is less than sixteen years of age only with the consent of the child's parent or, where the child is in a society's lawful custody, the society's consent, except where this Act provides otherwise.

(3) Exception — Subsections (1) and (2) do not apply where a service is provided to a child under Part IV (Young Offenders).

(4) Discharge from residential placement — A child who is placed in a residential placement with the consent referred to in subsection (2) may only be discharged from the placement,

(a) with the consent that would be required for a new residential placement; or

(b) where the placement is made under the authority of an agreement made under subsection 29(1) (temporary care agreements) or subsection 30(1) or (2) (special needs agreements), in accordance with section 33 (termination by notice).

(5) Transfer to another placement — A child who is placed in a residential placement with the consent referred to in subsection (2) shall not be transferred from one placement to another unless the consent that would be required for a new residential placement is given.

(6) Child's wishes — Before a child is placed in or discharged from a residential placement or transferred from one residential placement to another with the consent referred to in subsection (2), the service provider shall take the child's wishes into account, if they can be reasonably ascertained.

28. Counselling service: child twelve or older — A service provider may provide a counselling service to a child who is twelve years of age or older with the child's consent, and no other person's consent is required, but if the child is less than sixteen years of age the service provider shall discuss with the child at the earliest appropriate opportunity the desirability of involving the child's parent.

Temporary Care Agreements

29. (1) Temporary care agreement — A person who is temporarily unable to care adequately for a child in his or her custody, and the society having jurisdiction where the person resides, may make a written agreement for the society's care and custody of the child.

(2) Child's age — No temporary care agreement shall be made in respect of a child,

(a) who is sixteen years of age or older; or

(b) who is twelve years of age or older, unless the child is a party to the agreement.

(3) Exception: developmental disability — Clause (2)(b) does not apply where it has been determined on the basis of an assessment, not more than one year before the agreement is made, that the child does not have capacity to participate in the agreement because of a developmental disability.

(4) Duty of society — A society shall not make a temporary care agreement unless the society,

(a) has determined that an appropriate residential placement that is likely to benefit the child is available; and

(b) is satisfied that no less disruptive course of action, such as care in the child's own home, is appropriate for the child in the circumstances.

(5) Term of agreement limited — No temporary care agreement shall be made for a term exceeding six months, but the parties to a temporary care agreement may, with a Director's written approval, agree to extend it for a further period or periods if the total term of the agreement, as extended, does not exceed an aggregate of twelve months.

(6) Time limit — No temporary care agreement shall be made or extended so as to result in a child being in a society's care and custody, for a period exceeding,

(a) 12 months, if the child is less than 6 years of age on the day the agreement is entered into or extended; or

(b) 24 months, if the child is 6 years of age or older on the day the agreement is entered into or extended.

(6.1) Same — In calculating the period referred to in subsection (6), time during which a child has been in a society's care and custody,

   (a) as a society ward under paragraph 2 of subsection 57(1);

   (b) under a temporary care agreement under subsection 29(1); or

   (c) under a temporary order made under clause 51(2)(d),

shall be counted.

(6.2) Previous periods to be counted — The period referred to in subsection (6) shall include any previous periods that the child was in a society's care and custody as described in subsection (6.1) other than periods that precede a continuous period of five or more years that the child was not in a society's care and custody.

Transitional Provisions

Subsection 37(1) of 1999, c. 2, provides as follows:

> *(1) For the purposes of subsections 29(6), (6.1) and (6.2) of the* Child and Family Services Act, *as enacted by subsection 8(2) of this Act, no period that a child was in a society's care and custody before the day subsection 8(2) of this Act is proclaimed in force [i.e. before March 31, 2000], shall be counted.*

Subsection 37(2) of 1999, c. 2 further provides:

> *(2) Despite the proclamation of subsection 8(2) of this Act, subsection 29(6) of the* Child and Family Services Act, *as it read on the day before that proclamation, shall continue to apply with respect to a child who is in the care and custody of a society on the day of that proclamation so long as that child continues to be in the care and custody of a society.*

On the day before that proclamation, s. 29(6) read as follows:

> 29. *(6)* Twenty-four month rule — *No temporary care agreement shall be made or extended so as to result in a child being in a society's care and custody, whether under a temporary care agreement or under a temporary order or order for society wardship made under Part III (Child Protection), for a continuous period exceeding twenty-four months.*

(7) Authority to consent to medical treatment may be transferred — A temporary care agreement may provide that the society is entitled to consent to medical treatment for the child where a parent's consent would otherwise be required.

(8) Contents of temporary care agreement — A temporary care agreement shall include:

   1. A statement by all the parties to the agreement that the child's care and custody are transferred to the society.

   2. A statement by all the parties to the agreement that the child's placement is voluntary.

   3. A statement, by the person referred to in subsection (1), that he or she is temporarily unable to care for the child adequately and has discussed with the society alternatives to residential placement of the child.

   4. An undertaking by the person referred to in subsection (1) to maintain contact with the child and be involved in the child's care.

5. If it is not possible for the person referred to in subsection (1) to maintain contact with the child and be involved in the child's care, the person's designation of another named person who is willing to do so.

6. The name of the individual who is the primary contract between the society and the person referred to in subsection (1).

7. Such other provisions as are prescribed.

(9) Designation by advisory committee — Where the person referred to in subsection (1) does not give an undertaking under paragraph 4 or designate another person under paragraph 5 of subsection (8), an advisory committee that has jurisdiction may, in consultation with the society, name a suitable person who is willing to maintain contact with the child and be involved in the child's care.

(10) Variation of agreement — The parties to a temporary care agreement may vary the agreement from time to time in a manner that is consistent with this Part and the regulations made under it.

1999, c. 2, s. 8; 2001, c. 13, s. 5(5)

Special Needs Agreements

30. (1) Special needs agreement with society — A person who is unable to provide the services required by a child in his or her custody because the child has a special need, and a society having jurisdiction where the person resides, may with a Director's written approval make a written agreement for,

(a) the society's provision of services to meet the child's special need; and

(b) the society's supervision or care and custody of the child.

(2) Special needs agreement with Minister. — A person who is unable to provide the services required by a child in his or her custody because the child has a special need, and the Minister, may make a written agreement for,

(a) the Minister's provision of services to meet the child's special need; and

(b) the Minister's supervision or care and custody of the child.

(3) Term to be specified — A special needs agreement shall only be made for a specific period, but may be extended, with a Director's written approval in the case of an agreement with a society, for a further period or periods.

(4) s. 29(7-10) apply — Where a special needs agreement provides for a child's residential placement, subsections 29(7), (8), (9) and (10) (authority to consent to medical treatment, contents of agreement, variation) apply with necessary modifications, and subsection 29(4) (duty of society) applies to the society or the Minister, as the case may be, with necessary modifications.

31. (1) Society agreements with sixteen and seventeen year olds — A child who is sixteen years of age or older and is not in the care of his or her parent and has a special need, and the society having jurisdiction where the child resides, may with a Director's written approval make a written agreement for the society's provision of services to meet the child's special need.

(2) Idem: special needs agreement with Minister — A child who is sixteen years of age or older and is not in the care of his or her parent and has a special need, and the

Minister, may make a written agreement for the Minister's provision of services to meet the person's special need.

(3) Contents of agreements — An agreement made under subsection (1) or (2) shall contain the prescribed provisions.

(4) s. 29(10) applies — Subsection 29(10) (variation) applies to an agreement made under subsection (1) or (2).

Expiry and Termination of Agreements

32. Agreement expires at eighteen — No agreement made under section 29, 30 or 31 shall continue beyond the eighteenth birthday of the person who is its subject.

33. (1) Notice of termination of agreement — A party to an agreement made under section 29, 30 or 31 may terminate the agreement at any time by giving every other party written notice that the party wishes to terminate the agreement.

(2) When notice takes effect — Where notice is given under subsection (1), the agreement terminates on the expiry of five days, or such longer period not exceeding twenty-one days as the agreement specifies, after the day on which every other party has actually received the notice.

(3) Return of child, etc., by society — Where notice of a wish to terminate an agreement for care and custody made under subsection 29(1) or 30(1) is given by or to a society under subsection (1), the society shall as soon as possible, and in any event before the agreement terminates under subsection (2),

    (a) cause the child to be returned to the person who made the agreement, or to a person who has obtained an order for the child's custody since the agreement was made; or

    (b) where the society is of the opinion that the child would be in need of protection within the meaning of subsection 37(2) of Part III (Child Protection) if returned to the person referred to in clause (a), bring the child before the court under that Part to determine whether the child would be in need of protection in that case, and thereafter Part III applies to the child, with necessary modifications.

(4) Idem: Minister — Where notice of a wish to terminate an agreement for care and custody made under subsection 30(2) is given by or to the Minister under subsection (1), subsection (3) applies to the Minister, with necessary modifications.

(5) Idem: expiry of agreement — Where a temporary care agreement expires or is about to expire under subsection 29(6), and where a temporary care agreement or a special needs agreement that provides for care and custody expires or is about to expire according to its own terms and is not extended, the society or the Minister, as the case may be, shall before the agreement expires or as soon as practicable thereafter, but in any event within twenty-one days after the agreement expires,

    (a) cause the child to be returned to the person who made the agreement, or to a person who has obtained an order for the child's custody since the agreement was made; or

    (b) where the society or the Minister, as the case may be, is of the opinion that the child would be in need of protection within the meaning of subsection 37(2) of Part III (Child Protection) if returned to the person referred to in clause (a), bring the child before the court under that Part to determine whether the child would be in need of protection in that case, and thereafter Part III applies to the child, with necessary modifications.

Review by Residential Placement Advisory Committee

34. (1) Application — In this section, "residential placement" does not include,

(a) a placement made under the *Young Offenders Act* (Canada) or under Part IV (Young Offenders);

(b) commitment to a secure treatment program under Part VI (Extraordinary Measures); or

(c) a placement with a person who is neither a service provider nor a foster parent. *("placement en établissement")*

(2) Residential placement advisory committees — The Minister may establish residential placement advisory committees each consisting of,

(a) persons engaged in providing services;

(b) other persons who have demonstrated an informed concern for the welfare of children;

(c) one representative of the Ministry; and

(d) if the Minister wishes, another person or persons, including a representative of a band or native community, whom the Minister considers appropriate,

and shall specify the territorial jurisdiction of each advisory committee.

(3) Payments, etc., to members — The Minister may pay allowances and reasonable travelling expenses to any or all of the members of an advisory committee, and may authorize an advisory committee to hire support staff.

(4) Duties of committee — An advisory committee has a duty to advise, inform and assist parents, children and service providers with respect to the availability and appropriateness of residential services and alternatives to residential services, to conduct reviews under this section, and to name persons for the purpose of subsection 29(9) (contact with child under temporary care agreement), and has such further duties as are prescribed.

(5) Designation by Director — A Director may designate a building, group of buildings or part of a building in which residential services can be provided to ten or more children at a time as an institution for the purposes of this section.

(6) Mandatory review by committee — An advisory committee shall review,

(a) every residential placement in an institution of a child who resides within the advisory committee's jurisdiction, if the placement is intended to last or actually lasts ninety days or more,

(i) as soon as possible, but in any event within forty-five days of the day on which the child is placed in the institution,

(ii) unless the placement is reviewed under subclause (i), within twelve months of the establishment of the committee or within such longer period as the Minister allows, and

(iii) while the placement continues, at least once during each nine month period succeeding the review under subclause (i) or (ii);

(b) every residential placement of a child twelve years of age or older who objects to the placement and resides within the advisory committee's jurisdiction,

    (i) within the week immediately following the day that is fourteen days after the child is placed, and

    (ii) while the placement continues, at least once during each nine month period succeeding the review under subclause (i); and

(c) an existing or proposed residential placement of a child that the Minister refers to the advisory committee, within thirty days of the referral.

(7) Discretionary review — An advisory committee may at any time review or re-review, on a person's request or on its own initiative, an existing or proposed residential placement of a child who resides within the advisory committee's jurisdiction.

(8) Review to be informal, etc. — An advisory committee shall conduct a review under this section in an informal manner, in the absence of the public, and in the course of the review may,

(a) interview the child, members of the child's family and any representatives of the child and family;

(b) interview persons engaged in providing services and other persons who may have an interest in the matter or may have information that would assist the advisory committee;

(c) examine documents and reports that are presented to the committee; and

(d) examine records of the child and of members of the child's family, as defined in Part VIII (Confidentiality of and Access to Records), that are disclosed to the committee in accordance with that Part.

(9) Service providers to assist advisory committee — At an advisory committee's request, a service provider shall assist and co-operate with the advisory committee in its conduct of a review.

(10) What committee shall consider — In conducting a review, an advisory committee shall,

(a) determine whether the child has a special need;

(b) consider what programs are available for the child in the residential placement or proposed residential placement, and whether a program available to the child is likely to benefit the child;

(c) consider whether the residential placement or proposed residential placement is appropriate for the child in the circumstances;

(d) if it considers that a less restrictive alternative to the placement would be more appropriate for the child in the circumstances, specify that alternative;

(e) consider the importance of continuity in the child's care and the possible effect on the child of disruption of that continuity; and

(f) where the child is an Indian or native person, consider the importance, in recognition of the uniqueness of Indian and native culture, heritage and traditions, of preserving the child's cultural identity.

35. (1) Recommendations — An advisory committee that conducts a review shall advise,

    (a) the service provider;

(b) any representative of the child;

(c) the child's parent or, where the child is in a society's lawful custody, the society;

(d) the child, where it is reasonable to expect him or her to understand; and

(e) where the child is an Indian or native person, a representative chosen by the child's band or native community,

of its recommendations as soon as the review has been completed, and shall advise the child of his or her rights under section 36 if the child is twelve years of age or older.

(2) Report of review to Minister — An advisory committee that conducts a review shall, within thirty days of completing the review, make a report of its findings and recommendations to the Minister.

(3) Recommendation for less restrictive service — Where an advisory committee considers that the provision of a less restrictive service to a child would be more appropriate for the child than the residential placement, the advisory committee shall recommend in its report under subsection (2) that the less restrictive service be provided to the child.

(4) Additional reports at Minister's request — An advisory committee shall make a report of its activities to the Minister whenever the Minister requests it, in addition to making the reports required by subsection (2).

36. (1) Review by Child and Family Services Review Board — A child who is twelve years of age or older and is in a residential placement to which he or she objects may, if the placement has been reviewed by an advisory committee under section 34 and,

(a) the child is dissatisfied with the advisory committee's recommendation; or

(b) the advisory committee's recommendation is not followed,

apply to the Board for a determination of where he or she should remain or be placed.

(2) Duty of Board — The Board shall conduct a review with respect to an application made under subsection (1) and may do so by holding a hearing.

(3) Idem — The Board shall advise the child whether it intends to hold a hearing or not within ten days of receiving the child's application.

(4) Parties — The parties to a hearing under this section are,

(a) the child;

(b) the child's parent or, where the child is in a society's lawful custody, the society;

(c) where the child is an Indian or native person, a representative chosen by the child's band or native community; and

(d) any other persons that the Board specifies.

(5) Time for determination — The Board shall complete its review and make a determination within thirty days of receiving a child's application, unless,

(a) the Board holds a hearing with respect to the application; and

(b) the parties consent to a longer period for the Board's determination.

(6) Board's recommendation — After conducting a review under subsection (2), the Board may,

(a) order that the child be transferred to another residential placement, if the Board is satisfied that the other residential placement is available;

(b) order that the child be discharged from the residential placement; or

(c) confirm the existing placement.

PART III — CHILD PROTECTION

37. (1) Definitions — In this Part,

"child" does not include a child as defined in subsection 3(1) who is actually or apparently sixteen years of age or older, unless the child is the subject of an order under this Part; *("enfant")*

"child protection worker" means a Director, a local director or a person authorized by a Director or local director for the purposes of section 40 (commencing child protection proceedings); *("préposé à la protection de l'enfance")*

"extended family", when used in reference to a child, means the persons to whom the child is related by blood, marriage or adoption; *("famille élargie")*

"parent", when used in reference to a child, means each of,

(a) the child's mother,

(b) an individual described in one of paragraphs 1 to 6 of subsection 8(1) of the *Children's Law Reform Act*, unless it is proved on a balance of probabilities that he is not the child's natural father,

(c) the individual having lawful custody of the child,

(d) an individual who, during the twelve months before intervention under this Part, has demonstrated a settled intention to treat the child as a child of his or her family, or has acknowledged parentage of the child and provided for the child's support,

(e) an individual who, under a written agreement or a court order, is required to provide for the child, has custody of the child or has a right of access to the child, and

(f) an individual who has acknowledged parentage of the child in writing under section 12 of the *Children's Law Reform Act*,

but does not include a foster parent; *("père ou mère")*

"place of safety" means a foster home, a hospital, and a place or one of a class of places designated as such by a Director under subsection 17(2) of Part I (Flexible Services), but does not include,

(a) a place of secure custody as defined in Part IV (Young Offenders), or

(b) a place of secure temporary detention as defined in Part IV. *("lieu sûr")*

(2) Child in need of protection — A child is in need of protection where,

(a) the child has suffered physical harm, inflicted by the person having charge of the child or caused by or resulting from that person's,

(i) failure to adequately care for, provide for, supervise or protect the child, or

(ii) pattern of neglect in caring for, providing for, supervising or protecting the child.

(b) there is a risk that the child is likely to suffer physical harm inflicted by the person having charge of the child or caused by or resulting from that person's,

(i) failure to adequately care for, provide for, supervise or protect the child, or

(ii) pattern of neglect in caring for, providing for, supervising or protecting the child.

(c) the child has been sexually molested or sexually exploited, by the person having charge of the child or by another person where the person having charge of the child knows or should know of the possibility of sexual molestation or sexual exploitation and fails to protect the child;

(d) there is a risk that the child is likely to be sexually molested or sexually exploited as described in clause (c).

(e) the child requires medical treatment to cure, prevent or alleviate physical harm or suffering and the child's parent or the person having charge of the child does not provide, or refuses or is unavailable or unable to consent to, the treatment;

(f) the child has suffered emotional harm, demonstrated by serious,

  (i) anxiety,

  (ii) depression,

  (iii) withdrawal,

  (iv) self-destructive or aggressive behaviour, or

  (v) delayed development,

and there are reasonable grounds to believe that the emotional harm suffered by the child results from the actions, failure to act or pattern of neglect on the part of the child's parent or the person having charge of the child;

(f.1) the child has suffered emotional harm of the kind described in subclause (f)(i), (ii), (iii), (iv) or (v) and the child's parent or the person having charge of the child does not provide, or refuses or is unavailable or unable to consent to, services or treatment to remedy or alleviate the harm;

(g) there is a risk that the child is likely to suffer emotional harm of the kind described in subclause (f)(i), (ii), (iii), (iv) or (v) resulting from the actions, failure to act or pattern of neglect on the part of the child's parent or the person having charge of the child;

(g.1) there is a risk that the child is likely to suffer emotional harm of the kind described in subclause (f)(i), (ii), (iii), (iv) or (v) and that the child's parent or the person having charge of the child does not provide, or refuses or is unavailable or unable to consent to, services or treatment to prevent the harm.

(h) the child suffers from a mental, emotional or developmental condition that, if not remedied, could seriously impair the child's development and the child's parent or the person having charge of the child does not provide, or refuses or is unavailable or unable to consent to, treatment to remedy or alleviate the condition;

(i) the child has been abandoned, the child's parent has died or is unavailable to exercise his or her custodial rights over the child and has not made adequate provision for the child's care and custody, or the child is in a residential placement and the parent refuses or is unable or unwilling to resume the child's care and custody;

(j) the child is less than twelve years old and has killed or seriously injured another person or caused serious damage to another person's property, services or treatment are necessary to prevent a recurrence and the child's parent or the person having charge of the child does not provide, or refuses or is unavailable or unable to consent to, those services or treatment;

(k) the child is less than twelve years old and has on more than one occasion injured another person or caused loss or damage to another person's property, with the encouragement of the person having charge of the child or because of that person's failure or inability to supervise the child adequately; or

(l) the child's parent is unable to care for the child and the child is brought before the court with the parent's consent and, where the child is twelve years of age or older, with the child's consent, to be dealt with under this Part.

(3) Best interests of child — Where a person is directed in this Part to make an order or determination in the best interests of a child, the person shall take into consideration those of the following circumstances of the case that he or she considers relevant:

1. The child's physical, mental and emotional needs, and the appropriate care or treatment to meet those needs.

2. The child's physical, mental and emotional level of development.

3. The child's cultural background.

4. The religious faith, if any, in which the child is being raised.

5. The importance for the child's development of a positive relationship with a parent and a secure place as a member of a family.

6. The child's relationships by blood or through an adoption order.

7. The importance of continuity in the child's care and the possible effect on the child of disruption of that continuity.

8. The merits of a plan for the child's care proposed by a society, including a proposal that the child be placed for adoption or adopted, compared with the merits of the child remaining with or returning to a parent.

9. The child's views and wishes, if they can be reasonably ascertained.

10. The effects on the child of delay in the disposition of the case.

11. The risk that the child may suffer harm through being removed from, kept away from, returned to or allowed to remain in the care of a parent.

12. The degree of risk, if any, that justified the finding that the child is in need of protection.

13. Any other relevant circumstance.

(4) Where child an Indian or native person — Where a person is directed in this Part to make an order or determination in the best interests of a child and the child is an Indian or native person, the person shall take into consideration the importance, in recognition of the uniqueness of Indian and native culture, heritage and traditions, of preserving the child's cultural identity.

1999, c. 2, s. 9

Transitional Provision

Pursuant to 1999, c. 2, s. 37(5), section 37 of the Child and Family Services Act, *as it read on the day before the March 31, 2000 proclamation of 1999, c. 2, s. 9, continues to apply to any proceeding under Part III, including a status review proceeding, commenced before that date.*

On the day before the proclamation, section 37 read as follows:

37. (1) Definitions — Is this Part,

"child" does not include a child as defined in subsection 3(1) who is actually or apparently sixteen years of age or older, unless the child is the subject of an order under this Part; ("enfant")

"child protection worker" means a Director, a local director or a person authorized by a Director or local director for the purposes of section 40 (commencing child protection proceedings); ("préposé à la protection de l'enfance")

"extended family", when used in reference to a child, means the persons to whom the child is related by blood, marriage or adoption; ("famille élargie")

"parent", when used in reference to a child, means each of,

> *(a) the child's mother,*

> *(b) an individual described in one of paragraphs 1 to 6 of subsection 8(1) of the* Children's Law Reform Act, *unless it is proved on a balance of probabilities that he is not the child's natural father,*

> *(c) the individual having lawful custody of the child,*

> *(d) an individual who, during the twelve months before intervention under this Part, has demonstrated a settled intention to treat the child as a child of his or her family, or has acknowledged parentage of the child and provided for the child's support,*

> *(e) an individual who, under a written agreement or a court order, is required to provide for the child, has custody of the child or has a right of access to the child, and*

> *(f) an individual who has acknowledged parentage of the child in writing under section 12 of the* Children's Law Reform Act,

but does not include a foster parent; ("père ou mère")

"place of safety" means a foster home, a hospital and a place or one of a class of places designated as such by a Director under subsection 17(2) of Part I (Flexible Services), but does not include,

> *(a) a place of secure custody as defined in Part IV (Young Offenders), or*

> *(b) a place of secure temporary detention as defined in Part IV.*

("lieu sûr")

(2) **Child in need of protection** — *A child is in need of protection where,*

> *(a) the child has suffered physical harm inflicted by the person having charge of the child or caused by that person's failure to care and provide for or supervise and protect the child adequately;*

> *(b) there is a substantial risk that the child will suffer physical harm inflicted or caused as described in clause (a);*

> *(c) the child has been sexually molested or sexually exploited, by the person having charge of the child or by another person where the person having charge of the child knows or should know of the possibility of sexual molestation or sexual exploitation and fails to protect the child;*

> *(d) there is a substantial risk that the child will be sexually molested or sexually exploited as described in clause (c);*

> *(e) the child requires medical treatment to cure, prevent or alleviate physical harm or suffering and the child's parent or the person having charge of the child does not provide, or refuses or is unavailable or unable to consent to, the treatment;*

> *(f) the child has suffered emotional harm, demonstrated by severe,*

>> *(i) anxiety,*

>> *(ii) depression,*

>> *(iii) withdrawal, or*

(iv) self-destructive or aggressive behaviour,

and the child's parent or the person having charge of the child does not provide, or refuses or is unavailable or unable to consent to, services or treatment to remedy or alleviate the harm;

(g) there is a substantial risk that the child will suffer emotional harm of the kind described in clause (f), and the child's parent or the person having charge of the child does not provide, or refuses or is unavailable or unable to consent to, services or treatment to prevent the harm;

(h) the child suffers from a mental, emotional or developmental condition that, if not remedied, could seriously impair the child's development and the child's parent or the person having charge of the child does not provide, or refuses or is unavailable or unable to consent to, treatment to remedy or alleviate the condition;

(i) the child has been abandoned, the child's parent has died or is unavailable to exercise his or her custodial rights over the child and has not made adequate provision for the child's care and custody, or the child is in a residential placement and the parent refuses or is unable or unwilling to resume the child's care and custody;

(j) the child is less than twelve years old and has killed or seriously injured another person or caused serious damage to another person's property, services or treatment are necessary to prevent a recurrence and the child's parent or the person having charge of the child does not provide, or refuses or is unavailable or unable to consent to, those services or treatment;

(k) the child is less than twelve years old and has on more than one occasion injured another person or caused loss or damage to another person's property, with the encouragement of the person having charge of the child or because of that person's failure or inability to supervise the child adequately; or

(l) the child's parent is unable to care for the child and the child is brought before the court with the parent's consent and, where the child is twelve years of age or older, with the child's consent, to be dealt with under this Part.

(3) **Best interests of child** — Where a person is directed in this Part to make an order or determination in the best interests of a child, the person shall take into consideration those of the following circumstances of the case that he or she considers relevant:

1. The child's physical, mental and emotional needs, and the appropriate care or treatment to meet those needs.

2. The child's physical, mental and emotional level of development.

3. The child's cultural background.

4. The religious faith, if any, in which the child is being raised.

5. The importance for the child's development of a positive relationship with a parent and a secure place as a member of a family.

6. The child's relationships by blood or through an adoption order.

7. The importance of continuity in the child's care and the possible effect on the child of disruption of that continuity.

8. The merits of a plan for the child's care proposed by a society, including a proposal that the child be placed for adoption or adopted, compared with the merits of the child remaining with or returning to a parent.

9. The child's views and wishes, if they can be reasonably ascertained.

10. The effects on the child of delay in the disposition of the case.

11. The risk that the child may suffer harm through being removed from, kept away from, returned to or allowed to remain in the care of a parent.

12. *The degree of risk, if any, that justified the finding that the child is in need of protection.*

13. *Any other relevant circumstance.*

(4) Where child an Indian or native person — *Where a person is directed in this Part to make an order or determination in the best interests of a child and the child is an Indian or native person, the person shall take into consideration the importance, in recognition of the uniqueness of Indian and native culture, heritage and traditions, of preserving the child's cultural identity.*

Legal Representation

38. (1) Legal representation of child — A child may have legal representation at any stage in a proceeding under this Part.

(2) Court to consider issue — Where a child does not have legal representation in a proceeding under this Part, the court,

    (a) shall, as soon as practicable after the commencement of the proceeding; and

    (b) may, at any later stage in the proceeding,

determine whether legal representation is desirable to protect the child's interests.

(3) Direction for legal representation — Where the court determines that legal representation is desirable to protect a child's interests, the court shall direct that legal representation be provided for the child.

(4) Criteria — Where,

    (a) the court is of the opinion that there is a difference of views between the child and a parent or a society, and the society proposes that the child be removed from a person's care or be made a society or Crown ward under paragraph 2 or 3 of subsection 57(1);

    (b) the child is in the society's care and,

        (i) no parent appears before the court, or

        (ii) it is alleged that the child is in need of protection within the meaning of clause 37(2)(a), (c), (f), (f.1) or (h); or

    (c) the child is not permitted to be present at the hearing,

legal representation shall be deemed to be desirable to protect the child's interests, unless the court is satisfied, taking into account the child's views and wishes if they can be reasonably ascertained, that the child's interests are otherwise adequately protected.

(5) Where parent a minor — Where a child's parent is less than eighteen years of age, the Children's Lawyer shall represent the parent in a proceeding under this Part unless the court orders otherwise.

1994, c. 27, s. 43(2); 1999, c. 2, s. 10

Transitional Provision

Pursuant to 1999, c. 2, s. 37(5), section 38 of the Child and Family Services Act, *as it read on the day before the March 31, 2000 proclamation of 1999, c. 2, s. 10, continues to apply to any proceeding under Part III, including a status review proceeding, commenced before that date.*

On the day before the proclamation, section 38 read as follows:

38. (1) Legal representation of child — A child may have legal representation at any stage in a proceeding under this Part.

(2) Court to consider issue — Where a child does not have legal representation in a proceeding under this Part, the court,

> *(a) shall, as soon as practicable after the commencement of the proceeding, and*

> *(b) may, at any later stage in the proceeding,*

determine whether legal representation is desirable to protect the child's interests.

(3) Direction for legal representation — Where the court determines that legal representation is desirable to protect a child's interests, the court shall direct that legal representation be provided for the child.

(4) Criteria — Where,

> *(a) the court is of the opinion that there is a difference of views between the child and a parent or a society, and the society proposes that the child be removed fro a person's care or be made a society or Crown ward under paragraph 2 or 3 of subsection 57(1);*

> *(b) the child is in the society's care and,*

>> *(i) no parent appears before the court, or*

>> *(ii) it is alleged that the child is in need of protection within the meaning of clause 37(2)(a), (c), (f) or (h); or*

> *(c) the child is not permitted to be present at the hearing,*

legal representation shall be deemed to be desirable to protect the child's interests, unless the court is satisfied, taking into account the child's views and wishes if they can be reasonably ascertained, that the child's interests are otherwise adequately protected.

(5) Where parent a minor — Where a child's parent is less than eighteen years of age, the Children's Lawyer shall represent the parent in a proceeding under this Part unless the court orders otherwise.

Parties and Notice

39. (1) Parties — The following are parties to a proceeding under this Part:

1. The applicant.

2. The society having jurisdiction in the matter.

3. The child's parent.

4. Where the child is an Indian or a native person, a representative chosen by the child's band or native community.

(2) Director to be added — At any stage in a proceeding under this Part, the court shall add a Director as a party on his or her motion.

(3) Right to participate — Any person, including a foster parent, who has cared for the child continuously during the six months immediately before the hearing,

> (a) is entitled to the same notice of the proceeding as a party;

> (b) may be present at the hearing;

> (c) may be represented by a solicitor; and

> (d) may make submissions to the court,

but shall take no further part in the hearing without leave of the court.

(4) Child twelve or older — A child twelve years of age or more who is the subject of a proceeding under this Part is entitled to receive notice of the proceeding and to be present at the hearing, unless the court is satisfied that being present at the hearing would cause the child emotional harm and orders that the child not receive notice of the proceeding and not be permitted to be present at the hearing.

(5) Child under twelve — A child less than twelve years of age who is the subject of a proceeding under this Part is not entitled to receive notice of the proceeding or to be present at the hearing unless the court is satisfied that the child,

    (a) is capable of understanding the hearing; and

    (b) will not suffer emotional harm by being present at the hearing,

and orders that the child receive notice of the proceeding and be permitted to be present at the hearing.

(6) Child's participation — A child who is the applicant under subsection 64(4) (status review), receives notice of a proceeding under this Part or has legal representation in a proceeding is entitled to participate in the proceeding and to appeal under section 69 as if he or she were a party.

(7) Dispensing with notice — Where the court is satisfied that the time required for notice to a person might endanger the child's health or safety, the court may dispense with notice to that person.

Commencing Child Protection Proceedings

40. (1) Application — A society may apply to the court to determine whether a child is in need of protection.

(2) Warrant to apprehend child — A justice of the peace may issue a warrant authorizing a child protection worker to bring a child to a place of safety if the justice of the peace is satisfied on the basis of a child protection worker's sworn information that there are reasonable and probable grounds to believe that,

    (a) the child is in need of protection; and

    (b) a less restrictive course of action is not available or will not protect the child adequately.

(3) Idem — A justice of the peace shall not refuse to issue a warrant under subsection (2) by reason only that the child protection worker may bring the child to a place of safety under subsection (7).

(4) Order to produce or apprehend child — Where the court is satisfied, on a person's application upon notice to a society, that there are reasonable and probable grounds to believe that,

    (a) a child is in need of protection, the matter has been reported to the society, the society has not made an application under subsection (1), and no child protection worker has sought a warrant under subsection (2) or apprehended the child under subsection (7); and

    (b) the child cannot be protected adequately otherwise than by being brought before the court, the court may order,

    (c) that the person having charge of the child produce him or her before the court at the time and place named in the order for a hearing under subsection 47(1) to determine whether he or she is in need of protection; or

    (d) where the court is satisfied that an order under clause (c) would not protect the child adequately, that a child protection worker employed by the society bring the child to a place of safety.

(5) Child's name, location not required — It is not necessary, in an application under subsection (1), a warrant under subsection (2) or an order made under subsection (4), to describe the child by name or to specify the premises where the child is located.

(6) Authority to enter, etc. — A child protection worker authorized to bring a child to a place of safety by a warrant issued under subsection (2) or an order made under clause (4)(d) may at any time enter any premises specified in the warrant or order, by force if necessary, and may search for and remove the child.

(7) Apprehension without warrant — A child protection worker who believes on reasonable and probable grounds that,

    (a) a child is in need of protection; and

    (b) there would be a substantial risk to the child's health or safety during the time necessary to bring the matter on for a hearing under subsection 47(1) or obtain a warrant under subsection (2),

may without a warrant bring the child to a place of safety.

(8) Police assistance — A child protection worker acting under this section may call for the assistance of a peace officer.

(9) Consent to examine child — A child protection worker acting under subsection (7) or under a warrant issued under subsection (2) or an order made under clause (4)(d) may authorize the child's medical examination where a parent's consent would otherwise be required.

(10) Place of open temporary detention — Where a child protection worker who brings a child to a place of safety under this section believes on reasonable and probable grounds that no less restrictive course of action is feasible, the child may be detained in a place of safety that is a place of open temporary detention as defined in Part IV (Young Offenders).

(11) Right of entry, etc. — A child protection worker who believes on reasonable and probable grounds that a child referred to in subsection (7) is on any premises may without a warrant enter the premises, by force, if necessary, and search for and remove the child.

(12) Regulations re power of entry — A child protection worker authorized to enter premises under subsection (6) or (11) shall exercise the power of entry in accordance with the regulations.

(13) Peace officer has powers of child protection worker — Subsections (2), (6), (7), (10), (11) and (12) apply to a peace officer as if the peace officer were a child protection worker.

(14) Protection from personal liability — No action shall be instituted against a peace officer or child protection worker for any act done in good faith in the execution or intended execution of that person's duty under this section or for an alleged neglect or default in the execution in good faith of that duty.

1993, c. 27, Sched.

Special Cases of Apprehension of Children

41. (1) Warrant to apprehend child in care — A justice of the peace may issue a warrant authorizing a peace officer or child protection worker to bring a child to a place of safety if the justice of the peace is satisfied on the basis of a peace officer's or child protection worker's sworn information that,

(a) the child is actually or apparently under the age of sixteen years and has left or been removed from a society's lawful care and custody without its consent; and

(b) there are reasonable and probable grounds to believe that there is no course of action available other than bringing the child to a place of safety that would adequately protect the child.

(2) Idem — A justice of the peace shall not refuse to issue a warrant to a person under subsection (1) by reason only that the person may bring the child to a place of safety under subsection (4).

(3) No need to specify premises — It is not necessary in a warrant under subsection (1) to specify the premises where the child is located.

(4) Apprehension of child in care without warrant — A peace officer or child protection worker who believes on reasonable and probable grounds that,

(a) a child is actually or apparently under the age of sixteen years and has left or been removed from a society's lawful care and custody without its consent; and

(b) there would be a substantial risk to the child's health or safety during the time necessary to obtain a warrant under subsection (1),

may without a warrant bring the child to a place of safety.

(5) Apprehension of child absent from place of open temporary detention — Where a child is detained under this Part in a place of safety that has been designated as a place of open temporary detention as defined in Part IV (Young Offenders) and leaves the place without the consent of,

(a) the society having care, custody and control of the child; or

(b) the person in charge of the place of safety,

a peace officer, the person in charge of the place of safety or that person's delegate may apprehend the child without a warrant.

(6) Idem — A person who apprehends a child under subsection (5) shall,

(a) take the child to a place of safety to be detained until the child can be returned to the place of safety the child left; or

(b) return the child or arrange for the child to be returned to the place of safety the child left.

42. (1) Apprehension of child under twelve — A peace officer who believes on reasonable and probable grounds that a child actually or apparently under twelve years of age has committed an act in respect of which a person twelve years of age or older could be found guilty of an offence may apprehend the child without a warrant and on doing so,

    (a) shall return the child to the child's parent or other person having charge of the child as soon as practicable; or

    (b) where it is not possible to return the child to the parent or other person within a reasonable time, shall take the child to a place of safety to be detained there until the child can be returned to the parent or other person.

(2) Notice to parent, etc. — The person in charge of a place of safety in which a child is detained under subsection (1) shall make reasonable efforts to notify the child's parent or other person having charge of the child of the child's detention so that the child may be returned to the parent or other person.

(3) Where child not returned to parent, etc., within twelve hours — Where a child detained in a place of safety under subsection (1) cannot be returned to the child's parent or other person having charge of the child within twelve hours of being taken to the place of safety, the child shall be dealt with as if the child had been taken to a place of safety under subsection 40(7) and not apprehended under subsection (1).

1993, c. 27, Sched.

43. (1) Application — In this section, **"parent"** includes,

    (a) an approved agency that has custody of the child;

    (b) a person who has care and control of the child. *("père ou mère")*

(2) Warrant to apprehend runaway child — A justice of the peace may issue a warrant authorizing a peace officer or child protection worker to apprehend a child if the justice of the peace is satisfied on the basis of the sworn information of a parent of the child that,

    (a) the child is under the age of sixteen years;

    (b) the child has withdrawn from the parent's care and control without the parent's consent; and

    (c) the parent believes on reasonable and probable grounds that the child's health or safety may be at risk if the child is not apprehended.

(3) Idem — A person who apprehends a child under subsection (2) shall return the child to the child's parent as soon as practicable and where it is not possible to return the child to the parent within a reasonable time, take the child to a place of safety.

(4) Notice to parent, etc. — The person in charge of a place of safety to which a child is taken under subsection (3) shall make reasonable efforts to notify the child's parent that the child is in the place of safety so that the child may be returned to the parent.

(5) Where child not returned to parent within twelve hours — Where a child taken to a place of safety under subsection (3) cannot be returned to the child's parent within twelve hours of being taken to the place of safety, the child shall be dealt with as if the child had been taken to a place of safety under subsection 40(2) and not apprehended under subsection (2).

(6) Where custody enforcement proceedings more appropriate — A justice of the peace shall not issue a warrant under subsection (2) where a child has withdrawn from the care and control of one parent with the consent of another parent under circumstances where a proceeding under section 36 of the *Children's Law Reform Act* would be more appropriate.

(7) No need to specify premises — It is not necessary in a warrant under subsection (2) to specify the premises where the child is located.

(8) Child protection proceedings — Where a peace officer or child protection worker believes on reasonable and probable grounds that a child apprehended under this section is in need of protection and there may be a substantial risk to the health or safety of the child if the child were returned to the parent,

> (a) the peace officer or child protection worker may take the child to a place of safety under subsection 40(7); or

> (b) where the child has been taken to a place of safety under subsection (5), the child shall be dealt with as if the child had been taken there under subsection 40(7).

Power of Entry and Other Provisions for Special Cases of Apprehension

44. (1) Authority to enter, etc. — A person authorized to bring a child to a place of safety by a warrant issued under subsection 41(1) or 43(2) may at any time enter any premises specified in the warrant, by force, if necessary, and may search for and remove the child.

(2) Right of entry, etc. — A person authorized under subsection 41(4) or (5) or 42(1) who believes on reasonable and probable grounds that a child referred to in the relevant subsection is on any premises may without a warrant enter the premises, by force, if necessary, and search for and remove the child.

(3) Regulations re power of entry — A person authorized to enter premises under this section shall exercise the power of entry in accordance with the regulations.

(4) Police assistance — A child protection worker acting under section 41 or 43 may call for the assistance of a peace officer.

(5) Consent to examine child — A child protection worker who deals with a child under subsection 42(3) or 43(5) as if the child had been taken to a place of safety may authorize the child's medical examination where a parent's consent would otherwise be required.

(6) Place of open temporary detention — Where a person who brings a child to a place of safety under section 41 or 42 believes on reasonable and probable grounds that no less restrictive course of action is feasible, the child may be detained in a place of safety that is a place of open temporary detention as defined in Part IV (Young Offenders).

(7) Protection from personal liability — No action shall be instituted against a peace officer or child protection worker for any act done in good faith in the execution or intended execution of that person's duty under this section or section 41, 42 or 43 or for an alleged neglect or default in the execution in good faith of that duty.

Hearings and Orders

45. (1) Definition — In this section,

"**media**" means the press, radio and television media. ("*média*")

(2) Application — This section applies to hearings held under this Part, except hearings under section 76 (child abuse register).

Proposed Amendment — 45(2)

(2) Application — This section applies to hearings held under this Part.

1999, c. 2, s. 11 [Not in force at date of publication.]

(3) Hearings separate from criminal proceedings — A hearing shall be held separately from hearings in criminal proceedings.

(4) Hearings private unless court orders otherwise — A hearing shall be held in the absence of the public, subject to subsection (5), unless the court, after considering,

    (a) the wishes and interests of the parties; and

    (b) whether the presence of the public would cause emotional harm to a child who is a witness at or a participant in the hearing or is the subject of the proceeding,

orders that the hearing be held in public.

(5) Media representatives — Media representatives chosen in accordance with subsection (6) may be present at a hearing that is held in the absence of the public, unless the court makes an order excluding them under subsection (7).

(6) Idem — The media representatives who may be present at a hearing that is held in the absence of the public shall be chosen as follows:

    1. The media representatives in attendance shall choose not more than two persons from among themselves.

    2. Where the media representatives in attendance are unable to agree on a choice of persons, the court may choose not more than two media representatives who may be present at the hearing.

    3. The court may permit additional media representatives to be present at the hearing.

(7) Order excluding media representatives or prohibiting publication — The court may make an order,

    (a) excluding a particular media representative from all or part of a hearing;

    (b) excluding all media representatives from all or a part of a hearing; or

    (c) prohibiting the publication of a report of the hearing or a specified part of the hearing,

where the court is of the opinion that the presence of the media representative or representatives or the publication of the report, as the case may be, would cause emotional harm to a child who is a witness at or a participant in the hearing or is the subject of the proceeding.

(8) Prohibition: identifying child — No person shall publish or make public information that has the effect of identifying a child who is a witness at or a participant in a hearing or the subject of a proceeding, or the child's parent or foster parent or a member of the child's family.

(9) Idem: order re adult — The court may make an order prohibiting the publication of information that has the effect of identifying a person charged with an offence under this Part.

(10) Transcript — No person except a party or a party's solicitor shall be given a copy of a transcript of the hearing, unless the court orders otherwise.

46. (1) Time of detention limited — As soon as practicable, but in any event within five days after a child is brought to a place of safety under section 40 or subsection 79(6) or a homemaker remains or is placed on premises under subsection 78(2),

(a) the matter shall be brought before a court for a hearing under subsection 47(1) (child protection hearing);

(b) the child shall be returned to the person who last had charge of the child or, where there is an order for the child's custody that is enforceable in Ontario, to the person entitled to custody under the order; or

(c) a temporary care agreement shall be made under subsection 29(1) of Part II (Voluntary Access to Services).

(2) Idem: place of open temporary detention — Within twenty-four hours after a child is brought to a place of safety that is a place of open temporary detention, or as soon thereafter as is practicable, the matter shall be brought before a court for a hearing and the court shall,

(a) where it is satisfied that no less restrictive course of action is feasible, order that the child remain in the place of open temporary detention for a period or periods not exceeding an aggregate of thirty days and then be returned to the care and custody of the society;

(b) order that the child be discharged from the place of open temporary detention and returned to the care and custody of the society; or

(c) make an order under subsection 51(2) (temporary care and custody).

47. (1) Child protection hearing — Where an application is made under subsection 40(1) or a matter is brought before the court to determine whether the child is in need of protection, the court shall hold a hearing to determine the issue and make an order under section 57.

(2) Child's name, age, etc. — As soon as practicable, and in any event before determining whether a child is in need of protection, the court shall determine,

(a) the child's name and age;

(b) the religious faith, if any, in which the child is being raised;

(c) whether the child is an Indian or a native person and, if so, the child's band or native community; and

(d) where the child was brought to a place of safety before the hearing, the location of the place from which the child was removed.

(3) Where sixteenth birthday intervenes — Despite anything else in this Part, where the child was under the age of sixteen years when the proceeding was commenced or when the child was apprehended, the court may hear and determine the matter and make an order under this Part as if the child were still under the age of sixteen years.

48. (1) Territorial jurisdiction defined — In this section,

"territorial jurisdiction" means a society's territorial jurisdiction under subsection 15(2). (*"territoire"*)

(2) Place of hearing — A hearing under this Part with respect to a child shall be held in the territorial jurisdiction in which the child ordinarily resides, except that,

(a) where the child is brought to a place of safety before the hearing, the hearing shall be held in the territorial jurisdiction in which the place from which the child was removed is located;

(b) where the child is in a society's care under an order for society or Crown wardship under section 57, the hearing shall be held in the society's territorial jurisdiction; and

(c) where the child is the subject of an order for society supervision under section 57, the hearing may be held in the society's territorial jurisdiction or in the territorial jurisdiction in which the parent or other person with whom the child is placed resides.

(3) Transfer of proceeding — Where the court is satisfied at any stage of a proceeding under this Part that there is a preponderance of convenience in favour of conducting it in another territorial jurisdiction, the court may order that the proceeding be transferred to that other territorial jurisdiction and be continued as if it had been commenced there.

(4) Orders affecting society — The court shall not make an order placing a child in the care or under the supervision of a society unless the place where the court sits is within the society's territorial jurisdiction.

49. Power of court — The court may, on its own initiative, summon a person to attend before it, testify and produce any document or thing, and may enforce obedience to the summons as if it had been made in a proceeding under the *Family Law Act*.

1993, c. 27, Sched.

50. (1) Consideration of past conduct toward children — Despite anything in the *Evidence Act*, in any proceeding under this Part,

(a) the court may consider the past conduct of a person toward any child if that person is caring for or has access to or may care for or have access to a child who is the subject of the proceeding; and

(b) any oral or written statement or report that the court considers relevant to the proceeding, including a transcript, exhibit or finding or the reasons for a decision in an earlier civil or criminal proceeding, is admissible into evidence.

(2) Idem: order of presentation — In a hearing under subsection 47(1), evidence relating only to the disposition of the matter shall not be admitted before the court has determined that the child is in need of protection.

1999, c. 2, s. 12

Transitional Provision

Pursuant to 1999, c. 2, s. 37(5), section 50 of the Child and Family Services Act, *as it read on the day before the March 31, 2000 proclamation of 1999, c. 2, s. 12, continues to apply to any proceeding under Part III, including a status review proceeding, commenced before that date.*

On the day before the proclamation, section 50 read as follows:

> 50. (1) Evidence at hearing: past conduct toward children — *Despite anything in the* Evidence Act, *before ordering that a child be placed in or returned to the care and custody of a person other than a society, the court may consider that person's past conduct toward any child that is or has been in his or her care, and any oral or written statement or report that the*

court considers relevant, including a transcript, exhibit or finding in an earlier civil or criminal proceeding, may be admitted into evidence and shall be proved as the court directs.

(2) Idem: order of presentation — In a hearing under subsection 47(1), evidence relating only to the disposition of the matter shall not be admitted before the court has determined that the child is in need of protection.

51. (1) Adjournments — The court shall not adjourn a hearing for more than thirty days,

(a) unless all the parties present and the person who will be caring for the child during the adjournment consent; or

(b) if the court is aware that a party who is not present at the hearing objects to the longer adjournment.

(2) Custody during adjournment — Where a hearing is adjourned, the court shall make a temporary order for care and custody providing that the child,

(a) remain in or be returned to the care and custody of the person who had charge of the child immediately before intervention under this Part;

(b) remain in or be returned to the care and custody of the person referred to in clause (a), subject to the society's supervision and on such reasonable terms and conditions relating to the child's supervision as the court considers appropriate;

(c) be placed in the care and custody of a person other than the person referred to in clause (a), with the consent of that other person, subject to the society's supervision and on such reasonable terms and conditions relating to the child's supervision as the court considers appropriate; or

(d) remain or be placed in the care and custody of the society, but not be placed in,

(i) a place of secure custody as defined in Part IV (Young Offenders), or

(ii) a place of open temporary detention as defined in that Part that has not been designated as a place of safety.

(3) Criteria — The court shall not make an order under clause (2)(c) or (d) unless the court is satisfied that there are reasonable grounds to believe that there is a risk that the child is likely to suffer harm and that the child cannot be protected adequately by an order under clause (2)(a) or (b).

(4) Application of s. 62 — Where the court makes an order under clause (2)(d), section 62 (parental consents) applies with necessary modifications.

(5) Access — An order made under clause (2)(c) or (d) may contain provisions regarding any person's right of access to the child on such terms and conditions as the court considers appropriate.

(6) Power to vary — The court may at any time vary or terminate an order made under subsection (2).

(7) Evidence on adjournments — For the purpose of this section, the court may admit and act on evidence that the court considers credible and trustworthy in the circumstances.

1999, c. 2, s. 13

Transitional Provision

Pursuant to 1999, c. 2, s. 37(5), section 51 of the Child and Family Services Act, as it read on the day before the March 31, 2000 proclamation of 1999, c. 2, s. 13, continues to apply to any proceeding under Part III, including a status review proceeding, commenced before that date.

On the day before the proclamation, section 51 read as follows:

51. (1) Adjournments *— The court shall not adjourn a hearing for more than thirty days,*

(a) *unless all the parties present and the person who will be caring for the child during the adjournment consent; or*

(b) *if the court is aware that a party who is not present at the hearing objects to the longer adjournment.*

(2) Custody during adjournment *— Where a hearing is adjourned, the court shall make a temporary order for care and custody providing that the child,*

(a) *remain in or be returned to the care and custody of the person who had charge of the child immediately before intervention under this Part;*

(b) *remain in or be returned to the care and custody of the person referred to in clause (a), subject to the society's supervision and on such reasonable terms and conditions relating to the child's supervision as the court considers appropriate;*

(c) *be placed in the care and custody of a person other than the person referred to in clause (a), with the consent of that other person, subject to the society's supervision and on such reasonable terms and conditions relating to the child's supervision as the court considers appropriate; or*

(d) *remain or be placed in the care and custody of the society, but not be placed in,*

(i) *a place of secure custody as defined in Part IV (Young Offenders), or*

(ii) *a place of open temporary detention as defined in that Part that has not been designated as a place of safety.*

(3) Criteria *— The court shall not make an order under clause (2)(c) or (d) unless the court is satisfied that there are reasonable and probable grounds to believe that there is a substantial risk to the child's health or safety and that the child cannot be protected adequately by an order under clause (2)(a) or (b).*

(4) Application of s. 62 *— Where the court makes an order under clause (2)(d), section 62 (parental consents) applies with necessary modifications.*

(5) Access *— An order made under clause (2)(c) or (d) may contain provisions regarding any person's right of access to the child on such terms and conditions as the court considers appropriate.*

(6) Power to vary *— The court may at any time vary or terminate an order made under subsection (2).*

(7) Evidence on adjournments *— For the purpose of this section, the court may admit and act on evidence that the court considers credible and trustworthy in the circumstances.*

52. Delay: court to fix date — Where an application is made under subsection 40(1) or a matter is brought before the court to determine whether a child is in need of protection and the determination has not been made within three months after the commencement of the proceeding, the court,

(a) shall by order fix a date for the hearing of the application, and the date may be the earliest date that is compatible with the just disposition of the application; and

(b) may give such directions and make such orders with respect to the proceeding as are just.

53. (1) Reasons, etc — Where the court makes an order under this Part, the court shall give,

    (a) a statement of any terms or conditions imposed on the order;

    (b) a statement of every plan for the child's care proposed to the court;

    (c) a statement of the plan for the child's care that the court is applying in its decision; and

    (d) reasons for its decision, including,

        (i) a brief statement of the evidence on which the court bases its decision, and

        (ii) where the order has the effect of removing or keeping the child from the care of the person who had charge of the child immediately before intervention under this Part, a statement of the reasons why the child cannot be adequately protected while in the person's care.

(2) Idem — Clause (1)(b) does not require the court to identify a person with whom or a place where it is proposed that a child be placed for care and supervision.

Assessments

54. (1) Order for assessment — Where a child has been found to be in need of protection, the court may order that within a specified time,

    (a) the child; or

    (b) a parent or a person, except a foster parent, in whose charge the child has been or may be,

attend before and undergo an assessment by a specified person who is qualified, in the court's opinion, to perform medical, emotional, developmental, psychological, educational or social assessments and has consented to perform the assessment.

(2) Report — The person performing an assessment under subsection (1) shall make a written report of the assessment to the court within the time specified in the order, which shall not be more than thirty days unless the court is of the opinion that a longer assessment period is necessary.

(3) Copies of report — At least seven days before the court considers the report at a hearing, the court or, where the assessment was requested by a party, that party, shall provide a copy of the report to,

    (a) the person assessed, subject to subsections (4) and (5);

    (b) the child's solicitor or agent of record;

    (c) a parent appearing at the hearing, or the parent's solicitor of record;

    (d) the society caring for or supervising the child;

    (e) a Director, where he or she requests a copy;

    (f) where the child is an Indian or a native person, a representative chosen by the child's band or native community; and

    (g) any other person who, in the opinion of the court, should receive a copy of the report for the purposes of the case.

(4) Child under twelve — Where the person assessed is a child less than twelve years of age, the child shall not receive a copy of the report unless the court considers it desirable that the child receive a copy of the report.

(5) Child twelve or older — Where the person assessed is a child twelve years of age or more, the child shall receive a copy of the report, except that where the court is satisfied that disclosure of all or part of the report to the child would cause the child emotional harm, the court may withhold all or part of the report from the child.

(6) Assessment is evidence — The report of an assessment ordered under subsection (1) is evidence and is part of the court record of the proceeding.

(7) Inference from refusal — The court may draw any inference it considers reasonable from a person's refusal to undergo an assessment ordered under subsection (1).

(8) Report inadmissible — The report of an assessment ordered under subsection (1) is not admissible into evidence in any other proceeding except,

(a) a proceeding under this Part, including an appeal under section 69;

(b) a proceeding referred to in section 81; or

(c) a proceeding under the *Coroners Act*,

without the consent of the person or persons assessed.

1999, c. 2, s. 14

Transitional Provision

Pursuant to 1999, c. 2, s. 37(5), section 54 of the Child and Family Services Act, *as it read on the day before the March 31, 2000 proclamation of 1999, c. 2, s. 14, continues to apply to any proceeding under Part III, including a status review proceeding, commenced before that date.*

On the day before the proclamation, s. 54 read as follows:

54. (1) Order for assessment — Where a child has been found to be in need of protection, the court may order that within a specified time,

(a) the child; or

(b) a parent or a person, except a foster parent, in whose charge the child has been or may be,

attend before and undergo an assessment by a specified person who is qualified, in the court's opinion, to perform medical, emotional, developmental, psychological, educational or social assessments and has consented to perform the assessment.

(2) Report — The person performing an assessment under subsection (1) shall make a written report of the assessment to the court within the time specified in the order, which shall not be more than thirty days unless the court is of the opinion that a longer assessment period is necessary.

(3) Copies of report — At least seven days before the court considers the report at a hearing, the court or, where the assessment was requested by a party, that party, shall provide a copy of the report to,

(a) the person assessed, subject to subsections (4) and (5);

(b) the child's solicitor or agent of record;

(c) a parent appearing at the hearing, or the parent's solicitor of record;

(d) the society caring for or supervising the child;

(e) a Director, where he or she requests a copy;

(f) where the child is an Indian or a native person, a representative chosen by the child's band or native community; and

(g) any other person who, in the opinion of the court, should receive a copy of the report for the purposes of the case.

(4) Child under twelve — Where the person assessed is a child less than twelve years of age, the child shall not receive a copy of the report unless the court considers it desirable that the child receive a copy of the report.

(5) Child twelve or older — Where the person assessed is a child twelve years of age or more, the child shall receive a copy of the report, except that where the court is satisfied that disclosure of all or part of the report to the child would cause the child emotional harm, the court may withhold all or part of the report from the child.

(6) Assessment is evidence — The report of an assessment ordered under subsection (1) is evidence and is part of the court record of the proceeding.

(7) Inference from refusal — The court may draw any inference it considers reasonable from a person's refusal to undergo an assessment ordered under subsection (1).

(8) Report inadmissible: exceptions — The report of an assessment ordered under subsection (1) is not admissible into evidence in any other proceeding except,

(a) an appeal in the proceeding under section 69;

(b) a proceeding under the Corners Act; or

(c) a proceeding referred to in section 81 (recovery on child's behalf),

without the consent of the person or persons assessed.

55. Consent order: special requirements — Where a child is brought before the court on consent as described in clause 37(2)(l), the court shall, before making an order under section 57 that would remove the child from the parent's care and custody,

(a) ask whether,

(i) the society has offered the parent and child services that would enable the child to remain with the parent, and

(ii) the parent and, where the child is twelve years of age or older, the child has consulted independent legal counsel in connection with the consent; and

(b) be satisfied that,

(i) the parent and, where the child is twelve years of age or older, the child understands the nature and consequences of the consent,

(ii) every consent is voluntary, and

(iii) the parent and, where the child is twelve years of age or older, the child consents to the order being sought.

56. Society's plan for child — The court shall, before making an order under section 57 or 65, obtain and consider a plan for the child's care prepared in writing by the society and including,

(a) a description of the services to be provided to remedy the condition or situation on the basis of which the child was found to be in need of protection;

(b) a statement of the criteria by which the society will determine when its wardship or supervision is no longer required;

(c) an estimate of the time required to achieve the purpose of the society's intervention;

(d) where the society proposes to remove or has removed the child from a person's care,

    (i) an explanation of why the child cannot be adequately protected while in the person's care, and a description of any past efforts to do so, and

    (ii) a statement of what efforts, if any, are planned to maintain the child's contact with the person; and

(e) where the society proposes to remove or has removed the child from a person's care permanently, a description of the arrangements made or being made for the child's long-term stable placement.

57. (1) Order where child in need of protection — Where the court finds that a child is in need of protection and is satisfied that intervention through a court order is necessary to protect the child in the future, the court shall make one of the following orders, in the child's best interests:

1. **Supervision order** — That the child be placed with or returned to a parent or another person, subject to the supervision of the society, for a specified period of at least three and not more than twelve months.

2. **Society wardship** — That the child be made a ward of the society and be placed in its care and custody for a specified period not exceeding twelve months.

3. **Crown wardship** — That the child be made a ward of the Crown, until the wardship is terminated under section 65 or expires under subsection 71(1), and be placed in the care of the society.

4. **Consecutive orders of society wardship and supervision** — That the child be made a ward of the society under paragraph 2 for a specified period and then be returned to a parent or another person under paragraph 1, for a period or periods not exceeding an aggregate of twelve months.

(2) Court to inquire — In determining which order to make under subsection (1), the court shall ask the parties what efforts the society or another agency or person made to assist the child before intervention under this Part.

(3) Less disruptive alternatives preferred — The court shall not make an order removing the child from the care of the person who had charge of him or her immediately before intervention under this Part unless the court is satisfied that alternatives that are less disruptive to the child, including non-residential services and the assistance referred to in subsection (2), would be inadequate to protect the child.

(4) Community placement to be considered — Where the court decides that it is necessary to remove the child from the care of the person who had charge of him or her immediately before intervention under this Part, the court shall, before making an order for society or Crown wardship under paragraph 2 or 3 of subsection (1), consider whether it is possible to place the child with a relative, neighbour or other member of the child's community or extended family under paragraph 1 of subsection (1) with the consent of the relative or other person.

(5) Idem: where child an Indian or a native person — Where the child referred to in subsection (4) is an Indian or a native person, unless there is a substantial reason for placing the child elsewhere, the court shall place the child with,

    (a) a member of the child's extended family;

CFSA

(b) a member of the child's band or native community; or

(c) another Indian or native family.

(6) [Repealed 1999, c. 2, s. 15(2).]

(7) Idem — When the court has dispensed with notice to a person under subsection 39(7), the court shall not make an order for Crown wardship under paragraph 3 of subsection (1), or an order for society wardship under paragraph 2 of subsection (1) for a period exceeding thirty days, until a further hearing under subsection 47(1) has been held upon notice to that person.

(8) Terms and conditions of supervision order — Where the court makes a supervision order under paragraph 1 of subsection (1), the court may impose reasonable terms and conditions relating to the child's care and supervision on,

(a) the person with whom the child is placed or to whom the child is returned;

(b) the supervising society;

(c) the child; and

(d) any other person who participated in the hearing.

(9) Where no court order necessary — Where the court finds that a child is in need of protection but is not satisfied that a court order is necessary to protect the child in the future, the court shall order that the child remain with or be returned to the person who had charge of the child immediately before intervention under this Part.

1999, c. 2, s. 15

Transitional Provision

Pursuant to 1999, c. 2, s. 37(5), section 57 of the Child and Family Services Act, *as it read on the day before the March 31, 2000 proclamation of 1999, c. 2, s. 15, continues to apply to any proceeding under Part III, including a status review proceeding, commenced before that date.*

On the day before the proclamation, section 57 read as follows:

57. (1) *Order where child in need of protection— Where the court finds that a child is in need of protection and is satisfied that intervention through a court order is necessary to protect the child in the future, the court shall make one of the following orders, in the child's best interests:*

1. *Supervision order— That the child be placed with or returned to a parent or another person, subject to the supervision of the society, for a specified period of at least three and not more than twelve months.*

2. *Society wardship — That the child be made a ward of the society and be placed in its care and custody for a specified period not exceeding twelve months.*

3. *Crown wardship — That the child be made a ward of the Crown, until the wardship is terminated under section 65 or expires under subsection 71(1), and be placed in the care of the society.*

4. *Consecutive orders of society wardship and supervision— That the child be made a ward of the society under paragraph 2 for a specified period and then be returned to a parent or another person under paragraph 1, for a period or periods not exceeding an aggregate of twelve months.*

(2) *Court to inquire — In determining which order to make under subsection (1), the court shall ask the parties what efforts the society or another agency or person made to assist the child before intervention under this Part.*

(3) Less restrictive alternatives preferred — The court shall not make an order removing the child from the care of the person who had charge of him or her immediately before intervention under this Part unless the court is satisfied that less restrictive alternatives, including non-residential services and the assistance referred to in subsection (2),

 (a) have been attempted and have failed;

 (b) have been refused by the person having charge of the child; or

 (c) would be inadequate to protect the child.

(4) Community placement to be considered — Where the court decides that it is necessary to remove the child from the care of the person who had charge of him or her immediately before intervention under this Part, the court shall, before making an order for society or Crown wardship under paragraph 2 or 3 of subsection (1), consider whether it is possible to place the child with a relative, neighbour or other member of the child's community or extended family under paragraph 1 of subsection (1) with the consent of the relative or other person.

(5) Idem: where child an Indian or a native person — Where the child referred to in subsection (4) is an Indian or a native person, unless there is a substantial reason for placing the child elsewhere, the court shall place the child with,

 (a) a member of the child's extended family;

 (b) a member of the child's band or native community; or

 (c) another Indian or native family.

(6) Crown wardship order restricted — The court shall not make an order for Crown wardship under paragraph 3 of subsection (1) unless the court is satisfied that the circumstances justifying the order are unlikely to change within a reasonably foreseeable time not exceeding twenty-four months so that the child can be returned to the care of the person who had charge of him or her immediately before intervention under this Part.

(7) Idem — When the court has dispensed with notice to a person under subsection 39(7), the court shall not make an order for Crown wardship under paragraph 3 of subsection (1), or an order for society wardship under paragraph 2 of subsection (1) for a period exceeding thirty days, until a further hearing under subsection 47(1) has been held upon notice to that person.

(8) Terms and conditions of supervision order — Where the court makes a supervision order under paragraph 1 of subsection (1), the court may impose reasonable terms and conditions relating to the child's care and supervision on,

 (a) the person with whom the child is placed or to whom the child is returned;

 (b) the supervising society;

 (c) the child; and

 (d) any other person who participated in the hearing.

(9) Where no court order necessary — Where the court finds that a child is in need of protection but is not satisfied that a court order is necessary to protect the child in the future, the court shall order that the child remain with or be returned to the person who had charge of the child immediately before intervention under this Part.

Access

58. (1) Access order — The court may, in the child's best interests,

 (a) when making an order under this Part; or

 (b) upon an application under subsection (2),

make, vary or terminate an order respecting a person's access to the child or the child's access to a person, and may impose such terms and conditions on the order as the court considers appropriate.

(2) Who may apply — Where a child is in a society's care and custody or supervision,

    (a) the child;

    (b) any other person, including, where the child is an Indian or a native person, a representative chosen by the child's band or native community; or

    (c) the society,

may apply to the court at any time for an order under subsection (1).

(3) Notice — An applicant referred to in clause (2)(b) shall give notice of the application to the society.

(4) Idem — A society making or receiving an application under subsection (2) shall give notice of the application to,

    (a) the child, subject to subsections 39(4) and (5) (notice to child);

    (b) the child's parent;

    (c) the person caring for the child at the time of the application; and

    (d) where the child is an Indian or a native person, a representative chosen by the child's band or native community.

(5) Child over sixteen — No order respecting access to a person sixteen years of age or more shall be made under subsection (1) without the person's consent.

(6) Six-month period — No application shall be made under subsection (2) by a person other than a society within six months of,

    (a) the making of an order under section 57;

    (b) the disposition of a previous application by the same person under subsection (2);

    (c) the disposition of an application under section 64 (review); or

    (d) the final disposition or abandonment of an appeal from an order referred to in clause (a), (b) or (c),

whichever is later.

(7) No application where child placed for adoption — No person or society shall make an application under subsection (2) where the child,

    (a) is a Crown ward;

    (b) has been placed in a person's home by the society or by a Director for the purpose of adoption under Part VII (Adoption); and

    (c) still resides in that person's home.

59. (1) Access: where child removed from person in charge — Where an order is made under paragraph 1 or 2 of subsection 57(1) removing a child from the person who had charge of the child immediately before intervention under this Part, the court shall make an order for access by the person unless the court is satisfied that continued contact with him or her would not be in the child's best interests.

(2) Access: Crown ward — The court shall not make or vary an access order with respect to a Crown ward under section 58 (access) or section 65 (status review) unless the court is satisfied that,

(a) the relationship between the person and the child is beneficial and meaningful to the child; and

(b) the ordered access will not impair the child's future opportunities for a permanent or stable placement.

(3) Termination of access: Crown ward — The court shall terminate an access order with respect to a Crown ward if,

(a) the order is no longer in the best interests of the child; or

(b) the court is no longer satisfied that clauses (2)(a) and (b) apply with respect to that access.

1999, c. 2, s. 16

Transitional Provision

Pursuant to 1999, c. 2, s. 37(5), section 59 of the Child and Family Services Act, *as it read on the day before the March 31, 2000 proclamation of 1999, c. 2, s. 16, continues to apply to any proceeding under Part III, including a status review proceeding, commenced before that date.*

On the day before the proclamation, section 59 read as follows:

59. (1) Access: where child removed from person in charge — Where an order is made under paragraph 1 or 2 of subsection 57(1) removing a child from the person who had charge of the child immediately before intervention under this Part, the court shall make an order for access by the person unless the court is satisfied that continued contact with him or her would not be in the child's best interests.

(2) Idem: Crown ward — Where a child is made a Crown ward under paragraph 3 of subsection 57(1), the court shall not make an order for access by the person who had charge of the child immediately before intervention under this Part unless the court is satisfied that,

(a) permanent placement in a family setting has not been planned or is not possible, and the person's access will not impair the child's future opportunities for such placement;

(b) the child is at least twelve years of age and wishes to maintain contact with the person;

(c) the child has been or will be placed with a person who does not wish to adopt the child; or

(d) some other special circumstance justifies making an order for access.

(3) Termination of access to Crown ward — The court shall not terminate an order for access to a Crown ward unless the court is satisfied that the circumstances that justified the making of the order under subsection (2) no longer exist.

Payment Orders

60. (1) Order for payment by parent — Where the court places a child in the care of,

(a) a society; or

(b) a person other than the child's parent, subject to a society's supervision,

the court may order a parent or a parent's estate to pay the society a specified amount at specified intervals for each day the child is in the society's care or supervision.

(2) Criteria — In making an order under subsection (1), the court shall consider those of the following circumstances of the case that the court considers relevant:

1. The assets and means of the child and of the parent or the parent's estate.

2. The child's capacity to provide for his or her own support.

3. The capacity of the parent or the parent's estate to provide support.

4. The child's and the parent's age and physical and mental health.

5. The child's mental, emotional and physical needs.

6. Any legal obligation of the parent or the parent's estate to provide support for another person.

7. The child's aptitude for and reasonable prospects of obtaining an education.

8. Any legal right of the child to support from another source, other than out of public money.

(3) Order ends at eighteen — No order made under subsection (1) shall extend beyond the day on which the child attains the age of eighteen years.

(4) Power to vary — The court may vary, suspend or terminate an order made under subsection (1) where the court is satisfied that the circumstances of the child or parent have changed.

(5) Collection by municipality — The council of a municipality may enter into an agreement with the board of directors of a society providing for the collection by the municipality, on the society's behalf, of the amounts ordered to be paid by a parent under subsection (1).

(6) Enforcement — An order made against a parent under subsection (1) may be enforced as if it were an order for support made under Part III of the *Family Law Act*.

1993, c. 27, Sched.

Society and Crown Wardship

61. (1) Application — This section applies where a child is made a society or Crown ward under paragraph 2 or 3 of subsection 57(1).

(2) Placement — The society having care of a child shall choose a residential placement for the child that,

    (a) represents the least restrictive alternative for the child;

    (b) where possible, respects the religious faith, if any, in which the child is being raised;

    (c) where possible, respects the child's linguistic and cultural heritage;

    (d) where the child is an Indian or a native person, is with a member of the child's extended family, a member of the child's band or native community or another Indian or native family, if possible; and

    (e) takes into account the child's wishes, if they can be reasonably ascertained, and the wishes of any parent who is entitled to access to the child.

(3) Education — The society having care of a child shall ensure that the child receives an education that corresponds to his or her aptitudes and abilities.

(4) Placement outside or removal from Ontario — The society having care of a child shall not place the child outside Ontario or permit a person to remove the child from Ontario permanently unless a Director is satisfied that extraordinary circumstances justify the placement or removal.

(5) Rights of child, parent and foster parent — The society having care of a child shall ensure that,

(a) the child is afforded all the rights referred to in Part V (Rights of Children); and

(b) the wishes of any parent who is entitled to access to the child and, where the child is a Crown ward, of any foster parent with whom the child has lived continuously for two years are taken into account in the society's major decisions concerning the child.

(6) Change of placement — The society having care of a child may remove the child from a foster home or other residential placement where, in the opinion of a Director or local director, it is in the child's best interests to do so.

(7) Rights of foster parents in certain cases — Where a child is a Crown ward and has lived with a foster parent continuously for two years, the society shall not remove the child under subsection (6) without first giving the foster parent ten days notice of the proposed removal and of his or her right to a review under section 68.

(8) Time for review — Where a foster parent requests a review under section 68 within ten days of receiving a notice under subsection (7), the society shall not remove the child until the review and any further review by a Director have been completed and unless the society's board of directors or the Director, as the case may be, recommend that the child be removed.

(9) Exception where child at risk — Subsections (7) and (8) do not apply where, in the opinion of a Director or local director, there would be a risk that the child is likely to suffer harm during the time necessary for notice to the foster parent and a review under section 68.

(10) Review of certain placements — Sections 34, 35 and 36 (review by Residential Placement Advisory Committee, further review by Children's Services Review Board) of Part II (Voluntary Access to Services) apply to a residential placement made by a society.
1999, c. 2, s. 17

62. (1) Society ward: consent to medical treatment — Where a child is made a society ward under paragraph 2 of subsection 57(1), the society may consent to and authorize medical treatment for the child where a parent's consent would otherwise be required, unless the court orders that the parent shall retain any right that he or she may have to give or refuse consent to medical treatment for the child.

(2) Idem — The court shall not make an order under subsection (1) where failure to consent to necessary medical treatment was a ground for finding that the child was in need of protection.

(3) Court order — Where a parent referred to in an order made under subsection (1) refuses or is unavailable or unable to consent to medical treatment for the child and the court is satisfied that the treatment would be in the child's best interests, the court may authorize the society to consent to the treatment.

(4) Consent to child's marriage — Where a child is made a society ward under paragraph 2 of subsection 57(1), the child's parent retains any right that he or she may have under the *Marriage Act* to give or refuse consent to the child's marriage.

63. (1) Crown custodian of Crown wards — Where a child is made a Crown ward under paragraph 3 of subsection 57(1), the Crown has the rights and responsibilities of a parent for the purpose of the child's care, custody and control and has the right to give or refuse consent to medical treatment for the child where a parent's consent would otherwise be required, and the Crown's powers, duties and obligations in respect of the child, except those assigned to a Director by this Act or the regulations, shall be exercised and performed by the society caring for the child.

(2) Society custodian of society wards — Where a child is made a society ward under paragraph 2 of subsection 57(1), the society has the rights and responsibilities of a parent for the purpose of the child's care, custody and control.

Review

64. (1) Application — This section applies where a child is the subject of an order for society supervision, society wardship or Crown wardship under subsection 57(1).

(2) Society to seek status review — The society having care, custody or supervision of a child,

(a) may apply to the court at any tine, subject to subsection (9);

(b) where the order is for society supervision or society wardship, shall apply to the court before the expiry of the order, except under subsection 71(1) (age of eighteen); and

(c) where the society has removed the child from the care of a person with whom the child was placed under an order for society supervision, shall apply to the court within five days of the child's removal,

for review of the child's status.

(3) Application of subs. (2)(a, c) — Where a child is the subject of an order for society supervision under subsection 57(1), clauses (2)(a) and (c) also apply to the society that has jurisdiction in the county or district in which the parent or other person with whom the child is placed resides.

(4) Others may seek status review — An application for review of a child's status may be made on notice to the society by,

(a) the child, where the child is at least twelve years of age;

(b) any parent of the child, subject to subsection (5);

(c) the person with whom the child was placed under an order for society supervision; or

(d) where the child is an Indian or a native person, a representative chosen by the child's band or native community.

(5) Leave required in certain cases — Where the child is a Crown ward and has lived with the same foster parent continuously during the two years immediately before the application, an application under subsection (4) shall not be made by any parent of the child without the court's leave.

(6) Notice — A society making an application under subsection (2) or receiving notice of an application under subsection (4) shall give notice of the application to,

(a) the child, subject to subsections 39(4) and (5) (notice to child);

(b) the child's parent, unless the child is a Crown ward and is sixteen years of age or older;

(c) the person with whom the child was placed under an order for society supervision;

(d) a foster parent who has cared for the child continuously during the six months immediately before the application;

(e) where the child is an Indian or a native person, a representative chosen by the child's band or native community; and

(f) a Director, if the child is a Crown ward.

(7) Six-month period — No application shall be made under subsection (4) within six months of,

(a) the making of the original order under subsection 57(1);

(b) the disposition of a previous application by any person under subsection (4); or

(c) the final disposition or abandonment of an appeal from an order referred to in clause (a) or (b),

whichever is the latest.

(8) Exception — Subsection (7) does not apply where,

(a) the child is a society ward or the subject of an order for society supervision, or the child is a Crown ward and an order for access has been made under section 58; and

(b) the court is satisfied that a major element of the plan for the child's care that the court applied in its decision is not being carried out.

(9) No review where child placed for adoption — No person or society shall make an application under this section where the child,

(a) is a Crown ward;

(b) has been placed in a person's home by the society or by a Director for the purpose of adoption under Part VII; and

(c) still resides in that person's home.

(10) Interim care and custody — Where an application is made under this section, the child shall remain in the care and custody of the person or society having charge of the child, until the application is disposed of, unless the court is satisfied that the child's best interests require a change in the child's care and custody.

1999, c. 2, s. 18

65. (1) Court may vary, etc — Where an application for review of a child's status is made under section 64, the court may, in the child's best interests,

(a) vary or terminate the original order made under subsection 57(1), including a term or condition or a provision for access that is part of the order;

(b) order that the original order terminate on a specified future date; or

(c) make a further order or orders under section 57.

(2) Restriction — Where a child has been made a Crown ward under paragraph 3 of subsection 57(1), the court shall not make an order for society wardship under subsection (1).

(3) [Repealed 1999, c. 2, s. 19.]

1999, c. 2, s. 19

103

Transitional Provision

Pursuant to 1999, c. 2, s. 37(5), subsection 65(3) of the Child and Family Services Act, *as it read on the day before the March 31, 2000 proclamation of 1999, c. 2, s. 19, continues to apply to any proceeding under Part III, including a status review proceeding, commenced before that date.*

On the day before the repealing proclamation, subsection 65(3) read as follows:

65. (3) Criteria — *Before making an order under subsection (1), the court shall consider,*

(a) *whether the grounds on which the original order was made still exist;*

(b) *whether the plan for the child's care that the court applied in its decision is being carried out;*

(c) *what services have been provided or offered under this Act to the person who had charge of the child immediately before intervention under this Part;*

(d) *whether the person is satisfied with those services;*

(e) *whether the society is satisfied that the person has co-operated with the society and with any person or agency providing services;*

(f) *whether the person or the child requires further services;*

(g) *whether, where immediate termination of an order has been applied for but is not appropriate, a future date for termination of the order can be estimated; and*

(h) *what is the least restrictive alternative that is in the child's best interests.*

66. (1) Director's annual review of Crown wards — A Director or a person authorized by a Director shall, at least once during each calendar year, review the status of every child,

(a) who is a Crown ward;

(b) who was a Crown ward throughout the immediately preceding twenty-four months; and

(c) whose status has not been reviewed under this section or under section 65 during that time.

(2) Idem — After a review under subsection (1), the Director may direct the society to make an application for review of the child's status under subsection 64(2) or give any other direction that, in the Director's opinion, is in the child's best interests.

67. (1) Investigation by judge — The Minister may appoint a judge of the Court of Ontario to investigate a matter relating to a child in a society's care or the proper administration of this Part, and a judge who is appointed shall conduct the investigation and make a written report to the Minister.

(2) Powers of judge — For the purposes of an investigation under subsection (1), the judge has the powers of a commission under Part II of the *Public Inquiries Act*, and that Part applies to the investigation as if it were an inquiry under that Act.

1999, c. 2, s. 20

68. (1) Society review procedure — A society shall establish a written review procedure, which shall be approved by a Director, for hearing and dealing with complaints by any person regarding services sought or received from the society, and shall make the review procedure available to any person on request.

(2) **Idem** — A review procedure established under subsection (1), shall include an opportunity for the person making the complaint to be heard by the society's board of directors.

(3) **Further review by Director** — A person who makes a complaint and is not satisfied with the response of the society's board of directors may have the matter reviewed by a Director.

Appeals

69. (1) Appeal — An appeal from a court's order under this Part may be made to the Superior Court of Justice by,

(a) the child, if the child is entitled to participate in the proceeding under subsection 39(6) (child's participation);

(b) any parent of the child;

(c) the person who had charge of the child immediately before intervention under this Part;

(d) a Director or local director; or

(e) where the child is an Indian or a native person, a representative chosen by the child's band or native community.

(2) **Exception** — Subsection (1) does not apply to an order for an assessment under section 54.

(3) **Care and custody pending appeal** — Where a decision regarding the care and custody of a child is appealed under subsection (1), execution of the decision shall be stayed for the ten days immediately following service of the notice of appeal on the court that made the decision, and where the child is in the society's custody at the time the decision is made, the child shall remain in the care and custody of the society until,

(a) the ten day period of the stay has expired; or

(b) an order is made under subsection (4),

whichever is earlier.

(4) **Temporary order** — The Superior Court of Justice may, in the child's best interests, make a temporary order for the child's care and custody pending final disposition of the appeal, except an order placing the child in a place of secure custody as defined in Part IV (Young Offenders) or a place of secure temporary detention as defined in that Part that has not been designated as a place of safety, and the court may, on any party's motion before the final disposition of the appeal, vary or terminate the order or make a further order.

(5) **No extension where child placed for adoption** — No extension of the time for an appeal shall be granted where the child has been placed for adoption under Part VII (Adoption).

(6) **Further evidence** — The court may receive further evidence relating to events after the appealed decision.

(7) **Place of hearing** — An appeal under this section shall be heard in the county or district in which the order appealed from was made.

CFSA

(8) s. 45 applies — Section 45 (hearings private, etc.) applies with necessary modifications to an appeal under this section.

1999, c. 2, s. 35

Expiry of Orders

70. (1) Time limit — Subject to subsections (3) and (4), the court shall not make an order for society wardship under this Part that results in a child being a society ward for a period exceeding,

(a) 12 months, if the child is less than 6 years of age on the day the court makes an order for society wardship; or

(b) 24 months, if the child is 6 years of age or older on the day the court makes an order for society wardship.

(2) Same — In calculating the period referred to in subsection (1), time during which a child has been in a society's care and custody under,

(a) an agreement made under subsection 29(1) or 30(1) (temporary care or special needs agreement); or

(b) a temporary order made under clause 51(2)(d),

shall be counted.

(2.1) Previous periods to be counted — The period referred to in subsection (1) shall include any previous periods that the child was in a society's care and custody as a society ward or as described in subsection (2) other than periods that precede a continuous period of five or more years that the child was not in a society's care and custody.

(3) Idem — Where the period referred to in subsection (1) or (4) expires and,

(a) an appeal of an order made under subsection 57(1) has been commenced and is not yet finally disposed of; or

(b) the court has adjourned a hearing under section 65 (status review),

the period shall be deemed to be extended until the appeal has been finally disposed of and any new hearing ordered on appeal has been completed or an order has been made under section 65, as the case may be.

Transitional Provisions

Subsection 21(1) of 1999, c. 2, replaced subsections 70(1) and (2), and added subsection 70(2.1). Subsection 21(2) of 1999, c. 2 amended subsection 70(3).

Subsection 37(3) of 1999, c. 2, provides as follows:

(3) For the purposes of subsections 70(1), (2) and (2.1) of the Child and Family Services Act, *as enacted by subsection 21(1) of this Act, no period that a child was in a society's care and custody before the day subsection 21(1) of this Act is proclaimed in force [i.e. before March 31, 2000] shall be counted.*

Subsection 37(4) of 1999, c. 2, provides as follows:

(4) Despite the proclamation of subsections 21(1) and (2) of this Act, subsections 70(1), (2) and (3) of the Child and Family Services Act, *as they read on the day before that proclamation [i.e. before March 31, 2000], shall continue to apply with respect to a child who is in the care and custody of a society on the day of that proclamation so long as that child continues to be in the care and custody of a society.*

106

On the day before that proclamation, those subsections provided as follows:

70. (1) **Twenty-four month rule** — *Subject to subsection (3), the court shall not make an order under this Part that results in a child being a society ward for a continuous period exceeding twenty-four months.*

(2) **Idem** — *In the calculation of the twenty-four month period referred to in subsection (1), time during which a child is in a society's care,*

(a) *under an agreement made under subsection 29(1) or 30(1) (temporary care or special needs agreement) of Part II (Voluntary Access to Services); or*

(b) *under a temporary order made under clause 51(2)(d),*

shall be counted.

(3) **Idem** — *Where the twenty-four month period referred to in subsection (1) expires and,*

(a) *an appeal of an order made under subsection 57(1) has been commenced and is not yet finally disposed of; or*

(b) *the court has adjourned a hearing under section 65 (status review),*

the period shall be deemed to be extended until the appeal has been finally disposed of and any new hearing ordered on appeal has been completed or an order has been made under section 65, as the case may be.

(4) **Six month extension** — Subject to paragraphs 2 and 4 of subsection 57(1), the court may by order extend the period permitted under subsection (1) by a period not to exceed six months if it is in the child's best interests to do so.

1999, c. 2, s. 21

71. (1) **Expiry of orders** — An order under this Part expires when the child who is the subject of the order,

(a) attains the age of eighteen years; or

(b) marries,

whichever comes first.

(2) **Crown ward: continuing care** — Where an order for Crown wardship expires under subsection (1), the society may, with a Director's approval, continue to provide care and maintenance for the former Crown ward in accordance with the regulations.

Duty to Report

72. (1) **Duty to report child in need of protection** — Despite the provisions of any other Act, if a person, including a person who performs professional or official duties with respect to children, has reasonable grounds to suspect one of the following, the person shall forthwith report the suspicion and the information on which it is based to a society:

1. The child has suffered physical harm, inflicted by the person having charge of the child or caused by or resulting from that person's,

i. failure to adequately care for, provide for, supervise or protect the child, or

ii. pattern of neglect in caring for, providing for, supervising or protecting the child.

2. There is a risk that the child is likely to suffer physical harm inflicted by the person having charge of the child or caused by or resulting from that person's,

i. failure to adequately care for, provide for, supervise or protect the child, or

ii. pattern of neglect in caring for, providing for, supervising or protecting the child.

3. The child has been sexually molested or sexually exploited, by the person having charge of the child or by another person where the person having charge of the child knows or should know of the possibility of sexual molestation or sexual exploitation and fails to protect the child.

4. There is a risk that the child is likely to be sexually molested or sexually exploited as described in paragraph 3.

5. The child requires medical treatment to cure, prevent or alleviate physical harm or suffering and the child's parent or the person having charge of the child does not provide, or refuses or is unavailable or unable to consent to, the treatment.

6. The child has suffered emotional harm, demonstrated by serious,

    i. anxiety,

    ii. depression,

    iii. withdrawal,

    iv. self-destructive or aggressive behaviour, or

    v. delayed development,

and there are reasonable grounds to believe that the emotional harm suffered by the child results from the actions, failure to act or pattern of neglect on the part of the child's parent or the person having charge of the child.

7. The child has suffered emotional harm of the kind described in subparagraph i, ii, iii, iv or v of paragraph 6 and the child's parent or the person having charge of the child does not provide, or refuses or is unavailable or unable to consent to, services or treatment to remedy or alleviate the harm.

8. There is a risk that the child is likely to suffer emotional harm of the kind described in subparagraph i, ii, iii, iv or v of paragraph 6 resulting from the actions, failure to act or pattern of neglect on the part of the child's parent or the person having charge of the child.

9. There is a risk that the child is likely to suffer emotional harm of the kind described in subparagraph i, ii, iii, iv or v of paragraph 6 and that the child's parent or the person having charge of the child does not provide, or refuses or is unavailable or unable to consent to, services or treatment to prevent the harm.

10. The child suffers from a mental, emotional or developmental condition that, if not remedied, could seriously impair the child's development and the child's parent or the person having charge of the child does not provide, or refuses or is unavailable or unable to consent to, treatment to remedy or alleviate the condition.

11. The child has been abandoned, the child's parent has died or is unavailable to exercise his or her custodial rights over the child and has not made adequate provision for the child's care and custody, or the child is in a residential placement and the parent refuses or is unable or unwilling to resume the child's care and custody.

12. The child is less than 12 years old and has killed or seriously injured another person or caused serious damage to another person's property, services or treatment are necessary to prevent a recurrence and the child's parent or the person having charge of the child does not provide, or refuses or is unavailable or unable to consent to, those services or treatment.

13. The child is less than 12 years old and has on more than one occasion injured another person or caused loss or damage to another person's property, with the encouragement of the person having charge of the child or because of that person's failure or inability to supervise the child adequately.

(2) Ongoing duty to report — A person who has additional reasonable grounds to suspect one of the matters set out in subsection (1) shall make a further report under subsection (1) even if he or she has made previous reports with respect to the same child.

(3) Person must report directly — A person who has a duty to report a matter under subsection (1) or (2) shall make the report directly to the society and shall not rely on any other person to report on his or her behalf.

(4) Offence — A person referred to in subsection (5) is guilty of an offence if,

(a) he or she contravenes subsection (1) or (2) by not reporting a suspicion; and

(b) the information on which it was based was obtained in the course of his or her professional or official duties.

(5) Same — Subsection (4) applies to every person who performs professional or official duties with respect to children including,

(a) a health care professional, including a physician, nurse, dentist, pharmacist and psychologist;

(b) a teacher, school principal, social worker, family counsellor, priest, rabbi, member of the clergy, operator or employee of a day nursery and youth and recreation worker;

(c) a peace officer and a coroner;

(d) a solicitor; and

(e) a service provider and an employee of a service provider.

(6) Same — In clause (5)(b),

"youth and recreation worker" does not include a volunteer.

(6.1) Same — A director, officer or employee of a corporation who authorizes, permits or concurs in a contravention of an offence under subsection (4) by an employee of the corporation is guilty of an offence.

(6.2) Same — A person convicted of an offence under subsection (4) or (6.1) is liable to a fine of not more than $1,000.

(7) Section overrides privilege — This section applies although the information reported may be confidential or privileged, and no action for making the report shall be instituted against a person who acts in accordance with this section unless the person acts maliciously or without reasonable grounds for the suspicion.

(8) Exception: solicitor client privilege — Nothing in this section abrogates any privilege that may exist between a solicitor and his or her client.

1993, c. 27, Sched.; 1999, c. 2, s. 22

72.1 (1) Duty of society — A society that obtains information that a child in its care and custody is or may be suffering or may have suffered abuse shall forthwith report the information to a Director.

(2) Definition — In this section and sections 73 and 75, "**to suffer abuse**", when used in reference to a child, means to be in need of protection within the meaning of clause 37(2)(a), (c), (e), (f), (f.1) or (h).

Proposed Amendment — 72.1(2)

(2) Definition — In this section and section 73,

"**to suffer abuse**", when used in reference to a child, means to be in need of protection within the meaning of clause 37(2)(a), (c), (e), (f), (f.1) or (h).

1999, c. 2, s. 23(2) [Not in force at date of publication.]

1999, c. 2, s. 23(1)

Review Teams

73. (1) Definition — In this section, "**review team**" means a team established by a society under subsection (2). *("groupe d'étude")*

(2) Review teams — Every society shall establish a review team that includes,

(a) persons who are professionally qualified to perform medical, psychological, developmental, educational or social assessments; and

(b) at least one legally qualified medical practitioner.

(3) Chair — The members of a review team shall choose a chair from among themselves.

(4) Duty of team — Whenever a society refers the case of a child who may be suffering or may have suffered abuse to its review team, the review team or a panel of at least three of its members, designated by the chair, shall,

(a) review the case; and

(b) recommend to the society how the child may be protected.

(5) Disclosure to team permitted — Despite the provisions of any other Act, a person may disclose to a review team or to any of its members information reasonably required for a review under subsection (4).

(6) Subsection overrides privilege — Subsection (5) applies although the information disclosed may be confidential or privileged and no action for disclosing the information shall be instituted against a person who acts in accordance with subsection (5), unless the person acts maliciously or without reasonable grounds.

(7) Where child not to be returned without review or hearing — Where a society with a review team has information that a child placed in its care under subsection 51(2) (temporary care and custody) or subsection 57(1) (order where child in need of protection) may have suffered abuse, the society shall not return the child to the care of the person who had charge of the child at the time of the possible abuse unless,

(a) the society has,

(i) referred the case to its review team, and

(ii) obtained and considered the review team's recommendations; or

(b) the court has terminated the order placing the child in the society's care.

Court-Ordered Access to Records

74. (1) Definition — In this section and sections 74.1 and 74.2,

"**record**" means recorded information, regardless of physical form or characteristics.

(2) Motion or application, production of record — A Director or a society may at any time make a motion or an application for an order under subsection (3) or (3.1) for the production of a record or part of a record.

(3) Order — Where the court is satisfied that a record or part of a record that is the subject of a motion referred to in subsection (2) contains information that may be relevant to a proceeding under this Part and that the person in possession or control of the record has refused to permit a Director or the society to inspect it, the court may order that the person in possession or control of the record produce it or a specified part of it for inspection and copying by the Director, by the society or by the court.

(3.1) Same — Where the court is satisfied that a record or part of a record that is the subject of an application referred to in subsection (2) may be relevant to assessing compliance with one of the following and that the person in possession or control of the record has refused to permit a Director or the society to inspect it, the court may order that the person in possession or control of the record produce it or a specified part of it for inspection and copying by the Director, by the society or by the court:

1. An order under clause 51(2)(b) or (c) that is subject to supervision.

2. An order under clause 51(2)(c) or (d) with respect to access.

3. A supervision order under section 57.

4. An access order under section 58.

5. An order under section 65 with respect to access or supervision.

6. A restraining order under section 80.

(4) Court may examine record — In considering whether to make an order under subsection (3) or (3.1), the court may examine the record.

(5) Information confidential — No person who obtains information by means of an order made under subsection (3) or (3.1) shall disclose the information except,

(a) as specified in the order; and

(b) in testimony in a proceeding under this Part.

(6) Application: solicitor client privilege excepted — Subject to subsection (7), this section applies despite any other Act, but nothing in this section abrogates any privilege that may exist between a solicitor and his or her client.

(7) Matters to be considered by court — Where a motion or an application under subsection (2) concerns a record that is a clinical record within the meaning of section 35 of the *Mental Health Act*, subsection 35(6) (attending physician's statement, hearing) of that Act applies and the court shall give equal consideration to,

(a) the matters to be considered under subsection 35(7) of that Act; and

(b) the need to protect the child.

(8) Same — Where a motion or an application under subsection (2) concerns a record that is a record of a mental disorder within the meaning of section 183, that section applies and the court shall give equal consideration to,

    (a) the matters to be considered under subsection 183(6); and

    (b) the need to protect the child.

1999, c. 2, s. 24

74.1 (1) Warrant for access to record — The court or a justice of the peace may issue a warrant for access to a record or a specified part of it if the court or justice of the peace is satisfied on the basis of information on oath from a Director or a person designated by a society that there are reasonable grounds to believe that the record or part of the record is relevant to investigate an allegation that a child is or may be in need of protection.

(2) Authority conferred by warrant — The warrant authorizes the Director or the person designated by the society to,

    (a) inspect the record specified in the warrant during normal business hours or during the hours specified in the warrant;

    (b) make copies from the record in any manner that does not damage the record; and

    (c) remove the record for the purpose of making copies.

(3) Return of record — A person who removes a record under clause (2)(c) shall promptly return it after copying it.

(4) Admissibility of copies — A copy of a record that is the subject of a warrant under this section and that is certified as being a true copy of the original by the person who made the copy is admissible in evidence to the same extent as and has the same evidentiary value as the record.

(5) Duration of warrant — The warrant is valid for seven days.

(6) Execution — The Director or the person designated by the society may call on a peace officer for assistance in executing the warrant.

(7) Solicitor-client privilege — This section applies despite any other Act, but nothing in this section abrogates any privilege that may exist between a solicitor and his or her client.

(8) Matters to be considered — If a warrant issued under this section concerns a clinical record within the meaning of section 35 of the *Mental Health Act* and the warrant is challenged under subsection 35(6) (attending physician's statement, hearing) of that Act, equal consideration shall be given to,

    (a) the matters set out in subsection 35(7) of that Act; and

    (b) the need to protect the child.

(9) Same — If a warrant issued under this section concerns a record of a mental disorder within the meaning of section 183 and the warrant is challenged under section 183, equal consideration shall be given to,

    (a) the matters set out in subsection 183(6); and

    (b) the need to protect the child.

1999, c. 2, s. 25

74.2 (1) Telewarrant — Where a Director or a person designated by a society believes that there are reasonable grounds for the issuance of a warrant under section 74.1 and that it would be impracticable to appear personally before the court or a justice of the peace to make application for a warrant in accordance with section 74.1, the Director or person designated by the society may submit an information on oath by telephone or other means of telecommunication to a justice designated for the purpose by the Chief Justice of the Ontario Court of Justice.

(2) Same — The information shall,

(a) include a statement of the grounds to believe that the record or part of the record is relevant to investigate an allegation that a child is or may be in need of protection; and

(b) set out the circumstances that make it impracticable for the Director or person designated by the society to appear personally before a court or justice of the peace.

(3) Warrant to be issued — The justice may issue a warrant for access to the record or the specified part of it if the justice is satisfied that the application discloses,

(a) reasonable grounds to believe that the record or the part of a record is relevant to investigate an allegation that a child is or may be in need of protection; and

(b) reasonable grounds to dispense with personal appearance for the purpose of an application under section 74.1.

(4) Validity of warrant — A warrant issued under this section is not subject to challenge by reason only that there were not reasonable grounds to dispense with personal appearance for the purpose of an application under section 74.1.

(5) Application of provisions — Subsections 74.1(2) to (9) apply with necessary modifications with respect to a warrant issued under this section.

(6) Definition — In this section,

"justice" means justice of the peace, a judge of the Ontario Court of Justice or a judge of the Family Court of the Superior Court.

1999, c. 2, s. 26

Child Abuse Register

75. (1) Definitions — In this section and in section 76,

"Director" means the person appointed under subsection (2); *("directeur")*

"register" means the register maintained under subsection (5); *("registre")*

"registered person" means a person identified in the register, but does not include,

(a) a person who reports to a society under subsection 72(2) or (3) and is not the subject of the report, or

(b) the child who is the subject of a report. *("personne inscrite")*

(2) Director — The Minister may appoint an employee of the Ministry as Director for the purposes of this section.

(3) Duty of society — A society that receives a report under section 72 that a child, including a child in the society's care, is or may be suffering or may have suffered abuse shall forthwith verify the reported information, or ensure that the information is verified by another society, in the manner determined by the Director, and if the information is verified, the society that verified it shall forthwith report it to the Director in the prescribed form.

(4) Protection from liability — No action or other proceeding for damages shall be instituted against an officer or employee of a society, acting in good faith, for an act done in the execution or intended execution of the duty imposed on the society by subsection (3) or for an alleged neglect or default of that duty.

(5) Child abuse register — The Director shall maintain a register in the manner prescribed by the regulations for the purpose of recording information reported to the Director under subsection (3), but the register shall not contain information that has the effect of identifying a person who reports to a society under subsection 72(2) or (3) and is not the subject of the report.

(6) Register confidential — Despite any other Act, no person shall inspect, remove, alter or permit the inspection, removal or alteration of information maintained in the register, or disclose or permit the disclosure of information that the person obtained from the register, except as this section authorizes.

(7) Coroner's inquest, etc. — A person who is,

(a) a coroner, or a legally qualified medical practitioner or peace officer authorized in writing by a coroner, acting in connection with an investigation or inquest under the *Coroners Act*; or

(b) the Children's Lawyer or the Children's Lawyer's authorized agent,

may inspect, remove and disclose information in the register in accordance with his or her authority.

(8) Minister or Director may permit access to register — The Minister or the Director may permit,

(a) a person who is employed by,

(i) the Ministry,

(ii) a society, or

(iii) a recognized child protection agency outside Ontario; or

(b) a person who is providing or proposes to provide counselling or treatment to a registered person,

to inspect and remove information in the register and to disclose the information to a person referred to in subsection (7) or to another person referred to in this subsection, subject to such terms and conditions as the Director may impose.

(9) Director may disclose information — The Minister or the Director may disclose information in the register to a person referred to in subsection (7) or (8).

(10) Research — A person who is engaged in research may, with the Director's written approval, inspect and use the information in the register, but shall not,

(a) use or communicate the information for any purpose except research, academic pursuits or the compilation of statistical data; or

(b) communicate any information that may have the effect of identifying a person named in the register.

(11) Registered person — A child, a registered person or the child's or registered person's solicitor or agent may inspect only the information in the register that refers to the child or registered person.

(12) Physician — A legally qualified medical practitioner may, with the Director's written approval, inspect the information in the register that is specified by the Director.

(13) Amendment of register — The Director or an employee of the Ministry acting under the Director's authority,

(a) shall remove a name from or otherwise amend the register where the regulations require the removal or amendment; and

(b) may amend the register to correct an error.

(14) Register inadmissible: exceptions — The register shall not be admitted into evidence in a proceeding except,

(a) to prove compliance or non-compliance with this section;

(b) in a hearing or appeal under section 76;

(c) in a proceeding under the *Coroners Act*; or

(d) in a proceeding referred to in section 81 (recovery on child's behalf).

Proposed Repeal — 75.

75. [Repealed 1999, c. 2, s. 27. Not in force at date of publication.]

1994, c. 27, s. 43(2)

76. (1) Definition — In this section, **"hearing"** means a hearing held under clause (4)(b). *("audience")*

(2) Notice to registered person — Where an entry is made in the register, the Director shall forthwith give written notice to each registered person referred to in the entry indicating that,

(a) the person is identified in the register;

(b) the person or the person's solicitor or agent is entitled to inspect the information in the register that refers to or identifies the person; and

(c) the person is entitled to request that the Director remove the person's name from or otherwise amend the register.

(3) Request to amend register — A registered person who receives notice under subsection (2) may request that the Director remove the person's name from or otherwise amend the register.

(4) Director's response — On receiving a request under subsection (3), the Director may,

(a) grant the request; or

(b) hold a hearing, on ten days written notice to the parties, to determine whether to grant or refuse the request.

(5) Delegation — The Director may authorize another person to hold a hearing and exercise the Director's powers and duties under subsection (8).

(6) Procedure — The *Statutory Powers Procedure Act* applies to a hearing and a hearing shall be conducted in accordance with the prescribed practices and procedures.

(7) Hearing — The parties to a hearing are,

(a) the registered person;

(b) the society that verified the information referring to or identifying the registered person; and

(c) any other person specified by the Director.

(8) Director's decision — Where the Director determines, after holding a hearing, that the information in the register with respect to a registered person is in error or should not be in the register, the Director shall remove the registered person's name from or otherwise amend the register, and may order that the society's records be amended to reflect the Director's decision.

(9) Appeal to Divisional Court — A party to a hearing may appeal the Director's decision to the Divisional Court.

(10) Hearing private — A hearing or appeal under this section shall be held in the absence of the public and no media representative shall be permitted to attend.

(11) Publication — No person shall publish or make public information that has the effect of identifying a witness at or a participant in a hearing, or a party to a hearing other than a society.

(12) Record inadmissible: exception — The record of a hearing or appeal under this section shall not be admitted into evidence in any other proceeding except a proceeding under clause 85(1)(d) (confidentiality of register) or clause 85(1)(e) (amendment of society's records).

Proposed Repeal — 76.

76. [Repealed 1999, c. 2, s. 28. Not in force at date of publication.]

Powers of Director

77. (1) Director's power to transfer — A Director may direct, in the best interests of a child in the care or supervision of a society, that the child,

(a) be transferred to the care or supervision of another society; or

(b) be transferred from one placement to another placement designated by the Director.

(2) Criteria — In determining whether to direct a transfer under clause (1)(b), the Director shall take into account,

(a) the length of time the child has spent in the existing placement;

(b) the views of the foster parents; and

(c) the views and preferences of the child, where they are reasonably ascertainable.

Homemakers

78. (1) Definition — In this section, **"homemaker"** means a person who is approved by a Director or local director for the purposes of this section. (*"aide familiale"*)

(2) Homemaker may remain on premises — Where it appears to a person entering premises under section 40 or 44 that,

(a) a child who in the person's opinion is unable to care for himself or herself has been left on the premises without competent care or supervision; and

(b) no person having charge of the child is available or able to consent to the placement of a homemaker on the premises,

the person may, instead of taking the child to a place of safety,

(c) remain on the premises; or

(d) arrange with a society for the placement of a homemaker on the premises.

(3) Homemaker's authority — A homemaker who remains or is placed on premises under subsection (2) may enter and live there, carry on normal housekeeping activities that are reasonably necessary for the care of any child on the premises and exercise reasonable control and discipline over any such child.

(4) Protection from personal liability — No action shall be instituted against a homemaker who remains or is placed on premises under subsection (2) for,

(a) entering and living on the premises;

(b) anything done or omitted in connection with normal housekeeping activities on the premises;

(c) providing goods and services reasonably necessary for the care of any child on the premises; or

(d) the exercise of reasonable control and discipline over any child on the premises,

so long as the homemaker acts in good faith with reasonable care in the circumstances.

(5) Notice to person having charge of child — Where a homemaker remains or is placed on premises under subsection (2), the society shall forthwith notify or make reasonable efforts to notify the person last having charge of the child that a homemaker has been placed on the premises.

(6) Court order, etc. — Where a child with whom a homemaker has been placed under subsection (2),

(a) is found not to be in need of protection, the homemaker shall leave the premises; or

(b) is found to be in need of protection, the court may authorize the homemaker to remain on the premises until,

(i) a specified day not more than thirty days from the date of the order, or

(ii) a person who is entitled to custody of the child returns to care for the child,

whichever is sooner.

(7) Extension — Where no person returns to care for the child before the day specified in an order under clause (6)(b), the court may,

(a) extend the order; or

(b) hold a further hearing under section 47 and make an order under section 57.

Offences, Restraining Orders, Recovery on Child's Behalf

79. (1) Definition — In this section, **"abuse"** means a state or condition of being physically harmed, sexually molested or sexually exploited. *("mauvais traitements")*

(2) Child abuse — No person having charge of a child shall,

(a) inflict abuse on the child; or

(b) by failing to care and provide for or supervise and protect the child adequately,

(i) permit the child to suffer abuse, or

(ii) permit the child to suffer from a mental, emotional or developmental condition that, if not remedied, could seriously impair the child's development.

(3) Leaving child unattended — No person having charge of a child less than sixteen years of age shall leave the child without making provision for his or her supervision and care that is reasonable in the circumstances.

(4) Reverse onus — Where a person is charged with contravening subsection (3) and the child is less than ten years of age, the onus of establishing that the person made provision for the child's supervision and care that was reasonable in the circumstances rests with the person.

(5) Allowing child to loiter, etc. — No parent of a child less than sixteen years of age shall permit the child to,

(a) loiter in a public place between the hours of midnight and 6 a.m.; or

(b) be in a place of public entertainment between the hours of midnight and 6 a.m., unless the parent accompanies the child or authorizes a specified individual eighteen years of age or older to accompany the child.

(6) Police may take child home or to place of safety — Where a child who is actually or apparently less than sixteen years of age is in a place to which the public has access between the hours of midnight and 6 a.m. and is not accompanied by a person described in clause (5)(b), a peace officer may apprehend the child without a warrant and proceed as if the child has been apprehended under subsection 42(1).

(7) Child protection hearing — The court may, in connection with a case arising under subsection (2), (3) or (5), proceed under this Part as if an application had been made under subsection 40(1) (child protection proceeding) in respect of the child.

80. (1) Restraining order — Where the court finds that a child is in need of protection, the court may, instead of or in addition to making an order under subsection 57(1), make an order in the child's best interests restraining or prohibiting a person's access to or contact with the child, and may include in the order such directions as the court considers appropriate for implementing the order and protecting the child.

(2) Idem: notice — An order shall not be made under subsection (1) unless notice of the proceeding has been served personally on the person to be named in the order.

(3) Six month maximum — An order made under subsection (1) shall be in force for a specified period not exceeding six months.

(4) Extension, variation and termination — An application for the extension, variation or termination of an order made under subsection (1) may be made by,

    (a) the person who is the subject of the order;

    (b) the child;

    (c) the person having charge of the child;

    (d) a society;

    (e) a Director; or

    (f) where the child is an Indian or a native person, a representative chosen by the child's band or native community.

(5) Idem — Where an application is made under subsection (4), the court may, in the child's best interests,

    (a) extend the order for a further period or periods of six months; or

    (b) vary or terminate the order.

(6) Child in society's care not to be returned while order in force — Where a society has care of a child and an order made under subsection (1) prohibiting a person's access to the child is in force, the society shall not return the child to the care of,

    (a) the person named in the order; or

    (b) a person who may permit that person to have access to the child.

81. (1) Definition — In this section, **"to suffer abuse"**, when used in reference to a child, means to be in need of protection within the meaning of clause 37(2) (a), (c), (e), (f), (f.1) or (h). (*"subir de mauvais traitements"*)

(2) Recovery on child's behalf — When the Children's Lawyer is of the opinion that a child has a cause of action or other claim because the child has suffered abuse, the Children's Lawyer may, if he or she considers it to be in the child's best interests, institute and conduct proceedings on the child's behalf for the recovery of damages or other compensation.

(3) Idem: society — Where a child is in a society's care and custody, subsection (2) also applies to the society with necessary modifications.

1994, c. 27, s. 43(2); 1999, c. 2, s. 29

82. Prohibition — No person shall place a child in the care and custody of a society, and no society shall take a child into its care and custody, except,

    (a) in accordance with this Part; or

    (b) under an agreement made under subsection 29(1) or 30(1) (temporary care or special needs agreement) of Part II (Voluntary Access to Services).

83. Offence — Where a child is the subject of an order for society supervision, society wardship or Crown wardship under subsection 57(1), no person shall,

    (a) induce or attempt to induce the child to leave the care of the person with whom the child is placed by the court or by the society, as the case may be;

    (b) detain or harbour the child after the person or society referred to in clause (a) requires that the child be returned;

(c) interfere with the child or remove or attempt to remove the child from any place; or

(d) for the purpose of interfering with the child, visit or communicate with the person, referred to in clause (a).

84. Offence — No person shall,

(a) knowingly give false information in an application under this Part; or

(b) obstruct, interfere with or attempt to obstruct or interfere with a child protection worker or a peace officer who is acting under section 40, 41, 42, 43 or 44.

85. (1) Offences — A person who contravenes,

(a) an order for access made under subsection 58(1);

(b) [Repealed 1999, c. 2, s. 30(1).]

(c) subsection 74(5) (disclosure of information obtained by court order);

(d) subsection 75(6) or (10) (confidentiality of child abuse register);

(e) an order made under subsection 76(8) (amendment of society's records);

(f) subsection 79(3) or (5) (leaving child unattended, etc.);

(g) a restraining order made under subsection 80(1);

(h) section 82 (unauthorized placement);

(i) any provision of section 83 (interference with child, etc.); or

(j) clause 84(a) or (b),

and a director, officer or employee of a corporation who authorizes, permits or concurs in such a contravention by the corporation is guilty of an offence and on conviction is liable to a fine of not more than $1,000 or, to imprisonment for a term of not more than one year, or to both.

Proposed Amendment — 85(1)

(1) Offences — A person who contravenes,

(a) an order for access made under subsection 58(1);

(b) [Repealed 1999, c. 2, s. 30(1).]

(c) subsection 74(5) (disclosure of information obtained by court order);

(d) [Repealed 1999, c. 2, s. 30(2). Not in force at date of publication.]

(e) [Repealed 1999, c. 2, s. 30(3). Not in force at date of publication.]

(f) subsection 79(3) or (5) (leaving child unattended, etc.);

(g) a restraining order made under subsection 80(1);

(h) section 82 (unauthorized placement);

(i) any provision of section 83 (interference with child, etc.); or

(j) clause 84(a) or (b),

and a director, officer or employee of a corporation who authorizes, permits or concurs in such a contravention by the corporation is guilty of an offence and on conviction is liable to a fine of not more than $1,000 or to imprisonment for a term of not more than one year, or to both.

1999, c. 2, s. 30(2), (3) [Not in force at date of publication.]

(2) Idem — A person who contravenes subsection 79(2) (child abuse), and a director, officer or employee of a corporation who authorizes, permits or concurs in such a contravention by the corporation is guilty of an offence and on conviction is liable to a fine of not more than $2,000 or to imprisonment for a term of not more than two years, or to both.

(3) Idem — A person who contravenes subsection 45(8) or 76(11) (publication of identifying information) or an order prohibiting publication made under clause 45(7)(c) or subsection 45(9), and a director, officer or employee of a corporation who authorizes, permits or concurs in such a contravention by the corporation, is guilty of an offence and on conviction is liable to a fine of not more than $10,000 or to imprisonment for a term of not more than three years, or to both.

Proposed Amendment — 85(3)

(3) Idem — A person who contravenes subsection 45(8) (publication of identifying information) or an order prohibiting publication made under clause 45(7)(c) or subsection 45(9), and a director, officer or employee of a corporation who authorizes, permits or concurs in such a contravention by the corporation, is guilty of an offence and on conviction is liable to a fine of not more than $10,000 or to imprisonment for a term of not more than three years, or to both.

1999, c. 2, s. 30(5) [Not in force at date of publication.]

1999, c. 2, s. 30(1), (4)

Child's Religious Faith

86. (1) How child's religious faith determined — For the purposes of this section, a child shall be deemed to have the religious faith agreed upon by the child's parent, but where there is no agreement or the court cannot readily determine what the religious faith agreed upon is or whether any religious faith is agreed upon, the court may decide what the child's religious faith is, if any, on the basis of the child's circumstances.

(2) Child's wishes to be consulted — The court shall consider the child's views and wishes, if they can be reasonably ascertained, in determining what the child's religious faith is, if any.

(3) Religious faith of child — A Protestant child shall not be committed under this Part to the care of a Roman Catholic society or institution and a Roman Catholic child shall not be committed under this Part to a Protestant society or institution, and a Protestant child shall not be placed in a foster home with a Roman Catholic family and a Roman Catholic child shall not be placed in a foster home with a Protestant family, and, where a child committed under this Part is other than Protestant or Roman Catholic, the child shall be placed where practicable with a family of his of her own religious faith, if any.

(4) Where only one society — Subsection (3) does not apply to the commitment of a child to the care of a society in a municipality in which there is only one society.

(5) Director's discretion re foster placement — Where a society,

(a) is unable to place a child in a suitable foster home within a reasonable time because of the operation of subsection (3); and

(b) would be able to place the child in a suitable foster home but for the operation of subsection (3),

121

the society may apply to a Director who may order that subsection (3) does not apply to the child in respect of the placement.

Injunctions

87. (1) Injunction — The Superior Court of Justice may grant an injunction to restrain a person from contravening section 83, on the society's application.

(2) Variation, etc. — The court may vary or terminate an order made under subsection (1), on any person's application.

1999, c. 2, s. 35

PART IV — YOUNG OFFENDERS

88. Definitions — In this Part,

"bailiff" means a bailiff appointed under clause 90(1)(c); *("huissier")*

"Board" means the Custody Review Board established under subsection 96(1); *("Commission")*

"federal Act" means the *Young Offenders Act* (Canada); *("loi fédérale")*

"maximum security place of custody" means a place of secure custody in which the Minister has established a maximum security custody program; *("lieu de garde à sécurité maximale")*

"medium security place of custody" means a place of secure custody in which the Minister has established a medium security custody program; *("lieu de garde à sécurité moyenne")*

"place of open custody" means a place or facility designated as a place of open custody under subsection 24.1(1) of the federal Act and operated by or for the Minister; *("lieu de garde en milieu ouvert")*

"place of open temporary detention" means a place of temporary detention in which the Minister has established an open detention program; *("lieu de détention provisoire en milieu ouvert")*

"place of secure custody" means a place or facility designated for the secure containment or restraint of young persons under subsection 24.1(1) of the federal Act and operated by or for the Minister; *("lieu de garde en milieu fermé")*

"place of secure temporary detention" means a place of temporary detention in which the Minister has established a secure detention program; *("lieu de détention provisoire en milieu fermé")*

"place of temporary detention" means a place or facility designated as a place of temporary detention under subsection 7(1) of the federal Act and operated by or for the Minister; *("lieu de détention provisoire")*

"probation officer" means a probation officer appointed under clause 90(1)(b); *("agent de probation")*

"provincial director" means a provincial director appointed under clause 90(1)(a); *("directeur provincial")* "**services and programs**" means,

    (a) prevention programs,

    (b) pre-trial detention and supervision programs,

    (c) open and secure custody programs,

    (d) probation services,

    (e) programs for the administration and supervision of dispositions, and

    (f) other related services and programs; *("services et programmes")*

"**young person**" means a child as defined in subsection 3(1) who is, or, in the absence of evidence to the contrary, appears to be,

    (a) twelve years of age, or more, but

    (b) under sixteen years of age,

and includes a person sixteen years of age or more charged with having committed an offence while he or she was twelve years of age or more but under sixteen years of age. *("adolescent")*

Programs and Officers

89. (1) Services and programs — The Minister may,

    (a) establish, operate and maintain services and programs; and

    (b) make agreements with persons for the provision of services and programs,

for or on behalf of young persons for the purposes of the federal Act and the *Provincial Offences Act*, and may make payments for those services and programs out of legislative appropriations.

(2) Secure and open temporary detention programs — The Minister may establish,

    (a) secure temporary detention programs, in which restrictions are continuously imposed on the liberty of young persons by physical barriers, close staff supervision or limited access to the community; and

    (b) open temporary detention programs, in which restrictions that are less stringent than in a secure temporary detention program are imposed on the liberty of young persons,

in places of temporary detention.

(3) Maximum and medium security custody programs — The Minister may establish,

    (a) maximum security custody programs, in which restrictions are continuously imposed on the liberty of young persons by physical barriers, close staff supervision or limited access to the community; and

    (b) medium security custody programs, in which restrictions that are less stringent than in a maximum security custody program are imposed on the liberty of young persons,

in places of secure custody.

(4) Open custody programs — The Minister may establish open custody programs in places of open custody.

(5) Where locking up permitted — A place of secure custody and a place of secure temporary detention may be locked for the detention of young persons.

90. (1) Appointments by Minister — The Minister may appoint any person as,

(a) a provincial director, to perform any or all of the duties and functions of a provincial director,

(i) under the federal Act, and

(ii) under the regulations;

(b) a probation officer, to perform any or all of the duties and functions,

(i) of a youth worker under the federal Act, and

(ii) of a probation officer for the purpose of dealing with young persons under the *Provincial Offences Act*, and

(iii) of a probation officer under the regulations; and

(c) a bailiff, to perform any or all of the duties and functions of a bailiff under the regulations.

(2) Limitations, etc., on appointments — The Minister may set out in an appointment made under subsection (1) any conditions or limitations to which it is subject.

(3) Probation officer and bailiff have powers of peace officer — While performing their duties and functions, a probation officer appointed under clause (1)(b) and a bailiff appointed under clause (1)(c) have the powers of a peace officer.

(4) Remuneration and expenses — The remuneration and expenses of a person appointed under subsection (1) who is not a public servant under the *Public Service Act* shall be fixed by the Minister and shall be paid out of legislative appropriations.

91. (1) Approval of provincial director for provision of services to person over sixteen — With the approval of a provincial director, services may be provided under this Part to a person sixteen years of age or more who is a young person within the meaning of the federal Act but not within the meaning of young person as defined in section 88.

(2) Person deemed to be young person — A person who is the subject of an approval under subsection (1) shall be deemed to be a young person for the purposes of this Part.

92. Reports and information — A person in charge of a service or program provided under subsection 89(1), a person in charge of a place of temporary detention, open custody or secure custody, a bailiff and a probation officer,

(a) shall make the prescribed reports and furnish the prescribed information to the Minister, in the prescribed form and at the prescribed intervals; and

(b) shall make a report to the Minister whenever the Minister requests it, in the form and containing the information specified by the Minister.

Temporary Detention

93. (1) Open detention unless provincial director determines otherwise — A young person who is detained under the federal Act in a place of temporary detention shall be detained in a place of open temporary detention unless a provincial director determines under subsection (2) that the young person is to be detained in a place of secure temporary detention.

(2) Where secure detention available — A provincial director may detain a young person in a place of secure temporary detention if the circumstances described in paragraph 1 or 2 apply to the young person and if the provincial director is satisfied that it is necessary to detain the young person in a place of secure temporary detention to ensure the young person's attendance in court or to protect the public interest or safety:

1. The young person is charged with an offence for which an adult would be liable to imprisonment for five years or more and,

i. the offence includes causing or attempting to cause serious bodily harm to another person,

ii. the young person has, at any time, failed to appear in court when required to do so under the federal Act or escaped or attempted to escape from lawful detention, or

iii. the young person has, within the twelve months immediately preceding the offence on which the current charge is based, been convicted of an offence for which an adult would be liable to imprisonment for five years or more.

2. The young person is detained in a place of temporary detention and leaves or attempts to leave without the consent of the person in charge or is charged with having escaped or attempting to escape from lawful custody or being unlawfully at large under the *Criminal Code* (Canada).

(3) Idem — Despite subsection (1), a young person who is apprehended because he or she has left or has not returned to a medium security or maximum security place of custody may be detained in a place of secure temporary detention until he or she is returned to the first-named place of custody.

(4) Idem — Despite subsection (1), a young person who is detained under the federal Act in a place of temporary detention may be detained in a place of secure temporary detention for a period not exceeding twenty-four hours while a provincial director makes a determination in respect of the young person under subsection (2).

(5) Review by youth court — A young person who is being detained in a place of secure temporary detention and is brought before a youth court for a review under the *Criminal Code* (Canada) may request that the youth court review the level of his or her detention, and the youth court may confirm the provincial director's decision under subsection (2) or may direct that the young person be transferred to a place of open temporary detention.

Custody

94. (1) Medium rather than maximum security custody unless provincial director determines otherwise — A young person who is committed to secure custody under the federal Act shall be held in a medium security place of custody unless a provincial director determines under subsection (2) that the young person is to be held in a maximum security place of custody.

(2) Where maximum security custody available — A provincial director may place a young person in or transfer a young person to a maximum security place of custody if the young person is committed to secure custody under the federal Act for an offence for which an adult would be liable to imprisonment for five years or more and,

(a) the offence for which the young person is committed to secure custody includes causing or attempting to cause serious bodily harm to another person; or

CFSA

(b) the young person has, within the twelve months immediately preceding the offence for which he or she is committed to secure custody,

(i) been held in a maximum security place of custody, or

(ii) been found guilty of an offence for which an adult would be liable to imprisonment for five years or more,

where the provincial director is satisfied that it would not be appropriate to hold the young person in a medium security place of custody, having regard to,

(c) the young person's age and previous history;

(d) the circumstances of the commission of the offence for which the young person is committed to secure custody;

(e) the contents of a pre-disposition report;

(f) the needs of the young person; and

(g) the need to protect the public interest and safety.

(3) Transfer from maximum to medium security custody — A provincial director may transfer a young person from a maximum security place of custody to a medium security place of custody if the provincial director is satisfied that the transfer is justified because the young person has made sufficient progress or for some other appropriate reason.

(4) Reasons — A provincial director who makes a determination under this section shall give written reasons for the determination to the young person and to the persons in charge of the places of custody from and to which the young person is transferred.

95. Young persons in open custody — Where a young person is sentenced to a term of imprisonment for breach of probation under clause 75 (d) of the *Provincial Offences Act*, to be served in open custody as set out in section 103 of that Act,

(a) the young person shall be held in a place of open custody specified by a provincial director; and

(b) the provisions of section 35 (temporary release) of the federal Act apply with necessary modifications.

Custody Review Board

96. (1) Custody Review Board — The Custody Review Board is continued under the name Custody Review Board in English and Commission de révision des placements sous garde in French and shall have the powers and duties given to it by this Part and the regulations.

(2) Chair and vice-chairs — The Board shall be composed of the prescribed number of members who shall be appointed by the Lieutenant Governor in Council.

(3) Members — The Lieutenant Governor in Council may appoint a member of the Board as chair and may appoint one or more other members as vice-chairs.

(4) Term — A member of the Board shall hold office for the prescribed term.

(5) Quorum — The prescribed number of members of the Board are a quorum.

(6) Remuneration — The chair and vice-chairs and the other members of the Board shall be paid the daily allowances determined by the Lieutenant Governor in Council and are entitled to their reasonable and necessary travelling and living expenses while attending meetings or otherwise engaged in the work of the Board.

(7) Duties of Board — The Board shall conduct reviews under section 97 and perform such other duties as are assigned to it by the regulations.

97. (1) Application to Board — A young person may apply to the Board for a review of,

(a) a provincial director's decision to hold the young person in or transfer the young person to a maximum security place of custody;

(b) the particular place where the young person is held or to which the young person has been transferred;

(c) a provincial director's refusal to authorize the young person's temporary release under section 35 of the federal Act; or

(d) the young person's transfer from a place of open custody to a place of secure custody under subsection 24.2 (9) of the federal Act,

within thirty days of the decision, placement or transfer, as the case may be.

(2) Duty of Board — The Board shall conduct a review with respect to an application made under subsection (1) and may do so by holding a hearing.

(3) Idem — The Board shall advise the young person whether it intends to hold a hearing or not within ten days of receiving the young person's application.

(4) Procedure — The *Statutory Powers Procedure Act* does not apply to a hearing held under subsection (2).

(5) Idem — The Board shall complete its review and make a determination within thirty days of receiving a young person's application, unless,

(a) the Board holds a hearing with respect to the application; and

(b) the young person and the provincial director whose decision is being reviewed consent to a longer period for the Board's determination.

(6) Board's recommendations — After conducting a review under subsection (2), the Board may,

(a) recommend to the provincial director,

(i) that the young person be transferred to a medium security place of custody,

(ii) where the Board is of the opinion that the place where the young person is held or to which he or she has been transferred is not appropriate to meet the young person's needs, that the young person be transferred to another place,

(iii) that the young person's temporary release be authorized under section 35 of the federal Act, or

(iv) where the young person has been transferred under subsection 24.2(9) of the federal Act, that the young person be returned to a place of open custody; or

(b) confirm the decision, placement or transfer.

1993, c. 27, Sched.

Apprehension of Young Persons Who are Absent from Custody Without Permission

98. (1) Apprehension of young person absent from place of temporary detention — A peace officer, the person in charge of a place of temporary detention or that person's delegate, who believes on reasonable and probable grounds that a young person detained under the federal Act or the *Provincial Offences Act* in a place of temporary detention has left the place without the consent of the person in charge and fails or refuses to return there may apprehend the young person with or without a warrant and take the young person or arrange for the young person to be taken to a place of temporary detention.

(2) Idem: place of open custody — A peace officer, the person in charge of a place of open custody or that person's delegate, who believes on reasonable and probable grounds that a young person held in a place of open custody as described in section 95,

(a) has left the place without the consent of the person in charge and fails or refuses to return there; or

(b) fails or refuses to return to the place of open custody upon completion of a period of temporary release under clause 95 (b),

may apprehend the young person with or without a warrant and take the young person or arrange for the young person to be taken to a place of open custody or a place of temporary detention.

(3) Young person to be returned within forty-eight hours — A young person who is apprehended under this section shall be returned to the place from which he or she is absent within forty-eight hours after being apprehended unless the provincial director detains the young person in secure temporary detention under paragraph 2 of subsection 93(2).

(4) Warrant to apprehend young person — A justice of the peace who is satisfied on the basis of a sworn information that there are reasonable and probable grounds to believe that a young person held in a place of temporary detention or open custody,

(a) has left the place without the consent of the person in charge and fails or refuses to return there; or

(b) fails or refuses to return to a place of open custody upon completion of a period of temporary release under clause 95(b),

may issue a warrant authorizing a peace officer, the person in charge of the place of temporary detention or open custody or that person's delegate to apprehend the young person.

(5) Authority to enter, etc. — Where a person authorized to apprehend a young person under subsection (1) or (2) believes on reasonable and probable grounds that a young person referred to it the relevant subsection is on any premises the person may with or without a warrant enter the premises, by force, if necessary, and search for and remove the young person

(6) Regulations re exercise of power of entry — A person authorized to enter premise under subsection (5) shall exercise the power of entry in accordance with the regulations.

PART V — RIGHTS OF CHILDREN

99. Definition — In this Part, **"child in care"** means a child who is receiving residential services from a service provider and includes,

(a) a child who is in the care of a foster parent; and

(b) a child who is detained in a place of temporary detention, committed to secure or open custody under the *Young Offenders Act* (Canada), or held in a place of open custody under section 95 of Part IV (Young Offenders). *("enfant recevant des soins", "enfant qui reçoit des soins")*

Locking Up

100. (1) Locking up restricted — No service provider shall detain a child or permit a child to be detained in locked premises in the course of the provision of a service to the child, except as Part IV (Young Offenders) and Part VI (Extraordinary Measures) authorize.

(2) Application of subs. (1) — Subsection (1) does not prohibit the routine locking of premises for security at night.

Corporal Punishment

101. No corporal punishment — No service provider or foster parent shall inflict corporal punishment on a child or permit corporal punishment to be inflicted on a child in the course of the provision of a service to the child.

Office of Child and Family Service Advocacy

102. Office of Child and Family Service Advocacy — The Office of Child and Family Service Advocacy is continued under the name Office of Child and Family Service Advocacy in English and Bureau d'assistance à l'enfance et à la famille in French, to,

(a) co-ordinate and administer a system of advocacy, except for advocacy before a court, on behalf of children and families who receive or seek approved services or services purchased by approved agencies;

(b) advise the Minister on matters and issues concerning the interests of those children and families; and

(c) perform any similar functions given to it by this Act or the regulations or another Act or the regulations made under another Act.

Rights of Children in Care

103. (1) Rights of communication, etc. — A child in care has a right,

(a) to speak in private with, visit and receive visits from members of his or her family regularly, subject to subsection (2);

(b) to speak in private with and receive visits from,

(i) the child's solicitor,

129

(ii) another person representing the child, including an advocate appointed for the child by the Office of Child and Family Service Advocacy referred to in section 102,

(iii) the Ombudsman appointed under the *Ombudsman Act* and members of the Ombudsman's staff, and

(iv) a member of the Legislative Assembly of Ontario or of the Parliament of Canada; and

(c) to send and receive mail that is not read, examined or censored by another person, subject to subsection (3).

(2) When child a Crown ward — A child in care who is a Crown ward is not entitled as of right to speak with, visit or receive visits from a member of his or her family, except under an order for access made under Part III (Child Protection).

(3) Opening, etc., of mail to child — Mail to a child in care,

(a) may be opened by the service provider or a member of the service provider's staff in the child's presence and may be inspected for articles prohibited by the service provider;

(b) where the service provider believes on reasonable grounds that the contents of the mail may cause the child physical or emotional harm, may be examined or read by the service provider or a member of the service provider's staff in the child's presence, subject to clause (c);

(c) shall not be examined or read by the service provider or a member of the service provider's staff if it is to or from the child's solicitor; and

(d) shall not be censored or withheld from the child, except that articles prohibited by the service provider may be removed from the mail and withheld from the child.

104. Personal liberties — A child in care has a right,

(a) to have reasonable privacy and possession of his or her own personal property; and

(b) to receive the religious instruction and participate in the religious activities of his or her choice, subject to section 106.

105. (1) Plan of care — A child in care has a right to a plan of care designed to meet the child's particular needs, which shall be prepared within thirty days of the child's admission to the residential placement.

(2) Rights to care — A child in care has a right,

(a) to participate in the development of the child's individual plan of care and in any changes made to it;

(b) to receive meals that are well-balanced, of good quality and appropriate for the child;

(c) to be provided with clothing that is of good quality and appropriate for the child, given the child's size and activities and prevailing weather conditions;

(d) to receive medical and dental care, subject to section 106, at regular intervals and whenever required, in a community setting whenever possible;

(e) to receive an education that corresponds to the child's aptitudes and abilities, in a community setting whenever possible; and

(f) to participate in recreational and athletic activities that are appropriate for the child's aptitudes and interests, in a community setting whenever possible.

106. Parental consent, etc. — Subject to subsection 51(4) and sections 62 and 63 (temporary order, society and Crown wards) of Part III (Child Protection), the parent of a child in care retains any right that he or she may have,

(a) to direct the child's education and religious upbringing; and

(b) to give or refuse consent to medical treatment for the child.

107. Right to be heard — A child in care has a right to be consulted and to express his or her views, to the extent that is practical given the child's level of understanding, whenever significant decisions concerning the child are made, including decisions with respect to medical treatment, education and religion and decisions with respect to the child's discharge from the placement or transfer to another residential placement.

108. Right to be informed — A child in care has a right to be informed, in language suitable for the child's level of understanding, of,

(a) the child's rights under this Part;

(b) the internal complaints procedure established under subsection 109(1) and the further review available under section 110;

(c) the existence of the Office of Child and Family Service Advocacy referred to in section 102;

(d) the review procedures available for children twelve years of age or older under sections 34, 35 and 36 of Part II (Voluntary Access to Services);

(e) the review procedures available under section 97 of Part IV (Young Offenders), in the case of a child who is detained in a place of temporary detention, committed to secure or open custody under the *Young Offenders Act* (Canada), or held in a place of open custody under section 95 of Part IV (Young Offenders);

(f) the child's responsibilities while in the placement; and

(g) the rules governing day-to-day operation of the residential service, including disciplinary procedures,

upon admission to the residential placement, to the extent that is practical given the child's level of understanding.

Complaint and Review Procedures

109. (1) Internal complaints procedure — A service provider who provides residential services to children or places children in residential placements shall establish a written procedure, in accordance with the regulations, for hearing and dealing with complaints regarding alleged violations of the rights under this Part of children in care.

(2) Idem — A service provider shall conduct a review or ensure that a review is conducted, in accordance with the procedure established under subsection (1), on the complaint of,

(a) a child in care;

(b) the child's parent; or

(c) another person representing the child,

and shall seek to resolve the complaint.

110. (1) Further review — Where a person referred to in subsection 109(2) who makes a complaint and is not satisfied with the result of the review conducted under that subsection requests in writing that the Minister appoint a person to conduct a further review of the complaint, the Minister shall appoint a person who is not employed by the service provider to do so.

(2) Idem — A person appointed under subsection (1) shall review the complaint in accordance with the regulations and may, but is not required to, do so by holding a hearing.

(3) Procedure — The *Statutory Powers Procedure Act* does not apply to a hearing held under subsection (2).

(4) Powers of appointed person — A person appointed under subsection (1) has, for the purposes of the review, all the powers of a program supervisor appointed under subsection 5(2) of Part I (Flexible Services).

(5) Review and report within thirty days — A person appointed under subsection (1) shall, within thirty days after the day of the appointment, complete the review, set out in a report his or her findings and recommendations, including the reasons for not holding a hearing if none was held, and provide copies of the report to,

(a) the person who made the complaint;

(b) the service provider; and

(c) the Minister.

111. (1) Minister to advise persons affected of any decision — Where the Minister decides to take any action with respect to a complaint after receiving a report under subsection 110(5), the Minister shall advise the person who made the complaint and the service provider of the decision.

(2) Remedies preserved — The Minister's decision referred to in subsection (1) does not affect any other remedy that may be available.

PART VI — EXTRAORDINARY MEASURES

112. Definitions — In this Part,

"administrator" means the person in charge of a secure treatment program; *("administrateur")*

"intrusive procedure" means,

(a) a mechanical means of controlling behaviour,

(b) an aversive stimulation technique, or

(c) any other procedure that is prescribed as an intrusive procedure; *("technique d'ingérence")*

"mental disorder" means a substantial disorder of emotional processes, thought or cognition which grossly impairs a person's capacity to make reasoned judgments; *("trouble mental")*

"psychotropic drug" means a drug or combination of drugs prescribed as a psychotropic drug; *("psychotrope")*

"review team" means an interdisciplinary review team established under subsection 129(1); *("groupe d'étude")*

"secure isolation room" means a locked room approved under subsection 126(1) for use for the secure isolation of children; *("pièce d'isolement sous clef")*

"secure treatment program" means a program established or approved by the Minister under subsection 113(1). *("programme de traitement en milieu fermé")*

Secure Treatment Programs

113. (1) Minister may establish or approve programs — The Minister may,

    (a) establish, operate and maintain; or

    (b) approve,

programs for the treatment of children with mental disorders, in which continuous restrictions are imposed on the liberty of the children.

(2) Terms and conditions — The Minister may impose terms and conditions on an approval given under subsection (1) and may vary or amend the terms and conditions or impose new terms and conditions at any time.

(3) Admission of children — No child shall be admitted to a secure treatment program except by a court order under section 117 (commitment to secure treatment program) or under section 124 (emergency admission).

(4) Locking up permitted — The premises of a secure treatment program may be locked for the detention of children.

Commitment to Secure Treatment

114. (1) Who may apply for order for child's commitment — Any one of the following persons may, with the administrator's written consent, apply to the court for an order for the child's commitment to a secure treatment program:

    1. Where the child is less than sixteen years of age,

        i. the child's parent,

        ii. a person other than an administrator who is caring for the child, if the child's parent consents to the application, or

        iii. a society that has custody of the child under an order made under Part III (Child Protection).

    2. Where the child is sixteen years of age or more,

        i. the child,

        ii. the child's parent, if the child consents to the application,

        iii. a society that has custody of the child under an order made under Part III (Child Protection), if the child consents to the application, or

        iv. a physician.

(2) Time for hearing — Where an application is made under subsection (1), the court shall deal with the matter within ten days of the making of an order under subsection (6) (legal representation) or, where no such order is made, within ten days of the making of the application.

(3) Adjournments — The court may adjourn the hearing of an application but shall not adjourn it for more than thirty days unless the applicant and the child consent to the longer adjournment.

(4) Interim order — Where a hearing is adjourned, the court may make a temporary order for the child's commitment to a secure treatment program if the court is satisfied that the child meets the criteria for commitment set out in clauses 117(1)(a) to (f) and, where the child is less than twelve years old, the Minister consents to the child's admission.

(5) Evidence on adjournments — For the purpose of subsection (4), the court may admit and act on evidence that the court considers credible and trustworthy in the circumstances.

(6) Legal representation of child — Where an application is made under subsection (1) in respect of a child who does not have legal representation, the court shall, as soon as practicable and in any event before the hearing of the application, direct that legal representation be provided for the child.

(7) Hearing private — A hearing under this section shall be held in the absence of the public and no media representative shall be permitted to attend.

(8) Child entitled to be present — The child who is the subject of an application under subsection (1) is entitled to be present at the hearing unless,

(a) the court is satisfied that being present at the hearing would cause the child emotional harm; or

(b) the child, after obtaining legal advice, consents in writing to the holding of the hearing in his or her absence.

(9) Court may require child's presence — The court may require a child who has consented to the holding of the hearing in his or her absence under clause (8)(b) to be present at all or part of the hearing.

115. (1) Child may waive hearing of oral evidence — Where an application is made under subsection 114(1), the court shall deal with the matter by holding a hearing and shall hear oral evidence unless the child, after obtaining legal advice, consents in writing to the making of an order under subsection 117(1) without the hearing of oral evidence, and the consent is filed with the court.

(2) Court may hear oral evidence despite consent — The court may hear oral evidence although the child has given a consent under subsection (1).

(3) Time limitation — A child's consent under subsection (1) is not effective for more than the period referred to in subsection 118(1) (period of commitment).

116. (1) Assessment — The court may, at any time after an application is made under subsection 114(1), order that the child attend within a specified time for an assessment before a specified person who is qualified, in the court's opinion, to perform an assessment to assist the court to determine whether the child should be committed to a secure treatment program and has consented to perform the assessment.

(2) Report — The person performing an assessment under subsection (1) shall make a written report of the assessment to the court within the time specified in the order, which shall not be more than thirty days unless the court is of the opinion that a longer assessment period is necessary.

(3) Who may not perform assessment — The court shall not order an assessment to be performed by a person who provides services in the secure treatment program to which the application relates.

(4) Copies of report — The court shall provide a copy of the report to,

    (a) the applicant;

    (b) the child, subject to subsection (6);

    (c) the child's solicitor;

    (d) a parent appearing at the hearing;

    (e) a society that has custody of the child under an order made under Part III (Child Protection);

    (f) the administrator of the secure treatment program; and

    (g) where the child is an Indian or a native person, a representative chosen by the child's band or native community.

(5) Idem — The court may cause a copy of the report to be given to a parent who does not attend the hearing but is, in the court's opinion, actively interested in the proceedings.

(6) Court may withhold report from child — The court may withhold all or part of the report from the child where the court is satisfied that disclosure of all or part of the report to the child would cause the child emotional harm.

117. (1) Commitment to secure treatment: criteria — The court may order that a child be committed to a secure treatment program only where the court is satisfied that,

    (a) the child has a mental disorder;

    (b) the child has, as a result of the mental disorder, within the forty-five days immediately preceding,

        (i) the application under subsection 114(1),

        (ii) the child's detention or custody under the *Young Offenders Act* (Canada) or under the *Provincial Offences Act*, or

        (iii) the child's admission to a psychiatric facility under the *Mental Health Act* as an involuntary patient,

    caused or attempted to cause serious bodily harm to himself, herself or another person;

    (c) the child has,

        (i) within the twelve months immediately preceding the application, but on another occasion than that referred to in clause (b), caused, attempted to cause or by words or conduct made a substantial threat to cause serious bodily harm to himself, herself or another person, or

        (ii) in committing the act or attempt referred to in clause (b), caused or attempted to cause a person's death;

(d) the secure treatment program would be effective to prevent the child from causing or attempting to cause serious bodily harm to himself, herself or another person;

(e) treatment appropriate for the child's mental disorder is available at the place of secure treatment to which the application relates; and

(f) no less restrictive method of providing treatment appropriate for the child's mental disorder is appropriate in the circumstances.

(2) Where child under twelve — Where the child is less than twelve years old, the court shall not make an order under subsection (1) unless the Minister consents to the child's commitment.

(3) Additional requirement where applicant is physician — Where the applicant is a physician, the court shall not make an order under subsection (1) unless the court is satisfied that the applicant believes the criteria set out in that subsection are met.

118. (1) Period of commitment — The court shall specify in an order under subsection 117(1) the period not exceeding 180 days for which the child shall be committed to the secure treatment program.

(2) Where society is applicant — Where a child is committed to a secure treatment program on a society's application and the period specified in the court's order is greater than sixty days, the child shall be released on a day sixty days after the child's admission to the secure treatment program unless before that day,

(a) the child's parent consents to the child's commitment for a longer period; or

(b) the child is made a Crown or society ward under Part III (Child Protection),

but in no case shall the child be committed to the secure treatment program for longer than the period specified under subsection (1).

(3) How time calculated — In the calculation of a child's period of commitment, time spent in the secure treatment program before an order has been made under section 117 (commitment) or pending an application under section 120 (extension) shall be counted.

(4) Where order expires after eighteenth birthday — A person who is the subject of an order made under subsection 117(1) or 120(5) may be kept in the secure treatment program after attaining the age of eighteen years, until the order expires.

1993, c. 27, Sched.

119. (1) Reasons, etc. — Where the court makes an order under subsection 117(1) or 120(5), the court shall give,

(a) reasons for its decision;

(b) a statement of the plan, if any, for the child's care on release from the secure treatment program; and

(c) a statement of the less restrictive alternatives considered by the court, and the reasons for rejecting them.

(2) Plan for care on release — Where no plan for the child's care on release from the secure treatment program is available at the time of the order, the administrator shall, within ninety days of the date of the order, prepare such a plan and file it with the court.

Extension of Period of Commitment

120. (1) Who may apply for extension — Where a child is the subject of an order made under subsection 117(1) (commitment) or subsection (5),

(a) a person referred to in subsection 114 (1), with the administrator's written consent; or

(b) the administrator, with a parent's written consent or, where the child is in a society's lawful custody, the society's consent,

may, before the expiry of the period of commitment, apply for an order extending the child's commitment to the secure treatment program.

(2) Idem — Where a person is kept in the secure treatment program under subsection 118(4) after attaining the age of eighteen years,

(a) the person, with the written consent of the administrator;

(b) the person's parent, with the written consent of the person and the administrator;

(c) a physician, with the written consent of the administrator and the person; or

(d) the administrator, with the written consent of the person,

may, before the expiry of the period of commitment, apply for one further order extending the person's commitment to the secure treatment program.

(3) Child may be kept in program while application pending — Where an application is made under subsection (1) or (2), the child may be kept in the secure treatment program until the application is disposed of.

(4) ss. 114(3), (6–9), 115, 116 apply — Subsections 114(3), (6), (7), (8) and (9) (hearing) and sections 115 (child's waiver) and 116 (assessment) apply with necessary modifications to an application made under subsection (1) or (2).

(5) Criteria for extension — The court may make an order extending a child's commitment to a secure treatment program only where the court is satisfied that,

(a) the child has a mental disorder;

(b) the secure treatment program would be effective to prevent the child from causing or attempting to cause serious bodily harm to himself, herself or another person;

(c) no less restrictive method of providing treatment appropriate for the child's mental disorder is appropriate in the circumstances;

(d) the child is receiving the treatment proposed at the time of the original order under subsection 117(1), or other appropriate treatment; and

(e) there is an appropriate plan for the child's care on release from the secure treatment program.

(6) Period of extension — The court shall specify in an order under subsection (5) the period not exceeding 180 days for which the child shall be committed to the secure treatment program.

1993, c. 27, Sched.

CFSA

Release by Administrator

121. (1) Unconditional release by administrator — The administrator may release a child from a secure treatment program unconditionally where the administrator,

(a) has given the person with lawful custody of the child reasonable notice of the intention to release him or her; and

(b) is satisfied that,

(i) the child no longer requires the secure treatment program, and

(ii) there is an appropriate plan for the child's care on release from the secure treatment program.

(2) Conditional release — The administrator may release a child from a secure treatment program temporarily for medical or compassionate reasons, or for a trial placement in an open setting, for such period and on such terms and conditions as the administrator determines.

(3) Administrator may release despite court order — Subsections (1) and (2) apply despite an order made under subsection 117(1) (commitment) or 120(5) (extension).

Review of Commitment

122. (1) Review of commitment — Any one of the following persons may apply to the court for an order terminating an order made under subsection 117(1) (commitment) or 120(5) (extension):

1. The child, where the child is twelve years of age or more.

2. The child's parent.

3. The society having care, custody or supervision of the child.

(2) ss. 114(3), (6–9), 115, 116 apply — Subsections 114(3), (6), (7), (8) and (9) (hearing) and sections 115 (child's waiver) and 116 (assessment) apply with necessary modifications to an application made under subsection (1).

(3) Termination of order — The court shall make an order terminating a child's commitment unless the court is satisfied that,

(a) the child has a mental disorder;

(b) the secure treatment program would continue to be effective to prevent the child from causing or attempting to cause serious bodily harm to himself, herself or another person;

(c) no less restrictive method of providing treatment appropriate for the child's mental disorder is appropriate in the circumstances; and

(d) the child is receiving the treatment proposed at the time of the most recent order under subsection 117(1) or 120(5), or other appropriate treatment.

(4) Idem — In making an order under subsection (3), the court shall consider whether there is an appropriate plan for the child's care on release from the secure treatment program.

1993, c. 27, Sched.

123. ss. 120(3–6), 121, 122 apply — Subsections 120(3), (4), (5) and (6) and sections 121 and 122 apply with necessary modifications to a person who is eighteen years of age or older and committed to a secure treatment program as if the person were a child.

Emergency Admission

124. (1) Who may apply for emergency admission — Any one of the following persons may apply to the administrator for the emergency admission of a child to a secure treatment program:

1. Where the child is less than sixteen years of age,

i. the child's parent,

ii. a person who is caring for the child with a parent's consent,

iii. a child protection worker who has apprehended the child under section 40 of Part III (Child Protection), or

iv. a society that has custody of the child under an order made under Part III.

2. Where the child is sixteen years of age or more,

i. the child,

ii. the child's parent, if the child consents to the application,

iii. a society that has custody of the child under an order made under Part III (Child Protection), if the child consents to the application, or

iv. a physician.

(2) Criteria for admission — The administrator may admit a child to the secure treatment program on an application under subsection (1) for a period not to exceed thirty days where the administrator believes on reasonable grounds that,

(a) the child has a mental disorder;

(b) the child has, as a result of the mental disorder, caused, attempted to cause or by words or conduct made a substantial threat to cause serious bodily harm to himself, herself or another person;

(c) the secure treatment program would be effective to prevent the child from causing or attempting to cause serious bodily harm to himself, herself or another person;

(d) treatment appropriate for the child's mental disorder is available at the place of secure treatment to which the application relates; and

(e) no less restrictive method of providing treatment appropriate for the child's mental disorder is appropriate in the circumstances.

(3) Admission on consent — The administrator may admit the child under subsection (2) although the criterion set out in clause (2)(b) is not met, where,

(a) the other criteria set out in subsection (2) are met;

(b) the child, after obtaining legal advice, consents to his or her admission; and

(c) if the child is less than sixteen years of age, the child's parent or, where the child is in a society's lawful custody, the society consents to the child's admission.

(4) Where child under twelve — Where the child is less than twelve years old, the administrator shall not admit the child under subsection (2) unless the Minister consents to the child's admission.

(5) Additional requirement where applicant is physician — Where the applicant is a physician, the administrator shall not admit the child under subsection (2) unless the administrator is satisfied that the applicant believes the criteria set out in that subsection are met.

(6) Notices required — The administrator shall ensure that within twenty-four hours after a child is admitted to a secure treatment program under subsection (2),

> (a) the child is given written notice of his or her right to a review under subsection (9); and

> (b) the Office of Child and Family Service Advocacy and the Children's Lawyer are given notice of the child's admission.

(7) Mandatory advice — The Office of Child and Family Service Advocacy shall ensure that forthwith after the notice is received a person who is not employed by the secure treatment facility explains to the child his or her right to a review in language suitable for the child's level of understanding.

(8) Children's Lawyer to ensure child represented — The Children's Lawyer shall represent the child at the earliest possible opportunity, and in any event within five days after receiving a notice under subsection (6) unless the Children's Lawyer is satisfied that another person will provide legal representation for the child within that time.

(9) Application for review — Where a child is admitted to a secure treatment program under this section, any person, including the child, may apply to the Board for an order releasing the child from the secure treatment program.

(10) Child may be kept in program while application pending — Where an application is made under subsection (9), the child may be kept in the secure treatment program until the application is disposed of.

(11) Procedure — Subsections 114(7), (8) and (9) (hearing) and section 115 (waive oral evidence) apply with necessary modifications to an application made under subsection (9).

(12) Time for review — Where an application is made under subsection (9), the Board shall dispose of the matter within five days of the making of the application.

(13) Order — The Board shall make an order releasing the child from the secure treatment program unless the Board is satisfied that the child meets the criteria for emergency admission set out in clauses 124(2)(a) to (e).

1993, c. 27, Sched.; 1994, c. 27, s. 43(2)

Police Assistance

125. (1) Police may take child for secure treatment — A peace officer may take a child to a place where there is a secure treatment program,

> (a) for emergency admission, at the request of an applicant referred to in subsection 124(1); or

> (b) where an order for the child's commitment to the secure treatment program has been made under section 117.

(2) Apprehension of child who leaves — Where a child who has been admitted to a secure treatment program leaves the facility in which the secure treatment program is located without the consent of the administrator, a peace officer may apprehend the child with or without a warrant and return the child to the facility.

(3) Period of commitment — Where a child is returned to a facility under subsection (2), the time that the child was absent from the facility shall not be taken into account in calculating the period of commitment.

Secure Isolation

126. (1) Director's approval — A Director may approve a locked room that complies with the prescribed standards and is located in premises where an approved service or a service purchased by an approved agency is provided, for use for the secure isolation of children, on such terms and conditions as the Director determines.

(2) Withdrawal of approval — Where a Director is of the opinion that a secure isolation room is unnecessary or is being used in a manner that contravenes this Part or the regulations, the Director may withdraw the approval given under subsection (1) and shall give the affected service provider notice of the decision, with reasons.

127. (1) Prohibition — No service provider or foster parent shall isolate in a locked place a child who is in his or her care or permit the child to be isolated in a locked place, except in accordance with this section and the regulations.

(2) Secure treatment, secure custody and secure temporary detention — Subsection (1) does not prohibit the routine locking at night of rooms in the premises of secure treatment programs or in places of secure custody and places of secure temporary detention under Part IV (Young Offenders).

(3) Criteria for use of secure isolation — A child may be placed in a secure isolation room where,

    (a) in the service provider's opinion,

        (i) the child's conduct indicates that the child is likely, in the immediate future, to cause serious property damage or to cause another person serious bodily harm, and

        (ii) no less restrictive method of restraining the child is practicable; and

    (b) where the child is less than twelve years of age, a Director gives permission for the child to be placed in a secure isolation room because of exceptional circumstances.

(4) One hour limit — A child who is placed in a secure isolation room shall be released within one hour unless the person in charge of the premises approves the child's longer isolation in writing and records the reasons for not restraining the child by a less restrictive method.

(5) Continuous observation of child — The service provider shall ensure that a child who is placed in a secure isolation room is continuously observed by a responsible person.

(6) Review — Where a child is kept in a secure isolation room for more than one hour, the person in charge of the premises shall review the child's isolation at prescribed intervals.

(7) Release — A child who is placed in a secure isolation room shall be released as soon as the person in charge is satisfied that the child is not likely to cause serious property damage or serious bodily harm in the immediate future.

CFSA

(8) Maximum periods — In no event shall a child be kept in a secure isolation room for a period or periods that exceed an aggregate of eight hours in a given twenty-four period or an aggregate of twenty-four hours in a given week.

128. Review of use of secure isolation — A person in charge of premises containing a secure isolation room shall review,

    (a) the need for the secure isolation room; and

    (b) the prescribed matters,

every three months from the date on which the secure isolation room is approved under subsection 126 (1), shall make a written report of each review to a Director and shall make such additional reports as are prescribed.

Review Teams

129. (1) Review team — A service provider who is approved under subsection 130 (1) shall establish an interdisciplinary review team with the duty of reviewing and approving or refusing the proposed use of intrusive procedures.

(2) Idem — A review team shall consist of,

    (a) persons employed by the service provider; and

    (b) one person who is not employed by the service provider and is approved by the Minister,

and may also include a legally qualified medical practitioner.

(3) Panel — Any three members of a review team may review and approve or refuse the proposed use of an intrusive procedure.

(4) Report to service provider — A review team shall make a report to the service provider concerning every review conducted under subsection (3) and subsection 133 (1) (review of certain recommended procedures).

(5) Report to Minister — A review team shall make reports of its activities to the Minister at the prescribed intervals.

Unproclaimed Text — 130, 131

Intrusive Procedures

130. (1) Approval by Minister — The Minister may approve a service provider for the use of the intrusive procedures specified in the approval and may set out in the approval any conditions and limitations to which it is subject.

(2) Revocation, etc., of approval — The Minister may at any time revoke, suspend or amend an approval given under subsection (1) and shall give the affected service provider notice, with reasons, of the Minister's decision.

(3) Proclamation — *This section shall come into force on a day to be named by proclamation of the Lieutenant Governor.*

131. (1) Intrusive procedures restricted — No service provider shall use or permit the use of an intrusive procedure in respect of a child in the service provider's care, except in accordance with this section.

(2) Exception — Subsection (1) does not prohibit the use of restraints that are reasonably necessary for the secure transportation or transfer of a child who has been admitted to a secure treatment program under this Part, who is detained or has been committed to custody under the *Young Offenders Act* (Canada) or to whom section 95 of Part IV (Young Offenders) (open custody) applies.

(3) When service provider may use or permit intrusive procedure — A service provider who is approved under subsection 130 (1) may use or permit the use of an intrusive procedure in respect of a child in the service provider's care only,

(a) if the intrusive procedure is specified in the approval;

(b) in accordance with the conditions and limitations set out in the Minister's approval; and

(c) with the approval, obtained in advance and not more than thirty days before the intrusive procedure is used, of the service provider's review team.

(4) Criteria — A review team shall not approve the use of an intrusive procedure in respect of a child unless,

(a) if the child is sixteen years of age or more, the child consents to its use;

(b) if the child is less than sixteen years of age, the child's parent or, where the child is in a society's lawful custody, the society consents to its use;

(c) the child's behaviour warrants its use;

(d) at least one less intrusive alternative has been attempted without success in improving the child's behaviour;

(e) no other less intrusive alternative is practicable; and

(f) there are reasonable grounds to believe that the procedure would improve the child's behaviour.

(5) Idem — A review team shall not approve the use of an intrusive procedure in respect of a child who is less than sixteen years of age or lacks capacity within the meaning of section 4 without first considering the child's views and preferences, where they can be reasonably ascertained.

(6) Emergency — Where,

(a) a service provider who is approved under subsection 130 (1) believes on reasonable grounds that delay in the use of an intrusive procedure in respect of a child in the service provider's care would cause the child or another person serious mental or physical harm;

(b) the intrusive procedure is specified in the Minister's approval;

(c) if the child is sixteen years of age or more, the child consents to the use of the intrusive procedure or apparently does not have capacity; and

(d) if the child is less than sixteen years of age, the child's parent or, where the child is in a society's lawful custody, the society,

(i) consents to the use of the intrusive procedure, or

(ii) is not immediately available,

143

the service provider may use or permit the use of the intrusive procedure in respect of the child, in accordance with the conditions and limitations set out in the Minister's approval, during a period not exceeding seventy-two hours, without the approval of the review team, despite clause (3)(c).

(7) Idem — Where a service provider uses or permits the use of an intrusive procedure under subsection (6), the service provider shall seek the review team's approval as soon as possible, and in any event within seventy-two hours of the first use of the intrusive procedure, and shall not continue its use or permit its continued use in respect of the child unless the review team approves it.

(8) Proclamation — *This section shall come into force on a day to be named by proclamation of the Lieutenant Governor.*

Psychotropic Drugs

132. (1) Consents required for use of psychotropic drug — A service provider shall not administer or permit the administration of a psychotropic drug to a child in the service provider's care without,

> (a) if the child is sixteen years of age or more, the child's consent; or

> (b) if the child is less than sixteen years of age, the consent of the child's parent or, where the child is in a society's lawful custody, the society's consent.

(2) Idem — A consent referred to in subsection (1) shall identify the psychotropic drug clearly and shall specify,

> (a) what condition the psychotropic drug is intended to alleviate;

> (b) the range of intended dosages;

> (c) the risks and possible side effects associated with the psychotropic drug, and how they vary with different dosages; and

> (d) the frequency with which and the period of time during which the psychotropic drug is to be administered.

(3) Child's views and preferences — A service provider shall not administer or permit the administration of a psychotropic drug to a child in the service provider's care who is less than sixteen years of age or lacks capacity within the meaning of section 4 without first considering the child's views and preferences, where they can be reasonably ascertained, except under subsection (4).

Unproclaimed Text — 132(4), (5)

(4) Emergency — Where,

> (a) a service provider believes on reasonable grounds that,

>> (i) delay in the administration of a psychotropic drug to a child in the service provider's care would cause the child or another person serious mental or physical harm, and

>> (ii) no less restrictive course of action would prevent the harm;

> (b) if the child is sixteen years of age or more, the child apparently does not have capacity; and

(c) if the child is less than sixteen years of age, the child's parent or, where the child is in a society's lawful custody, the society, is not immediately available,

the service provider may administer or permit the administration of the psychotropic drug to the child during a period not exceeding seventy-two hours without the consent referred to in subsection (1).

(5) **Idem** — Where a service provider administers or permits the administration of a psychotropic drug under subsection (4), the service provider shall seek the consent referred to in subsection (1) as soon as possible, and in any event within seventy-two hours of the first administration of the psychotropic drug, and shall not continue its administration or permit its continued administration to the child unless the consent is given.

(6) **Proclamation** — *Subsections (4) and (5) shall come into force on a day to be named by proclamation of the Lieutenant Governor.*

Additional Duty of Review Teams

133. (1) **Review of certain recommended procedures** — Where it is recommended that a child in the care of or regularly receiving services from a service provider who has established a review team undergo,

(a) non-therapeutic medical or chemical experimentation;

(b) psychosurgery;

(c) non-therapeutic sterilization; or

(d) electro-convulsive therapy,

three members of the review team shall review the matter and advise the child's parent or, where the child is in a society's lawful custody, the society, and the service provider of the review team's opinion as to the appropriateness of the recommendation.

(2) **Panel to include medical practitioner** — One of the members of the review team acting under subsection (1) shall be a legally qualified medical practitioner.

(3) **Prohibition** — No procedure referred to in subsection (1) shall be carried out in premises where an approved service or a service purchased by an approved agency is provided.

Professional Advisory Board

134. (1) **Professional Advisory Board** — The Minister may establish a Professional Advisory Board, composed of physicians and other professionals who,

(a) have special knowledge in the use of intrusive procedures and psychotropic drugs;

(b) have demonstrated an informed concern for the welfare and interests of children; and

(c) are not employed by the Ministry.

(2) **Chair** — The Minister shall appoint one of the members of the Professional Advisory Board as its chair.

(3) **Duties of Board** — The Professional Advisory Board shall, at the Minister's request,

(a) advise the Minister on,

(i) prescribing procedures as intrusive procedures, and

145

(ii) making, amending, suspending and revoking approvals under section 130;

(b) investigate and review the use of intrusive procedures and psychotropic drugs and make recommendations to the Minister; and

(c) review the practices and procedures of service providers with respect to,

(i) secure isolation,

(ii) intrusive procedures, and

(iii) psychotropic drugs,

and make recommendations to the Minister.

135. Request for review — Any person may request that the Minister refer the matter of the use of secure isolation or an intrusive procedure in respect of a child, or the administration of a psychotropic drug to a child, to the Professional Advisory Board for investigation and review.

PART VII — ADOPTION

136. (1) Definitions — In this Part,

"licensee" means the holder of a licence issued under Part IX (Licensing) to place children for adoption; *("titulaire de permis")*

"relative", when used in reference to a child, means the child's grandparent, great-uncle, great-aunt, uncle or aunt, whether by blood, marriage or adoption; *("parent")*

"spouse" has the same meaning as in Parts I and II of the *Human Rights Code. ("conjoint")*

(2) Best interests of child — Where a person is directed in this Part to make an order or determination in the best interests of a child, the person shall take into consideration those of the following circumstances of the case that he or she considers relevant:

1. The child's physical, mental and emotional needs, and the appropriate care or treatment to meet those needs.

2. The child's physical, mental and emotional level of development.

3. The child's cultural background.

4. The religious faith, if any, in which the child is being raised.

5. The importance for the child's development of a positive relationship with a parent and a secure place as a member of a family.

6. The child's relationships by blood or through an adoption order.

7. The importance of continuity in the child's care and the possible effect on the child of disruption of that continuity.

8. The child's views and wishes, if they can be reasonably ascertained.

9. The effects on the child of delay in the disposition of the case.

10. Any other relevant circumstance.

(3) Where child an Indian or native person — Where a person is directed in this Part to make an order or determination in the best interests of a child and the child is an Indian or native person, the person shall take into consideration the importance, in recognition of the uniqueness of Indian and native culture, heritage and traditions, of preserving the child's cultural identity.

Consent to Adoption

137. (1) Definition — In this section, **"parent"**, when used in reference to a child, means each of,

(a) the child's mother;

(b) an individual described in one of paragraphs 1 to 6 of subsection 8(1) of the *Children's Law Reform Act*, unless it is proved on a balance of probabilities that he is not the child's natural father;

(c) the individual having lawful custody of the child;

(d) an individual who, during the twelve months before the child is placed for adoption under this Part, has demonstrated a settled intention to treat the child as a child of his or her family, or has acknowledged parentage of the child and provided for the child's support;

(e) an individual who, under a written agreement or court order, is required to provide for the child, has custody of the child or has a right of access to the child; and

(f) an individual who has acknowledged parentage of the child in writing under section 12 of the *Children's Law Reform Act*,

but does not include a licensee or a foster parent. *("père ou mère")*

(2) Consent of parent, etc. — An order for the adoption of a child who is less than sixteen years of age, or is sixteen years of age or more but has not withdrawn from parental control, shall not be made without,

(a) the written consent of every parent; or

(b) where the child has been made a Crown ward under Part III (Child Protection), the written consent of a Director.

(3) Idem — A consent under clause (2)(a) shall not be given before the child is seven days old.

(4) Idem — Where a child is being placed for adoption by a society or licensee, a consent under clause (2)(a) shall not be given until,

(a) the society or licensee has advised the parent of his or her right,

(i) to withdraw the consent under subsection (8),

(ii) to be informed, on his or her request, whether an adoption order has been made in respect of the child, and

(iii) to obtain non-identifying information under section 166 and to participate in the adoption disclosure register maintained under clause 163(2)(a); and

(b) the society or licensee has given the parent an opportunity to seek counselling and independent legal advice with respect to the consent.

(5) Custody of child — Where,

(a) a child is being placed for adoption by a society or licensee;

(b) every consent required under subsection (2) has been given and has not been withdrawn under subsection (8); and

147

(c) the twenty-one day period referred to in subsection (8) has expired,

the rights and responsibilities of the child's parents with respect to the child's custody, care and control are transferred to the society or licensee, until the consent is withdrawn under subsection 139(1) (late withdrawal with leave of court) or an order is made for the child's adoption under section 146.

(6) Consent of person to be adopted — An order for the adoption of a person who is seven years of age or more shall not be made without the person's written consent.

(7) Idem — A consent under subsection (6) shall not be given until the person has had an opportunity to obtain counselling and independent legal advice with respect to the consent.

(8) Withdrawal of consent — A person who gives a consent under subsection (2) or (6) may withdraw it in writing within twenty-one days after the consent is given and where that person had custody of the child immediately before giving the consent, the child shall be returned to him or her as soon as the consent is withdrawn.

(9) Dispensing with person's consent — The court may dispense with a person's consent required under subsection (6) where the court is satisfied that,

(a) obtaining the consent would cause the person emotional harm; or

(b) the person is not able to consent because of a developmental disability.

(10) Consent of applicant's spouse — An adoption order shall not be made on the application of a person who is a spouse without the written consent of the other spouse.

(11) Consents by minors: role of Children's Lawyer — Where a person who gives a consent under clause (2)(a) is less than eighteen years of age, the consent is not valid unless the Children's Lawyer is satisfied that the consent is fully informed and reflects the person's true wishes.

(12) Affidavits of execution — An affidavit of execution in the prescribed form shall be attached to a consent and a withdrawal of a consent under this section.

(13) Form of foreign consents — A consent required under this section that is given outside Ontario and whose form does not comply with the requirements of subsection (12) and the regulations is not invalid for that reason alone, if its form complies with the laws of the jurisdiction where it is given.

1994, c. 27, s. 43(2); 2001, c. 13, s. 5(6)

138. Dispensing with consent — The court may dispense with a consent required under section 137 for the adoption of a child, except the consent of the child or of a Director, where the court is satisfied that,

(a) it is in the child's best interests to do so; and

(b) the person whose consent is required has received notice of the proposed adoption and of the application to dispense with consent, or a reasonable effort to give the notice has been made.

139. (1) Late withdrawal of consent — The court may permit a person who gave a consent to the adoption of a child under section 137 to withdraw the consent after the twenty-one day period referred to in subsection 137(8) where the court is satisfied that it is in the child's best interests to do so, and where that person had custody of the child immediately before giving the consent, the child shall be returned to him or her as soon as the consent is withdrawn.

(2) Exception: child placed for adoption — Subsection (1) does not apply where the child has been placed with a person for adoption and remains in that person's care.

Placement for Adoption

140. (1) Duty of society — A society shall make all reasonable efforts to secure the adoption of,

(a) every child who has been made a Crown ward under Part III (Child Protection) and is in the society's care and custody; and

(b) at the request of a Director or of another society, any child who has been made a Crown ward and is in that society's care and custody.

(2) When society may place child for adoption — No society shall place a child for adoption until,

(a) any outstanding order of access to the child made under subsection 58(1) of Part III has been terminated;

(b) where the child is a Crown ward, the time for commencing an appeal of the order of Crown wardship or of an order under subsection 65(1) of Part III (status review) has expired; or

(c) where the child is a Crown ward, any appeal of an order referred to in clause (b) has been finally disposed of or abandoned,

whichever is the latest.

(3) Where child an Indian or native person — Where a child to be placed for adoption is an Indian or native person, the society shall give the child's band or native community thirty days written notice of its intention to place the child for adoption.

141. (1) Only societies and licensees may place children, etc — No person except a society or licensee shall,

(a) place a child with another person for adoption; or

(b) take, send or attempt to take or send a child who is a resident of Ontario out of Ontario to be placed for adoption.

(2) Only societies, etc., may bring children into Ontario — No person except a society or a licensee whose licence contains a term permitting the licensee to act under this subsection shall bring a child who is not a resident of Ontario into Ontario to be placed for adoption.

(3) Licensee to notify Director of placement — No licensee except a licensee exempted under subsection (5) shall,

(a) place a child with another person for adoption; or

(b) take, send or attempt to take or send a child who is a resident of Ontario out of Ontario to be placed for adoption,

without first notifying a Director of the proposed placement.

(4) Director's approval required — No person shall receive a child for adoption, except from a society or from a licensee exempted under subsection (5), without first receiving a Director's approval of the placement under clause 142(2)(a).

(5) Designation of licensee — A Director may designate a licensee that is an agency as exempt from the requirements of subsections (3) and (4).

(6) Placements to be registered — A society or licensee who places a child with another person for adoption shall register the placement in the prescribed manner within thirty days of placing the child.

(7) Idem: Director — A Director who becomes aware of any placement for adoption of a child that has not been registered under subsection (6) shall forthwith register the placement in the prescribed manner.

(8) Exception: family adoptions — Subsections (1), (2), (3), (4), (6) and (7) do not apply to,

(a) the placement for adoption of a child with the child's relative, the child's parent or a spouse of the child's parent; or

(b) the taking or sending of a child out of Ontario for adoption by the child's relative, the child's parent or a spouse of the child's parent.

142. (1) Adoption homestudy — A licensee who notifies a Director of a proposed placement under subsection 141(3) shall at the same time provide the Director with a report of an adoption homestudy of the person with whom placement is proposed, prepared by a person who, in the opinion of the Director or a local director, is qualified to make an adoption homestudy.

(2) Director's approval — A Director who receives a report under subsection (1) shall consider it and, as soon as possible,

(a) approve the proposed placement; or

(b) refuse to approve the placement and give notice of the refusal to the licensee and the person with whom placement is proposed.

(3) Right to hearing — Where a Director gives notice under clause (2)(b), the licensee and the person with whom placement is proposed are entitled to a hearing before the Board.

(3.1) Application of other sections — Sections 197, 199, 201 and 202 of Part IX (Licensing) apply to the hearing with necessary modifications and for that purpose references to the Tribunal shall be deemed to be references to the Board.

(3.2) Extension of time — If the Board is satisfied that there are reasonable grounds for the licensee or the person with whom placement is proposed to apply for an extension of the time fixed for requiring the hearing and for the Board to grant relief, it may,

(a) extend the time either before or after the expiration of the time; and

(b) give the directions that it considers proper as a result of extending the time.

(3.3) Recording of evidence — The evidence taken before the Board at the hearing shall be recorded.

(4) Placement outside Canada — A Director shall not approve the proposed placement of a child outside Canada unless the Director is satisfied that a prescribed special circumstance justifies the placement.

(5) Terms and conditions — A Director may approve a proposed placement under clause (2)(a) subject to any terms and conditions that the Director considers appropriate, including supervision of the placement by,

(a) a specified society, licensee or person; or

(b) in the case of a placement outside Ontario, a specified child protection agency recognized in the jurisdiction of the placement.

(6) Right to hearing — Where a Director imposes a term or condition on an approval under subsection (5), the licensee and the person with whom placement is proposed are entitled to a hearing before the Board.

(7) Application of other sections — Sections 198, 199, 201 and 202 of Part IX (Licensing) apply to the hearing with necessary modifications and for that purpose references to the Tribunal shall be deemed to be references to the Board.

1993, c. 27, Sched.; 1999, c. 12, Sched. G, s. 16(2), (3)

143. (1) Access orders terminate — Where a child is placed for adoption by a society or licensee, every order respecting access to the child is terminated, except an order made under Part III (Child Protection).

(2) No interference, etc., with child in placement — Where a child has been placed for adoption by a society or licensee and no adoption order has been made, no person shall,

(a) interfere with the child; or

(b) for the purpose of interfering with the child, visit or communicate with the child or with the person with whom the child has been placed.

Director's Review

144. (1) Review by Director — Where,

(a) a society makes a decision refusing to place a child with a person, including a foster parent who is caring for the child, for adoption; or

(b) a society or licensee makes a decision to remove a child who has been placed with a person for adoption,

a Director may review the decision of the society or licensee and may,

(c) confirm the decision, giving written reasons for doing so; or

(d) rescind the decision and do anything further that the society or licensee may do under this Part with respect to the child's placement.

(2) Idem — A Director who reviews a decision under subsection (1) shall take into account the importance of continuity in the child's care.

145. (1) Notice to Director — Where a child has been placed for adoption under this Part, no order for the child's adoption has been made and,

(a) the person with whom the child is placed asks the society or licensee that placed the child to remove the child; or

(b) the society or licensee proposes to remove the child from the person with whom the child was placed,

the society or licensee shall notify a Director.

(2) Idem — Where no order for a child's adoption has been made and a year has expired since,

>   (a) the earlier of the child's placement for adoption or the giving of the most recent consent under clause 137(2)(a); or

>   (b) the most recent review under subsection (3),

whichever is later, the society or licensee shall notify a Director, unless the child is a Crown ward.

(3) Director's review — A Director who receives notice under subsection (1) or (2) shall review the child's status and may, in the child's best interests,

>   (a) where the child is in the care of the person with whom the child was placed for adoption, confirm the child's placement or do anything the society or licensee that placed the child may do with respect to the child's placement or further placement;

>   (b) where the child was placed for adoption by a licensee, direct the licensee to place the child in the care and custody of a specified society;

>   (c) where the child is in the care, custody and control of a society, direct the society to bring the child before the court under Part III to determine whether the child is in need of protection;

>   (d) where the child leaves or is removed from the care of the person with whom the child was placed for adoption, do anything the society or licensee that placed the child may do with respect to the child's further placement; or

>   (e) where a parent who gave consent under clause 137(2)(a) and had charge of the child at the time the consent was given agrees to resume the child's care and custody, direct the society or licensee that placed the child to return the child to the parent.

(4) Deemed withdrawal of consent — Where a Director directs a society or licensee to return a child to a parent under clause (3)(e), the parent's consent under clause 137(2)(a) shall be deemed to be withdrawn.

Adoption Orders

146. (1) Adoption of child — The court may make an order for the adoption of a child who is less than sixteen years of age, or is sixteen years of age or more but has not withdrawn from parental control, and,

>   (a) has been placed for adoption by a society or licensee; or

>   (b) has been placed for adoption by a person other than a society or licensee and has resided with the applicant for at least two years,

in the child's best interests, on the application of the person with whom the child is placed.

(2) Family adoption — The court may make an order for the adoption of a child, in the child's best interests, on the application of,

>   (a) a relative of the child;

>   (b) the child's parent; or

>   (c) the spouse of the child's parent.

(3) Adoption of adult, etc. — The court may make an order for the adoption of,

>   (a) a person eighteen years of age or more; or

(b) a child who is sixteen years of age or more and has withdrawn from parental control,

on another person's application.

(4) Who may apply — An application under this section may only be made,

(a) by one individual;

(b) jointly, by two individuals who are spouses of one another; or

(c) by any other individuals that the court may allow, having regard to the best interests of the child.

(5) Residency requirement — The court shall not make an order under this section for the adoption of, or on the application of, a person who is not a resident of Ontario.

1999, c. 6, s. 6

147. Where applicant a minor — The court shall not make an order under section 146 on the application of a person who is less than eighteen years of age unless the court is satisfied that special circumstances justify making the order.

148. Where order not to be made — Where the court has made an order,

(a) dispensing with a consent under section 138; or

(b) refusing to permit the late withdrawal of a consent under subsection 139(1),

the court shall not make an order under section 146, until,

(c) the time for commencing an appeal of the order has expired; or

(d) any appeal of the order has been finally disposed of or abandoned,

whichever is later.

149. (1) Director's statement — Where an application is made for an order for the adoption of a child under subsection 146(1), a Director shall, before the hearing, file a written statement with the court indicating,

(a) that the child has resided with the applicant for at least six months or, in the case of an application under clause 146(1)(b), for at least two years and, in the Director's opinion, it would be in the child's best interests to make the order;

(b) in the case of an application under clause 146(1)(a), that for specified reasons it would be in the child's best interests, in the Director's opinion, to make the order although the child has resided with the applicant for less than six months; or

(c) that the child has resided with the applicant for at least six months or, in the case of an application under clause 146(1)(b), for at least two years and, in the Director's opinion, it would not be in the child's best interests to make the order,

and referring to any additional circumstances that the Director wishes to bring to the court's attention.

(2) Local director may make statement — Where a child was placed by a society and has resided with the applicant for at least six months, the statement under subsection (1) may be made and filed by the local director.

(3) Amendment of statement, etc. — The Director or local director, as the case may be, may amend the statement referred to in subsection (1) at any time and may attend at the hearing and make submissions.

153

(4) Where recommendation negative — Where the statement under subsection (1) indicates that, in the Director's or local director's opinion, it would not be in the child's best interests to make the order, a copy of the statement shall be filed with the court and served on the applicant at least thirty days before the hearing.

(5) Reports of child's adjustment — The statement under subsection (1) shall be based on a report of the child's adjustment in the applicant's home, prepared by,

(a) the society that placed the child or has jurisdiction where the child is placed; or

(b) a person approved by the Director or local director.

(6) Family adoptions: court may require statement — Where an application is made for an order for the adoption of a child under subsection 146(2), the court may order that subsections (1), (3), (4) and (5) shall apply to the application.

1993, c. 27, Sched.

150. (1) Place of hearing — An application for an adoption order shall be heard and dealt with in the county or district in which,

(a) the applicant; or

(b) the person to be adopted,

resides at the time the application is filed.

(2) Transfer of proceeding — Where the court is satisfied at any stage of an application for an adoption order that there is a preponderance of convenience in favour of conducting it in another county or district, the court may order that it be transferred to that other county or district and be continued as if it had been commenced there.

151. (1) Hearing in private — An application for an adoption order shall be heard and dealt with in the absence of the public.

(2) Court files private — No person shall have access to the court file concerning an application for an adoption order, except,

(a) the court and authorized court employees;

(b) the parties and their solicitors and agents; and

(c) a Director and a local director.

(3) Stale applications — Where an application for an adoption order is not heard within twelve months of the day on which the applicant signed it,

(a) the court shall not hear the application unless the court is satisfied that it is just to do so; and

(b) the applicant may make another application.

(4) No right to notice — No person,

(a) who has given a consent under clause 137(2)(a) and has not withdrawn it;

(b) whose consent has been dispensed with under section 138; or

(c) who is a parent of a Crown ward who is placed for adoption,

is entitled to receive notice of an application under section 146.

152. (1) Power of court — The court may, on its own initiative, summon a person to attend before it, testify and produce any document or thing, and may enforce obedience to the summons as if it had been made in a proceeding under the *Family Law Act*.

(2) Duty of court — The court shall not make an order for the adoption of a child under subsection 146(1) or (2) unless the court is satisfied that,

(a) every person who has given a consent under section 137 understands the nature and effect of the adoption order; and

(b) every applicant understands and appreciates the special role of an adoptive parent.

(3) Participation of child — Where an application is made for an order for the adoption of a child under subsection 146(1) or (2), the court shall,

(a) inquire into the child's capacity to understand and appreciate the nature of the application; and

(b) consider the child's views and wishes, if they can be reasonably ascertained,

and where it is practical to do shall hear the child.

(4) Participation of adult, etc. — Where an application is made for an order for the adoption of a person under subsection 146(3), the court shall consider the person's views and wishes and, on request, hear the person.

1993, c. 27, Sched.

153. (1) Change of name — Where the court makes an order under section 146, the court may, at the request of the applicant or applicants and, where the person adopted is twelve years of age or more, with the person's written consent,

(a) change the person's surname to a surname that the person could have been given if he or she had been born to the applicant or applicants; and

(b) change the person's given name.

(2) When child's consent not required — A child's consent to a change of name under subsection (1) is not required where the child's consent was dispensed with under subsection 137(9).

Interim Orders

154. (1) Interim order — Where an application is made for an order for the adoption of a child under subsection 146(1) or (2), the court, after considering the statement made under subsection 149(1), may postpone the determination of the matter and make an interim order in the child's best interests placing the child in the applicant's care and custody for a specified period not exceeding one year.

(2) Terms and conditions — The court may make an order under subsection (1) subject to any terms and conditions that the court considers appropriate respecting,

(a) the child's maintenance and education;

(b) supervision of the child; and

(c) any other matter the court considers advisable in the child's best interests.

(3) Not an adoption order — An order under subsection (1) is not an adoption order.

(4) Consents required — Sections 137 and 138 (consents to adoption) apply to an order under subsection (1) with necessary modifications.

(5) Departure from Ontario — Where an applicant takes up residence outside Ontario after obtaining an order under subsection (1), the court may nevertheless make an adoption order under subsection 146(1) or (2) where the statement made under subsection 149(1) indicates that, in the Director's or local director's opinion, it would be in the child's best interests to make the order.

155. Successive adoption orders — An adoption order under subsection 146(1) or (2) or an interim custody order under subsection 154(1) may be made in respect of a person who is the subject of an earlier adoption order.

Appeals

156. (1) Appeal: adoption order — An appeal from a court's order under section 146 may be made to the Superior Court of Justice by,

(a) the applicant for the adoption order; and

(b) the Director or local director who made the statement under subsection 149(1).

(2) Idem: dispensing with consent — An appeal from a court's order under section 138 dispensing with a consent may be made to the Superior Court of Justice by,

(a) the persons referred to in subsection (1); and

(b) the person whose consent was dispensed with.

(3) Idem: late withdrawal of consent — An appeal from a court's order under subsection 139(1) permitting the late withdrawal of a consent may be made to the Superior Court of Justice by,

(a) the persons referred to in subsection (1); and

(b) the person who gave the consent.

(4) No extension of time for appeal — No extension of the time for an appeal shall be granted.

(5) Place of hearing — An appeal under this section shall be heard in the county or district in which the order appealed from was made.

(6) Hearing in private — An appeal under this section shall be heard in the absence of the public.

1999, c. 2, s. 35

Effect of Adoption Order

157. Order final — An adoption order under section 146 is final and irrevocable, subject only to section 156 (appeals), and shall not be questioned or reviewed in any court by way of injunction, declaratory judgment, *certiorari*, *mandamus*, prohibition, *habeas corpus* or application for judicial review.

158. (1) Definition — In this section, **"adopted child"** means a person who was adopted in Ontario. *("enfant adopté")*

(2) Status of adopted child — For all purposes of law, as of the date of the making of an adoption order,

> (a) the adopted child becomes the child of the adoptive parent and the adoptive parent becomes the parent of the adopted child; and

> (b) the adopted child ceases to be the child of the person who was his or her parent before the adoption order was made and that person ceases to be the parent of the adopted child, except where the person is the spouse of the adoptive parent,

as if the adopted child had been born to the adoptive parent.

(3) How relationships determined — The relationship to one another of all persons, including the adopted child, the adoptive parent, the kindred of the adoptive parent, the parent before the adoption order was made and the kindred of that former parent shall for all purposes be determined in accordance with subsection (2).

(4) Reference in will or other document — In any will or other document made at any time before or after the 1st day of November, 1985, and whether the maker of the will or document is alive on that day or not, a reference to a person or group or class of persons described in terms of relationship by blood or marriage to another person shall be deemed to refer to or include, as the case may be, a person who comes within the description as a result of an adoption, unless the contrary is expressed.

(5) Application of section — This section applies and shall be deemed always to have applied with respect to any adoption made under any Act heretofore in force, but not so as to affect,

> (a) any interest in property or right of the adopted child that has indefeasibly vested before the date of the making of an adoption order; and

> (b) any interest in property or right that has indefeasibly vested before the 1st day of November, 1985.

(6) Exception — Subsections (2) and (3) do not apply for the purposes of the laws relating to incest and the prohibited degrees of marriage to remove a person from a relationship that would have existed but for those subsections.

159. Effect of foreign adoption — An adoption effected according to the law of another jurisdiction, before or after the 1st day of November, 1985, has the same effect in Ontario as an adoption under this Part.

160. (1) No order for access by birth parent, etc — Where an order for the adoption of a child has been made under this Part no court shall make an order under this Part for access to the child by,

> (a) a birth parent; or

> (b) a member of a birth parent's family.

(2) Definition — In this section,

"birth parent" has the same meaning as in section 166. *("père ou mère de sang")*

Records, Confidentiality and Disclosure

161. Parent to be informed on request — At the request of a person whose consent to an adoption was required under clause 137(2)(a) or a predecessor of that provision and was given or was dispensed with, any society or the licensee that placed the child for adoption shall inform the person whether an order has been made for the child's adoption.

162. (1) Definition — In this section,

"court" includes the Superior Court of Justice. *("tribunal")*

(2) Papers to be sealed up — Subject to subsections (3) and 167(6), the documents used upon an application for an adoption order under this Part or a predecessor of this Part shall be sealed up together with a certified copy of the original order and filed in the office of the court by the proper officer of the court, and shall not be open for inspection except upon an order of the court or the written direction of the Registrar of Adoption Information appointed under subsection 163(1).

(3) Transmission of order — Within thirty days after an adoption order is made under this Part, the proper officer of the court shall cause a sufficient number of certified copies of it to be made, under the seal of the proper certifying authority, and shall transmit,

(a) the original order to be the adoptive parent;

(b) one certified copy to the Registrar of Adoption Information;

(c) one certified copy to the Registrar General under the *Vital Statistics Act*, or, if the adopted child was born outside Ontario, two certified copies;

(d) if the adopted child is an Indian, one certified copy to the Registrar under the *Indian Act* (Canada).

1999, c.2, s. 35

Registrar of Adoption Information

163. (1) Registrar of Adoption Information — The Minister may appoint an employee of the Ministry as Registrar of Adoption Information for the purposes of this section and sections 164 to 174.

(2) Duties of Registrar — The Registrar shall,

(a) maintain a register for the purposes of section 167;

(b) ensure that counselling is provided to persons who receive identifying information from the Registrar;

(c) ensure that counselling is made available to persons who receive non-identifying information from the Registrar, who are or may wish to be named in the register, or who are concerned that they may be affected by the disclosure of identifying information;

(d) have searches conducted in accordance with subsection 169(3).

(3) Delegation of Registrar's powers and duties — The Registrar may, in writing, authorize other employees of the Ministry to exercise any or all of the Registrar's powers and perform any or all of the Registrar's duties.

(4) Counselling — The counselling referred to in this section and in sections 166 (disclosure of non-identifying information), 167 (adoption disclosure register) and 170 (persons adopted outside Ontario) shall be provided by persons who are, in the opinion of the Registrar or a local director, qualified to do so.

164. Confidentiality rules apply — Sections 165 to 174 apply regardless of when the adoption order was made.

Confidentiality of Adoption Records

165. (1) Adoption information confidential — Despite any other Act, after an adoption order is made, no person shall inspect, remove, alter or permit the inspection, removal or alteration of information that relates to the adoption and is kept,

(a) by the Ministry;

(b) by a society or licensee; or

(c) in the adoption disclosure register maintained under clause 163(2)(a),

or disclose or permit the disclosure of such information that the person obtained from the records of the Ministry, including the register, or from the records of a society or licensee.

(2) Exceptions — Subsection (1) does not apply to,

(a) the disclosure of information by a person who obtained it before the adoption order was made, if the information was obtained in accordance with this Act and the regulations or with the consent of the person to whom the information relates;

(b) the disclosure of non-identifying information in accordance with section 166 or 170 (persons adopted outside Ontario);

(c) the disclosure of identifying information in accordance with section 167 (adoption disclosure register) or 170;

(d) the disclosure of identifying or non-identifying information in accordance with section 168 (disclosure to protect health, safety or welfare);

(e) the disclosure of information in accordance with an order of the Board under subsection 172(10);

(f) the routine maintenance and updating of records by the Ministry or a society or licensee;

(g) the release by the Registrar of Adoption Information of a copy of an adoption order to,

(i) the adoptive parent,

(ii) the adopted person or any other person if, in the Registrar's opinion, it is desirable that he or she receive a copy of the adoption order, or

(iii) a governmental authority that requires the copy to issue a birth certificate, passport or visa;

(h) the inspection, by a person named in subsection (3), of information kept by the Ministry or a society or licensee, or the disclosure of such information to such a person;

(i) the disclosure of information to a person who is engaged in research, in accordance with subsection (4).

CFSA

(3) Persons entitled to share information — Clause (2)(h) applies in respect of:

1. The Minister.

2. The Registrar of Adoption Information.

3. A Director, or an employee of the Ministry who has a Director's written authority.

4. A local director, or an employee of a society who has the local director's written authority.

5. A licensee who is an individual, a director of a licensee that is a corporation, or an employee of a licensee who has the licensee's written authority.

6. A child protection or child placement agency that is recognized in another jurisdiction.

(4) Research — A person who is engaged in research may, with the written approval of the Registrar of Adoption Information or, in the case of information kept by a society, with the local director's written approval, inspect and use information that relates to adoptions, but shall not,

(a) use or communicate the information for any purpose except research, academic pursuits or the compilation of statistical data; or

(b) communicate any identifying information.

(5) Privacy — The *Freedom of Information and Protection of Privacy Act* does not apply to information that relates to an adoption.

Disclosure of Non-Identifying Information

166. (1) Definition — In this section and in sections 167 to 174, **"Registrar"** means the Registrar of Adoption Information appointed under subsection 163(1). *("registrateur")*

(2) Idem — In this section and in sections 163, 165 and 167 to 174,

"identifying information" means information whose disclosure, alone or in combination with other information, will in the circumstances reveal the identity of the person to whom it relates; *("renseignements identificatoires")*

"non-identifying information" means information that is not identifying information. *("renseignements non indentificatoires")*

(3) Idem — In this section and in sections 167, 168 and 169,

"adopted person" means a person who was adopted in Ontario; *("personne adoptée")*

"birth grandparent" means any parent of a birth parent; *("grand-père our grand-mère de sang")*

"birth parent" means an adopted person's biological mother or father, and includes a person whose consent to another person's adoption was required under clause 137(2)(a) or a predecessor of that provision and was given or was dispensed with; *("père ou mère de sang")*

"birth sibling" means a child of the same birth parent as an adopted person, and includes the birth parent's adopted child and a person whom the birth parent has demonstrated a settled intention to treat as a child of his or her family; *("frère ou soeur de sang")*

"register" means the register maintained under clause 163(2)(a). *("registre")*

(4) Who may request information — Each of the following persons may make a request to the Registrar for non-identifying information that relates to an adoption:

1. The adopted person, if he or she has attained the age of eighteen years or has the written consent of an adoptive parent.

2. An adoptive parent.

3. A birth parent or birth grandparent.

4. A birth sibling who has attained the age of eighteen years.

5. A person who is a member of a prescribed class, if the person has the written consent of the adopted person and the adopted person would be entitled to make the request or, if not, the written consent of an adoptive parent.

6. Any other person if, in the Registrar's opinion, it is desirable that the person be able to request non-identifying information as if he or she were a birth parent.

(5) Disclosure of information — When a person makes a request under subsection (4), the Registrar shall do one of the following:

1. Disclose to the person all the relevant non-identifying information in the Ministry's possession that relates to the adoption.

2. Forward that information to a society or licensee for disclosure to the person in accordance with subsection (7).

3. If the person lives outside Ontario, disclose that information to a child protection or child placement agency that is recognized in the jurisdiction where the person lives, or to an individual in that jurisdiction who, in the Registrar's opinion, is qualified to provide counselling.

4. Refer the person's request to a society or licensee that has the relevant information.

(6) Counselling — When the Registrar discloses information under subsection (5), he or she shall also ensure that counselling is made available to the person receiving the information.

(7) Information forwarded to society or licensee — When the Registrar forwards information to a society or licensee under subsection (5), the society or licensee shall disclose it to the person who requested it and shall also make counselling available to him or her.

(8) Societies and licensees — Subsections (4), (5), (6) and (7) also apply with necessary modifications to societies and licensees.

(9) Further disclosure — A person who receives information under subsection (5) or (7) may disclose it to any person.

Adoption Disclosure Register

167. (1) Disclosure of identifying information — After an adoption order is made in Ontario, identifying information that relates to the adoption may be disclosed in accordance with this section or section 168 (disclosure to protect health, safety or welfare).

(2) Who may apply to be named in register — Each of the following persons may apply to a society or to the Registrar to be named in the register:

1. An adopted person who has attained the age of eighteen years.

2. The birth parent or birth grandparent of an adopted person.

3. The birth sibling of an adopted person, if the birth sibling has attained the age of eighteen years.

4. Any other person if, in the Registrar's opinion, it is desirable that the person be named in the register as if he or she were a birth parent.

(3) Society to forward application — A society that receives an application shall promptly send it to the Registrar.

(4) Entry in register, etc — On receiving an application, the Registrar shall enter the applicant's name in the register and then make a search to determine whether the adopted person and his or her birth parent, birth grandparent or birth sibling or a person described in paragraph 4 of subsection (2) are both named in the register.

(5) Further consents — If the Registrar determines that an adopted person and his or her birth parent, birth grandparent or birth sibling or a person described in paragraph 4 of subsection (2) are both named in the register, the Registrar shall, after ensuring that each of them receives counselling, give both persons an opportunity to consent in writing to the disclosure of information in accordance with subsections (8) and (9).

(6) Registrar to compile relevant material — If both persons give the further consent referred to in subsection (5), the Registrar shall compile the material described in paragraphs 1, 2 and 3:

1. All relevant identifying information from the records of the Ministry and of societies and licensees.

2. If the adopted person requests it, copies of the documents referred to in subsection 162(2) (court file).

3. If the adopted person requests it, an extract of information from his or her original birth registration kept by the Registrar General under the *Vital Statistics Act*.

(7) Idem — The compiled material shall include only information that pertains to the adopted person or the other person named in the register and shall not include a copy of the adopted person's original birth registration.

(8) Disclosure by Registrar — The Registrar shall ensure that the compiled material is promptly disclosed to the adopted person and also to the other person named in the register, separately and in accordance with one or more of the methods described in subsection (9).

(9) Idem — The Registrar may,

(a) make the compiled material available to the adopted person or the other person named in the register, or to both, first ensuring that each person to whom the material is made available receives counselling;

(b) forward the compiled material to a society that he or she considers appropriate to undertake disclosure to the adopted person or the other person named in the register, or to both;

(c) if the adopted person or the other person named in the register lives outside Ontario, forward the compiled material to a child protection or child placement agency that is recognized in the jurisdiction where the person lives, or to an individual in that jurisdiction, but only if the Registrar is satisfied that the person will receive appropriate counselling.

(10) Exception: further consent — If a person whose further consent to disclosure would be required is named in the register but has died, cannot be found despite a discreet and reasonable search that has continued for at least six months, or appears to lack capacity as defined in subsection 4(1), the Registrar may disclose information to the other person named in the register in accordance with subsection (9) without the first-named person's further consent.

(11) Duty of society — A society that receives compiled material under clause (9)(b) shall promptly make it available to the adopted person or the other person named in the register, or both, as the case may be, first ensuring that each person to whom the material is made available receives counselling.

(12) Additional information — If the society's records contain identifying information that pertains to the adopted person or the other person named in the register and that is not included in the compiled material, that society shall disclose the information in the same manner as the compiled material.

(13) Duty of society — A society shall provide counselling to persons who receive identifying information from the society, and shall make counselling available to persons who are named or may wish to be named in the register or who are concerned that they may be affected by the disclosure of identifying information.

(14) Further disclosure — A person who is named in the register and receives information under subsection (9), (10), (11) or (12) may disclose it to any person.

Disclosure to Protect Health, Safety or Welfare

168. (1) Disclosure to protect health, safety or welfare — The Registrar may disclose identifying or non-identifying information that relates to an adoption to any person if, in the Registrar's opinion, the health, safety or welfare of that person or of any other person requires the disclosure.

(2) Application of subs. (1) — Subsection (1) applies whether the adoption order was made in Ontario or elsewhere.

(3) Further disclosure — A person who receives information under this section in the course of his or her professional or official duties may disclose it further only for the purpose of protecting a person's health, safety or welfare.

(4) Idem — A person who receives information under this section otherwise than as described in subsection (3) may disclose it to any person.

Searches

169. (1) Request for search by Registrar — An adopted person who has attained the age of eighteen years may ask the Registrar to search on his or her behalf for a specific person in one of the following categories:

1. A person whose consent to the adoption was required under clause 137(2)(a) or a predecessor of that provision and was given or was dispensed with.

2. A person who has acknowledged that he is the adopted person's biological father.

3. A parent of a person described in paragraph 1 or 2.

4. A birth sibling of the adopted person who has also attained the age of eighteen years.

(2) Idem, member of prescribed class — A person who is a member of a prescribed class may ask the Registrar to search on his or her behalf for a specific adopted person who has attained the age of eighteen years.

(3) Duty of Registrar — The Registrar shall have a discreet and reasonable search made for the person mentioned in the request, and shall seek to ascertain whether that person wishes to be named in the register.

(4) Exception re disclosure — If the Registrar discovers that the person mentioned in the request has died or appears to lack capacity as defined in subsection 4(1), or if the person cannot be found despite a discreet and reasonable search that has continued for at least six months, the Registrar may disclose information to the person who made the request, in accordance with section 167, as if both persons were named in the register.

Persons Adopted Outside Ontario

170. (1) Definitions — In this section,

"adopted person" means a person who was adopted outside Ontario; *("personne adoptée")*

"birth parent" means an adopted person's biological mother or father, or a person whose consent to another person's adoption was given or dispensed with; *("père ou mère de sang")*

"birth grandparent" means any parent of a birth parent; *("grand-père ou grand-mère de sang")*

"birth sibling" means a child of the same birth parent as an adopted person, and includes the birth parent's adopted child and a person whom the birth parent has demonstrated a settled intention to treat as a child of his or her family; *("frère ou soeur de sang")*

"out of province adoption" means an adoption where the adoption order was made outside Ontario. *("adoption hors province")*

(2) Who may request non-identifying information — Each of the following persons may make a request to the Registrar for non-identifying information that relates to an out of province adoption:

1. The adopted person, if he or she has attained the age of eighteen years or has the written consent of an adoptive parent.

2. An adoptive parent.

3. A birth parent or birth grandparent.

4. A birth sibling who has attained the age of eighteen years.

5. Any other person if, in the opinion of the Registrar or local director, it is desirable that the person receive non-identifying information as if he or she were a birth parent.

(3) Disclosure of information — When a person makes a request under subsection (2), the Registrar shall disclose to the person all the relevant non-identifying information in the Ministry's possession that relates to the adoption.

(4) Counselling — When the Registrar discloses information under subsection (3), he or she shall also ensure that counselling is made available to the person receiving the information, to the extent that it is feasible to do so.

(5) Societies and licensees — Subsections (2), (3) and (4) also apply with necessary modifications to societies and licensees.

(6) Disclosure of identifying information to agency outside Ontario — If identifying information that relates to an out of province adoption is kept by the Ministry or by a society, the Registrar may provide the information to a child protection or child placement agency that is recognized in another jurisdiction, for disclosure in accordance with the laws of that jurisdiction.

(7) Further disclosure — A person who receives information under this section may disclose it to any person.

Refusal of Information

171. (1) Refusal to disclose non-identifying information — The disclosure of non-identifying information that a person would otherwise be entitled to receive under section 166 or 170 may be refused,

    (a) by the Registrar if, in his or her opinion, the disclosure might result in serious physical or emotional harm to any person;

    (b) by a society if, in the local director's opinion, the disclosure might result in serious physical or emotional harm to any person;

    (c) by a licensee if, in the Registrar's opinion, the disclosure might result in serious physical or emotional harm to any person.

(2) Refusal to disclose identifying information — The disclosure of identifying information that a person would otherwise be entitled to receive under section 167 may be refused by the Registrar or by a society if, in the Registrar's opinion, the disclosure might result in serious physical or emotional harm to any person.

(3) Notice of refusal — When the disclosure of information is refused under this section, the Registrar or local director, as the case may be, shall promptly give the person seeking the information notice of the refusal, the reason for it and the person's right to a review under section 172.

Review

172. (1) Review by Child and Family Services Review Board — A person who is refused information in accordance with section 171 may, within twenty days of receiving notice of the decision, request that the Board review the matter.

(2) Duty of Board — The Board shall conduct a review with respect to the request, following the prescribed procedures.

(3) Hearings — Unless the parties to a review agree otherwise, the Board shall hold a hearing.

(4) Parties — The parties to a review are,

    (a) the person who requested the review;

    (b) the person who gave notice of the decision to withhold the information.

(5) Registrar to be added — At any stage in a review, the Board shall add the Registrar as a party on his or her request.

(6) Information need not be disclosed in course of review — The Board may examine the information without disclosing it to the person who requested the review.

(7) Idem, evidence and submissions — The Board may receive any evidence and submissions without disclosing them to the person who requested the review, and when the Board holds a hearing it may hear any part of the evidence and submissions in that person's absence.

(8) Lawyer or agent not to be excluded — When the Board acts under subsection (6) or (7), the lawyer or agent of the person who requested the review is nevertheless entitled to examine the information and to be present, to cross-examine witnesses and to make submissions, or to examine the evidence and submissions and respond to them, as the case may be, on condition that the lawyer or agent undertakes not to reveal the information, evidence and submissions to his or her client.

(9) Time for decision — The Board shall complete its review and make a decision within ninety days of receiving notice of the request, unless the parties consent to a longer period.

(10) Board's decision — After conducting a review, the Board may make an order requiring the Registrar, society or licensee, as the case may be, to disclose all or part of the information to the person, or may make an order confirming the refusal.

(11) Conditions — The Board may include conditions in its order.

(12) Written decision with reasons — Whether the Board holds a hearing or not, it shall give its decision in writing, with reasons.

Information in Court File

173. (1) Application — This section applies to court proceedings that relate to decisions made by the Board under section 172 or by the Registrar, local directors or licensees under sections 165, 166, 167, 168, 169, 170 and 171.

(2) Examination of identifying information in court file — Unless the court orders otherwise, only the court may examine identifying information that is in the court file and comes from the records of the Ministry or of a society or licensee.

(3) Disclosure of information — No person shall, without the court's permission, disclose identifying information described in subsection (2) that he or she obtained from the court file.

Fees and Expenses

174. Fees and expenses — The Registrar, societies and licensees may charge the prescribed fees for services provided under clause 165(2)(g) and sections 166, 167, 169 and 170, and may charge up to the prescribed amounts for expenses incurred in providing services under sections 166, 167, 169 and 170.

Offences

175. No payments for adoption — No person, whether before or after a child's birth, shall give, receive or agree to give or receive a payment or reward of any kind in connection with,

(a) the child's adoption or placement for adoption;

(b) a consent under section 137 to the child's adoption; or

(c) negotiations or arrangements with a view to the child's adoption,

except for,

(d) the prescribed expenses of a licensee, or such greater expenses as are approved by a Director;

(e) proper legal fees and disbursements; and

(f) a subsidy paid by an approved agency or by the Minister to an adoptive parent or to a person with whom a child is placed for adoption.

176. (1) Offence — A person who contravenes subsection 141(1), (2) or (3) (placement for adoption) and a director, officer or employee of a corporation who authorizes, permits or concurs in such a contravention by the corporation is guilty of an offence, whether an order is subsequently made for the child's adoption or not, and on conviction is liable to a fine of not more than $2,000 or to imprisonment for a term of not more than two years, or to both.

(2) Idem — A person who contravenes subsection 141(4) (receiving child) is guilty of an offence and on conviction is liable to a fine of not more than $2,000 or to imprisonment for a term of not more than two years, or to both.

(3) Idem — A person who contravenes subsection 143(2) (interference with child) is guilty of an offence and on conviction is liable to a fine of not more than $1,000 or to imprisonment for a term of not more than one year, or to both.

(4) Idem — A person who contravenes section 175 and a director, officer or employee of a corporation who authorizes, permits or concurs in such a contravention by the corporation is guilty of an offence and on conviction is liable to a fine of not more than $25,000 or to imprisonment for a term of not more than three years, or to both.

(5) Limitation period — A proceeding under subsection (1), (2) or (4) shall not be commenced after the expiration of two years after the date on which the offence was, or is alleged to have been, committed.

Injunction

177. (1) Injunction — The Superior Court of Justice may grant an injunction to restrain a person from contravening subsection 143(2), on the society's or licensee's application.

(2) Variation, etc. — The Court may vary or terminate an order made under subsection (1), on any person's application.

1999, c.2, s. 35

PART VIII — CONFIDENTIALITY OF AND ACCESS TO RECORDS

Unproclaimed Text — 178

178. (1) Definitions — In this Part,

"family", when used in reference to a person, means,

(a) the person's parents and children, and

(b) the person's spouse within the meaning of Part II of the *Family Law Act*; (*"famille"*)

"record", when used in reference to a person, means all recorded information, regardless of physical form or characteristics, that,

(a) relates to the person,

(b) is recorded in connection with the provision of an approved service, or a service purchased by an approved agency, to the person or a member of the person's family, and

(c) is under the control of a service provider. (*"dossier"*)

(2) Proclamation — *This section shall come into force on a day to be named by proclamation of the Lieutenant Governor.*

179.

Unproclaimed Text — 179(1)

(1) Exception: information in existing records — This Part does not apply to information recorded before the day this Part comes into force.

(2) Exception: certain kinds of records — This Part does not apply to a record,

Unproclaimed Text — 179(2)(a)

(a) obtained by means of an order made under subsection 74(3) of Part III (child abuse investigation);

Proposed Repeal — 179(2)(a)

(a) obtained by means of an order made under subsection 74(3) or (3.1) or a warrant obtained under section 74.1 or 74.2.

1999, c. 2, s. 31 [Not in force at date of publication.]

Unproclaimed Text — 179(2)(b)

(b) in the register maintained under subsection 75(5) of Part III (child abuse register);

Proposed Repeal — 179(2)(b)

(b) [Repealed 1999, c. 2, s. 31. Not in force at date of publication.]

1999, c. 2, s. 31 [Not in force at date of publication.]

(c) that relates to the adoption of a child under Part VII;

(d) in the adoption disclosure register maintained under clause 163(2)(a) of Part VII;

Unproclaimed Text — 179(2)(e)

(e) that relates to a patient and whose disclosure without the patient's consent would contravene a regulation made under the *Health Disciplines Act*;

Unproclaimed Text — 179(2)(f)

(f) that is a clinical record within the meaning of subsection 35(1) of the *Mental Health Act*;

Unproclaimed Text — 179(2)(g)

(g) that is a medical record kept by a hospital that is approved under the *Public Hospitals Act*.

(3) Proclamation — *Subsection (1) and clauses 2(a), (b), (c), (e), (f) and (g) shall come into force on a day to be named by proclamation of the Lieutenant Governor.*

Unproclaimed Text — 180–182

Disclosure of Records

180. (1) Prohibition — No service provider or employee of a service provider shall disclose a person's record to any person, except in accordance with section 181 (disclosure with consent), 182 (disclosure without consent) or 183 (access by subject and parents) or subsection 188(4) (review by Board).

(2) Exception — Subsection (1) does not prevent the disclosure of a person's record that is,

    (a) required or permitted by,

        (i) another Act or a regulation made under another Act, or

        (ii) an order of a court; or

    (b) permitted by the *Young Offenders Act* (Canada).

(3) Proclamation — *This section shall come into force on a day to be named by proclamation of the Lieutenant Governor.*

181. (1) Consent to disclosure: child under sixteen — A service provider may disclose the record of a child under the age of sixteen years, with the written consent of the child's parent or, where the child is in a society's lawful custody, the society's written consent.

(2) Exception: child's counselling records — Subsection (1) does not apply to a record created in connection with the provision of counselling services to a child under section 28 of Part II (Voluntary Access to Services), which may be disclosed only with the child's written consent.

(3) Consent to disclosure: person over sixteen — A service provider may disclose the record of a person who is sixteen years of age or older with that person's written consent.

CFSA

(4) Requirements for consent — A consent given under subsection (1), (2) or (3) to the disclosure of a person's record shall specify,

    (a) what information is to be disclosed;

    (b) the purpose of the disclosure;

    (c) to whom the record is to be disclosed;

    (d) whether the consent authorizes the further disclosure of the record by the person referred to in clause (c), and, if so, to whom and for what purposes; and

    (e) the period of time during which the consent remains effective, unless revoked.

(5) When revocation of consent effective — The revocation of a consent given under subsection (1), (2) or (3) is effective when it is delivered to the service provider in writing or the service provider otherwise obtains actual notice of it.

(6) Proclamation — *This section shall come into force on a day to be named by proclamation of the Lieutenant Governor.*

182. (1) Disclosure without consent — A service provider may disclose a person's record without any consent referred to in section 181,

    (a) to persons who provide approved services as employees or agents of the service provider;

    (b) to a foster parent, if the person is a child who is in the foster parent's care;

    (c) to employees, officers and professional advisors of the service provider who require access to the person's record for the performance of their duties;

    (d) to a society, if the person is a child who is in the society's care under,

        (i) an order made under Part III (Child Protection), or

        (ii) a temporary care agreement or special needs agreement made under Part II (Voluntary Access to Services), unless the agreement provides otherwise;

    (e) to a peace officer, if the service provider believes on reasonable grounds that,

        (i) failure to disclose the person's record is likely to cause the person or another person physical or emotional harm, and

        (ii) the need for disclosure is urgent;

    (f) to a person who is providing medical treatment to the person whose record is concerned, if the service provider believes on reasonable grounds that,

        (i) failure to disclose the record is likely to cause the person whose record is concerned physical or emotional harm, and

        (ii) the need for disclosure is urgent; or

    (g) to a review team for the purposes of section 73 of Part III (Child Protection).

(2) Idem: research — A service provider may, with a Director's written approval obtained in accordance with the regulations, disclose a person's record to a person engaged in research, but that persons shall not,

    (a) use or communicate information from the record for any purpose except research, academic pursuits or the compilation of statistical data; or

    (b) communicate any information that may have the effect of identifying a person whose record is disclosed.

(3) Mandatory disclosure — A service provider shall disclose a person's record without any consent referred to in section 181,

(a) to a program supervisor; or

(b) to a Director,

who requests its disclosure.

(4) Prohibition — A program supervisor or Director shall not use or communicate information from a person's record obtained under subsection (3) for any purpose outside the scope of his or her duties.

(5) Notice of disclosure without consent — A service provider who discloses a person's record under clause (1)(e) or (f) shall promptly give written notice of the disclosure to the person whose record was disclosed.

(6) Proclamation — *This section shall come into force on a day to be named by proclamation of the Lieutenant Governor.*

183. (1) Definition — In this section, **"record of a mental disorder"** means a record or a part of a record made about a person concerning a substantial disorder of emotional processes, thought or cognition of the person which grossly impairs the person's capacity to make reasoned judgments. *("dossier relatif à un trouble mental")*

(2) Disclosure pursuant to summons — A service provider shall disclose, transmit or permit the examination of a record of a mental disorder pursuant to a summons, order, direction, notice or similar requirement in respect of a matter in issue or that may be in issue in a court of competent jurisdiction or under any Act unless a physician states in writing that he or she believes that to do so,

(a) is likely to result in harm to the treatment or recovery of the person to whom the record relates; or

(b) is likely to result in,

(i) injury to the mental condition of another person, or

(ii) bodily harm to another person.

(3) Hearing to be held — The court before which a matter described in subsection (2) is in issue on motion or, where a disclosure, transmittal or examination is not required by a court, the Divisional Court on motion shall determine whether the record referred to in the physician's statement should be disclosed, transmitted or examined.

(4) Idem — A motion under subsection (3) shall be on notice to the physician and shall be held in the absence of the public.

(5) Consideration of court — In a motion under subsection (3), the court shall consider whether or not the disclosure, transmittal or examination of the record referred to in the physician's statement is likely to have a result described in clause (2)(a) or (b) and for the purpose the court may examine the record.

(6) Order of court — The court shall not order that the record referred to in the physician's statement be disclosed, transmitted or examined if the court is satisfied that a result described in clause (2)(a) or (b) is likely unless satisfied that to do so is essential in the interests of justice.

CFSA

(7) Return of record to service provider — Where a record of a mental disorder is required under this section, the clerk of the court or body in which it is admitted in evidence or, if not so admitted, the person to whom the record is transmitted shall return the record to the service provider forthwith after the determination of the matter in issue in respect of which the record was required.

Unproclaimed Text — 184–191

Access to Records

184. (1) Right of access to personal records — Subject to subsection (2) and section 185, a person who is twelve years of age or older has a right to and shall on request be given access to,

(a) his or her own records;

(b) the records of his or her child who is under the age of sixteen years; and

(c) the records of a child who is in his or her lawful custody or charge and is under the age of sixteen years.

(2) Exception: child's counselling records — Clauses (1)(b) and (c) do not apply to a record created in connection with the provision of counselling services to a child under section 28 of Part II (Voluntary Access to Services), which may be disclosed to the child's parent only with the child's written consent.

(3) Restriction by parent, etc. — Any parent of a child, if the child is under the age of sixteen years, may designate specific information that is contained in the child's record and relates to the parent as information that shall not be disclosed to the child, and the service provider shall not disclose the designated information to the child.

(4) Child's access to records — The consent of a child's parent is not required for the child's access to a record under subsection (1).

(5) Proclamation — *This section shall come into force on a day to be named by proclamation of the Lieutenant Governor.*

185. (1) Where access may be refused — A service provider may refuse to give a person referred to in subsection 184(1) access to all or part of his or her record where the person is a child under the age of sixteen years and the service provider is of the opinion that access to all or part of the record would cause the child physical or emotional harm.

(2) Information that may be withheld — A service provider may withhold from a person referred to in subsection 184(1) the name of another person and other information relating to that other person where the service provider is of the opinion that disclosure is likely to result in physical or emotional harm to that other person.

(3) Idem: informants — A service provider may withhold from a person referred to in subsection 184(1) the name of an individual who has provided information in the person's record but is not engaged in providing services.

(4) Idem: assessments — A service provider may withhold from a person referred to in subsection 184(1) the contents of a medical, emotional, developmental, psychological, educational or social assessment performed by a person who is not employed by the service provider, but may not withhold that person's name.

(5) Proclamation — *This section shall come into force on a day to be named by proclamation of the Lieutenant Governor.*

186. (1) Duty of service provider — Where a person referred to in subsection 184(1) requests access to a record, the service provider shall, within thirty days of receiving the request,

(a) give the person access to the record;

(b) notify the person that the service provider refuses to give him or her access to part of the record, stating the reasons for the refusal, and give the person access to the rest of the record;

(c) notify the person that the service provider refuses to give him or her access to the record, stating the reasons for the refusal; or

(d) notify the person that this Part does not apply to the record or that the record does not exist, if that is the case.

(2) Notice of right of review — A notice of a refusal of access under clause (1)(b) or (c) shall contain a statement of the person's right to request a review of the matter under subsection 188(1).

(3) Proclamation — *This section shall come into force on a day to be named by proclamation of the Lieutenant Governor.*

187. (1) Right to have record corrected — A person who has a right to access to a record under subsection 184(1) also has a right to have errors or omissions in the record corrected.

(2) Duty of service provider — Where a person referred to in subsection (1) requests that a service provider correct an error or omission in a record, the service provider shall, within thirty days of receiving the request,

(a) make the correction as requested, and give notice of the correction to every person to whom the service provider has disclosed the record;

(b) notify the person that the service provider refuses to make the correction as requested, stating the reasons for the refusal, and note the request and response on the record; or

(c) notify the person that this Part does not apply to the record or that the record does not exist, if that is the case.

(3) Notice of right of review — A notice of refusal to make a correction under clause (2)(b) shall contain a statement of the person's right to request a review of the matter under subsection 188(1).

(4) Proclamation. — *This section shall come into force on a day to be named by proclamation of the Lieutenant Governor.*

Review

188. (1) Right to review: refusal of access or correction — A person referred to in subsection 184(1) or 187(1) whose request for access to or correction of a record is refused in whole or in part may, within twenty days of receiving notice of the refusal, request that the Board review the matter.

(2) Idem: unauthorized disclosure — A person who believes that a service provider may have disclosed his or her record without authority may, within twenty days of becoming aware of the possible unauthorized disclosure, request that the Board review the matter.

(3) Duty of Board — Where the Board receives notice of a request for review under subsection (1) or (2), it shall review the matter, following the prescribed procedures, and may do so by holding a hearing.

(4) Board may examine record — In conducting a review requested under subsection (1) or (2), the Board may examine the record in question.

(5) Decision of Board — On completing a review requested under subsection (1), the Board may,

(a) order the service provider to give the person access to all or part of the record;

(b) order the service provider to make a correction to the record and give the notice referred to in clause 187(2)(a); or

(c) if it is satisfied that the refusal appealed from is justified, confirm the refusal,

and shall provide a copy of its decision to the person who requested the review, the service provider and the Minister.

(6) Idem — On completing a review requested under subsection (2), the Board,

(a) shall, unless it is satisfied that no disclosure or no unauthorized disclosure of the person's record took place, declare that the disclosure was unauthorized;

(b) may order the service provider to change its procedures for the maintenance and disclosure of persons' records, or to desist from a particular disclosure practice; and

(c) where it is satisfied that an unauthorized disclosure took place, may recommend to the Minister that the service provider's approval under Part I (Flexible Services), if any, be revoked or, where the service provider is a licensee, that the licence be revoked under Part IX (Licensing),

and shall provide a copy of its decision to the person who requested the review, the service provider and the Minister.

(7) Proclamation — *This section shall come into force on a day to be named by proclamation of the Lieutenant Governor.*

General

189. (1) Access, etc., to be noted on record — Every disclosure of all or part of a person's record and every correction to a person's record shall be noted on and forms part of the record.

(2) Exception — Subsection (1) does not apply to routine use of a person's record by a service provider and the service provider's employees or, where the service provider is the Minister, the Minister's employees engaged in providing services.

(3) Proclamation — *This section shall come into force on a day to be named by proclamation of the Lieutenant Governor.*

190. (1) Protection from liability for disclosure — Where a service provider discloses a person's record in accordance with this Part, no action or other proceeding shall be instituted against the service provider or anyone acting under the service provider's authority,

(a) if this Part requires the disclosure; or

(b) if this Part permits the disclosure and the service provider has reasonable grounds to believe the information contained in the record to be accurate.

(2) Proclamation — *This section shall come into force on a day to be named by proclamation of the Lieutenant Governor.*

191. (1) Code of record-keeping procedures — Every service provider shall establish and follow a written code of procedure for the creation, maintenance and disclosure of persons' records.

(2) Idem — A code of procedure referred to in subsection (1) shall contain,

(a) a description of the types of information that may be recorded and the purposes for which information may be recorded;

(b) a requirement that information, wherever possible, be collected from or confirmed by the person to whom it relates;

(c) a requirement that no more information be recorded than is actually necessary for the provision of the service in question; and

(d) the prescribed provisions.

(3) Retention, storage and destruction schedules — Every service provider shall retain, store and destroy persons' records in accordance with the prescribed schedules.

(4) Proclamation — *This section shall come into force on a day to be named by proclamation of the Lieutenant Governor.*

PART IX — LICENSING

192. Definitions — In this Part,

"children's residence" means,

(a) a parent model residence where five or more children not of common parentage, or

(b) a staff model residence where three or more children not of common parentage,

live and receive residential care, and includes a foster home or other home or institution that is supervised or operated by a society, but does not include,

(c) a house licensed under the *Private Hospitals Act*,

(d) a day nursery as defined in the *Day Nurseries Act*,

(e) a recreational camp under the *Health Protection and Promotion Act*,

(f) a home for special care under the *Homes for Special Care Act*,

(g) a school or private school as defined in the *Education Act*,

(h) a hostel intended for short term accommodation,

(i) a hospital that receives financial aid from the Government of Ontario, or

(j) a group home or similar facility that receives financial assistance from the Minister of Correctional Services but receives no financial assistance from the Minister under this Act; *("foyer pour enfants")*

CFSA

"non-profit agency" means a corporation without share capital that has objects of a charitable nature and,

(a) to which Part III of the *Corporations Act* applies, or

(b) that is incorporated by or under a general or special Act of the Parliament of Canada; *("agence sans but lucratif")*

"parent model residence" means a building, group of buildings or part of a building where not more than two adult persons live and provide care for children on a continuous basis; *("foyer de type familial")*

"staff model residence" means a building, group of buildings or part of a building where adult persons are employed to provide care for children on the basis of scheduled periods of duty. *("foyer avec rotation de personnel")*

Where Licence Required

193. (1) Licence required to operate children's residence, etc. — No person shall,

(a) establish, operate or maintain a children's residence; or

(b) provide, directly or indirectly, residential care for three or more children not of common parentage in places that are not children's residences,

except under the authority of a licence issued by a Director under this Part.

(2) Idem: placement for adoption — No person other than a society shall place a child for adoption, except under the authority of a licence issued by a Director under this Part.

(3) Issuing licence — Subject to section 195, a person who applies for a licence in accordance with this Part and the regulations and pays the prescribed fee is entitled to be issued a licence by a Director, subject to any terms and conditions imposed by the Director.

(4) Idem — Despite subsection (3),

(a) a licence shall not be issued to a partnership or association of persons; and

(b) a licence to place a child for adoption shall only be issued to an individual or a non-profit agency.

(5) Renewal of licence — Subject to section 196, a licensee who applies for renewal of the licence in accordance with this Part and the regulations and pays the prescribed fee is entitled to have the licence renewed by a Director, subject to any terms and conditions imposed by the Director.

(6) Provisional licence or renewal — Where an applicant for a licence or renewal of a licence does not meet all the requirements for the issuing or renewal of the licence and requires time to meet them, a Director may, subject to such terms and conditions as the Director may prescribe, issue a provisional licence for the period that the Director considers necessary to give the applicant time to meet the requirements.

(7) Not transferable — A licence is not transferable.

(8) Placements must be in accord with Act and regulations — No licensee shall place a child in a residential placement except in accordance with this Act and the regulations.

Powers of Program Supervisor

194. (1) Powers of program supervisor — For the purpose of ensuring compliance with this Act and the regulations a program supervisor may, at all reasonable times, upon producing proper identification, enter,

(a) the premises of a licensee;

(b) a children's residence; or

(c) a place where a child receives residential care,

and may inspect the facilities, the services provided, the books of account and the records relating to the services, and make copies of those books and records or remove them from the premises to copy them as may be reasonably required.

(2) Offence — No person shall hinder, obstruct or attempt to hinder or obstruct a program supervisor in the performance of the program supervisor's duties or knowingly give false information about the premises or services to a program supervisor.

(3) Idem — No licensee or person in charge of premises referred to in clause (1) (a), (b) or (c) shall refuse to give a program supervisor access to the books and records referred to in subsection (1) or refuse to give a program supervisor information about the premises or services that the program supervisor reasonably requires.

(4) Regulations re exercise of power of entry — A program supervisor shall exercise the power of entry set out in subsection (1) in accordance with the regulations.

Refusal and Revocation

195. Grounds for refusal — A Director may refuse to issue a licence where, in the Director's opinion,

(a) the applicant or an employee of the applicant, or, where the applicant is a corporation, an officer or director of the corporation is not competent to carry on the activity for which the licence is required in a responsible manner in accordance with this Act and the regulations;

(b) the past conduct of the applicant or an employee of the applicant or, where the applicant is a corporation, of an officer or director of the corporation, affords reasonable grounds for belief that the activity for which the licence is required will not be carried on in a responsible manner in accordance with this Act and the regulations; or

(c) the premises in which the applicant proposes to establish, operate and maintain a children's residence or to provide residential care, as the case may be, do not comply with the requirements of this Part and the regulations.

196. Refusal to renew; revocation — A Director may refuse to renew or may revoke a licence where, in the Director's opinion,

(a) the licensee or an employee of the licensee, or where the licensee is a corporation, an officer or director of the corporation has contravened or has knowingly permitted a person under his or her control or direction or associated with him or her to contravene,

(i) this Act or the regulations,

(ii) another Act, or the regulations made under another Act, that applies to the activity for which the licence is required, or

177

(iii) a term or condition of the licence;

(b) the premises where the children's residence is located or the residential care is provided do not comply with the requirements of this Part and the regulations;

(c) the activity for which the licence is required is carried on in a manner that is prejudicial to the children's health, safety or welfare;

(d) a person has made a false statement in the application for the licence or for its renewal, or in a report or document required to be furnished by this Act or the regulations, or by another Act or the regulations made under another Act that applies to the activity for which the licence is required; or

(e) a change has occurred in the employees, officers or directors of the applicant that would, if the applicant were applying for the licence in the first instance, afford grounds under clause 195 (b) for refusing to issue the licence.

Hearing by Tribunal

197. (1) Notice of proposal —

[Editor's Note: Section 16(5) of the Red Tape Reduction Act, 1999, S.O. 1999, c. 12, Schedule G. provides that despite the replacement of the Child and Family Services Review Board (the "Board") with the Licence Appeal Tribunal (the "Tribunal"), members of the Board immediately before subsection 16(4) comes into force shall be members of the Tribunal for the purpose of performing the duties of the Tribunal with respect to proceedings before the Board that were commenced before that subsection comes into force.]

Where a Director proposes to refuse to issue a licence under section 195 or to refuse to renew or to revoke a licence under section 196, the Director shall cause notice of the proposal, together with written reasons, to be served on the applicant or licensee, who may require a hearing.

(2) Request for hearing — A notice under subsection (1) shall inform the applicant or licensee that the applicant or licensee is entitled to a hearing by the Tribunal if he, she or it mails or delivers to the Director and to the Tribunal, within ten days after the notice under subsection (1) is served, a written request for a hearing.

(3) Powers of Director where no hearing required — Where an applicant or licensee does not require a hearing under subsection (2), the Director may carry out the proposal.

(4) Powers of Tribunal where hearing required — Where an applicant or licensee requires a hearing under subsection (2), the Tribunal shall appoint a time for and hold a hearing and may, on hearing the matter,

(a) order the Director to carry out the proposal; or

(b) order the Director to take such other action as the Tribunal considers appropriate, in accordance with this Part and the regulations,

and the Tribunal may substitute its opinion for that of the Director.

1999, c. 12, Sched. G, s. 16(4)

198. (1) Review of terms of licence by Tribunal — A licensee who is dissatisfied with the terms and conditions prescribed by a Director under subsection 193 (3), (5) or (6) is entitled to a hearing by the Tribunal if the licensee mails or delivers to the Director and to the Tribunal, within fifteen days after receiving the licence, a written request for a hearing.

(2) Powers of Tribunal — Where a licensee requires a hearing under subsection (1), the Tribunal shall appoint a time for and hold a hearing and may, on hearing the matter,

(a) confirm any or all of the terms and conditions;

(b) strike out any or all of the terms and conditions; or

(c) impose such other terms and conditions as the Tribunal considers appropriate.

(3) Receipt of licence — For the purposes of subsection (1), a licensee shall be deemed to receive the licence on the tenth day after the day of its mailing, unless the licensee establishes that he, she or it did not receive it or did not, through absence, accident, illness or another cause beyond the licensee's control, acting in good faith, receive the licence until a later date.

1999, c. 12, Sched. G, s. 16(4)

199. (1) [Repealed 1999, c. 12, Sched. G, s. 16(6).]

(2) Continuation of licence pending renewal — Subject to section 200, where a licensee has applied for renewal of the licence and paid the prescribed fee within the prescribed time or, if no time is prescribed, before the licence expires, the licence shall be deemed to continue,

(a) until the renewal is granted; or

(b) where the licensee is served with notice that the Director proposes to refuse to grant the renewal, until the time for requiring a hearing has expired and, where a hearing is required, until the Tribunal has made its decision.

1999, c. 12, Sched. G, s. 16(6), (7)

200. (1) Provisional suspension of licence — A Director may, by causing notice to be served on a licensee, provisionally and without a hearing suspend the licence where, in the Director's opinion, the manner in which the children's residence is operated, residential care is provided or children are placed for adoption, as the case may be, is an immediate threat to the health, safety or welfare of the children.

(2) Contents of notice — A notice served under subsection (1) shall contain a statement of the grounds for suspending the licence.

(3) When suspension takes effect — A provisional suspension takes effect on the date that the licensee receives the notice.

(4) s. 197 (2-4) apply — Where a notice is served under subsection (1), subsections 197 (2), (3) and (4) apply with necessary modifications.

201. (1) Parties — The Director, the applicant or licensee who requires the hearing and any other persons that the Tribunal specifies are parties to a proceeding under this Part.

(2) Members with prior involvement — A member of the Tribunal who has taken part before a hearing in any investigation or consideration of its subject matter, including a review under section 188 of Part VIII (Confidentiality of and Access to Records) that relates to the applicant or licensee, shall not take part in the hearing.

(3) Discussion of subject matter of hearing — A member of the Tribunal who takes part in a hearing shall not communicate with any person, except another member, a solicitor who is not the solicitor of any party, or an employee of the Tribunal, about the subject matter of the hearing, unless all parties are notified and given an opportunity to participate.

(4) When Tribunal seeks independent legal advice — The Tribunal may seek independent legal advice about the subject matter of a hearing and, if it does so, shall disclose the nature of the advice to the parties to enable them to respond.

(5) Examination of documentary evidence — A party to a proceeding under this Part shall be given an opportunity, before the hearing, to examine any written or documentary evidence that will be produced and any report whose contents will be given in evidence at the hearing.

(6) [Repealed 1999, c. 12, Sched. G, s. 16(8).]

(7) Only members at hearing to participate in decision, etc. — No member of the Tribunal shall participate in a decision of the Tribunal under this Part unless he or she was present throughout the hearing and heard the evidence and argument of the parties and, unless the parties consent, the Tribunal shall not make a decision under this Part unless all the members who were present at the hearing participate in the decision.

(8) Final decision of Tribunal within ninety days — Despite section 21 of the *Statutory Powers Procedure Act*, the Tribunal shall make a final decision and notify the parties of it within ninety days from the day the Tribunal receives the applicant's or licensee's request for a hearing under subsection 197 (2) or 198 (1).

1999, c. 12, Sched. G, s. 16(7)–(9)

Appeal

202. (1) Appeal — An appeal lies to the Divisional Court from the Tribunal's decision under this Part.

(2) Record to be filed in the court — Where notice of an appeal is served under this section, the Tribunal shall forthwith file with the court the record of the proceeding in which the decision appealed from was made.

(3) Minister entitled to be heard — The Minister is entitled to be heard, by counsel or otherwise, on the argument of an appeal under this section.

1999, c. 12, Sched. G, s. 16(10), (11)

Delivery of Licence and Records

203. (1) Records and licence to be handed over to Minister — A licensee whose licence is revoked or who ceases to carry on the activity for which the licence is required shall deliver up to the Minister the licence and all the records in the licensee's possession or control that relate to the children to whom services were being provided.

(2) Removal of children — Where a licence to operate a children's residence or to provide residential care is suspended or revoked, the parent of every child in the children's residence or other place where residential care is provided shall arrange for the child's removal from the residence or other place as soon as is practicable, having regard to the child's best interests, and the Minister may assist in finding an alternative placement for the child.

Occupation by Minister

204. (1) Order for Minister's occupation — The Minister may, where a Director's proposal to revoke or not to renew a licence under subsection 197 (1) or notice of provisional suspension under subsection 198 (1) has been served on a licensee who operates a children's residence or provides residential care and the matter has not yet been finally disposed of, apply without notice to the Superior Court of Justice for an order,

(a) authorizing the Minister to occupy and operate the children's residence or the premises where the residential care is provided, pending the outcome of the proceeding until alternative accommodation may be found for the children who are being cared for; and

(b) directing the sheriff to assist the Minister as may be necessary in occupying the premises.

(2) Where court may make order — The court may make an order referred to subsection (1) where it is satisfied that the health, safety or welfare of the children being cared for require it.

(3) Interim management — Where an order has been made under subsection (2), the Minister may, despite sections 25 and 39 of the *Expropriations Act*, immediately occupy and operate or arrange for the occupation and operation of the premises for a period not exceeding six months.

1999, c. 2, s. 35

Injunctions

205. (1) Injunction — A Director may apply to the Superior Court of Justice for an order enjoining any person from,

(a) contravening subsection 193(1) (licence requirement); or

(b) carrying on an activity for which a licence is required while the licence is provisionally suspended under section 200.

(2) Idem — Any person may apply to the court for an order varying or discharging an order made under subsection (1).

1999, c. 2, s. 35

Offences

206. (1) Offence — Every person who,

(a) contravenes subsection 193(1);

(b) contravenes a term or condition of a licence relating to the maximum number of children to be cared for in a children's residence or other place where residential care is provided under the authority of a licence;

(c) causes a child to be cared for in a children's residence operated by a person who is not licensed under this Part, or in another place where residential care is provided by a person who is required to be but is not licensed to provide residential care under this Part; or

(d) is a child's parent or a person under a legal duty to provide for the child and permits the child to be cared for in a children's residence or other place referred to in clause (c),

CFSA

and every director, officer or employee of a corporation who authorizes, permits or concurs in such an act by the corporation is guilty of an offence and on conviction is liable to a fine of not more than $1,000 for each day on which the offence continues or to imprisonment for a term of not more than one year, or to both.

(2) Idem — Every person who,

(a) knowingly contravenes subsection 194(2) or (3) (obstructing program supervisor, etc.);

(b) knowingly furnishes false information in an application under this Part or in a statement, report or return required to be furnished under this Part or the regulations; or

(c) fails to comply with an order or direction made by a court under this Part,

and every director, officer or employee of a corporation who authorizes, permits or concurs in such a contravention, furnishing or failure by the corporation is guilty of an offence and on conviction is liable to a fine of not more than $2,000.

Child and Family Services Review Board

207. (1) Child and Family Services Review Board — The Child and Family Services Review Board is continued under the name Child and Family Services Review Board in English and Commission de révision des services à l'enfance et à la famille in French.

(2) Idem — The Board is composed of the prescribed number of members appointed by the Lieutenant Governor in Council and has the powers and duties given to it by this Act and the regulations.

(3) Chair and vice-chairs — The Lieutenant Governor in Council may appoint a member of the Board as chair and may appoint one or more other members as vice-chairs.

(4) Term — A member of the Board shall hold office for the prescribed term.

(5) Quorum — The prescribed number of members of the Board are a quorum.

(6) Remuneration — The chair and vice-chairs and the other members of the Board shall be paid the daily allowances determined by the Lieutenant Governor in Council and are entitled to their reasonable and necessary travelling and living expenses while attending meetings or otherwise engaged in the work of the Board.

PART X — INDIAN AND NATIVE CHILD AND FAMILY SERVICES

208. Definition — In this Part, **"customary care"** means the care and supervision of an Indian or native child by a person who is not the child's parent, according to the custom of the child's band or native community. *("soins conformes aux traditions")*

209. Designation of native communities — The Minister may designate a community, with the consent of its representatives, as a native community for the purposes of this Act.

210. Agreements with bands and native communities — The Minister may make agreements with bands and native communities, and any other parties whom the bands or native communities choose to involve, for the provision of services.

211. (1) Designation of child and family service authority — A band or native community may designate a body as an Indian or native child and family service authority.

(2) Agreements, etc. — Where a band or native community has designated an Indian or native child and family service authority, the Minister,

(a) shall, at the band's or native community's request, enter into negotiations for the provision of services by the child and family service authority;

(b) may enter into agreements with the child and family service authority and, if the band or native community agrees, any other person, for the provision of services; and

(c) may designate the child and family service authority, with its consent and if it is an approved agency, as a society under subsection 15(2) of Part I (Flexible Services).

212. Subsidy for customary care — Where a band or native community declares that an Indian or native child is being cared for under customary care, a society or agency may grant a subsidy to the person caring for the child.

213. Consultation with bands and native communities — A society or agency that provides services or exercises powers under this Act with respect to Indian or native children shall regularly consult with their bands or native communities about the provision of the services or the exercise of the powers and about matters affecting the children, including,

(a) the apprehension of children and the placement of children in residential care;

(b) the placement of homemakers and the provision of other family support services;

(c) the preparation of plans for the care of children;

(d) status reviews under Part III (Child Protection);

(e) temporary care and special needs agreements under Part II (Voluntary Access to Services);

(f) adoption placements;

(g) the establishment of emergency houses; and

(h) any other matter that is prescribed.

PART XI — REGULATIONS

214. (1) Regulations: Part I (Flexible Services) — The Lieutenant Governor in Council may make regulations for the purposes of Part I,

1. prescribing additional powers and duties of Directors and program supervisors;

2. prescribing reports to be made and information to be furnished under subsection 5(5), their form and the intervals at which they are to be made or furnished;

3. governing the exercise of the power of entry set out in subsection 6(1);

4. governing the management and operation of approved agencies or any class of them;

5. governing the provision of approved services or any class of them;

6. exempting designated approved agencies or approved services or any class of them from any provision of this Act or the regulations for a specified period or periods;

6.1 respecting the composition of boards of approved agencies or classes of approved agencies, requiring board members to undertake training programs and prescribing those programs;

7. governing the accommodation, facilities and equipment to be provided,

    i. in buildings in which approved services are provided, and

    ii. in the course of the provision of approved services;

8. further defining "service", "child development service", "child treatment service", "child welfare service", "community support service" and "young offenders service";

9. defining "prevention service";

10. governing the establishment, management, operation, location, construction, alteration and renovation of buildings, or any class of them, in which approved services are provided;

11. prescribing procedures and conditions of eligibility for the admission of children and other persons to and their discharge from places where approved services are provided;

12. prescribing the qualifications, powers and duties of persons employed in providing approved services or any class of approved services;

12.1 prescribing classes of persons employed or to be employed in providing approved services or any class of approved services who must undertake training, prescribing that training and prescribing the circumstances under which that training must be undertaken.

13. governing the residential placement of children and prescribing procedures for placements, discharge, assessments and case management;

14. requiring and prescribing medical and other related or ancillary services for the care and treatment of children and other persons in places where services or any class of them are provided;

15. governing applications by agencies for approval under subsections 8(1) and 9(1) and establishing criteria for approval;

16. governing applications by approved agencies for payments under this Part, prescribing the method, time, manner, terms and conditions of payments and providing for the suspension and withholding of payments and for the making of deductions from payments;

17. prescribing the manner of computing the amount of financial assistance for the purposes of sections 8 and 9, prescribing classes of payments for the purposes of those sections and determining the amounts of payments;

18. governing the transfer and assignment of the assets of approved agencies acquired with financial assistance from the Province of Ontario, or of any class of such assets, for the purposes of subsection 10(3), and prescribing classes of such assets;

19. requiring approved agencies to provide the prescribed information to the prescribed persons, and prescribing the information and the persons;

20. prescribing the accounts and records to be kept by approved agencies, the claims, returns and reports to be made and budgets to be submitted to the Minister and the methods, time and manner in which they shall be made or submitted;

21. requiring service providers, or any class of service providers, to keep records, and prescribing the form and content of those records;

22. providing for the recovery, by an approved agency or by the Minister, from the person or persons in whose charge a child is or has been or from the estate of that person or persons of amounts paid by the agency for the child's care and maintenance,

and prescribing the circumstances and the manner in which such a recovery may be made;

23. providing for the recovery of payments made to approved agencies under this Part and the regulations;

24. prescribing provisions to be included in the by-laws of approved agencies, or any class of them, for the purpose of subsection 13(2);

25. prescribing the number of band or native community representatives on the boards of directors of agencies or any class of them, the manner of their appointment and their terms, for the purpose of subsection 13(3);

26. prescribing forms and providing for their use;

27. prescribing fees or classes of fees that may be charged for services and the terms and conditions under which a fee may be charged;

28. [Repealed 1999, c. 2, s. 32(2).]

29. providing for an executive committee of the board of directors of a society, its composition, quorum, powers and duties;

30. prescribing a system for determining,

    i. the amounts of payments under subsection 19(2) (payments by Minister), and

    ii. a society's estimated expenditures.

    iii. [Repealed 1999, c. 2, s. 32(3).]

31. [Repealed 1999, c. 2, s. 32(3).]

32. governing the construction, alteration, renovation, extension, furnishing and equipping of homes operated or supervised by societies, other than children's residences as defined in Part IX (Licensing), where residential care is provided to children.

(2) Idem — A regulation made under paragraph 6.1, 12.1, 18, 24 or 25 of subsection (1) (boards of approved agencies, training of persons providing approved services, transfer of assets, prescribed provisions in agency by-laws, band or native community representatives) may be general or specific in its application.

(3) Idem — A regulation made under paragraph 17 or 30 of subsection (1) (financial assistance for the purposes of sections 8 and 9, amounts of payments to societies) is, if it so provides, effective with reference to a period before it is filed.

(4) Idem — The Minister shall prescribe,

    (a) standards of services; and

    (b) procedures and practices to be followed by societies,

for the purposes of subsection 15(4).

1999, c. 2, s. 32

215. Regulations: Part II (Voluntary Access to Services) — The Lieutenant Governor in Council may make regulations for the purposes of Part II,

    (a) defining "counselling";

    (b) prescribing provisions to be contained in agreements made under section 29 (temporary care agreements) and sections 30 and 31 (special needs agreements);

    (c) requiring that residential placements with or by service providers be made in accordance with written agreements, and prescribing their form and contents;

(d) prescribing practices, procedures and further duties for advisory committees;

(e) further defining "special need" and "developmental disability".

2001, c. 13, s. 5(7)

216. Regulations: Part III (Child Protection) — The Lieutenant Governor in Council may make regulations for the purposes of Part III,

(a) governing the exercise of the powers of entry set out in subsections 40(6) and (11) and section 44;

(b) assigning to a Director any powers, duties or obligations of the Crown with respect to Crown wards;

(c) prescribing the care and maintenance that may be provided to a former Crown ward under subsection 71(2), and the terms and conditions on which the care and maintenance may be provided;

(c.1) respecting the format of warrants under sections 74.1 and 74.2 and the procedures to be followed in applying for, issuing, receiving and filing warrants of different formats;

(c.2) prescribing manners of applying for a warrant under section 74.2, including a manner other than submitting an information on oath, setting out the circumstances under which those manners may be used and providing for any additional requirements that must be met if those manners are used.

(d) prescribing the form in which reports are to be made under subsection 75(3);

Proposed Repeal — 216(d)

(d) [Repealed 1999, c. 2, s. 33(2). Not in force at date of publication.]

(e) respecting the manner in which the register referred to in subsection 75(5) is to be kept;

Proposed Repeal — 216(e)

(e) [Repealed 1999, c. 2, s. 33(2). Not in force at date of publication.]

(f) requiring the removal of a name from the register referred to in subsection 75(5), or the amendment of the register, under specified circumstances, and specifying those circumstances;

Proposed Repeal — 216(f)

(f) [Repealed 1999, c. 2, s. 33(2). Not in force at date of publication.]

(g) prescribing practices and procedures for hearings held under clause 76(4)(b) (amendment of register);

Proposed Repeal — 216(g)

(g) [Repealed 1999, c. 2, s. 33(2). Not in force at date of publication.]

(h) prescribing forms and providing for their use.

1993, c. 27, Sched.; 1999, c. 2, s. 33(1)

217. (1) Regulations: Part IV (Young Offenders) — The Lieutenant Governor in Council may make regulations for the purposes of Part IV,

(a) governing the establishment, operation, maintenance, management and use of places of temporary detention, open custody and secure custody and other services and programs provided under subsection 89(1);

(b) governing the establishment and operation of and the accommodation, equipment and services to be provided in any premises or class of premises established, operated, maintained or designated for the purposes of the federal Act or for providing services or programs under subsection 89(1);

(c) prescribing additional duties and functions of,

    (i) probation officers, and

    (ii) provincial directors;

(d) prescribing the duties and functions of bailiffs;

(e) prescribing the qualifications of probation officers;

(f) prescribing additional duties and functions of persons in charge of places of temporary detention, open custody and secure custody;

(g) prescribing reports to be made and information to be furnished under section 92, their form and the intervals at which they are to be made or furnished;

(h) governing the conduct, discipline, rights and privileges of young persons in places of temporary detention, open custody or secure custody or any class of them or in a service or program provided under subsection 89(1);

(i) prescribing procedures for the admission of young persons to and their discharge from places of temporary detention, open custody or secure custody or any class of them or premises in which a service or program is provided under subsection 89(1);

(j) prescribing classes of payment by way of provincial aid for the establishment, operation or maintenance of places of temporary detention, open custody or secure custody, the methods of determining the payments, the manner and time of making them, the terms and conditions of such payments and the circumstances under which such payments may be suspended or withheld or deductions may be made from them;

(k) prescribing the number of members of the Board, their terms of office and the number of members that is a quorum;

(l) prescribing additional powers, duties and procedures of the Board;

(m) governing the exercise of the power of entry given under subsection 98(5);

(n) respecting any matter considered necessary or advisable to carry out effectively the intent and purpose of Part IV.

(2) Idem — A regulation made under clause (1)(j) (classes of payment by way of provincial aid) is, if it so provides, effective with reference to a period before it is filed.

218. Regulations: Part V (Rights of Children) — The Lieutenant Governor in Council may make regulations for the purposes of Part V,

(a) governing internal complaints procedures to be established under section 109;

(b) establishing procedures for reviews under section 110;

(c) prescribing additional functions of the Office of Child and Family Service Advocacy.

219. Regulations: Part VI (Extraordinary Measures) — The Lieutenant Governor in Council may make regulations for the purposes of Part VI,

(a) prescribing procedures for the admission of persons to and their discharge from secure treatment programs;

(b) prescribing standards for secure treatment programs;

(c) prescribing standards for secure isolation rooms;

(d) prescribing procedures to be followed when a child is placed in or released from a secure isolation room;

(e) prescribing the frequency of reviews under subsection 127(6);

(f) prescribing matters to be reviewed and prescribing additional reports under section 128;

(g) prescribing procedures as intrusive procedures;

(h) prescribing the intervals at which reports are to be made by review teams under subsection 129(5);

(i) prescribing drugs, combinations of drugs or classes of drugs as psychotropic drugs;

(j) prescribing forms and requiring their use.

220. (1) Regulations: Part VII (Adoption) — The Lieutenant Governor in Council may make regulations for the purposes of Part VII,

(a) prescribing the form of an affidavit of execution for the purposes of subsection 137(12);

(b) prescribing the manner in which placements are to be registered under subsection 141(6);

(c) prescribing special circumstances for the purposes of subsection 142(4) (placement outside Canada);

(d) prescribing forms and providing for their use;

(e) further defining "identifying information" and "non-identifying information" for the purposes of sections 163 to 174;

(f) prescribing classes of persons for the purposes of paragraph 5 of subsection 166(4) (persons who may request non-identifying information);

(g) prescribing classes of persons for the purposes of subsection 169(2) (search by Registrar);

(h) prescribing additional powers, duties and procedures for the Board under section 172;

(i) prescribing fees and amounts for the purposes of section 174;

(j) prescribing expenses that may be charged under clause 175(d), classes of such expenses and the terms and conditions under which such expenses or classes of expenses may be charged.

(2) Idem — Regulations made under clause (1)(i) may prescribe different fees and amounts for the Registrar, for societies and for licensees.

1993, c. 27, Sched.

221. Regulations: Part VIII (Confidentiality of and Access to Records) — The Lieutenant Governor in Council may make regulations for the purposes of Part VIII,

(a) prescribing the manner in which a Director's approval is to be obtained under subsection 182(2) (disclosure for research);

(b) prescribing review procedures for the Board under subsection 188(3);

(c) prescribing provisions for the purposes of subsection 191(2) (service providers' codes of procedure);

(d) prescribing retention, storage and destruction schedules for the purposes of subsection 191(3).

222. Regulations: Part IX (Licensing) — The Lieutenant Governor in Council may make regulations for the purposes of Part IX,

(a) governing the establishment, management, operation and use of children's residences, and other premises where residential care is provided under the authority of a licence;

(b) defining "common parentage" for the purposes of the definition of "children's residence" in section 192 and clause 193(1)(b);

(c) governing the issuing, renewal and expiry of licences and prescribing fees payable by an applicant for a licence or its renewal;

(d) governing the exercise of the power of entry set out in subsection 194(1);

(e) governing the establishment of and the accommodation, facilities, equipment and services to be provided in,

(i) children's residences, and

(ii) other premises where residential care is provided under the authority of a licence,

or any class of them;

(f) exempting designated,

(i) children's residences,

(ii) other premises where residential care is provided under the authority of a licence, or

(iii) persons placing children for adoption,

or any class of them, from any provision of this Part or the regulations for a prescribed period, and prescribing the period;

(g) prescribing the accounts and records to be kept by licensees;

(h) prescribing the qualifications, powers and duties of persons supervising children in,

(i) children's residences, or

(ii) other premises where residential care is provided under the authority of a licence,

or any class of them;

(i) governing procedures for the admission to and discharge of children from,

(i) children's residences, or

(ii) other premises where residential care is provided under the authority of a licence,

CFSA

189

or any class of them;

(j) requiring the operators of children's residences or persons who provide residential care or place children for adoption under the authority of a licence to provide the prescribed information and to make the prescribed returns and reports, and prescribing the information, returns and reports;

(k) prescribing the number of members of the Board, their terms of office and the number of members that is a quorum;

(l) prescribing additional powers, duties and procedures of the Board;

(m) governing the placement of children for adoption;

(n) prescribing rules and standards governing the placement of children by licensees for adoption;

(o) providing for the inspection of the records of persons licensed to place children for adoption;

(p) governing the qualifications of persons or classes of persons employed by persons licensed to place children for adoption;

(q) requiring persons licensed to place children for adoption to be bonded or to submit letters of credit in the prescribed form and terms and with the prescribed collateral security, prescribing the form, terms and collateral security and providing for the forfeiture of bonds and letters of credit and the disposition of the proceeds;

(r) prescribing forms and providing for their use.

223. Regulations: Part X (Indian and Native Child and Family Services) — The Lieutenant Governor in Council may make regulations for the purposes of Part X,

(a) exempting an Indian or native child and family service authority, a band or native community or specified persons or classes of persons, including persons caring for children under customary care, from any provision of this Act or the regulations;

(b) prescribing matters requiring consultation between societies or agencies and bands or native communities for the purposes of clause 213(h).

PART XII — MISCELLANEOUS

224. (1) Review of Act — The Minister shall periodically conduct a review of this Act or those provisions of it specified by the Minister.

(2) Beginning of review — The Minister shall inform the public when a review under this section begins and what provisions of this Act are included in the review.

(3) Written report — The Minister shall prepare a written report respecting the review and shall make that report available to the public.

(4) Period for review — The first review shall be completed and the report made available to the public within five years after the day this section comes into force.

(5) Same — Each subsequent review shall be completed and the report made available to the public within five years after the day the report on the previous review has been made available to the public

1999, c. 2, s. 34

ONT. REG. 71 — REGISTER

made under the *Child and Family Services Act*
R.R.O. 1990, Reg. 71, as am. O. Reg. 213/00.

1. [Repealed O. Reg. 213/00, s. 1.]

2. (1) A society that receives information under section 72 of the Act concerning the abuse of a child shall enquire of the Director who maintains the register established under subsection 75 (5) of the Act, within three days after receiving the information, to determine whether any person referred to in the information has been previously identified in the register.

(2) A society that makes a report of verified information concerning the abuse of a child under subsection 75 (3) of the Act to the Director shall make the report within fourteen days after the information is verified by the society unless the Director extends the period of time.

(3) Upon receiving an inquiry from a society under subsection (1), the Director shall forthwith notify the society whether any person referred to in the information received by the society under section 72 of the Act has been previously identified in the register, the date of any such prior identification and the society or other agency that reported the prior identification.

(4) A report by a society to the Director of verified information concerning the abuse of a child made under subsection 75 (3) of the Act shall be in Form 1.

(5) Where a case concerning the abuse of a child has been reported by a society under subsection 75 (3) of the Act and the case is not closed by the society, the society shall make a further report in Form 2 to the Director within four months after making of the original report under subsection 75 (3) of the Act.

(6) Where a case is not closed, a society shall make a subsequent report to the Director in Form 2 on each anniversary of the original report until the case is closed by the society.

(7) [Repealed O. Reg. 213/00, s. 2.]

(8) [Repealed O. Reg. 213/00, s. 2.]

3. (1) The Director shall record information reported to the register under subsection 75 (3) of the Act in Form 3.

(2) The Director shall maintain information in the register established under subsection 75 (5) of the Act for at least twenty-five years from the date of the recording of the information unless the information has been previously expunged or amended pursuant to a decision by the Director.

4. (1) Every society shall ensure that each child in care of the society is given a medical and dental examination as soon as is practical after the admission of the child to care.

(2) Every society shall ensure that each child who is in care of the society is given a medical examination and dental examination at least once a year.

(3) Every society shall keep a record of each medical examination and dental examination of each child admitted into care by the society.

(4) Every society shall ensure that the treatment recommended as a result of a medical examination or dental examination of a child admitted into care by the society is carried out within the times recommended.

(5) Psychological and psychiatric assessments or treatment or both shall be provided for each child in the care of a society in accordance with the needs of the child where the society is of the opinion that the behaviour and condition of the child indicate that an assessment or treatment or both is necessary in the circumstances.

(6) The results of each assessment and treatment carried out under subsection (5) shall be recorded by the society.

5. (1) No society that admits a child into care shall place the child in a foster home or other home unless the child has previously visited the home at least ten days before the placement.

(2) Subsection (1) does not apply where it is not practical in the circumstances to have the child visit the home at least ten days before the placement.

(3) Every society shall ensure that each child placed in a foster home or other home by the society is visited by a social worker,

(a) within seven days after the child's admission to the home;

(b) at least once within thirty days of the placement; and

(c) at least once every three months after the visit referred to in clause (b),

or at such other interval as the local director directs.

6. Every society that receives an application to adopt or board a child that is in the care of the society shall, within thirty days after receiving the application, begin an investigation of the applicant and the home of the applicant.

7. (1) Every society shall open and maintain a separate file with respect to,

(a) each person who is a parent within the meaning of subsection 137 (1) of the Act who relinquishes a child to the society for adoption;

(b) each prospective adoptive parent;

(c) each child who is placed or who is intended to be placed for adoption by the society; and

(d) each foster parent who provides services to the society in connection with an adoption.

(2) The society shall review each file referred to in subsection (1) and bring the file up to date at least every six months until the file is closed.

(3) The society shall permanently retain a record of the contents of each file referred to in subsection (1).

SCHEDULE [FORMS]

Form 1 — Report to Child Abuse Register

Ministry of Community and Social Services Ontario Please print clearly or type	**Form 1** *Child and Family Services Act*	**Report to Child Abuse Register** Ministry use only Jurisdiction no. / File no.

A. Child (Corrections to Form 1 to be made on Form 2)

Last name | First name(s) | Sex | Birthdate or approximate age Y M D

Also known as

B. Alleged Abuser(s) (Corrections to Form 1 to be made on Form 2)

(1) Last name | First name(s) | Sex | Birthdate or approximate age Y M D

Also known as

Mailing address (include postal code)

Relationship to child
- ☐ Father   ☐ Mother   ☐ C.L. parent
- ☐ Stepfather   ☐ Stepmother   ☐ Grandparent
- ☐ Foster father   ☐ Foster mother   ☐ Sibling
- ☐ Uncle   ☐ Aunt   ☐ Other (specify)

(2) Last name | First name(s) | Sex | Birthdate or approximate age Y M D

Also known as

Mailing address (include postal code)

Relationship to child
- ☐ Father   ☐ Mother   ☐ C.L. parent
- ☐ Stepfather   ☐ Stepmother   ☐ Grandparent
- ☐ Foster father   ☐ Foster mother   ☐ Sibling
- ☐ Uncle   ☐ Aunt   ☐ Other (specify)

(3) Last name | First name(s) | Sex | Birthdate or approximate age Y M D

Also known as

Mailing Address (include postal code)

Relationship to child
- ☐ Father   ☐ Mother   ☐ C.L. parent
- ☐ Stepfather   ☐ Stepmother   ☐ Grandparent
- ☐ Foster father   ☐ Foster mother   ☐ Sibling
- ☐ Uncle   ☐ Aunt   ☐ Other (specify)

C. Parents of Child (if other than above)

Last name | First name(s) | Names and ages of siblings or other children if helpful for tracking

Also known as | Sex | Approx age | Relationship to child

Mailing address (include postal code)

Last name | First name(s)

Also known as | Sex | Approx | Relationship to child

Mailing address (include postal code)

D. Persons with whom child living at time of incident (if other than above)

Last name | First name(s) | Sex | Approx age | Relationship to child

Also known as | Mailing address (include postal code)

Last name | First name(s) | Sex | Approx age | Relationship to child

Also known as | Mailing address (include postal code)

E. Abuse

Date of incident Y M D | Date unknown | Episodic/ongoing From (date) | Reported to CAS Y M D | Place of incident
- ☐ Child's home
- ☐ Other (specify)

Source of report (do not identify informant)
- ☐ Victim   ☐ Relative   ☐ Professional (specify)
- ☐ Parent   ☐ Neighbour/friend   ☐ Other (specify)

Did or should parent(s) or caretaker(s) know of and permit or fail to prevent abuse? ☐ No ☐ Yes (elaborate) and also register under Section "B (3)" "Alleged Abusers".

Type of Abuse (Check ANY that apply)
- ☐ Physical   ☐ Emotional   ☐ Sexual   ☐ Failure to provide

Indicate the overall degree of abuse
- ☐ Mild   ☐ Moderate   ☐ Severe

0488 (11/86) front

CFSA Regs

Form 1

Ont. Reg. 71 — Register

Indicators (Check ANY that apply)   ☐ Fatal Injury (date of death)

☐ Abrasions	☐ Fractures	☐ Pregnancy	☐ Withdrawal	☐ No visible injuries (elaborate)
☐ Cuts	☐ Burns/Scalding	☐ Anxiety	☐ Developmental Delays	
☐ Welts	☐ Malnutrition	☐ Depression	☐ Self destructive aggressive behaviour	
☐ Bruises	☐ Other physical illness	☐ Irritation, pain, injury to genital area		☐ Other behavioural or physical (specify)
☐ Poisoning (specify)	☐ Mental, emotional or developmental condition requiring treatment (specify)	☐ Other indicators of sexual molestation or exploitation (specify)		

Brief explanation of occurrence(s) (including a statement describing frequency and duration)

F. Action taken on behalf of child

☐ Treated Outside Hospital

Examined by ☐ Physician   ☐ Reg. nurse   ☐ Social Worker

Hospitalized ☐ For assessment   ☐ For treatment   ☐ As place of safety

Child apprehended   **Other children apprehended**

☐ No ☐ Yes   ☐ No ☐ Yes   Number

CAS request to court

☐ Supervision order   Length requested

☐ Society wardship   Length requested

☐ Crown wardship

☐ Not yet known

Court hearing

Held on   Adjourned to

Disposition (if known)

CAS agreement with decision   ☐ No   ☐ Yes

G. Current situation

Child's present whereabouts

☐ At home   ☐ In hospital   ☐ In CAS care   ☐ Placed elsewhere (specify)

Elaborate if necessary

Alleged abuser(s)

☐ Still in home

☐ Child still in his/her care

☐ Living elsewhere

☐ In hospital (address)

☐ In prison   (address)

☐ Whereabouts unknown

☐ Unidentified

Action relating to alleged abuser(s)

Police Involvement

☐ None

☐ Informal contact   ☐ Police investigation

☐ Joint investigation with CAS

☐ Charges laid   ☐ pending

State charges

Adjourned to (date if known)

Disposition of case   ☐ Not yet known

Alleged abuser(s)/parents informed by CAS of report to

☐ Register   ☐ Not informed (please elaborate)

Regional and/or Area Office involved?

☐ No   ☐ Yes

Additional Comments

Previous CAS involvement with family

☐ No ☐ Yes (specify)

Previous abuse report to Ministry

☐ By this Society

☐ By another Society (specify)

☐ Register (post June 15, 1979)

Date

Send letter of notification to alleged abuser

☐ Directly   ☐ c/o CAS   ☐ Other (specify)

In other language (specify)

Reporting Society	Referred to another Society/child welfare authority	Date of referral y m d
Caseworker(s) (type name(s))	Signature of Local Director (type name and sign)	Date
	OR Authorized designate (type name and sign)	Date

0468 (11/85) Reverse

Form 2 — Follow-up Report to Child Abuse Register

Ministry of Community and Social Services Ontario	Form 2 Child and Family Services Act	Follow-up Report to Child Abuse Register

Ministry use only

Jurisdiction no. File no.

Please print clearly or type

☐ 4 month follow-up ☐ Annual Report, Year 1,2,3 ☐ Other ☐ Final Report

Child (Corrections to Form 1 to be made on Form 2)

Last name	First name(s)	Sex	Birthdate or approximate age (y, m, d)

Also known as

Alleged abuser(s) (Corrections to Form 1 to be made on Form 2)

1. Last name | First name(s) | Sex | Birthdate or approximate age (y, m, d)

Also known as

Mailing address (include postal code)

Relationship to child

☐ Father ☐ Mother ☐ C.L. parent
☐ Stepfather ☐ Stepmother ☐ Grandparent
☐ Foster father ☐ Foster mother ☐ Sibling
☐ Uncle ☐ Aunt ☐ Other (specify)

2. Last name | First name(s) | Sex | Birthdate or approximate age (y, m, d)

Also known as

Mailing address (include postal code)

Relationship to child

☐ Father ☐ Mother ☐ C.L. parent
☐ Stepfather ☐ Stepmother ☐ Grandparent
☐ Foster father ☐ Foster mother ☐ Sibling
☐ Uncle ☐ Aunt ☐ Other (specify)

3. Last name | First name(s) | Sex | Birthdate or approximate age (y, m, d)

Also known as

Mailing address (include postal code)

Relationship to child

☐ Father ☐ Mother ☐ C.L. parent
☐ Stepfather ☐ Stepmother ☐ Grandparent
☐ Foster father ☐ Foster mother ☐ Sibling
☐ Uncle ☐ Aunt ☐ Other (specify)

Action taken on behalf of child - update

Child apprehended Other children apprehended

☐ No change

☐ No ☐ Yes ☐ No ☐ Yes Number

CAS request to court

☐ Supervision order Length requested
☐ Society wardship Length requested
☐ Crown wardship
☐ Not yet known

Court hearing

Held on Adjourned to

Disposition (if known)

CAS agreement with decision ☐ No ☐ Yes

Current situation - update

☐ No change

Child's present whereabouts

☐ At home ☐ In hospital ☐ In CAS care ☐ Placed elsewhere (specify)

Elaborate if necessary

Alleged abuser(s)

☐ Still in home
☐ Child still in his/her care
☐ Living elsewhere
☐ In hospital
☐ In prison
☐ Whereabouts unknown
☐ Still unidentified

Action relating to alleged abuser(s)
Police involvement
☐ None
☐ Informal contact ☐ Police investigation
☐ Joint investigation with CAS
☐ Charges laid ☐ pending
State charges

Adjourned to (date if known)

Disposition of case, specifics of sentence, if applicable

195

Causative factors

Present level of condition

Parents	Deterioration		Improvement		Unchanged
	Slight	Significant	Slight	Significant	
☐ heavy child care responsibilities	☐	☐	☐	☐	☐
☐ lack of support system	☐	☐	☐	☐	☐
☐ marital difficulties	☐	☐	☐	☐	☐
☐ lack of knowledge of child care/development	☐	☐	☐	☐	☐
☐ physical violence/corporal punishment acceptable	☐	☐	☐	☐	☐
☐ different cultural/sub-cultural/religious norms	☐	☐	☐	☐	☐
☐ alcohol/drug abuse	☐	☐	☐	☐	☐
☐ physical/mental illness	☐	☐	☐	☐	☐
☐ personality disorder/sociopathic	☐	☐	☐	☐	☐
☐ intellectual limitations	☐	☐	☐	☐	☐
☐ abused in childhood	☐	☐	☐	☐	☐
☐ emotionally deprived in childhood	☐	☐	☐	☐	☐
☐ other	☐	☐	☐	☐	☐

Child

	Slight	Significant	Slight	Significant	Unchanged
☐ unwanted	☐	☐	☐	☐	☐
☐ premature	☐	☐	☐	☐	☐
☐ handicapped	☐	☐	☐	☐	☐
☐ behaviour problem/provocative	☐	☐	☐	☐	☐
☐ other	☐	☐	☐	☐	☐

Environment

	Slight	Significant	Slight	Significant	Unchanged
☐ housing	☐	☐	☐	☐	☐
☐ unemployment	☐	☐	☐	☐	☐
☐ finances	☐	☐	☐	☐	☐
☐ social isolation	☐	☐	☐	☐	☐
☐ other	☐	☐	☐	☐	☐

Services provided	By	For	Unavailable	Rejected
☐ psychiatric/psychological assessment				
☐ psychiatric treatment				
☐ counselling				
☐ medical treatment				
☐ public health nurse				
☐ parent education courses				
☐ parents anonymous/self help group				
☐ volunteer visitor/parent aide				
☐ professional child care worker				
☐ day care				
☐ homemaker				
☐ material needs/financial assistance				
☐ housing				
☐ employment				
☐ child taken into care				
☐ other				

Elaborate on any of the above information

Reporting society	Date

Caseworker(s) (type name(s))   Signature(s)

Form 3 — Child Abuse Register

| Ministry of Community and Social Services Ontario | Form 3 *Child and Family Services Act* | **Child Abuse Register** |

Child

Last name	First name(s)		
Known as (if applicable)		Sex	Birthdate or approx. age (y, m, d)	File No.

Alleged Abuser

Last name	First name(s)	Relationship to child
Known as (if applicable)		Sex	Birthdate or approx. age (y, m, d)	
Mailing address			

Incident

| Date (y, m, d) | Date Not Known | Episodic/ongoing From (Date) | Date reported to CAS (y, m, d) | Previous abuse report to Ministry ☐ No ☐ Yes | Date(s) (y, m, d) | By: |

Reporting Society

Name of Society	Form 1 signed by:	Registered by:
		Child Abuse Registrar
Name(s) of caseworker(s)	Dated (y, m, d)	Date (y, m, d)

0460 (12/85) Front

197

No letter sent: ☐ address unknown   ☐ abuser unidentified

Date letter sent (y, m, d)

☐ Direct   ☐ c/o CAS   ☐ Other   Other language

Date letter returned (y, m, d)   Disposition of returned letter

Inspected as per the *Child and Family Services Act* Clause 76(2)(b) by:

Signature   Date (y, m, d)

Witnessed by

0460 (12/85) Reverse

ONT. REG. 70 — GENERAL

made under the *Child and Family Services Act*

R.R.O. 1990, Reg. 70, as am. O. Reg. 139/91; 239/92; 683/92; 161/93; 400/93; 50/94; 509/94; 539/94; 763/94; 225/95 483/97; 199/99; 45/00; 303/01; 77/02.

[Note: only Forms 8–12 are reproduced here.]

. . . . .

SCHEDULE — [FORMS]

. . . . .

Form 8 — Information in Support of a Warrant to Apprehend and Return a Child in Care

Ontario Court .... Court file no. ....(Provincial Division) .... at ....(address)

This is the Information of ....(Name of informant) of ....(address)

I am a ❏ peace officer

❏ child protection worker employed by ....

I have reasonable and probable grounds to believe that ....(name of child) who is a child actually or apparently under the age of sixteen years has left or been removed from the lawful care of ....(name of society) without the consent of the society.

I have reasonable and probable grounds to believe and do believe that there is no course of action available other than bringing the child to a place of safety that would protect the child adequately, for the following reasons:

    Set out reasons ....*(Do not complete if not applicable)*

I have reasonable and probable grounds to believe that the child may be found at:

    ....(address(es) street and number).................................. (municipality)

    Sworn (or affirmed) before me this .... day of ...., 19 .... at the .... of ....(Signature of informant) in the .... of ....(A justice of the peace in and for the Province of Ontario)

O. Reg. 683/92, s. 2.

Form 9 — Warrant to Apprehend and Return a Child Who Has Withdrawn From a Parent's Control

Ontario Court (Provincial Division)

Court file no.

at ....

...................................(address)

TO ALL CHILD PROTECTION WORKERS AND PEACE OFFICERS IN THE PROVINCE OF ONTARIO:

On the basis of an Information under subsection 43 (2) of the *Child and Family, Services Act*, which information is laid before me on oath of ....,

❏ a parent of the child named or described on the back of this warrant,

❏ an authorized officer of an approved agency that has custody of the child,

❏ a person who has care and control of the child,

I am satisfied that the child is under sixteen years of age.

I am also satisfied, on the basis of that information, that the child has withdrawn from the care and control of a person described above without that person's consent. I am also satisfied, on the basis of that information, that the person described above believes on reasonable and probable grounds that the child's health or safety may be at risk if the child is not apprehended.

I am further satisfied, on the basis of that information, that the child has not withdrawn from the care and control of one parent with the consent of another parent in circumstances where a proceeding under section 36 of the *Children's Law Reform Act* would be more appropriate.

Check this box only if child's whereabouts are known

❏ I am further satisfied, on the basis of that Information, that the child may now be found at (*Give a municipal address or a precise description of the premises where the child may be found.*)

....

....

....

....

I THEREFORE AUTHORIZE YOU to return the child to the child's parent ....(name) at ....(address) as soon as practicable and, where it is not possible to return the child to the parent within a reasonable time, to take the child to a place of safety as defined in the *Child and Family Services Act*.

This warrant further authorizes you to enter by force if necessary and to search ....(Name and location of premises) and to remove the child from it.

This Warrant expires on the .... day of ...., 19 ....

..........(Date)..................................(Signature of justice of the peace)

...................................(City, town, etc. where this Warrant signed) ....
(Print or type name of justice of the peace)

Insert all available information

.... Full name of child
.... Birth date (d,m,y) .... Sex
.... Aliases or nicknames
.... Residential address .... Telephone number
.... Present location of child .... Telephone number
.... Height .... Weight .... Hair colour ....
Hair style .... Eye colour .... Complexion
.... Other features
.... Name and address of person to be contacted for further information
.... Telephone number.

Form 10 — Information in Support of a Warrant to Apprehend and Return a Child Who Has Withdrawn From a Parent's Control

Ontario Court (Provincial Division)

Court file no.

at ....(address)

This is the Information of .... of (Name of informant) .... (address)

1. I am ❑ a parent of

❑ an authorized officer of an approved agency that has custody of

❑ a person who has care and control of

.................................(name of child) who was born on ....(date)

2. On or about the .... day of ....(name of child) withdrew from my care and control without consent by: ....(describe circumstances)

3. I have reasonable and probable grounds to believe and do believe that if ....(child's name) is not apprehended his/her health or safety may be at risk, for the following reasons:

(set out reasons) ....

....

....

....

4. ....(name of child) has not withdrawn from the care and control of one parent with the consent of another parent in circumstances where a proceeding under section 36 of the *Children's Law Reform Act* would be more appropriate.

(Do not complete if not applicable)

5. I have reasonable and probable grounds to believe that ....(name of child) may be found at ....(address) ....(street and number) ....(municipality)

Sworn (or affirmed) before me this .... day of ...., 19 .... at the .... of ....(Signature of informant) in the

.... of ....(A justice of the peace
in and for the Province of Ontario) O. Reg. 683/92, s.3

Form 11 — Information to Obtain a Warrant of Apprehension and Return of a Young Person
(Section 98 of the Act)

This is the information of ....(Name) ....(Address)
....(Occupation) who says that he/she has reasonable and probable grounds to believe and does believe that on or about the .... day of
.........., 19 ....

   ❏ male

   ❏ female ....(Surname) ....(Given names)
..........(Birthdate) (d,m,y)

   ❏ a young person detained under the *Young Offenders Act* (Canada) or the *Provincial Offences Act*

OR

   ❏ a young person held in a place of open custody under clause 75 (d) of the *Provincial Offences Act* at ....(Name of place of temporary detention or open custody) ....(Address)

1. ❏ left the said place of temporary detention or open custody prior to release there-from and without the consent of .... (Name and position)

   ❏ the person in charge of the place of temporary detention *OR*

   ❏ the person in charge of the place of open custody and failed or refused to return there

OR

2. failed or refused to return to the said place of open custody upon completion of a period of temporary release contrary to Part IV of the *Child and Family Services Act.*

And that he/she may be found at ....(Name and location of premises)

And that I am a person who has authority to apprehend the said young person.

Sworn (or affirmed) before me, this .... day of ...., 19 .... at .... in the
....

...................................(Signature of informant)

...................................(Address)

...................................(Justice of the Peace)

Note: This information to be used only for the issuance of a warrant of apprehension and return of a young person under Part IV of the *Child and Family Services Act* O. Reg. 683/92, s.4.

Form 12 — Warrant of Apprehension and Return of a Young Person

(Section 98 of the Act)

To all peace officers in the Province of Ontario:

Whereas on the information upon oath of ....

I am satisfied that there are reasonable and probable grounds to believe that on or about the .... day of ...., 19 ....

Young Person (give all known information) ....(Name) ....(Birthdate) (d,m,y) ....(Sex)

....(Residence or location)

Physical Description

(Height)	(Weight)	(Hair colour)	(Hair style)	(Eye colour)

(Complexion) ....

(Other features) ....

❏ a young person detained under the *Young Offenders Act* (Canada) or *Provincial Offences Act*

OR

❏ a young person held in a place of open custody under clause 75 (d) of the *Provincial Offences Act* at ....(Name of place of temporary detention or open custody) ....(Address)

1. ❏ left the said place of temporary detention or open custody prior to discharge therefrom and without the consent of ....(Name and position)

❏ the person in charge of the place of temporary detention

OR

❏ the person in charge of the place of open custody and failed or refused to return there

OR

2. failed or refused to return to the said place of open custody upon completion of a period of temporary release contrary to Part IV of the *Child and Family Services Act*.

This warrant authorizes you under the said Act to apprehend, hold and return the said young person to ....(Name of place of temporary detention, open custody) and further authorizes you to enter by force if necessary and to search ....(Name of location of premises) and to remove the young person therefrom.

.........(Date).........(Place).........(Justice of the Peace)

This warrant expires on ....(Date)

Note: For further information about the young person contact:

...................................(Name)

...................................(Position and Telephone No.)

. . . . .

203

ONT. REG 206/00 — PROCEDURES, PRACTICES AND STANDARDS OF SERVICE FOR CHILD PROTECTION CASES

made under the *Child and Family Services Act*
O. Reg. 206/00

1. In this Regulation,

"child" has the same meaning as in Part III of the Act;

"Child Protection Fast Track Information System" means the database containing information extracted from the records kept by societies respecting children and families with whom the society has had contact in connection with the society's function under clause 15(3)(a) of the Act;

"Risk Assessment Model" means the Ministry of Community and Social Services publication titled "Risk Assessment Model for Child Protection in Ontario" and dated March 2000.

2. Within 24 hours after receiving information that a child is or may be in need of protection, a society shall,

(a) record the information it received;

(b) rate the information it received in accordance with the rating criteria contained in the publication of the Ontario Association of Children's Aid Societies titled "Ontario Child Welfare ELIGIBILITY SPECTRUM" and dated March 2000;

(c) record the rating made under clause (b) and the reasons for the rating;

(d) search the Child Protection Fast Track Information System for information that may be relevant in determining whether or not there are reasonable and probable grounds to believe that the child or any other child in the same family is in need of protection;

(e) record the information that may be relevant found under clause (d);

(f) decide, in accordance with the Risk Assessment Model, whether or not a full child protection investigation should be initiated with respect to the child and any other child in the same family;

(g) record the decision made under clause (f);

(h) if the decision made under clause (f) is that a full child protection investigation should be initiated,

(i) determine, in accordance with the Risk Assessment Model, the time within which a child protection worker should first meet with the child who is, or the children who are, the subject of the investigation, and

(ii) develop, in accordance with the Risk Assessment Model, a plan for carrying out the investigation; and

(i) record the determination made under subclause (h)(i) and the plan developed under subclause (h)(ii);

205

3. A society shall ensure that,

(a) when a child protection worker first meets with the child who is, or any of the children who are, the subject of a full child protection investigation, the worker conducts a safety assessment in accordance with the Risk Assessment Model and takes the actions that are immediately necessary to protect the child or children, as the case may be; and

(b) as soon as possible and no later than 24 hours after the first meeting referred to in clause (a), the worker records the safety assessment conducted under clause (a) and the actions, if any, the worker has taken under clause (a) to protect the child or children, as the case may be.

4. (1) After completing a full child protection investigation, a society shall,

(a) record the findings of the investigation;

(b) determine, in accordance, with the Risk Assessment Model, whether or not there are reasonable and probable grounds to believe that the child who was, or any of the children who were, the subject of the investigation is in need of protection; and

(c) record the determination made under clause (b) and the reasons for it.

(2) If the determination made by the society under clause (1)(b) is that there are reasonable and probable grounds to believe that the child who was, or any of the children who were, the subject of the investigation is in need of protection, the society shall,

(a) carry out, in accordance with the Risk Assessment Model, a risk assessment and an assessment of other child protection issues;

(b) develop and carry out, in accordance with the Risk Assessment Model, a plan for reducing the risk of future harm to the child who is, or the children who are, believed to be in need of protection; and

(c) record the assessments carried out under clause (a), the plan developed under clause (b) and the steps taken to implement the plan.

(3) The society shall repeat the tasks it is required to perform under clauses (2)(a), (b) and (c) at least every six months until it determines, in accordance with the Risk Assessment Model, that the child is, or the children are, as the case may be, no longer eligible for child protection services.

(4) When the society determines that the child is, or the children are, as the case may be, no longer eligible for child protection services, the society shall,

(a) review its most recent assessments under clause (2)(a) and its most recent plan under clause (2)(b); and

(b) record the review.

5. This Regulation comes into force on the day section 1 of the *Child and Family Services Amendment Act (Child Welfare Reform), 1999* comes into force.

CHILDREN'S LAW REFORM ACT

R.S.O. 1990, c. C.12 [ss. 77–84 not in force at date of publication.], as am. S.O. 1992, c. 32, s. 4; 1993, c. 27, Sched.; 1996, c. 2, s. 63; 1996, c. 25, s. 3; 1998, c. 26, s. 101; 1999, c. 6, s. 7; 2000, c. 33, s. 21 [Not in force at date of publication.]; 2001, c. 9, Sched. B, s. 4.

PART I — EQUAL STATUS OF CHILDREN

1. (1) Rule of parentage — Subject to subsection (2), for all purposes of the law of Ontario a person is the child of his or her natural parents and his or her status as their child is independent of whether the child is born within or outside marriage.

(2) Exception for adopted children — Where an adoption order has been made, section 158 or 159 of the *Child and Family Services Act* applies and the child is the child of the adopting parents as if they were the natural parents.

(3) Kindred relationships — The parent and child relationships as determined under subsections (1) and (2) shall be followed in the determination of other kindred relationships flowing therefrom.

(4) Common law distinction of legitimacy abolished — Any distinction at common law between the status of children born in wedlock and born out of wedlock is abolished and the relationship of parent and child and kindred relationships flowing therefrom shall be determined for the purposes of the common law in accordance with this section.

2. (1) Rule of construction — For the purposes of construing any instrument, Act or regulation, unless the contrary intention appears, a reference to a person or group or class of persons described in terms of relationship by blood or marriage to another person shall be construed to refer to or include a person who comes within the description by reason of the relationship of parent and child as determined under section 1.

(2) Application — Subsection (1) applies to,

(a) any Act of the Legislature or any regulation, order or by-law made under an Act of the Legislature enacted or made before, on or after the 31st day of March, 1978; and

(b) any instrument made on or after the 31st day of March, 1978.

PART II — ESTABLISHMENT OF PARENTAGE

3. Court under ss. 4 to 7 — The court having jurisdiction for the purposes of sections 4 to 7 is,

(a) the Family Court, in the areas where it has jurisdiction under subsection 21.1(4) of the *Courts of Justice Act*;

(b) the Superior Court of Justice, in the rest of Ontario.

1996, c. 25, s. 3(1); 2001, c. 9, Sched. B, s. 4(7)

4. (1) Application for declaration — Any person having an interest may apply to a court for a declaration that a male person is recognized in law to be the father of a child or that a female person is the mother of a child.

(2) Declaration of paternity recognized at law — Where the court finds that a presumption of paternity exists under section 8 and unless it is established, on the balance of probabilities, that the presumed father is not the father of the child, the court shall make a declaratory order confirming that the paternity is recognized in law.

(3) Declaration of maternity — Where the court finds on the balance of probabilities that the relationship of mother and child has been established, the court may make a declaratory order to that effect.

(4) Idem — Subject to sections 6 and 7, an order made under this section shall be recognized for all purposes.

5. (1) Application for declaration of paternity where no presumption — Where there is no person recognized in law under section 8 to be the father of a child, any person may apply to the court for a declaration that a male person is his or her father, or any male person may apply to the court for a declaration that a person is his child.

(2) Limitation — An application shall not be made under subsection (1) unless both the persons whose relationship is sought to be established are living.

(3) Declaratory order — Where the court finds on the balance of probabilities that the relationship of father and child has been established, the court may make a declaratory order to that effect and, subject to sections 6 and 7, the order shall be recognized for all purposes.

6. Reopening on new evidence — Where a declaration has been made under section 4 or 5 and evidence becomes available that was not available at the previous hearing, the court may, upon application, discharge or vary the order and make such other orders or directions as are ancillary thereto.

7. Appeal — An appeal lies from an order under section 4 or 5 or a decision under section 6 in accordance with the rules of the court.

8. (1) Recognition in law of parentage — Unless the contrary is proven on a balance of probabilities, there is a presumption that a male person is, and he shall be recognized in law to be, the father of a child in any one of the following circumstances:

1. The person is married to the mother of the child at the time of the birth of the child.

2. The person was married to the mother of the child by a marriage that was terminated by death or judgment of nullity within 300 days before the birth of the child or by divorce where the decree *nisi* was granted within 300 days before the birth of the child.

3. The person marries the mother of the child after the birth of the child and acknowledges that he is the natural father.

4. The person was cohabiting with the mother of the child in a relationship of some permanence at the time of the birth of the child or the child is born within 300 days after they ceased to cohabit.

5. The person has certified the child's birth, as the child's father, under the *Vital Statistics Act* or a similar Act in another jurisdiction in Canada.

6. The person has been found or recognized in his lifetime by a court of competent jurisdiction in Canada to be the father of the child.

(2) Where marriage void — For the purpose of subsection (1), where a man and woman go through a form of marriage with each other, in good faith, that is void and cohabit, they shall be deemed to be married during the time they cohabit and the marriage shall be deemed to be terminated when they cease to cohabit.

(3) Conflicting presumptions — Where circumstances exist that give rise to a presumption or presumptions of paternity by more than one father under subsection (1), no presumption shall be made as to paternity and no person is recognized in law to be the father.

9. Admissibility in evidence of acknowledgment against interest — A written acknowledgment of parentage that is admitted in evidence in any civil proceeding against the interest of the person making the acknowledgment is proof, in the absence of evidence to the contrary, of the fact.

10. (1) Approved blood tests — Upon the application of a party in a civil proceeding in which the court is called upon to determine the parentage of a child, the court may give the party leave to obtain blood tests of such persons as are named in the order granting leave and to submit the results in evidence.

(2) Conditions attached — Leave under subsection (1) may be given subject to such terms and conditions as the court thinks proper.

(3) Inference from refusal — Where leave is given under subsection (1) and a person named therein refuses to submit to the blood test, the court may draw such inferences as it thinks appropriate.

(4) Consent to procedure — The *Health Care Consent Act, 1996* applies to the blood test as if it were treatment under that Act.

1992, c. 32, s. 4; 1996, c. 2, s. 63

11. Regulations for blood tests — The Lieutenant Governor in Council may make regulations governing blood tests for which leave is given by a court under section 10 including, without limiting the generality of the foregoing,

(a) the method of taking blood samples and the handling, transportation and storage thereof;

(b) the conditions under which a blood sample may be tested;

(c) designating persons or facilities or classes thereof who are authorized to conduct blood tests for the purposes of section 10;

(d) prescribing procedures respecting the admission of reports of blood tests in evidence;

(e) prescribing forms for the purpose of section 10 and this section and providing for their use.

12. (1) Statutory declaration of parentage — A person may file in the office of the Registrar General a statutory declaration, in the form prescribed by the regulations, affirming that he or she is the father or mother, as the case may be, of a child.

(2) Idem — Two persons may file in the office of the Registrar General a statutory declaration, in the form prescribed by the regulations, jointly affirming that they are the father and mother of a child.

13. Copies of statutory declarations under *Vital Statistics Act* — Upon application and upon payment of the fee prescribed under the *Vital Statistics Act*, any person who has an interest, furnishes substantially accurate particulars and satisfies the Registrar General as to the reason for requiring it may obtain from the Registrar General a certified copy of a statutory declaration filed under section 12.

14. (1) Filing of court decisions respecting parentage — Every registrar or clerk of a court in Ontario shall furnish the Registrar General with a statement in the form prescribed by the regulations respecting each order or judgment of the court that confirms or makes a finding of parentage.

(2) Inspection by public — Upon application and upon payment of the fee prescribed under the *Vital Statistics Act*, any person may inspect a statement respecting an order or judgment filed under subsection (1) and obtain a certified copy thereof from the Registrar General.

1993, c. 27, Sched.

15. Certified copies as evidence — A certificate certifying a copy of a document to be a true copy, obtained under section 12, 13 or 14, purporting to be signed by the Registrar General or Deputy Registrar General or on which the signature of either is lithographed, printed or stamped is, without proof of the office or signature of the Registrar General or Deputy Registrar General, receivable in evidence as proof, in the absence of evidence to the contrary, of the filing and contents of the document for all purposes in any action or proceeding.

16. Duties of Registrar General — Nothing in this Act shall be construed to require the Registrar General to amend a registration showing parentage other than in recognition of an order made under section 4, 5 or 6.

17. Regulations for forms — The Lieutenant Governor in Council may make regulations prescribing forms for the purposes of this Part.

PART III — CUSTODY, ACCESS AND GUARDIANSHIP
INTERPRETATION

18. (1) Definitions — In this Part,

"court" means the Ontario Court of Justice, the Family Court or the Superior Court of Justice; ("tribunal")

"extra-provincial order" means an order, or that part of an order, of an extra-provincial tribunal that grants to a person custody of or access to a child; ("ordonnance extraprovinciale")

"extra-provincial tribunal" means a court or tribunal outside Ontario that has jurisdiction to grant to a person custody of or access to a child; ("tribunal extraprovincial") "**separation agreement**" means an agreement that is a valid separation agreement under Part IV of the *Family Law Act*. ("accord de séparation")

(2) **Child** — A reference in this Part to a child is a reference to the child while a minor.
1996, c. 25, s. 3(2); 2001, c. 9, Sched. B, s. 4(7), (8)

19. Purposes — The purposes of this Part are,

(a) to ensure that applications to the courts in respect of custody of, incidents of custody of, access to and guardianship for children will be determined on the basis of the best interests of the children;

(b) to recognize that the concurrent exercise of jurisdiction by judicial tribunals of more than one province, territory or state in respect of the custody of the same child ought to be avoided, and to make provision so that the courts of Ontario will, unless there are exceptional circumstances, refrain from exercising or decline jurisdiction in cases where it is more appropriate for the matter to be determined by a tribunal having jurisdiction in another place with which the child has a closer connection;

(c) to discourage the abduction of children as an alternative to the determination of custody rights by due process; and

(d) to provide for the more effective enforcement of custody and access orders and for the recognition and enforcement of custody and access orders made outside Ontario.

Custody and Access

20. (1) Father and mother entitled to custody — Except as otherwise provided in this Part, the father and the mother are equally entitled to custody of the child.

(2) **Rights and responsibilities** — A person entitled to custody of a child has the rights and responsibilities of a parent in respect of the person of the child and must exercise those rights and responsibilities in the best interests of the child.

(3) **Authority to act** — Where more than one person is entitled to custody of a child, any one of them may exercise the rights and accept the responsibilities of a parent on behalf of them in respect of the child.

(4) **Where parents separate** — Where the parents of a child live separate and apart and the child lives with one of them with the consent, implied consent or acquiescence of the other of them, the right of the other to exercise the entitlement of custody and the incidents of custody, but not the entitlement to access, is suspended until a separation agreement or order otherwise provides.

Proposed Addition — 20(4a)

(4a) **Duty of separated parents** — Where the parents of a child live separate and apart and the child is in the custody of one of them and the other is entitled to access under the terms of a separation agreement or order, each shall, in the best interests of the child, encourage and support the child's continuing parent-child relationship with the other.
R.S.O. 1990, c. C.12, s. 77 [Not in force at date of publication.]

(5) **Access** — The entitlement to access to a child includes the right to visit with and be visited by the child and the same right as a parent to make inquiries and to be given information as to the health, education and welfare of the child.

CLRA

(6) Marriage of child — The entitlement to custody of or access to a child terminates on the marriage of the child.

(7) Entitlement subject to agreement or order — Any entitlement to custody or access or incidents of custody under this section is subject to alteration by an order of the court or by separation agreement.

21. Application for order — A parent of a child or any other person may apply to a court for an order respecting custody of or access to the child or determining any aspect of the incidents of custody of the child.

22. (1) Jurisdiction — A court shall only exercise its jurisdiction to make an order for custody of or access to a child where,

> (a) the child is habitually resident in Ontario at the commencement of the application for the order;

> (b) although the child is not habitually resident in Ontario, the court is satisfied,

>> (i) that the child is physically present in Ontario at the commencement of the application for the order,

>> (ii) that substantial evidence concerning the best interests of the child is available in Ontario,

>> (iii) that no application for custody of or access to the child is pending before an extra-provincial tribunal in another place where the child is habitually resident,

>> (iv) that no extra-provincial order in respect of custody of or access to the child has been recognized by a court in Ontario,

>> (v) that the child has a real and substantial connection with Ontario, and

>> (vi) that, on the balance of convenience, it is appropriate for jurisdiction to be exercised in Ontario.

(2) Habitual residence — A child is habitually resident in the place where he or she resided,

> (a) with both parents;

> (b) where the parents are living separate and apart, with one parent under a separation agreement or with the consent, implied consent or acquiescence of the other or under a court order; or

> (c) with a person other than a parent on a permanent basis for a significant period of time,

whichever last occurred.

(3) Abduction — The removal or withholding of a child without the consent of the person having custody of the child does not alter the habitual residence of the child unless there has been acquiescence or undue delay in commencing due process by the person from whom the child is removed or withheld.

23. Serious harm to child — Despite sections 22 and 41, a court may exercise its jurisdiction to make or to vary an order in respect of the custody of or access to a child where,

> (a) the child is physically present in Ontario; and

(b) the court is satisfied that the child would, on the balance of probabilities, suffer serious harm if,

(i) the child remains in the custody of the person legally entitled to custody of the child,

(ii) the child is returned to the custody of the person legally entitled to custody of the child, or

(iii) the child is removed from Ontario.

24. (1) Merits of application for custody or access — The merits of an application under this Part in respect of custody of or access to a child shall be determined on the basis of the best interests of the child.

Proposed Amendment — 24(1)

(1) Merits of application for custody or access — The merits of an application or motion under this Part in respect of custody of or access to a child shall be determined on the basis of the best interests of the child.

R.S.O. 1990, c. C.12, s. 78(1) [Not in force at date of publication.]

(2) Best interests of child — In determining the best interests of a child for the purposes of an application under this Part in respect of custody of or access to a child, a court shall consider all the needs and circumstances of the child including,

(a) the love, affection and emotional ties between the child and,

(i) each person entitled to or claiming custody of or access to the child,

(ii) other members of the child's family who reside with the child, and

(iii) persons involved in the care and upbringing of the child;

(b) the views and preferences of the child, where such views and preferences can reasonably be ascertained;

(c) the length of time the child has lived in a stable home environment;

(d) the ability and willingness of each person applying for custody of the child to provide the child with guidance and education, the necessaries of life and any special needs of the child;

(e) any plans proposed for the care and upbringing of the child;

(f) the permanence and stability of the family unit with which it is proposed that the child will live; and

(g) the relationship by blood or through an adoption order between the child and each person who is party to the application.

Proposed Amendment — 24(2)

(2) Best interests of child — In determining the best interests of a child for the purpose of an application or motion under this Part in respect of custody of or access to a child, a court shall consider all the child's needs and circumstances, including,

(a) the love, affection and emotional ties between the child and,

(i) each person seeking custody or access,

(ii) other members of the child's family residing with him or her, and

(iii) persons involved in the child's care and upbringing;

(b) the child's views and preferences, if they can reasonably be ascertained;

(c) the length of time the child has lived in a stable home environment;

(d) the ability of each person seeking custody or access to act as a parent;

(e) the ability and willingness of each person seeking custody to provide the child with guidance, education and necessities of life and to meet any special needs of the child;

(f) any plans proposed for the child's care and upbringing;

(g) the permanence and stability of the family unit with which it is proposed that the child will live; and

(h) the relationship, by blood or through an adoption order, between the child and each person who is a party to the application or motion.

R.S.O. 1990, c. C.12, s. 78(2) [Not in force at date of publication.]

(3) Past conduct — The past conduct of a person is not relevant to a determination of an application under this Part in respect of custody of or access to a child unless the conduct is relevant to the ability of the person to act as a parent of a child.

Proposed Amendment — 24(3)

(3) Domestic violence to be considered — In assessing a person's ability to act as a parent, the court shall consider the fact that the person has at any time committed violence against his or her spouse, same-sex partner or child, against his or her child's parent or against another member of the person's household.

R.S.O. 1990, c. C.12, s. 78(2) [Not in force at date of publication.] [Amended 1999, c. 6, s. 7(1).]

Proposed Addition — 24(3.1), (4)

(3.1) Definitions — In subsection (3),

"same-sex partner" means either of two persons of the same sex who live together in a conjugal relationship outside marriage; ("partenaire de même sexe")

"spouse" means,

(a) a spouse as defined in section 1 of the *Family Law Act*, or

(b) either of two persons of the opposite sex who live together in a conjugal relationship outside marriage. ("conjoint")

R.S.O. 1990, c. C.12, s. 78(2) [Not in force at date of publication.][Amended 1999, c. 6, s. 7(2).]

(4) Restrictions on consideration of other past conduct — Other than the conduct referred to in subsection (3), a person's past conduct may be considered only if the court is satisfied that it is relevant to the person's ability to act as a parent.

R.S.O. 1990, c. C.12, s. 78(2) [Not in force at date of publication.]

25. Declining jurisdiction — A court having jurisdiction under this Part in respect of custody or access may decline to exercise its jurisdiction where it is of the opinion that it is more appropriate for jurisdiction to be exercised outside Ontario.

26. (1) Delay — Where an application under this Part in respect of custody of or access to a child has not been heard within six months after the commencement of the proceedings, the clerk or local registrar of the court shall list the application for the court and give notice to the parties of the date and time when and the place where the court will fix a date for the hearing of the application.

(2) Directions — At a hearing of a matter listed by the clerk or local registrar in accordance with subsection (1), the court by order may fix a date for the hearing of the application and may give such directions in respect of the proceedings and make such order in respect of the costs of proceedings as the court considers appropriate.

(3) Early date — Where the court fixes a date under subsection (2), the court shall fix the earliest date that, in the opinion of the court, is compatible with a just disposition of the application.

27. Effect of divorce proceedings — Where an action for divorce is commenced under the *Divorce Act* (Canada), any application under this Part in respect of custody of or access to a child that has not been determined is stayed except by leave of the court.

Custody and Access — Orders

28. Powers of court — The court to which an application is made under section 21,

(a) by order may grant the custody of or access to the child to one or more persons;

(b) by order may determine any aspect of the incidents of the right to custody or access; and

(c) may make such additional order as the court considers necessary and proper in the circumstances.

Proposed Addition — 28a

28a (1) Application to fix times or days of access — If an order in respect of access to a child provides for a person's access to the child without specifying times or days, a party to the order may apply to the court that made it to vary it by specifying times or days.

(2) Order — The court may vary the order by specifying the times or days agreed to by the parties, or the times or days the court considers appropriate if the parties do not agree.

(3) Separation agreements — Subsection (1) also applies, with necessary modifications, in respect of a separation agreement under section 54 of the *Family Law Act* or a predecessor of that section that provides for a person's access to a child without specifying times or days.

(4) Exception — Subsection (1) does not apply in respect of orders made under the *Divorce Act* (Canada) or a predecessor of that Act.
R.S.O. 1990, c. C.12, s. 79 [Not in force at date of publication.]

29. Order varying an order — A court shall not make an order under this Part that varies an order in respect of custody or access made by a court in Ontario unless there has been a material change in circumstances that affects or is likely to affect the best interests of the child.

CLRA

Proposed Amendment — 29

29. (1) Order varying an order — A court shall not make an order under this Part that varies an order in respect of custody or access made by a court in Ontario unless there has been a material change in circumstances that affects or is likely to affect the best interests of the child.

(2) Exception — Subsection (1) does not apply in respect of orders made under subsection 28a(2) (fixing times or days of access) or 34a(2) or (6) (access enforcement, etc.).

R.S.O. 1990, c. C.12, s. 80 [Not in force at date of publication.]

Custody and Access — Assistance to Court

30. (1) Assessment of needs of child — The court before which an application is brought in respect of custody of or access to a child, by order, may appoint a person who has technical or professional skill to assess and report to the court on the needs of the child and the ability and willingness of the parties or any of them to satisfy the needs of the child.

(2) When order may be made — An order may be made under subsection (1) on or before the hearing of the application in respect of custody of or access to the child and with or without a request by a party to the application.

(3) Agreement by parties — The court shall, if possible, appoint a person agreed upon by the parties, but if the parties do not agree the court shall choose and appoint the person.

(4) Consent to act — The court shall not appoint a person under subsection (1) unless the person has consented to make the assessment and to report to the court within the period of time specified by the court.

(5) Attendance for assessment — In an order under subsection (1), the court may require the parties, the child and any other person who has been given notice of the proposed order, or any of them, to attend for assessment by the person appointed by the order.

(6) Refusal to attend — Where a person ordered under this section to attend for assessment refuses to attend or to undergo the assessment, the court may draw such inferences in respect of the ability and willingness of any person to satisfy the needs of the child as the court considers appropriate.

(7) Report — The person appointed under subsection (1) shall file his or her report with the clerk and local registrar of the court.

(8) Copies of report — The clerk or local registrar of the court shall give a copy of the report to each of the parties and to counsel, if any, representing the child.

(9) Admissibility of report — The report mentioned in subsection (7), is admissible in evidence in the application.

(10) Assessor may be witness — Any of the parties, and counsel, if any, representing the child, may require the person appointed under subsection (1) to attend as a witness at the hearing of the application.

(11) Directions — Upon motion, the court by order may give such directions in respect of the assessment as the court considers appropriate.

(12) Fees and expenses — The court shall require the parties to pay the fees and expenses of the person appointed under subsection (1).

(13) Idem, proportions or amounts — The court shall specify in the order the proportions or amounts of the fees and expenses that the court requires each party to pay.

(14) Idem, serious financial hardship — The court may relieve a party from responsibility for payment of any of the fees and expenses of the person appointed under subsection (1) where the court is satisfied that payment would cause serious financial hardship to the party.

Proposed Amendment — 30(14)

(14) Idem, serious financial hardship — The court may require one party to pay all the fees and expenses of the person appointed under subsection (1) if the court is satisfied that payment would cause the other party or parties serious financial hardship.

R.S.O. 1990, c. C.12, s. 81 [Not in force at date of publication.]

(15) Other expert evidence — The appointment of a person under subsection (1) does not prevent the parties or counsel representing the child from submitting other expert evidence as to the needs of the child and the ability and willingness of the parties or any of them to satisfy the needs of the child.

31. (1) Mediation — Upon an application for custody of or access to a child, the court, at the request of the parties, by order may appoint a person selected by the parties to mediate any matter specified in the order.

(2) Consent to act — The court shall not appoint a person under subsection (1) unless the person,

(a) has consented to act as mediator, and

(b) has agreed to file a report with the court within the period of time specified by the court.

(3) Duty of mediator — It is the duty of a mediator to confer with the parties and endeavour to obtain an agreement in respect of the matter.

(4) Form of report — Before entering into mediation on the matter, the parties shall decide whether,

(a) the mediator is to file a full report on the mediation, including anything that the mediator considers relevant to the matter in mediation; or

(b) the mediator is to file a report that either sets out the agreement reached by the parties or states only that the parties did not reach agreement on the matter.

(5) Filing of report — The mediator shall file his or her report with the clerk or local registrar of the court in the form decided upon by the parties under subsection (4).

(6) Copies of report — The clerk or local registrar of the court shall give a copy of the report to each of the parties and to counsel, if any, representing the child.

(7) Admissions made in the course of mediation — Where the parties have decided that the mediator's report is to be in the form described in clause (4)(b), evidence of anything said or of any admission or communication made in the course of the mediation is not admissible in any proceeding except with the consent of all parties to the proceeding in which the order was made under subsection (1).

217

(8) Fees and expenses — The court shall require the parties to pay the fees and expenses of the mediator.

(9) Idem, proportions or amounts — The court shall specify in the order the proportions or amounts of the fees and expenses that the court requires each party to pay.

(10) Idem, serious financial hardship — The court may relieve a party from responsibility for payment of any of the fees and expenses of the mediator where the court is satisfied that payment would cause serious financial hardship to the party.

Proposed Amendment — 31(10)

(10) Idem, serious financial hardship — The court may require one party to pay all the mediator's fees and expenses if the court is satisfied that payment would cause the other party or parties serious financial hardship.

R.S.O. 1990, c. C.12, s. 82 [Not in force at date of publication.]

32. (1) Further evidence — Where a court is of the opinion that it is necessary to receive further evidence from a place outside Ontario before making a decision, the court may send to the Attorney General, Minister of Justice or similar officer of the place outside Ontario such supporting material as may be necessary together with a request,

(a) that the Attorney General, Minister of Justice or similar officer take such action as may be necessary in order to require a named person to attend before the proper tribunal in that place and produce or give evidence in respect of the subject-matter of the application; and

(b) that the Attorney General, Minister of Justice or similar officer or the tribunal send to the court a certified copy of the evidence produced or given before the tribunal.

(2) Cost of obtaining evidence — A court that acts under subsection (1) may assess the cost of so acting against one or more of the parties to the application or may deal with such cost as costs in the cause.

33. (1) Referral to court — Where the Attorney General receives from an extra-provincial tribunal a request similar to that referred to in section 32 and such supporting material as may be necessary, it is the duty of the Attorney General to refer the request and the material to the proper court.

(2) Obtaining evidence — A court to which a request is referred by the Attorney General under subsection (1) shall require the person named in the request to attend before the court and produce or give evidence in accordance with the request.

Custody and Access — Enforcement

34. (1) Supervision of custody or access — Where an order is made for custody of or access to a child, a court may give such directions as it considers appropriate for the supervision of the custody or access by a person, a children's aid society or other body.

(2) Consent to act — A court shall not direct a person, a children's aid society or other body to supervise custody or access as mentioned in subsection (1) unless the person, society or body has consented to act as supervisor.

Proposed Addition — 34a

34a (1) Motion to enforce right of access — A person in whose favour an order has been made for access to a child at specific times or on specific days and who claims that a person in whose favour an order has been made for custody of the child has wrongfully denied him or her access to the child may make a motion for relief under subsection (2) to the court that made the access order.

(2) Order for relief — If the court is satisfied that the responding party wrongfully denied the moving party access to the child, the court may, by order,

(a) require the responding party to give the moving party compensatory access to the child for the period agreed to by the parties, or for the period the court considers appropriate if the parties do not agree;

(b) require supervision as described in section 34;

(c) require the responding party to reimburse the moving party for any reasonable expenses actually incurred as a result of the wrongful denial of access;

(d) appoint a mediator in accordance with section 31 as if the motion were an application for access.

(3) Period of compensatory access — A period of compensatory access shall not be longer than the period of access that was wrongfully denied.

(4) What constitutes wrongful denial of access — A denial of access is wrongful unless it is justified by a legitimate reason such as one of the following:

1. The responding party believed on reasonable grounds that the child might suffer physical or emotional harm if the right of access were exercised.

2. The responding party believed on reasonable grounds that he or she might suffer physical harm if the right of access were exercised.

3. The responding party believed on reasonable grounds that the moving party was impaired by alcohol or a drug at the time of access.

4. The moving party failed to present himself or herself to exercise the right of access within one hour of the time specified in the order or the time otherwise agreed on by the parties.

5. The responding party believed on reasonable grounds that the child was suffering from an illness of such a nature that it was not appropriate in the circumstances that the right of access be exercised.

6. The moving party did not satisfy written conditions concerning access that were agreed to by the parties or that form part of the order for access.

7. On numerous occasions during the preceding year, the moving party had, without reasonable notice and excuse, failed to exercise the right of access.

8. The moving party had informed the responding party that he or she would not seek to exercise the right of access on the occasion in question.

(5) Motion re failure to exercise of right of access, etc. — A person in whose favour an order has been made for custody of a child and who claims that a person in whose favour an order has been made for access to the child has, without reasonable notice and excuse, failed to exercise the right of access or to return the child as the order

CLRA

219

requires, may make a motion for relief under subsection (6) to the court that made the access order.

(6) Order for relief — If the court is satisfied that the responding party, without reasonable notice and excuse, failed to exercise the right of access or to return the child as the order requires, the court may, by order,

(a) require supervision as described in section 34;

(b) require the responding party to reimburse the moving party for any reasonable expenses actually incurred as a result of the failure to exercise the right of access or to return the child as the order requires;

(c) appoint a mediator in accordance with section 31 as if the motion were an application for access.

(7) Speedy hearing — A motion under subsection (1) or (5) shall be heard within ten days after it has been served.

(8) Limitation — A motion under subsection (1) or (5) shall not be made more than thirty days after the alleged wrongful denial or failure.

(9) Oral evidence only — The motion shall be determined on the basis of oral evidence only, unless the court gives leave to file an affidavit.

(10) Scope of evidence at hearing limited — At hearing of the motion, unless the court orders otherwise, evidence shall be admitted only if it is directly related to,

(a) the alleged wrongful denial of access or failure to exercise the right of access or return the child as the order requires; or

(b) the responding party's reasons for the denial or failure.

(11) Separation agreement may be filed with court — A person who is a party to a separation agreement made under section 54 of the *Family Law Act* or a predecessor of that section may file the agreement with the clerk of the Ontario Court of Justice or of the Family Court, together with the person's affidavit stating that the agreement is in effect and has not been set aside or varied by a court or agreement.

(12) Effect of filing — When a separation agreement providing for access to a child at specific times or on specific days is filed in this manner, subsections (1) and (5) apply as if the agreement were an order of the court where it is filed.

(13) Motion made in bad faith — If the court is satisfied that a person has made a motion under subsection (1) or (5) in bad faith, the court may prohibit him or her from making further motions without leave of the court.

(14) Idem — Subsections (1) and (5) do not apply in respect of orders made under the *Divorce Act* (Canada) or a predecessor of that Act.

(15) Application — Subsections (1) and (5) do not apply in respect of a denial of access or a failure to exercise a right of access or to return a child as the order or agreement requires that takes place before the day this section comes into force.

R.S.O. 1990, c. C.12, s. 83 [Not in force at date of publication.][Amended 2001, c. 9, Sched. B, s. 4(8), (9).]

35. (1) Order restraining harassment — On application, a court may make an interim or final order restraining a person from molesting, annoying or harassing the applicant or children in the applicant's lawful custody and may require the person to enter into the recognizance or post the bond that the court considers appropriate.

Proposed Amendment — s. 35(1)

(1) Order restraining harassment — On application, a court may make an interim or final order restraining a person from molesting, annoying or harassing the applicant or children in the applicant's lawful custody, or from communicating with the applicant or children, except as the order provides, and may require the person to enter into the recognizance that the court considers appropriate.

R.S.O. 1990, c. C.12, s. 84. [Not in force at date of publication.]

(2) Offence — A person who contravenes a restraining order is guilty of an offence and on conviction is liable to either or both a fine of $5,000 and imprisonment for a term of not more than three months for a first offence and not more than two years for a subsequent offence.

Proposed Repeal — 35(2)

(2) [Repealed 2000, c. 33, s. 21(1). Not in force at date of publication.]

(3) Arrest without warrant — A police officer may arrest without warrant a person the police officer believes on reasonable and probable grounds to have contravened a restraining order.

(4) Existing orders — Subsections (2) and (3) also apply in respect of contraventions committed after those subsections come into force, of restraining orders made under a predecessor of this section.

Proposed Repeal — 35.

35. [Repealed 2000, c. 33, s. 21(2). Not in force at date of publication.]

[Editor's note: Subsection 21(3) of S.O. 2000, c. 33 provides that despite the repeal of subsection 35(2) of the Children's Law Reform Act, any prosecution begun under that subsection before its repeal shall continue as if it were still in force. Subsection 21(4) of S.O. 2000, c. 33 provides that despite the repeal of section 35 of the Children's Law Reform Act, any proceeding begun under that section before its repeal shall continue as if that section were still in force and any order made under that section before its repeal or pursuant to clause 21(4)(a) of S.O. 2000, c. 33 after the repeal of section 35 of the Children's Law Reform Act remains in force until it terminates by its own terms or is rescinded or terminated by a court.]

36. (1) Order where child unlawfully withheld — Where a court is satisfied upon application by a person in whose favour an order has been made for custody of or access to a child that there are reasonable and probable grounds for believing that any person is unlawfully withholding the child from the applicant, the court by order may authorize the applicant or someone on his or her behalf to apprehend the child for the purpose of giving effect to the rights of the applicant to custody or access, as the case may be.

CLRA

(2) Order to locate and take child — Where a court is satisfied upon application that there are reasonable and probable grounds for believing,

(a) that any person is unlawfully withholding a child from a person entitled to custody of or access to the child;

(b) that a person who is prohibited by court order or separation agreement from removing a child from Ontario proposes to remove the child or have the child removed from Ontario; or

(c) that a person who is entitled to access to a child proposes to remove the child or to have the child removed from Ontario and that the child is not likely to return,

the court by order may direct a police force, having jurisdiction in any area where it appears to the court that the child may be, to locate, apprehend and deliver the child to the person named in the order.

(3) Application without notice — An order may be made under subsection (2) upon an application without notice where the court is satisfied that it is necessary that action be taken without delay.

(4) Duty to act — The police force directed to act by an order under subsection (2) shall do all things reasonably able to be done to locate, apprehend and deliver the child in accordance with the order.

(5) Entry and search — For the purpose of locating and apprehending a child in accordance with an order under subsection (2), a member of a police force may enter and search any place where he or she has reasonable and probable grounds for believing that the child may be with such assistance and such force as are reasonable in the circumstances.

(6) Time — An entry or a search referred to in subsection (5) shall be made only between 6 a.m. and 9 p.m. standard time unless the court, in the order, authorizes entry and search at another time.

(7) Expiration of order — An order made under subsection (2) shall name a date on which it expires, which shall be a date not later than six months after it is made unless the court is satisfied that a longer period of time is necessary in the circumstances.

(8) When application may be made — An application under subsection (1) or (2) may be made in an application for custody or access or at any other time.

37. (1) Application to prevent unlawful removal of child — Where a court, upon application, is satisfied upon reasonable and probable grounds that a person prohibited by court order or separation agreement from removing a child from Ontario proposes to remove the child from Ontario, the court in order to prevent the removal of the child from Ontario may make an order under subsection (3).

(2) Application to ensure return of child — Where a court, upon application, is satisfied upon reasonable and probable grounds that a person entitled to access to a child proposes to remove the child from Ontario and is not likely to return the child to Ontario, the court in order to secure the prompt, safe return of the child to Ontario may make an order under subsection (3).

(3) Order by court — An order mentioned in subsection (1) or (2) may require a person to do any one or more of the following:

1. Transfer specific property to a named trustee to be held subject to the terms and conditions specified in the order.

2. Where payments have been ordered for the support of the child, make the payments to a specified trustee subject to the terms and conditions specified in the order.

3. Post a bond, with or without sureties, payable to the applicant in such amount as the court considers appropriate.

4. Deliver the person's passport, the child's passport and any other travel documents of either of them that the court may specify to the court or to an individual or body specified by the court.

(4) Idem, Ontario Court of Justice — The Ontario Court of Justice shall not make an order under paragraph 1 of subsection (3).

(5) Terms and conditions — In an order under paragraph 1 of subsection (3), the court may specify terms and conditions for the return or the disposition of the property as the court considers appropriate.

(6) Safekeeping — A court or an individual or body specified by the court in an order under paragraph 4 of subsection (3) shall hold a passport or travel document delivered in accordance with the order in safekeeping in accordance with any directions set out in the order.

(7) Directions — In an order under subsection (3), a court may give such directions in respect of the safekeeping of the property, payments, passports or travel documents as the court considers appropriate.

2001, c. 9, Sched. B, s. 4(8)

38. (1) Contempt of orders of Ontario Court of Justice — In addition to its powers in respect of contempt, the Ontario Court of Justice may punish by fine or imprisonment, or both, any wilful contempt of or resistance to its process or orders in respect of custody of or access to a child, but the fine shall not in any case exceed $5,000 nor shall the imprisonment exceed ninety days.

(2) Conditions of imprisonment — An order for imprisonment under subsection (1) may be made conditional upon default in the performance of a condition set out in the order and may provide for the imprisonment to be served intermittently.

2001, c. 9, Sched. B, s. 4(8)

39. (1) Information as to address — Where, upon application to a court, it appears to the court that,

(a) for the purpose of bringing an application in respect of custody or access under this Part; or

(b) for the purpose of the enforcement of an order for custody or access,

the proposed applicant or person in whose favour the order is made has need to learn or confirm the whereabouts of the proposed respondent or person against whom the order referred to in clause (b) is made, the court may order any person or public body to provide the court with such particulars of the address of the proposed respondent or person against whom the order referred to in clause (b) is made as are contained in the records in the cus-

CLRA

tody of the person or body, and the person or body shall give the court such particulars as are contained in the records and the court may then give the particulars to such person or persons as the court considers appropriate.

(2) Exception — A court shall not make an order on an application under subsection (1) where it appears to the court that the purpose of the application is to enable the applicant to identify or to obtain particulars as to the identity of a person who has custody of a child, rather than to learn or confirm the whereabouts of the proposed respondent or the enforcement of an order for custody or access.

(3) Compliance with order — The giving of information in accordance with an order under subsection (1) shall be deemed for all purposes not to be a contravention of any Act or regulation or any common law rule of confidentiality.

(4) Section binds Crown — This sections binds the Crown in right of Ontario.

Custody and Access — Extra-Provincial Matters

40. Interim powers of court — Upon application, a court,

(a) that is satisfied that a child has been wrongfully removed to or is being wrongfully retained in Ontario; or

(b) that may not exercise jurisdiction under section 22 or that has declined jurisdiction under section 25 or 42,

may do any one or more of the following:

1. Make such interim order in respect of the custody or access as the court considers is in the best interests of the child.

2. Stay the application subject to,

    i. the condition that a party to the application promptly commence a similar proceeding before an extra-provincial tribunal, or

    ii. such other conditions as the court considers appropriate.

3. Order a party to return the child to such place as the court considers appropriate and, in the discretion of the court, order payment of the cost of the reasonable travel and other expenses of the child and any parties to or witnesses at the hearing of the application.

41. (1) Enforcement of extra-provincial orders — Upon application by any person in whose favour an order for the custody of or access to a child has been made by an extra-provincial tribunal, a court shall recognize the order unless the court is satisfied,

(a) that the respondent was not given reasonable notice of the commencement of the proceeding in which the order was made;

(b) that the respondent was not given an opportunity to be heard by the extra-provincial tribunal before the order was made;

(c) that the law of the place in which the order was made did not require the extra-provincial tribunal to have regard for the best interests of the child;

(d) that the order of the extra-provincial tribunal is contrary to public policy in Ontario; or

(e) that, in accordance with section 22, the extra-provincial tribunal would not have jurisdiction if it were a court in Ontario.

(2) Effect of recognition of order — An order made by an extra-provincial tribunal that is recognized by a court shall be deemed to be an order of the court and enforceable as such.

(3) Conflicting orders — A court presented with conflicting orders made by extra-provincial tribunals for the custody of or access to a child that, but for the conflict, would be recognized and enforced by the court under subsection (1) shall recognize and enforce the order that appears to the court to be most in accord with the best interests of the child.

(4) Further orders — A court that has recognized an extra-provincial order may make such further orders under this Part as the court considers necessary to give effect to the order.

42. (1) Superseding order, material change in circumstances — Upon application, a court by order may supersede an extra-provincial order in respect of custody of or access to a child where the court is satisfied that there has been a material change in circumstances that affects or is likely to affect the best interests of the child and,

(a) the child is habitually resident in Ontario at the commencement of the application for the order; or

(b) although the child is not habitually resident in Ontario, the court is satisfied,

(i) that the child is physically present in Ontario at the commencement of the application for the order,

(ii) that the child no longer has a real and substantial connection with the place where the extra-provincial order was made,

(iii) that substantial evidence concerning the best interests of the child is available in Ontario,

(iv) that the child has a real and substantial connection with Ontario, and

(v) that, on the balance of convenience, it is appropriate for jurisdiction to be exercised in Ontario.

(2) Declining jurisdiction — A court may decline to exercise its jurisdiction under this section where it is of the opinion that it is more appropriate for jurisdiction to be exercised outside Ontario.

43. Superseding order, serious harm — Upon application, a court by order may supersede an extra-provincial order in respect of custody of or access to a child if the court is satisfied that the child would, on the balance of probability, suffer serious harm if,

(a) the child remains in the custody of the person legally entitled to custody of the child;

(b) the child is returned to the custody of the person entitled to custody of the child; or

(c) the child is removed from Ontario.

44. True copy of extra-provincial order — A copy of an extra-provincial order certified as a true copy by a judge, other presiding officer or registrar of the tribunal that made the order or by a person charged with keeping the orders of the tribunal is proof, in the absence of evidence to the contrary, of the making of the order, the content of the order and the appointment and signature of the judge, presiding officer, registrar or other person.

CLRA

45. Court may take notice of foreign law — For the purposes of an application under this Part, a court may take notice, without requiring formal proof, of the law of a jurisdiction outside Ontario and of a decision of an extra-provincial tribunal.

46. (1) Definition — In this section,

"convention" means the Convention on the Civil Aspects of International Child Abduction, set out in the Schedule to this section.

(2) Convention on Civil Aspects of International Child Abduction — On, from and after the 1st day of December, 1983, except as provided in subsection (3), the convention is in force in Ontario and the provisions thereof are law in Ontario.

(3) Exception — The Crown is not bound to assume any costs resulting under the convention from the participation of legal counsel or advisers or from court proceedings except in accordance with the *Legal Aid Services Act, 1998*.

(4) Central Authority — The Ministry of the Attorney General shall be the Central Authority for Ontario for the purpose of the convention.

(5) Application to court — An application may be made to a court in pursuance of a right or an obligation under the convention.

(6) Request to ratify convention — The Attorney General shall request the Government of Canada to submit a declaration to the Ministry of Foreign Affairs of the Kingdom of the Netherlands, declaring that the convention extends to Ontario.

(7) Regulations — The Lieutenant Governor in Council may make such regulations as the Lieutenant Governor in Council considers necessary to carry out the intent and purpose of this section.

(8) Conflict — Where there is a conflict between this section and any other enactment, this section prevails.

CONVENTION ON THE CIVIL ASPECTS OF INTERNATIONAL CHILD ABDUCTION
(November 1980) 19 I.L.M. 1501

The States signatory to the present Convention,

Firmly convinced that the interests of children are of paramount importance in matters relating to their custody,

Desiring to protect children internationally from the harmful effects of their wrongful removal or retention and to establish procedures to ensure their prompt return to the State of their habitual residence, as well as to secure protection for rights of access,

Have resolved to conclude a Convention to this effect and have agreed upon the following provisions:

Chapter I — Scope of the Convention

Article 1

The objects of the present Convention are:

(a) to secure the prompt return of children wrongfully removed to or retained in any Contracting State; and

(b) to ensure that rights of custody and of access under the law of one Contracting State are effectively respected in the other Contracting States.

Article 2

Contracting States shall take all appropriate measures to secure within their territories the implementation of the objects of the Convention. For this purpose they shall use the most expeditious procedures available.

Article 3

The removal or the retention of a child is to be considered wrongful where:

(a) it is in breach of rights of custody attributed to a person, an institution or any other body, either jointly or alone, under the law of the State in which the child was habitually resident immediately before the removal or retention; and

(b) at the time of removal or retention those rights were actually exercised, either jointly or alone, or would have been so exercised but for the removal or retention.

The rights of custody mentioned in sub-paragraph (a) above, may arise in particular by operation of law or by reason of a judicial or administrative decision, or by reason of an agreement having legal effect under the law of that State.

Article 4

The Convention shall apply to any child who was habitually resident in a Contracting State immediately before any breach of custody or access rights. The Convention shall cease to apply when the child attains the age of 16 years.

Article 5

For the purposes of this Convention:

(a) "rights of custody" shall include rights relating to the care of the person of the child and, in particular, the right to determine the child's place of residence;

(b) "rights of access" shall include the right to take a child for a limited period of time to a place other than the child's habitual residence.

Chapter II — Central Authorities

Article 6

A Contracting State shall designate a Central Authority to discharge the duties which are imposed by the Convention upon such authorities.

Federal States, States with more than one system of law or States having autonomous territorial organizations shall be free to appoint more than one Central Authority and to specify the territorial extent of their powers. Where a State has appointed more than one Central Authority, it shall designate the Central Authority to which applications may be addressed for transmission to the appropriate Central Authority within that State.

Article 7

Central Authorities shall co-operate with each other and promote co-operation amongst the competent authorities in their respective States to secure the prompt return of children and to achieve the other objects of this Convention.

In particular, either directly or through any intermediary, they shall take all appropriate measures:

(a) to discover the whereabouts of a child who has been wrongfully removed or retained;

(b) to prevent further harm to the child or prejudice to interested parties by taking or causing to be taken provisional measures;

CLRA

(c) to secure the voluntary return of the child or to bring about an amicable resolution of the issues;

(d) to exchange, where desirable, information relating to the social background of the child;

(e) to provide information of a general character as to the law of their State in connection with the application of the Convention;

(f) to initiate or facilitate the institution of judicial or administrative proceedings with a view to obtaining the return of the child and, in a proper case, to make arrangements for organizing or securing the effective exercise of rights of access;

(g) where the circumstances so require, to provide or facilitate the provision of legal aid and advice, including the participation of legal counsel and advisers;

(h) to provide such administrative arrangements as may be necessary and appropriate to secure the safe return of the child;

(i) to keep each other informed with respect to the operation of this Convention and, as far as possible, to eliminate any obstacles to its application.

Chapter III — Return of Children

Article 8

Any person, institution or other body claiming that a child has been removed or retained in breach of custody rights may apply either to the Central Authority of the child's habitual residence or to the Central Authority of any other Contracting State for assistance in securing the return of the child.

The application shall contain:

(a) information concerning the identity of the applicant, of the child and of the person alleged to have removed or retained the child;

(b) where available, the date of birth of the child;

(c) the grounds on which the applicant's claim for return of the child is based;

(d) all available information relating to the whereabouts of the child and the identity of the person with whom the child is presumed to be.

The application may be accompanied or supplemented by:

(e) an authenticated copy of any relevant decision or agreement;

(f) a certificate or an affidavit emanating from a Central Authority, or other competent authority of the State of the child's habitual residence, or from a qualified person, concerning the relevant law of that State;

(g) any other relevant document.

Article 9

If the Central Authority which receives an application referred to in Article 8 has reason to believe that the child is in another Contracting State, it shall directly and without delay transmit the application to the Central Authority of that Contracting State and inform the requesting Central Authority, or the applicant, as the case may be.

Article 10

The Central Authority of the State where the child is shall take or cause to be taken all appropriate measures in order to obtain the voluntary return of the child.

Article 11

The judicial or administrative authorities of Contracting States shall act expeditiously in proceedings for the return of children.

If the judicial or administrative authority concerned has not reached a decision within six weeks from the date of commencement of the proceedings, the applicant or the Central Authority of the requested State, on its own initiative or if asked by the Central Authority of the requesting State, shall have the right to request a statement of the reasons for the delay. If a reply is received by the Central Authority of the requested State, that Authority shall transmit the reply to the Central Authority of the requesting State, or to the applicant, as the case may be.

Article 12

Where a child has been wrongfully removed or retained in terms of Article 3 and, at the date of commencement of the proceedings before the judicial or administrative authority of the Contracting State where the child is, a period of less than one year has elapsed from the date of the wrongful removal or retention, the authority concerned shall order the return of the child forthwith.

The judicial or administrative authority, even where the proceedings have been commenced after the expiration of the period of one year referred to in the preceding paragraph, shall also order the return of the child, unless it is demonstrated that the child is now settled in its new environment.

Where the judicial or administrative authority in the requested State has reason to believe that the child has been taken to another State, it may stay the proceedings or dismiss the application for the return of the child.

Article 13

Despite the provisions of the preceding Article, the judicial or administrative authority of the requested State is not bound to order the return of the child if the person, institution or other body which opposes its return establishes that:

    (a) the person, institution or other body having the care of the person of the child was not actually exercising the custody rights at the time of removal or retention, or had consented to or subsequently acquiesced in the removal or retention; or

    (b) there is a grave risk that his or her return would expose the child to physical or psychological harm or otherwise place the child in an intolerable situation.

The judicial or administrative authority may also refuse to order the return of the child if it finds that the child objects to being returned and has attained an age and degree of maturity at which it is appropriate to take account of its views.

In considering the circumstances referred to in this Article, the judicial and administrative authorities shall take into account the information relating to the social background of the child provided by the Central Authority or other competent authority of the child's habitual residence.

Article 14

In ascertaining whether there has been a wrongful removal or retention within the meaning of Article 3, the judicial or administrative authorities of the requested State may take notice directly of the law of, and of judicial or administrative decisions, formally recognized or not in the State of the habitual residence of the child, without recourse to the specific procedures for the proof of that law or for the recognition of foreign decisions which would otherwise be applicable.

Article 15

The judicial or administrative authorities of a Contracting State may, prior to the making of an order for the return of the child, request that the applicant obtain from the authorities of the State of the habitual residence of the child a decision or other determination that the removal or retention was wrongful within the meaning of Article 3 of the Convention, where such a decision or determination may be obtained in that State. The Central Authorities of the Contracting States shall so far as practicable assist applicants to obtain such a decision or determination.

Article 16

After receiving notice of a wrongful removal or retention of a child in the sense of Article 3, the judicial or administrative authorities of the Contracting State to which the child has been removed or in which it has been retained shall not decide on the merits of rights of custody until it has been determined that the child is not to be returned under this Convention or unless an application under this Convention is not lodged within a reasonable time following receipt of the notice.

Article 17

The sole fact that a decision relating to custody has been given in or is entitled to recognition in the requested State shall not be a ground for refusing to return a child under this Convention, but the judicial or administrative authorities of the requested State may take account of the reasons for that decision in applying this Convention.

Article 18

The provisions of this Chapter do not limit the power of a judicial or administrative authority to order the return of the child at any time.

Article 19

A decision under this Convention concerning the return of the child shall not be taken to be a determination on the merits of any custody issue.

Article 20

The return of the child under the provisions of Article 12 may be refused if this would not be permitted by the fundamental principles of the requested State relating to the protection of human rights and fundamental freedoms.

Chapter IV — Rights of Access

Article 21

An application to make arrangements for organizing or securing the effective exercise of rights of access may be presented to the Central Authorities of the Contracting States in the same way as an application for the return of a child.

The Central Authorities are bound by the obligations of co-operation which are set forth in Article 7 to promote the peaceful enjoyment of access rights and the fulfilment of any conditions to which the exercise of those rights may be subject. The Central Authorities shall take steps to remove, as far as possible, all obstacles to the exercise of such rights.

The Central Authorities, either directly or through intermediaries, may initiate or assist in the institution of proceedings with a view to organizing or protecting these rights and securing respect for the conditions to which the exercise of these rights may be subject.

Chapter V — General Provisions

Article 22

No security, bond or deposit, however described, shall be required to guarantee the payment of costs and expenses in the judicial or administrative proceedings falling within the scope of this Convention.

Article 23

No legalization or similar formality may be required in the context of this Convention.

Article 24

Any application, communication or other document sent to the Central Authority of the requested State shall be in the original language, and shall be accompanied by a translation into the official language or one of the official languages of the requested State or, where that is not feasible, a translation into French or English.

However, a Contracting State may, by making a reservation in accordance with Article 42, object to the use of either French or English, but not both, in an application, communication or other document sent to its Central Authority.

Article 25

Nationals of the Contracting States and persons who are habitually resident within those States shall be entitled in matters concerned with the application of this Convention to legal aid and advice in any other Contracting State on the same conditions as if they themselves were nationals of and habitually resident in that State.

Article 26

Each Central Authority shall bear its own costs in applying this Convention.

Central Authorities and other public services of Contracting States shall not impose any charges in relation to applications submitted under this Convention. In particular, they may not require any payment from the applicant towards the costs and expenses of the proceeding or, where applicable, those arising from the participation of legal counsel or advisers. However, they may require the payment of the expenses incurred or to be incurred in implementing the return of the child.

However, a Contracting State may, by making a reservation in accordance with Article 42, declare that it shall not be bound to assume any costs referred to in the preceding paragraph resulting from the participation of legal counsel or advisers or from court proceedings, except insofar as those costs may be covered by its system of legal aid and advice.

Upon ordering the return of a child or issuing an order concerning rights of access under this Convention, the judicial or administrative authorities may, where appropriate, direct the person who removed or retained the child, or who prevented the exercise of rights of access, to pay necessary expenses incurred by or on behalf of the applicant, including travel expenses, any costs incurred or payments made for locating the child, the costs of legal representation of the applicant, and those of returning the child.

Article 27

When it is manifest that the requirements of this Convention are not fulfilled or that the application is otherwise not well founded, a Central Authority is not bound to accept the application. In that case, the Central Authority shall forthwith inform the applicant or the Central Authority through which the application was submitted, as the case may be, of its reasons.

Article 28

A Central Authority may require that the application be accompanied by a written authorization empowering it to act on behalf of the applicant, or to designate a representative to act.

Article 29

This Convention shall not preclude any person, institution or body who claims that there has been a breach of custody or access rights within the meaning of Article 3 or 21 from applying directly to the judicial or administrative authorities of a Contracting State, whether or not under the provisions of this Convention.

Article 30

Any application submitted to the Central Authorities or directly to the judicial or administrative authorities of a Contracting State in accordance with the terms of this Convention, together

CLRA

with documents and other information appended thereto or provided by a Central Authority, shall be admissible in the courts or administrative authorities of the Contracting States.

Article 31

In relation to a State which in matters of custody of children has two or more systems of law applicable in different territorial units:

(a) a reference to habitual residence in that State shall be construed as referring to habitual residence in a territorial unit of that State;

(b) a reference to the law of the State of habitual residence shall be construed as referring to the law of the territorial unit in that State where the child habitually resides.

Article 32

In relation to a State which in matters of custody of children has two or more systems of law applicable to different categories of persons, any reference to the law of that State shall be construed as referring to the legal system specified by the law of that State.

Article 33

A State within which different territorial units have their own rules of law in respect of custody of children shall not be bound to apply this Convention where a State with a unified system of law would not be bound to do so.

Article 34

This Convention shall take priority in matters within its scope over the *Convention of 5 October 1961 concerning the powers of authorities and the law applicable in respect of the protection of minors*, as between Parties to both Conventions. Otherwise the present Convention shall not restrict the application of an international instrument in force between the State of origin and the State addressed or other law of the State addressed for the purposes of obtaining the return of a child who has been wrongfully removed or retained or of organizing access rights.

Article 35

This Convention shall apply as between Contracting States only to wrongful removals or retentions occurring after its entry into force in those States.

Where a declaration has been made under Article 39 or 40, the reference in the preceding paragraph to a Contracting State shall be taken to refer to the territorial unit or units in relation to which this Convention applies.

Article 36

Nothing in this Convention shall prevent two or more Contracting States, in order to limit the restrictions to which the return of the child may be subject, from agreeing among themselves to derogate from any provisions of this Convention which may imply such a restriction.

Chapter VI — Final Clauses

Article 37

The Convention shall be open for signature by the States which were Members of the Hague Conference on Private International Law at the time of its Fourteenth Session.

It shall be ratified, accepted or approved and the instruments of ratification, acceptance or approval shall be deposited with the Ministry of Foreign Affairs of the Kingdom of the Netherlands.

Article 38

Any other State may accede to the Convention.

The instrument of accession shall be deposited with the Ministry of Foreign Affairs of the Kingdom of the Netherlands.

The Convention shall enter into force for a State acceding to it on the first day of the third calendar month after the deposit of its instrument of accession.

The accession will have effect only as regards the relations between the acceding State and such Contracting States as will have declared their acceptance of the accession. Such a declaration will also have to be made by any Member State ratifying, accepting or approving the Convention after an accession. Such declaration shall be deposited at the Ministry of Foreign Affairs of the Kingdom of the Netherlands; this Ministry shall forward, through diplomatic channels, a certified copy to each of the Contracting States.

The Convention will enter into force as between the acceding State and the State that has declared its acceptance of the accession on the first day of the third calendar month after the deposit of the declaration of acceptance.

Article 39

Any State may, at the time of signature, ratification, acceptance, approval or accession, declare that the Convention shall extend to all the territories for the international relations of which it is responsible, or to one or more of them. Such a declaration shall take effect at the time the Convention enters into force for that State.

Such declaration, as well as a subsequent extension, shall be notified to the Ministry of Foreign Affairs of the Kingdom of the Netherlands.

Article 40

If a Contracting State has two or more territorial units in which different systems of law are applicable in relation to matters dealt with in this Convention, it may at the time of signature, ratification, acceptance, approval or accession declare that this Convention shall extend to all its territorial units or only to one or more of them and may modify this declaration by submitting another declaration at any time.

Any such declaration shall be notified to the Ministry of Foreign Affairs of the Kingdom of the Netherlands and shall state expressly the territorial units to which the Convention applies.

Article 41

Where a Contracting State has a system of government under which executive, judicial and legislative powers are distributed between central and other authorities within that State, its signature or ratification, acceptance or approval of, or accession to this Convention, or its making of any declaration in terms of Article 40 shall carry no implication as to the internal distribution of powers within that State.

Article 42

Any State may, not later than the time of ratification, acceptance, approval or accession, or at the time of making a declaration in terms of Article 39 or 40, make one or both of the reservations provided for in Article 24 and Article 26, third paragraph. No other reservation shall be permitted.

Any State may at any time withdraw a reservation it has made. The withdrawal shall be notified to the Ministry of Foreign Affairs of the Kingdom of the Netherlands.

The reservation shall cease to have effect on the first day of the third calendar month after the notification referred to in the preceding paragraph.

Article 43

The Convention shall enter into force on the first day of the third calendar month after the deposit of the third instrument of ratification, acceptance, approval or accession referred to in Articles 37 and 38.

CLRA

Thereafter the Convention shall enter into force:

1. for each State ratifying, accepting, approving or acceding to it subsequently, on the first day of the third calendar month after the deposit of its instrument of ratification, acceptance, approval or accession;

2. for any territory or territorial unit to which the Convention has been extended in conformity with Article 39 or 40, on the first day of the third calendar month after the notification referred to in that Article.

Article 44

The Convention shall remain in force for five years from the date of its entry into force in accordance with the first paragraph of Article 43 even for States which subsequently have ratified, accepted, approved it or acceded to it. If there has been no denunciation, it shall be renewed tacitly every five years.

Any denunciation shall be notified to the Ministry of Foreign Affairs of the Kingdom of the Netherlands at least six months before the expiry of the five year period. It may be limited to certain of the territories or territorial units to which the Convention applies.

The denunciation shall have effect only as regards the State which has notified it. The Convention shall remain in force for the other Contracting States.

Article 45

The Ministry of Foreign Affairs of the Kingdom of the Netherlands shall notify the States Members of the Conference, and the States which have acceded in accordance with Article 38, of the following:

1. the signatures and ratifications, acceptances and approvals referred to in Article 37;

2. the accessions referred to in Article 38;

3. the date on which the Convention enters into force in accordance with Article 43;

4. the extensions referred to in Article 39;

5. the declarations referred to in Articles 38 and 40;

6. the reservations referred to in Article 24 and Article 26, third paragraph, and the withdrawals referred to in Article 42;

7. the denunciations referred to in Article 44.

Done at The Hague on the 25th day of October, 1980.

1998, c. 26, s. 101

Guardianship

47. (1) Appointment of guardian — Upon application by a child's parent or by any other person, on notice to the Children's Lawyer, a court may appoint a guardian of the child's property.

(2) Responsibility of guardian — A guardian of the property of a child has charge of and is responsible for the care and management of the property of the child.

2001, c. 9, Sched. B, s. 4(1)

48. (1) Parents as guardians — As between themselves and subject to any court order or any agreement between them, the parents of a child are equally entitled to be appointed by a court as guardians of the property of the child.

(2) Parent and other person — As between a parent of a child and a person who is not a parent of the child, the parent has a preferential entitlement to be appointed by a court as a guardian of the property of the child.

(3) More than one guardian — A court may appoint more than one guardian of the property of a child.

(4) Guardians jointly responsible — Where more than one guardian is appointed of the property of a child, the guardians are jointly responsible for the care and management of the property of the child.

49. Criteria — In deciding an application for the appointment of a guardian of the property of a child, the court shall consider all the circumstances, including,

    (a) the ability of the applicant to manage the property of the child;

    (b) the merits of the plan proposed by the applicant for the care and management of the property of the child; and

    (c) the views and preferences of the child, where such views and preferences can reasonably be ascertained.

2001, c. 9, Sched. B, s. 4(2)

50. Effect of appointment — The appointment of a guardian by a court under this Part has effect in all parts of Ontario.

51. (1) Payment of debt due to child if no guardian — If no guardian of a child's property has been appointed, a person who is under a duty to pay money or deliver personal property to the child discharges that duty, to the extent of the amount paid or the value of the personal property delivered, subject to subsection (1.1), by paying money or delivering personal property to,

    (a) the child, if the child has a legal obligation to support another person;

    (b) a parent with whom the child resides; or

    (c) a person who has lawful custody of the child.

(1.1) Same — The total of the amount of money paid and the value of personal property delivered under subsection (1) shall not exceed the prescribed amount or, if no amount is prescribed, $10,000.

(2) Money payable under judgment — Subsection (1) does not apply in respect of money payable under a judgment or order of a court.

(3) Receipt for payment — A receipt or discharge for money or personal property not in excess of the amount or value set out in subsection (1) received for a child by a parent with whom the child resides or a person who has lawful custody of the child has the same validity as if a court had appointed the parent or the person as a guardian of the property of the child.

(4) Responsibility for money or property — A parent with whom a child resides or a person who has lawful custody of a child who receives and holds money or personal property referred to in subsection (1) has the responsibility of a guardian for the care and management of the money or personal property.

CLRA

(5) Regulations — The Lieutenant Governor in Council may, by regulation, prescribe an amount for the purpose of subsection (1.1).

2001, c. 9, Sched. B, s. 4(3), (4)

52. Accounts — A guardian of the property of a child may be required to account or may voluntarily pass the accounts in respect of the care and management of the property of the child in the same manner as a trustee under a will may be required to account or may pass the accounts in respect of the trusteeship.

53. Transfer of property to child — A guardian of the property of a child shall transfer to the child all property of the child in the care of the guardian when the child attains the age of eighteen years.

54. Management fees and expenses — A guardian of the property of a child is entitled to payment of a reasonable amount for fees for and expenses of management of the property of the child.

55. (1) Bond by guardian — A court that appoints a guardian of the property of a child shall require the guardian to post a bond, with or without sureties, payable to the child in such amount as the court considers appropriate in respect of the care and management of the property of the child.

(2) Where parent appointed guardian — Subsection (1) does not apply where the court appoints a parent of a child as guardian of the property of the child and the court is of the opinion that it is appropriate not to require the parent to post a bond.

56. Where child has support obligation — Upon application by a child who has a legal obligation to support another person, the court that appointed a guardian of the property of the child or a co-ordinate court by order shall end the guardianship for the child.

57. (1) Removal of guardian — A guardian of the property of a child may be removed by a court for the same reasons for which a trustee may be removed.

(2) Resignation of guardian — A guardian of the property of a child, with the permission of a court, may resign as guardian upon such conditions as the court considers appropriate.

58. Notice to Estate Registrar for Ontario — A notice of every application to a court for appointment of a guardian of the property of a child shall be transmitted by the clerk or local registrar of the court to the Estate Registrar for Ontario.

1993, c. 27, Sched.

Disposition of Property

59. (1) Court order re property of child — Upon application by a child's parent or by any other person, on notice to the Children's Lawyer, the Superior Court of Justice by order may require or approve, or both,

(a) the disposition or encumbrance of all or part of the interest of the child in land;

(b) the sale of the interest of the child in personal property; or

(c) the payment of all or part of any money belonging to the child or of the income from any property belonging to the child, or both.

(2) Criteria — An order shall be made under subsection (1) only where the Court is of the opinion that the disposition, encumbrance, sale or payment is necessary or proper for the support or education of the child or will substantially benefit the child.

(3) Conditions — An order under subsection (1) may be made subject to such conditions as the Court considers appropriate.

(4) Limitation — The Court shall not require or approve a disposition or encumbrance of the interest of a child in land contrary to a term of the instrument by which the child acquired the interest.

(5) Execution of documents — The Court, where it makes an order under subsection (1), may order that the child or another person named in the order execute any documents necessary to carry out the disposition, encumbrance, sale or payment.

(6) Directions — The Court by order may give such directions as it considers necessary for the carrying out of an order made under subsection (1).

(7) Validity of documents — Every document executed in accordance with an order under this section is as effectual as if the child by whom it was executed was eighteen years of age or, if executed by another person in accordance with the order, as if the child had executed it and had been eighteen years of age at the time.

(8) Liability — No person incurs or shall be deemed to incur liability by making a payment in accordance with an order under clause (1)(c).

2001, c. 9, Schcd. B, s. 4(5)

60. (1) Order for maintenance where power of appointment in favour of children — Upon application by or with the consent of a person who has an estate for life in property with power to devise or appoint the property to one or more of his or her children, the Superior Court of Justice may order that such part of the proceeds of the property as the Court considers proper be used for the support, education or benefit of one or more of the children.

(2) Idem — An order may be made under subsection (1) whether or not,

    (a) there is a gift over in the event that there are no children to take under the power; or

    (b) any person could dispose of the property in the event that there are no children to take under the power.

2001, c. 9, Sched. B, s. 4(7)

Testamentary Custody and Guardianship

61. (1) Custody, appointment by will — A person entitled to custody of a child may appoint by will one or more persons to have custody of the child after the death of the appointor.

(2) Guardianship, appointment by will — A guardian of the property of a child may appoint by will one or more persons to be guardians of the property of the child after the death of the appointor.

CLRA

(3) Appointment by minor — An unmarried parent who is a minor may make an appointment mentioned in subsection (1) or (2) by a written appointment signed by the parent.

(4) Limitation — An appointment under subsection (1), (2) or (3) is effective only,

(a) if the appointor is the only person entitled to custody of the child or who is the guardian of the property of the child, as the case requires, on the day immediately before the appointment is to take effect; or

(b) if the appointor and any other person entitled to custody of the child or who is the guardian of the property of the child, as the case requires, die at the same time or in circumstances that render it uncertain which survived the other.

(5) Where more than one appointment — Where two or more persons are appointed to have custody of or to be guardians of the property of a child by appointors who die as mentioned in clause (4)(b), only the appointments of the persons appointed by both or all of the appointors are effective.

(6) Consent of appointee — No appointment under subsection (1), (2) or (3) is effective without the consent of the person appointed.

(7) Expiration of appointment — An appointment under subsection (1), (2) or (3) for custody of a child or guardianship of the property of a child expires ninety days after the appointment becomes effective or, where the appointee applies under this Part for custody of the child or guardianship of the property of the child within the ninety-day period, when the application is disposed of.

(8) Application or order under ss. 21, 47 — An appointment under this section does not apply to prevent an application for or the making of an order under section 21 or 47.

(9) Application — This section applies in respect of,

(a) any will made on or after the 1st day of October, 1982; and

(b) any will made before the 1st day of October, 1982, if the testator is living on that day.

Procedure

62. (1) Joinder of proceedings — An application under this Part may be made in the same proceeding and in the same manner as an application under the *Family Law Act*, or in another proceeding.

(2) Nature of order — An application under this Part may be an original application or for the variance of an order previously given or to supersede an order of an extra-provincial tribunal.

(3) Parties — The parties to an application under this Part in respect of a child shall include,

(a) the mother and the father of the child;

(b) a person who has demonstrated a settled intention to treat the child as a child of his or her family;

(c) a person who had the actual care and upbringing of the child immediately before the application; and

238

(d) any other person whose presence as a party is necessary to determine the matters in issue.

(4) Combining of applications — Where, in an application under this Part, it appears to the court that it is necessary or desirable in the best interests of the child to have other matters first or simultaneously determined, the court may direct that the application stand over until such other proceedings are brought or determined as the court considers appropriate, subject to section 26.

(5) Where identity of father not known — Where there is no presumption of paternity and the identity of the father is not known or is not reasonably capable of being ascertained, the court may order substituted service or may dispense with service of documents upon the father in the proceeding.

63. (1) Application or response by minor — A minor who is a parent may make an application under this Part without a next friend and may respond without a litigation guardian.

(2) Consent by minor — A consent in respect of a matter provided for by this Part is not invalid by reason only that the person giving the consent is a minor.

64. (1) Child entitled to be heard — In considering an application under this Part, a court where possible shall take into consideration the views and preferences of the child to the extent that the child is able to express them.

(2) Interview by court — The court may interview the child to determine the views and preferences of the child.

(3) Recording — The interview shall be recorded.

(4) Counsel — The child is entitled to be advised by and to have his or her counsel, if any, present during the interview.

65. Where child is sixteen or more years old — Nothing in this Part abrogates the right of a child of sixteen or more years of age to withdraw from parental control.

66. All proceedings in one court — Except as otherwise provided, where an application is made to a court under this Part, no person who is a party to the proceeding shall make an application under this Part to any other court in respect of a matter in issue in the proceeding, but the court may order that the proceeding be transferred to a court having other jurisdiction where, in the opinion of the court, the court having other jurisdiction is more appropriate to determine the matters in issue that should be determined at the same time.

67. (1) Consent orders — Upon the consent of the parties in an application under this Part, the court may make any order that the court is otherwise empowered to make by this Part, subject to the duty of the court to have regard to the best interests of the child.

(2) Incorporation of contract in order — Any matter provided for in this Part and in a domestic contract as defined in the *Family Law Act* may be incorporated in an order made under this Part.

CLRA

68. Part subject to contracts — Where a domestic contract as defined in the *Family Law Act* makes provision in respect of a matter that is provided for in this Part, the contract prevails except as otherwise provided in Part IV of the *Family Law Act*.

69. Jurisdiction of Superior Court of Justice — This Part does not deprive the Superior Court of Justice of its *parens patriae* jurisdiction.

2001, c. 9, Sched. B, s. 4(7)

70. [Repealed 2001, c. 9, Sched. B, s. 4(6).]

71. (1) Place of application for interim order — An application for an interim order shall be made to the court in which the original proceeding was taken.

(2) Place of application to vary order — An application under this Part to vary an order may be made to the court in which the original proceeding was taken or to a co-ordinate court in another part of Ontario.

72. Interim order — In a proceeding under this Part, the court may make such interim order as the court considers appropriate.

73. Appeal from Ontario Court of Justice — An appeal from an order of the Ontario Court of Justice under this Part lies to the Superior Court of Justice.

2001, c. 9, Sched. B, s. 4(7), (8)

74. Order effective pending appeal — An order under this Part is effective even if an appeal is taken from the order, unless the court that made the order or the court to which the appeal is taken orders otherwise.

75. (1) Rule of construction — For the purposes of construing any instrument, Act or regulation, unless the contrary intention appears, a reference to a guardian with respect to the person of a child shall be construed to refer to custody of the child and a reference to a guardian with respect to property of a child shall be construed to refer to guardianship of the property of the child.

(2) Application — Subsection (1) applies to any instrument, any Act of the Legislature or any regulation, order or by-law made under an Act of the Legislature enacted or made before, on or after the 1st day of October, 1982.

76. [Repealed 2001, c. 9, Sched. B, s. 4(6).]

PART IV — AMENDMENTS

[Editor's note: The following sections amend previous sections of this Act, but had not been proclaimed in force at the date of publication. The amendments have been incorporated into the affected sections as shaded text indicating that the shaded material was not in force at the date of publication.]

Unproclaimed text — Proposed Amendments

77. *Section 20 is amended by adding the following subsection:*

(4a) Duty of separated parents — Where the parents of a child live separate and apart and the child is in the custody of one of them and the other is entitled to access under the terms of a separation agreement or order, each shall, in the best interests of the child, encourage and support the child's continuing parent-child relationship with the other.

78. (1) *Subsection 24 (1) is amended by inserting after "application" in the first line "or motion".*

(2) *Subsections 24(2) and (3) are repealed and the following substituted:*

(2) Best interests of child — In determining the best interests of a child for the purpose of an application or motion under this Part in respect of custody of or access to a child, a court shall consider all the child's needs and circumstances, including,

(a) the love, affection and emotional ties between the child and,

(i) each person seeking custody or access,

(ii) other members of the child's family residing with him or her, and

(iii) persons involved in the child's care and upbringing;

(b) the child's views and preferences, if they can reasonably be ascertained;

(c) the length of time the child has lived in a stable home environment;

(d) the ability of each person seeking custody or access to act as a parent;

(e) the ability and willingness of each person seeking custody to provide the child with guidance, education and necessities of life and to meet any special needs of the child;

(f) any plans proposed for the child's care and upbringing;

(g) the permanence and stability of the family unit with which it is proposed that the child will live; and

(h) the relationship, by blood or through an adoption order, between the child and each person who is a party to the application or motion.

(3) Domestic violence to be considered — In assessing a person's ability to act as a parent, the court shall consider the fact that the person has at any time committed violence against his or her spouse, same-sex partner or child, against his or her child's parent or against another member of the person's household.

(3.1) Definitions — In subsection (3),

"same-sex partner" means either of two persons of the same sex who live together in a conjugal relationship outside marriage; ("partenaire de même sexe")

"spouse" means,

(a) a spouse as defined in section 1 of the *Family Law Act*, or

(b) either of two persons of the opposite sex who live together in a conjugal relationship outside marriage. ("conjoint")

(4) Restrictions on consideration of other past conduct — Other than the conduct referred to in subsection (3), a person's past conduct may be considered only if the court is satisfied that it is relevant to the person's ability to act as a parent.

1999, c. 6, s. 7

CLRA

79. *This Act is amended by adding the following section:*

28a (1) Application to fix times or days of access — If an order in respect of access to a child provides for a person's access to the child without specifying times or days, a party to the order may apply to the court that made it to vary it by specifying times or days.

(2) Order — The court may vary the order by specifying the times or days agreed to by the parties, or the times or days the court considers appropriate if the parties do not agree.

(3) Separation agreements — Subsection (1) also applies, with necessary modifications, in respect of a separation agreement under section 54 of the *Family Law Act* or a predecessor of that section that provides for a person's access to a child without specifying times or days.

(4) Exception — Subsection (1) does not apply in respect of orders made under the *Divorce Act* (Canada) or a predecessor of that Act.

80. *Section 29 is amended by adding the following subsection:*

(2) Exception — Subsection (1) does not apply in respect of orders made under subsection 28a(2) (fixing times or days of access) or 34a(2) or (6) (access enforcement, etc.).

81. *Subsection 30(14) is repealed and the following substituted:*

(14) Idem, serious financial hardship — The court may require one party to pay all the fees and expenses of the person appointed under subsection (1) if the court is satisfied that payment would cause the other party or parties serious financial hardship.

82. *Subsection 31(10) is repealed and the following substituted:*

(10) Idem, serious financial hardship — The court may require one party to pay all the mediator's fees and expenses if the court is satisfied that payment would cause the other party or parties serious financial hardship.

83. *This Act is further amended by adding the following section:*

34a (1) Motion to enforce right of access — A person in whose favour an order has been made for access to a child at specific times or on specific days and who claims that a person in whose favour an order has been made for custody of the child has wrongfully denied him or her access to the child may make a motion for relief under subsection (2) to the court that made the access order.

(2) Order for relief — If the court is satisfied that the responding party wrongfully denied the moving party access to the child, the court may, by order,

(a) require the responding party to give the moving party compensatory access to the child for the period agreed to by the parties, or for the period the court considers appropriate if the parties do not agree;

(b) require supervision as described in section 34;

(c) require the responding party to reimburse the moving party for any reasonable expenses actually incurred as a result of the wrongful denial of access;

(d) appoint a mediator in accordance with section 31 as if the motion were an application for access.

(3) Period of compensatory access — A period of compensatory access shall not be longer than the period of access that was wrongfully denied.

(4) What constitutes wrongful denial of access — A denial of access is wrongful unless it is justified by a legitimate reason such as one of the following:

1. The responding party believed on reasonable grounds that the child might suffer physical or emotional harm if the right of access were exercised.

2. The responding party believed on reasonable grounds that he or she might suffer physical harm if the right of access were exercised.

3. The responding party believed on reasonable grounds that the moving party was impaired by alcohol or a drug at the time of access.

4. The moving party failed to present himself or herself to exercise the right of access within one hour of the time specified in the order or the time otherwise agreed on by the parties.

5. The responding party believed on reasonable grounds that the child was suffering from an illness of such a nature that it was not appropriate in the circumstances that the right of access be exercised.

6. The moving party did not satisfy written conditions concerning access that were agreed to by the parties or that form part of the order for access.

7. On numerous occasions during the preceding year, the moving party had, without reasonable notice and excuse, failed to exercise the right of access.

8. The moving party had informed the responding party that he or she would not seek to exercise the right of access on the occasion in question.

(5) Motion re failure to exercise of right of access, etc. — A person in whose favour an order has been made for custody of a child and who claims that a person in whose favour an order has been made for access to the child has, without reasonable notice and excuse, failed to exercise the right of access or to return the child as the order requires, may make a motion for relief under subsection (6) to the court that made the access order.

(6) Order for relief — If the court is satisfied that the responding party, without reasonable notice and excuse, failed to exercise the right of access or to return the child as the order requires, the court may, by order,

(a) require supervision as described in section 34;

(b) require the responding party to reimburse the moving party for any reasonable expenses actually incurred as a result of the failure to exercise the right of access or to return the child as the order requires;

(c) appoint a mediator in accordance with section 31 as if the motion were an application for access.

(7) Speedy hearing — A motion under subsection (1) or (5) shall be heard within ten days after it has been served.

(8) Limitation — A motion under subsection (1) or (5) shall not be made more than thirty days after the alleged wrongful denial or failure.

(9) Oral evidence only — The motion shall be determined on the basis of oral evidence only, unless the court gives leave to file an affidavit.

(10) Scope of evidence at hearing limited — At hearing of the motion, unless the court orders otherwise, evidence shall be admitted only if it is directly related to,

(a) the alleged wrongful denial of access or failure to exercise the right of access or return the child as the order requires; or

(b) the responding party's reasons for the denial or failure.

(11) Separation agreement may be filed with court — A person who is a party to a separation agreement made under section 54 of the *Family Law Act* or a predecessor of that section may file the agreement with the clerk of the Ontario Court of Justice or of the Fam-

CLRA

ily Court, together with the person's affidavit stating that the agreement is in effect and has not been set aside or varied by a court or agreement.

(12) **Effect of filing** — When a separation agreement providing for access to a child at specific times or on specific days is filed in this manner, subsections (1) and (5) apply as if the agreement were an order of the court where it is filed.

(13) **Motion made in bad faith** — If the court is satisfied that a person has made a motion under subsection (1) or (5) in bad faith, the court may prohibit him or her from making further motions without leave of the court.

(14) **Idem** — Subsections (1) and (5) do not apply in respect of orders made under the *Divorce Act* (Canada) or a predecessor of that Act.

(15) **Application** — Subsections (1) and (5) do not apply in respect of a denial of access or a failure to exercise a right of access or to return a child as the order or agreement requires that takes place before the day this section comes into force.

2001, c. 9, Sched. B, s. 4(8), (9)

84. *Subsection 35 (1) is repealed and the following substituted:*

(1) Order restraining harassment — On application, a court may make an interim or final order, restraining a person from molesting, annoying or harassing the applicant or children in the applicant's lawful custody, or from communicating with the applicant or children, except as the order provides, and may require the person to enter into the recognizance that the court considers appropriate.

85. *Sections 77 to 84 do not come into force until a day to be named by proclamation of the Lieutenant Governor.*

ONT. REG. 72 — FORMS

made under the *Children's Law Reform Act*
R.R.O. 1990, Reg. 72

1. A declaratory order under section 4 or 5 of the Act may contain a recital in Form 1.

2. (1) A statutory declaration affirming parentage under subsection 12(1) of the Act shall be in Form 2.

(2) A joint statutory declaration affirming parentage under subsection 12(2) of the Act shall be in Form 3.

3. A finding of parentage in an order or judgement that is to be referred to in a statement furnished under section 14 of the Act may be in Form 4.

4. A statement furnished under section 14 of the Act respecting an order or judgment that confirms or makes a finding or parentage shall be in Form 5.

SCHEDULE [FORMS]

The text in square brackets has been editorially added by Carswell and does not form part of the text of the legislation.

Form 1

Children's Law Reform Act

— Recital for Order under Section 4 or 5 of Act

Upon the application of . . . .

for an order declaring that . . . .

is the (father or mother) of) . . . .(name of child)

and upon . . . .

. . . .

and it appearing that . . . .(name of child)

was born on the .... day of ...., 19 ...., at .... (place of birth)

and the birth is registered as number . . . .

Registration Number . . . .(to be filled in by Registrar General)

Form 2

Children's Law Reform Act

— Declaration Affirming Parentage

I, ...(name in full), of the ....(status of municipality)

of ....(name of municipality), in the ....(regional municipality, county or district)

of ...., in the .... (province or state)

of .... solemnly declare that I am the mother/father of

...................................(surname of child) .... (given names)

a ....(male/female) child born on ....(date)

at ....(place)

Birth registration number (if known) ....

My date of birth is ....

My place of birth is ....

My social insurance number is ....

and I make this solemn declaration conscientiously believing it to be true and knowing that it is of the same force and effect as if made under oath:

Declared before me	)
	)
at the	)
	)
of	)
	)
this...................................day of	)
	) . . . .
..................................., 19..........	) (signature of deponent) .
	)
. . . .	)
A Commissioner, etc.	)

Registration Number . . . .
(to be filled in by Registrar General)

Form 3

Children's Law Reform Act

— Joint Declaration Affirming Parentage

1. I, ... (mother's name in full), of the .... (status of municipality)

of ....(name of municipality), in the .... (regional municipality, county or district)

of ...., in the................................(province or state)

of .... solemnly declare that I am the mother of

.... (surname of child) (given names)

a .... (male/female) child born on .... (date)

at .... (place)

Birth registration number (if known) ....

My social insurance number is ....

2. I, ... (father's name in full), of the .... (status of municipality)

of .... (name of municipality), in the .... (regional municipality, county or district)

of ...., in the.................................. (province or state)

of .... solemnly declare that I am the father of

the child referred to in paragraph 1.

My social insurance number is ....

and we make this solemn declaration conscientiously believing it to be true and knowing that it is of the same force and effect as if made under oath:

at the ....)

of ....)

this .... day of)

.................................)..................................(signature of father)

................................, 19 ....)

.... A Commissioner, etc.)

Severelly declared before me)	
)	
at the . . . .)	. . . .
)	(signature of mother)
)	
of . . . .)	
)	
this.................................day of)	
)	. . . .
................................, 19..........)	(signature of father)
)	
. . . .)	
A Commissioner, etc.)	

Form 4

Children's Law Reform Act

— Finding of Parentage

This court finds that a relationship of parentage has been established and,
(a) that the father is,

. . . .
(surname)

. . . .
(given names)

. . . .
(address)

. . . .
(date of birth)

. . . .
(social insurance number)
(b) that the mother is,

. . . .
(surname)

. . . .
(given names)

. . . .
(address)

. . . .
(date of birth)

. . . .
(social insurance number)
(c) and that the child is,

. . . .
(surname)

. . . .
(given names)

. . . .
(sex)

. . . .
(date of birth)

. . . .
(place of birth)

. . . .

(birth registration number)

Registration Number . . . .

(to be filled in by Registrar General)

Form 5

Children's Law Reform Act
— Statement of Finding of Parentage

In the ...., file number ....

Nature of proceeding ....

Parties ....

Date or Order or Judgment ....

Entry Numbe ....

I, ..., registrar/clerk of the above court hereby state that the order/judgment in the above-mentioned matter confirms or makes a finding of parentage setting out the following particulars:

Father: Surname ....

Given name(s) ....

Address ....

Birth date ....

Social Insurance Number ....

Mother: Surname ....

Given name(s) ....

Address ....

Birth date ....

Social Insurance Number ....

Child: Surname ....

Given name(s) ....

Sex ....

Birth date ....

Place of Birth ....

Birth Registration number ....

Signature: .... Date: ....

CREDITORS' RELIEF ACT

R.S.O. 1990, c. C.45, as am. S.O. 1994, c. 27, s. 44; 1996, c. 31, s. 67.

[Note: only sections 3 and 4 are reproduced here.]

. . . . .

3. (1) Attachment to be for benefit of all creditors — A creditor who attaches a debt shall be deemed to do so for the benefit of all creditors of the debtor as well as for the creditor's own benefit.

(2) To whom to be paid — Payment of the debt shall be made to the sheriff for the county in which the debtor resides or, if the debtor resides outside the Province, to the sheriff for the county in which the proceeding that gave rise to the judgment was commenced.

(3) Garnishment in courts and specified — This section does not apply to a debt attached by garnishment in the Small Claims Court, the Ontario Court (Provincial Division) or the Unified Family Court unless, before the amount recovered by garnishment is actually received by the creditor, an execution against the property of the debtor is placed in the hands of the sheriff for the county.

(4) Money paid to sheriff who has no execution in hand — Where money is paid to a sheriff in whose hands there is no execution against the property of the debtor and there is in the hands of the sheriff for another county an execution against the property of the debtor, the court on the application of the last-mentioned sheriff or of a creditor or of the debtor may direct, on such terms as to costs and otherwise as seem just, that such money be paid over to the last-mentioned sheriff to be distributed by him or her as if such money had then been paid to him or her by the garnishee, and the court shall fix the compensation to be paid to the sheriff by whom the money was received from the garnishee for his or her services.

(5) Money paid into specified courts — Where money recovered by garnishment is paid into the Small Claims Court, the Ontario Court (Provincial Division) or the Unified Family Court, the sheriff is entitled to demand and receive it from the clerk of the court for the purpose of distributing it under this Act, except in so far as the priority created by subsection 4(1) applies to the money.

(6) Right of attaching creditor to share with other creditors — An attaching creditor is entitled to share in respect of that creditor's claim against the debtor in any distribution made under this Act, but that creditor's share shall not exceed the amount recovered by that creditor's garnishment proceedings unless that creditor has in due time placed an execution or a certificate given under this Act in the sheriff's hands.

(7) Sheriff's right to recover attached debt — If money referred to in subsection (5) is received by the attaching creditor, the sheriff may recover it from that creditor.

(8) Clerk not liable — The clerk of the Small Claims Court, the Ontario Court (Provincial Division) or the Unified Family Court is not liable for making payment to the creditor unless, at the time of payment, the clerk has notice that there is an execution against the property of the debtor in the sheriff's hands.

4. (1) Priority for support orders — A support or maintenance order has priority over other judgment debts regardless of when an enforcement process is issued or served,

> (a) if the order is for periodic payments, in the amount of the arrears owing under the order at the time of seizure or attachment; and

> (b) if the order is for a lump sum payment, in the amount of the lump sum.

(2) Support orders rank equally — Support or maintenance orders rank equally with one another.

(3) Enforcement process — Process for the enforcement of a support or maintenance order shall be identified on its face as being for support or maintenance.

(4) Crown bound — Subsection (1) binds the Crown in right of Ontario.

1996, c. 31, s. 67.

. . . . .

CRIMINAL CODE

An Act respecting the criminal law

R.S.C. 1985, c. C-46, as am. R.S.C. 1985, c. 2 (1st Supp.), ss. 1–3; R.S.C. 1985, c.
11 (1st Supp.), s. 2; R.S.C. 1985, c. 27 (1st Supp.), ss. 1–187, 203; R.S.C. 1985, c.
31 (1st Supp.), s. 61; R.S.C. 1985, c. 47 (1st Supp.), s. 1; R.S.C. 1985, c. 51 (1st
Supp.), s. 1; R.S.C. 1985, c. 52 (1st Supp.), ss. 1–3; R.S.C. 1985, c. 1 (2nd Supp.),
s. 213; R.S.C. 1985, c. 24 (2nd Supp.), ss. 45–47; R.S.C. 1985, c. 27 (2nd Supp.), s.
10; R.S.C. 1985, c. 35 (2nd Supp.), s. 34; R.S.C. 1985, c. 10 (3rd Supp.), ss. 1, 2;
R.S.C. 1985, c. 19 (3rd Supp.), ss. 1–16; R.S.C. 1985, c. 30 (3rd Supp.), ss. 1, 2;
R.S.C. 1985, c. 34 (3rd Supp.), ss. 9–13; R.S.C. 1985, c. 1 (4th Supp.), ss. 13–18,
45; R.S.C. 1985, c. 23 (4th Supp.), ss. 1–8; R.S.C. 1985, c. 29 (4th Supp.), s. 17;
R.S.C. 1985, c. 30 (4th Supp.), s. 45; R.S.C. 1985, c. 31 (4th Supp.), ss. 94–97;
R.S.C. 1985, c. 32 (4th Supp.), ss. 55–62; R.S.C. 1985, c. 40 (4th Supp.), s. 2;
R.S.C. 1985, c. 42 (4th Supp.), ss. 1–8; R.S.C. 1985, c. 50 (4th Supp.), s. 1; S.C.
1989, c. 2, s. 1; 1990, c. 15, s. 1; 1990, c. 16, ss. 2–7; 1990, c. 17, ss. 7–15; 1990,
c. 44, s. 15; 1991, c. 1, s. 28; 1991, c. 4, ss. 1, 2; 1991, c. 28, ss. 6–12; 1991, c.
40, ss. 1–41; 1991, c. 43, ss. 1–10 [s. 10(8) not in force at date of publication.];
1992, c. 1, s. 58; 1992, c. 11, ss. 14–18; 1992, c. 20, ss. 199–204, 215, 216, 228,
229; 1992, c. 21, s. 9; 1992, c. 22, s. 12; 1992, c. 27, s. 90; 1992, c. 38; 1992, c.
41; 1992, c. 47, ss. 68–72; 1992, c. 51, ss. 32–43, 67; 1993, c. 7; 1993, c. 25, ss.
93–96; 1993, c. 28, s. 78 (Sched. III, items 25–37); 1993, c. 34, s. 59(1); 1993, c.
37; 1993, c. 40; 1993, c. 45; 1993, c. 46; 1994, c. 12, s. 1; 1994, c. 13, s. 7; 1994,
c. 38, ss. 14, 25; 1994, c. 44, ss. 1–84; 1995, c. 5, s. 25(1)(g); 1995, c. 19, ss.
37–41; 1995, c. 22, ss. 1–12, 14, 15, 19–24 [s. 6 (as it enacts ss. 718.3(5),
747–747.8 of the *Criminal Code*) not in force at date of publication.]; 1995, c. 27,
ss. 1, 3; 1995, c. 29, ss. 39, 40; 1995, c. 32, s. 33; 1995, c. 39, ss. 138–157,
188–190 [s. 139 (as it amends s. 97 of the *Criminal Code*) to come into force
January 1, 2003 if not proclaimed in force sooner.]; 1995, c. 42, ss. 73–78, 86, 87;
1996, c. 8, s. 32; 1996, c. 16, s. 60; 1996, c. 19, ss. 65–76, 93.3; 1996, c. 31, ss.
68–72; 1996, c. 34, ss. 1–8 [ss. 1, 2(1), 3–5 not in force at date of publication.];
1997, c. 2; 1997, c. 9, s. 124 [Not in force at date of publication.]; 1997, c. 16, ss.
1–7; 1997, c. 17, ss. 1–10; 1997, c. 18, ss. 2–115, 139.1, 140, 141 [ss. 106, 107 not
in force at date of publication.]; 1997, c. 17, ss. 1–10; 1997, c. 23, ss. 1–20, 26, 27;
1997, c. 30, ss. 1–3; 1997, c. 39, ss. 1–3; 1998, c. 7, ss. 2, 3; 1998, c. 9, ss. 2–8;
1998, s. 15, s. 20; 1998, c. 30, ss. 14, 16; 1998, c. 34, ss. 8, 9, 11; 1998, c. 35, ss.
119–121; 1998, c. 37, ss. 15–24; 1999, c. 2, s. 47; 1999, c. 3, ss. 25–58; 1999, c. 5,
ss. 1–47, 51, 52; 1999, c. 17, s. 120; 1999, c. 18, ss. 92–95; 1999, c. 25; 1999, c.
28, ss. 155, 156; 1999, c. 31, ss. 67–69; 1999, c. 32, ss. 1–6; 1999, c. 33, s. 346;
1999, c. 35, s. 11; 2000, c. 1, s. 9; 2000, c. 2; 2000, c. 10, ss. 13–24; 2000, c. 12,
ss. 91–95; 2000, c. 17, s. 89; 2000, c. 24, ss. 42–46; 2000, c. 25; 2001, c. 26, s.
294 [Not in force at date of publication.]; 2001, c. 27, ss. 244–247 [s. 245 not in
force at date of publication.]; 2001, c. 32, ss. 1–46.1, 81(2) [ss. 1(1), (6), 3, 9(1),
12(5), 31(3), 44: (Fr.)][s. 81(2) conditions not yet satisfied.]; 2001, c. 37; 2001, c.
41, ss. 2–23, 31–34, 80, 126, 130(7.1), 133(1), (2), (5), (8)–(11), (13)–(19), 143 [s.

143 conditions not yet satisfied.]; 2002, c. 1, ss. 175–186; 2002, c. 7, ss. 137–150 [Not in force at date of publication.]; 2002, c. 13, ss. 1–86 [ss. 5(1), 16, 86: (Fr.)] [ss. 24–46, 48, 59, 72, 79, 89, 90 to come into force July 23, 2003.]; 2002, c. 22, ss. 324–327, 409(2)(b) [ss. 324–327 not in force at date of publication.] [s. 326 repealed 2002, c. 22, s. 409(2)(a); s. 327 repealed 2002, c. 22, s. 409(6).].

[Note: only sections 57(2), 127 and 282–286 are reproduced here.]

. . . . .

57.

. . . . .

(2) False statement in relation to passport — Every one who, while in or out of Canada, for the purpose of procuring a passport for himself or any other person or for the purpose of procuring any material alteration or addition to any such passport, makes a written or an oral statement that he knows is false or misleading

    (a) is guilty of an indictable offence and liable to imprisonment for a term not exceeding two years; or

    (b) is guilty of an offence punishable on summary conviction.

. . . . .

127. (1) Disobeying order of court — Every one who, without lawful excuse, disobeys a lawful order made by a court of justice or by a person or body of persons authorized by any Act to make or give the order, other than an order for the payment of money, is, unless a punishment or other mode of proceeding is expressly provided by law, guilty of an indictable offence and liable to imprisonment for a term not exceeding two years.

(2) Attorney General of Canada may act — Where the order referred to in subsection (1) was made in proceedings instituted at the instance of the Government of Canada and conducted by or on behalf of that Government, any proceedings in respect of a contravention of or conspiracy to contravene that order may be instituted and conducted in like manner.

. . . . .

282. (1) Abduction in contravention of custody order — Every one who, being the parent, guardian or person having the lawful care or charge of a person under the age of fourteen years, takes, entices away, conceals, detains, receives or harbours that person, in contravention of the custody provisions of a custody order in relation to that person made by a court anywhere in Canada, with intent to deprive a parent or guardian or any other person who has the lawful care or charge of that person, of the possession of that person is guilty of

    (a) an indictable offence and is liable to imprisonment for a term not exceeding ten years; or

    (b) an offence punishable on summary conviction.

(2) Where no belief in validity of custody order — Where a count charges an offence under subsection (1) and the offence is not proven only because the accused did not believe that there was a valid custody order but the evidence does prove an offence under section 283, the accused may be convicted of an offence under section 283.

1993, c. 45, s. 4

283. (1) Abduction — Every one who, being the parent, guardian or person having the lawful care or charge of a person under the age of fourteen years, takes, entices away, conceals, detains, receives or harbours that person, whether or not there is a custody order in relation to that person made by a court anywhere in Canada, with intent to deprive a parent or guardian, or any other person who has the lawful care or charge of that person, of the possession of that person, is guilty of

    (a) an indictable offence and is liable to imprisonment for a term not exceeding ten years; or

    (b) an offence punishable on summary conviction.

(2) Consent required — No proceedings may be commenced under subsection (1) without the consent of the Attorney General or counsel instructed by him for that purpose.

1993, c. 45, s. 5

284. Defence — No one shall be found guilty of an offence under sections 281 to 283 if he establishes that the taking, enticing away, concealing, detaining, receiving or harbouring of any young person was done with the consent of the parent, guardian or other person having the lawful possession, care or charge of that young person.

285. Defence — No one shall be found guilty of an offence under sections 280 to 283 if the court is satisfied that the taking, enticing away, concealing, detaining, receiving or harbouring of any young person was necessary to protect the young person from danger of imminent harm or if the person charged with the offence was escaping from danger of imminent harm.

1993, c. 45, s. 6

286. No defence — In proceedings in respect of an offence under sections 280 to 283, it is not a defence to any charge that a young person consented to or suggested any conduct of the accused.

. . . . .

DIVORCE ACT

R.S.C. 1985, c. 3 (2nd Supp.), as am. R.S.C. 1985, c. 27 (2nd Supp.), s. 10; S.C. 1990, c. 18, ss. 1, 2; 1992, c. 51, s. 46; 1993, c. 8, ss. 1–5; 1993, c. 28, s. 78 (Sched. III, items 41–43) [Amended 1998, c. 15, ss. 22, 23; 1999, c. 3, (Sched., item 11).]; 1997, c. 1, ss. 1–15; 1998, c. 30, s. 15(f); 1999, c. 3, s. 61; 1999, c. 31, s. 74 (Fr.); 2002, c. 7, ss. 158–160 [Not in force at date of publication.]; 2002, c. 8, s. 183(1)(i) [Not in force at date of publication.].

Short Title

1. Short title — This Act may be cited as the *Divorce Act*.

Interpretation

2. (1) Definitions — In this Act,

"age of majority", in respect of a child, means the age of majority as determined by the laws of the province where the child ordinarily resides, or, if the child ordinarily resides outside of Canada, eighteen years of age;

"appellate court", in respect of an appeal from a court, means the court exercising appellate jurisdiction with respect to that appeal;

"applicable guidelines", means

(a) where both spouses or former spouses are ordinarily resident in the same province at the time an application for a child support order or a variation order in respect of a child support order is made, or the amount of a child support order is to be recalculated pursuant to section 25.1, and that province has been designated by an order made under subsection (5), the laws of the province specified in the order, and

(b) in any other case, the Federal Child Support Guidelines;

"child of the marriage" means a child of two spouses or former spouses who, at the material time,

(a) is under the age of majority and who has not withdrawn from their charge, or

(b) is the age of majority or over and under their charge but unable, by reason of illness, disability or other cause, to withdraw from their charge or to obtain the necessaries of life;

"child support order", means an order made under subsection 15.1(1);

"corollary relief proceeding" means a proceeding in a court in which either or both former spouses seek a child support order, a spousal support order or a custody order;

"court", in respect of a province, means

(a) for the Province of Ontario, the Superior Court of Justice,

257

(a.1) for the Province of Prince Edward Island or Newfoundland, the trial division of the Supreme Court of the Province,

(b) for the Province of Quebec, the Superior Court,

(c) for the Province of Nova Scotia and British Columbia, the Supreme Court of the Province,

(d) for the Province of New Brunswick, Manitoba, Saskatchewan or Alberta, the Court of Queen's Bench for the Province, and

(e) for the Yukon Territory or the Northwest Territories, the Supreme Court of the territory, and in Nunavut, the Nunavut Court of Justice,

---

Proposed Amendment — 2(1) "court" (e)

(e) for Yukon or the Northwest Territories, the Supreme Court, and in Nunavut, the Nunavut Court of Justice,

2002, c. 7, s. 158 [Not in force at date of publication.]

---

and includes such other court in the province the judges of which are appointed by the Governor General as is designated by the Lieutenant Governor in Council of the province as a court for the purposes of this Act;

"custody" includes care, upbringing and any other incident of custody;

"custody order" means an order made under subsection 16(1);

"divorce proceeding" means a proceeding in a court in which either or both spouses seek a divorce alone or together with a child support order, a spousal support order or a custody order;

"Federal Child Support Guidelines" means the guidelines made under section 26.1;

"provincial child support service" means any service, agency or body designated in an agreement with a province under subsection 25.1(1);

"spousal support order" means an order made under subsection 15.2(1);

"spouse" means either of a man or woman who are married to each other;

"support order" means a child support order or a spousal support order;

"variation order" means an order made under subsection 17(1);

"variation proceeding" means a proceeding in a court in which either or both former spouses seek a variation order.

(2) Child of the marriage — For the purposes of the definition "child of the marriage" in subsection (1), a child of two spouses or former spouses includes

(a) any child for whom they both stand in the place of parents; and

(b) any child of whom one is the parent and for whom the other stands in the place of a parent.

(3) Term not restrictive — The use of the term "application" to describe a proceeding under this Act in a court shall not be construed as limiting the name under which and the form and manner in which that proceeding may be taken in that court, and the name, manner and form of the proceeding in that court shall be such as is provided for by the rules regulating the practice and procedure in that court.

(4) Idem — The use in section 21.1 of the terms "affidavit" and "pleadings" to describe documents shall not be construed as limiting the name that may be used to refer to those documents in a court and the form of those documents, and the name and form of the documents shall be such as is provided for by the rules regulating the practice and procedure in that court.

(5) Provincial child support guidelines — The Governor in Council may, by order, designate a province for the purposes of the definition **"applicable guidelines"** in subsection (1) if the laws of the province establish comprehensive guidelines for the determination of child support that deal with the matters referred to in section 26.1. The order shall specify the laws of the province that constitute the guidelines of the province.

(6) Amendments included — The guidelines of a province referred to in subsection (5) include any amendments made to them from time to time.

R.S.C. 1985, c. 27 (2nd Supp.), s. 10 (Sched., items 7(1) and (2)); 1990, c. 18, s. 1; 1992, c. 51, s. 46; 1993, c. 28, s. 78 (Sched. III, item 41) [Repealed 1999, c. 3, (Sched., item 11).]; 1997, c. 1, s. 1; 1998, c. 30, s. 15(f); 1999, c. 3, s. 61

Jurisdiction

3. (1) Jurisdiction in divorce proceedings — A court in a province has jurisdiction to hear and determine a divorce proceeding if either spouse has been ordinarily resident in the province for at least one year immediately preceding the commencement of the proceeding.

(2) Jurisdiction where two proceedings commenced on different days — Where divorce proceedings between the same spouses are pending in two courts that would otherwise have jurisdiction under subsection (1) and were commenced on different days and the proceeding that was commenced first is not discontinued within thirty days after it was commenced, the court in which a divorce proceeding was commenced first has exclusive jurisdiction to hear and determine any divorce proceeding then pending between the spouses and the second divorce proceeding shall be deemed to be discontinued.

(3) Jurisdiction where two proceedings commenced on same day — Where divorce proceedings between the same spouses are pending in two courts that would otherwise have jurisdiction under subsection (1) and were commenced on the same day and neither proceeding is discontinued within thirty days after it was commenced, the Federal Court — Trial Division has exclusive jurisdiction to hear and determine any divorce proceeding then pending between the spouses and the divorce proceedings in those courts shall be transferred to the Federal Court — Trial Division on the direction of that Court.

Proposed Amendment — 3(3)

(3) Jurisdiction where two proceedings commenced on same day — Where divorce proceedings between the same spouses are pending in two courts that would otherwise have jurisdiction under subsection (1) and were commenced on the same day and neither proceeding is discontinued within thirty days after it was commenced, the Federal Court has exclusive jurisdiction to hear and determine any divorce proceeding then pending between the spouses and the divorce proceedings in those courts shall be transferred to the Federal Court on the direction of that Court.

2002, c. 8, s. 183(1)(i) [Not in force at date of publication.]

4. (1) Jurisdiction in corollary relief proceedings — A court in a province has jurisdiction to hear and determine a corollary relief proceeding if

    (a) either former spouse is ordinarily resident in the province at the commencement of the proceeding; or

    (b) both former spouses accept the jurisdiction of the court.

(2) Jurisdiction where two proceedings commenced on different days — Where corollary relief proceedings between the same former spouses and in respect of the same matter are pending in two courts that would otherwise have jurisdiction under subsection (1) and were commenced on different days and the proceeding that was commenced first is not discontinued within thirty days after it was commenced, the court in which a corollary relief proceeding was commenced first has exclusive jurisdiction to hear and determine any corollary relief proceeding then pending between the former spouses in respect of that matter and the second corollary relief proceeding shall be deemed to be discontinued.

(3) Jurisdiction where two proceedings commenced on same day — Where proceedings between the same former spouses and in respect of the same matter are pending in two courts that would otherwise have jurisdiction under subsection (1) and were commenced on the same day and neither proceeding is discontinued within thirty days after it was commenced, the Federal Court — Trial Division has exclusive jurisdiction to hear and determine any corollary relief proceeding then pending between the former spouses in respect of that matter and the corollary relief proceedings in those courts shall be transferred to the Federal Court — Trial Division on the direction of that Court.

Proposed Amendment — 4(3)

(3) Jurisdiction where two proceedings commenced on same day — Where proceedings between the same former spouses and in respect of the same matter are pending in two courts that would otherwise have jurisdiction under subsection (1) and were commenced on the same day and neither proceeding is discontinued within thirty days after it was commenced, the Federal Court has exclusive jurisdiction to hear and determine any corollary relief proceeding then pending between the former spouses in respect of that matter and the corollary relief proceedings in those courts shall be transferred to the Federal Court on the direction of that Court.

    2002, c. 8, s. 183(1)(i) [Not in force at date of publication.]

                                                1993, c. 8, s. 1

5. (1) Jurisdiction in variation proceedings — A court in a province has jurisdiction to hear and determine a variation proceeding if

    (a) either former spouse is ordinarily resident in the province at the commencement of the proceeding; or

    (b) both former spouses accept the jurisdiction of the court.

(2) Jurisdiction where two proceedings commenced on different days — Where variation proceedings between the same former spouses and in respect of the same matter are pending in two courts that would otherwise have jurisdiction under subsection (1) and were commenced on different days and the proceeding that was commenced first is not discontinued within thirty days after it was commenced, the court in which a variation proceeding was commenced first has exclusive jurisdiction to hear and determine any variation proceeding then pending between the former spouses in respect of that matter and the second variation proceeding shall be deemed to be discontinued.

(3) Jurisdiction where two proceedings commenced on same day — Where variation proceedings between the same former spouses and in respect of the same matter are pending in two courts that would otherwise have jurisdiction under subsection (1) and were commenced on the same day and neither proceeding is discontinued within thirty days after it was commenced, the Federal Court — Trial Division has exclusive jurisdiction to hear and determine any variation proceeding then pending between the former spouses in respect of that matter and the variation proceedings in those courts shall be transferred to the Federal Court — Trial Division on the direction of that Court.

Proposed Amendment — 5(3)

(3) Jurisdiction where two proceedings commenced on same day — Where variation proceedings between the same former spouses and in respect of the same matter are pending in two courts that would otherwise have jurisdiction under subsection (1) and were commenced on the same day and neither proceeding is discontinued within thirty days after it was commenced, the Federal Court has exclusive jurisdiction to hear and determine any variation proceeding then pending between the former spouses in respect of that matter and the variation proceedings in those courts shall be transferred to the Federal Court on the direction of that Court.

2002, c. 8, s. 183(1)(i) [Not in force at date of publication.]

6. (1) Transfer of divorce proceeding where custody application — Where an application for an order under section 16 is made in a divorce proceeding to a court in a province and is opposed and the child of the marriage in respect of whom the order is sought is most substantially connected with another province, the court may, on application by a spouse or on its own motion, transfer the divorce proceeding to a court in that other province.

(2) Transfer of corollary relief proceeding where custody application — Where an application for an order under section 16 is made in a corollary relief proceeding to a court in a province and is opposed and the child of the marriage in respect of whom the order is sought is most substantially connected with another province, the court may, on application by a former spouse or on its own motion, transfer the corollary relief proceeding to a court in that other province.

(3) Transfer of variation proceeding where custody application — Where an application for a variation order in respect of a custody order is made in a variation proceeding to a court in a province and is opposed and the child of the marriage in respect of whom the variation order is sought is most substantially connected with another province, the court may, on application by a former spouse or on its own motion, transfer the variation proceeding to a court in that other province.

(4) Exclusive jurisdiction — Notwithstanding sections 3 to 5, a court in a province to which a proceeding is transferred under this section has exclusive jurisdiction to hear and determine the proceeding.

7. Exercise of jurisdiction by judge — The jurisdiction conferred on a court by this Act to grant a divorce shall be exercised only by a judge of the court without a jury.

Divorce

8. (1) Divorce — A court of competent jurisdiction may, on application by either or both spouses, grant a divorce to the spouse or spouses on the ground that there has been a breakdown of their marriage.

(2) Breakdown of marriage — Breakdown of a marriage is established only if

(a) the spouses have lived separate and apart for at least one year immediately preceding the determination of the divorce proceeding and were living separate and apart at the commencement of the proceeding; or

(b) the spouse against whom the divorce proceeding is brought has, since celebration of the marriage,

(i) committed adultery, or

(ii) treated the other spouse with physical or mental cruelty of such a kind as to render intolerable the continued cohabitation of the spouses.

(3) Calculation of period of separation — For the purposes of paragraph (2)(a),

(a) spouses shall be deemed to have lived separate and apart for any period during which they lived apart and either of them had the intention to live separate and apart from the other; and

(b) a period during which spouses have lived separate and apart shall not be considered to have been interrupted or terminated

(i) by reason only that either spouse has become incapable of forming or having an intention to continue to live separate and apart or of continuing to live separate and apart of the spouse's own volition, if it appears to the court that the separation would probably have continued if the spouse had not become so incapable, or

(ii) by reason only that the spouses have resumed cohabitation during a period of, or periods totalling, not more than ninety days with reconciliation as its primary purpose.

9. (1) Duty of legal advisor — It is the duty of every barrister, solicitor, lawyer or advocate who undertakes to act on behalf of a spouse in a divorce proceeding

(a) to draw to the attention of the spouse the provisions of this Act that have as their object the reconciliation of spouses, and

(b) to discuss with the spouse the possibility of the reconciliation of the spouses and to inform the spouse of the marriage counselling or guidance facilities known to him or her that might be able to assist the spouses to achieve a reconciliation,

unless the circumstances of the case are of such a nature that it would clearly not be appropriate to do so.

(2) Idem — It is the duty of every barrister, solicitor, lawyer or advocate who undertakes to act on behalf of a spouse in a divorce proceeding to discuss with the spouse the advisability of negotiating the matters that may be the subject of a support order or a custody order and to inform the spouse of the mediation facilities known to him or her that might be able to assist the spouses in negotiating those matters.

(3) Clarification — Every document presented to a court by a barrister, solicitor, lawyer or advocate that formally commences a divorce proceeding shall contain a statement by him or her certifying that he or she has complied with this section.

10. (1) Duty of court, reconciliation — In a divorce proceeding, it is the duty of the court, before considering the evidence, to satisfy itself that there is no possibility of the reconciliation of the spouses, unless the circumstances of the case are of such a nature that it would clearly not be appropriate to do so.

(2) Adjournment — Where at any stage in a divorce proceeding it appears to the court from the nature of the case, the evidence or the attitude of either or both spouses that there is a possibility of the reconciliation of the spouses, the court shall

(a) adjourn the proceeding to afford the spouses an opportunity to achieve a reconciliation; and

(b) with the consent of the spouses or in the discretion of the court, nominate

(i) a person with experience or training in marriage counselling or guidance, or

(ii) in special circumstances, some other suitable person, to assist the spouses to achieve a reconciliation.

(3) Resumption — Where fourteen days have elapsed from the date of any adjournment under subsection (2), the court shall resume the proceeding on the application of either or both spouses.

(4) Nominee not competent or compellable — No person nominated by a court under this section to assist spouses to achieve a reconciliation is competent or compellable in any legal proceedings to disclose any admission or communication made to that person in his or her capacity as a nominee of the court for that purpose.

(5) Evidence not admissible — Evidence of anything said or of any admission or communication made in the course of assisting spouses to achieve a reconciliation is not admissible in any legal proceedings.

11. (1) Duty of court, bars — In a divorce proceeding, it is the duty of the court

(a) to satisfy itself that there has been no collusion in relation to the application for a divorce and to dismiss the application if it finds that there was collusion in presenting it;

(b) to satisfy itself that reasonable arrangements have been made for the support of any children of the marriage, having regard to the applicable guidelines, and, if such arrangements have not been made, to stay the granting of the divorce until such arrangements are made; and

(c) where a divorce is sought in circumstances described in paragraph 8(2)(b), to satisfy itself that there has been no condonation or connivance on the part of the spouse bringing the proceeding, and to dismiss the application for a divorce if that spouse has condoned or connived at the act or conduct complained of unless, in the opinion of the court, the public interest would be better served by granting the divorce.

(2) Revival — Any act or conduct that has been condoned is not capable of being revived so as to constitute a circumstance described in paragraph 8(2)(b).

(3) Condonation — For the purposes of this section, a continuation or resumption of cohabitation during a period of, or periods totalling, not more than ninety days with reconciliation as its primary purpose shall not be considered to constitute condonation.

(4) Definition of "collusion" — In this section, **"collusion"** means an agreement or conspiracy to which an applicant for a divorce is either directly or indirectly a party for the purpose of subverting the administration of justice, and includes any agreement, understanding or arrangement to fabricate or suppress evidence or to deceive the court, but does not include an agreement to the extent that it provides for separation between the parties, financial support, division of property or the custody of any child of the marriage.

1997, c. 1, s. 1.1

12. (1) Effective date generally — Subject to this section, a divorce takes effect on the thirty-first day after the day on which the judgment granting the divorce is rendered.

(2) Special circumstances — Where, on or after rendering a judgment granting a divorce,

> (a) the court is of the opinion that by reason of special circumstances the divorce should take effect earlier than the thirty-first day after the day on which the judgment is rendered, and

> (b) the spouses agree and undertake that no appeal from the judgment will be taken, or any appeal from the judgment that was taken has been abandoned,

the court may order that the divorce takes effect at such earlier time as it considers appropriate.

(3) Effective date where appeal — A divorce in respect of which an appeal is pending at the end of the period referred to in subsection (1), unless voided on appeal, takes effect on the expiration of the time fixed by law for instituting an appeal from the decision on that appeal or any subsequent appeal, if no appeal has been instituted within that time.

(4) Certain extensions to be counted — For the purposes of subsection (3), the time fixed by law for instituting an appeal from a decision on an appeal includes any extension thereof fixed pursuant to law before the expiration of that time or fixed thereafter on an application instituted before the expiration of that time.

(5) No late extensions of time for appeal — Notwithstanding any other law, the time fixed by law for instituting an appeal from a decision referred to in subsection (3) may not be extended after the expiration of that time, except on an application instituted before the expiration of that time.

(6) Effective date where decision of Supreme Court of Canada — A divorce in respect of which an appeal has been taken to the Supreme Court of Canada, unless voided on the appeal, takes effect on the day on which the judgment on the appeal is rendered.

(7) Certificate of divorce — Where a divorce takes effect in accordance with this section, a judge or officer of the court that rendered the judgment granting the divorce or, where that judgment has been appealed, of the appellate court that rendered the judgment on the final appeal, shall, on request, issue to any person a certificate that a divorce granted under this Act dissolved the marriage of the specified persons effective as of a specified date.

(8) Conclusive proof — A certificate referred to in subsection (7), or a certified copy thereof, is conclusive proof of the facts so certified without proof of the signature or authority of the person appearing to have signed the certificate.

13. Legal effect throughout Canada — On taking effect, a divorce granted under this Act has legal effect throughout Canada.

14. Marriage dissolved — On taking effect, a divorce granted under this Act dissolves the marriage of the spouses.

COROLLARY RELIEF

Interpretation

15. Definition of "spouse" — In section 15.1 to 16, **"spouse"** has the meaning assigned by subsection 2(1), and includes a former spouse.

1997, c. 1, s. 2

Child Support Orders

15.1 (1) Child support order — A court of competent jurisdiction may, on application by either or both spouses, make an order requiring spouse to pay for the support of any or all children of the marriage.

(2) Interim order — Where an application is made under subsection (1), the court may, on application by either or both spouses, make an interim order requiring a spouse to pay for the support of any or all children of the marriage, pending the determination of the application under subsection (1).

(3) Guidelines apply — A court making an order under subsection (1) or an interim order under subsection (2) shall do so in accordance with the applicable guidelines.

(4) Terms and conditions — The court may make an order under subsection (1) or an interim order under subsection (2) for a definite or indefinite period or until a specified event occurs, and may impose terms, conditions or restrictions in connection with the order or interim order as it thinks fit and just.

(5) Court may take agreement, etc., into account — Notwithstanding subsection (3), a court may award an amount that is different from the amount that would be determined in accordance with the applicable guidelines if the court is satisfied

(a) that special provisions in an order, a judgment or a written agreement respecting the financial obligations of the spouses, or the division or transfer of their property, directly or indirectly benefit a child, or that special provisions have otherwise been made for the benefit of a child; and

(b) that the application of the applicable guidelines would result in an amount of child support that is inequitable given those special provisions.

(6) Reasons — Where the court award, pursuant to subsection (5), an amount that is different from the amount that would be determined in accordance with the applicable guidelines, the court shall record its reasons for having done so.

(7) Consent orders — Notwithstanding subsection (3), a court may award an amount that is different from the amount that would be determined in accordance with the applicable guidelines on the consent of both spouses if it is satisfied that reasonable arrangements have been made for the support of the child to whom the order relates.

(8) Reasonable arrangements — For the purposes of subsection (7), in determining whether reasonable arrangements have been made for the support of a child, the court shall have regard to the applicable guidelines. However, the court shall not consider the arrangements to be unreasonable solely because the amount of support agreed to is not the same as the amount that would otherwise have been determined in accordance with the applicable guidelines.

1997, c. 1, s. 2

Spousal Support Orders

15.2 (1) Spousal support order — A court of competent jurisdiction may, on application by either or both spouses, make an order requiring a spouse to secure or pay, or to secure and pay, such lump sum or periodic sums, or such lump sum and periodic sums, as the court thinks reasonable for the support of the other spouse.

(2) Interim order — Where an application is made under subsection (1), the court may, on application by either or both spouses, make an interim order requiring a spouse to secure or pay, or to secure and pay, such lump sum or periodic sums, or such lump sum and periodic sums, as the court thinks reasonable for the support of the other spouse, pending the determination of the application under subsection (1).

(3) Terms and conditions — The court may make an order under subsection (1) or an interim order under subsection (2) for a definite or indefinite period or until a specified event occurs, and may impose terms, conditions or restrictions in connection with the order as it thinks fit and just.

(4) Factors — In making an order under subsection (1) or an interim order under subsection (2), the court shall take into consideration the condition, means, needs and other circumstances of each spouse, including

(a) the length of time the spouses cohabited;

(b) the functions performed by each spouse during cohabitation; and

(c) any order, agreement or arrangement relating to support of either spouse.

(5) Spousal misconduct — In making an order under subsection (1) or an interim order under subsection (2), the court shall not take into consideration any misconduct of a spouse in relation to the marriage.

(6) Objectives of spousal support order — An order made under subsection (1) or an interim order under subsection (2) that provides for the support of a spouse should

(a) recognize any economic advantages or disadvantages to the spouses arising from the marriage or its breakdown;

(b) apportion between the spouses any financial consequences arising from the care of any child of the marriage over and above any obligation for the support of any child of the marriage;

(c) relieve any economic hardship of the spouses arising from the breakdown of the marriage; and

(d) in so far as practicable, promote the economic self-sufficiency of each spouse within a reasonable period of time.

1997, c. 1, s. 2

Priority

15.3 (1) Priority to child support — Where a court is considering an application for a child support order and an application for a spousal support order, the court shall give priority to child support in determining the applications.

(2) Reasons — Where, as a result of giving priority to child support, the court is unable to make a spousal support order or the court makes a spousal support order in an amount that is less than it otherwise would have been, the court shall record its reasons for having done so.

(3) Consequences of reduction or termination of child support order — Where, as a result of giving priority to child support, a spousal support order was not made, or the amount of a spousal support order is less than it otherwise would have been, any subsequent reduction or termination of that child support constitutes a change of circumstances for the purposes of applying for a spousal support order, or a variation order in respect of the spousal support order, as the case may be.

1997, c. 1, s. 2

Custody Orders

16. (1) Order for custody — A court of competent jurisdiction may, on application by either or both spouses or by any other person, make an order respecting the custody of or the access to, or the custody of and access to, any or all children of the marriage.

(2) Interim order for custody — Where an application is made under subsection (1), the court may, on application by either or both spouses or by any other person, make an interim order respecting the custody of or the access to, or the custody of and access to, any or all children of the marriage pending determination of the application under subsection (1).

(3) Application by other person — A person, other than a spouse, may not make an application under subsection (1) or (2) without leave of the court.

(4) Joint custody or access — The court may make an order under this section granting custody of, or access to, any or all children of the marriage to any one or more persons.

(5) Access — Unless the court orders otherwise, a spouse who is granted access to a child of the marriage has the right to make inquiries, and to be given information, as to the health, education and welfare of the child.

(6) Terms and conditions — The court may make an order under this section for a definite or indefinite period or until the happening of a specified event and may impose such other terms, conditions or restrictions in connection therewith as it thinks fit and just.

(7) Order respecting change of residence — Without limiting the generality of subsection (6), the court may include in an order under this section a term requiring any person who has custody of a child of the marriage and who intends to change the place of residence of that child to notify, at least thirty days before the change or within such other period before the change as the court may specify, any person who is granted access to that child of the change, the time at which the change will be made and the new place of residence of the child.

(8) Factors — In making an order under this section, the court shall take into consideration only the best interests of the child of the marriage as determined by reference to the condition, means, needs and other circumstances of the child.

(9) Past conduct — In making an order under this section, the court shall not take into consideration the past conduct of any person unless the conduct is relevant to the ability of that person to act as a parent of a child.

(10) Maximum contact — In making an order under this section, the court shall give effect to the principle that a child of the marriage should have as much contact with each spouse as is consistent with the best interests of the child and, for that purpose, shall take into consideration the willingness of the person for whom custody is sought to facilitate such contact.

Variation, Rescission or Suspension of Orders

17. (1) Order for variation, rescission or suspension — A court of competent jurisdiction may make an order varying, rescinding or suspending, prospectively or retroactively,

(a) a support order or any provision thereof on application by either or both former spouses; or

(b) a custody order or any provision thereof on application by either or both former spouses or by any other person.

(2) Application by other person — A person, other than a former spouse, may not make an application under paragraph (1)(b) without leave of the court.

(3) Terms and conditions — The court may include in a variation order any provision that under this Act could have been included in the order in respect of which the variation order is sought.

(4) Factors for child support order — Before the court makes a variation order in respect of a child support order, the court shall satisfy itself that a change of circumstances as provided for in the applicable guidelines has occurred since the making of the child support order or the last variation order made in respect of that order.

(4.1) Factors for spousal support order — Before the court makes a variation order in respect of a spousal support order, the court shall satisfy itself that a change in the condition, means, needs or other circumstances of either former spouse has occurred since the making of the spousal support order or the last variation order made in respect of that order, and, in making the variation order, the court shall take that change into consideration.

(5) Factors for custody order — Before the court makes a variation order in respect of a custody order, the court shall satisfy itself that there has been a change in the condition, means, needs or other circumstances of the child of the marriage occurring since the making of the custody order or the last variation order made in respect of that order, as the case may be, and, in making the variation order, the court shall take into consideration only the best interests of the child as determined by reference to that change.

(6) Conduct — In making a variation order, the court shall not take into consideration any conduct that under this Act could not have been considered in making the order in respect of which the variation order is sought.

(6.1) Guidelines apply — A court making a variation order in respect of a child support order shall do so in accordance with the applicable guidelines.

(6.2) Court may take agreement, etc., into account — Notwithstanding subsection (6.1), in making a variation order in respect of a child support order, a court may award an amount that is different from the amount that would be determined in accordance with the applicable guidelines if the court is satisfied

(a) that special provisions in an order, a judgment or a written agreement respecting the financial obligations of the spouses, or the division or transfer of their property, directly or indirectly benefit a child, or that special provisions have otherwise been made for the benefit of a child; and

(b) that the application of the applicable guidelines would result in an amount of child support that is inequitable given those special provisions.

(6.3) Reasons — Where the court awards, pursuant to subsection (6.2), an amount that is different from the amount that would be determined in accordance with the applicable guidelines, the court shall record its reasons for having done so.

(6.4) Consent orders — Notwithstanding subsection (6.1), a court may award an amount that is different from the amount that would be determined in accordance with the applicable guidelines on the consent of both spouses if it is satisfied that reasonable arrangements have been made for the support of the child to whom the order relates.

(6.5) Reasonable arrangements — For the purposes of subsection (6.4), in determining whether reasonable arrangements have been made for the support of a child, the court shall have regard to the applicable guidelines. However, the court shall not consider the arrangements to be unreasonable solely because the amount of support agreed to is not the same as the amount that would otherwise have been determined in accordance with the applicable guidelines.

(7) Objectives of variation order varying spousal support order — A variation order varying a spousal support order should

(a) recognize any economic advantages or disadvantages to the former spouse arising from the marriage or its breakdown;

(b) apportion between the former spouses any financial consequences arising from the care of any child of the marriage over and above any obligation for the support of any child of the marriage;

(c) relieve any economic hardship of the former spouses arising from the breakdown of the marriage; and

(d) in so far as practicable, promote the economic self-sufficiency of each former spouse within a reasonable period of time.

(8) [Repealed 1997, c. 1, s. 5(5).]

(9) Maximum contact — In making a variation order varying a custody order, the court shall give effect to the principle that a child of the marriage should have as much contact with each former spouse as is consistent with the best interests of the child and, for that purpose, where the variation order would grant custody of the child to a person who does not currently have custody, the court shall take into consideration the willingness of that person to facilitate such contact.

(10) Limitation — Notwithstanding subsection (1), where a spousal support order provides for support for a definite period or until a specified event occurs, a court may not, on an application instituted after the expiration of that period or the occurrence of the event, make a variation order for the purpose of resuming that support unless the court is satisfied that

(a) a variation order is necessary to relieve economic hardship arising from a change described in subsection (4.1) that is related to the marriage; and

(b) the changed circumstances, had they existed at the time of the making of the spousal support order or the last variation order made in respect of that order, as the case may be, would likely have resulted in a different order.

(11) Copy of order — Where a court makes a variation order in respect of a support order or a custody order made by another court, it shall send a copy of the variation order, certified by a judge or officer of the court, to that other court.

1997, c. 1, ss. 4, 5

17.1 Variation order by affidavit, etc. — Where both former spouses are ordinarily resident in different provinces, a court of competent jurisdiction may, in accordance with any applicable rules of the court, make a variation order pursuant to subsection 17(1) on the basis of the submissions of the former spouses, whether presented orally before the court or by means of affidavits or any means of telecommunication, if both former spouses consent thereto.

1993, c. 8, s. 2

Provisional Orders

18. (1) Definitions — In this section and section 19,

"Attorney General", in respect of a province, means

(a) for the Yukon Territory, the member of the Council of the Yukon Territory designated by the Commissioner of the Yukon Territory,

> **Proposed Amendment — 18(1) "Attorney General" (a)**
>
> (a) for Yukon, the member of the Executive Council of Yukon designated by the Commissioner of Yukon,
>
> 2002, c. 7, s. 159 [Not in force at date of publication.]

(b) for the Northwest Territories, the member of the Council of the Northwest Territories designated by the Commissioner of the Northwest Territories,

(b.1) for Nunavut, the member of the Executive Council of Nunavut designated by the Commissioner of Nunavut, and

(c) for the other provinces, the Attorney General of the province,

and includes any person authorized in writing by the member or Attorney General to act for the member or Attorney General in the performance of a function under this section or section 19;

"provisional order" means an order made pursuant to subsection (2).

(2) Provisional order — Notwithstanding paragraph 5(1)(a) and subsection 17(1), where an application is made to a court in a province for a variation order in respect of a support order and

(a) the respondent in the application is ordinarily resident in another province, and has not accepted the jurisdiction of the court, or both former spouses have not consented to the application of section 17.1 in respect of the matter, and

(b) in the circumstances of the case, the court is satisfied that the issues can be adequately determined by proceeding under this section and section 19,

the court shall make a variation order with or without notice to and in the absence of the respondent, but such order is provisional only and has no legal effect until it is confirmed in a proceeding under section 19 and, where so confirmed, it has legal effect in accordance with the terms of the order confirming it.

(3) Transmission — Where a court in a province makes a provisional order, it shall send to the Attorney General for the province

(a) three copies of the provisional order certified by a judge or officer of the court;

(b) a certified or sworn document setting out or summarizing the evidence given to the court; and

(c) a statement giving any available information respecting the identification, location, income and assets of the respondent.

(4) Idem — On receipt of the documents referred to in subsection (3), the Attorney General shall send the documents to the Attorney General for the province in which the respondent is ordinarily resident.

(5) Further evidence — Where, during a proceeding under section 19, a court in a province remits the matter back for further evidence to the court that made the provisional order, the court that made the order shall, after giving notice to the applicant, receive further evidence.

(6) Transmission — Where evidence is received under subsection (5), the court that received the evidence shall forward to the court that remitted the matter back a certified or sworn document setting out or summarizing the evidence, together with such recommendations as the court that received the evidence considers appropriate.

1993, c. 8, s. 2; 1993, c. 28, s. 78 (Sched. III, item 43); 1997, c. 1, s. 6

19. (1) Transmission — On receipt of any documents sent pursuant to subsection 18(4), the Attorney General for the province in which the respondent is ordinarily resident shall send the documents to a court in the province.

(2) Procedure — Subject to subsection (3), where documents have been sent to a court pursuant to subsection (1), the court shall serve on the respondent a copy of the documents and a notice of a hearing respecting confirmation of the provisional order and shall proceed with the hearing, in the absence of the applicant, taking into consideration the certified or sworn document setting out or summarizing the evidence given to the court that made the provisional order.

(3) Return to Attorney General — Where documents have been sent to a court pursuant to subsection (1) and the respondent apparently is outside the province and is not likely to return, the court shall send the documents to the Attorney General for that province, together with any available information respecting the location and circumstances of the respondent.

(4) Idem — On receipt of any documents and information sent pursuant to subsection (3), the Attorney General shall send the documents and information to the Attorney General for the province of the court that made the provisional order.

(5) Right of respondent — In a proceeding under this section, the respondent may raise any matter that might have been raised before the court that made the provisional order.

(6) Further evidence — Where, in a proceeding under this section, the respondent satisfies the court that for the purpose of taking further evidence or for any other purpose it is necessary to remit the matter back to the court that made the provisional order, the court may so remit the matter and adjourn the proceeding for that purpose.

(7) Order of confirmation or refusal — Subject to subsection (7.1), at the conclusion of a proceeding under this section, the court shall make an order

    (a) confirming the provisional order without variation;

    (b) confirming the provisional order with variation; or

    (c) refusing confirmation of the provisional order.

(7.1) Guidelines apply — A court making an order under subsection (7) in respect of a child support order shall do so in accordance with the applicable guidelines.

(8) Further evidence — The court, before making an order confirming the provisional order with variation or an order refusing confirmation of the provisional order, shall decide whether to remit the matter back for further evidence to the court that made the provisional order.

(9) Interim order for support of children — Where a court remits a matter pursuant to this section in relation to a child support order, the court may, pending the making of an order under subsection (7), make an interim order in accordance with the applicable guidelines requiring a spouse to pay for the support of any or all children of the marriage.

(9.1) Interim order for support of spouse — Where a court remits a matter pursuant to this section in relation to a spousal support order, the court may make an interim order requiring a spouse to secure or pay, or to secure and pay, such lump sum or periodic sums, or such lump sum and periodic sums, as the court thinks reasonable for the support of the other spouse, pending the making of an order under subsection (7).

(10) Terms and conditions — The court may make an order under subsection (9) or (9.1) for a definite or indefinite period or until a specified event occurs, and may impose terms, conditions or restrictions in connection with the order as it thinks fit and just.

(11) Provisions applicable — Subsection 17(4), (4.1) and (6) to (7) apply, with such modifications as the circumstances require, in respect of an order made under subsection (9) or (9.1) as if it were a variation order referred to in those subsections.

(12) Report and filing — On making an order under subsection (7), the court in a province shall

    (a) send a copy of the order, certified by a judge or officer of the court, to the Attorney General for that province, to the court that made the provisional order and, where that court is not the court that made the support order in respect of which the provisional order was made, to the court that made the support order;

    (b) where an order is made confirming the provisional order with or without variation, file the order in the court; and

(c) where an order is made confirming the provisional order with variation or refusing confirmation of the provisional order, give written reasons to the Attorney General for that province and to the court that made the provisional order.

1993, c. 8, s. 4; 1997, c. 1, s. 7

20. (1) Definition of court — In this section, "court", in respect of a province, has the meaning assigned by subsection 2(1) and includes such other court having jurisdiction in the province as is designated by the Lieutenant Governor in Council of the province as a court for the purposes of this section.

(2) Legal effect throughout Canada — Subject to subsection 18(2), an order made under any of sections 15.1 to 17 or subsection 19(7), (9) or (9.1) has legal effect throughout Canada.

(3) Enforcement — An order that has legal effect throughout Canada pursuant to subsection (2) may be

(a) registered in any court in a province and enforced in like manner as an order of that court; or

(b) enforced in a province in any other manner provided for by the laws of that province, including its laws respecting reciprocal enforcement between the province and a jurisdiction outside Canada.

(4) Variation of orders — Notwithstanding subsection (3), a court may only vary an order that has legal effect throughout Canada pursuant to subsection (2) in accordance with this Act.

1997, c. 1, s. 8

20.1 (1) Assignment of order — A support order may be assigned to

(a) any minister of the Crown for Canada designated by the Governor in Council;

(b) any minister of the Crown for a province, or any agency in a province, designated by the Lieutenant Governor in Council of the province;

(c) any member of the Council of the Yukon Territory, or any agency in the Yukon Territory, designated by the Commissioner of the Yukon Territory;

Proposed Amendment — 20.1(1)(c)

(c) any member of the Legislative Assembly of Yukon, or any agency in Yukon, designated by the Commissioner of Yukon;

2002, c. 7, s. 160 [Not in force at date of publication.]

(d) any member of the Council of the Northwest Territories, or any agency in the Northwest Territories, designated by the Commissioner of the Northwest Territories; or

(e) any member of the Legislative Assembly of Nunavut, or any agency in Nunavut, designated by the Commissioner of Nunavut.

(2) Rights — A minister, member or agency referred to in subsection (1) to whom an order is assigned is entitled to the payments due under the order, and has the same right to be notified of, and to participate in, proceedings under this Act to vary, rescind, suspend or enforce the order as the person who would otherwise be entitled to the payments.

1993, c. 28, s. 78 (Sched. III, item 43.1) [As enacted by 1998, c. 15, s. 23.]; 1997, c. 1, s. 9

Appeals

21. (1) Appeal to appellate court — Subject to subsections (2) and (3), an appeal lies to the appellate court from any judgment or order, whether final or interim, rendered or made by a court under this Act.

(2) Restriction on divorce appeals — No appeal lies from a judgment granting a divorce on or after the day on which the divorce takes effect.

(3) Restriction on order appeals — No appeal lies from an order made under this Act more than thirty days after the day on which the order was made.

(4) Extension — An appellate court or a judge thereof may, on special grounds, either before or after the expiration of the time fixed by subsection (3) for instituting an appeal, by order extend that time.

(5) Powers of appellate court — The appellate court may

(a) dismiss the appeal; or

(b) allow the appeal and

(i) render the judgment or make the order that ought to have been rendered or made, including such order or such further or other order as it deems just, or

(ii) order a new hearing where it deems it necessary to do so to correct a substantial wrong or miscarriage of justice.

(6) Procedure on appeals — Except as otherwise provided by this Act or the rules or regulations, an appeal under this section shall be asserted, heard and decided according to the ordinary procedure governing appeals to the appellate court from the court rendering the judgment or making the order being appealed.

General

21.1 (1) Definition of "spouse" — In this section, "spouse" has the meaning assigned by subsection 2(1) and includes a former spouse.

(2) Affidavit re removal of barriers to religious remarriage — In any proceedings under this Act, a spouse (in this section referred to as the "deponent") may serve on the other spouse and file with the court an affidavit indicating

(a) that the other spouse is the spouse of the deponent;

(b) the date and place of the marriage, and the official character of the person who solemnized the marriage;

(c) the nature of any barriers to the remarriage of the deponent within the deponent's religion the removal of which is within the other spouse's control;

(d) where there are any barriers to the remarriage of the other spouse within the other spouse's religion the removal of which is within the deponent's control, that the deponent

(i) has removed those barriers, and the date and circumstances of that removal, or

(ii) has signified a willingness to remove those barriers, and the date and circumstances of that signification;

(e) that the deponent has, in writing, requested the other spouse to remove all of the barriers to the remarriage of the deponent within the deponent's religion the removal of which is within the other spouse's control;

(f) the date of the request described in paragraph (e); and

(g) that the other spouse, despite the request described in paragraph (e), has failed to remove all of the barriers referred to in that paragraph.

(3) Powers of court where barriers not removed — Where a spouse who has been served with an affidavit under subsection (2) does not

(a) within fifteen days after that affidavit is filed with the court or within such longer period as the court allows, serve on the deponent and file with the court an affidavit indicating that all of the barriers referred to in paragraph (2)(e) have been removed, and

(b) satisfy the court, in any additional manner that the court may require, that all of the barriers referred to in paragraph (2)(e) have been removed,

the court may, subject to any terms that the court considers appropriate,

(c) dismiss any application filed by that spouse under this Act, and

(d) strike out any other pleadings and affidavits filed by that spouse under this Act.

(4) Special case — Without limiting the generality of the court's discretion under subsection (3), the court may refuse to exercise its powers under paragraphs (3)(c) and (d) where a spouse who has been served with an affidavit under subsection (2)

(a) within fifteen days after that affidavit is filed with the court or within such longer period as the court allows, serves on the deponent and files with the court an affidavit indicating genuine grounds of a religious or conscientious nature for refusing to remove the barriers referred to in paragraph (2)(e); and

(b) satisfies the court, in any additional manner that the court may require, that the spouse has genuine grounds of a religious or conscientious nature for refusing to remove the barriers referred to in paragraph (2)(e).

(5) Affidavits — For the purposes of this section, an affidavit filed with the court by a spouse must, in order to be valid, indicate the date on which it was served on the other spouse.

(6) Where section does not apply — This section does not apply where the power to remove the barrier to religious remarriage lies with a religious body or official.

1990, c. 18, s. 2

22. (1) Recognition of foreign divorce — A divorce granted, on or after the coming into force of this Act, pursuant to a law of a country or subdivision of a country other than Canada by a tribunal or other authority having jurisdiction to do so shall be recognized for all purposes of determining the marital status in Canada of any person, if either former spouse was ordinarily resident in that country or subdivision for at least one year immediately preceding the commencement of proceedings for the divorce.

(2) Idem — A divorce granted, after July 1, 1968, pursuant to a law of a country or subdivision of a country other than Canada by a tribunal or other authority having jurisdiction to do so, on the basis of the domicile of the wife in that country or subdivision determined as if she were unmarried and, if she was a minor, as if she had attained the age of majority, shall be recognized for all purposes of determining the marital status in Canada of any person.

(3) Other recognition rules preserved — Nothing in this section abrogates or derogates from any other rule of law respecting the recognition of divorces granted otherwise than under this Act.

23. (1) Provincial laws of evidence — Subject to this or any other Act of Parliament, the laws of evidence of the province in which any proceedings under this Act are taken, including the laws of proof of service of any document, apply to such proceedings.

(2) Presumption — For the purposes of this section, where any proceedings are transferred to the Federal Court — Trial Division under subsection 3(3) or 5(3), the proceedings shall be deemed to have been taken in the province specified in the direction of the Court to be the province with which both spouses or former spouses, as the case may be, are or have been most substantially connected.

Proposed Amendment — 23(2)

(2) Presumption — For the purposes of this section, where any proceedings are transferred to the Federal Court under subsection 3(3) or 5(3), the proceedings shall be deemed to have been taken in the province specified in the direction of the Court to be the province with which both spouses or former spouses, as the case may be, are or have been most substantially connected.

2002, c. 8, s. 183(1)(i) [Not in force at date of publication.]

---

24. Proof of signature or office — A document offered in a proceeding under this Act that purports to be certified or sworn by a judge or an officer of a court shall, unless the contrary is proved, be proof of the appointment, signature or authority of the judge or officer and, in the case of a document purporting to be sworn, of the appointment, signature or authority of the person before whom the document purports to be sworn.

25. (1) Definition of "competent authority" — In this section, **"competent authority"**, in respect of a court, or appellate court, in a province means the body, person or group of persons ordinarily competent under the laws of that province to make rules regulating the practice and procedure in that court.

(2) Rules — Subject to subsection (3), the competent authority may make rules applicable to any proceedings under this Act in a court, or appellate court, in a province, including, without limiting the generality of the foregoing, rules

    (a) regulating the practice and procedure in the court, including the addition of persons as parties to the proceedings;

    (b) respecting the conduct and disposition of any proceedings under this Act without an oral hearing;

    (b.1) respecting the application of section 17.1 in respect of proceedings for a variation order;

    (c) regulating the sittings of the court;

    (d) respecting the fixing and awarding of costs;

    (e) prescribing and regulating the duties of officers of the court;

    (f) respecting the transfer of proceedings under this Act to or from the court; and

    (g) prescribing and regulating any other matter considered expedient to attain the ends of justice and carry into effect the purposes and provisions of this Act.

(3) Exercise of power — The power to make rules for a court or appellate court conferred by subsection (2) on a competent authority shall be exercised in the like manner and subject to the like terms and conditions, if any, as the power to make rules for that court conferred on that authority by the laws of the province.

(4) Not statutory instruments — Rules made pursuant to this section by a competent authority that is not a judicial or quasi-judicial body shall be deemed not to be statutory instruments within the meaning and for the purposes of the *Statutory Instruments Act*.

1993, c. 8, s. 5

25.1 (1) Agreements with provinces — With the approval of the Governor in Council, the Minister of Justice may, on behalf of the Government of Canada, enter into an agreement with a province authorizing a provincial child support service designated in the agreement to

(a) assist courts in the province in the determination of the amount of child support; and

(b) recalculate, at regular intervals, in accordance with the applicable guidelines, the amount of child support orders on the basis of updated income information.

(2) Effect of recalculation — Subject to subsection (5), the amount of a child support order as recalculated pursuant to this section shall for all purposes be deemed to be the amount payable under the child support order.

(3) Liability — The former spouse against whom a child support order was made becomes liable to pay the amount as recalculated pursuant to this section thirty-one days after both former spouses to whom the order relates are notified of the recalculation in the manner provided for in the agreement authorizing the recalculation.

(4) Right to vary — Where either or both former spouses to whom a child support order relates do not agree with the amount of the order as recalculated pursuant to this section, either former spouse may, within thirty days after both former spouses are notified of the recalculation in the manner provided for in the agreement authorizing the recalculation, apply to a court of competent jurisdiction for an order under subsection 17(1).

(5) Effect of application — Where an application is made under subsection (4), the operation of subsection (3) is suspended pending the determination of the application, and the child support order continues in effect.

(6) Withdrawal of application — Where an application made under subsection (4) is withdrawn before the determination of the application, the former spouse against whom the order was made becomes liable to pay the amount as recalculated pursuant to this section on the day on which the former spouse would have become liable had the application not been made.

1997, c. 1, s. 10

26. (1) Regulations — The Governor in Council may make regulations for carrying the purposes and provisions of this Act into effect and, without limiting the generality of the foregoing, may make regulations

(a) respecting the establishment and operation of a central registry of divorce proceedings in Canada; and

(b) providing for uniformity in the rules made pursuant to section 25.

(2) Regulations prevail — Any regulations made pursuant to subsection (1) to provide for uniformity in the rules prevail over those rules.

26.1 (1) Guidelines — The Governor in Council may establish guidelines respecting the making of orders for child support, including, but without limiting the generality of the fore-going, guidelines

(a) respecting the way in which the amount of an order for child support is to be determined;

(b) respecting the circumstances in which discretion may be exercised in the making of an order for child support;

(c) authorizing a court to require that the amount payable under an order for child support be paid in periodic payments, in a lump sum or in a lump sum and periodic payments;

(d) authorizing a court to require that the amount payable under an order for child support be paid or secured, or paid and secured, in the manner specified in the order;

(e) respecting the circumstances that give rise to the making of a variation order in respect of a child support order;

(f) respecting the determination of income for the purposes of the application of the guidelines;

(g) authorizing a court to impute income for the purposes of the application of the guidelines; and

(h) respecting the production of income information and providing for sanctions when that information is not provided.

(2) The guidelines shall be based on the principle that spouses have a joint financial obligation to maintain the children of the marriage in accordance with their relative abilities to contribute to the performance of that obligation.

(3) Definition of "order for child support" — In subsection (1) **"order for child support"** means

(a) an order or interim order made under section 15.1;

(b) a variation order in respect of a child support order; or

(c) an order or an interim order made under section 19.

1997, c. 1, s. 11

27. (1) Fees — The Governor in Council may, by order, authorize the Minister of Justice to prescribe a fee to be paid by any person to whom a service is provided under this Act or the regulations.

(2) Agreements — The Minister of Justice may, with the approval of the Governor in Council, enter into an agreement with the government of any province respecting the collection and remittance of any fees prescribed pursuant to subsection (1).

28. Review and report — The Minister of Justice shall undertake a comprehensive review of the provisions and operation of the Federal Child Support Guidelines and the determination of child support under this Act and shall cause a report on the review to be laid before each House of Parliament within five years after the coming into force of this section.

1997, c. 1, s. 12

29. [Repealed 1997, c. 1, s. 12.]

30. [Repealed 1997, c. 1, s. 12.]

31. [Repealed 1997, c. 1, s. 12.]

Transitional Provisions

32. Proceedings based on facts arising before commencement of Act — Proceedings may be commenced under this Act notwithstanding that the material facts or circumstances giving rise to the proceedings or to jurisdiction over the proceedings occurred wholly or partly before the day on which this Act comes into force.

Divorce Act, R.S. 1970, c. D-8

33. Proceedings commenced before commencement of Act — Proceedings commenced under the *Divorce Act*, chapter D-8 of the Revised Statutes of Canada, 1970, before the day on which this Act comes into force and not finally disposed of before that day shall be dealt with and disposed of in accordance with that Act as it read immediately before that day, as though it had not been repealed.

1997, c. 1, s. 13

34. (1) Variation and enforcement of orders previously made — Subject to subsection (1.1), any order made under subsection 11(1) of the *Divorce Act*, chapter D-8 of the Revised Statutes of Canada, 1970, including any order made pursuant to section 33 of this Act, and any order to the like effect made corollary to a decree of divorce granted in Canada before July 2, 1968 or granted on or after that day pursuant to subsection 22(2) of that Act may be varied, rescinded, suspended or enforced in accordance with sections 17 to 20, other than subsection 17(10), of this Act as if

(a) the order were a support order or custody order, as the case may be; and

(b) in subsections 17(4), (4.1) and (5), the words **"or the last order made under subsection 11(2) of the *Divorce Act*, chapter D-8 of the Revised Statutes of Canada, 1970, varying that order"** were added immediately before the words **"or the last variation order made in respect of that order"**.

(1.1) Combined orders — Where an application is made under subsection 17(1) to vary an order referred to in subsection (1) that provides a single amount of money for the combined support of one or more children and a former spouse, the court shall rescind the order and treat the application as an application for a child support order and an application for a spousal support order.

(2) Enforcement of interim orders — Any order made under section 10 of the *Divorce Act*, chapter D-8 of the Revised Statutes of Canada, 1970, including any order made pursuant to section 33 of this Act, may be enforced in accordance with section 20 of this Act as if it were an order made under subsection 15.1(1) or 15.2(1) or section 16 of this Act, as the case may be.

(3) Assignment of orders previously made — Any order for the maintenance of a spouse or child of the marriage made under section 10 or 11 of the *Divorce Act*, chapter D-8 of the Revised Statutes of Canada, 1970, including any order made pursuant to section 33 of this Act, and any order to the like effect made corollary to a decree of divorce granted in Canada before July 2, 1968 or granted on or after that day pursuant to subsection 22(2) of that Act may be assigned to any minister, member or agency designated pursuant to section 20.1

1997, c. 1, s. 14

35. Procedural laws continued — The rules and regulations made under the *Divorce Act*, chapter D-8 of the Revised Statutes of Canada, 1970, and the provisions of any other law or of any rule, regulation or other instrument made thereunder respecting any matter in relation to which rules may be made under subsection 25(2) that were in force in Canada or any province immediately before the day on which this Act comes into force and that are not inconsistent with this Act continue in force as though made or enacted by or under this Act until they are repealed or altered by rules or regulations made under this Act or are, by virtue of the making of rules or regulations under this Act, rendered inconsistent with those rules or regulations.

Divorce Act, R.S. 1985, c. 3 (2nd Supp.)

35.1 (1) Variation and enforcement of support orders previously made — Subject to subsection (2), any support order made under this Act before the coming into force of this section may be varied, rescinded, suspended or enforced in accordance with sections 17 to 20 as if the support order were a child support order or a spousal support order, as the case may be.

(2) Combined orders — Where an application is made under subsection 17(1) to vary a support order made under this Act before the coming into force of this section that provides for the combined support of one or more children and a former spouse, the court shall rescind the order and treat the application as an application for a child support order and an application for a spousal support order.

(3) Assignment of orders previously made — Any support order made under this Act before the coming into force of this section may be assigned to any minister, member or agency designated pursuant to section 20.1

1997, c. 1, s. 15

Commencement

36 [1]**Commencement** — This Act shall come into force on a day to be fixed by proclamation.

---

[1][Note: Act in force June 1, 1986, *see* SI/86-70.]

CAN. REG. 86-547 — CENTRAL REGISTRY OF DIVORCE PROCEEDINGS FEE ORDER

made under the *Divorce Act, 1985*

Order prescribing the fee to be paid by any person to whom a service is provided under the central registry of divorce proceedings regulations

SOR/86-547

Divorce Regs

1. Short title — This Order may be cited as the *Central Registry of Divorce Proceedings Fee Order.*

2. (1) Fee — Subject to subsection (2), the fee to be paid by a person who files an application for divorce and in respect of whom a service is provided under section 5 of the *Central Registry of Divorce Proceedings Regulations* is $10 per application.

(2) No fee shall be paid by a person who receives legal aid from a province in respect of the person's application for divorce where, pursuant to the law of the province, payment by that person of the fees established by the province for filing an application for divorce is waived.

CAN. REG. 86-600 — CENTRAL REGISTRY OF DIVORCE PROCEEDINGS REGULATIONS

made under the *Divorce Act, 1985*

Regulations respecting the establishment and operation of a central registry of divorce proceedings in canada

SOR/86-600

1. Short title — These Regulations may be cited as the *Central Registry of Divorce Proceedings Regulations*.

2. Interpretation — In these Regulations,

"Act" means the *Divorce Act, 1985*; *(Loi)*

"application for divorce" means an application referred to in subsection 8(1) of the Act; *(demande de divorce)*

"central registry" means the central registry of divorce proceedings established under subsection 3(1); *(Bureau d'enregistrement)*

"registrar" means the chief administrative officer of a court and includes the registrar, prothonotary or clerk of the court; *(greffier)*

"registration form" means the registration of divorce proceeding form set out in the schedule. *(formulaire d'enregistrement)*

3. (1) Establishment of Central Registry — A central registry of divorce proceedings is hereby established and shall be located in the city of Ottawa in the Province of Ontario.

(2) A record of pending divorce proceedings in Canada shall be maintained in the central registry and shall consist of the information contained in the registration of divorce proceedings forms received at the central registry.

4. Operation of Central Registry — On the day that an application for divorce is filed, the registrar of the court in which the application is filed shall, on receipt of the fee prescribed in the *Central Registry of Divorce Proceedings Fee Order*

(a) assign to the application a number, to be known as a divorce registry number, that next follows in sequence the number assigned to the last preceding application for divorce filed in that court; and

(b) in respect of the application, complete Part I of the registration form and send it to the central registry.

5. (1) On receipt of Part I of a registration form sent pursuant to section 4, an officer of the central registry shall

(a) check if the divorce registry number of the form is in the numerical sequence and if not, advise the appropriate registrar thereof, in writing, and request that within seven days thereafter the central registry be

(i) informed of the reason for the lack of numerical sequence, or

(ii) provided with the missing form or forms; and

(b) enter the information contained in the registration form in the record referred to in subsection 3(2).

(2) Where the record referred to in subsection 3(2), indicates that two divorce proceedings are pending between the spouses referred to in a registration form, an officer of the central registry shall send written notification to that effect, including the information contained in the record in respect of those proceedings

(a) to the registrar of each court in which the applications for a divorce have been filed by the spouses, where the applications were not filed on the same day; or

(b) to the registrar of each court in which the applications for a divorce have been filed by the spouses and the Registry of the Federal Court, where the applications were filed on the same day.

(3) Where the record, referred to in subsection 3(2) indicates that no other divorce proceedings are pending between the spouses referred to in a registration form, an officer of the central registry shall send written notification to that effect to the registrar of the court in which the application for divorce has been filed.

(4) A notification referred to in subsections (2) and (3) may be in the form of an endorsement on the relevant registration form or a separate notice.

6. On receipt of a notification pursuant to subsection 5(2) or (3), a registrar of a court shall

(a) place the notification with the relevant application for divorce; and

(b) where two divorce proceedings are pending between the spouses referred to in the notification, inform the spouse who filed the application for divorce in the court of the other application.

7. Within seven days after the discontinuance of a divorce proceeding or the taking effect of the dismissal or judgment in respect of a divorce proceeding, the appropriate registrar shall complete Part II of the relevant registration form and send it to the central registry.

8. On receipt of Part II of a registration form sent pursuant to section 7, an officer of the central registry shall enter the information contained in the form in the record referred to in subsection 3(2).

SCHEDULE [1]

(Sections 4, 5, 7 and 8)

Schedule Sections 4, 5, 7 and 8 — Registration of Divorce Proceeding Form

| SCHEDULE
(Sections 4, 5, 7 and 8)
GOVERNMENT OF CANADA
**REGISTRATION OF DIVORCE
PROCEEDING FORM**
(The Divorce Act, 1985) | ANNEXE
(articles 4, 5, 7 et 8)
GOUVERNEMENT DU CANADA
**FORMULAIRE D'ENREGISTREMENT
D'UNE ACTION EN DIVORCE**
(Loi de 1985 sur le divorce) |

Canada

PART I – PARTIE I

THIS COPY IS TO BE COMPLETED AND SENT TO THE CENTRAL REGISTRY OF DIVORCE PROCEEDINGS, OTTAWA, ON THE DAY THE APPLICATION IS FILED.
À REMPLIR ET À TRANSMETTRE AU BUREAU D'ENREGISTREMENT DES ACTIONS EN DIVORCE, À OTTAWA, LE JOUR MÊME DU DÉPÔT DE LA DEMANDE DE DIVORCE.

Court No / N° du tribunal   Divorce Registry No / N° d'enregistrement

1. PLACE AND PROVINCE APPLICATION FILED
LIEU ET PROVINCE DU DÉPÔT DE LA DEMANDE

2. DATE APPLICATION FILED
DATE DU DÉPÔT DE LA DEMANDE   Day / Jour   Month / Mois   19

3. APPLICANT(S) / DEMANDE DEPOSÉE PAR
1 ☐ Husband / Mari   2 ☐ Wife / Femme   3 ☐ Joint / Les deux

	HUSBAND – MARI	WIFE – FEMME
4. FULL NAMES NOM (print or type) (dactylographier ou écrire en lettres moulées)	Surname / Nom Given name(s) / Prénom(s)	Maiden Surname / Nom de jeune fille Given name(s) / Prénom(s)
5. DATE OF BIRTH DATE DE NAISSANCE	Day / Jour Month / Mois 19	Day / Jour Month / Mois 19
6. MARITAL STATUS AT TIME OF MARRIAGE ÉTAT MATRIMONIAL LORS DU MARIAGE	1 ☐ Never married / Jamais marié 2 ☐ Widowed / Veuf 3 ☐ Divorced / Divorcé	1 ☐ Never married / Jamais mariée 2 ☐ Widowed / Veuve 3 ☐ Divorced / Divorcée

7. DATE OF MARRIAGE
DATE DU MARIAGE   Day / Jour   Month / Mois   19

8. MARRIAGE BREAKDOWN BY REASON OF
FAIT ÉTABLISSANT L'ÉCHEC DU MARIAGE
1 ☐ Separation for not less than 1 year / Séparation d'au moins 1 an
2 ☐ Adultery / Adultère
3 ☐ Physical cruelty / Cruauté physique
4 ☐ Mental cruelty / Cruauté mentale

Signature of registrar
Signature du greffier   Day / Jour   Month / Mois   19

PART II – PARTIE II

THIS COPY IS TO BE COMPLETED AND SENT TO THE CENTRAL REGISTRY OF DIVORCE PROCEEDINGS, OTTAWA, WITHIN 7 DAYS AFTER A DIVORCE PROCEEDING IS DISCONTINUED OR WITHIN 7 DAYS AFTER THE TAKING EFFECT OF THE DISMISSAL OF A DIVORCE PROCEEDING OR A JUDGMENT RENDERED IN RESPECT OF A DIVORCE PROCEEDING.
À REMPLIR ET À TRANSMETTRE AU BUREAU D'ENREGISTREMENT DES ACTIONS EN DIVORCE, À OTTAWA, DANS LES 7 JOURS QUI SUIVENT L'ABANDON D'UNE ACTION EN DIVORCE OU LA PRISE D'EFFET DU REJET OU DU JUGEMENT CONCERNANT UNE ACTION EN DIVORCE.

9. 1 ☐ ANSWER FILED / DÉFENSE DÉPOSÉE   2 ☐ NOT FILED / NON DÉPOSÉE

10. 1 ☐ NOTICE OF DISCONTINUANCE / AVIS D'ABANDON   2 ☐ INFORMAL DISCONTINUANCE / ABANDON INFORMEL   DATE   Day / Jour   Month / Mois   19

11. 1 ☐ DIVORCE WITHOUT A HEARING / DIVORCE SANS AUDITION   2 ☐ UNCONTESTED HEARING / DEMANDE NON CONTESTÉE   3 ☐ CONTESTED HEARING / DEMANDE CONTESTÉE

12. 1 ☐ APPLICATION DISMISSED / DEMANDE REJETÉE   2 ☐ DIVORCE NOT GRANTED / DIVORCE NON ACCORDÉ   3 ☐ DIVORCE GRANTED / DIVORCE ACCORDÉ ▶ Date divorce took effect – Date où le divorce a pris effet   Day / Jour   Month / Mois   19

13. 1 ☐ CHILDREN OF THE MARRIAGE / ENFANTS À CHARGE   2 ☐ NO CHILDREN OF THE MARRIAGE / AUCUN ENFANT À CHARGE

14. 1 ☐ CUSTODY ORDER / ORDONNANCE DE GARDE   2 ☐ NO CUSTODY ORDER / AUCUNE ORDONNANCE DE GARDE

CUSTODY GRANTED TO. GARDE ACCORDÉE	BIRTHDATES OF THE CHILDREN OF THE MARRIAGE – DATE DE NAISSANCE DE CHACUN DES ENFANTS À CHARGE (Day, Month, Year) (Jour, Mois, Année)
THE HUSBAND / AU MARI	
THE WIFE / À LA FEMME	
THE HUSBAND AND WIFE, JOINTLY / AU MARI ET À LA FEMME, CONJOINTEMENT	
TO A PERSON OTHER THAN THE HUSBAND OR THE WIFE / À UNE PERSONNE AUTRE QUE LE MARI OU LA FEMME	

Signature of registrar
Signature du greffier   Day / Jour   Month / Mois   19

IIIC-388 (05/24)

CAN. REG. 97-175 — FEDERAL CHILD SUPPORT GUIDELINES

made under the *Divorce Act*

SOR/97-175, as am. SOR/97-563; SOR/99-136; SOR/2000-337; SOR/2000-390 (Fr.); SOR/2001-292.

Federal Child Support Guidelines

Objectives

1. Objectives — The objectives of these Guidelines are

(a) to establish a fair standard of support for children that ensures that they continue to benefit from the financial means of both spouses after separation;

(b) to reduce conflict and tension between spouses by making the calculation of child support orders more objective;

(c) to improve the efficiency of the legal process by giving courts and spouses guidance in setting the levels of child support orders and encouraging settlement; and

(d) to ensure consistent treatment of spouses and children who are in similar circumstances.

Interpretation

2. (1) Definitions — The definitions in this subsection apply in these Guidelines.

"Act" means the *Divorce Act*.

"child" means a child of the marriage.

"income" means the annual income determined under sections 15 to 20.

"order assignee" means a minister, member or agency referred to in subsection 20.1(1) of the Act to whom a child support order is assigned in accordance with that subsection.

"spouse" has the meaning assigned by subsection 2(1) of the Act, and includes a former spouse.

"table" means a federal child support table set out in Schedule I.

(2) Income Tax Act — Words and expressions that are used in sections 15 to 21 and that are not defined in this section have the meanings assigned to them under the *Income Tax Act*.

(3) Most current information — Where, for the purposes of these Guidelines, any amount is determined on the basis of specified information, the most current information must be used.

(4) Application of Guidelines — In addition to child support orders, these Guidelines apply, with such modifications as the circumstances require, to

(a) interim orders under subsections 15.1(2) and 19(9) of the Act;

(b) orders varying a child support order;

(c) orders referred to in subsection 19(7) of the Act; and

(d) recalculations under paragraph 25.1(1)(b) of the Act.

(5) Recalculations — For greater certainty, the provisions of these Guidelines that confer a discretionary power on a court do not apply to recalculations under paragraph 25.1(1)(b) of the Act by a provincial child support service.

Amount of Child Support

3. (1) Presumptive rule — Unless otherwise provided under these Guidelines, the amount of a child support order for children under the age of majority is

(a) the amount set out in the applicable table, according to the number of children under the age of majority to whom the order relates and the income of the spouse against whom the order is sought; and

(b) the amount, if any, determined under section 7.

(2) Child the age of majority or over — Unless otherwise provided under these Guidelines, where a child to whom a child support order relates is the age of majority or over, the amount of the child support order is

(a) the amount determined by applying these Guidelines as if the child were under the age of majority; or

(b) if the court considers that approach to be inappropriate, the amount that it considers appropriate, having regard to the condition, means, needs and other circumstances of the child and the financial ability of each spouse to contribute to the support of the child.

(3) Applicable table — The applicable table is

(a) if the spouse against whom an order is sought resides in Canada

(i) the table for the province in which that spouse ordinarily resides at the time the application for the child support order, or for a variation order in respect of a child support order, is made or the amount is to be recalculated under section 25.1 of the Act,

(ii) where the court is satisfied that the province in which that spouse ordinarily resides has changed since the time described in subparagraph (i), the table for the province in which the spouse ordinarily resides at the time of determining the amount of support, or

(iii) where the court is satisfied that, in the near future after determination of the amount of support, that spouse will ordinarily reside in a given province other than the province in which the spouse ordinarily resides at the time of that determination, the table for the given province; and

(b) if the spouse against whom an order is sought resides outside of Canada, or if the residence of that spouse is unknown, the table for the province where the other spouse ordinarily resides at the time the application for the child support order or for a variation order in respect of a child support order is made or the amount is to be recalculated under section 25.1 of the Act.

(SOR/97-563, s. 1)

4. Incomes over $150,000 — Where the income of the spouse against whom a child support order is sought is over $150,000, the amount of a child support order is

(a) the amount determined under section 3; or

(b) if the court considers that amount to be inappropriate,

(i) in respect of the first $150,000 of the spouse's income, the amount set out in the applicable table for the number of children under the age of majority to whom the order relates;

(ii) in respect of the balance of the spouse's income, the amount that the court considers appropriate, having regard to the condition, means, needs and other circumstances of the children who are entitled to support and the financial ability of each spouse to contribute to the support of the children; and

(iii) the amount, if any, determined under section 7.

5. Spouse in place of a parent — Where the spouse against whom a child support order is sought stands in the place of a parent for a child, the amount of a child support order is, in respect of that spouse, such amount as the court considers appropriate, having regard to these Guidelines and any other parent's legal duty to support the child.

6. Medical and dental insurance — In making a child support order, where medical or dental insurance coverage for the child is available to either spouse through his or her employer or otherwise at a reasonable rate, the court may order that coverage be acquired or continued.

7. (1) Special or extraordinary expenses — In a child support order the court may, on either spouse's request, provide for an amount to cover all or any portion of the following expenses, which expenses may be estimated, taking into account the necessity of the expense in relation to the child's best interests and the reasonableness of the expense in relation to the means of the spouses and those of the child and to the family's spending pattern prior to the separation:

(a) child care expenses incurred as a result of the custodial parent's employment, illness, disability or education or training for employment;

(b) that portion of the medical and dental insurance premiums attributable to the child;

(c) health-related expenses that exceed insurance reimbursement by at least $100 annually, including orthodontic treatment, professional counselling provided by a psychologist, social worker, psychiatrist or any other person, physiotherapy, occupational therapy, speech therapy and prescription drugs, hearing aids, glasses and contact lenses;

(d) extraordinary expenses for primary or secondary school education or for any other educational programs that meet the child's particular needs;

(e) expenses for post-secondary education; and

(f) extraordinary expenses for extracurricular activities.

Divorce Regs

(2) Sharing of expense — The guiding principle in determining the amount of an expense referred to in subsection (1) is that the expense is shared by the spouses in proportion to their respective incomes after deducting from the expense, the contribution, if any, from the child.

(3) Subsidies, tax deductions, etc. — In determining the amount of an expense referred to in subsection (1), the court must take into account any subsidies, benefits or income tax deductions or credits relating to the expense, and any eligibility to claim a subsidy, benefit or income tax deduction or credit relating to the expense.

SOR/2000-337, s. 1

8. Split custody — Where each spouse has custody of one or more children, the amount of a child support order is the difference between the amount that each spouse would otherwise pay if a child support order were sought against each of the spouses.

9. Shared custody — Where a spouse exercises a right of access to, or has physical custody of, a child for not less than 40 per cent of the time over the course of a year, the amount of the child support order must be determined by taking into account

> (a) the amounts set out in the applicable tables for each of the spouses;

> (b) the increased costs of shared custody arrangements; and

> (c) the conditions, means, needs and other circumstances of each spouse and of any child for whom support is sought.

10. (1) Undue hardship — On either spouse's application, a court may award an amount of child support that is different from the amount determined under any of sections 3 to 5, 8 or 9 if the court finds that the spouse making the request, or a child in respect of whom the request is made, would otherwise suffer undue hardship.

(2) Circumstances that may cause undue hardship — Circumstances that may cause a spouse or child to suffer undue hardship include the following:

> (a) the spouse has responsibility for an unusually high level of debts reasonably incurred to support the spouses and their children prior to the separation or to earn a living;

> (b) the spouse has unusually high expenses in relation to exercising access to a child;

> (c) the spouse has a legal duty under a judgment, order or written separation agreement to support any person;

> (d) the spouse has a legal duty to support a child, other than a child of the marriage, who is

> > (i) under the age of majority, or

> > (ii) the age of majority or over but is unable, by reason of illness, disability or other cause, to obtain the necessaries of life; and

> (e) the spouse has a legal duty to support any person who is unable to obtain the necessaries of life due to an illness or disability.

(3) Standards of living must be considered — Despite a determination of undue hardship under subsection (1), an application under that subsection must be denied by the court if it is of the opinion that the household of the spouse who claims undue hardship would, after determining the amount of child support under any of sections 3 to 5, 8 or 9, have a higher standard of living than the household of the other spouse.

(4) Standards of living test — In comparing standards of living for the purpose of subsection (3), the court may use the comparison of household standards of living test set out in Schedule II.

(5) Reasonable time — Where the court awards a different amount of child support under subsection (1), it may specify, in the child support order, a reasonable time for the satisfaction of any obligation arising from circumstances that cause undue hardship and the amount payable at the end of that time.

(6) Reasons — Where the court makes a child support order in a different amount under this section, it must record its reasons for doing so.

Elements of a Child Support Order

11. Form of payments — The court may require in a child support order that the amount payable under the order be paid in periodic payments, in a lump sum or in a lump sum and periodic payments.

12. Security — The court may require in the child support order that the amount payable under the order be paid or secured, or paid and secured, in the manner specified in the order.

13. Information to be specified in order — A child support must include the following information:

(a) the name and birth date of each child to whom the order relates;

(b) the income of any spouse whose income is used to determine the amount of the child support order;

(c) the amount determined under paragraph 3(1)(a) for the number of children to whom the order relates;

(d) the amount determined under paragraph 3(2)(b) for a child the age of majority or over;

(e) the particulars of any expense described in subsection 7(1), the child to whom the expense relates, and the amount of the expense or, where that amount cannot be determined, the proportion to be paid in relation to the expense; and

(f) the date on which the lump sum or first payment is payable and the day of the month or other time period on which all subsequent payments are to be made.

Variation of Child Support Orders

14. Circumstances for variation — For the purposes of subsection 17(4) of the Act, any one of the following constitutes a change of circumstances that gives rise to the making of a variation order in respect of a child support order:

(a) in the case where the amount of child support includes a determination made in accordance with the applicable table, any change in circumstances that would result in a different child support order or any provision thereof;

(b) in the case where the amount of child support does not include a determination made in accordance with a table, any change in the condition, means, needs or other circumstances of either spouse or of any child who is entitled to support; and

(c) in the case of an order made before May 1, 1997, the coming into force of section 15.1 of the Act, enacted by section 2 of chapter 1 of the Statutes of Canada, (1997).

(SOR/97-563, s. 2); SOR/2000-337, s. 2

Income

15. (1) Determination of annual income — Subject to subsection (2), a spouse's annual income is determined by the court in accordance with sections 16 to 20.

(2) Agreement — Where both spouses agree in writing on the annual income of a spouse, the court may consider that amount to be the spouse's income for the purposes of these Guidelines if the court thinks that the amount is reasonable having regard to the income information provided under section 21.

16. Calculation of annual income — Subject to sections 17 to 20, a spouse's annual income is determined using the sources of income set out under the heading "Total income" in the T1 General form issued by the Canada Customs and Revenue Agency and is adjusted in accordance with Schedule III.

SOR/2000-337, s. 3

17. (1) Pattern of income — If the court is of the opinion that the determination of a spouse's annual income under section 16 would not be the fairest determination of that income, the court may have regard to the spouse's income over the last three years and determine an amount that is fair and reasonable in light of any pattern of income, fluctuation in income or receipt of non-recurring amount during those years.

(2) Non-recurring losses — Where a spouse has incurred a non-recurring capital or business investment loss, the court may, if it is of the opinion that the determination of the spouse's annual income under section 16 would not provide the fairest determination of the annual income, choose not to apply sections 6 and 7 of Schedule III, and adjust the amount of the loss, including related expenses and carrying charges and interest expenses, to arrive at such amount as the court considers appropriate.

SOR/2000-337, s. 4

18. (1) Shareholder, director or officer — Where a spouse is a shareholder, director or officer of a corporation and the court is of the opinion that the amount of the spouse's annual income as determined under section 16 does not fairly reflect all the money available to the spouse for the payment of child support, the court may consider the situations described in section 17 and determine the spouse's annual income to include

(a) all or part of the pre-tax income of the corporation, and of any corporation that is related to that corporation, for the most recent taxation year; or

(b) an amount commensurate with the services that the spouse provides to the corporation, provided that the amount does not exceed the corporation's pre-tax income.

(2) Adjustment to corporation's pre-tax income — In determining the pre-tax income of a corporation for the purposes of subsection (1), all amounts paid by the corporation as salaries, wages or management fees, or other payments or benefits, to or on behalf of persons with whom the corporation does not deal at arm's length must be added to the pre-tax income, unless the spouse establishes that the payments were reasonable in the circumstances.

19. (1) Imputing income — The court may impute such amount of income to a spouse as it considers appropriate in the circumstances, which circumstances include the following:

(a) the spouse is intentionally under-employed or unemployed, other than where the under-employment or unemployment is required by the needs of a child of the marriage or any child under the age of majority or by the reasonable educational or health needs of the spouse;

(b) the spouse is exempt from paying federal or provincial income tax;

(c) the spouse lives in a country that has effective rates of income tax that are significantly lower than those in Canada;

(d) it appears that income has been diverted which would affect the level of child support to be determined under these Guidelines;

(e) the spouse's property is not reasonably utilized to generate income;

(f) the spouse has failed to provide income information when under a legal obligation to do so;

(g) the spouse unreasonably deducts expenses from income;

(h) the spouse derives a significant portion of income from dividends, capital gains or other sources that are taxed at a lower rate than employment or business income or that are exempt from tax; and

(i) the spouse is a beneficiary under a trust and is or will be in receipt of income or other benefits from the trust.

(2) Reasonableness of Expenses — For the purpose of paragraph (1)(g), the reasonableness of an expense deduction is not solely governed by whether the deduction is permitted under the *Income Tax Act*.

SOR/2000-337, s. 5

20. Non-resident — Where a spouse is a non-resident of Canada, the spouse's annual income is determined as though the spouse were a resident of Canada.

Income Information

21. (1) Obligation of applicant — A spouse who is applying for a child support order and whose income information is necessary to determine the amount of the order must include the following with the application:

(a) a copy of every personal income tax return filed by the spouse for each of the three most recent taxation years;

(b) a copy of every notice of assessment and re-assessment issued to the spouse for each of the three most recent taxation years;

(c) where the spouse is an employee, the most recent statement of earnings indicating the total earnings paid in the year to date, including overtime or, where such a statement is not provided by the employer, a letter from the spouse's employer setting out that information including the spouse's rate of annual salary or remuneration;

(d) where the spouse is self-employed, for the three most recent taxation years

(i) the financial statements of the spouse's business or professional practice, other than a partnership, and

Divore Regs

(ii) a statement showing a breakdown of all salaries, wages, management fees or other payments or benefits paid to, or on behalf of, persons or corporations with whom the spouse does not deal at arm's length;

(e) where the spouse is a partner in a partnership, confirmation of the spouse's income and draw from, and capital in, the partnership for its three most recent taxation years;

(f) where the spouse controls a corporation, for its three most recent taxation years

(i) the financial statements of the corporation and its subsidiaries, and

(ii) a statement showing a breakdown of all salaries, wages, management fees or other payments or benefits paid to, or on behalf of, persons or corporations with whom the corporation, and every related corporation, does not deal at arm's length;

(g) where the spouse is a beneficiary under a trust, a copy of the trust settlement agreement and copies of the trust's three most recent financial statements; and

(h) in addition to any income information that must be included under paragraphs (c) to (g), where the spouse receives income from employment insurance, social assistance, a pension, workers compensation, disability payments or any other source, the most recent statement of income indicating the total amount of income from the applicable source during the current year, or if such a statement is not provided, a letter from the appropriate authority stating the required information.

(2) Obligation of respondent — A spouse who is served with an application for a child support order and whose income information is necessary to determine the amount of the order, must, within 30 days after the application is served if the spouse resides in Canada or the United States or within 60 days if the spouse resides elsewhere, or such other time limit as the court specifies, provide the court, as well as the other spouse or the order assignee, as the case may be, with the documents referred to in subsection (1).

(3) Special expenses or undue hardship — Where, in the course of proceedings in respect of an application for a child support order, a spouse requests an amount to cover expenses referred to in subsection 7(1) or pleads undue hardship, the spouse who would be receiving the amount of child support must, within 30 days after the amount is sought or undue hardship is pleaded if the spouse resides in Canada or the United States or within 60 days if the spouse resides elsewhere, or such other time limit as the court specifies, provide the court and the other spouse with the documents referred to in subsection (1).

(4) Income over $ 150,000 — Where, in the course of proceedings in respect of an application for a child support order, it is established that the income of the spouse who would be paying the amount of child support is greater than $150,000, the other spouse must, within 30 days after the income is established to be greater than $150,000 if the other spouse resides in Canada or the United States or within 60 days if the other spouse resides elsewhere, or such other time limit as the court specifies, provide the court and the spouse with the documents referred to in subsection (1).

(5) Making of rules not precluded — Nothing in this section precludes the making of rules by a competent authority, within the meaning of section 25 of the Act, respecting the disclosure of income information that is considered necessary for the purposes of the determination of an amount of a child support order.

SOR/2000-337, s. 6

22. (1) Failure to comply — Where a spouse fails to comply with section 21, the other spouse may apply

(a) to have the application for a child support order set down for a hearing, or move for judgment; or

(b) for an order requiring the spouse who failed to comply to provide the court, as well as the other spouse or order assignee, as the case may be, with the required documents.

(2) Costs of the proceedings — Where a court makes an order under paragraph (1)(a) or (b), the court may award costs in favour of the other spouse up to an amount that fully compensates the other spouse for all costs incurred in the proceedings.

23. Adverse inference — Where the court proceeds to a hearing on the basis of an application under paragraph 22(1)(a), the court may draw an adverse inference against the spouse who failed to comply and impute income to that spouse in such amount as it considers appropriate.

24. Failure to comply with court order — Where a spouse fails to comply with an order issued on the basis of an application under paragraph 22(1)(b), the court may

(a) strike out any of the spouse's pleadings;

(b) make a contempt order against the spouse;

(c) proceed to a bearing, in the course of which it may draw an adverse inference against the spouse and impute income to that spouse in such amount as it considers appropriate; and

(d) award costs in favour of the other spouse up to an amount that fully compensates the other spouse for all costs incurred in the proceedings.

25. (1) Continuing obligation to provide income information — Every spouse against whom a child support order has been made must, on the written request of the other spouse or the order assignee, not more than once a year after the making of the order and as long as the child is a child within the meaning of these Guidelines, provide that other spouse or the order assignee with

(a) the documents referred to in subsection 21(1) for any of the three most recent taxation years for which the spouse has not previously provided the documents;

(b) as applicable, any current information, in writing, about the status of any expenses included in the order pursuant to subsection 7(1); and

(c) as applicable, any current information, in writing, about the circumstances relied on by the court in a determination of undue hardship.

(2) Below minimum income — Where a court has determined that the spouse against whom a child support order is sought does not have to pay child support because his or her income level is below the minimum amount required for application of the tables, that spouse must, on the written request of the other spouse, not more than once a year after the determination and as long as the child is a child within the meaning of these Guidelines, provide the other spouse with the documents referred to in subsection 21(1) for any of the three most recent taxation years for which the spouse has not previously provided the documents.

(3) Obligation of receiving spouse — Where the income information of the spouse in favour of whom a child support order is made is used to determine the amount of the order, the spouse must, not more than once a year after the making of the order and as long as the child is a child within the meaning of these Guidelines, on the written request of the other spouse, provide the other spouse with the documents and information referred to in subsection (1).

(4) Information requests — Where a spouse or an order assignee requests information from the other spouse under any of subsections (1) to (3) and the income information of the requesting spouse is used to determine the amount of the child support order, the requesting spouse or order assignee must include the documents and information referred to in subsection (1) with the request.

SOR/97-563, s. 3

(5) Time limit — A spouse who receives a request made under any of subsections (1) to (3) must provide the required documents within 30 days after the request's receipt if the spouse resides in Canada or the United States and within 60 days after the request's receipt if the spouse resides elsewhere.

(6) Deemed receipt — A request made under any of subsections (1) to (3) is deemed to have been received 10 days after it is sent.

(7) Failure to comply — A court may, on application by either spouse or an order assignee, where the other spouse has failed to comply with any of subsections (1) to (3)

(a) consider the other spouse to be in contempt of court and award costs in favour of the applicant up to an amount that fully compensates the applicant for all costs incurred in the proceedings; or

(b) make an order requiring the other spouse to provide the required documents to the court, as well as to the spouse or order assignee, as the case may be.

(8) Unenforceable provision — A provision in a judgment, order or agreement purporting to limit a spouse's obligation to provide documents under this section is unenforceable.

26. Provincial child support services — A spouse or an order assignee may appoint a provincial child support service to act on their behalf for the purposes of requesting and receiving income information under any of subsections 25(1) to (3), as well as for the purposes of an application under subsection 25(7).

Coming Into Force

27. Coming into force — These Guidelines come into force on May 1, 1997.

. . . . .

SCHEDULE II — COMPARISON OF HOUSEHOLD STANDARDS OF LIVING TEST
(Subsection 10(4))

1. Definitions — The definitions in this section apply in this Schedule.

"average tax rate" [Repealed SOR/2000-337, s. 7(1).]

"child" means a child of the marriage or a child who

(a) is under the age of majority; or

(b) is the age of majority or over but is unable, by reason of illness, disability or other cause to obtain the necessaries of life.

"household" means a spouse and any of the following persons residing with the spouse

(a) any person who has a legal duty to support the spouse or whom the spouse has a legal duty to support;

(b) any person who shares living expenses with the spouse or from whom the spouse otherwise receives an economic benefit as a result of living with that person, if the court considers it reasonable for that person to be considered part of the household; and

(c) any child whom the spouse or the person described in paragraph (a) or (b) has a legal duty to support.

"taxable income" means the annual taxable income determined using the calculations required to determine "Taxable Income" in the T1 General form issued by the Canada Customs and Revenue Agency.

SOR/97-563, s. 11; SOR/2000-337, s. 7

2. Test — The comparison of household standards of living test is as follows:

Step 1

Establish the annual income of each person in each household by applying the formula

$$A - B$$

where

A is the person's income determined under sections 15 to 20 of these Guidelines, and

B is the federal and provincial taxes payable on the person's taxable income.

Where the information on which to base the income determination is not provided, the court may impute income in the amount it considers appropriate.

Step 2

Adjust the annual income of each person in each household by

(a) deducting the following amounts, calculated on an annual basis:

(i) any amount relied on by the court as a factor that resulted in a determination of undue hardship, except any amount attributable to the support of a member of the household that is not incurred due to a disability or serious illness of that member,

(ii) the amount that would otherwise be payable by the person in respect of a child to whom the order relates, if the pleading of undue hardship was not made,

(A) under the applicable table, or

(B) as is considered by the court to be appropriate, where the court considers the table amount to be inappropriate,

(iii) any amount of support that is paid by the person under a judgment, order or written separation agreement, except

    (A) an amount already deducted under subparagraph (i), and

    (B) an amount paid by the person in respect of a child to whom the order referred to in subparagraph (ii) relates; and

SOR/97-563, s. 11

(b) adding the following amounts, calculated on an annual basis:

    (i) any amount that would otherwise be receivable by the person in respect of a child to whom the order relates, if the pleading of undue hardship was not made,

        (A) under the applicable table, or

        (B) as is considered by the court to be appropriate, where the court considers the table amount to be inappropriate,

        SOR/97-563, s. 11

    (ii) any amount of child support that the person has received for any child under a judgment, order or written separation agreement.

Step 3

Add the amounts of adjusted annual income for all the persons in each household to determine the total household income for each household.

Step 4

Determine the applicable low-income measures amount for each household based on the following:

(Low-income Measures)	
Household Size	**Low-income Measures Amount**
One person 1 adult	$10,382
Two persons	
2 adults	$14,535
1 adult and 1 child	$14,535
Three persons	
3 adults	$18,688
2 adults and 1 child	$17,649
1 adult and 2 children	$17,649
Four persons	
4 adults	$22,840
3 adults and 1 child	$21,802
2 adults and 2 children	$20,764
1 adult and 3 children	$20,764
Five persons	
5 adults	$26,993
4 adults and 1 child	$25,955
3 adults and 2 children	$24,917
2 adults and 3 children	$23,879
1 adult and 4 children	$23,879
Six persons	

(Low-income Measures)	
Household Size	**Low-income Measures Amount**
6 adults	$31,145
5 adults and 1 child	$30,108
4 adults and 2 children	$29,070
3 adults and 3 children	$28,031
2 adults and 4 children	$26,993
1 adult and 5 children	$26,993
Seven persons	
7 adults	$34,261
6 adults and 1 child	$33,222
5 adults and 2 children	$32,184
4 adults and 3 children	$31,146
3 adults and 4 children	$30,108
2 adults and 5 children	$29,070
1 adult and 6 children	$29,070
Eight persons	
8 adults	$38,413
7 adults and 1 child	$37,375
6 adults and 2 children	$36,337
5 adults and 3 children	$35,299
4 adults and 4 children	$34,261
3 adults and 5 children	$33,222
2 adults and 6 children	$32,184
1 adult and 7 children	$32,184

Divorce Regs

Step 5

Divide the household income amount (Step 3) by the low-income measures amount (Step 4) to get a household income ratio for each household.

Step 6

Compare the household income ratios. The household that has the higher ratio has the higher standard of living.

SCHEDULE III

(Section 16)

Adjustments to Income

1. Employment expenses — Where the spouse is an employee, the spouse's applicable employment expenses described in the following provisions of the *Income Tax Act* are deducted:

(a) [Repealed SOR/2000-337, s. 8(1).]

(b) paragraph 8(1)(d) concerning expenses of teacher's exchange fund contribution;

(c) paragraph 8(1)(e) concerning expenses of railway employees;

(d) paragraph 8(1)(f) concerning sales expenses;

299

(e) paragraph 8(1)(g) concerning transport employee's expenses;

(f) paragraph 8(1)(h) concerning travel expenses;

(f.1) paragraph 8(1)(h.1) concerning motor vehicle travel expenses;

(g) paragraph 8(1)(i) concerning dues and other expenses of performing duties;

(h) paragraph 8(1)(j) concerning motor vehicle and aircraft costs;

(i) paragraph 8(1)(l.1) concerning *Canada Pension Plan* contributions and *Employment Insurance Act* premiums paid in respect of another employee who acts as an assistant or substitute for the spouse;

(j) paragraph 8(1)(n) concerning salary reimbursement;

(k) paragraph 8(1)(o) concerning forfeited amounts;

(l) paragraph 8(1)(p) concerning musical instrument costs; and

(m) paragraph 8(1)(q) concerning artists' employment expenses.

SOR/97-563, s. 12; SOR/2000-337, s. 8

2. Child support — Deduct any child support received that is included to determine total income in the T1 General form issued by the Canada Customs and Revenue Agency.

SOR/97-563, s. 13; SOR/2000-337, s. 9

3. (1) Spousal support — To calculate income for the purpose of determining an amount under an applicable table, deduct the spousal support received from the other spouse.

(2) Special or extraordinary expenses — To calculate income for the purpose of determining an amount under section 7 of these Guidelines, deduct the spousal support paid to the other spouse.

4. Social assistance — Deduct any amount of social assistance income that is not attributable to the spouse.

SOR/2000-337, s. 10

5. Dividends from taxable Canadian corporations — Replace the taxable amount of dividends from taxable Canadian corporations received by the spouse by the actual amount of those dividends received by the spouse.

6. Capital gains and capital losses — Replace the taxable capital gains realized in a year by the spouse by the actual amount of capital gains realized by the spouse in excess of the spouse's actual capital losses in that year.

7. Business investment losses — Deduct the actual amount of business investment losses suffered by the spouse during the year.

8. Carrying charges — Deduct the spouse's carrying charges and interest expenses that are paid by the spouse and that would be deductible under the *Income Tax Act*.

9. Net self-employment income — Where the spouse's net self-employment income is determined by deducting an amount for salaries, benefits, wages or management fees, or other payments, paid to or on behalf of persons with whom the spouse does not deal at arm's length, include that amount, unless the spouse establishes that the payments were necessary to earn the self-employment income and were reasonable in the circumstances.

10. Additional amount — Where the spouse reports income from self-employment that, in accordance with sections 34.1 and 34.2 of the *Income Tax Act*, includes an additional amount earned in a prior period, deduct the amount earned in the prior period, net of reserves.

SOR/2000-337, s. 11

11. Capital cost allowance for property — Include the spouse's deduction for an allowable capital cost allowance with respect to real property.

12. Partnership income — Where the spouse earns income through a partnership or sole proprietorship, deduct any amount included in income that is properly required by the partnership or sole proprietorship for purposes of capitalization.

SOR/97-563, s. 14

13. (1) Employee stock options — Where the spouse has received, as an employee benefit, options to purchase shares of a Canadian-controlled private corporation, or a publicly traded corporation that is subject to the same tax treatment with reference to stock options as a Canadian-controlled private corporation, and has exercised those options during the year, add the difference between the value of the shares at the time the options are exercised and the amount paid by the spouse for the shares, and any amount paid by the spouse to acquire the options to purchase the shares, to the income for the year in which the options are exercised.

(2) Disposal of shares — If the spouse has disposed of the shares during a year, deduct from the income for that year the difference determined under subsection (1).

SOR/2000-337, s. 12; SOR/2001-292, s. 1

Divorce Regs

DOMESTIC VIOLENCE PROTECTION ACT, 2000

S.O. 2000, c. 33 [Not in force at date of publication.], as am. S.O. 2002, c. 18, Sched. A, s. 6.

1. (1) Definitions — In this Act,

"applicant" means an applicant for an intervention order or an emergency intervention order; *("requérant")*

"child" mans a person under the age of 18; *("enfant")*

"cohabit" means to live together in a conjugal relationship, whether within or outside marriage; *("cohabiter")*

"court" means the Superior Court of Justice; *("tribunal")*

"designated judge or justice" means a judge of the Ontario Court of Justice or justice of the peace designated under section 13; *("juge désigné")*

"prescribed" means prescribed by regulations made under this Act; *("prescrit")*

"relative" means any person related to another person by blood, marriage or adoption; *("parent")*

"residence" includes a residence that a person has vacated due to domestic violence; *("résidence")*

"respondent" means the respondent to an application for an intervention order or an emergency intervention order; *("intimé")*

"weapon" means weapon as defined in the *Criminal Code* Canada. *("arme")*

(2) Domestic violence — For the purposes of this Act, domestic violence means the following acts or omissions committed against an applicant's relative or any child:

1. An assault that consists of the intentional application of force that causes the applicant to fear for his or her safety, but does not include any act committed in self-defence.

2. An intentional or reckless act or omission that causes bodily harm or damage to property.

3. An act or omission or threatened act or omission that causes the applicant to fear for his or her safety.

4. Forced physical confinement, without lawful authority.

5. Sexual assault, sexual exploitation or sexual molestation, or the threat of sexual assault, sexual exploitation or sexual molestation.

6. A series of acts which collectively causes the applicant to fear for his or her safety, including following, contacting, communicating with, observing or recording any person.

(3) Same — Domestic violence may be found to have occurred for the purposes of this Act whether or not, in respect of any act or omission described in subsection (2), a charge has been laid or dismissed or withdrawn or a conviction has been or could be obtained.

2. (1) Applicants — Subject to subsection (2), the following persons may apply for an intervention order or an emergency intervention order:

1. A spouse or former spouse, within the meaning of Part III of the *Family Law Act*, of the respondent.

2. A same-sex partner or former same-sex partner, within the meaning of Part III of the *Family Law Act*, of the respondent.

3. A person who is cohabiting with the respondent, or who has cohabited with the respondent for any period of time, whether or not they are cohabiting at the time of the application.

4. A person who is or was in a dating relationship with the respondent.

5. A relative of the respondent who resides with the respondent.

(2) Age restriction — A person must be at least 16 years old to apply for, or be the respondent to an application for, an intervention order or an emergency intervention order.

3. (1) Intervention order — On application with notice to the respondent, the court may make a temporary or final intervention order if it is satisfied on a balance of probabilities that,

(a) domestic violence has occurred; and

(b) a person or property may be at risk of harm or damage.

2000, c. 33, s. 3(1)

(2) Content of order — An intervention order may contain any or all of the following provisions that the court considers appropriate in the circumstances for the protection of any person or property that may be at risk of harm or damage or for the assistance of the applicant or any child:

1. Restraining the respondent from attending at or near, or entering, any place that is attended regularly by the applicant, a relative of the applicant, any child or any other specified person, including a residence, property business, school or place of employment.

2. Restraining the respondent from engaging in any specified conduct that is threatening, annoying or harassing to the applicant, a relative of the applicant, any child or any other specified person.

3. Requiring the respondent to vacate the applicant's residence, either immediately or within a specified period of time.

4. Requiring a peace officer, within a specified period of time, to accompany the applicant, respondent or a specified person to the applicant's residence and supervise the removal of that person's or another named person's belongings.

5. Restraining the respondent from contacting or communicating with the applicant or any other specified person, directly or indirectly.

6. Restraining the respondent from following the applicant or any other specified person from place to place, or from being within a specified distance of the applicant or other specified person.

7. Requiring a peace officer to seize,

     i. any weapons where the weapons have been used or have been threatened to be used to commit domestic violence, and

     ii. any documents that authorize the respondent to own, possess or control a weapon described in subparagraph i.

8. Granting the applicant exclusive possession of the residence shared by the applicant and the respondent, regardless of ownership.

9. Requiring the respondent to pay the applicant compensation for monetary losses suffered by the applicant or any child as a direct result of the domestic violence, the amount of which may be summarily determined by the court, including loss of earnings or support, medical or dental expenses, out-of-pocket expenses for injuries sustained, moving and accommodation expenses and the costs, including legal fees, of an application under this Act.

10. Granting the applicant or respondent temporary possession and exclusive use of specified personal property.

11. Restraining the respondent from taking, converting, damaging or otherwise dealing with property in which the applicant has an interest.

12. Requiring the respondent to attend specified counselling.

13. Recommending that a child attend specified counselling at the respondent's expense.

(3) Other proceedings — An application under this section shall contain a summary of all previous and current court proceedings and orders affecting the applicant and respondent, including all applications and orders under this Act.

(4) Terms — Subject to subsection (5), any provision of an intervention order described in subsection (2) may be subject to such terms as the court considers appropriate, including a term that specifies the period of time for which the provision shall be in force.

(5) Same — A provision of an intervention order described in paragraph 7 of subsection (2) shall cease to be in force if an order or final determination with respect to the respondent's ownership, possession or control of weapon is made under the *Criminal Code* (Canada) or the *Firearms Act* (Canada)

(6) Enforcement — A provision of an intervention order described in paragraph 1, 2, 3, 4, 5, 6, 7 or 8 of subsection (2) shall be enforced by peace officers under the *Criminal Code* (Canada).

(7) Same — A provision of an intervention order described in paragraph 9, 10, 11, 12 or 13 of subsection (2) may be secured by a requirement that the respondent,

     (a) post a bond in the form and amount that the court considers appropriate; or

     (b) enter into a recognizance in a form acceptable to the court.

Domestic
Violence

4. (1) Emergency intervention order — On application, without notice to the respondent, the court or a designated judge or justice may make an emergency intervention order if the court or designated judge or justice is satisfied on a balance of probabilities that,

> (a) domestic violence has occurred;

> (b) a person or property is at risk of harm or damage; and

> (c) the matter must be dealt with on an urgent and temporary basis for the protection of the person or property that is at risk of harm or damage.

(2) Other proceedings — An application under this section shall contain a summary of all previous and current court proceedings and orders affecting the applicant and respondent, including all applications and orders under this Act.

(2.1) Use of telecommunication — An application to a designated judge or justice under subsection (1) may be made and adjudicated by telephone or by a means of telecommunication that produces a writing.

(2.2) Same — Despite any other Act, for the purposes of subsection (2.1),

> (a) evidence may be provided, under oath,

> > (i) by telephone, or

> > (ii) by a means of telecommunication that produces a writing; and

> (b) when evidence is provided as described in subclause (a)(i) or (ii), the oath may be administered by telephone.

(3) Contents of emergency intervention order — An emergency intervention order may only contain a provision that the court could include in an intervention order under paragraph 1, 2, 3, 4, 5, 6 or 7 of subsection 3(2) which the court or designated judge or justice considers appropriate in the circumstances for the urgent protection of a person or property that is at risk of harm or damage.

(4) Terms — Subject to subsection (5), any provision of an emergency intervention order may be subject to such terms as the court or designated judge or justice, as the case may be, considers appropriate, including a term that specifies the period of time for which the provision shall be in force.

(5) Same — A provision of an emergency intervention order described in paragraph 7 of subsection 3(2) shall cease to be in force if an order or final determination with respect to the respondent's ownership, possession or control of weapons is made under the *Criminal Code* (Canada) or the *Firearms Act* (Canada).

(6) Enforcement — A provision of an emergency intervention order shall be enforced by peace officers under the *Criminal Code* (Canada).

(7) Emergency intervention order prevails over civil orders — An emergency intervention order prevails over any order made under the *Children's Law Reform Act*, the *Divorce Act* (Canada) or the *Family Law Act* against or affecting the applicant or respondent or any child.

(8) Right to hearing — Every emergency intervention order shall,

> (a) advise the applicant and the respondent that they are entitled to a hearing before the court for the purpose of asking for the variation or termination of the emergency intervention order if either one requests a hearing within 30 days after the respondent is served with the order; and

(b) set out the procedures to be followed in order to make the request.

(9) Designated judge or justice's order sent to court for review — Upon making an emergency intervention order, a designated judge or justice shall promptly forward a copy of the order and all supporting documentation, including any reasons for the order, to the court.

2002, c. 18, Sched. A, s. 6(1)

4.1 (1) Emergency intervention orders available in designated locations according to prescribed schedules — In a location that is designated by a regulation made under clause 19(1)(b.1), a designated judge or justice shall be available to hear applications under section 4 on the basis of the schedule prescribed for that location under clause 19(1)(b.2).

(2) Purpose of subs. (1) — The purpose of subsection (1) is to facilitate proceeding in phases towards the goal of making emergency intervention orders available on a 24-hour a day basis seven days a week throughout Ontario.

2002, c. 18, Sched. A, s. 6(2)

5. (1) Request for hearing — Upon receiving a request for a hearing in respect of an emergency intervention order from the applicant or respondent within the required 30-day period, the clerk of the court shall set a date for the hearing of the matter, which shall be not later than 14 days after the date the court received the request for the hearing.

(2) Confirmation or order for hearing — If a request for a hearing in respect of an emergency intervention order made by a designated judge or justice is not made by the applicant or respondent within the required 30-day period, a judge of the court shall review the emergency intervention order and the supporting documentation, without holding a hearing, and,

    (a) shall confirm the order if he or she is satisfied that there was evidence before the designated judge or justice to support the granting of the order; or

    (b) shall order a hearing of the matter if the judge is not satisfied that there was evidence before the designated judge or justice to support the granting of the order or is not satisfied that the evidence before the designated judge or justice supported one or more of the provisions contained in the order.

(3) Notice of confirmation — If the judge confirms the emergency intervention order under clause (2)(a), the confirmed emergency intervention order shall be deemed, for all purposes, to be an intervention order made by the court and the clerk of the court shall notify the applicant and respondent of the confirmation.

(4) Notice of hearing under subs. (1) — If a date for a hearing of the matter is set under subsection (1), the clerk of the court shall notify the applicant and respondent of the date of the hearing.

(5) Notice of hearing under subs. (2) — If a hearing of the matter is ordered under subsection (2), the clerk of the court shall notify the applicant and respondent of the date of the hearing, which shall be not later than 14 days after the date of the order under subsection (2).

(6) If no request for hearing re court order — If no request is made within the required 30-day period in respect of an emergency intervention order made by the court, the emergency intervention order shall be deemed, for all purposes, to be an intervention order made by the court on the day after the expiry of the required 30-day period.

(7) Order not stayed by request for hearing — An emergency intervention order that is the subject of a request for a hearing by the applicant or respondent remains in force and is not stayed by the making of the request.

6. (1) Powers at court at hearing — At a hearing set or ordered under section 5, the court may confirm, vary or terminate the emergency intervention order and section 3, including paragraphs 8 to 13 of subsection 3(2), applies to the hearing and the order with necessary modifications.

(2) Same — A hearing under this section shall be a new hearing and, in addition to any new evidence brought before the court, the court shall consider the evidence that was before the designated judge or justice or court that made the emergency intervention order.

(3) Confirmed or varied order deemed to be court order — If the court confirms or varies the emergency intervention order, the confirmed or varied emergency intervention order shall be deemed, for all purposes, to be an intervention order made by the court.

7. (1) Service — An intervention order made by the court under section 3 or 6 shall be served on the respondent,

    (a) by a peace officer, if the court so directs;

    (b) by the applicant's counsel or agent;

    (c) by the court, if the applicant was unrepresented before the court; or

    (d) in any other prescribed manner.

(2) Same — An emergency intervention order shall be served on the respondent in the prescribed manner.

(3) Substituted service — If the court is satisfied at any time that service cannot be effected by a means described in subsection (1) or (2), it may make an order for substituted service on the respondent, whether or not any attempt has yet been made to serve the respondent.

(4) Same — If a designated judge or justice is satisfied at any time that service cannot be effected by a means described in subsection (2), he or she may make an order for substituted service on the respondent, whether or not any attempt has yet been made to serve the respondent.

(5) Sunday service — Despite section 124 of the *Courts of Justice Act*, an emergency intervention order may be served on a Sunday without leave of the court.

2002, c. 18, Sched. A, s. 6(3)

8. (1) Orders immediately effective — An intervention order and an emergency intervention order are effective immediately upon being made.

(2) Not enforceable without service or notice — Despite subsection (1), an intervention order or an emergency intervention order is not enforceable against the respondent unless the respondent,

    (a) has been served with the order; or

    (b) has received notice of the order.

9. (1) Motion to vary or terminate order — The applicant or respondent to an intervention order may make a motion to the court at any time, upon notice to the other party, to vary or terminate the order.

(2) Order to vary or terminate — If the court is satisfied, upon a motion under subsection (1), that there has been a material change in circumstances since the intervention order was made, the court may vary or terminate the order.

(3) Order not stayed by motion — The intervention order that is the subject of a motion under this section remains in force and is not stayed by the bringing of the motion.

10. (1) Civil orders to be considered — In a review of an emergency intervention order by a judge under subsection 5(2), at a hearing under section 6 or on a motion to vary or terminate an intervention order under section 9, the judge shall consider any outstanding orders made under the *Children's Law Reform Act* or the *Family Law Act* against or affecting the applicant or respondent or any child and may, if he or she considers it appropriate and if it is authorized under the Act under which each such order is made, vary, amend or rescind any of those orders under the Act under which it is made to the extent necessary in order to provide protection under an intervention order.

(2) Same — In a review of an emergency intervention order by a judge under subsection 5(2), at a hearing under section 6 or on a motion to vary or terminate an intervention order under section 9, the judge shall consider any outstanding orders made under the *Divorce Act*, (Canada) against or affecting the applicant or respondent or any child and may consider whether it would be appropriate under the *Divorce Act* (Canada) to vary, amend or rescind any of those orders.

11. Appeal — An appeal from an intervention order may be made to the Divisional Court.

12. (1) Property ownership not affected by order — Except as provided by paragraph 7 or 11 of subsection 3(2), an intervention order or an emergency intervention order does not in any manner affect the title to or an ownership interest in any real or personal property jointly held by the applicant and respondent or solely held by one of them.

(2) Exclusive possession of leased residence — Where a residence is leased by a respondent pursuant to an oral, written or implied agreement and an applicant who is to a party to the lease is granted exclusive possession of that residence as permitted by paragraph 8 of subsection 3(2), no landlord shall evict the applicant solely because the applicant is not a party to the lease.

(3) Same — On the request of an applicant mentioned in subsection (2), the landlord shall advise the applicant of the status of the lease and serve the applicant with notice of any claim against the respondent arising from the lease and the applicant, at his or her option, may assume the responsibilities of the respondent under the lease.

13. Designated judges, justices of the peace — The Chief Justice of the Ontario Court of Justice shall designate the judges of the Ontario Court of Justice and justices of the peace who may hear applications under section 4.

2002, c. 18, Sched. A, s. 6(4)

14. Protection from personal liability — No action or other proceeding shall be instituted against a peace officer, clerk of the court or any other person for any act done in good faith or for any alleged neglect or default in good faith, in the execution or intended execution of,

(a) the person's duty under this Act; or

(b) the person's duty to carry out the provisions of an order made under this Act.

15. No other rights of action affected — An application for an intervention order or an emergency intervention order under this Act is in addition to and does not diminish any existing right of action for the applicant or for any other victim of domestic violence.

16. (1) Prohibition — No person shall, in making an application or motion under this Act, commit perjury or public mischief within the meaning of the *Criminal Code* (Canada).

(2) Enforcement — Subsection (1) shall be enforced by peace officers under the *Criminal Code*.

17. (1) Rules of court — Subject to the approval of the Lieutenant Governor in Council, the Family Rules Committee may make rules under section 68 of the *Courts of Justice Act* in relation to the practice and procedure in proceedings under this Act, including rules,

(a) governing applications for intervention orders and emergency intervention orders;

(b) governing the procedures for requesting a hearing in respect of an emergency intervention order;

(c) governing the procedures for conducting a hearing described in clause (b);

(d) governing the service of any order made under this Act and any notice required to be given under this Act, but not prescribing a manner of serving intervention orders and emergency intervention orders for the purpose of section 7;

(e) prescribing the contents of intervention orders and emergency intervention orders;

(f) prescribing forms.

(2) Rules to provide expeditious access to judicial system — The rules of court applicable to the practice and procedure in proceedings under this Act shall be designed to provide applicants and respondents expeditious access to the judicial system.

(3) No fees for application, etc. — No fee may be prescribed under the *Administration of Justice Act* for any application, request or motion under this Act.

2002, c. 18, Sched. A, s. 6(5)

18. (1) Attorney General may require rules — The Attorney General may require that the Family Rules Committee make, amend or revoke a rule that it has the authority to make, amend or revoke, as described in section 17.

(2) Regulation may be made if rule is not — If the Family Rules Committee does not make, amend or revoke a rule as required by the Attorney General within 60 days after receiving the Attorney General's requirement in writing, the Lieutenant Governor in Council may make a regulation that carries out the intent of the Attorney General's requirement.

(3) Regulation prevails over rule — A regulation made under subsection (2) may amend or revoke a rule of court and, in the event of a conflict between a regulation made under subsection (2) and the rules of the court, the regulation prevails.

19. (1) Regulations — The Lieutenant Governor in Council may make regulations,

(a) respecting the seizure, retention, return or disposal of items required to be seized pursuant to a provision in an intervention order or an emergency intervention order described in paragraph 7 of subsection 3(2), including authorizing the court or a designated judge or justice to issue a warrant authorizing the entry and search of a dwelling or other place;

(b) governing methods of applying to a designated judge or justice for an emergency intervention order;

(b.1) designating locations for the purpose of section 4.1;

(b.2) prescribing a schedule for a location designated under clause (b.1);

(c) prescribing manners of serving intervention orders and emergency intervention orders for the purpose of section 7;

(d) requiring the court or a designated judge or justice to send a copy of an order made under this Act to any person specified by the regulations;

(e) respecting any matter that the Lieutenant Governor in Council considers necessary or advisable to carry out effectively the intent and purpose of this Act.

(2) Different application to different areas of Ontario — A regulation made under subsection 18(2) or subsection (1) may contain different rules, requirements and provisions for different areas of Ontario.

(3) Schedule — A schedule prescribed under clause (1)(b.2) may provide for availability on a 24-hour a day basis seven days a week or on any other basis.

2002, c. 18, Sched. A, s. 6(6), (7)

CONSEQUENTIAL AMENDMENTS

20. Courts of Justice Act — **(1)** The Schedule to section 21.8 of the *Courts of Justice Act*, as enacted by the Statutes of Ontario, 1994, chapter 12, section 8 and amended by 1996, chapter 31, section 65 and 1999, chapter 6, section 18, is amended by adding the following paragraph:

1.1 Proceedings under the *Domestic Violence Protection Act, 2000*, except for matters heard by designated judges or justices as that Act permits.

(2) Section 68 of the Act, as amended by the Statutes of Ontario, 1996, chapter 25, section 9 and 1998, chapter 20, Schedule a, section 22, is amended by adding the following subsection:

(5) Domestic Violence Protection Act, 2000 — Despite paragraph 1.1 of the Schedule to section 21.8, the rule-making authority of the Family Rules Committee extends to the entire *Domestic Violence Protection Act, 2000*, including the activities of designated judges and justices.

2002, c. 18, Sched. A, s. 6(8)

21. (1) Repeal of s. 35(2) of Children's Law Reform Act — Subsection 35(2) of the *Children's Law Reform Act* is repealed.

(2) Repeal of s. 35 of Children's Law Reform Act — Section 35 of the Act, as amended by subsection (1), is repealed.

(3) Transition — Despite the repeal of subsection 35(2) of the Act, any prosecution begun under that subsection before its repeal shall continue as if it were still in force.

(4) Same — Despite the repeal of section 35 of the Act,

(a) any proceedings begun under that section before its repeal shall continue as if section 35 were still in force; and

(b) any order made under section 35 before its repeal or pursuant to clause (a), after its repeal, remains in force until it terminates by its own terms or is rescinded or terminated by a court.

22. (1) Repeal of s. 46(2) of Family Law Act — Subsection 46(2) of the *Family Law Act* is repealed.

(2) Repeal of s. 46 of *Family Law Act* — Section 46 of the Act, as amended by the Statutes of Ontario, 1999, chapter 6, section 25 and by subsection (1) of this Act, is repealed.

(3) Transition — Despite the repeal of subsection 46(2) of the Act, any prosecution begun under that subsection before its repeal shall continue as if it were still in force.

(4) Same — Despite the repeal of section 46 of the Act,

(a) any proceeding begun under that section before its repeal shall continue as if section 46 were still in force; and

(b) any order made under section 46 before its repeal or pursuant to clause (a), after its repeal, remains in force until it terminates by its own terms or is rescinded or terminated by a court.

COMMENCEMENT AND SHORT TITLE

23. Commencement — This Act comes into force on a day to be named by proclamation of the Lieutenant Governor.

24. Short title — The short title of this Act is the *Domestic Violence Protection Act, 2000.*

EVIDENCE ACT

R.S.O. 1990, c. E.23, as am. S.O. 1993, c. 27, Sched.; 1995, c. 6, s. 6; 1996, c. 25, s. 5; 1998, c. 18, Sched. B, s. 7; 1998, c. 18, Sched. G, s. 50; 1999, c. 12, Sched. B, s. 7; 2000, c. 26, Sched. A, s. 7; 2001, c. 9, Sched. B, s. 8; 2002, c. 8, Sched. I, s. 10 [Not in force at date of publication.]; 2002, c. 17, Sched. F, s. 1; 2002, c. 18, Sched. A, s. 8 [Not in force at date of publication.].

. . . . .

8. (1) Evidence of parties — The parties to an action and the persons on whose behalf it is brought, instituted, opposed or defended are, except as hereinafter otherwise provided, competent and compellable to give evidence on behalf of themselves or of any of the parties, and the husbands and wives of such parties and persons are, except as hereinafter otherwise provided, competent and compellable to give evidence on behalf of any of the parties.

(2) Evidence of husband and wife — Without limiting the generality of subsection (1), a husband or a wife may in an action give evidence that he or she did or did not have sexual intercourse with the other party to the marriage at any time or within any period of time before or during the marriage.

. . . . .

10. Evidence in proceedings in consequence of adultery — The parties to a proceeding instituted in consequence of adultery and the husbands and wives of such parties are competent to give evidence in such proceedings, but no witness in any such proceeding, whether a party to the suit or not, is liable to be asked or bound to answer any question tending to show that he or she is guilty of adultery, unless such witness has already given evidence in the same proceeding in disproof of his or her alleged adultery.

11. Communications made during marriage — A husband is not compellable to disclose any communication made to him by his wife during the marriage, nor is a wife compellable to disclose any communication made to her by her husband during the marriage.

. . . . .

18. (1) Presumption of competency — A person of any age is presumed to be competent to give evidence.

(2) Challenge, examination — When a person's competence is challenged, the judge, justice or other presiding officer shall examine the person.

(3) Exception — However, if the judge, justice or other presiding officer is of the opinion that the person's ability to give evidence might be adversely affected if he or she examined the person, the person may be examined by counsel instead.

1995, c. 6, s. 6(1)

. . . . .

ONT. REG. 655/00 — FAMILY CASE MANAGEMENT RULES FOR THE SUPERIOR COURT OF JUSTICE IN TORONTO

made under the *Courts of Justice Act*

O. Reg. 655/00, as am. O. Reg. 201/01; 448/01; 335/02.

Rule 1 — Application and Interpretation of Rules

1.01 Family Case Management Rules — **(1) Scope** — These rules apply to proceedings in the Superior Court of Justice that are commenced in the part of the City of Toronto that was known as the City of Toronto before January 1, 1998 and belong to the following categories:

1. Proceedings under the *Children's Law Reform Act*, the *Divorce Act* (Canada), the *Family Law Act*, the *Family Responsibility and Support Arrears Enforcement Act, 1996*, the *Marriage Act* and the *Reciprocal Enforcement of Support Orders Act*.

2. Proceedings for the interpretation or enforcement of a marriage contract, cohabitation agreement, separation agreement or paternity agreement.

3. Proceedings for relief by way of constructive or resulting trust or a monetary award as compensation for unjust enrichment between persons who have cohabited.

4. Proceedings for the enforcement of a support order.

(2) Rules of Civil Procedure — The Rules of Civil Procedure also apply to proceedings to which these rules apply, but these rules prevail in the event of conflict.

(3) Time — A time prescribed under these rules or the Rules of Civil Procedure may be extended only by order of the case management judge.

(4) Format of documents — The forms prescribed in these rules and notices and orders referred to in these rules may be single spaced, may bear the short title of the proceeding and need not have a backsheet.

(5) Registrar's notices — Notices sent by the registrar under these rules may be printed on coloured paper.

1.02 Purpose — The purpose of these rules is to establish a case management system that reduces unnecessary cost and delay in family litigation, facilitates early and fair settlements and brings proceedings expeditiously to a just determination while allowing sufficient time for the conduct of the proceeding.

1.03 Definitions — In these rules,

"applicant" includes a petitioner, a plaintiff, a respondent who makes a claim and a defendant who makes a counterclaim, crossclaim or third or subsequent party claim; *("requérant")*

"case management judge" means the judge assigned to manage a proceeding under these rules; *("juge responsable de la gestion de la cause")*

"defence" includes an answer; *("défense")*

"originating document" means a notice of application, a petition, statement of claim, notice of action, counterclaim, claim by respondent, counterpetition, crossclaim or third or subsequent party claim; *("document introductif")*

"respondent" includes a defendant. *("intimé")*

1.04 Matters Not Provided For — If matters are not provided for in these rules, the practice shall be determined by analogy to them.

Rule 2 — General Procedure

2.01 Commencement of Proceeding — (1) **Case information statement** — On filing an originating document, the applicant shall file in duplicate a case information statement (Form 1).

(2) **Statement mandatory** — The registrar shall not accept an originating document without the case information statement.

2.02 Assignment of Proceedings to Case Management — (1) **Registrar's duty** — The registrar shall assign all proceedings to case management.

(2) **Warning** — When an originating document is issued or filed, the registrar shall attach to it a warning that the proceeding will be subject to case management by the court, and shall give the applicant a copy of the warning for service on each respondent.

2.03 Timetable — (1) **Prepared by registrar** — On the commencement of a proceeding, the registrar shall give the applicant a timetable showing that the proceeding shall be set down for hearing within 230 days.

(2) **Given to client** — The applicant's solicitor shall give a copy of the timetable forthwith to his or her client.

(3) **Service** — The case information statement, the timetable, the warning and the originating document shall be served together.

2.04 Failure to Comply with Timetable — (1) **Powers of registrar** — If a party fails to comply with a timetable, the registrar shall serve a notice on the parties that the proceeding will be dismissed without further notice unless, within 30 days after service of the notice, a party,

(a) sets the proceeding down for trial;

(b) files minutes of settlement; or

(c) requests a case conference.

(2) Dismissal after 30 days — If no party takes a step referred to in clause (1)(a), (b) or (c) within 30 days after service of the notice, the registrar shall dismiss the proceeding with costs.

(3) Registrar to serve dismissal order — The registrar shall serve the order on the parties by mail, and the solicitor for a party shall immediately give a copy of the order to his or her client and file proof that this has been done.

2.05 Defence of Proceeding — **(1) Case information statement with defence** — The respondent shall serve and file a case information statement (Form 1) with any defence.

(2) Refusal to accept defence — The registrar shall not accept a defence without the case information statement.

2.06 Consolidation or Hearing Together of Related Proceedings — **(1) Consolidation** — Where the court orders, under the Rules of Civil Procedure, that a proceeding to which these rules apply be consolidated with a proceeding to which they would not otherwise apply, these rules apply to the consolidated proceeding.

(2) Hearing together — Where the court orders, under the Rules of Civil Procedure, that a proceeding to which these rules apply be heard at the same time as or immediately before or after a proceeding to which they would not otherwise apply, the case management judge may order that these rules apply to the other proceeding.

(3) Service of case management documents — Where a proceeding becomes subject to these rules under subrule (1) or (2), the applicant in the proceeding originally subject to these rules shall forthwith serve the case information statements, timetable and warning on every party to the other proceeding who is not also a party to the proceeding originally subject to these rules.

Rule 3 — Case Management Judge and Case Conference

3.01 Case Management Judge — **(1) Assignment** — A case management judge shall be assigned to a proceeding the first time one of the following events occurs:

    1. A party makes a motion on notice to another party and confirms in accordance with subrule (6) that the motion will be argued.

    2. A party requests a case conference.

(2) Duties — The case management judge shall deal with all matters that arise in the proceeding before the hearing, including all motions, case conferences and pre-trial conferences.

(3) Substitution — A substitute case management judge may be assigned to a proceeding at any time.

(4) Informal motion procedure — A motion may be made to the case management judge, depending on the practical requirements of the situation,

    (a) with or without supporting material or a motion record;

    (b) by attendance, conference call, telephone call or telephone transmission, or in writing; and

    (c) in the absence of the public, if the case management judge is of the opinion that it is impractical to have the motion heard in public.

Fam. Case
Mgmt. Tor.

(5) Motion without material — Where a motion is made without supporting material or a motion record,

   (a) a case management motion form (Form 2) signed by the moving party's solicitor shall be submitted to the case management judge before the motion is heard;

   (b) a case management motion form signed by the responding party's solicitor may be submitted to the case management judge before the motion is heard;

   (c) the case management judge shall record the disposition of the motion on the form;

   (d) the registrar shall send a copy of the disposition of the motion to the parties unless the case management judge directs that a copy need not be sent; and

   (e) no formal order need be prepared, signed or entered unless the case management judge directs it.

(6) Confirmation of motion — A party who makes a motion on notice to another party shall confirm with the registrar that the motion will be argued, by filing a confirmation (Form 3) not later than 2 p.m. two days before the hearing date.

(7) Effect of failure to confirm — If no confirmation is filed in accordance with subrule (6), the motion shall not be heard, except by order of a judge.

(8) Powers on own initiative — The case management judge may, on his or her own initiative, require a hearing, case conference or conference call to deal with any matter arising in connection with case management, including a failure to comply with these rules or the Rules of Civil Procedure.

(9) Powers generally — The case management judge may,

   (a) extend or abridge a time prescribed under an order, these rules or the Rules of Civil Procedure;

   (b) adjourn a case conference;

   (c) delegate his or her authority to another judge;

   (d) set aside an order made by the registrar under these rules;

   (e) direct a reference under the Rules of Civil Procedure; and

   (f) make orders, impose terms and give directions as necessary to carry out the purpose of these rules.

(10) Motion for leave to appeal — Despite subrule (2), a motion for leave to appeal from an order of the case management judge shall be made to another judge.

(11) Not to preside at hearing — The case management judge shall not preside at the hearing of the proceeding.

3.02 Case Conference — (1) Scheduled on request — The registrar shall schedule a case conference at a party's request.

(2) Notice and confirmation — When a case conference is scheduled at a party's request, the party shall,

   (a) immediately serve a case conference notice (Form 4) on every other party; and

   (b) confirm with the registrar that the conference is to take place, by filing, not later than 2 p.m. two days before the scheduled date, a confirmation (Form 3), failing which the registrar shall cancel the conference.

(3) Case memorandum — Each party shall serve a case memorandum and file it with proof of service, not later than two days before a case conference, unless the case management judge directs that a party need not file a case memorandum.

(4) Duties of judge — At the conference, the case management judge shall,

(a) identify the issues, and note those that are contested and those that are not contested;

(b) explore methods (including alternative dispute resolution methods) to resolve the contested issues;

(c) if possible, secure the parties' agreement to a specific schedule of events in the proceeding, within the 230-day timetable within which the proceeding is to be set down for hearing;

(d) review and, if necessary, amend the timetable for the proceeding;

(e) set a date for the next appearance in court, unless the proceeding is disposed of at the conference; and

(f) complete a memorandum of outstanding issues.

(5) Parties to attend personally if directed — The parties shall attend the conference personally if the case management judge so directs.

(6) Counsel — Counsel attending the conference shall be the counsel who will appear at the hearing, shall have authority to deal with the matters referred to in subrule (4) and shall be fully acquainted with the facts and legal issues.

(7) Powers of judge — At the conference, the case management judge may, where appropriate,

(a) make a procedural order;

(b) make an order for interim relief;

(c) on consent of the parties, refer any issue for alternative dispute resolution;

(d) convene a pre-trial conference;

(e) convene a hearing; and

(f) give directions.

(8) Subsequent conferences — Subsequent conferences may be convened on the case management judge's initiative or at the request of a party.

(9) Amending timetable — A party seeking to amend the timetable for the proceeding at a case conference shall notify the other parties of the proposed amendment and the reason for it before requesting the conference and, where the other parties consent to the proposed amendment, the consent shall be filed.

Rule 4 — Steps Before Hearing

4.01 Pre-trial Conference — (1) Action on trial list — Counsel shall, within 30 days after an action is placed on the trial list, make arrangements with the registrar for a pre-trial conference, failing which the registrar shall set a date and the conference shall take place on that date unless the case management judge orders otherwise.

(2) Case memorandum — The applicant, or any other party by direction of the case management judge or by agreement of the parties, shall serve and file with proof of service a case memorandum and a record for the hearing (containing all pleadings, financial statements and net family property statements and all other material the party considers necessary for the pre-trial conference), not later than 10 days before the conference.

(3) Other parties to deliver memoranda — Every other party shall serve and file with proof of service a case memorandum containing any other material the party considers necessary for the pre-trial conference, not later than five days before the conference.

(4) Expert reports — A party's case memorandum shall also contain a copy of all expert reports intended for use at the hearing and, in the case of an expert who has not yet provided a report, a summary of the evidence that the expert is expected to give at the hearing.

(5) Expert reports not disclosed — An expert report that was not served or in respect of which a summary of evidence was not provided at the pre-trial conference may be introduced at the hearing only with permission of the presiding judge, on any terms he or she considers appropriate, and the judge shall give permission to introduce the report unless prejudice will result that cannot be compensated for by costs or an adjournment.

(6) Confirmation of conference — The parties shall confirm with the registrar that the pre-trial conference will take place, by jointly filing a confirmation (Form 3) not later than 2 p.m. two days before the scheduled date, failing which the registrar shall cancel the conference.

4.02 Preparation for Hearing — (1) Completion before pre-trial conference — All forms of discovery and disclosure before a hearing required or permitted by the Rules of Civil Procedure shall be completed before the pre-trial conference, and a party may not require further discovery or disclosure without an order.

(2) No motions after pre-trial conference — No motion may be made after a pre-trial conference, except with the permission of the case management judge.

Rule 5 — Family Case Management Advisory Committee

5.01 Family Case Management Advisory Committee — (1) Establishment — There shall be a Family Case Management Advisory Committee for the Superior Court of Justice in Toronto, to monitor the operation of these rules and to recommend to the appropriate authorities, including the Family Rules Committee, changes in policies and procedures necessary to facilitate case management.

(2) Composition — The committee shall consist of,

   (a) two judges of the Superior Court of Justice, chosen by the court's regional senior judge for the Toronto region;

   (b) two persons chosen by the Advocates' Society;

   (c) two persons chosen by the Canadian Bar Association — Ontario;

   (d) two persons chosen by the County of York Law Association; and

   (e) two persons employed in the administration of the courts, chosen by the Regional Director of Courts Administration for the Toronto region.

Rule 6 — Citation

6.01 Short Title — These rules may be cited as the Family Case Management Rules for the Superior Court of Justice in Toronto.

6.02 Commencement — These rules comes into force on December 31, 2000.

6.03 Revocation — (1) These rules are revoked on December 31, 2003.

(2) Ontario Regulation 704/91 is revoked on December 31, 2000.

O. Reg. 448/01, s. 1; 335/02, s. 1

Form 1

Courts of Justice Act

Court file no ....
Ontario
Superior Court of Justice
Toronto Family Law
SHORT TITLE OF CASE
and

Case Information Statement

This Form Filed By

❏ applicant/petitioner/plaintiff
❏ respondent/defendant — give name..........
❏ other — specify kind of party and give name..........

Order Sought by Person Filing This Form

Divorce Act

❏ divorce
❏ child support
❏ spousal support
❏ custody
❏ access
❏ other — specify
....

Family Law Act

❏ child support
❏ spousal support
❏ same-sex partner support
❏ property — equalize

❏ excl. possession
❏ restraining order
❏ other — specify

....

Children's Law Reform Act

❏ custody
❏ access
❏ paternity declaration
❏ other — specify

....

Other

❏ constructive/resulting trust
❏ partition/sale
❏ annulment
❏ other — specify

....

Person Filing This Form

❏ Married — date: .... Separated — date: ....
❏ Not married — cohabited from: .... Separated — date: ....
Birth date: .... Social insurance no.: ....
Employer — name, address and telephone: ....

Other Party

Birth date: .... Social insurance no.: ....
Employer — name, address and telephone: ....

Children

Name and birth date: ....
Name and birth date: ....

This Person's Lawyer

(If no lawyer, give person's name, address for service, telephone and fax numbers.)
Name and firm: ....
Address: ....
Telephone: .... Fax: .... Date: ....

O. Reg. 201/01, s. 1

Form 2

Courts of Justice Act

Court file no ....
Ontario
Superior Court of Justice
Toronto Family Law
SHORT TITLE OF CASE
and

Family Law Case Management Motion Form

BEFORE JUSTICE .... *(if applicable)*
TO BE HEARD ON ....

This Form Filed By

❏ applicant/petitioner/plaintiff
❏ defendant/respondent
❏ other — specify

Motion Made:

❏ for a consent order/judgment
❏ on notice to all persons — opposition expected
❏ on notice to all persons — unopposed
❏ without notice

Order Sought:

(Attach separate sheet if necessary; do not alter this form.)

Statute(s) and Rule(s) Relied On:

(statute name and section, rule number)

Method of Hearing Requested:

❏ in writing only
❏ personal attendance
❏ conference call*
* *Date and time for conference call must be arranged in advance with Family Law Office*

Material Relied On:

❏ Continuing Record tabs ....
❏ material attached
❏ see attached list *(specify affidavits; if transcripts, highlight relevant sections)*

This Person's Lawyer

(If no lawyer, give person's name, address for service, telephone and fax numbers.)

Name and firm: ....

phone and fax: ....

Other Person's Lawyer

Name and firm: ....

phone and fax: ....

Dated: ....

Court file no ....

Ontario

Superior Court of Justice

Toronto Family Law

SHORT TITLE OF CASE

and

Family Law Case Management Motion Form — Page 2

Disposition by Case Management Judge

❏ See issues sheet

❏ Order as follows:

NEXT APPEARANCE DATE: ....

NEXT APPEARANCE BY CONFERENCE CALL   [Y]   [N]

CONTINUING RECORD REQUIRED   [Y]   [N]

CASE MEMORANDUM REQUIRED   [Y]   [N]

CLIENTS TO ATTEND   [Y]   [N]

TIME ESTIMATE ON NEXT APPEARANCE .... minutes

❏ No formal order necessary

❏ Registrar to send copy of this page to parties

❏ S.D.O. to issue

❏ Formal order to be prepared by ....

❏ No copy of disposition to be sent to parties

Date ....

Judge's name ....

Judge's Signature ....

For use by court office only

To: .... To: ....

Firm: .... Firm: ....

Fax: .... Fax: ....

Form 3
Courts of Justice Act

Court file no ....

Ontario

Superior Court of Justice

Toronto Family Law

Short title .... and ....

(If applicable:) Moving Party .... Responding party ....

I, ..., COUNSEL FOR THE .... CONFIRM THAT I HAVE:

❑ DISCUSSED WITH ...., OPPOSING COUNSEL, THE MATTERS REFERRED TO BELOW AND CONFIRM,

OR

❑ I HAVE BEEN UNABLE TO CONFIRM WITH OPPOSING COUNSEL BECAUSE.................................

....

    (A) THE MOTION/CONFERENCE IS PROCEEDING ON .... AS SCHEDULED

    (B) THE MOTION IS PROCEEDING BY WAY OF:

        ❑ ARGUMENT ON ALL ISSUES

        ❑ ARGUMENT ON THE ISSUES DESCRIBED IN PARAGRAPH (C) BELOW

        ❑ CONSENT ORDER

        ❑ ADJOURNMENT ON CONSENT FROM .... TO ....

        ❑ OPPOSED ADJOURNMENT TO BE REQUESTED BY ....

    (C) THE ARGUMENT WILL PROCEED ON THE FOLLOWING ISSUES:

    (D) THE FOLLOWING MOTION RECORDS SHOULD BE READ BY THE JUDGE:

    (E) TIME ESTIMATE:.

        ....*(moving party)* + ... *(responding party)* = ... *(total)*

    (F) JUSTICE .... IS ASSIGNED TO THIS MATTER.

.... *(Date and time)*

.... *(Counsel's name — please print)*

..........*(Counsel's signature)*

..........*(Phone number)*

..........*(Fax number) (No transmittal page necessary)*

TO: FAMILY LAW OFFICE

FACSIMILE 327-6137

(Confirmation only — no filings will be accepted)

Form 4

Courts of Justice Act

Court file no ....

Ontario

Superior Court of Justice

Toronto Family Law

SHORT TITLE OF CASE

Case Conference Notice

TO: *(name of party or counsel)*.................................

At the request of

❑ the case management judge

❑ the petitioner/plaintiff/applicant

❑ the respondent/defendant

your attendance at a case conference at 393 University Ave., Toronto, is required on *(date and time)* .... to deal with the following matters:

Factual Information for Case Management Judge

(to be completed by all counsel)

COUNSEL COMPLETING THIS FORM

    (name and address)

ACTING FOR:

    ❑ petitioner/plaintiff/applicant

    ❑ defendant/respondent

    ❑ other

DETAILS OF RELATIONSHIP:

    Date of marriage or start of cohabitation

    Date of separation

    Children: *(name, date of birth)*

OUTSTANDING ISSUES:

STATUS OF LEGAL PROCEEDINGS:

Are discoveries complete?

Are productions complete?

What needs to be done before case can be listed for trial?

(Attach financial statements and net family property statements where appropriate to case conference.)

TABLE OF CONCORDANCE

Family Law Act, 1986	Family Law Act	Family Law Act, 1986	Family Law Act
S.O. 1986, c. 4	R.S.O. 1990, c. F-3	S.O. 1986, c. 4	R.S.O. 1990, c. F-3
1(1)	1(1)	34(3–6)	34(3–6)
1(2)	1(2)	35(1)	35(1)
2(1,2)	2(1,2)	35(2–6)	35(2–6)
2(3)	2(3)	36–43	36–43
2(4–11)	2(4–11)	44(1,2)	44(1,2)
3	3	44(3–9)	44(3–9)
4(1)	4(1)	45	45
4(2)	4(2)	46(1)	46(1)
4(3–5)	4(3–5)	46(2)	46(2)
5	5	46(3,4)	46(3,4)
6(1–5)	6(1–5)	47	47
6(6)	6(6)	48	48
6(6a)	6(7)	49(1)	49(1)
6(7)	6(8)	49(2)	49(2)
6(8)	6(9)	50–58	50–58
6–9	6(10)	59(1)	59(1)
6(10–19)	6(11–20)	59(2–5)	59(2–5)
7–16	7–16	60–69	60–69
17	17	70(1)	70(1)
18–23	18–23	70(2)	—
24(1–4)	24(1–4)	70(3,4)	70(2,3)
24(5)	24(5)	71(1)	—
24(6,7)	24(6,7)	71(2)	—
25–32	25–32	71(3,4)	—
33(1–5)	33(1–5)	72	—
33(6)	33(6)	73	—
33(7–10)	33(7–10)	74	—
34(1)	34(1)	75	—
34(2)	34(2)	76,77	—

FLA

FAMILY LAW ACT

R.S.O. 1990, c. F.3, as am. 1992, c. 32, s. 12; 1993, c. 27, Sched.; 1997, c. 20; 1997, c. 25, Sched. E, s. 1; 1998, c. 26, s. 102; 1999, c. 6, s. 25; 2000, c. 4, s. 12; 2000, c. 33, s. 22 [Not in force at date of publication.]; 2002, c. 17, Sched. F, s. 1; 2002, c. 24, Sched. B, ss. 25, item 9, 37 [Not in force at date of publication.].

Preamble

Whereas it is desirable to encourage and strengthen the role of the family; and whereas for that purpose it is necessary to recognize the equal position of spouses as individuals within marriage and to recognize marriage as a form of partnership; and whereas in support of such recognition it is necessary to provide in law for the orderly and equitable settlement of the affairs of the spouses upon the breakdown of the partnership, and to provide for other mutual obligations in family relationships, including the equitable sharing by parents of responsibility for their children; *Therefore, Her Majesty, by and with the advice and consent of the Legislative Assembly of the Province of Ontario, enacts as follows:*

1. (1) Definitions — In this Act,

"child" includes a person whom a parent has demonstrated a settled intention to treat as a child of his or her family, except under an arrangement where the child is placed for valuable consideration in a foster home by a person having lawful custody;

"child support guidelines" means the guidelines established by the regulations made under subsections 69(2) and (3);

"cohabit" means to live together in a conjugal relationship, whether within or outside marriage;

"court" means the Ontario Court (Provincial Division), the Unified Family Court or the Ontario Court (General Division);

"domestic contract" means a domestic contract as defined in Part IV (Domestic Contracts);

"parent" includes a person who has demonstrated a settled intention to treat a child as a child of his or her family, except under an arrangement where the child is placed for valuable consideration in a foster home by a person having lawful custody;

"paternity agreement" means a paternity agreement as defined in Part IV (Domestic Contracts);

"spouse" means either of a man and woman who,

(a) are married to each other, or

(b) have together entered into a marriage that is voidable or void, in good faith on the part of a person relying on this clause to assert any right.

(2) Polygamous marriages — In the definition of "spouse", a reference to marriage includes a marriage that is actually or potentially polygamous, if it was celebrated in a jurisdiction whose system of law recognizes it as valid.

1997, c. 20, s. 1; 1999, c. 6, s. 25(1)

2. (1) Staying application — If, in an application under this Act, it appears to the court that for the appropriate determination of the spouses' affairs it is necessary or desirable to have other matters determined first or simultaneously, the court may stay the application until another proceeding is brought or determined as the court considers appropriate.

(2) All proceedings in one court — Except as this Act provides otherwise, no person who is a party to an application under this Act shall make another application under this Act to another court, but the court may order that the proceeding be transferred to a court having other jurisdiction where, in the first court's opinion, the other court is more appropriate to determine the matters in issue that should be determined at the same time.

(3) Applications in Ontario Court (General Division) — In the Ontario Court (General Division), an application under this Act may be made by action or application.

(4) Statement re removal of barriers to remarriage — A party to an application under section 7 (net family property), 10 (questions of title between spouses), 33 (support), 34 (powers of court) or 37 (variation) may serve on the other party and file with the court a statement, verified by oath or statutory declaration, indicating that,

    (a) the author of the statement has removed all barriers that are within his or her control and that would prevent the other spouse's remarriage within that spouse's faith; and

    (b) the other party has not done so, despite a request.

(5) Idem — Within ten days after service of the statement, or within such longer period as the court allows, the party served with a statement under subsection (4) shall serve on the other party and file with the court a statement, verified by oath or statutory declaration, indicating that the author of the statement has removed all barriers that are within his or her control and that would prevent the other spouse's remarriage within that spouse's faith.

(6) Dismissal, etc. — When a party fails to comply with subsection (5),

    (a) if the party is an applicant, the proceeding may be dismissed;

    (b) if the party is a respondent, the defence may be struck out.

(7) Exception — Subsections (5) and (6) do not apply to a party who does not claim costs or other relief in the proceeding.

(8) Extension of times — The court may, on motion, extend a time prescribed by this Act if it is satisfied that,

    (a) there are apparent grounds for relief;

    (b) relief is unavailable because of delay that has been incurred in good faith; and

    (c) no person will suffer substantial prejudice by reason of the delay.

(9) Incorporation of contract in order — A provision of a domestic contract in respect of a matter that is dealt with in this Act may be incorporated in an order made under this Act.

(10) Act subject to contracts — A domestic contract dealing with a matter that is also dealt with in this Act prevails unless this Act provides otherwise.

(11) Registration of orders — An order made under this Act that affects real property does not affect the acquisition of an interest in the real property by a person acting in good faith without notice of the order, unless the order is registered in the proper land registry office.

3. (1) Mediation — In an application under this Act, the court may, on motion, appoint a person whom the parties have selected to mediate any matter that the court specifies.

(2) Consent to act — The court shall appoint only a person who,

(a) has consented to act as mediator; and

(b) has agreed to file a report with the court within the period of time specified by the court.

(3) Duty of mediator — The mediator shall confer with the parties, and with the children if the mediator considers it appropriate to do so, and shall endeavour to obtain an agreement between the parties.

(4) Full or limited report — Before entering into mediation, the parties shall decide whether,

(a) the mediator is to file a full report on the mediation, including anything that he or she considers relevant; or

(b) the mediator is to file a limited report that sets out only the agreement reached by the parties or states only that the parties did not reach agreement.

(5) Filing and copies of report — The mediator shall file with the clerk or registrar of the court a full or limited report, as the parties have decided, and shall give a copy to each of the parties.

(6) Admissions, etc., in the course of mediation — If the parties have decided that the mediator is to file a limited report, no evidence of anything said or of any admission or communication made in the course of the mediation is admissible in any proceeding, except with the consent of all parties to the proceeding in which the mediator was appointed.

(7) Fees and expenses — The court shall require the parties to pay the mediator's fees and expenses and shall specify in the order the proportions or amounts of the fees and expenses that each party is required to pay.

(8) Idem, serious financial hardship — The court may require one party to pay all the mediator's fees and expenses if the court is satisfied that payment would cause the other party or parties serious financial hardship.

PART I — FAMILY PROPERTY

4. (1) Definitions — In this Part,

"court" means a court as defined in subsection 1 (1), but does not include the Ontario Court (Provincial Division);

"matrimonial home" means a matrimonial home under section 18 and includes property that is a matrimonial home under that section at the valuation date;

"net family property" means the value of all the property, except property described in subsection (2), that a spouse owns on the valuation date, after deducting,

(a) the spouse's debts and other liabilities, and

(b) the value of property, other than a matrimonial home, that the spouse owned on the date of the marriage, after deducting the spouse's debts and other liabilities, calculated as of the date of the marriage;

"property" means any interest, present or future, vested or contingent, in real or personal property and includes,

(a) property over which a spouse has, alone or in conjunction with another person, a power of appointment exercisable in favour of himself or herself,

(b) property disposed of by a spouse but over which the spouse has, alone or in conjunction with another person, a power to revoke the disposition or a power to consume or dispose of the property, and

(c) in the case of a spouse's rights under a pension plan that have vested, the spouse's interest in the plan including contributions made by other persons;

"valuation date" means the earliest of the following dates:

1. The date the spouses separate and there is no reasonable prospect that they will resume cohabitation.

2. The date a divorce is granted.

3. The date the marriage is declared a nullity.

4. The date one of the spouses commences an application based on subsection 5 (3) (improvident depletion) that is subsequently granted.

5. The date before the date on which one of the spouses dies leaving the other spouse surviving.

(2) Excluded property — The value of the following property that a spouse owns on the valuation date does not form part of the spouse's net family property:

1. Property, other than a matrimonial home, that was acquired by gift or inheritance from a third person after the date of the marriage.

2. Income from property referred to in paragraph 1, if the donor or testator has expressly stated that it is to be excluded from the spouse's net family property.

3. Damages or a right to damages for personal injuries, nervous shock, mental distress or loss of guidance, care and companionship, or the part of a settlement that represents those damages.

4. Proceeds or a right to proceeds of a policy of life insurance, as defined in the *Insurance Act*, that are payable on the death of the life insured.

5. Property, other than a matrimonial home, into which property referred to in paragraphs 1 to 4 can be traced.

6. Property that the spouses have agreed by a domestic contract is not to be included in the spouse's net family property.

(3) Onus of proof re deductions and exclusions — The onus of proving a deduction under the definition of "net family property" or an exclusion under subsection (2) is on the person claiming it.

(4) Close of business — When this section requires that a value be calculated as of a given date, it shall be calculated as of close of business on that date.

(5) Net family property not to be less than zero — If a spouse's net family property as calculated under subsections (1), (2) and (4) is less than zero, it shall be deemed to be equal to zero.

5. (1) Equalization of net family properties — When a divorce is granted or a marriage is declared a nullity, or when the spouses are separated and there is no reasonable prospect that they will resume cohabitation, the spouse whose net family property is the lesser of the two net family properties is entitled to one-half the difference between them.

(2) Idem — When a spouse dies, if the net family property of the deceased spouse exceeds the net family property of the surviving spouse, the surviving spouse is entitled to one-half the difference between them.

(3) Improvident depletion of spouse's net family property — When spouses are co-habiting, if there is a serious danger that one spouse may improvidently deplete his or her net family property, the other spouse may on an application under section 7 have the difference between the net family properties divided as if the spouses were separated and there were no reasonable prospect that they would resume cohabitation.

(4) No further division — After the court has made an order for division based on subsection (3), neither spouse may make a further application under section 7 in respect of their marriage.

(5) Idem — Subsection (4) applies even though the spouses continue to cohabit, unless a domestic contract between the spouses provides otherwise.

(6) Variation of share — The court may award a spouse an amount that is more or less than half the difference between the net family properties if the court is of the opinion that equalizing the net family properties would be unconscionable, having regard to,

   (a) a spouse's failure to disclose to the other spouse debts or other liabilities existing at the date of the marriage;

   (b) the fact that debts or other liabilities claimed in reduction of a spouse's net family property were incurred recklessly or in bad faith;

   (c) the part of a spouse's net family property that consists of gifts made by the other spouse;

   (d) a spouse's intentional or reckless depletion of his or her net family property;

   (e) the fact that the amount a spouse would otherwise receive under subsection (1), (2) or (3) is disproportionately large in relation to a period of cohabitation that is less than five years;

   (f) the fact that one spouse has incurred a disproportionately larger amount of debts or other liabilities than the other spouse for the support of the family;

   (g) a written agreement between the spouses that is not a domestic contract; or

   (h) any other circumstance relating to the acquisition, disposition, preservation, maintenance or improvement of property.

(7) Purpose — The purpose of this section is to recognize that child care, household management and financial provision are the joint responsibilities of the spouses and that inherent in the marital relationship there is equal contribution, whether financial or otherwise, by the spouses to the assumption of these responsibilities, entitling each spouse to the equalization of the net family properties, subject only to the equitable considerations set out in subsection (6).

6. (1) Election: spouse's will — When a spouse dies leaving a will, the surviving spouse shall elect to take under the will or to receive the entitlement under section 5.

FLA

(2) Idem: spouse's intestacy — When a spouse dies intestate, the surviving spouse shall elect to receive the entitlement under Part II of the *Succession Law Reform Act* or to receive the entitlement under section 5.

(3) Idem: spouse's partial intestacy — When a spouse dies testate as to some property and intestate as to other property, the surviving spouse shall elect to take under the will and to receive the entitlement under Part II of the *Succession Law Reform Act*, or to receive the entitlement under section 5.

(4) Property outside estate — A surviving spouse who elects to take under the will or to receive the entitlement under Part II of the *Succession Law Reform Act*, or both in the case of a partial intestacy, shall also receive the other property to which he or she is entitled because of the first spouse's death.

(5) Gifts by will — The surviving spouse shall receive the gifts made to him or her in the deceased spouse's will in addition to the entitlement under section 5 if the will expressly provides for that result.

(6) Insurance, etc. — Where a surviving spouse,

    (a) is the beneficiary,

        (i) of a policy of life insurance, as defined in the *Insurance Act*, that was taken out on the life of the deceased spouse and owned by the deceased spouse or was taken out on the lives of a group of which he or she was a member, or

        (ii) of a lump sum payment provided under a pension or similar plan on the death of the deceased spouse; and

    (b) elects or has elected to receive the entitlement under section 5,

the payment under the policy or plan shall be credited against the surviving spouse's entitlement under section 5, unless a written designation by the deceased spouse provides that the surviving spouse shall receive payment under the policy or plan in addition to the entitlement under section 5.

(7) Idem — If a surviving spouse,

    (a) elects or has elected to receive the entitlement under section 5; and

    (b) receives payment under a life insurance policy or a lump sum payment provided under a pension or similar plan that is in excess of the entitlement under section 5,

and there is no written designation by the deceased spouse described in subsection (6), the deceased spouse's personal representative may recover the excess amount from the surviving spouse.

(8) Effect of election to receive entitlement under section 5 — When a surviving spouse elects to receive the entitlement under section 5, the gifts made to him or her in the deceased spouse's will are revoked and the will shall be interpreted as if the surviving spouse had died before the other, unless the will expressly provides that the gifts are in addition to the entitlement under section 5.

(9) Idem — When a surviving spouse elects to receive the entitlement under section 5, the spouse shall be deemed to have disclaimed the entitlement under Part II of the *Succession Law Reform Act*.

(10) Manner of making election — The surviving spouse's election shall be in the form prescribed by the regulations made under this Act and shall be filed in the office of the Estate Registrar for Ontario within six months after the first spouse's death.

(11) Deemed election — If the surviving spouse does not file the election within that time, he or she shall be deemed to have elected to take under the will or to receive the entitlement under the *Succession Law Reform Act*, or both, as the case may be, unless the court, on application, orders otherwise.

(12) Priority of spouse's entitlement — The spouse's entitlement under section 5 has priority over,

(a) the gifts made in the deceased spouse's will, if any, subject to subsection (13);

(b) a person's right to a share of the estate under Part II (Intestate Succession) of the *Succession Law Reform Act*;

(c) an order made against the estate under Part V (Support of Dependants) of the *Succession Law Reform Act*, except an order in favour of a child of the deceased spouse.

(13) Exception — The spouse's entitlement under section 5 does not have priority over a gift by will made in accordance with a contract that the deceased spouse entered into in good faith and for valuable consideration, except to the extent that the value of the gift, in the court's opinion, exceeds the consideration.

(14) Distribution within six months of death restricted — No distribution shall be made in the administration of a deceased spouse's estate within six months of the spouse's death, unless,

(a) the surviving spouse gives written consent to the distribution; or

(b) the court authorizes the distribution.

(15) Idem, notice of application — No distribution shall be made in the administration of a deceased spouse's death after the personal representative has received notice of an application under this Part, unless,

(a) the applicant gives written consent to the distribution; or

(b) the court authorizes the distribution.

(16) Extension of limitation period — If the court extends the time for a spouse's application based on subsection 5 (2), any property of the deceased spouse that is distributed before the date of the order and without notice of the application shall not be brought into the calculation of the deceased spouse's net family property.

(17) Exception — Subsections (14) and (15) do not prohibit reasonable advances to dependants of the deceased spouse for their support.

(18) Definition — In subsection (17), "dependant" has the same meaning as in Part V of the *Succession Law Reform Act*.

(19) Liability of personal representative — If the personal representative makes a distribution that contravenes subsection (14) or (15), the court makes an order against the estate under this Part and the undistributed portion of the estate is not sufficient to satisfy the order, the personal representative is personally liable to the applicant for the amount that was distributed or the amount that is required to satisfy the order, whichever is less.

FLA

(20) Order suspending administration — On motion by the surviving spouse, the court may make an order suspending the administration of the deceased spouse's estate for the time and to the extent that the court decides.

7. (1) Application to court — The court may, on the application of a spouse, former spouse or deceased spouse's personal representative, determine any matter respecting the spouses' entitlement under section 5.

(2) Personal action; estates — Entitlement under subsections 5 (1), (2) and (3) is personal as between the spouses but,

(a) an application based on subsection 5 (1) or (3) and commenced before a spouse's death may be continued by or against the deceased spouse's estate; and

(b) an application based on subsection 5 (2) may be made by or against a deceased spouse's estate.

(3) Limitation — An application based on subsection 5 (1) or (2) shall not be brought after the earliest of,

(a) two years after the day the marriage is terminated by divorce or judgment of nullity;

(b) six years after the day the spouses separate and there is no reasonable prospect that they will resume cohabitation;

(c) six months after the first spouse's death.

8. Statement of property — In an application under section 7, each party shall serve on the other and file with the court, in the manner and form prescribed by the rules of the court, a statement verified by oath or statutory declaration disclosing particulars of,

(a) the party's property and debts and other liabilities,

(i) as of the date of the marriage,

(ii) as of the valuation date, and

(iii) as of the date of the statement;

(b) the deductions that the party claims under the definition of "net family property";

(c) the exclusions that the party claims under subsection 4 (2); and

(d) all property that the party disposed of during the two years immediately preceding the making of the statement, or during the marriage, whichever period is shorter.

9. (1) Powers of court — In an application under section 7, the court may order,

(a) that one spouse pay to the other spouse the amount to which the court finds that spouse to be entitled under this Part;

(b) that security, including a charge on property, be given for the performance of an obligation imposed by the order;

(c) that, if necessary to avoid hardship, an amount referred to in clause (a) be paid in instalments during a period not exceeding ten years or that payment of all or part of the amount be delayed for a period not exceeding ten years; and

(d) that, if appropriate to satisfy an obligation imposed by the order,

(i) property be transferred to or in trust for or vested in a spouse, whether absolutely, for life or for a term of years, or

(ii) any property be partitioned or sold.

(2) Financial information, inspections — The court may, at the time of making an order for instalment or delayed payments or on motion at a later time, order that the spouse who has the obligation to make payments shall,

(a) furnish the other spouse with specified financial information, which may include periodic financial statements; and

(b) permit inspections of specified property of the spouse by or on behalf of the other spouse, as the court directs.

(3) Variation — If the court is satisfied that there has been a material change in the circumstances of the spouse who has the obligation to make instalment or delayed payments, the court may, on motion, vary the order, but shall not vary the amount to which the court found the spouse to be entitled under this Part.

(4) Ten-year period — Subsections (3) and 2 (8) (extension of times) do not permit the postponement of payment beyond the ten-year period mentioned in clause (1) (c).

10. (1) Determination of questions of title between spouses — A person may apply to the court for the determination of a question between that person and his or her spouse or former spouse as to the ownership or right to possession of particular property, other than a question arising out of an equalization of net family properties under section 5, and the court may,

(a) declare the ownership or right to possession;

(b) if the property has been disposed of, order payment in compensation for the interest of either party;

(c) order that the property be partitioned or sold for the purpose of realizing the interests in it; and

(d) order that either or both spouses give security, including a charge on property, for the performance of an obligation imposed by the order,

and may make ancillary orders or give ancillary directions.

(2) Estates — An application based on subsection (1) may be made by or continued against the estate of a deceased spouse.

11. (1) Operating business or farm — An order made under section 9 or 10 shall not be made so as to require or result in the sale of an operating business or farm or so as to seriously impair its operation, unless there is no reasonable alternative method of satisfying the award.

(2) Idem — To comply with subsection (1), the court may,

(a) order that one spouse pay to the other a share of the profits from the business or farm; and

(b) if the business or farm is incorporated, order that one spouse transfer or have the corporation issue to the other shares in the corporation.

12. Orders for preservation — In an application under section 7 or 10, if the court considers it necessary for the protection of the other spouse's interests under this Part, the court may make an interim or final order,

(a) restraining the depletion of a spouse's property; and

FLA

(b) for the possession, delivering up, safekeeping and preservation of the property.

13. Variation and realization of security — If the court has ordered security or charged a property with security for the performance of an obligation under this Part, the court may, on motion,

(a) vary or discharge the order; or

(b) on notice to all persons having an interest in the property, direct its sale for the purpose of realizing the security or charge.

14. Presumptions — The rule of law applying a presumption of a resulting trust shall be applied in questions of the ownership of property between husband and wife, as if they were not married, except that,

(a) the fact that property is held in the name of spouses as joint tenants is proof, in the absence of evidence to the contrary, that the spouses are intended to own the property as joint tenants; and

(b) money on deposit in the name of both spouses shall be deemed to be in the name of the spouses as joint tenants for the purposes of clause (a).

15. Conflict of laws — The property rights of spouses arising out of the marital relationship are governed by the internal law of the place where both spouses had their last common habitual residence or, if there is no place where the spouses had a common habitual residence, by the law of Ontario.

16. (1) Application of Part — This Part applies to property owned by spouses,

(a) whether they were married before or after the 1st day of March, 1986; and

(b) whether the property was acquired before or after that day.

(2) Application of s. 14 — Section 14 applies whether the event giving rise to the presumption occurred before or after the 1st day of March, 1986.

PART II — MATRIMONIAL HOME

17. Definitions — In this Part,

"court" means a court as defined in subsection 1 (1) but does not include the Ontario Court (Provincial Division);

"property" means real or personal property.

18. (1) Matrimonial home — Every property in which a person has an interest and that is or, if the spouses have separated, was at the time of separation ordinarily occupied by the person and his or her spouse as their family residence is their matrimonial home.

(2) Ownership of shares — The ownership of a share or shares, or of an interest in a share or shares, of a corporation entitling the owner to occupy a housing unit owned by the corporation shall be deemed to be an interest in the unit for the purposes of subsection (1).

(3) Residence on farmland, etc. — If property that includes a matrimonial home is normally used for a purpose other than residential, the matrimonial home is only the part of the property that may reasonably be regarded as necessary to the use and enjoyment of the residence.

19. (1) Possession of matrimonial home — Both spouses have an equal right to possession of a matrimonial home.

(2) Idem — When only one of the spouses has an interest in a matrimonial home, the other spouse's right of possession,

    (a) is personal as against the first spouse; and

    (b) ends when they cease to be spouses, unless a separation agreement or court order provides otherwise.

20. (1) Designation of matrimonial home — One or both spouses may designate property owned by one or both of them as a matrimonial home, in the form prescribed by the regulations made under this Act.

(2) Contiguous property — The designation may include property that is described in the designation and is contiguous to the matrimonial home.

(3) Registration — The designation may be registered in the proper land registry office.

(4) Effect of designation by both spouses — On the registration of a designation made by both spouses, any other property that is a matrimonial home under section 18 but is not designated by both spouses ceases to be a matrimonial home.

(5) Effect of designation by one spouse — On the registration of a designation made by one spouse only, any other property that is a matrimonial home under section 18 remains a matrimonial home.

(6) Cancellation of designation — The designation of a matrimonial home is cancelled, and the property ceases to be a matrimonial home, on the registration or deposit of,

    (a) a cancellation, executed by the person or persons who made the original designation, in the form prescribed by the regulations made under this Act;

    (b) a decree absolute of divorce or judgment of nullity;

    (c) an order under clause 23 (e) cancelling the designation; or

    (d) proof of death of one of the spouses.

(7) Revival of other matrimonial homes — When a designation of a matrimonial home made by both spouses is cancelled, section 18 applies again in respect of other property that is a matrimonial home.

21. (1) Alienation of matrimonial home — No spouse shall dispose of or encumber an interest in a matrimonial home unless,

    (a) the other spouse joins in the instrument or consents to the transaction;

    (b) the other spouse has released all rights under this Part by a separation agreement;

    (c) a court order has authorized the transaction or has released the property from the application of this Part; or

    (d) the property is not designated by both spouses as a matrimonial home and a designation of another property as a matrimonial home, made by both spouses, is registered and not cancelled.

FLA

(2) Setting aside transaction — If a spouse disposes of or encumbers an interest in a matrimonial home in contravention of subsection (1), the transaction may be set aside on an application under section 23, unless the person holding the interest or encumbrance at the time of the application acquired it for value, in good faith and without notice, at the time of acquiring it or making an agreement to acquire it, that the property was a matrimonial home.

(3) Proof that property not a matrimonial home — For the purpose of subsection (2), a statement by the person making the disposition or encumbrance,

> (a) verifying that he or she is not, or was not, a spouse at the time of the disposition or encumbrance;

> (b) verifying that the person is a spouse who is not separated from his or her spouse and that the property is not ordinarily occupied by the spouses as their family residence;

> (c) verifying that the person is a spouse who is separated from his or her spouse and that the property was not ordinarily occupied by the spouses, at the time of their separation, as their family residence;

> (d) where the property is not designated by both spouses as a matrimonial home, verifying that a designation of another property as a matrimonial home, made by both spouses, is registered and not cancelled; or

> (e) verifying that the other spouse has released all rights under this Part by a separation agreement,

shall, unless the person to whom the disposition or encumbrance is made had notice to the contrary, be deemed to be sufficient proof that the property is not a matrimonial home.

(4) Idem, attorney's personal knowledge — The statement shall be deemed to be sufficient proof that the property is not a matrimonial home if it is made by the attorney of the person making the disposition or encumbrance, on the basis of the attorney's personal knowledge.

(5) Liens arising by operation of law — This section does not apply to the acquisition of an interest in property by operation of law or to the acquisition of a lien under section 48 of the *Legal Aid Services Act, 1998.*

1998, c. 26, s. 102

22. (1) Right of redemption and to notice — When a person proceeds to realize upon a lien, encumbrance or execution or exercises a forfeiture against property that is a matrimonial home, the spouse who has a right of possession under section 19 has the same right of redemption or relief against forfeiture as the other spouse and is entitled to the same notice respecting the claim and its enforcement or realization.

(2) Service of notice — A notice to which a spouse is entitled under subsection (1) shall be deemed to be sufficiently given if served or given personally or by registered mail addressed to the spouse at his or her usual or last known address or, if none, the address of the matrimonial home, and, if notice is served or given by mail, the service shall be deemed to have been made on the fifth day after the day of mailing.

(3) Idem: power of sale — When a person exercises a power of sale against property that is a matrimonial home, sections 33 and 34 of the *Mortgages Act* apply and subsection (2) does not apply.

(4) Payments by spouse — If a spouse makes a payment in exercise of the right conferred by subsection (1), the payment shall be applied in satisfaction of the claim giving rise to the lien, encumbrance, execution or forfeiture.

(5) Realization may continue in spouse's absence — Despite any other Act, when a person who proceeds to realize upon a lien, encumbrance or execution or exercises a forfeiture does not have sufficient particulars of a spouse for the purpose and there is no response to a notice given under subsection (2) or under section 33 of the *Mortgages Act*, the realization or exercise of forfeiture may continue in the absence and without regard to the interest of the spouse and the spouse's rights under this section end on the completion of the realization or forfeiture.

1993, c. 27, Sched.

23. Powers of court respecting alienation — The court may, on the application of a spouse or person having an interest in property, by order,

(a) determine whether or not the property is a matrimonial home and, if so, its extent;

(b) authorize the disposition or encumbrance of the matrimonial home if the court finds that the spouse whose consent is required,

(i) cannot be found or is not available,

(ii) is not capable of giving or withholding consent, or

(iii) is unreasonably withholding consent,

subject to any conditions, including provision of other comparable accommodation or payment in place of it, that the court considers appropriate;

(c) dispense with a notice required to be given under section 22;

(d) direct the setting aside of a transaction disposing of or encumbering an interest in the matrimonial home contrary to subsection 21 (1) and the revesting of the interest or any part of it on the conditions that the court considers appropriate; and

(e) cancel a designation made under section 20 if the property is not a matrimonial home.

24. (1) Order for possession of matrimonial home — Regardless of the ownership of a matrimonial home and its contents, and despite section 19 (spouse's right of possession), the court may on application, by order,

(a) provide for the delivering up, safekeeping and preservation of the matrimonial home and its contents;

(b) direct that one spouse be given exclusive possession of the matrimonial home or part of it for the period that the court directs and release other property that is a matrimonial home from the application of this Part;

(c) direct a spouse to whom exclusive possession of the matrimonial home is given to make periodic payments to the other spouse;

(d) direct that the contents of the matrimonial home, or any part of them,

(i) remain in the home for the use of the spouse given possession, or

(ii) be removed from the home for the use of a spouse or child;

(e) order a spouse to pay for all or part of the repair and maintenance of the matrimonial home and of other liabilities arising in respect of it, or to make periodic payments to the other spouse for those purposes;

FLA

(f) authorize the disposition or encumbrance of a spouse's interest in the matrimonial home, subject to the other spouse's right of exclusive possession as ordered; and

(g) where a false statement is made under subsection 21 (3), direct,

(i) the person who made the false statement, or

(ii) a person who knew at the time he or she acquired an interest in the property that the statement was false and afterwards conveyed the interest,

to substitute other real property for the matrimonial home, or direct the person to set aside money or security to stand in place of it, subject to any conditions that the court considers appropriate.

(2) **Temporary or interim order** — The court may, on motion, make a temporary or interim order under clause (1) (a), (b), (c), (d) or (e).

(3) **Order for exclusive possession: criteria** — In determining whether to make an order for exclusive possession, the court shall consider,

(a) the best interests of the children affected;

(b) any existing orders under Part I (Family Property) and any existing support orders;

(c) the financial position of both spouses;

(d) any written agreement between the parties;

(e) the availability of other suitable and affordable accommodation; and

(f) any violence committed by a spouse against the other spouse or the children.

(4) **Best interests of child** — In determining the best interests of a child, the court shall consider,

(a) the possible disruptive effects on the child of a move to other accommodation; and

(b) the child's views and preferences, if they can reasonably be ascertained.

(5) **Offence** — A person who contravenes an order for exclusive possession is guilty of an offence and upon conviction is liable,

(a) in the case of a first offence, to a fine of not more than $5,000 or to imprisonment for a term of not more than three months, or to both; and

(b) in the case of a second or subsequent offence, to a fine of not more than $10,000 or to imprisonment for a term of not more than two years, or to both.

(6) **Arrest without warrant** — A police officer may arrest without warrant a person the police officer believes on reasonable and probable grounds to have contravened an order for exclusive possession.

(7) **Existing orders** — Subsections (5) and (6) also apply in respect of contraventions, committed on or after the 1st day of March, 1986, of orders for exclusive possession made under Part III of the *Family Law Reform Act*, being chapter 152 of the Revised Statutes of Ontario, 1980.

25. (1) Variation of possessory order — On the application of a person named in an order made under clause 24 (1) (a), (b), (c), (d) or (e) or his or her personal representative, if the court is satisfied that there has been a material change in circumstances, the court may discharge, vary or suspend the order.

(2) Variation of conditions of sale — On the motion of a person who is subject to conditions imposed in an order made under clause 23 (b) or (d) or 24 (1) (g), or his or her personal representative, if the court is satisfied that the conditions are no longer appropriate, the court may discharge, vary or suspend them.

(3) Existing orders — Subsections (1) and (2) also apply to orders made under the corresponding provisions of Part III of the *Family Law Reform Act*, being chapter 152 of the Revised Statutes of Ontario, 1980.

26. (1) Joint tenancy in matrimonial home — If a spouse dies owning an interest in a matrimonial home as a joint tenant with a third person and not with the other spouse, the joint tenancy shall be deemed to have been severed immediately before the time of death.

(2) Sixty-day period after spouse's death — Despite clauses 19 (2) (a) and (b) (termination of spouse's right of possession), a spouse who has no interest in a matrimonial home but is occupying it at the time of the other spouse's death, whether under an order for exclusive possession or otherwise, is entitled to retain possession against the spouse's estate, rent free, for sixty days after the spouse's death.

27. Registration of order — Orders made under this Part or under Part III of the *Family Law Reform Act*, being chapter 152 of the Revised Statutes of Ontario, 1980 are registrable against land under the *Registry Act* and the *Land Titles Act*.

28. (1) Application of Part — This Part applies to matrimonial homes that are situated in Ontario.

(2) Idem — This Part applies,

 (a) whether the spouses were married before or after the 1st day of March, 1986; and

 (b) whether the matrimonial home was acquired before or after that day.

PART III — SUPPORT OBLIGATIONS

29. Definitions — In this Part,

"dependant" means a person to whom another has an obligation to provide support under this Part;

"same-sex partner" means either of two persons of the same sex who have cohabited,

 (a) continuously for a period of not less than three years, or

 (b) in a relationship of some permanence, if they are the natural or adoptive parents of a child. ("partenaire de même sexe")

"spouse" means a spouse as defined in subsection 1 (1), and in addition includes either of a man and woman who are not married to each other and have cohabited,

 (a) continuously for a period of not less than three years, or

 (b) in a relationship of some permanence, if they are the natural or adoptive parents of a child.

1999, c. 6, s. 25(2)

FLA

30. Obligation of spouses for support — Every spouse and every same-sex partner has an obligation to provide support for himself or herself and for the other spouse or same-sex partner, in accordance with need, to the extent that he or she is capable of doing so.

1999, c. 6, s. 25(3)

31. (1) Obligation of parent to support child — Every parent has an obligation to provide support for his or her unmarried child who is a minor or is enrolled in a full time program of education, to the extent that the parent is capable of doing so.

(2) Idem — The obligation under subsection (1) does not extend to a child who is sixteen years of age or older and has withdrawn from parental control.

1997, c. 20, s. 2

32. Obligation of child to support parent — Every child who is not a minor has an obligation to provide support, in accordance with need, for his or her parent who has cared for or provided support for the child, to the extent that the child is capable of doing so.

33. (1) Order for support — A court may, on application, order a person to provide support for his or her dependants and determine the amount of support.

(2) Applicants — An application for an order for the support of a dependant may be made by the dependant or the dependant's parent.

Proposed Addition — 33(2.1)

(2.1) Same — The *Limitations Act, 2002* applies to an application made by the dependant's parent or by an agency referred to in subsection (3) as if it were made by the dependant himself or herself.

2002, c. 24, Sched. B, s. 37 [Not in force at date of publication.]

(3) An application for an order for the support of a dependant who is the respondent's spouse, same-sex partner or child may also be made by one of the following agencies,

    (a) the Ministry of Community and Social Services in the name of the Minister;

    (b) a municipality, excluding a lower-tier municipality in a regional municipality;

    (c) a district social services administration board under the *District Social Services Administration Boards Act;*

    (d) a band approved under section 15 of the *General Welfare Assistance Act*; or

    (e) a delivery agent under the *Ontario Works Act, 1997,*

if the agency is providing or has provided a benefit under the *Family Benefits Act*, assistance under the *General Welfare Assistance Act* or the *Ontario Works Act, 1997* or income support under the *Ontario Disability Support Program Act, 1997* in respect of the dependant's support, or if an application for such a benefit or assistance has been made to the agency by or on behalf of the dependant.

(4) Setting aside domestic contract — The court may set aside a provision for support or a waiver of the right to support in a domestic contract or paternity agreement and may determine and order support in an application under subsection (1) although the contract or agreement contains an express provision excluding the application of this section,

    (a) if the provision for support or the waiver of the right to support results in unconscionable circumstances;

(b) if the provision for support is in favour of or the waiver is by or on behalf of a dependant who qualifies for an allowance for support out of public money; or

(c) if there is default in the payment of support under the contract or agreement at the time the application is made.

(5) Adding party — In an application the court may, on a respondent's motion, add as a party another person who may have an obligation to provide support to the same dependant.

(6) Idem — In an action in the Ontario Court (General Division), the defendant may add as a third party another person who may have an obligation to provide support to the same dependant.

(7) Purposes of order for support of child — An order for the support of a child should,

(a) recognize that each parent has an obligation to provide support for the child;

(b) apportion the obligation according to the child support guidelines.

(8) Purposes of order for support of spouse — An order for the support of a spouse or same-sex partner should,

(a) recognize the spouse's or same-sex partner's contribution to the relationship and the economic consequences of the relationship for the spouse or same-sex partner;

(b) share the economic burden of child support equitably;

(c) make fair provision to assist the spouse or same-sex partner to become able to contribute to his or her own support; and

(d) relieve financial hardship, if this has not been done by orders under Parts I (Family Property) and II (Matrimonial Home).

(9) Determination of amount — In determining the amount and duration, if any, of support for a spouse, same-sex partner or parent in relation to need, the court shall consider all the circumstances of the parties, including,

(a) the dependant's and respondent's current assets and means;

(b) the assets and means that the dependant and respondent are likely to have in the future;

(c) the dependant's capacity to contribute to his or her own support;

(d) the respondent's capacity to provide support;

(e) the dependant's and respondent's age and physical and mental health;

(f) the dependant's needs, in determining which the court shall have regard to the accustomed standard of living while the parties resided together;

(g) the measures available for the dependant to become able to provide for his or her own support and the length of time and cost involved to enable the dependant to take those measures;

(h) any legal obligation of the respondent or dependant to provide support for another person;

(i) the desirability of the dependant or respondent remaining at home to care for a child;

(j) a contribution by the dependant to the realization of the respondent's career potential;

(k) [Repealed 1997, c. 20, s. 3(3).]

(l) if the dependant is a spouse or same-sex partner,

    (i) the length of time the dependant and respondent cohabited,

    (ii) the effect on the spouse's or same-sex partner's earning capacity of the responsibilities assumed during cohabitation,

    (iii) whether the spouse or same-sex partner has undertaken the care of a child who is of the age of eighteen years or over and unable by reason of illness, disability or other cause to withdraw from the charge of his or her parents,

    (iv) whether the spouse or same-sex partner has undertaken to assist in the continuation of a program of education for a child eighteen years of age or over who is unable for that reason to withdraw from the charge of his or her parents,

    (v) in the case of a spouse, any housekeeping, child care or other domestic service performed by the spouse for the family, as if the spouse were devoting the time spent in performing that service in remunerative employment and were contributing the earnings to the family's support,

    (v.1) in the case of a same-sex partner, any housekeeping, child care or other domestic service performed by the same-sex partner for the respondent or the respondent's family, as if the same-sex partner were devoting the time spent in performing that service in remunerative employment and were contributing the earnings to the support of the respondent or the respondent's family.

    (vi) the effect on the spouse's or same-sex partner's earnings and career development of the responsibility of caring for a child; and

(m) any other legal right of the dependant to support, other than out of public money.

(10) Conduct — The obligation to provide support for a spouse or same-sex partner exists without regard to the conduct of either spouse or same-sex partner, but the court may in determining the amount of support have regard to a course of conduct that is so unconscionable as to constitute an obvious and gross repudiation of the relationship.

(11) Application of child support guidelines — A court making an order for the support of a child shall do so in accordance with the child support guidelines.

(12) Exception: special provisions — Despite subsection (11), a court may award an amount that is different from the amount that would be determined in accordance with the child support guidelines if the court is satisfied,

(a) that special provisions in an order or a written agreement respecting the financial obligations of the parents, or the division or transfer of their property, directly or indirectly benefit a child, or that special provisions have otherwise been made for the benefit of a child; and

(b) that the application of the child support guidelines would result in an amount of child support that is inequitable given those special provisions.

(13) Reasons — Where the court awards, under subsection (12), an amount that is different from the amount that would be determined in accordance with the child support guidelines, the court shall record its reasons for doing so.

(14) Exception: consent orders — Despite subsection (11), a court may award an amount that is different from the amount that would be determined in accordance with the child support guidelines on the consent of both parents if the court is satisfied that,

(a) reasonable arrangements have been made for the support of the child to whom the order relates; and

(b) where support for the child is payable out of public money, the arrangements do not provide for an amount less than the amount that would be determined in accordance with the child support guidelines.

(15) Reasonable arrangements — For the purposes of clause (14)(a), in determining whether reasonable arrangements have been made for the support of a child,

(a) the court shall have regard to the child support guidelines; and

(b) the court shall not consider the arrangements to be unreasonable solely because the amount of support agreed to is not the same as the amount that would otherwise have been determined in accordance with the child support guidelines.

1997, c. 20, s. 3; 1997, c. 25, Sched. E, s. 1; 1999, c. 6, s. 25(4)–(10); 2002, c. 17, Sched. F, s. 1

34. (1) Powers of court — In an application under section 33, the court may make an interim or final order,

(a) requiring that an amount be paid periodically, whether annually or otherwise and whether for an indefinite or limited period, or until the happening of a specified event;

(b) requiring that a lump sum be paid or held in trust;

(c) requiring that property be transferred to or in trust for or vested in the dependant, whether absolutely, for life or for a term of years;

(d) respecting any matter authorized to be ordered under clause 24 (1) (a), (b), (c), (d) or (e) (matrimonial home);

(e) requiring that some or all of the money payable under the order be paid into court or to another appropriate person or agency for the dependant's benefit;

(f) requiring that support be paid in respect of any period before the date of the order;

(g) requiring payment to an agency referred to in subsection 33 (3) of an amount in reimbursement for a benefit or assistance referred to in that subsection, including a benefit or assistance provided before the date of the order;

(h) requiring payment of expenses in respect of a child's prenatal care and birth;

(i) requiring that a spouse or same-sex partner who has a policy of life insurance as defined in the *Insurance Act* designate the other spouse or same-sex partner or a child as the beneficiary irrevocably;

(j) requiring that a spouse or same-sex partner who has an interest in a pension plan or other benefit plan designate the other spouse or same-sex partner or a child as beneficiary under the plan and not change that designation; and

(k) requiring the securing of payment under the order, by a charge on property or otherwise.

(2) Limitation on jurisdiction of Ontario Court (Provincial Division) — The Ontario Court (Provincial Division) shall not make an order under clause (1) (b), (c), (i), (j) or (k) except for the provision of necessities or to prevent the dependant from becoming or continuing to be a public charge, and shall not make an order under clause (d).

FLA

(3) Assignment of support — An order for support may be assigned to an agency referred to in subsection 33 (3).

(3.1) Same — An agency referred to in subsection 33(3) to whom an order for support is assigned is entitled to the payments due under the order and has the same right to be notified of and to participate in proceedings under this Act to vary, rescind, suspend or enforce the order as the person who would otherwise be entitled to the payments.

(4) Support order binds estate — An order for support binds the estate of the person having the support obligation unless the order provides otherwise.

(5) Indexing of support payments — In an order made under clause (1) (a), other than an order for the support of a child, the court may provide that the amount payable shall be increased annually on the order's anniversary date by the indexing factor, as defined in subsection (6), for November of the previous year.

(6) Definition — The indexing factor for a given month is the percentage change in the Consumer Price Index for Canada for prices of all items since the same month of the previous year, as published by Statistics Canada.

1997, c. 20, s. 4; 1999, c. 6, s. 25(11)

35. (1) Domestic contract, etc., may be filed with court — A person who is a party to a domestic contract or paternity agreement may file the contract or agreement with the clerk of the Ontario Court (Provincial Division) or of the Unified Family Court together with the person's affidavit stating that the contract or agreement is in effect and has not been set aside or varied by a court or agreement.

(2) Effect of filing — A provision for support or maintenance contained in a contract or agreement that is filed in this manner,

    (a) may be enforced;

    (b) may be varied under section 37; and

    (c) except in the case of a provision for the support of a child, may be increased under section 38,

as if it were an order of the court where it is filed.

(3) Setting aside available — Subsection 33 (4) (setting aside in unconscionable circumstances, etc.) applies to a contract or agreement that is filed in this manner.

(4) Enforcement available despite waiver — Subsection (1) and clause (2)(a) apply despite an agreement to the contrary.

(5) Existing contracts, etc. — Subsections (1) and (2) also apply to contracts and agreements made before the 1st day of March, 1986.

(6) Existing arrears — Clause (2) (a) also applies to arrears accrued before the 1st day of March, 1986.

1997, c. 20, s. 5

36. (1) Effect of divorce proceeding — When a divorce proceeding is commenced under the *Divorce Act* (Canada), an application for support under this Part that has not been adjudicated is stayed, unless the court orders otherwise.

(2) Arrears may be included in order — The court that deals with a divorce proceeding under the *Divorce Act* (Canada) may determine the amount of arrears owing under an order for support made under this Part and make an order respecting that amount at the same time as it makes an order under the *Divorce Act* (Canada).

(3) Idem — If a marriage is terminated by divorce or judgment of nullity and the question of support is not adjudicated in the divorce or nullity proceedings, an order for support made under this Part continues in force according to its terms.

37. (1) Application for variation — An application to the court for variation of an order made or confirmed under this Part may be made by,

    (a) a dependant or respondent named in the order;

    (b) a parent of a dependant referred to in clause (a);

    (c) the personal representative of a respondent referred to in clause (a); or

    (d) an agency referred to in subsection 33(3).

(2) Powers of court: spouse and parent support — In the case of an order for support of a spouse, same-sex partner or parent, if the court is satisfied that there has been a material change in the dependant's or respondent's circumstances or that evidence not available on the previous hearing has become available, the court may,

    (a) discharge, vary or suspend a term of the order, prospectively or retroactively;

    (b) relieve the respondent from the payment of part or all of the arrears or any interest due on them; and

    (c) make any other order under section 34 that the court considers appropriate in the circumstances referred to in section 33.

(2.1) Powers of court: child support — In the case of an order for support of a child, if the court is satisfied that there has been a change in circumstances within the meaning of the child support guidelines or that evidence not available on the previous hearing has become available, the court may,

    (a) discharge, vary or suspend a term of the order, prospectively or retroactively;

    (b) relieve the respondent from the payment of part or all of the arrears or any interest due them; and

    (c) make any other order for the support of a child that the court could make on an application under section 33.

(2.2) Application of child support guidelines — A court making an order under subsection (2.1) shall do so in accordance with the child support guidelines.

(2.3) Exception: special provisions — Despite subsection (2.2), a court may award an amount that is different from the amount that would be determined in accordance with the child support guidelines if the court is satisfied,

    (a) that special provisions in an order or a written agreement respecting the financial obligations of the parents, or the division or transfer of their property, directly or indirectly benefit a child, or that special provisions have otherwise been made for the benefit of a child; and

    (b) that the application of the child support guidelines would result in an amount of child support that is inequitable given those special provisions.

FLA

(2.4) Reasons — Where the court awards, under subsection (2.3), an amount that is different from the amount that would be determined in accordance with the child support guidelines, the court shall record its reasons for doing so.

(2.5) Exception: consent orders — Despite subsection (2.2), a court may award an amount that is different from the amount that would be determined in accordance with the child support guidelines on the consent of both parents if the court is satisfied that,

(a) reasonable arrangements have been made for the support of the child to whom the order relates; and

(b) where support for the child is payable out of public money, the arrangements do not provide for an amount less than the amount that would be determined in accordance with the child support guidelines.

(2.6) Reasonable arrangements — For the purposes of clause (2.5)(a), in determining whether reasonable arrangements have been made for the support of a child,

(a) the court shall have regard to the child support guidelines; and

(b) the court shall not consider the arrangements to be unreasonable solely because the amount of support agreed to is not the same as the amount that would otherwise have been determined in accordance with the child support guidelines.

(3) Limitation on applications for variation — No application for variation shall be made within six months after the making of the order for support or the disposition of another application for variation in respect of the same order, except by leave of the court.

1997, c. 20, s. 6; 1999, c. 6, s. 25(12)

38. (1) Non-application to orders for child support — This section does not apply to an order for the support of a child.

(2) Application to have existing order indexed — If an order made or confirmed under this Part is not indexed under subsection 34(5), the dependant, or an agency referred to in subsection 33(3), may apply to the court to have the order indexed in accordance with subsection 34(5).

(3) Power of court — The court shall, unless the respondent shows that his or her income, assets and means have not increased sufficiently to permit the increase, order that the amount payable be increased by the indexing factor, as defined in subsection 34(6), for November of the year before the year in which the application is made and be increased in the same way annually thereafter on the anniversary date of the order under this section.

1997, c. 20, s. 7

38.1 (1) Priority to child support — Where a court is considering an application for the support of a child and an application for the support of a spouse or same-sex partner, the court shall give priority to the support of the child in determining the applications.

(2) Reasons — Where as a result of giving priority to the support of a child, the court is unable to make an order for the support of a spouse or same-sex partner or the court makes an order for the support of a spouse or same-sex partner in an amount less than it otherwise would have, the court shall record its reasons for doing so.

(3) Consequences of reduction or termination of child support — Where as a result of giving priority to the support of a child, an order for the support of a spouse or same-sex partner is not made or the amount of the order for the support of a spouse or same-

partner is less than it otherwise would have been, any material reduction or termination of the support for the child constitutes a material change of circumstances for the purposes of an application for the support of the spouse or same-sex partner or for variation of an order for the support of the spouse or same-sex partner.

(4) Non-application of limitation — Subsection 50(1) does not apply to an action or application for the support of a spouse or same-sex partner in the circumstances set out in subsection (3).

Proposed Repeal — 38.1(4)

(4) [Repealed 2002, c. 24, Sched. B, s. 25, item 9. Not in force at date of publication.]

1997, c. 20, s. 8; 1999, c. 6, s. 25(13)-(16)

39. (1) Existing orders — Sections 36 to 38 also apply to orders for maintenance or alimony made before the 31st day of March, 1978 or in proceedings commenced before the 31st day of March, 1978 and to orders for support made under Part II of the *Family Law Reform Act*, being chapter 152 of the Revised Statutes of Ontario, 1980.

(2) Combined support orders — Where an application is made under section 37 to vary an order that provides a single amount of money for the combined support of one or more children and a spouse or same-sex partner, the court shall rescind the order and treat the application as an application for an order for the support of a child and an application for an order for the support of a spouse or same-sex partner.

(3) Existing proceedings — Where an application for the support of a child, including an application under section 37 to vary an order for the support of a child, is made before the day the *Uniform Federal and Provincial Child Support Guidelines Act, 1997* comes into force and the court has not considered any evidence in the application, other than in respect of an interim order, before that day, the proceeding shall be deemed to be an application under the *Family Law Act* as amended by the *Uniform Federal and Provincial Child Support Guidelines Act*, 1997, subject to such directions as the court considers appropriate.

1997, c. 20, s. 9; 1999, c. 6, s. 25(17)

40. Restraining orders — The court may, on application, make an interim or final order restraining the depletion of a spouse's or same-sex partner's property that would impair or defeat a claim under this Part.

1999, c. 6, s. 25(18)

41. Financial statement — In an application under section 33 or 37, each party shall serve on the other and file with the court a financial statement verified by oath or statutory declaration in the manner and form prescribed by the rules of the court.

42. (1) Order for return by employer — In an application under section 33 or 37, the court may order the employer of a party to the application to make a written return to the court showing the party's wages or other remuneration during the preceding twelve months.

(2) Return as evidence — A return purporting to be signed by the employer may be received in evidence as proof, in the absence of evidence to the contrary, of its contents.

(3) Order for access to information — The court may, on motion, make an order under subsection (4) if it appears to the court that, in order to make an application under section 33 or 37, the moving party needs to learn or confirm the proposed respondent's whereabouts.

FLA

(4) Idem — The order shall require the person or public body to whom it is directed to provide the court or the moving party with any information that is shown on a record in the person's or public body's possession or control and that indicates the proposed respondent's place of employment, address or location.

(5) Crown bound — This section binds the Crown in right of Ontario.

43. (1) Arrest of absconding debtor — If an application is made under section 33 or 37 and the court is satisfied that the respondent is about to leave Ontario and that there are reasonable grounds for believing that the respondent intends to evade his or her responsibilities under this Act, the court may issue a warrant for the respondent's arrest for the purpose of bringing him or her before the court.

(2) Bail — Section 150 (interim release by justice of the peace) of the *Provincial Offences Act* applies with necessary modifications to an arrest under the warrant.

44. (1) Provisional orders — In an application under section 33 or 37 in the Ontario Court (Provincial Division) or the Unified Family Court, the court shall proceed under this section, whether or not the respondent in the application files a financial statement, if,

(a) the respondent fails to appear;

(b) it appears to the court that the respondent resides in a locality in Ontario that is more than 150 kilometres away from the place where the court sits; and

(c) the court is of the opinion, in the circumstances of the case, that the issues can be adequately determined by proceeding under this section.

(2) Idem — If the court determines that it would be proper to make a final order, were it not for the respondent's failure to appear, the court shall make an order for support that is provisional only and has no effect until it is confirmed by the Ontario Court (Provincial Division) or the Unified Family Court sitting nearest the place where the respondent resides.

(3) Transmission for hearing — The court that makes a provisional order shall send to the court in the locality in which the respondent resides copies of such documents and records, certified in such manner, as are prescribed by the rules of the court.

(4) Show cause — The court to which the documents and records are sent shall cause them to be served upon the respondent, together with a notice to file with the court the financial statement required by section 41, and to appear and show cause why the provisional order should not be confirmed.

(5) Confirmation of order — At the hearing, the respondent may raise any defence that might have been raised in the original proceeding, but if the respondent fails to satisfy the court that the order ought not to be confirmed, the court may confirm the order without variation or with the variation that the court considers proper having regard to all the evidence.

(6) Adjournment for further evidence — If the respondent appears before the court and satisfies the court that for the purpose of a defence or for the taking of further evidence or otherwise it is necessary to remit the case to the court where the applicant resides, the court may remit the case and adjourn the proceeding for that purpose.

(7) Where order not confirmed — If the respondent appears before the court and the court, having regard to all the evidence, is of the opinion that the order ought not to be confirmed, the court shall remit the case to the court sitting where the order was made with a statement of the reasons for doing so, and the court sitting where the order was made shall dispose of the application in accordance with the statement.

(8) Certificates as evidence — A certificate certifying copies of documents or records for the purpose of this section and purporting to be signed by the clerk of the court is, without proof of the clerk's office or signature, admissible in evidence in a court to which it is transmitted under this section as proof, in the absence of evidence to the contrary, of the copy's authenticity.

(9) Right of appeal — No appeal lies from a provisional order made under this section, but a person bound by an order confirmed under this section has the same right of appeal as he or she would have had if the order had been made under section 34.

45. (1) Pledging credit for necessities — During cohabitation, a spouse or same-sex partner has authority to render himself or herself and his or her spouse or same-sex partner jointly and severally liable to a third party for necessities of life, unless the spouse or same-sex partner has notified the third party that he or she has withdrawn the authority.

(2) Liability for necessities of minor — If a person is entitled to recover against a minor in respect of the provision of necessities for the minor, every parent who has an obligation to support the minor is liable for them jointly and severally with the minor.

(3) Recovery between persons jointly liable — If persons are jointly and severally liable under this section, their liability to each other shall be determined in accordance with their obligation to provide support.

(4) Common law supplanted — This section applies in place of the rules of common law by which a wife may pledge her husband's credit.

1999, c. 6, s. 25(19)

46. (1) Order restraining harassment — On application, a court may make an interim or final order restraining the applicant's spouse, same-sex partner or former spouse or same-sex partner from molesting, annoying or harassing the applicant or children in the applicant's lawful custody, or from communicating with the applicant or children, except as the order provides, and may require the applicant's spouse, same-sex partner or former spouse or same-sex partner to enter into the recognizance that the court considers appropriate.

(2) Offence — A person who contravenes a restraining order is guilty of an offence and upon conviction is liable,

(a) in the case of a first offence, to a fine of not more than $5,000 or to imprisonment for a term of not more than three months, or to both; and

(b) in the case of a second or subsequent offence, to a fine of not more than $10,000 or to imprisonment for a term of not more than two years, or to both.

Proposed Repeal — 46(2)

(2) [Repealed 2000, c. 33, s. 22(1). Not in force at date of publication.]

[Editor's Note: Section 23 of S.O. 2000, c. 33 provides that on a day to be named by proclamation of the Lieutenant Governor, subsection 46(2) of the Family Law Act, R.S.O. 1990, c. F.3 is repealed by subsection 22(1) of S.O. 2000, c. 33. Subsection 22(3) of S.O. 2000, c. 33 provides, however, that despite the repeal of subs. 46(2) of the Family Law Act, any prosecu-

FLA

tion begun under that subsection before its repeal shall continue as if that subsection were still in force.]

(3) Arrest without warrant — A police officer may arrest without warrant a person the police officer believes on reasonable and probable grounds to have contravened a restraining order.

(4) Existing orders — Subsections (2) and (3) also apply in respect of contraventions, committed, on or after the 1st day of March, 1986, of restraining orders made under Part II of the *Family Law Reform Act*, being chapter 152 of the Revised Statutes of Ontario, 1980.

Proposed Repeal — 46.

46. [Repealed 2000, c. 33, s. 22(2). Not in force at date of publication.]

[Editor's Note: Section 23 of S.O. 2000, c. 33 provides that on a day to be named by proclamation of the Lieutenant Governor, s. 46 of the Family Law Act, R.S.O. 1990, c. F.3 is repealed by subsection 22(2) of S.O. 2000, c. 33. Subsection 22(4) of S.O. 2000, c. 33 provides, however, that despite the repeal of s. 46 of the Family Law Act, any prosecution begun under that section before its repeal shall continue as if that subsection were still in force.]
1999, c. 6, s. 25(20)

47. Application for custody — The court may direct that an application for support stand over until an application for custody under the *Children's Law Reform Act* has been determined.

48. Appeal from Ontario Court (Provincial Division) — An appeal lies from an order of the Ontario Court (Provincial Division) under this Part to the Ontario Court (General Division).

49. (1) Contempt of orders of Ontario Court (Provincial Division) — In addition to its powers in respect of contempt, the Ontario Court (Provincial Division) may punish by fine or imprisonment, or by both, any wilful contempt of or resistance to its process, rules or orders under this Act, but the fine shall not exceed $5,000 nor shall the imprisonment exceed ninety days.

(2) Conditions of imprisonment — An order for imprisonment under subsection (1) may be conditional upon default in the performance of a condition set out in the order and may provide for the imprisonment to be served intermittently.

50. (1) Limitation — No action or application for an order for the support of a spouse or same-sex partner shall be brought under this Part after two years from the day the spouses or same-sex partners separate.

(2) Idem — If the spouses or same-sex partners provided for support on separation in a domestic contract, subsection (1) does not apply and no action or application for an order for the support of a spouse or same-sex partner shall be brought after default under the contract has subsisted for two years.

Proposed Repeal — 50

50. [Repealed 2002, c. 24, Sched. B, s. 25, item 9. Not in force at date of publication.]

1999, c. 6, s. 25(21), (22)

PART IV — DOMESTIC CONTRACTS

51. Definitions — In this Part,

"cohabitation agreement" means an agreement entered into under section 53;

"domestic contract" means a marriage contract, separation agreement or cohabitation agreement;

"marriage contract" means an agreement entered into under section 52;

"paternity agreement" means an agreement entered into under section 59;

"separation agreement" means an agreement entered into under section 54.

52. (1) Marriage contracts — A man and a woman who are married to each other or intend to marry may enter into an agreement in which they agree on their respective rights and obligations under the marriage or on separation, on the annulment or dissolution of the marriage or on death, including,

(a) ownership in or division of property;

(b) support obligations;

(c) the right to direct the education and moral training of their children, but not the right to custody of or access to their children; and

(d) any other matter in the settlement of their affairs.

(2) Rights re matrimonial home excepted — A provision in a marriage contract purporting to limit a spouse's rights under Part II (Matrimonial Home) is unenforceable.

53. (1) Cohabitation agreements — Two persons of the opposite sex or the same sex who are cohabiting or intend to cohabit and who are not married to each other may enter into an agreement in which they agree on their respective rights and obligations during cohabitation, or on ceasing to cohabit or on death, including,

(a) ownership in or division of property;

(b) support obligations;

(c) the right to direct the education and moral training of their children, but not the right to custody of or access to their children; and

(d) any other matter in the settlement of their affairs.

(2) Effect of marriage on agreement — If the parties to a cohabitation agreement marry each other, the agreement shall be deemed to be a marriage contract.

1999, c. 6, s. 25(23)

FLA

54. Separation agreements — Two persons of the opposite sex or the same sex who cohabited and are living separate and apart may enter into an agreement in which they agree on their respective rights and obligations, including,

(a) ownership in or division of property;

(b) support obligations;

(c) the right to direct the education and moral training of their children;

(d) the right to custody of and access to their children; and

(e) any other matter in the settlement of their affairs.

1999, c. 6, s. 25(24)

55. (1) Form of contract — A domestic contract and an agreement to amend or rescind a domestic contract are unenforceable unless made in writing, signed by the parties and witnessed.

(2) Capacity of minor — A minor has capacity to enter into a domestic contract, subject to the approval of the court, which may be given before or after the minor enters into the contract.

(3) Guardian of property — If a mentally incapable person has a guardian of property other than his or her own spouse, the guardian may enter into a domestic contract or give any waiver or consent under this Act on the person's behalf, subject to the approval of the court, given in advance.

(4) P.G.T. — In all other cases of mental incapacity, th Public Guardian and Trustee has power to act on the person's behalf in accordance with subsection (3).

1992, c. 32, s. 12

56. (1) Contracts subject to best interests of child — In the determination of a matter respecting the education, moral training or custody of or access to a child, the court may disregard any provision of a domestic contract pertaining to the matter where, in the opinion of the court, to do so is in the best interests of the child.

(1.1) Contracts subject to child support guidelines — In the determination of a matter respecting the support of a child, the court may disregard any provision of a domestic contract or paternity agreement pertaining to the matter where the provision is unreasonable having regard to the child support guidelines, as well as to any other provision relating to support of the child in the contract or agreement.

(2) Clauses requiring chastity — A provision in a domestic contract to take effect on separation whereby any right of a party is dependent upon remaining chaste is unenforceable, but this subsection shall not be construed to affect a contingency upon marriage or cohabitation with another.

(3) Idem — A provision in a domestic contract made before the 1st day of March, 1986 whereby any right of a party is dependent upon remaining chaste shall be given effect as a contingency upon marriage or cohabitation with another.

(4) Setting aside domestic contract — A court may, on application, set aside a domestic contract or a provision in it,

(a) if a party failed to disclose to the other significant assets, or significant debts or other liabilities, existing when the domestic contract was made;

(b) if a party did not understand the nature or consequences of the domestic contract; or

(c) otherwise in accordance with the law of contract.

(5) Barriers to remarriage — The court may, on application, set aside all or part of a separation agreement or settlement, if the court is satisfied that the removal by one spouse of barriers that would prevent the other spouse's remarriage within that spouse's faith was a consideration in the making of the agreement or settlement.

(6) Idem — Subsection (5) also applies to consent orders, releases, notices of discontinuance and abandonment and other written or oral arrangements.

(7) Application of subss. (4, 5, 6) — Subsections (4), (5) and (6) apply despite any agreement to the contrary.

1997, c. 20, s. 10

57. Rights of donors of gifts — If a domestic contract provides that specific gifts made to one or both parties may not be disposed of or encumbered without the consent of the donor, the donor shall be deemed to be a party to the contract for the purpose of enforcement or amendment of the provision.

58. Contracts made outside Ontario — The manner and formalities of making a domestic contract and its essential validity and effect are governed by the proper law of the contract, except that,

(a) a contract of which the proper law is that of a jurisdiction other than Ontario is also valid and enforceable in Ontario if entered into in accordance with Ontario's internal law;

(b) subsection 33 (4) (setting aside provision for support or waiver) and section 56 apply in Ontario to contracts for which the proper law is that of a jurisdiction other than Ontario; and

(c) a provision in a marriage contract or cohabitation agreement respecting the right to custody of or access to children is not enforceable in Ontario.

59. (1) Paternity agreements — If a man and a woman who are not spouses enter into an agreement for,

(a) the payment of the expenses of a child's prenatal care and birth;

(b) support of a child; or

(c) funeral expenses of the child or mother,

on the application of a party, or a children's aid society, to the Ontario Court (Provincial Division) or the Unified Family Court, the court may incorporate the agreement in an order, and Part III (Support Obligations) applies to the order in the same manner as if it were an order made under that Part.

(1.1) Child support guidelines — A court shall not incorporate an agreement for the support of a child in an order under subsection (1) unless the court is satisfied that the agreement is reasonable having regard to the child support guidelines, as well as to any other provision relating to support of the child in the agreement.

(2) Absconding respondent — If an application is made under subsection (1) and a judge of the court is satisfied that the respondent is about to leave Ontario and that there are reasonable grounds to believe that the respondent intends to evade his or her responsibilities under the agreement, the judge may issue a warrant in the form prescribed by the rules of the court for the respondent's arrest.

(3) Bail — Section 150 (interim release by justice of the peace) of the *Provincial Offences Act* applies with necessary modifications to an arrest under the warrant.

(4) Capacity of minor — A minor has capacity to enter into an agreement under subsection (1) that is approved by the court, whether the approval is given before or after the minor enters into the agreement.

(5) Application to existing agreements — This section applies to paternity agreements that were made before the 1st day of March, 1986.

1997, c. 20, s. 11

60. (1) Application of Act to existing contracts — A domestic contract validly made before the 1st day of March, 1986 shall be deemed to be a domestic contract for the purposes of this Act.

(2) Contracts entered into before the 1st day of March, 1986 — If a domestic contract was entered into before the 1st day of March, 1986 and the contract or any part would have been valid if entered into on or after that day, the contract or part is not invalid for the reason only that it was entered into before that day.

(3) Idem — If property is transferred, under an agreement or understanding reached before the 31st day of March, 1978, between spouses who are living separate and apart, the transfer is effective as if made under a domestic contract.

PART V — DEPENDANTS' CLAIM FOR DAMAGES

61. (1) Right of dependants to sue in tort — If a person is injured or killed by the fault or neglect of another under circumstances where the person is entitled to recover damages, or would have been entitled if not killed, the spouse, as defined in Part III (Support Obligations), same-sex partner, as defined in Part III (Support Obligations), children, grandchildren, parents, grandparents, brothers and sisters of the person are entitled to recover their pecuniary loss resulting from the injury or death from the person from whom the person injured or killed is entitled to recover or would have been entitled if not killed, and to maintain an action for the purpose in a court of competent jurisdiction.

(2) Damages in case of injury — The damages recoverable in a claim under subsection (1) may include,

    (a) actual expenses reasonably incurred for the benefit of the person injured or killed;

    (b) actual funeral expenses reasonably incurred;

    (c) a reasonable allowance for travel expenses actually incurred in visiting the person during his or her treatment or recovery;

    (d) where, as a result of the injury, the claimant provides nursing, housekeeping or other services for the person, a reasonable allowance for loss of income or the value of the services; and

    (e) an amount to compensate for the loss of guidance, care and companionship that the claimant might reasonably have expected to receive from the person if the injury or death had not occurred.

(3) Contributory negligence — In an action under subsection (1), the right to damages is subject to any apportionment of damages due to contributory fault or neglect of the person who was injured or killed.

(4) Limitations of actions — No action shall be brought under subsection (1) after the expiration of two years from the time the cause of action arose.

Proposed Repeal — 61(4)

(4) [Repealed 2002, c. 24, Sched. B, s. 25, item 9. Not in force at date of publication.]

1999, c. 6, s. 25(25)

62. (1) Offer to settle for global sum — The defendant may make an offer to settle for one sum of money as compensation for his or her fault or neglect to all plaintiffs, without specifying the shares into which it is to be divided.

(2) Apportionment — If the offer is accepted and the compensation has not been otherwise apportioned, the court may, on motion, apportion it among the plaintiffs.

(3) Payment before apportionment — The court may direct payment from the fund before apportionment.

(4) Payment may be postponed — The court may postpone the distribution of money to which minors are entitled.

63. Assessment of damages, insurance — In assessing damages in an action brought under this Part, the court shall not take into account any sum paid or payable as a result of the death or injury under a contract of insurance.

PART VI — AMENDMENTS TO THE COMMON LAW

64. (1) Unity of legal personality abolished — For all purposes of the law of Ontario, a married person has a legal personality that is independent, separate and distinct from that of his or her spouse.

(2) Capacity of married person — A married person has and shall be accorded legal capacity for all purposes and in all respects as if he or she were an unmarried person and, in particular, has the same right of action in tort against his or her spouse as if they were not married.

(3) Purpose of subss. (1, 2) — The purpose of subsections (1) and (2) is to make the same law apply, and apply equally, to married men and married women and to remove any difference in it resulting from any common law rule or doctrine.

65. Actions between parent and child — No person is disentitled from bringing an action or other proceeding against another for the reason only that they are parent and child.

66. Recovery for pre-natal injuries — No person is disentitled from recovering damages in respect of injuries for the reason only that the injuries were incurred before his or her birth.

FLA

67. Domicile of minor — The domicile of a person who is a minor is,

(a) if the minor habitually resides with both parents and the parents have a common domicile, that domicile;

(b) if the minor habitually resides with one parent only, that parent's domicile;

(c) if the minor resides with another person who has lawful custody of him or her, that person's domicile; or

(d) if the minor's domicile cannot be determined under clause (a), (b) or (c), the jurisdiction with which the minor has the closest connection.

68. [Repealed 2000, c. 4, s. 12.]

General

69. (1) Regulations — The Lieutenant Governor in Council may make regulations respecting any matter referred to as prescribed by the regulations.

(2) Same — The Lieutenant Governor in Council may make regulations establishing,

(a) guidelines respecting the making of orders for child support under this Act; and

(b) guidelines that may be designated under subsection 2(5) of the *Divorce Act* (Canada).

(3) Same — Without limiting the generality of subsection (2), guidelines may be established under subsection (2),

(a) respecting the way in which the amount of an order for child support is to be determined;

(b) respecting the circumstances in which discretion may be exercised in the making of an order for child support;

(c) respecting the circumstances that give rise to the making of a variation order in respect of an order for the support of a child;

(d) respecting the determination of income for the purposes of the application of the guidelines;

(e) authorizing a court to impute income for the purposes of the application of the guidelines;

(f) respecting the production of income information and providing for sanctions when that information is not provided.

1997, c. 20, s. 12

70. (1) Application of ss. 5-8 — Sections 5 to 8 apply unless,

(a) an application under section 4 of the *Family Law Reform Act*, being chapter 152 of the Revised Statutes of Ontario, 1980 was adjudicated or settled before the 4th day of June, 1985; or

(b) the first spouse's death occurred before the 1st day of March, 1986.

(2) Application of Part II — Part II (Matrimonial Home) applies unless a proceeding under Part III of the *Family Law Reform Act*, being chapter 152 of the Revised Statutes of Ontario, 1980 to determine the rights between spouses in respect of the property concerned was adjudicated or settled before the 4th day of June, 1985.

(3) **Interpretation of existing contracts** — A separation agreement or marriage contract that was validly made before the 1st day of March, 1986 and that excludes a spouse's property from the application of sections 4 and 8 of the *Family Law Reform Act*, being chapter 152 of the Revised Statutes of Ontario, 1980,

(a) shall be deemed to exclude that property from the application of section 5 of this Act; and

(b) shall be read with necessary modifications.

FLA

ONT. REG. 367 — DESIGNATION OF MATRIMONIAL HOME — FORMS

made under the *Family Law Act*

R.R.O. 1990, Reg. 367

1. A designation of a matrimonial home under subsection 20(1) of the Act shall be in Form. 1.

O. Reg. 95/86, s. 1.

2. A cancellation of a designation of a matrimonial home under clause 20(6)(a) of the Act shall be in Form 2.

O. Reg. 95/86, s. 2.

SCHEDULE [FORMS]

The text in square brackets has been editorially added by Carswell and does not form part of the text of the legislation.

Form 1 — Designation of Matrimonial Home

Form 1 — Designation of Matrimonial Home
Form 1

Family Law Act

DESIGNATION OF MATRIMONIAL HOME

Province of Ontario

Document General
Form 4 — Land Registration Reform Act

D

FOR OFFICE USE ONLY	(1) Registry ☐ Land Titles ☐	(2) Page 1 of pages
	(3) Property Identifier(s) Block Property	Additional See Schedule ☐
	(4) Nature of Document	
	Designation of matrimonial home (Family Law Act, s. 20)	
	(5) Consideration	
	Not applicable ------------------- Dollars $ -------------------	
	(6) Description	

New Property Identifiers   Additional See Schedule ☐

Executions   Additional See Schedule ☐

(7) This Document Contains   (a) Redescription New Easement Plan/Sketch ☐   (b) Schedule for: Description ☐ Parties ☐ Additional Other ☐

(8) This Document provides as follows:

(Check appropriate box and strike out inapplicable paragraph)

☐ The parties signing in box 10, who are spouses of each other, designate the property described in box 6 as a matrimonial home.

☐ The party signing in box 10, who is the spouse of _____ ,
(name)

designates the property described in box 6 as a matrimonial home.

Continued on Schedule ☐

(9) This Document relates to instrument number(s)
Not applicable ---

(10) Party(ies) (Set out Status or Interest) Name(s)	Signature(s)	Date of Signature Y M D

(11) Address for Service

(12) Party(ies) (Set out Status or Interest) Name(s)	Signature(s)	Date of Signature Y M D
Not applicable -------------------		

(13) Address for Service   Not applicable -------------------

(14) Municipal Address of Property	(15) Document Prepared by:	FOR OFFICE USE ONLY	Fees and Tax	
			Registration Fee	
			Total	

O. Reg. 95/86, Form 1

Form 2 — Cancellation of Designation of Matrimonial Home

Form 2 — Cancellation of Designation of Matrimonial Home

Family Law Act

Document General

Form 4 — Land Registration Reform Act

D

(1) Registry ☐ Land Titles ☐	(2) Page 1 of pages

(3) Property Identifier(s) Block Property	Additional: See Schedule ☐

(4) Nature of Document

Cancellation of designation of matrimonial home
(Family Law Act, s. 20)

(5) Consideration

Not applicable   Dollars $

(6) Description

FOR OFFICE USE ONLY

New Property Identifiers   Additional: See Schedule ☐

Executions   Additional: See Schedule ☐

(7) This Document Contains: (a) Redescription New Easement Plan/Sketch ☐   (b) Schedule for: Description ☐   Additional Parties ☐   Other ☐

(8) This Document provides as follows:

(Check appropriate box and strike out inapplicable paragraph)

☐ The parties signing in box 10, who are spouses of each other, cancel the designation by them of the property described in box 6 as a matrimonial home in the instrument referred to in box 9.

☐ The party signing in box 10, who is the spouse of _____ ,

(name)

cancels the designation of the property described in box 6 as a matrimonial home in the instrument referred to in box 9.   Continued on Schedule ☐

(9) This Document relates to instrument number(s)

(10) Party(ies) (Set out Status or Interest) Name(s)	Signature(s)	Date of Signature Y M D

(11) Address for Service

(12) Party(ies) (Set out Status or Interest) Name(s)	Signature(s)	Date of Signature Y M D
Not applicable		

(13) Address for Service   Not applicable

(14) Municipal Address of Property	(15) Document Prepared by:	Fees and Tax
		Registration Fee
		Total

FOR OFFICE USE ONLY

ONT. REG. 368 — ELECTION OF SURVIVING SPOUSE

made under the *Family Law Act*

R.R.O. 1990, Reg. 368

1. An election made under section 6 of the Act shall be in Form 1.

SCHEDULE

Form 1 — Election Under The Family Law Act/Choix Du Conjoint Fait En Vertu De La Loi Sur Le Droit de La Famille

Form 1
Formule 1

ELECTION UNDER THE *FAMILY LAW ACT*
CHOIX DU CONJOINT FAIT EN VERTU DE LA LOI SUR LE DROIT DE LA FAMILLE

	Court File No./*Dossier de la cour n°*

This election is filed by (solicitors)/*Déposé par (avocats)*

Name of deceased/*Nom du défunt* Surname/*Nom de famille*	Given name(s)/*Prénom(s)*

Last address of deceased/*Dernière adresse du défunt*   Street or postal address/*Rue et numéro ou adresse postale*   City, town, etc./*Cité, ville, etc.*

Date of death/*Date du décès*   Day, month, year/*Jour, mois, année*

Surviving spouse/*Conjoint survivant* Surname/*Nom de famille*	Given name(s)/*Prénom(s)*

Address of spouse/*Adresse du conjoint*   Street or postal address/*Rue et numéro ou adresse postale*   City, town, etc./*Cité, ville, etc.*   Postal Code/*Code postal*

I, ... the surviving spouse, elect:
Je soussigné(e)   (Please print)/(*Écrire en caractères d'imprimerie*)   *conjoint survivant, fais le choix suivant :*

☐ to receive the entitlement under section 5 of the *Family Law Act*;
jouir du droit prévu à l'article 5 de la Loi sur le droit de la famille;

    OR (check one box only)/
OU (cocher une seule case)

☐ to receive the entitlement under the will, or under Part II of the *Succession Law Reform Act*, if there is an intestacy, or both, if there is a partial intestacy./
bénéficier des dispositions testamentaires; s'il n'y a pas de testament, jouir du droit prévu à la partie II de la Loi portant réforme du droit des successions; s'il s'agit d'une succession en partie testamentaire et en partie sans testament, se prévaloir de ces deux options.

....
    Signature of surviving spouse/*Signature du conjoint survivant*   Date

NOTE: THIS ELECTION HAS IMPORTANT EFFECTS ON YOUR RIGHTS. YOU SHOULD HAVE LEGAL ADVICE BEFORE SIGNING IT.

REMARQUE: LE PRÉSENT CHOIX ENTRAÎNERA DES EFFECTS IMPORTANTS SUR VOS DROITS. VOUS DEVRIEZ OBTENIR DES CONSEILS JURIDIQUES AVANT DE LE SIGNER.
    O. Reg. 606/86, Form 1.; Régl. de l'Ont. 606/86, formule 1.

ONT. REG. 391/97 — CHILD SUPPORT GUIDELINES

made under the *Family Law Act*

O. Reg. 391/97, as am. O. Reg. 26/00 [Amended O. Reg. 126/00.]; 446/01.

Objectives

1. Objectives — The objectives of these guidelines are,

(a) to establish a fair standard of support for children that ensures that they benefit from the financial means of their parents and, in the case of divorce, from the financial means of both spouses after separation;

(b) to reduce conflict and tension between parents or spouses by making the calculation of child support more objective;

(c) to improve the efficiency of the legal process by giving courts, and parents and spouses, guidance in setting the levels of child support and encouraging settlement; and

(d) to ensure consistent treatment of parents or spouses and their children who are in similar circumstances.

Interpretation

2. (1) Definitions — The definitions in this subsection apply in these guidelines. "child" means,

(a) a child who is a dependant under the Act, or

(b) in cases where the *Divorce Act* (Canada) applies, a child of the marriage under that Act; ("enfant")

"income" means the annual income determined under sections 15 to 20; ("revenu")

"order assignee" means,

(a) an agency to whom an order is assigned under subsection 34(3) of the Act , or

(b) a minister, member or agency referred to in subsection 20.1(1) of the *Divorce Act* (Canada) to whom an order or the support of a child is assigned in accordance with hat subsection; ("cessionnaire de la créance alimentaire")

"parent", in a case to which the Act applies, means a parent to whom section 31 of the Act applies; ("pére ou mére")

"spouse", in a case to which the *Divorce Act* (Canada) applies, has the meaning assigned by subsection 2 of that Act, and includes a former spouse; ("époux")

"table" means,

(a) if the parent or spouse against whom an order is sought ordinarily resides in Ontario at the time of the application, the Child Support Table for Ontario set out in Schedule I to this Regulation,

(b) if the parent or spouse against whom an order is sought ordinarily resides elsewhere in Canada, the table set out in the Federal Child Support Guidelines for the province or territory in which the parent or spouse ordinarily resides at the time of the application,

(c) if the court is satisfied that the province or territory in which the parent or spouse against whom an order is sought ordinarily resides has changed since the time of the application, the table set out in the Federal Child Support Guidelines for the province or territory in which the parent or spouse ordinarily resides at the time the amount of support is determined,

(d) if the court is satisfied that the parent or spouse against whom an order is sought will, in the near future after the amount of support is determined, ordinarily reside in another province or territory than the one in which he or she ordinarily resides at the time the amount of support is determined, the table set out in the Federal Child Support Guidelines for that other province or territory,

(e) if the parent or spouse against whom an order is sought ordinarily resides outside of Canada or if the ordinary residence of the parent or spouse is unknown,

(i) the Child support Table for Ontario set out in Schedule I to this Regulation if the other parent or spouse applying for the order resides in Ontario, or

(ii) the table set out in the Federal Child Support Guidelines for the province or territory in which the parent or spouse applying for the order ordinarily resides. ("table")

(2) Income Tax Act (Canada) — Words and expressions that are used in sections 15 to 21 and that are not defined in this section have the meanings assigned to them under the *Income Tax Act* (Canada).

(3) Most current information — Where, for the purposes of these guideline, any amount is determined on the basis of specified information, the most current information must be used.

(4) Application of guidelines — In addition to their application to orders for support of a child, these guidelines apply, with such modifications as the circumstances require, to

(a) interim orders under subsection 34 (1) of the Act or subsections 15.1 (2) and 19 (9) of the *Divorce Act* (Canada);

(b) orders varying a child support order; and

(c) orders referred to in subsection 19 (7) of the *Divorce Act* (Canada).

O. Reg. 446/01, s. 1

Amount of Child Support

3. (1) Presumptive rule — Unless otherwise provided under these guidelines, the amount of an order for the support of a child for children under the age of majority is,

(a) the amount set out in the applicable table, according to the number of children under the age of majority to whom the order relates and the income of the parent or spouse against whom the order is sought; and

(b) the amount, if any, determined under section 7.

(2) Child the age of majority or over — Unless otherwise provided under these guidelines, where a child to whom an order for the support of a child relates is the age of majority or over, the amount of an order for the support of a child is,

(a) the amount determined by applying these guidelines as if the child were under the age of majority; or

(b) if the court considers that approach to be inappropriate, the amount that it considers appropriate, having regard to the condition, means, needs and other circumstances of the child and the financial ability of each parent or spouse to contribute to the support of the child.

4. Incomes over $150,000 — Where the income of the parent or spouse against whom an order for the support of a child is sought is over $150,000, the amount of an order for the support of a child is,

(a) the amount determined under section 3; or

(b) if the court considers that amount to be inappropriate,

(i) in respect of the first $150,000 of the parent's or spouse's income, the amount set out in the table for the number of children under the age of majority to whom the order relates,

(ii) in respect of the balance of the parent's or spouse's income, the amount that the court considers appropriate, having regard to the condition, means, needs and other circumstances of the children who are entitled to support and the financial ability of each parent or spouse to contribute to the support of the children, and

(iii) the amount, if any, determined under section 7.

5. Spouse in place of a parent — Where the spouse against whom an order for the support of a child is sought stands in the place of a parent for a child or the parent is not a natural or adoptive parent of the child, the amount of the order is, in respect of that parent or spouse, such amount as the court considers appropriate, having regard to these guidelines and any other parent's legal duty to support the child.

6. Medical and dental insurance — In making an order for the support of a child, where medical or dental insurance coverage for the child is available to either parent or spouse through his or her employer or otherwise at a reasonable rate, the court may order that coverage be acquired or continued.

7. (1) Special or extraordinary expenses — In an order for the support of a child, the court may, on the request of either parent or spouse or of an applicant under section 33 of the Act, provide for an amount to cover all or any portion of the following expenses, which expenses may be estimated, taking into account the necessity of the expense in relation to the child's best interests and the reasonableness of the expense in relation to the means of the parents or spouses and those of the child and to the spending pattern of the parents or spouses in respect of the child during cohabitation:

(a) child care expenses incurred as a result of the custodial parent's employment, illness, disability or education or training for employment;

(b) that portion of the medical and dental insurance premiums attributable to the child;

(c) health-related expenses that exceed insurance reimbursement by at least $100 annually, including orthodontic treatment, professional counselling provided by a psychologist, social worker, psychiatrist or any other person, physiotherapy, occupational therapy, speech therapy, prescription drugs, hearing aids, glasses and contact lenses;

(d) extraordinary expenses for primary or secondary school education or for any educational programs that meet the child's particular needs;

(e) expenses for post-secondary education; and

(f) extraordinary expenses for extracurricular activities.

(2) Sharing of expense — The guiding principle in determining the amount of an expense referred to in subsection (1) is that the expense is shared by the parents or spouses in proportion to their respective incomes after deducting from the expense, the contribution, if any, from the child.

(3) Subsidies, tax deductions, etc. — In determining the amount of an expense referred to in subsection (1), the court must take into account any subsidies, benefits or income tax deductions or credits relating to the expense, and any eligibility to claim a subsidy, benefit or income tax deduction or credit relating to the expense.

O. Reg. 446/01, s. 2

8. Split custody — Where each parent or spouse has custody of one or more children, the amount of an order for the support of a child is the difference between the amount that each parent or spouse would otherwise pay if such an order were sought against each of the parents or spouses.

9. Shared custody — Where a parent or spouse exercises a right of access to, or has physical custody of, a child for not less than 40 per cent of the time over the course of a year, the amount of the order for the support of a child must be determined by taking into account

(a) the amounts set out in the applicable tables for each of the parents or spouses;

(b) the increased costs of shared custody arrangements; and

(c) the condition, means, needs and other circumstances of each parent or spouse and of any child for whom support is sought.

10. (1) Undue hardship — On the application of either spouse or an applicant under section 33 of the Act, a court may award an amount of child support that is different from the amount determined under any of sections 3 to 5, 8 or 9 if the court finds that the parent or spouse making the request, or a child in respect of whom the request is made, would otherwise suffer undue hardship.

(2) Circumstances that may cause undue hardship — Circumstances that may cause a parent, spouse or child to suffer undue hardship include,

(a) the parent or spouse has responsibility for an unusually high level of debts reasonably incurred to support the parents or spouses and their children during cohabitation or to earn a living;

(b) the parent or spouse has unusually high expenses in relation to exercising access to a child;

(c) the parent or spouse has a legal duty under a judgment, order or written separation agreement to support any person;

(d) the spouse has a legal duty to support a child, other than a child of the marriage, who is

    (i) under the age of majority, or

    (ii) the age of majority or over but is unable, by reason of illness, disability or other cause, to obtain the necessaries of life;

(e) the parent has a legal duty to support a child, other than the child who is the subject of this application, who is under the age of majority or who is enrolled in a full time course of education;

(f) the parent or spouse has a legal duty to support any person who is unable to obtain the necessaries of life due to an illness or disability.

(3) Standards of living must be considered — Despite a determination of undue hardship under subsection (1), an application under that subsection must be denied by the court if it is of the opinion that the household of the parent or spouse who claims undue hardship would, after determining the amount of child support under any of sections 3 to 8, 8 or 9 have a higher standard of living than the household of the other parent or spouse.

(4) Standards of living test — In comparing standards of living for the purpose of subsection (3), the court may use the comparison of household standards of living test set out in Schedule II.

(5) Reasonable time — Where the court awards a different amount of child support under subsection (1), it may specify, in the order for child support, a reasonable time for the satisfaction of any obligation arising from circumstances that cause undue hardship and the amount payable at the end of that time.

(6) Reasons — Where the court makes an order for the support of a child in a different amount under this section, it must record its reason for doing so.

Elements of an Order for the Support of a Child

11. Form of payments — Where these guidelines apply to orders made under the *Divorce Act* (Canada) section 34 of the Act applies.

12. Security — The court may require in the order for the support of a child that the amount payable under the order be paid or secured, or paid and secured, in the manner specified in the order.

13. Information to be specified in order — An order for the support of a child must include,

(a) the name and birth date of each child to whom the order relates;

(b) the income of any parent or spouse whose income is used to determine the amount of the order.

(c) The amount determined under clause 3 (1) (a) for the number of children to whom the order relates;

(d) The amount determined under clause 3 (2) (b) for a child the age of majority or over;

373

(e) The particulars of any expense described in subsection 7 (1), the child to whom the expense relates and the amount of the expense or, where that amount cannot be determined, the proportion to be paid in relation to the expense; and

(f) The date on which the lump sum or first payment is payable and the day of the month or other time period on which all subsequent payments are to be made.

Variation of Orders for the Support of a Child

14. Circumstances for variation — For the purposes of subsection 37(2.2) of the Act and subsection 17(4) of the *Divorce Act* (Canada), any one of the following constitutes a change of circumstances that gives rise to the making of a variation order:

1. In the case where the amount of child support includes a determination made in accordance with the table, any change in circumstances that would result in a different order for the support of a child or any provision thereof.
2. In the case where the amount of child support does not include a determination made in accordance with a table, any change in the condition, means, needs or other circumstances of either parent or spouse or of any child who is entitled to support.
3. In the case of an order made under the *Divorce Act* (Canada) before May 1, 1997, the coming into force of section 15.1 of that Act, enacted by section 2 of chapter 1 of the Statutes of Canada, (1997).
4. In the case of an order made under the Act, the coming into force of subsection 33 (11) of the Act.

O. Reg. 446/01, s. 3

Income

15. (1) Determination of annual income — Subject to subsection (2), a parent's or spouse's annual income is determined by the court in accordance with sections 16 to 20.

(2) Agreement — Where both parents or spouses agree in writing on the annual income of a parent or spouse, the court may consider that amount to be the parent's or spouse's income for the purposes of these guidelines if the court thinks that the amount is reasonable having regard to the income information provided under section 21.

16. Calculation of annual income — Subject to sections 17 to 20, a parent's or spouse's annual income is determined using the sources of income set out under the heading "Total income" in the T1 General form issued by the Canada Customs and Revenue Agency and is adjusted in accordance with Schedule III.

O. Reg. 446/01, s. 4

17. (1) Pattern of income — If the court is of the opinion that the determination of a parent's or spouse's annual income under section 16 would not be the fairest determination of that income, the court may have regard to the parent's or spouse's income over the last three years and determine an amount that is fair and reasonable in light of any pattern of income, fluctuation in income or receipt of a non-recurring amount during those years.

(2) Non-recurring losses — Where a parent or spouse has incurred a non-recurring capital or business investment loss, the court may, if it is of the opinion that the determination of the parent's or spouse's annual income under section 16 would not provide the fairest determination of the annual income, choose not to apply sections 6 and 7 of Schedule III, and adjust the amount of the loss, including related expenses and carrying charges and interest expenses, to arrive at such amount as the court considers appropriate.

O. Reg. 446/01, s. 5

18. (1) Shareholder, director or officer — Where a parent or spouse is a shareholder, director or officer of a corporation and the court is of the opinion that the amount of the parent's or spouse's annual income as determined under section 16 does not fairly reflect all the money available to the parent or spouse for the payment of child support, the court may consider the situations described in section 17 and determine the parent's or spouse's annual income to include,

(a) all or part of the pre-tax income of the corporation, and of any corporation that is related to that corporation, for the most recent taxation year; or

(b) an amount commensurate with the services that the parent or spouse provides the corporation, provided that the amount does not exceed the corporation's pre-tax income.

(2) Adjustment to corporation's pre-tax income — In determining the pre-tax income of a corporation for the purposes of subsection (1), all amounts paid by the corporation as salaries, wages or management fees, or other payments or benefits, to or on behalf of person with whom the corporation does not deal at arm's length must be added to the pre-tax income, unless the parent or spouse establishes that the payments were reasonable in the circumstances.

19. (1) Imputing income — The court may impute such amount of income to a parent or spouse as it considers appropriate in the circumstances, which circumstances include,

(a) the parent or spouse is intentionally under-employed or unemployed, other than where the under- employment or unemployment is required by the needs of any child or by the reasonable educational or health needs of the parent or spouse;

(b) the parent or spouse is exempt from paying federal or provincial income tax;

(c) the parent or spouse lives in a country that has effective rates of income tax that are significantly lower than those in Canada;

(d) it appears that income has been diverted which would affect the level of child support to be determined under these guidelines;

(e) the parent's or spouse's property is not reasonably utilized to generate income;

(f) the parent or spouse has failed to provide income information when under a legal obligation to do so;

(g) the parent or spouse unreasonably deducts expenses from income;

(h) the parent or spouse derives a significant portion of income from dividends, capital gains or other sources that are taxed at a lower rate than employment or business income or that are exempt from tax; and

(i) the parent or spouse is a beneficiary under a trust and is or will be in receipt of income or other benefits from the trust.

(2) Reasonableness of expenses — For the purpose of clause (1) (g), the reasonableness of an expense deduction is not solely governed by whether the deduction is permitted under the *Income Tax Act* (Canada).

O. Reg. 446/01, s. 6

20. Non-resident — Where a parent or spouse is a non-resident of Canada, the parent's or spouse's annual income is determined s though the parent or spouse were a resident of Canada.

Income Information

21. (1) Obligation of applicant — A parent or spouse who is applying for an order for the support of a child and whose income information is necessary to determine the amount of the order must include with the application,

(a) a copy of every personal income tax return filed by the parent or spouse for each of the three most recent taxation years;

(b) a copy of every notice of assessment and reassessment issued to the parent or spouse for each of the three most recent taxation years;

(c) where the parent or spouse is an employee, the most recent statement of earnings indicating the total earnings paid in the year to date, including overtime, or, where such a statement is not provided by the employer, a letter from the parent's or spouse's employer setting out that information including the parent's or spouse's rate of annual salary or remuneration;

(d) where the parent or spouse is self-employed, for the three most recent taxation years,

(i) the financial statements of the parent's or spouse's business or professional practice, other than a partnership, and

(ii) a statement showing a breakdown of all salaries, wages, management fees or other payments or benefit paid to, or on behalf of, persons or corporations with whom the parent or spouse does not deal at arm's length;

(e) where the parent or spouse is a partner in partnership, confirmation of the parent's or spouse's income and draw from, and capital in, the partnership for its three most recent taxation years;

(f) where the parent or spouse controls a corporation, for its three most recent taxation years,

(i) the financial statements of the corporation and its subsidiaries, and

(ii) a statement showing a breakdown of all salaries, wages, management fees or other payments or benefits paid to, or on behalf of, persons or corporations with whom the corporation, and every related corporation, does not deal at arm's length;

(g) where the parent or spouse is a beneficiary under a trust, a copy of the trust settlement agreement and copies of the trust's three most recent financial statements; and

(h) in addition to any information that must be included under clauses (c) to (g), where the parent or spouse receives income from employment insurance, social assistance, a pension, workers compensation, disability payments or any other source, the most recent statement of income indicating the total amount of income from the applicable source during the current year or, if such a statement is not provided, a letter from the appropriate authority stating the required information.

(2) Obligation of respondent — A parent or spouse who is served with an application for an order for the support of a child and whose income information is necessary to determine the amount of the order, must, within 30 days after the application is served if the parent or spouse resides in Canada or the United States or within 60 days if the parent or spouse resides elsewhere, or such other time limit as the court specifies, provide the court, as well as the other spouse, an applicant under section 33 of the Act or the order assignee with the documents referred to in subsection (1).

(3) **Special expenses or undue hardship** — Where, in the course of proceedings in respect of an application for an order for the support of a child, a parent or spouse requests an amount to cover expenses referred to in subsection 7 (1) or pleads undue hardship, the parent or spouse who would be receiving the amount of child support must, within 30 days after the amount is sought or undue hardship is pleaded if the parent or spouse resides in Canada or the United States or within 60 days if the parent or spouse resides elsewhere, or such other time limit as the court specifies, provide the court and the other parent or spouse with the documents referred to in subsection (1).

(4) **Income over $150,000** — Where, in the course of proceedings in respect of an application for an order for the support of a child, it is established that the income of the parent or spouse who would be paying the amount of child support is greater than $150,000, the other parent or spouse must, within 30 days after the income is established to be greater than $150,000 if the other parent or spouse resides in Canada or the United States or within 60 days if the other parent or spouse resides elsewhere, or such other time limit as the court specifies, provide the court and the other parent or spouse with the documents referred to in subsection (1).

O. Reg. 446/01, s. 7

22. (1) Failure to comply — Where a parent or spouse fails to comply with section 21, the other spouse, an applicant under section 33 of the Act or an order assignee may apply,

(a) to have the application for an order for the support of a child set down for a hearing, or move for judgment; or

(b) for an order requiring the parent or spouse who failed to comply to provide the court, as well as the other parent or spouse or order assignee, as the case may be, with the required documents.

(2) **Costs of the proceedings** — Where a court makes an order under clause (1) (a) or (b), the court may award costs in favour of the other spouse, the applicant under section 33 of the Act or an order assignee up to an amount that fully compensates the other spouse, the applicant or order assignee for all costs incurred in the proceedings.

23. Adverse inference — Where the court proceeds to a hearing on the basis of an application under clause 22 (1) (a), the court may draw an adverse inference against the parent or spouse who failed to comply and impute income to that parent or spouse in such amount as it considers appropriate.

24. Failure to comply with court order — Where a parent or spouse fails to comply with an order issued on the basis of an application under clause 22 (1) (b), the court may,

(a) strike out any of the parent's or spouse's pleadings;

(b) make a contempt order against the parent or spouse;

(c) proceed to a hearing, in the course of which it may draw an adverse inference against the parent or spouse and impute income to that parent or spouse in such amount as it considers appropriate; and

(d) award costs in favour of the other spouse, an applicant under section 33 of the Act or an order assignee up to an amount that fully compensates the other spouse, the applicant or assignee for all costs incurred in the proceedings.

25. (1) Continuing obligation to provide income information — Every parent or spouse against whom an order for the support of a child has been made must, on the written request of the other spouse or the person or agency entitled to payment under the order not more than once a year after the making of the order and as long as the child is a child within the meaning of these guidelines, provide that other spouse, or the person or agency entitled to payment under the order, with,

(a) the documents referred to in subsection 21 (1) for any of the three most recent taxation years for which the parent or spouse has not previously provided the documents;

(b) as applicable, any current information in writing, about the status of any expenses included in the order pursuant to subsection 7 (1); and

(c) as applicable, any current information, in writing, about the circumstances relied on by the court in a determination of undue hardship.

(2) Below minimum income — Where a court has determined that the parent or spouse against whom an order for the support of a child is sought does not have to pay child support because his or her income level is below the minimum amount required for application of the tables, that parent or spouse must, on the written request of the other spouse or the applicant under section 33 of the Act, not more than once a year after the determination and as long as the child is a child within the meaning of these guidelines, provide the other spouse or the applicant with the documents referred to in subsection 21 (1) for any of the three most recent taxation years for which the parent or spouse has not previously provided the documents.

(3) Obligation of receiving parent or spouse — Where the income information of the parent or spouse in favour of whom an order for the support of a child is made is used to determine the amount of the order, the parent or spouse must, not more than once a year after the making of the order and as long as the child is a child within the meaning of these guidelines, on the written request of the other parent or spouse, provide the other parent or spouse with the documents and information referred to in subsection (1).

(4) Information requests — Where a parent or spouse requests information from the other parent or spouse under any of subsections (1) to (3) and the income information of the requesting parent or spouse is used to determine the amount of the order for the support of a child, the requesting parent or spouse must include the documents and information referred to in subsection (1) with the request.

(5) Time limit — A parent or spouse who receives a request made under any of subsections (1) to (3) must provide the required documents within 30 days after the request's receipt if the parent or spouse resides in Canada or the United States and within 60 days after the request's receipt if the parent or spouse resides elsewhere.

(6) Deemed receipt — A request made under any of subsection (1) to (3) is deemed to have been received 10 days after it is sent.

(7) Failure to comply — A court may, on application by either spouse, an applicant under section 33 of the Act or an order assignee, where the parent or spouse has failed to comply with any of subsections (1) to (3),

    (a) consider the parent or spouse to be in contempt of court and award costs in favour of the applicant up to an amount that fully compensates the applicant for all costs incurred in the proceedings; or

    (b) make an order requiring the parent or spouse to provide the required documents to the court, as well as to the spouse, order assignee or applicant under section 33 of the Act, as the case may be.

(8) Unenforceable provision — A provision in a judgment, order or agreement purporting to limit a parent's or spouse's obligation to provide documents under this section is unenforceable.

Coming into Force

26. Coming into Force — **(1)** These guidelines come into force with respect to cases to which the *Family Law Act* applies on the day the *Uniform Federal and Provincial Child Support Guidelines Act, 1997* is proclaimed in force.

(2) These guidelines come into force with respect to cases to which the *Divorce Act* (Canada) applies on the day these guidelines are specified by order of the Governor in Council as "applicable guidelines" within the meaning of that Act under subsection 2 (5) of that Act.

SCHEDULE I
(Subsection 2(1))

Child Support Table for Ontario

Notes:

1. The child support table for Ontario sets out the amount of monthly child support payments for Ontario on the basis of the annual income of the parent or spouse ordered to pay child support (the "support payor") and the number of children for whom a table amount is payable. Refer to these guidelines to determine whether special measures apply.

2. There is a threshold level of income below which no amount of child support is payable. Child support amounts are specified for incomes up to $150,000 per year. Refer to section 4 of these guidelines to determine the amount of child support payments for support payors with annual incomes over $150,000.

3. Income is set out in the table in intervals of $1,000. Monthly amounts are determined by adding the basic amount and the amount calculated by multiplying the applicable percentage by the portion of the income that exceeds the lower amount within that interval of income.

4. The amounts in the tables are based on economic studies of average spending on children in families at different income levels in Canada. They are calculated on the basis that child support payments are no longer taxable in the hands of the receiving parent and no longer deductible by the paying parent. They are calculated using a mathematical formula and generated by a computer program.

5. The formula referred to in note 4 sets support amounts to reflect average expenditures on children by a parent or spouse with a particular number of children and level of income. The calculation is based on the support payor's income. The formula uses the basic personal amount for non-refundable tax credits to recognize personal expense, and takes other federal and provincial income taxes and credits into account. Federal Child Tax benefits and Goods and Services Tax credits for children are excluded from the calculation. At lower income levels, the formula sets the amounts to take into account the combined impact of taxes and child support payments on the support payor's limited disposable income.

Schedule I

Federal Child Support Tables/Tables federales de pensions alimentaires pour enfants		Province: Ontario No. of Children/N BRE d'enfants: One/Un	

Income/ Revenu ($)		Monthly Award/ Paiement mensuel $	
From/De	To/A	Basic Amount/ Montant de base	Plus (%)	of Income over/du revenu depassant
---	---	---	---	---
0	6729	0		
6730	6999	0	5.00	6730
7000	7999	14	4.81	7000
8000	8999	62	0.86	8000
9000	9999	70	0.86	9000
10000	10999	79	0.86	10000
11000	11999	87	0.86	11000
12000	12999	96	0.86	12000
13000	13999	105	0.86	13000
14000	14999	113	0.68	14000
15000	15999	120	0.68	15000
16000	16999	127	0.68	16000
17000	17999	134	0.68	17000
18000	18999	140	0.72	18000
19000	19999	148	1.50	19000
20000	20999	163	1.50	20000
21000	21999	178	1.50	21000
22000	22999	192	1.06	22000
23000	23999	203	0.95	23000
24000	24999	213	0.95	24000
25000	25999	222	0.95	25000
26000	26999	232	0.88	26000
27000	27999	240	0.88	27000
28000	28999	249	0.88	28000
29000	29999	258	0.80	29000
30000	30999	266	0.71	30000
31000	31999	273	0.76	31000
32000	32999	281	0.83	32000
33000	33999	289	0.83	33000
34000	34999	297	0.79	34000
35000	35999	305	0.78	35000
36000	36999	313	0.81	36000
37000	37999	321	0.81	37000
38000	38999	329	0.81	38000
39000	39999	337	0.81	39000
40000	40999	345	0.84	40000

Federal Child Support Tables/Tables federales de pensions alimentaires pour enfants		Province: Ontario No. of Children/N BRE d'enfants: One/Un	

Income/ Revenu ($)		Monthly Award/ Paiement mensuel $	

From/De	To/A	Basic Amount/ Montant de base	Plus (%)	of Income over/du revenu depassant
41000	41999	354	0.84	41000
42000	42999	362	0.84	42000
43000	43999	371	0.84	43000
44000	44999	379	0.84	44000
45000	45999	387	0.84	45000
46000	46999	396	0.84	46000
47000	47999	404	0.84	47000
48000	48999	413	0.84	48000
49000	49999	421	0.84	49000
50000	50999	429	0.84	50000
51000	51999	436	0.84	51000
52000	52999	446	0.76	52000
53000	53999	454	0.72	53000
54000	54999	461	0.72	54000
55000	55999	468	0.73	55000
56000	56999	475	0.80	56000
57000	57999	483	0.80	57000
58000	58999	492	0.80	58000
59000	59999	500	0.75	59000
60000	60999	507	0.74	60000
61000	61999	514	0.74	61000
62000	62999	522	0.74	62000
63000	63999	529	0.70	63000
64000	64999	536	0.67	64000
65000	65999	543	0.51	65000
66000	66999	548	0.52	66000
67000	67999	553	0.55	67000
68000	68999	559	0.64	68000
69000	69999	565	0.67	69000
70000	70999	572	0.67	70000
71000	71999	578	0.67	71000
72000	72999	685	0.67	72000
73000	73999	592	0.67	73000
74000	74999	599	0.67	74000
75000	75999	605	0.67	75000
76000	76999	612	0.67	76000

Federal Child Support Tables/Tables federales de pensions alimentaires pour enfants				Province: Ontario No. of Children/N BRE d'enfants: One/Un
Income/ Revenu ($)		**Monthly Award/ Paiement mensuel $**		
From/De	To/A	Basic Amount/ Montant de base	Plus (%)	of Income over/du revenu depassant
77000	77999	619	0.67	77000
78000	78999	625	0.67	78000
79000	79999	632	0.67	79000
80000	80999	639	0.67	80000
81000	81999	645	0.67	81000
82000	82999	652	0.67	82000
83000	83999	659	0.67	83000
84000	84999	666	0.67	84000
85000	85999	672	0.67	85000
86000	86999	679	0.67	86000
87000	87999	686	0.67	87000
88000	88999	692	0.67	88000
89000	89999	699	0.67	89000
90000	90999	706	0.67	90000
91000	91999	712	0.67	91000
92000	92999	719	0.67	92000
93000	93999	726	0.67	93000
94000	94999	733	0.67	94000
95000	95999	739	0.67	95000
96000	96999	746	0.67	96000
97000	97999	753	0.67	97000
98000	98999	759	0.67	98000
99000	99999	766	0.67	99000
100000	100999	773	0.67	100000
101000	101999	779	0.67	101000
102000	102999	786	0.67	102000
103000	103999	793	0.67	103000
104000	104999	799	0.67	104000
105000	105999	806	0.67	105000
106000	106999	813	0.67	106000
107000	107999	820	0.67	107000
108000	108999	826	0.67	108000
109000	109999	833	0.67	109000
110000	110999	840	0.67	110000
111000	111999	846	0.67	111000
112000	112999	853	0.67	112000

Federal Child Support Tables/Tables federales de pensions alimentaires pour enfants				Province: Ontario No. of Children/N BRE d'enfants: One/Un
Income/ Revenu ($)		**Monthly Award/ Paiement mensuel $**		
From/De	To/A	Basic Amount/ Montant de base	Plus (%)	of Income over/du revenu depassant
113000	113999	860	0.67	113000
114000	114999	866	0.67	114000
115000	115999	873	0.67	115000
116000	116999	880	0.67	116000
117000	117999	887	0.67	117000
118000	118999	893	0.67	118000
119000	119999	900	0.67	119000
120000	120999	907	0.67	120000
121000	121999	913	0.67	121000
122000	122999	920	0.67	122000
123000	123999	927	0.67	123000
124000	124999	933	0.67	124000
125000	125999	940	0.67	125000
126000	126999	947	0.67	126000
127000	127999	954	0.67	127000
128000	128999	960	0.67	128000
129000	129999	967	0.67	129000
130000	130999	974	0.67	130000
131000	131999	980	0.67	131000
132000	132999	987	0.67	132000
133000	133999	994	0.67	133000
134000	134999	1000	0.67	134000
135000	135999	1007	0.67	135000
136000	136999	1014	0.67	136000
137000	137999	1020	0.67	137000
138000	138999	1027	0.67	138000
139000	139999	1034	0.67	139000
140000	140999	1041	0.67	140000
141000	141999	1047	0.67	141000
142000	142999	1054	0.67	142000
143000	143999	1061	0.67	143000
144000	144999	1067	0.67	144000
145000	145999	1074	0.67	145000
146000	146999	1081	0.67	146000
147000	147999	1087	0.67	147000
148000	148999	1094	0.67	148000

Federal Child Support Tables/Tables federales de pensions alimentaires pour enfants
Province: Ontario
No. of Children/N^{BRE} d'enfants: One/Un

Income/ Revenu ($)		Monthly Award/ Paiement mensuel $		
From/De	To/A	Basic Amount/ Montant de base	Plus (%)	of Income over/du revenu depassant
149000	149999	1101	0.67	149000

Federal Child Support Tables/Tables federales de pensions alimentaires pour enfants
Province: Ontario
No. of Children/N^{BRE} d'enfants: One/Un

Income/ Revenu ($)		Monthly Award/ Paiement mensuel $		
From/De	To/A	Basic Amount/ Montant de base	Plus (%)	of Income over/du revenu depassant
150000	or greater/ ou plus	1108	0.67	150000

Federal Child Support Tables/Tables federales de pensions alimentaires pour enfants
Province: Ontario
No. of Children/N^{BRE} d'enfants: Two/Deux

Income/ Revenu ($)		Monthly Award/ Paiement mensuel $		
From/De	To/A	Basic Amount/ Montant de base	Plus (%)	of Income over/du revenu depassant
0	6729	0		
6730	6999	0	5.42	6730
7000	7999	15	5.23	7000
8000	8999	67	3.54	8000
9000	9999	102	1.65	9000
10000	10999	119	2.86	10000
11000	11999	147	2.90	11000
12000	12999	176	2.21	12000
13000	13999	198	1.24	13000
14000	14999	211	1.24	14000
15000	15999	223	1.24	15000
16000	16999	236	1.24	16000
17000	17999	248	1.24	17000
18000	18999	260	1.24	18000
19000	19999	273	1.24	19000
20000	20999	285	1.24	20000
21000	21999	297	1.24	21000
22000	22999	310	1.24	22000
23000	23999	322	1.80	23000
24000	24999	340	1.96	24000

Federal Child Support Tables/Tables federales de pensions alimentaires pour enfants
Province: Ontario
No. of Children/N^{BRE} d'enfants: Two/Deux

Income/ Revenu ($)		Monthly Award/ Paiement mensuel $		
From/De	To/A	Basic Amount/ Montant de base	Plus (%)	of Income over/du revenu depassant
25000	25999	360	1.95	25000
26000	26999	379	1.85	26000
27000	27999	398	1.85	27000
28000	28999	416	1.66	28000
29000	29999	433	1.25	29000
30000	30999	446	1.10	30000
31000	31999	456	1.15	31000
32000	32999	468	1.26	32000
33000	33999	481	1.26	33000
34000	34999	493	1.26	34000
35000	35999	506	1.26	35000
36000	36999	518	1.30	36000
37000	37999	531	1.30	37000
38000	38999	544	1.26	38000
39000	39999	557	1.26	39000
40000	40999	570	1.31	40000
41000	41999	583	1.31	41000
42000	42999	596	1.31	42000
43000	43999	609	1.31	43000
44000	44999	622	1.31	44000

Federal Child Support Tables/Tables federales de pensions alimentaires pour enfants				Province: Ontario No. of Children/N BRE d'enfants: Two/Deux
Income/ Revenu ($)		Monthly Award/ Paiement mensuel $		
From/De	To/A	Basic Amount/ Montant de base	Plus (%)	of Income over/du revenu depassant
45000	45999	635	1.31	45000
46000	46999	648	1.31	46000
47000	47999	661	1.31	47000
48000	48999	674	1.31	48000
49000	49999	687	1.31	49000
50000	50999	700	1.31	50000
51000	51999	713	1.31	51000
52000	52999	726	1.22	52000
53000	53999	739	1.17	53000
54000	54999	750	1.17	54000
55000	55999	762	1.18	55000
56000	56999	774	1.25	56000
57000	57999	786	1.25	57000
58000	58999	799	1.25	58000
59000	59999	811	1.16	59000
60000	60999	823	1.15	60000
61000	61999	834	1.15	61000
62000	62999	846	1.15	62000
63000	63999	857	1.10	63000
64000	64999	868	1.07	64000
65000	65999	879	0.91	65000
66000	66999	888	0.91	66000
67000	67999	897	0.94	67000
68000	68999	907	1.02	68000
69000	69999	917	1.04	69000
70000	70999	927	1.04	70000
71000	71999	938	1.04	71000
72000	72999	948	1.04	72000
73000	73999	959	1.04	73000
74000	74999	969	1.04	74000
75000	75999	979	1.04	75000
76000	76999	990	1.04	76000
77000	77999	1000	1.04	77000
78000	78999	1011	1.04	78000
79000	79999	1021	1.04	79000
80000	80999	1031	1.04	80000

Federal Child Support Tables/Tables federales de pensions alimentaires pour enfants				Province: Ontario No. of Children/N BRE d'enfants: Two/Deux
Income/ Revenu ($)		Monthly Award/ Paiement mensuel $		
From/De	To/A	Basic Amount/ Montant de base	Plus (%)	of Income over/du revenu depassant
81000	81999	1042	1.04	81000
82000	82999	1052	1.04	82000
83000	83999	1063	1.04	83000
84000	84999	1073	1.04	84000
85000	85999	1084	1.04	85000
86000	86999	1094	1.04	86000
87000	87999	1104	1.04	87000
88000	88999	1115	1.04	88000
89000	89999	1125	1.04	89000
90000	90999	1136	1.04	90000
91000	91999	1146	1.04	91000
92000	92999	1156	1.04	92000
93000	93999	1167	1.04	93000
94000	94999	1177	1.04	94000
95000	95999	1188	1.04	95000
96000	96999	1198	1.04	96000
97000	97999	1209	1.04	97000
98000	98999	1219	1.04	98000
99000	99999	1229	1.04	99000
100000	100999	1240	1.04	100000
101000	101999	1250	1.04	101000
102000	102999	1261	1.04	102000
103000	103999	1271	1.04	103000
104000	104999	1281	1.04	104000
105000	105999	1292	1.04	105000
106000	106999	1302	1.04	106000
107000	107999	1313	1.04	107000
108000	108999	1323	1.04	108000
109000	109999	1334	1.04	109000
110000	110999	1344	1.04	110000
111000	111999	1354	1.04	111000
112000	112999	1365	1.04	112000
113000	113999	1375	1.04	113000
114000	114999	1386	1.04	114000
115000	115999	1396	1.04	115000
116000	116999	1406	1.04	116000

Federal Child Support Tables/Tables federales de pensions alimentaires pour enfants				Province: Ontario No. of Children/N BRE d'enfants: Two/Deux
Income/ Revenu ($)		Monthly Award/ Paiement mensuel $		
From/De	To/A	Basic Amount/ Montant de base	Plus (%)	of Income over/du revenu depassant
117000	117999	1417	1.04	117000
118000	118999	1427	1.04	118000
119000	119999	1438	1.04	119000
120000	120999	1448	1.04	120000
121000	121999	1459	1.04	121000
122000	122999	1469	1.04	122000
123000	123999	1479	1.04	123000
124000	124999	1490	1.04	124000
125000	125999	1500	1.04	125000
126000	126999	1511	1.04	126000
127000	127999	1521	1.04	127000
128000	128999	1531	1.04	128000
129000	129999	1542	1.04	129000
130000	130999	1552	1.04	130000
131000	131999	1563	1.04	131000
132000	132999	1573	1.04	132000
133000	133999	1584	1.04	133000
134000	134999	1594	1.04	134000

Federal Child Support Tables/Tables federales de pensions alimentaires pour enfants				Province: Ontario No. of Children/N BRE d'enfants: Two/Deux
Income/ Revenu ($)		Monthly Award/ Paiement mensuel $		
From/De	To/A	Basic Amount/ Montant de base	Plus (%)	of Income over/du revenu depassant
135000	135999	1604	1.04	135000
136000	136999	1615	1.04	136000
137000	137999	1625	1.04	137000
138000	138999	1636	1.04	138000
139000	139999	1646	1.04	139000
140000	140999	1656	1.04	140000
141000	141999	1667	1.04	141000
142000	142999	1677	1.04	142000
143000	143999	1688	1.04	143000
144000	144999	1698	1.04	144000
145000	145999	1709	1.04	145000
146000	146999	1719	1.04	146000
147000	147999	1729	1.04	147000
148000	148999	1740	1.04	148000
149000	149999	1750	1.04	149000
150000	or greater/ ou plus	1761	1.04	150000

Federal Child Support Tables/Tables federales de pensions alimentaires pour enfants				Province: Ontario No. of Children/N BRE d'enfants: Three/Trois
Income/ Revenu ($)		Monthly Award/ Paiement mensuel $		
From/De	To/A	Basic Amount/ Montant de base	Plus (%)	of Income over/du revenu depassant
0	6729	0		
6730	6999	0	5.83	6730
7000	7999	16	5.65	7000
8000	8999	72	3.95	8000
9000	9999	112	2.06	9000

Federal Child Support Tables/Tables federales de pensions alimentaires pour enfants				Province: Ontario No. of Children/N BRE d'enfants: Three/Trois
Income/ Revenu ($)		Monthly Award/ Paiement mensuel $		
From/De	To/A	Basic Amount/ Montant de base	Plus (%)	of Income over/du revenu depassant
10000	10999	132	3.27	10000
11000	11999	165	3.32	11000
12000	12999	198	3.20	12000
13000	13999	230	3.20	13000
14000	14999	262	3.20	14000

Federal Child Support Tables/Tables federales de pensions alimentaires pour enfants			Province: Ontario No. of Children/N ᴮᴿᴱ d'enfants: Three/Trois		Federal Child Support Tables/Tables federales de pensions alimentaires pour enfants			Province: Ontario No. of Children/N ᴮᴿᴱ d'enfants: Three/Trois
Income/ Revenu ($)		Monthly Award/ Paiement mensuel $			Income/ Revenu ($)		Monthly Award/ Paiement mensuel $	
From/De	To/A	Basic Amount/ Montant de base	Plus (%)	of Income over/du revenu depassant	From/De	To/A	Basic Amount/ Montant de base	Plus (%)	of Income over/du revenu depassant
15000	15999	294	2.81	15000	51000	51999	934	1.68	51000
16000	16999	323	1.68	16000	52000	52999	950	1.59	52000
17000	17999	339	1.68	17000	53000	53999	966	1.54	53000
18000	18999	356	1.68	18000	54000	54999	982	1.54	54000
19000	19999	373	1.68	19000	55000	55999	997	1.55	55000
20000	20999	390	1.68	20000	56000	56999	1013	1.61	56000
21000	21999	407	1.68	21000	57000	57999	1029	1.61	57000
22000	22999	424	1.68	22000	58000	58999	1045	1.61	58000
23000	23999	440	1.68	23000	59000	59999	1061	1.50	59000
24000	24999	457	1.68	24000	60000	60999	1076	1.47	60000
25000	25999	474	1.67	25000	61000	61999	1091	1.47	61000
26000	26999	491	1.54	26000	62000	62999	1105	1.47	62000
27000	27999	506	1.88	27000	63000	63999	1120	1.43	63000
28000	28999	525	2.20	28000	64000	64999	1134	1.39	64000
29000	29999	547	2.14	29000	65000	65999	1148	1.22	65000
30000	30999	568	2.09	30000	66000	66999	1160	1.22	66000
31000	31999	589	2.14	31000	67000	67999	1173	1.24	67000
32000	32999	611	2.28	32000	68000	68999	1185	1.32	68000
33000	33999	633	1.64	33000	69000	69999	1198	1.34	69000
34000	34999	650	1.60	34000	70000	70999	1212	1.34	70000
35000	35999	666	1.60	35000	71000	71999	1225	1.34	71000
36000	36999	682	1.60	36000	72000	72999	1238	1.34	72000
37000	37999	698	1.66	37000	73000	73999	1252	1.34	73000
38000	38999	715	1.66	38000	74000	74999	1265	1.34	74000
39000	39999	732	1.66	39000	75000	75999	1279	1.34	75000
40000	40999	748	1.72	40000	76000	76999	1292	1.34	76000
41000	41999	765	1.70	41000	77000	77999	1305	1.34	77000
42000	42999	782	1.68	42000	78000	78999	1319	1.34	78000
43000	43999	799	1.68	43000	79000	79999	1332	1.34	79000
44000	44999	816	1.68	44000	80000	80999	1346	1.34	80000
45000	45999	833	1.68	45000	81000	81999	1359	1.34	81000
46000	46999	850	1.68	46000	82000	82999	1372	1.34	82000
47000	47999	866	1.68	47000	83000	83999	1386	1.34	83000
48000	48999	883	1.68	48000	84000	84999	1399	1.34	84000
49000	49999	900	1.68	49000	85000	85999	1413	1.34	85000
50000	50999	917	1.68	50000	86000	86999	1426	1.34	86000

| Federal Child Support Tables/Tables federales de pensions alimentaires pour enfants | | | | Province: Ontario No. of Children/N ^{BRE} d'enfants: Three/Trois | Federal Child Support Tables/Tables federales de pensions alimentaires pour enfants | | | | Province: Ontario No. of Children/N ^{BRE} d'enfants: Three/Trois |

Income/ Revenu ($)		Monthly Award/ Paiement mensuel $			Income/ Revenu ($)		Monthly Award/ Paiement mensuel $		
From/De	To/A	Basic Amount/ Montant de base	Plus (%)	of Income over/du revenu depassant	From/De	To/A	Basic Amount/ Montant de base	Plus (%)	of Income over/du revenu depassant
87000	87999	1439	1.34	87000	120000	120999	1881	1.34	120000
88000	88999	1453	1.34	88000	121000	121999	1895	1.34	121000
89000	89999	1466	1.34	89000	122000	122999	1908	1.34	122000
90000	90999	1480	1.34	90000	123000	123999	1922	1.34	123000
91000	91999	1493	1.34	91000	124000	124999	1935	1.34	124000
92000	92999	1506	1.34	92000	125000	125999	1948	1.34	125000
93000	93999	1520	1.34	93000	126000	126999	1962	1.34	126000
94000	94999	1533	1.34	94000	127000	127999	1975	1.34	127000
95000	95999	1546	1.34	95000	128000	128999	1988	1.34	128000
96000	96999	1560	1.34	96000	129000	129999	2002	1.34	129000
97000	97999	1573	1.34	97000	130000	130999	2015	1.34	130000
98000	98999	1587	1.34	98000	131000	131999	2029	1.34	131000
99000	99999	1600	1.34	99000	132000	132999	2042	1.34	132000
100000	100999	1613	1.34	100000	133000	133999	2055	1.34	133000
101000	101999	1627	1.34	101000	134000	134999	2069	1.34	134000
102000	102999	1640	1.34	102000	135000	135999	2082	1.34	135000
103000	103999	1654	1.34	103000	136000	136999	2096	1.34	136000
104000	104999	1667	1.34	104000	137000	137999	2109	1.34	137000
105000	105999	1680	1.34	105000	138000	138999	2122	1.34	138000
106000	106999	1694	1.34	106000	139000	139999	2136	1.34	139000
107000	107999	1707	1.34	107000	140000	140999	2149	1.34	140000
108000	108999	1721	1.34	108000	141000	141999	2163	1.34	141000
109000	109999	1734	1.34	109000	142000	142999	2176	1.34	142000
110000	110999	1747	1.34	110000	143000	143999	2189	1.34	143000
111000	111999	1761	1.34	111000	144000	144999	2203	1.34	144000
112000	112999	1774	1.34	112000	145000	145999	2216	1.34	145000
113000	113999	1788	1.34	113000	146000	146999	2230	1.34	146000
114000	114999	1801	1.34	114000	147000	147999	2243	1.34	147000
115000	115999	1814	1.34	115000	148000	148999	2256	1.34	148000
116000	116999	1828	1.34	116000	149000	149999	2270	1.34	149000
117000	117999	1841	1.34	117000		or greater/ ou plus			
118000	118999	1855	1.34	118000					
119000	119999	1868	1.34	119000	150000	ou plus	2283	1.34	150000

Federal Child Support Tables/Tables federales de pensions alimentaires pour enfants			Province: Ontario No. of Children/N ᴮᴿᴱ d'enfants: Four/Quatre		Federal Child Support Tables/Tables federales de pensions alimentaires pour enfants			Province: Ontario No. of Children/N ᴮᴿᴱ d'enfants: Four/Quatre
Income/ Revenu ($)		Monthly Award/ Paiement mensuel $			Income/ Revenu ($)		Monthly Award/ Paiement mensuel $	
From/De	To/A	Basic Amount/ Montant de base	Plus (%)	of Income over/du revenu depassant	From/De	To/A	Basic Amount/ Montant de base	Plus (%)	of Income over/du revenu depassant
---	---	---	---	---	---	---	---	---	---
0	6729	0			41000	41999	914	2.02	41000
6730	6999	0	6.25	6730	42000	42999	934	2.02	42000
7000	7999	17	6.06	7000	43000	43999	954	2.02	43000
8000	8999	78	4.37	8000	44000	44999	975	2.02	44000
9000	9999	121	2.48	9000	45000	45999	995	1.99	45000
10000	10999	146	3.69	10000	46000	46999	1015	1.99	46000
11000	11999	183	3.74	11000	47000	47999	1034	1.99	47000
12000	12999	220	3.62	12000	48000	48999	1054	1.99	48000
13000	13999	256	3.62	13000	49000	49999	1074	1.99	49000
14000	14999	293	3.62	14000	50000	50999	1094	1.99	50000
15000	15999	329	3.62	15000	51000	51999	1114	1.99	51000
16000	16999	365	3.62	16000	52000	52999	1134	1.89	52000
17000	17999	401	3.34	17000	53000	53999	1153	1.84	53000
18000	18999	435	2.05	18000	54000	54999	1171	1.84	54000
19000	19999	455	2.05	19000	55000	55999	1189	1.85	55000
20000	20999	476	2.05	20000	56000	56999	1208	1.90	56000
21000	21999	496	2.05	21000	57000	57999	1227	1.90	57000
22000	22999	517	2.05	22000	58000	58999	1246	1.90	58000
23000	23999	537	2.05	23000	59000	59999	1265	1.77	59000
24000	24999	558	2.05	24000	60000	60999	1283	1.74	60000
25000	25999	578	2.04	25000	61000	61999	1300	1.74	61000
26000	26999	598	1.88	26000	62000	62999	1317	1.74	62000
27000	27999	617	1.88	27000	63000	63999	1335	1.69	63000
28000	28999	636	1.88	28000	64000	64999	1352	1.66	64000
29000	29999	655	1.66	29000	65000	65999	1368	1.48	65000
30000	30999	672	1.37	30000	66000	66999	1383	1.48	66000
31000	31999	685	2.33	31000	67000	67999	1398	1.50	67000
32000	32999	709	2.50	32000	68000	68999	1413	1.56	68000
33000	33999	733	2.50	33000	69000	69999	1428	1.58	69000
34000	34999	758	2.50	34000	70000	70999	1444	1.58	70000
35000	35999	783	2.51	35000	71000	71999	1460	1.58	71000
36000	36999	809	2.58	36000	72000	72999	1476	1.58	72000
37000	37999	834	2.03	37000	73000	73999	1492	1.58	73000
38000	38999	855	1.95	38000	74000	74999	1508	1.58	74000
39000	39999	874	1.96	39000	75000	75999	1523	1.58	75000
40000	40999	894	2.02	40000	76000	76999	1539	1.58	76000

Federal Child Support Tables/Tables federales de pensions alimentaires pour enfants				Province: Ontario No. of Children/N BRE d'enfants: Four/Quatre	Federal Child Support Tables/Tables federales de pensions alimentaires pour enfants				Province: Ontario No. of Children/N BRE d'enfants: Four/Quatre
Income/ Revenu ($)		Monthly Award/ Paiement mensuel $			Income/ Revenu ($)		Monthly Award/ Paiement mensuel $		
From/De	To/A	Basic Amount/ Montant de base	Plus (%)	of Income over/du revenu depassant	From/De	To/A	Basic Amount/ Montant de base	Plus (%)	of Income over/du revenu depassant
77000	77999	1555	1.58	77000	113000	113999	2125	1.58	113000
78000	78999	1571	1.58	78000	114000	114999	2141	1.58	114000
79000	79999	1587	1.58	79000	115000	115999	2157	1.58	115000
80000	80999	1603	1.58	80000	116000	116999	2172	1.58	116000
81000	81999	1618	1.58	81000	117000	117999	2188	1.58	117000
82000	82999	1634	1.58	82000	118000	118999	2204	1.58	118000
83000	83999	1650	1.58	83000	119000	119999	2220	1.58	119000
84000	84999	1666	1.58	84000	120000	120999	2236	1.58	120000
85000	85999	1682	1.58	85000	121000	121999	2252	1.58	121000
86000	86999	1698	1.58	86000	122000	122999	2267	1.58	122000
87000	87999	1713	1.58	87000	123000	123999	2283	1.58	123000
88000	88999	1729	1.58	88000	124000	124999	2299	1.58	124000
89000	89999	1745	1.58	89000	125000	125999	2315	1.58	125000
90000	90999	1761	1.58	90000	126000	126999	2331	1.58	126000
91000	91999	1777	1.58	91000	127000	127999	2347	1.58	127000
92000	92999	1793	1.58	92000	128000	128999	2362	1.58	128000
93000	93999	1808	1.58	93000	129000	129999	2378	1.58	129000
94000	94999	1824	1.58	94000	130000	130999	2394	1.58	130000
95000	95999	1840	1.58	95000	131000	131999	2410	1.58	131000
96000	96999	1856	1.58	96000	132000	132999	2426	1.58	132000
97000	97999	1872	1.58	97000	133000	133999	2442	1.58	133000
98000	98999	1888	1.58	98000	134000	134999	2457	1.58	134000
99000	99999	1903	1.58	99000	135000	135999	2473	1.58	135000
100000	100999	1919	1.58	100000	136000	136999	2489	1.58	136000
101000	101999	1935	1.58	101000	137000	137999	2505	1.58	137000
102000	102999	1951	1.58	102000	138000	138999	2521	1.58	138000
103000	103999	1967	1.58	103000	139000	139999	2537	1.58	139000
104000	104999	1983	1.58	104000	140000	140999	2552	1.58	140000
105000	105999	1998	1.58	105000	141000	141999	2568	1.58	141000
106000	106999	2014	1.58	106000	142000	142999	2584	1.58	142000
107000	107999	2030	1.58	107000	143000	143999	2600	1.58	143000
108000	108999	2046	1.58	108000	144000	144999	2616	1.58	144000
109000	109999	2062	1.58	109000	145000	145999	2631	1.58	145000
110000	110999	2077	1.58	110000	146000	146999	2647	1.58	146000
111000	111999	2093	1.58	111000	147000	147999	2663	1.58	147000
112000	112999	2109	1.58	112000	148000	148999	2679	1.58	148000

Federal Child Support Tables/Tables federales de pensions alimentaires pour enfants			Province: Ontario No. of Children/N BRE d'enfants: Four/Quatre	
Income/ Revenu ($)		**Monthly Award/ Paiement mensuel $**		
From/De	To/A	Basic Amount/ Montant de base	Plus (%)	of Income over/du revenu depassant
149000	149999	2695	1.58	149000

Federal Child Support Tables/Tables federales de pensions alimentaires pour enfants			Province: Ontario No. of Children/N BRE d'enfants: Four/Quatre	
Income/ Revenu ($)		**Monthly Award/ Paiement mensuel $**		
From/De	To/A	Basic Amount/ Montant de base	Plus (%)	of Income over/du revenu depassant
150000	or greater/ ou plus	2711	1.58	150000

Federal Child Support Tables/Tables federales de pensions alimentaires pour enfants			Province: Ontario No. of Children/N BRE d'enfants: Five/Cinq	
Income/ Revenu ($)		**Monthly Award/ Paiement mensuel $**		
From/De	To/A	Basic Amount/ Montant de base	Plus (%)	of Income over/du revenu depassant
0	6729	0		
6730	6999	0	6.25	6730
7000	7999	17	6.06	7000
8000	8999	78	4.37	8000
9000	9999	121	2.48	9000
10000	10999	146	3.69	10000
11000	11999	183	3.74	11000
12000	12999	220	3.62	12000
13000	13999	256	3.62	13000
14000	14999	293	3.62	14000
15000	15999	329	3.62	15000
16000	16999	365	3.62	16000
17000	17999	401	3.62	17000
18000	18999	437	3.62	18000
19000	19999	474	3.62	19000
20000	20999	510	3.62	20000
21000	21999	546	3.62	21000
22000	22999	582	3.54	22000
23000	23999	618	2.35	23000
24000	24999	641	2.35	24000

Federal Child Support Tables/Tables federales de pensions alimentaires pour enfants			Province: Ontario No. of Children/N BRE d'enfants: Five/Cinq	
Income/ Revenu ($)		**Monthly Award/ Paiement mensuel $**		
From/De	To/A	Basic Amount/ Montant de base	Plus (%)	of Income over/du revenu depassant
25000	25999	665	2.34	25000
26000	26999	688	2.17	26000
27000	27999	710	2.17	27000
28000	28999	731	2.17	28000
29000	29999	753	1.92	29000
30000	30999	772	1.58	30000
31000	31999	788	1.64	31000
32000	32999	805	1.83	32000
33000	33999	823	2.07	33000
34000	34999	844	2.68	34000
35000	35999	870	2.69	35000
36000	36999	897	2.77	36000
37000	37999	925	2.77	37000
38000	38999	953	2.77	38000
39000	39999	980	2.78	39000
40000	40999	1008	2.86	40000
41000	41999	1037	2.35	41000
42000	42999	1060	2.27	42000
43000	43999	1083	2.27	43000
44000	44999	1106	2.27	44000

Federal Child Support Tables/Tables federales de pensions alimentaires pour enfants				Province: Ontario No. of Children/N BRE d'enfants: Five/Cinq	Federal Child Support Tables/Tables federales de pensions alimentaires pour enfants				Province: Ontario No. of Children/N BRE d'enfants: Five/Cinq
Income/ Revenu ($)		Monthly Award/ Paiement mensuel $			Income/ Revenu ($)		Monthly Award/ Paiement mensuel $		
From/De	To/A	Basic Amount/ Montant de base	Plus (%)	of Income over/du revenu depassant	From/De	To/A	Basic Amount/ Montant de base	Plus (%)	of Income over/du revenu depassant
45000	45999	1129	2.27	45000	81000	81999	1835	1.79	81000
46000	46999	1151	2.27	46000	82000	82999	1853	1.79	82000
47000	47999	1174	2.27	47000	83000	83999	1870	1.79	83000
48000	48999	1197	2.26	48000	84000	84999	1888	1.79	84000
49000	49999	1219	2.24	49000	85000	85999	1906	1.79	85000
50000	50999	1242	2.24	50000	86000	86999	1924	1.79	86000
51000	51999	1264	2.24	51000	87000	87999	1942	1.79	87000
52000	52999	1287	2.14	52000	88000	88999	1960	1.79	88000
53000	53999	1308	2.09	53000	89000	89999	1978	1.79	89000
54000	54999	1329	2.09	54000	90000	90999	1995	1.79	90000
55000	55999	1350	2.10	55000	91000	91999	2013	1.79	91000
56000	56999	1371	2.15	56000	92000	92999	2031	1.79	92000
57000	57999	1392	2.15	57000	93000	93999	2049	1.79	93000
58000	58999	1414	2.15	58000	94000	94999	2067	1.79	94000
59000	59999	1435	1.99	59000	95000	95999	2085	1.79	95000
60000	60999	1455	1.97	60000	96000	96999	2103	1.79	96000
61000	61999	1475	1.97	61000	97000	97999	2120	1.79	97000
62000	62999	1494	1.97	62000	98000	98999	2138	1.79	98000
63000	63999	1514	1.92	63000	99000	99999	2156	1.79	99000
64000	64999	1533	1.88	64000	100000	100999	2174	1.79	100000
65000	65999	1552	1.69	65000	101000	101999	2192	1.79	101000
66000	66999	1569	1.69	66000	102000	102999	2210	1.79	102000
67000	67999	1586	1.71	67000	103000	103999	2228	1.79	103000
68000	68999	1603	1.77	68000	104000	104999	2245	1.79	104000
69000	69999	1620	1.79	69000	105000	105999	2263	1.79	105000
70000	70999	1638	1.79	70000	106000	106999	2281	1.79	106000
71000	71999	1656	1.79	71000	107000	107999	2299	1.79	107000
72000	72999	1674	1.79	72000	108000	108999	2317	1.79	108000
73000	73999	1692	1.79	73000	109000	109999	2335	1.79	109000
74000	74999	1710	1.79	74000	110000	110999	2353	1.79	110000
75000	75999	1728	1.79	75000	111000	111999	2370	1.79	111000
76000	76999	1745	1.79	76000	112000	112999	2388	1.79	112000
77000	77999	1763	1.79	77000	113000	113999	2406	1.79	113000
78000	78999	1781	1.79	78000	114000	114999	2424	1.79	114000
79000	79999	1799	1.79	79000	115000	115999	2442	1.79	115000
80000	80999	1817	1.79	80000	116000	116999	2460	1.79	116000

FLA Regs

Federal Child Support Tables/Tables federales de pensions alimentaires pour enfants		Province: Ontario No. of Children/N ᴮᴿᴱ d'enfants: Five/Cinq		
Income/ Revenu ($)		Monthly Award/ Paiement mensuel $		
From/De	To/A	Basic Amount/ Montant de base	Plus (%)	of Income over/du revenu depassant
117000	117999	2478	1.79	117000
118000	118999	2495	1.79	118000
119000	119999	2513	1.79	119000
120000	120999	2531	1.79	120000
121000	121999	2549	1.79	121000
122000	122999	2567	1.79	122000
123000	123999	2585	1.79	123000
124000	124999	2603	1.79	124000
125000	125999	2620	1.79	125000
126000	126999	2638	1.79	126000
127000	127999	2656	1.79	127000
128000	128999	2674	1.79	128000
129000	129999	2692	1.79	129000
130000	130999	2710	1.79	130000
131000	131999	2728	1.79	131000
132000	132999	2745	1.79	132000
133000	133999	2763	1.79	133000
134000	134999	2781	1.79	134000

Federal Child Support Tables/Tables federales de pensions alimentaires pour enfants		Province: Ontario No. of Children/N ᴮᴿᴱ d'enfants: Five/Cinq		
Income/ Revenu ($)		Monthly Award/ Paiement mensuel $		
From/De	To/A	Basic Amount/ Montant de base	Plus (%)	of Income over/du revenu depassant
135000	135999	2799	1.79	135000
136000	136999	2817	1.79	136000
137000	137999	2835	1.79	137000
138000	138999	2853	1.79	138000
139000	139999	2870	1.79	139000
140000	140999	2888	1.79	140000
141000	141999	2906	1.79	141000
142000	142999	2924	1.79	142000
143000	143999	2942	1.79	143000
144000	144999	2960	1.79	144000
145000	145999	2978	1.79	145000
146000	146999	2995	1.79	146000
147000	147999	3013	1.79	147000
148000	148999	3031	1.79	148000
149000	149999	3049	1.79	149000
150000	or greater/ ou plus	3067	1.79	150000

Federal Child Support Tables/Tables federales de pensions alimentaires pour enfants		Province: Ontario No. of Children/N ᴮᴿᴱ d'enfants: Six or more/Six ou plus		
Income/ Revenu ($)		Monthly Award/ Paiement mensuel $		
From/De	To/A	Basic Amount/ Montant de base	Plus (%)	of Income over/du revenu depassant
0	6729	0		
6730	6999	0	6.25	6730
7000	7999	17	6.06	7000
8000	8999	78	437	8000
9000	9999	121	2.48	9000

Federal Child Support Tables/Tables federales de pensions alimentaires pour enfants		Province: Ontario No. of Children/N ᴮᴿᴱ d'enfants: Six or more/Six ou plus		
Income/ Revenu ($)		Monthly Award/ Paiement mensuel $		
From/De	To/A	Basic Amount/ Montant de base	Plus (%)	of Income over/du revenu depassant
10000	10999	146	3.69	10000
11000	11999	183	3.74	11000
12000	12999	220	3.62	12000
13000	13999	256	3.62	13000
14000	14999	293	3.62	14000

Federal Child Support Tables/Tables federales de pensions alimentaires pour enfants			Province: Ontario No. of Children/N ᴮᴿᴱ d'enfants: Six or more/Six ou plus
Income/ Revenu ($)		**Monthly Award/ Paiement mensuel $**	
From/De To/A	Basic Amount/ Montant de base	Plus (%)	of Income over/du revenu depassant
15000 15999	329	3.62	15000
16000 16999	365	3.62	16000
17000 17999	401	3.62	17000
18000 18999	437	3.62	18000
19000 19999	474	3.62	19000
20000 20999	510	3.62	20000
21000 21999	546	3.62	21000
22000 22999	582	3.62	22000
23000 23999	618	3.62	23000
24000 24999	655	3.62	24000
25000 25999	691	3.59	25000
26000 26999	727	3.20	26000
27000 27999	759	3.20	27000
28000 28999	791	3.20	28000
29000 29999	823	2.74	29000
30000 30999	850	2.10	30000
31000 31999	871	2.18	31000
32000 32999	893	2.15	32000
33000 33999	914	2.05	33000
34000 34999	935	2.05	34000
35000 35999	955	2.06	35000
36000 36999	976	2.58	36000
37000 37999	1002	2.93	37000
38000 38999	1031	2.93	38000
39000 39999	1060	2.94	39000
40000 40999	1090	3.03	40000
41000 41999	1120	3.03	41000
42000 42999	1151	3.03	42000
43000 43999	1181	3.03	43000
44000 44999	1211	3.03	44000
45000 45999	1241	2.53	45000
46000 46999	1267	2.49	46000
47000 47999	1292	2.49	47000
48000 48999	1316	2.49	48000
49000 49999	1341	2.49	49000
50000 50999	1366	2.49	50000

Federal Child Support Tables/Tables federales de pensions alimentaires pour enfants			Province: Ontario No. of Children/N ᴮᴿᴱ d'enfants: Six or more/Six ou plus
Income/ Revenu ($)		**Monthly Award/ Paiement mensuel $**	
From/De To/A	Basic Amount/ Montant de base	Plus (%)	of Income over/du revenu depassant
51000 51999	1391	2.49	51000
52000 52999	1416	2.36	52000
53000 53999	1439	2.30	53000
54000 54999	1462	2.30	54000
55000 55999	1485	2.31	55000
56000 56999	1508	2.35	56000
57000 57999	1532	2.35	57000
58000 58999	1555	2.35	58000
59000 59999	1579	2.19	59000
60000 60999	1601	2.15	60000
61000 61999	1622	2.15	61000
62000 62999	1644	2.15	62000
63000 63999	1665	2.10	63000
64000 64999	1686	2.07	64000
65000 65999	1707	1.87	65000
66000 66999	1726	1.87	66000
67000 67999	1744	1.88	67000
68000 68999	1763	1.94	68000
69000 69999	1783	1.96	69000
70000 70999	1802	1.96	70000
71000 71999	1822	1.96	71000
72000 72999	1841	1.96	72000
73000 73999	1861	1.96	73000
74000 74999	1881	1.96	74000
75000 75999	1900	1.96	75000
76000 76999	1920	1.96	76000
77000 77999	1939	1.96	77000
78000 78999	1959	1.96	78000
79000 79999	1978	1.96	79000
80000 80999	1998	1.96	80000
81000 81999	2018	1.96	81000
82000 82999	2037	1.96	82000
83000 83999	2057	1.96	83000
84000 84999	2076	1.96	84000
85000 85999	2096	1.96	85000
86000 86999	2115	1.96	86000

FLA Regs

| Federal Child Support Tables/Tables federales de pensions alimentaires pour enfants | | | | Province: Ontario No. of Children/N ᴮᴿᴱ d'enfants: Six or more/Six ou plus | | Federal Child Support Tables/Tables federales de pensions alimentaires pour enfants | | | | Province: Ontario No. of Children/N ᴮᴿᴱ d'enfants: Six or more/Six ou plus |
| Income/ Revenu ($) | | Monthly Award/ Paiement mensuel $ | | | Income/ Revenu ($) | | Monthly Award/ Paiement mensuel $ | | |
From/De	To/A	Basic Amount/ Montant de base	Plus (%)	of Income over/du revenu depassant	From/De	To/A	Basic Amount/ Montant de base	Plus (%)	of Income over/du revenu depassant
87000	87999	2135	1.96	87000	120000	120999	2781	1.96	120000
88000	88999	2155	1.96	88000	121000	121999	2801	1.96	121000
89000	89999	2174	1.96	89000	122000	122999	2820	1.96	122000
90000	90999	2194	1.96	90000	123000	123999	2840	1.96	123000
91000	91999	2213	1.96	91000	124000	124999	2859	1.96	124000
92000	92999	2233	1.96	92000	125000	125999	2879	1.96	125000
93000	93999	2253	1.96	93000	126000	126999	2899	1.96	126000
94000	94999	2272	1.96	94000	127000	127999	2918	1.96	127000
95000	95999	2292	1.96	95000	128000	128999	2938	1.96	128000
96000	96999	2311	1.96	96000	129000	129999	2957	1.96	129000
97000	97999	2331	1.96	97000	130000	130999	2977	1.96	130000
98000	98999	2350	1.96	98000	131000	131999	2996	1.96	131000
99000	99999	2370	1.96	99000	132000	132999	3016	1.96	132000
100000	100999	2390	1.96	100000	133000	133999	3036	1.96	133000
101000	101999	2409	1.96	101000	134000	134999	3055	1.96	134000
102000	102999	2429	1.96	102000	135000	135999	3075	1.96	135000
103000	103999	2448	1.96	103000	136000	136999	3094	1.96	136000
104000	104999	2468	1.96	104000	137000	137999	3114	1.96	137000
105000	105999	2487	1.96	105000	138000	138999	3133	1.96	138000
106000	106999	2507	1.96	106000	139000	139999	3153	1.96	139000
107000	107999	2527	1.96	107000	140000	140999	3173	1.96	140000
108000	108999	2546	1.96	108000	141000	141999	3192	1.96	141000
109000	109999	2566	1.96	109000	142000	142999	3212	1.96	142000
110000	110999	2585	1.96	110000	143000	143999	3231	1.96	143000
111000	111999	2605	1.96	111000	144000	144999	3251	1.96	144000
112000	112999	2624	1.96	112000	145000	145999	3270	1.96	145000
113000	113999	2644	1.96	113000	146000	146999	3290	1.96	146000
114000	114999	2664	1.96	114000	147000	147999	3310	1.96	147000
115000	115999	2683	1.96	115000	148000	148999	3329	1.96	148000
116000	116999	2703	1.96	116000	149000	149999	3349	1.96	149000
117000	117999	2722	1.96	117000		or greater/			
118000	118999	2742	1.96	118000					
119000	119999	2761	1.96	119000	150000	ou plus	3368	1.96	150000

SCHEDULE II

(Subsection 10(4))

Comparison of Household Standards of Living Test

1. Definitions — The definitions in this section apply in this Schedule.

"average tax rate" [Revoked O. Reg. 446/01, s. 8(1).]

"child" means,

> (a) in cases where the *Divorce Act* (Canada) applies, a child of the marriage or a child who,

>> (i) is under the age of majority, or

>> (ii) is the age of majority or over but is unable, by reason of illness, disability or other cause to obtain the necessaries of life, or

> (b) in cases where the Act applies, a child who is a dependant under the Act; ("enfant")

"household" means a parent or spouse and any of the following persons residing with him or her,

> (a) any person who has a legal duty to support the parent or spouse or whom the parent or spouse has a legal duty to support,

> (b) any person who shares living expenses with the parent or spouse or from whom the parent or spouse otherwise receives an economic benefit as a result of living with that person, if the court considers it reasonable for that person to be considered part of the household, and

> (c) any child whom the parent or spouse or the person described in clause (a) or (b) has legal duty to support; ("ménage")

"taxable income" means the annual taxable income determined using the calculations required to determine "Taxable Income" in the T1 General form issued by the Canada Customs and Revenue Agency. ("revenu imposable")

2. Test — The comparison of household standards of living test is as follows:

Step 1: Establish the annual income of each person in each household by applying the formula

$$A - B$$

where

A   is the person's income determined under sections 15 to 20 of these guidelines, and

B   is the federal and provincial taxes payable on the person's taxable income. Where the information on which to base the income determination is not provided, the court may impute income in the amount it considers appropriate.

395

Step 2: Adjust the annual income of each person in each household by

    (a) deducting the following amounts, calculated on an annual basis:

        (i) any amount relied on by the court as a factor that resulted in a determination of undue hardship, except any amount attributable to the support of a member of the household that is not incurred due to a disability or serious illness of that member,

        (ii) the amount that would otherwise be payable by the person in respect of a child to whom the order relates, if the pleading of undue hardship was not made,

            (A) under the applicable table, or

            (B) as considered by the court to be appropriate, where the court considers the table amount to be inappropriate,

        (iii) any amount of support that is paid by the person under a judgment, order or written separation agreement, except,

            (A) an amount already deducted under subclause (i), and

            (B) an amount paid by the person in respect of a child to whom the order referred to in subclause (ii) relates; and

    (b) adding the following amounts, calculated on an annual basis:

        (i) any amount that would otherwise be receivable by the person in respect of a child to whom the order relates, if the pleading of undue hardship was not made,

            (A) under the applicable table, or

            (B) as considered by the court to be appropriate, where the court considers the table amount to be inappropriate, and

        (ii) any amount of child support that the person has received for any child under a judgment, order or written separation agreement.

Step 3: Add the amounts of adjusted annual income for all the persons in each household to determine the total household income for each household.

Step 4: Determine the applicable low-income measures amount for each household based on the following:

(Low-income Measures)

Household Size	Low-income Measures Amount
One person 1 adult	$10,382
Two persons	
2 adults	$14,535
1 adult and 1 child	$14,535
Three persons	
3 adults	$18,688
2 adults and 1 child	$17,649
1 adult and 2 children	$17,649
Four persons	
4 adults	$22,840
3 adults and 1 child	$21,802
2 adults and 2 children	$20,764
1 adult and 3 children	$20,764
Five persons	
5 adults	$26,993
4 adults and 1 child	$25,955

(Low-income Measures)

Household Size	Low-income Measures Amount
3 adults and 2 children	$24,917
2 adults and 3 children	$23,879
1 adult and 4 children	$23,879
Six persons	
6 adults	$31,145
5 adults and 1 child	$30,108
4 adults and 2 children	$29,070
3 adults and 3 children	$28,031
2 adults and 4 children	$26,993
1 adult and 5 children	$26,993
Seven persons	
7 adults	$34,261
6 adults and 1 child	$33,222
5 adults and 2 children	$32,184
4 adults and 3 children	$31,146
3 adults and 4 children	$30,108
2 adults and 5 children	$29,070
1 adult and 6 children	$29,070
Eight persons	
8 adults	$38,413
7 adults and 1 child	$37,375
6 adults and 2 children	$36,337
5 adults and 3 children	$35,299
4 adults and 4 children	$34,261
3 adults and 5 children	$33,222
2 adults and 6 children	$32,184
1 adult and 7 children	$32,184

Step 5: Divide the household income amount (Step 3) by the low-income measures amount (Step 4) to get a household income ratio for each household.

Step 6: Compare the household income ratios. The household that has the higher ration has the higher standard of living.

O. Reg. 446/01, ss. 8, 9

SCHEDULE III

(Section 16)

Adjustments to Income

1. Employment expenses — Where the parent or spouse is an employee, the parent's or spouse's applicable employment expense described in the following provisions of the *Income Tax Act* (Canada) are deducted:

(a) [Revoked O. Reg. 446/01, s. 10(1).]

(b) paragraph 8(1)(d) concerning expenses of teacher's exchange fund contribution;

(c) paragraph 8(1)(e) concerning expenses of railway employees;

(d) paragraph 8(1)(f) concerning sales expenses;

(e) paragraph 8(1)(g) concerning transport employee's expenses;

(f) paragraph 8(1)(h) concerning travel expenses;

(f.1) paragraph 8(1)(h.1) concerning motor vehicle travel expenses;

(g) paragraph 8(1)(i) concerning dues and other expenses of performing duties;

(h) paragraph 8(1)(j) concerning motor vehicle and aircraft costs;

(i) paragraph 8(1)(l.1) concerning *Canada Pension Plan* contributions and *Employment Insurance Act* (Canada) premiums paid in respect of another employee who acts as an assistant or substitute for the parent or spouse;

(j) paragraph 8(1)(n) concerning salary reimbursement;

(k) paragraph 8(1)(o) concerning forfeited amounts;

(l) paragraph 8(1)(p) concerning musical instrument costs; and

(m) paragraph 8(1)(q) concerning artists' employment expenses.

2. Child support — Deduct any child support received that is included to determine total income in the T1 General form issued by the Canada Customs and Revenue Agency.

3. (1) Support other than child support — To calculate income for the purpose of determining an amount under an applicable table, deduct the support, not including child support, received from the other parent or spouse.

(2) Special or extraordinary expenses — To calculate income for the purpose of determining an amount under section 7 of these guidelines, deduct the support, not including child support, paid to the other parent or spouse.

4. Social assistance — Deduct any amount of social assistance income that is not attributable to the parent or spouse.

5. Dividends from taxable Canadian corporations — Replace the taxable amount of dividends from taxable Canadian corporations received by the parent or spouse by the actual amount of those dividends received by the parent or spouse.

6. Capital gains and capital losses — Replace the taxable capital gains realized in a year by the parent or spouse by the actual amount of capital gains realized by the parent or spouse in excess of the parent or spouse's actual capital losses in that year.

7. Business investment losses — Deduct the actual amount of business investment losses suffered by the parent or spouse during the year.

8. Carrying charges — Deduct the parent's or spouse's carrying charges and interest expenses that are paid by the parent or spouse and that would be deductible under the *Income Tax Act* (Canada).

9. Net self-employment income — Where the parent's or spouse's net self-employment income is determined by deducting an amount for salaries, benefits, wages or management fees, or other payments, paid to or on behalf of person with whom the parent or spouse does not deal at arm's length, include that amount, unless the parent or spouse establishes that the payments were necessary to earn the self-employment income and were reasonable in the circumstances.

10. Additional amount — Where the parent or spouse reports income from self-employment that, in accordance with sections 34.1 and 34.2 of the *Income Tax Act* (Canada), includes an additional amount earned in a prior period, deduct the amount earned in the prior period, net of reserves.

11. Capital cost allowance for property — Include the parent or spouse's deduction for an allowable capital cost allowance with respect to real property.

12. Partnership or sole proprietorship income — Where the parent or spouse earns income through a partnership or sole proprietorship, deduct any amount included in income that is properly required by the partnership or sole proprietorship for purposes of capitalization.

13. (1) Employee stock options — Where the parent or spouse has received, as an employee benefit, options to purchase shares of a Canadian-controlled private corporation or a publicly traded corporation that is subject to the same tax treatment with reference to stock options as a Canadian-controlled private corporation, and has exercised those options during the year, add the difference between the value of the shares at the time the options are exercised and the amount paid by the parent or spouse for the shares and any amount paid by the parent or spouse to acquire the options to purchase the shares, to the income for the year in which the options are exercised.

(2) Disposal of shares — If the parent or spouse has disposed of the shares during a year, deduct from the income for that year the difference determined under subsection (1).

O. Reg. 26/00, s. 1; 446/01, s. 10

Ont. Reg. 114/99 — Family Law Rules (Superior Court of Justice and Ontario Court of Justice)[2]

made under the *Courts of Justice Act*

O. Reg. 114/99 [Corrected Gazette 8/5/99 Vol. 132:19.], as am. O. Reg. 441/99; 544/99; 250/00; 202/01; 337/02; 56/03; 91/03; 92/03.

Rule 1 — General

1. Short Title — **(1)** These rules may be cited as the *Family Law Rules*.

---

[2]Notice to the Profession Family Law Rules

The *Family Law Rules*, O. Reg. 114/99, is a new set of rules for family law cases in Superior Court of Justice, Family Court and Ontario Court of Justice locations. As a result of a delay in Family Court expansion, please note the revised implementation schedule for the new rules.

The Family Law rules will come into effect on September 15, 1999, as originally scheduled, in the following locations:

(a) all sites of the Ontario Court of Justice that are not affected by Family Court expansion and

(b) the Superior Court of Justice, Family Court site in London.

In the sites listed below, the *Family Law Rules* will come into effect on November 15, 1999. Until then, the rules of procedure that are currently in effect will continue to govern.

(a) all sites designated as expansion sites for the Superior Court of Justice, Family Court, namely:

(i) St. Catharines

(ii) York Region (Newmarket)

(iii) Durham Region (Whitby/Oshawa)

(iv) Peterborough

(v) Cobourg

(vi) Lindsay

(vii) Muskoka County

(viii) Ottawa–Carleton

(ix) L'Orignal

(x) Cornwall

(xi) Brockville

(xii) Perth

and

(b) the existing Family Court sites of Hamilton–Wentworth, Simcoe County, Kingston, and Napanee

(2) Cases and Courts to Which Rules Apply — These rules apply to all family law cases in the Family Court of the Superior Court of Justice and in the Ontario Court of Justice, whether started before, on or after the day when these rules take effect,

 (a) under,

   (i) the *Change of Name Act*,

   (ii) Parts III, VI and VII of the *Child and Family Services Act*,

   (iii) the *Children's Law Reform Act*, except sections 59 and 60,

   (iv) the *Divorce Act* (Canada)

   (v) the *Family Law Act*, except Part V,

   (vi) the *Family Responsibility and Support Arrears Enforcement Act, 1996*,

   (vii) sections 6 and 9 of the *Marriage Act*, and

   (viii) the *Interjurisdictional Support Orders Act*;

 (b) for the interpretation, enforcement or variation of a marriage contract, cohabitation agreement, separation agreement or paternity agreement;

 (c) for a constructive or resulting trust or a monetary award as compensation for unjust enrichment between persons who have cohabited; and

 (d) for annulment of a marriage or a declaration of validity or invalidity of a marriage.

(2.1) Appeals — Despite subrule (2), rule 38 (appeals) applies to the Superior Court of Justice and the Divisional Court.

(3) Case Management in Family Court of Superior Court of Justice — Despite subrule (2), rule 39 (case management in the Family Court of the Superior Court of Justice) applies only to cases in the Family Court of the Superior Court of Justice, which has jurisdiction in the following municipalities:

Regional Municipality of Durham
County of Frontenac
County of Haliburton
City of Hamilton
County of Lanark
United Counties of Leeds and Grenville
County of Lennox and Addington
County of Middlesex
Territorial District of Muskoka
The part of The Regional Municipality of Niagara that was the County of Lincoln as it existed on December 31, 1969
County of Northumberland
City of Ottawa
County of Peterborough
United Counties of Prescott and Russell
County of Simcoe
United Counties of Stormont, Dundas and Glengarry
City of Kawartha Lakes
Regional Municipality of York

(4) Case Management in Ontario Court of Justice — Despite subrule (2), rule 40 (case management in the Ontario Court of Justice) applies only to cases in the Ontario Court of Justice.

(5) Family Law Case Combined with Other Matter — If a case in the court combines a family law case to which these rules apply with another matter to which these rules would not otherwise apply, the parties may agree or the court on motion may order that these rules apply to the combined case or part of it.

(6) Conditions and Directions — When making an order, the court may impose conditions and give directions as appropriate.

(7) Matters not Covered in Rules — If these rules do not cover a matter adequately, the court may give directions, and the practice shall be decided by analogy to these rules, by reference to the *Courts of Justice Act* and the Act governing the case and, if the court considers it appropriate, by reference to the Rules of Civil Procedure.

(8) Failure to Follow Rules or Obey Order — The court may deal with a failure to follow these rules, or a failure to obey an order in the case or a related case, by making any order that it considers necessary for a just determination of the matter, on any conditions that the court considers appropriate, including,

    (a) an order for costs;

    (b) an order dismissing a claim made by a party who has wilfully failed to follow the rules or obey the order.

(9) Use of Forms — The forms authorized by these rules and set out in the Appendix of Forms shall be used where applicable and may be adjusted as needed to fit the situation.

(10) Format of Written Documents — Every written document in a case,

    (a) shall be legibly typed or printed;

    (b) shall be on white paper, or on white or nearly white paper with recycled paper content; and

    (c) may appear on one or both sides of the page.

(11) Practice Directions, etc. — A practice direction, notice, memorandum or guide for the conduct of cases in any area shall be,

    (a) approved in advance by the Chief Justice or Chief Judge of the court;

    (b) filed with the secretary of the Family Rules Committee; and

    (c) published in the *Ontario Reports*.

(12) Old Practice Directions, etc. — Practice directions, notices, memoranda and guides that were issued before these rules take effect no longer apply.

(13) Transitional Provision — If a case was started before these rules take effect, the court may, on motion, order that the case or a step in the case be carried on under the rules that applied before these rules take effect.

(14) Transition — Old Forms — A form in use under the rules that applied before these rules take effect may continue to be used, if it contains substantially the same information as the form required by these rules, until April 19, 2000.

O. Reg. 441/99, s. 1; 544/99, s.1; 202/01, s. 1; 56/03, s. 1

Rule 2 — Interpretation

2. (1) Definitions — In these rules,

"address" means a person's street or municipal address, mailing address, telephone number, fax number and electronic mail address;

"appellant" means a person who starts an appeal;

"applicant" means a person who starts an application;

"application" means, as the context requires, the document that starts a case or the procedure by which new cases are brought to the court for a final order or provisional order;

"bond" includes a recognizance, and expressions that refer to the posting of a bond include the act of entering into a recognizance;

"case" means an application or any other method allowed in law for bringing a matter to the court for a final order or provisional order, and includes all motions, enforcements and appeals;

"change", when used to refer to an order or agreement, means to vary, suspend or discharge, or a variation, suspension or discharge (depending on whether the word is used as a verb or as a noun);

"child" means a child as defined in the Act governing the case or, if not defined in that Act, a person under the age of 18 years, and in a case under the *Divorce Act* (Canada) includes a "child of the marriage" within the meaning of that Act;

"child protection case" means a case under Part III of the *Child and Family Services Act*;

"clerk" means a person who has the authority of a clerk or a registrar of the court;

"contempt motion" means a motion for a contempt order;

"contempt order" means an order finding a person in contempt of court;

"continuing record" means the record containing all the written documents in a case that are filed with the court, as continuously updated as required by these rules, but does not include a trial record;

"corporation" *French version only.*

"court" means the court in which a case is being heard;

"default hearing" means a hearing under section 41 of the *Family Responsibility and Support Arrears Enforcement Act, 1996* in which a payor is required to come to court to explain why payment has not been made as required by a support order;

"Director of the Family Responsibility Office" means the Director of the Family Responsibility Office under the *Family Responsibility and Support Arrears Enforcement Act, 1996*, and "Director" has the same meaning, unless the context requires otherwise;

"document" means information, sound or images recorded by any method;

"enforcement" means the use of one or more remedies mentioned in rule 26 (enforcement of orders) to enforce an order;

"file" means to file with proof of service in the court office in the municipality,

    (a) where the case or enforcement is started, or

    (b) to which the case or enforcement is transferred;

"final order" means an order, other than a temporary order, that decides a claim in an application, including,

    (a) an order made on motion that changes a final order,

    (b) a judgment, and

    (c) an order that decides a party's rights, in an issue between the parties or between a party and a non-party;

"government agency" means the Crown, a Crown agency, a municipal government or agency, a children's aid society or any other public body;

"income source" has the same meaning as in the *Family Responsibility and Support Arrears Enforcement Act, 1996*;

"lawyer" means a lawyer licensed to practise in Ontario;

"legal aid rate" means the rate payable by the Ontario Legal Aid Plan on an account submitted by a lawyer for copying in the lawyer's office;

"mail", when used as a noun, means ordinary or regular mail, and when used as a verb means to send by ordinary or regular mail;

"municipality" means a county, district, district municipality, regional municipality, the City of Toronto or a municipal corporation formed from the amalgamation of all the municipalities of a county, district, district municipality or regional municipality, and includes,

    (a) an Indian reserve within the territorial area of a municipality, and

    (b) the part of The Regional Municipality of Niagara that was the County of Lincoln as it existed on December 31, 1969;

"on motion" means on motion of a party or a person having an interest in the case;

"payment order" means a temporary or final order, but not a provisional order, requiring a person to pay money to another person, including,

    (a) an order to pay an amount under Part I or II of the *Family Law Act* or the corresponding provisions of a predecessor Act,

    (b) a support order,

    (c) a support deduction order,

    (d) an order under section 60 or subsection 154(2) of the *Child and Family Services Act*, or under the corresponding provision of a predecessor Act,

    (e) a payment order made under rules 26 to 32 (enforcement measures) or under section 41 of the *Family Responsibility and Support Arrears Enforcement Act, 1996*,

    (f) a fine for contempt of court,

    (g) an order of forfeiture of a bond or recognizance,

    (h) an order requiring a party to pay the fees and expenses of,

        (i) an assessor, mediator or other expert named by the court, or

        (ii) a person conducting a blood test to help determine a child's parentage, and

    (i) the costs and disbursements in a case;

"payor" means a person required to pay money under an order or agreement, and includes the estate trustee of a payor who died;

"periodic payment" means an amount payable at regular intervals and includes an amount payable in instalments;

"property claim" means a claim,

(a) under Part I of the *Family Law Act*,

(b) for a constructive or resulting trust, or

(c) for a monetary award as compensation for unjust enrichment;

"provisional order" means an order that is not effective until confirmed by a court;

"recipient" means a person entitled to receive money or costs under a payment order or agreement, including,

(a) a guardian or person with custody of a child who is entitled to money for the child's benefit under an order,

(b) in the case of a support order made under the *Family Law Act*, an agency referred to in subsection 33(3) of that Act,

(c) in the case of a support order made under the *Divorce Act* (Canada), an agency referred to in subsection 20.1(1) of that Act,

(d) a children's aid society entitled to money under an order made under section 60 or subsection 154(2) of the *Child and Family Services Act*, or the corresponding provision in a predecessor Act,

(e) an assessor, mediator or other expert entitled to fees and expenses from the party named in the order, and

(f) the estate trustee of a person who was entitled to money under an order at the time of his or her death;

"Registrar General" means the Registrar General under the *Vital Statistics Act*;

"respondent" means a person against whom a claim is made in an application, answer or appeal;

"special party" means a party who is a child or who is or appears to be mentally incapable for the purposes of the *Substitute Decisions Act, 1992* in respect of an issue in the case and who, as a result, requires legal representation, but does not include a child in a custody, access, child protection, adoption or child support case;

"support deduction order" means a support deduction order as defined in section 1 of the *Family Responsibility and Support Arrears Enforcement Act, 1996*;

"support order" means an order described in subsection 34(1) of the *Family Law Act* or a support order as defined in subsection 2(1) of the *Divorce Act* (Canada) or in section 1 of the *Family Responsibility and Support Arrears Enforcement Act, 1996*;

"temporary order" means an order that says it is effective only for a limited time, and includes an interim order;

"transcript" includes an electronic recording;

"trial" includes a hearing;

"uncontested trial" means a trial at which only the party making the claim provides evidence and submissions.

(2) Primary Objective — The primary objective of these rules is to enable the court to deal with cases justly.

(3) Dealing with Cases Justly — Dealing with a case justly includes,

(a) ensuring that the procedure is fair to all parties;

(b) saving expense and time;

(c) dealing with the case in ways that are appropriate to its importance and complexity; and

(d) giving appropriate court resources to the case while taking account of the need to give resources to other cases.

(4) Duty to Promote Primary Objective — The court is required to apply these rules to promote the primary objective, and parties and their lawyers are required to help the court to promote the primary objective.

(5) Duty to Manage Cases — The court shall promote the primary objective by active management of cases, which includes,

(a) at an early stage, identifying the issues, and separating and disposing of those that do not need full investigation and trial;

(b) encouraging and facilitating use of alternatives to the court process;

(c) helping the parties to settle all or part of the case;

(d) setting timetables or otherwise controlling the progress of the case;

(e) considering whether the likely benefits of taking a step justify the cost;

(f) dealing with as many aspects of the case as possible on the same occasion; and

(g) if appropriate, dealing with the case without parties and their lawyers needing to come to court, on the basis of written documents or by holding a telephone or video conference.

O. Reg. 544/99, s. 2

Rule 3 — Time

3. (1) Counting Days — In these rules or an order, the number of days between two events is counted as follows:

1. The first day is the day after the first event.

2. The last day is the day of the second event.

(2) Counting Days — Short Periods — If a rule or order provides a period of less than seven days for something to be done, Saturdays, Sundays and other days when all court offices are closed do not count as part of the period.

(3) Day when Court Offices Closed — If the last day of a period of time under these rules or an order falls on a day when court offices are closed, the period ends on the next day they are open.

(4) Counting Days — Examples — The following are examples of how time is counted under these rules:

1. Notice of a motion must be served not later than four days before the motion date (see subrule 14(11)). Saturday and Sunday are not counted, because the notice pe-

riod is less than seven days (see subrule (2)). Service on the day set out in the left column below is in time for the motion to be heard on the day set out in the right column below.

Service on	Motion may be heard on the following
Monday	Friday
Tuesday	Monday
Wednesday	Tuesday
Thursday	Wednesday
Friday	Thursday
Saturday	Friday
Sunday	Friday

2. A respondent who is served with an application in Canada has 30 days to serve an answer (see subrule 10(1)). A respondent who is served with an application on October 1 is in time if the answer is served on or before October 31. A respondent served on November 1 is in time if the answer is served on or before December 1.

3. If the last day for doing something under these rules or an order is New Year's Day, January 1, which is a day when court offices are closed, the time expires on January 2. If January 2 is a Saturday, Sunday or other day when court offices are closed, the time expires on January 3. If January 3 is a day when court offices are closed, the time expires on January 4.

(5) Order to Lengthen or Shorten Time — The court may make an order to lengthen or shorten any time set out in these rules or an order, except that it may lengthen a time set out in subrule 33(1) (timetable for child protection cases) only if the best interests of the child require it.

(6) Written Consent to Change Time — The parties may, by consent in writing, change any time set out in these rules, except that they may not change a time set out in,

    (a) clause 14 (11)(c) (confirmation of motion);

    (b) subrules 17 (14) and (14.1) (confirmation of conference, late briefs);

    (c) subrule 33 (1) (timetable for child protection cases);

    (d) rule 39 (case management in Family Court of Superior Court of Justice); or

    (e) rule 40 (case management in Ontario Court of Justice).

(7) Late Documents Refused by Court Office — The staff at a court office shall refuse to accept a document that a person asks to file after,

    (a) the time specified in these rules; or

    (b) the later time specified in a consent under subrule (6), a statute that applies to the case, or a court order.

O. Reg. 544/99, s. 3; 202/01, s. 2

Rule 4 — Representation

4. (1) Representation for a Party — A party may,

    (a) appear without a lawyer or other representative;

    (b) be represented by a lawyer; or

(c) be represented by a person who is not a lawyer, but only if the court gives permission in advance.

(2) Private Representation of Special Party — The court may authorize a person to represent a special party if the person is,

(a) appropriate for the task; and

(b) willing to act as representative.

(3) Public Law Officer to Represent Special Party — If there is no appropriate person willing to act as a special party's representative, the court may authorize the Children's Lawyer or the Public Guardian and Trustee to act as representative, but only with that official's consent.

(4) Service of Authorization to Represent — An order under subrule (2) or (3) shall be served immediately, by the person who asked for the order or by any other person named by the court,

(a) on the representative; and

(b) on every party in the case.

(5) Representation of Party who Dies — If a party dies after the start of a case, the court may make the estate trustee a party instead, on motion without notice.

(6) Authorizing Representative for Party who Dies — If the party has no estate trustee, the court may authorize an appropriate person to act as representative, with that person's consent, given in advance.

(7) Lawyer for Child — In a case that involves a child who is not a party, the court may authorize a lawyer to represent the child, and then the child has the rights of a party, unless the court orders otherwise.

(8) Child's Rights Subject to Statute — Subrule (7) is subject to section 38 (legal representation of child, protection hearing) and subsection 114(6) (legal representation of child, secure treatment hearing) of the *Child and Family Services Act*.

(9) Choice of Lawyer — A party appearing without a lawyer may choose a lawyer by,

(a) serving on every other party and filing a notice of change in representation (Form 4) containing the lawyer's consent to act; or

(b) having a lawyer come to court on the party's behalf.

(10) Change in Representation — Except as subrule (10.1) provides, a party represented by a lawyer may, by serving on every other party and filing a notice of change in representation (Form 4),

(a) change lawyers; or

(b) appear without a lawyer.

(10.1) Exception, Child Protection Case Scheduled for Trial — In a child protection case that has been scheduled for trial or placed on a trial list, a party may act under clause (10)(b) only with the court's permission, obtained in advance by motion made with notice.

(11) Notice of Change in Representation — A notice of change in representation shall,

(a) contain the party's address for service, if the party wants to appear without a lawyer; or

(b) show the name and address of the new lawyer, if the party wants to change lawyers.

(12) Lawyer's Removal from the Case — A lawyer may make a motion for an order to be removed from the case, with notice to the client and to,

(a) the Children's Lawyer, if the client is a child;

(b) the Public Guardian and Trustee, if the client is or appears to be mentally incapable in respect of an issue in the case.

(13) Notice of Motion to Remove Lawyer — Notice of a motion to remove a lawyer shall also be served on the other parties to the case, but the evidence in support of the motion shall not be served on them, shall not be put into the continuing record and shall not be kept in the court file after the motion is heard.

(14) Affidavit in Support of Motion to Remove Lawyer — The affidavit in support of the motion shall indicate what stage the case is at, the next event in the case and any scheduled dates.

(15) Contents and Service of Order Removing Lawyer — The order removing the lawyer from the case shall,

(a) set out the client's last known address for service; and

(b) be served on all other parties, served on the client by mail, fax or electronic mail at the client's last known address and filed immediately.

O. Reg. 91/03, s. 1

Rule 5 — Where a Case Starts and is to be Heard

5. (1) Where Case Starts — Subject to sections 21.8 and 21.11 of the *Courts of Justice Act* (territorial jurisdiction — Family Court), a case shall be started,

(a) in the municipality where a party resides;

(b) if the case deals with custody of or access to a child, in the municipality where the child ordinarily resides, except for cases described in,

(i) section 22 (jurisdiction of an Ontario court) of the *Children's Law Reform Act*, and

(ii) subsection 48(2) (place for child protection hearing) and subsection 150(1) (place for adoption proceeding) of the *Child and Family Services Act*; or

(c) in a municipality chosen by all parties, but only with the court's permission given in advance in that municipality.

(2) Starting Case — Danger to Child or Party — Subject to sections 21.8 and 21.11 of the *Courts of Justice Act*, if there is immediate danger that a child may be removed from Ontario or immediate danger to a child's or party's health or safety, a party may start a case in any municipality and a motion may be heard in that municipality, but the case shall be transferred to a municipality referred to in subrule (1) immediately after the motion is heard, unless the court orders otherwise.

(3) Clerk to Refuse Documents if Case in Wrong Place — The clerk shall refuse to accept an application for filing unless,

(a) the case is started in the municipality where a party resides;

(b) the case deals with custody of or access to a child and is started in the municipality where the child ordinarily resides;

(c) the case is started in a municipality chosen by all parties and the order permitting the case to be started there is filed with the application; or

(d) the lawyer or party asking to file the application says in writing that the case is one that is permitted by clause (1)(b) or subrule (2) to be started in that municipality.

(4) Place for Steps Other than Enforcement — All steps in the case, other than enforcement, shall take place in the municipality where the case is started or transferred.

(5) Place for Enforcement — Payment Orders — All steps in enforcement of a payment order, including a motion to suspend a support deduction order, shall take place,

(a) in the municipality where the recipient resides;

(b) if the recipient does not reside in Ontario, in the municipality where the order is filed with the court for enforcement;

(c) if the person enforcing the order consents, in the municipality where the payor resides; or

(d) in a motion under section 26 (income source dispute) of the *Family Responsibility and Support Arrears Enforcement Act, 1996*, in the municipality where the income source resides.

(6) Place for Enforcement — Other Orders — All steps in the enforcement of an order other than a payment order shall take place,

(a) if the order involves custody of or access to a child,

(i) in the municipality where the child ordinarily resides, or

(ii) if the child does not ordinarily reside in Ontario, in the municipality to which the child has the closest connection;

(b) if the order involves property, in the municipality where the person enforcing the order resides or the municipality where the property is located; or

(c) in a municipality chosen by all parties, but only with the court's permission given in advance in that municipality.

(7) Alternative Place for Enforcement — Order Enforced by Contempt Motion — An order, other than a payment order, that is being enforced by a contempt motion may also be enforced in the municipality in which the order was made.

(8) Transfer to Another Municipality — If it is substantially more convenient to deal with a case or any step in the case in another municipality, the court may, on motion, order that the case or step be transferred there.

(9) Change of Place for Child Protection Case — Notice of a motion under subsection 48(3) of the *Child and Family Services Act* to transfer a case to a place within the jurisdiction of another children's aid society shall be served on the parties and the other children's aid society, with the evidence in support of the motion.

Rule 6 — Service of Documents

6. (1) Methods of Service — Service of a document under these rules may be carried out by regular service or by special service in accordance with this rule, unless an Act, rule or order provides otherwise.

(2) Regular Service — Regular service of a document on a person is carried out by,

    (a) mailing a copy to the person's lawyer or, if none, to the person;

    (b) sending a copy by courier to the person's lawyer or, if none, to the person;

    (c) depositing a copy at a document exchange to which the person's lawyer belongs;

    (d) faxing a copy to the person's lawyer or, if none, to the person; or

    (e) carrying out special service.

(3) Special Service — Special service of a document on a person is carried out by,

    (a) leaving a copy,

        (i) with the person to be served,

        (ii) if the person is or appears to be mentally incapable in respect of an issue in the case, with the person and with the guardian of the person's property or, if none, with the Public Guardian and Trustee,

        (iii) if the person is a child, with the child and with the child's lawyer, if any,

        (iv) if the person is a corporation, with an officer, director or agent of the corporation, or with a person at any place of business of the corporation who appears to be managing the place, or

        (v) if the person is a children's aid society, with an officer, director or employee of the society;

    (b) leaving a copy with the person's lawyer of record in the case, or with a lawyer who accepts service in writing on a copy of the document;

    (c) mailing a copy to the person, together with an acknowledgment of service in the form of a prepaid return postcard (Form 6), all in an envelope that is addressed to the person and has the sender's return address (but service under this clause is not valid unless the return postcard, signed by the person, is filed in the continuing record); or

    (d) leaving a copy at the person's place of residence, in an envelope addressed to the person, with anyone who appears to be an adult person resident at the same address and, on the same day or on the next, mailing another copy to the person at that address.

(4) Special Service — Documents that Could Lead to Imprisonment — Special service of the following documents shall be carried out only by a method set out in subclause (3)(a), unless the court orders otherwise:

    1. A notice of contempt motion.

    2. A summons to witness.

    3. A notice of motion or notice of default hearing in which the person to be served faces a possibility of imprisonment.

(5) Regular Service at Address on Latest Document — Regular service may be carried out at the address for service shown on the latest document filed by the person to be served.

(6) Notice of Address Change — A party whose address for service changes shall immediately serve notice of the change on the other parties and file it.

(7) Service Outside Business Hours — If a document is served by any method after 4 p.m. on a day when court offices are open or at any time on a day when they are not open, service is effective on the next day when they are open.

(8) Hours of Fax Service — Service of a document by fax may be carried out only before 4 p.m. on a day when court offices are open, unless the parties consent or the court orders otherwise.

(9) Effective Date, Service by Mail — Service of a document by mail is effective on the fifth day after it was mailed.

(10) Effective Date, Service by Courier — Service of a document by courier is effective on the day after the courier picks it up.

(11) Effective Date, Service by Document Exchange — Service by deposit at a document exchange is effective only if the copy deposited and an additional copy of the document are date-stamped by the document exchange in the presence of the person depositing the copy, and then service is effective on the day after the date on the stamp.

(12) Information to be Included with Document Served by Fax — A document that is served by fax shall show, on its first page,

    (a) the sender's name, address, telephone number and fax number;

    (b) the name of the person or lawyer to be served;

    (c) the date and time of the fax;

    (d) the total number of pages faxed; and

    (e) the name and telephone number of a person to contact in case of transmission difficulties.

(13) Maximum Length of Document that may be Faxed — Service of a document or documents relating to a single step in a case may be carried out by fax only if the total number of pages (including any cover page or back sheet) is not more than 16, unless the parties consent in advance or the court orders otherwise.

(14) Documents that may not be Faxed — A trial record, appeal record, factum or book of authorities may not be served by fax at any time unless the person to be served consents in advance.

(15) Substituted Service — The court may, on motion without notice, order that a document be served by substituted service, using a method chosen by the court, if the party making the motion,

    (a) provides detailed evidence showing,

        (i) what steps have been taken to locate the person to be served, and

        (ii) if the person has been located, what steps have been taken to serve the document on that person; and

    (b) shows that the method of service could reasonably be expected to bring the document to the person's attention.

(16) Service not Required — The court may, on motion without notice, order that service is not required if,

(a) reasonable efforts to locate the person to be served have not been or would not be successful; and

(b) there is no method of substituted service that could reasonably be expected to bring the document to the person's attention.

(17) Service by Advertisement — If the court orders service by advertisement, Form 6A shall be used.

(18) Approving Irregular Service — When a document has been served by a method not allowed by these rules or by an order, the court may make an order approving the service if the document,

(a) came to the attention of the person to be served; or

(b) would have come to the person's attention if the person had not been evading service.

(19) Proof of Service — Service of a document may be proved by,

(a) an acceptance or admission of service, written by the person to be served or the person's lawyer;

(b) an affidavit of service (Form 6B);

(c) the return postcard mentioned in clause (3)(c); or

(d) the date stamp on a copy of the document served by deposit at a document exchange.

Rule 7 — Parties

7. (1) Who are Parties — Case — A person who makes a claim in a case or against whom a claim is made in a case is a party to the case.

(2) Who are Parties — Motion — For purposes of a motion only, a person who is affected by a motion is also a party, but this does not apply to a child affected by a motion relating to custody, access, child protection, adoption or child support.

(3) Persons who must be Named as Parties — A person starting a case shall name,

(a) as an applicant, every person who makes a claim;

(b) as a respondent,

(i) every person against whom a claim is made, and

(ii) every other person who should be a party to enable the court to decide all the issues in the case.

(4) Parties in Cases Involving Children — In any of the following cases, every parent or other person who has care and control of the child involved, except a foster parent under the *Child and Family Services Act*, shall be named as a party, unless the court orders otherwise:

1. A case about custody of or access to a child.

2. A child protection case.

3. A secure treatment case (Part VI of the *Child and Family Services Act*).

(5) Party Added by Court Order — The court may order that any person who should be a party shall be added as a party, and may give directions for service on that person.

(6) Permanent Case Name and Court File Number — The court file number given to a case and the description of the parties as applicants and respondents in the case shall remain the same on a motion to change an order, a status review application, an enforcement or an appeal, no matter who starts it, with the following exceptions:

1. In an enforcement of a payment order, the parties may be described instead as payors, recipients and garnishees.

2. In an appeal, the parties shall also be described as appellants and respondents.

3. When a case is transferred to another municipality, it may be given a new court file number.

Rule 8 — Starting a Case

8. (1) Filing an Application — To start a case, a person shall file an application (Form 8, 8A, 8B, 8C, 8D or 8D.1) and, if required, a summary of court cases (Form 8E).

(2) Change to Order or Agreement — by Motion — A party who wants to ask the court to change an order or agreement shall do so only by a motion under rule 15 (except in a status review application under the *Child and Family Services Act*, to which that rule does not apply).

(3) Claims in Application — An application may contain,

(a) a claim against more than one person; and

(b) more than one claim against the same person.

(4) Court Date Set when Application Filed — When an application is filed, the clerk shall,

(a) set a court date, except as provided by subrule 39(7) (case management, standard track); and

(b) seal the application with the court seal.

(5) Service of Application — The application shall be served immediately on every other party, and special service shall be used unless the party is listed in subrule (6).

(6) Service on Officials, Agencies, etc. — The application may be served by regular service,

(a) on a foster parent, at the foster parent's residence;

(b) on a representative of a band or native community, by serving the chief or other person who appears to be in charge of its management;

(c) on any of the following persons, at their place of business:

1. A Director appointed under section 5 of the *Child and Family Services Act*.

2. A local director appointed under section 16 of the *Child and Family Services Act*.

3. An administrator in charge of a secure treatment program under Part VI of the *Child and Family Services Act*.

4. A children's aid society.

5. The Minister of Community and Social Services.

6. An agency referred to in subsection 33(3) of the *Family Law Act* or subsection 20.1(1) of the *Divorce Act* (Canada).

7. The Director of the Family Responsibility Office.

8. The Children's Lawyer.

9. The Public Guardian and Trustee.

10. The Registrar General.

(7) Serving Protection Application on Child — In a child protection case in which the child is entitled to notice, the application shall be served on the child by special service.

(8) Serving Secure Treatment Application on Child — An application for secure treatment (Part VI of the *Child and Family Services Act*) shall be served on the child by special service.

(9) Serving Application on Child's Lawyer — If an order has been made for legal representation of a child under section 38 or subsection 114(6) of the *Child and Family Services Act* or under subrule 4(7), the applicant, or another party directed by the court, shall serve all documents in the continuing record and any status review application on the child's lawyer by regular service.

(10) Serving Protection Application Before Start of Case — If a child is brought to a place of safety (section 40, 42 or 43 of the *Child and Family Services Act*) or a homemaker remains or is placed on premises (subsection 78(2) of that Act), an application may be served without being sealed by the clerk, if it is filed on or before the court date.

(11) Application not Served on or Before Court Date — If an application is not served on a respondent on or before the court date, at the applicant's request the clerk shall set a new court date for that respondent and the applicant shall make the necessary change to the application and serve it immediately on that respondent.

O. Reg. 337/02, s. 1

Rule 9 — Continuing Record

9. (1) How Continuing Record Created — A person starting a case shall,

(a) prepare the continuing record of the case, to be the court's permanent record of the case;

(b) serve it on all other parties; and

(c) before filing it, add to it the affidavits of service or other documents proving service of the continuing record under clause (b).

(2) Duty to Keep Up Continuing Record — Once the continuing record has been filed, the parties, under the clerk's supervision, are responsible for adding to it all documents that are filed in the case.

(3) Form and Cover — The continuing record shall have a red front cover and be in a form that allows documents to be added to it as this rule requires.

(4) Three-hole Format — All documents in the continuing record shall be punched in standard three-hole format.

(5) Contents — The following requirements apply to the contents of the continuing record:

1. First, there shall be a section labelled "Contents", containing a cumulative table of contents which shall be updated every time a document is filed. The cumulative table of contents shall list every document filed, indicating the tab or page number of the record where the document is found, the kind of document, which party filed it, the date of the document and the date it was filed. For an affidavit or transcript of evidence, the name of the person who gave the affidavit or the evidence shall also be shown.

2. After the first section, there shall be a section labelled "Endorsements" containing 10 blank sheets (or more if necessary), on which the judge dealing with any step in the case shall note the disposition of that step and the date. The court's file copy of each order made in the case shall be put into the endorsement section after the endorsement pages. If the continuing record has more than one volume, the endorsement section shall be only in the first one.

3. Next there shall be a section labelled "Documents", containing every document filed in the case arranged in order, with the most recent one at the back. The documents shall be numbered consecutively.

4. If 100 or more sheets have been put into the documents section of a volume of the continuing record, the person filing the next document shall create a new volume. The volume shall be numbered on its front cover and shall contain separate contents and documents sections as provided in paragraphs 1 and 3.

(6) Written Reasons for Order — If the court gives written reasons for making an order,

(a) they may be endorsed on the continuing record by hand, or the endorsement may be a short note saying that written reasons are being given separately;

(b) the clerk shall add a copy of the reasons to the endorsements section of the continuing record; and

(c) the clerk shall send a copy to the parties by mail, fax or electronic mail.

(7) Party's Duty to Keep Up Continuing Record — A party serving documents shall,

(a) serve and file any documents that are not already in the continuing record; and

(b) serve with the documents an updated cumulative table of contents that lists the documents being filed.

(8) No Service or Filing of Documents Already in Continuing Record — A party shall not serve or file any document that is already in the continuing record, despite any requirement in these rules that the document be served and filed.

(9) Documents Referred to by Number in Continuing Record — A party who is relying on a document in the continuing record shall refer to it by its tab or page number in the continuing record.

(10) Documents not to be Removed from Continuing Record — No document shall be removed from the continuing record, except by order.

(11) Use of Continuing Record for Matters after the Case Ends — If the court has made a final order, any existing continuing record for the case shall continue to be used,

(a) for an enforcement of the order, if the enforcement is started at the court office where the continuing record is kept;

(b) for a motion to change the order, if the motion is started at the court office where the continuing record is kept;

(c) for a status review of a child protection order, if the status review application is started at the court office where the continuing record is kept.

(12) Appeal — If a final order is appealed, only the notice of appeal and the order of the appeal court (and no other appeal document) shall be added to the continuing record.

(13) Transfer of Continuing Record if Case Transferred — If the court transfers a case to another municipality the clerk shall, on request, transfer the continuing record to the clerk at the court office in the other municipality, and the continuing record shall be used there as if the case had started in the other municipality.

(14) Transfer of Continuing Record on Request — If a person takes a step referred to in subrule (11) in another municipality, the clerk shall, on request, transfer the continuing record to the other municipality and then,

(a) the continuing record may be used as if the case had started in the other municipality; or

(b) a new continuing record may be started there.

(15) Continuing Record for Confirmation of Support Order — When a provisional support order or a provisional change to a support order is sent to a court in Ontario for confirmation,

(a) if the provisional order or change was made in Ontario, the clerk shall send the continuing record to the court office where the confirmation is to take place and the respondent shall update it as this rule requires; and

(b) if the provisional order or change was not made in Ontario, the clerk shall prepare the continuing record and the respondent shall update it as this rule requires.

(16) Transitional Provision — This rule applies to cases started before these rules come into effect, in the following manner:

1. Any party may at any time prepare, serve and file the continuing record as described in subrule (1). This rule then applies to all documents filed afterward.

2. If neither party has filed the continuing record in accordance with paragraph 1, the first party who files a document after these rules come into effect shall start the continuing record as described in subrule (1). This rule then applies to all documents filed afterward.

3. Despite paragraph 2, the court may free a party from the obligation to start the continuing record, and give other directions about the form and contents of the record for the case.

O. Reg. 544/99, s. 4

Rule 10 — Answering a Case

10. (1) Serving and Filing Answer — A person against whom an application is made shall serve an answer (Form 10, 33B or 33B.1) on every other party and file it within 30 days after being served with the application.

(2) Time for Answer — Application Served Outside Canada or U.S.A. — If an application is served outside Canada or the United States of America, the time for serving and filing an answer is 60 days.

(2.1) Exception — Placement for Adoption — In an application to dispense with a parent's consent before adoption placement, (Form 8D.1), the time for serving the answer is,

(a) 20 days, if the application is served in Canada or the United States of America;

(b) 40 days, if the application is served outside Canada or the United States of America.

(3) Answer May Include Claim — A respondent may include in the answer,

(a) a claim against the applicant;

(b) a claim against any other person, who then also becomes a respondent in the case.

(4) Answer by Added Respondent — Subrules (1) to (3) apply to a respondent added under subrule (3), except that the time for serving and filing an answer is 14 days after service on the added respondent, or 30 days if the added respondent is served outside Canada or the United States of America.

(5) No Answer or Answer Struck Out — If a respondent does not serve and file an answer as this rule requires, or if the answer is struck out by an order,

(a) the respondent is not entitled to any further notice of steps in the case (except as subrule 25(13) (service of order) provides);

(b) the respondent is not entitled to participate in the case in any way;

(c) the court may deal with the case in the respondent's absence; and

(d) the clerk may set a date for an uncontested trial.

(6) Reply — A party may, within 10 days after being served with an answer, serve and file a reply (Form 10A) in response to a claim made in the answer.

O. Reg. 337/02, s. 2; 91/03, s. 2

Rule 11 — Amending an Application, Answer or Reply

11. (1) Amending Application without Court's Permission — An applicant may amend the application without the court's permission as follows:

1. If no answer has been filed, by serving and filing an amended application in the manner set out in rule 8 (starting a case).

2. If an answer has been filed, by serving and filing an amended application in the manner set out in rule 8 and also filing the consent of all parties to the amendment.

(2) Amending Answer without Court's Permission — A respondent may amend the answer without the court's permission as follows:

1. If the application has been amended, by serving and filing an amended answer within 14 days after being served with the amended application.

2. If the application has not been amended, by serving and filing an amended answer and also filing the consent of all parties to the amendment.

(2.1) Child Protection, Amendments Without Court's Permission — In a child protection case, if a significant change relating to the child happens after the original document is filed,

(a) the applicant may serve and file an amended application, an amended plan of care or both; and

(b) the respondent may serve and file an amended answer and plan of care.

(3) Amending Application or Answer with Court's Permission — On motion, the court shall give permission to a party to amend an application, answer or reply, unless the amendment would disadvantage another party in a way for which costs or an adjournment could not compensate.

(4) How Amendment is Shown — An amendment shall be clearly shown by underlining all changes, and the rule or order permitting the amendment and the date of the amendment shall be noted in the margin of each amended page.

91/03, s. 3

Rule 12 — Withdrawing, Combining or Splitting Cases

12. (1) Withdrawing Application, Answer or Reply — A party who does not want to continue with all or part of a case may withdraw all or part of the application, answer or reply by serving a notice of withdrawal (Form 12) on every other party and filing it.

(2) Withdrawal — Special Party's Application, Answer or Reply — A special party's application, answer or reply may be withdrawn (whether in whole or in part) only with the court's permission, and the notice of motion for permission shall be served on every other party and on,

(a) the Children's Lawyer, if the special party is a child;

(b) the Public Guardian and Trustee, if the special party is not a child.

(3) Costs Payable on Withdrawal — A party who withdraws all or part of an application, answer or reply shall pay the costs of every other party in relation to the withdrawn application, answer, reply or part, up to the date of the withdrawal, unless the court orders or the parties agree otherwise.

(4) Costs on Withdrawal by Government Agency — Despite subrule (3), if the party is a government agency, costs are in the court's discretion.

(5) Combining and Splitting Cases — If it would be more convenient to hear two or more cases, claims or issues together or to split a case into two or more separate cases, claims or issues, the court may, on motion, order accordingly.

(6) Splitting Divorce from Other Issues — The court may, on motion, make an order splitting a divorce from the other issues in a case if,

(a) neither spouse will be disadvantaged by the order; and

(b) reasonable arrangements have been made for the support of any children of the marriage.

Rule 13 — Financial Statements

13. (1) Financial Statement with Application, Answer or Motion — If an application, answer or notice of motion contains a claim for support, a property claim, or a claim for exclusive possession of the matrimonial home and its contents,

(a) the party making the claim shall serve and file a financial statement (Form 13 or 13.1) with the document that contains the claim; and

(b) the party against whom the claim is made shall serve and file a financial statement within the time for serving and filing an answer, reply or affidavit in response to the motion, whether the party is serving an answer, reply or affidavit in response to the motion or not.

(1.1) Form 13 for Support Claim Without Property Claim — If the application, answer or notice of motion contains a claim for support but does not contain a property claim or a claim for exclusive possession of the matrimonial home and its contents, the financial statement used by the parties under these rules shall be in Form 13.

(1.2) Form 13.1 for Property Claim With or Without Support Claim — If the application, answer or notice of motion contains a property claim or a claim for exclusive possession of the matrimonial home and its contents, the financial statement used by the parties under these rules shall be in Form 13.1, whether a claim for support is also included or not.

(1.3) Exception, Certain Support Claims — If the only claim for support contained in the application, answer or notice of motion is a claim for child support in the amount specified in the table of the applicable child support guidelines, the party making the claim is not required to file a financial statement, unless the application, answer or notice of motion also contains a property claim or a claim for exclusive possession of the matrimonial home and its contents.

(1.4) Transition — A person who files a financial statement or a new financial statement on or after April 28, 2003, is required to use Form 13 or Form 13.1, as the case may be, as made by Ontario Regulation 92/03, even if the case was started before April 28, 2003.

(2) Claim for Payment Order under CFSA — If an application, answer or notice of motion contains a claim for a payment order under section 60 of the *Child and Family Services Act*, clause (1)(a) does not apply to the children's aid society but clause (1)(b) applies to the party against whom the claim is made.

(3) Financial Statements in Custody Cases — If an application, answer or notice of motion contains a claim for custody of or access to a child and this rule does not otherwise require the parties to serve and file financial statements, the court may order each party to serve and file a financial statement in Form 13 within the time decided by the court.

(4) Financial Statement with Motion to Change Support — The following requirements apply if a motion contains a claim for a change in a support order or agreement:

1. The party making the motion shall serve and file a financial statement with the notice of motion.

2. The party against whom the claim is made shall serve and file a financial statement as soon as possible after being served with the notice of motion, but in any event no later than two days before the motion date. Any affidavit in response to the motion shall be served and filed at the same time as the financial statement.

(5) No Financial Statement from Assignee — The assignee of a support order is not required to serve and file a financial statement under subrule (4).

(6) Full Disclosure in Financial Statement — A party who serves and files a financial statement shall,

(a) make full and frank disclosure of the party's financial situation;

(b) attach any documents to prove the party's income that the financial statement requires;

(c) follow the instructions set out in the form; and

(d) fully complete all portions of the statement.

(7) Income Tax Documents Required — The clerk shall not accept a party's financial statement for filing unless,

(a) copies of the party's income tax returns and notices of assessment for the three previous taxation years are attached as the form requires;

(b) the financial statement contains the party's signed direction to the Canada Customs and Revenue Agency (Form 13A) for disclosure of the party's income and deduction printouts; or

(c) the financial statement contains a sworn statement that the party is not required to file an income tax return because of the *Indian Act* (Canada).

(8) No Financial Statement by Consent — Spousal Support in Divorce — Parties to a claim for spousal support under the *Divorce Act* (Canada) do not need to serve and file financial statements if they file a consent,

(a) agreeing not to serve and file financial statements; or

(b) agreeing to a specified amount of support, or to no support.

(9) No Financial Statement by Consent — Change in Support — Parties to a consent motion for a change in support do not need to serve and file financial statements if they file a consent agreeing not to serve and file them.

(10) Documents not to be Filed without Financial Statement — The clerk shall not accept an application, answer, reply, notice of motion or affidavit in response for filing without a financial statement if these rules require the document to be filed with a financial statement.

(11) Additional Financial Information — If a party believes that another party's financial statement does not contain enough information for a full understanding of the other party's financial circumstances,

(a) the party shall ask the other party to give the necessary additional information; and

(b) if the other party does not give it within seven days, the court may, on motion, order the other party to give the information or to serve and file a new financial statement.

(12) Updating Financial Statement — Before any case conference, motion, settlement conference or trial, each party shall update the information in any financial statement that is more than 30 days old by serving and filing,

(a) a new financial statement; or

(b) an affidavit saying that the information in the last statement has not changed and is still true.

(12.1) Minor Changes — If there have been minor changes but no major changes to the information in a party's past statement, the party may serve and file, instead of a new financial statement, an affidavit with details of the changes.

(12.2) Time for Updating — The material described in subrules (12) and (12.1) shall be served and filed as follows:

1. For a case conference or settlement conference requested by a party, the requesting party shall serve and file at least seven days before the conference date and the other party shall serve and file at least four days before that date.

2. For a case conference or settlement conference that is not requested by a party, the applicant shall serve and file at least seven days before the conference date and the respondent shall serve and file at least four days before that date.

3. For a motion, the party making the motion shall serve and file at least seven days before the motion date and the other party shall serve and file at least four days before that date.

4. For a trial, the applicant shall serve and file at least seven days before the trial date and the respondent shall serve and file at least four days before that date.

(13) Questioning on Financial Statement — A party may be questioned under rule 20 on a financial statement provided under this rule, but only after a request for information has been made under clause (11)(a).

(14) Net Family Property Statement — Each party to a property claim under Part I of the *Family Law Act* shall serve and file a net family property statement (Form 13B) or, if the party has already served a net family property statement, an affidavit saying that the information in that statement has not changed and is still true,

(a) not less than seven days before a settlement conference; and

(b) not more than 30 days and not less than seven days before a trial.

(15) Correcting and Updating Statement or Answer — As soon as a party discovers that information in the party's financial statement or net family property statement or in a response the party gave under this rule is incorrect or incomplete, or that there has been a material change in the information provided, the party shall immediately serve on every other party to the claim and file the correct information or a new statement containing the correct information, together with any documents substantiating it.

(16) Order to File Statement — If a party has not served and filed a financial statement or net family property statement or information as required by this rule or an Act, the court may, on motion without notice, order the party to serve and file the document or information and, if it makes that order, shall also order the party to pay costs.

(17) Failure to Obey Order to File Statement or Give Information — If a party does not obey an order to serve and file a financial statement or net family property statement or to give information as this rule requires, the court may,

(a) dismiss the party's case;

(b) strike out any document filed by the party;

(c) make a contempt order against the party;

(d) order that any information that should have appeared on the statement may not be used by the party at the motion or trial;

(e) make any other appropriate order.

O. Reg. 544/99, s. 5; 202/01, s. 3; 92/03, s. 1

Rule 14 — Motions

14. (1) When to Make Motion — A person who wants any of the following may make a motion:

1. A temporary order for a claim made in an application.

2. Directions on how to carry on the case.

3. A change in an order or agreement (but not a change in a final order in a child protection case that is reviewable under section 64 of the *Child and Family Services Act*).

(2) Who May Make Motion — A motion may be made by a party to the case or by a person with an interest in the case.

(3) Parties to Motion — A person who is affected by a motion is also a party, for purposes of the motion only, but this does not apply to a child affected by a motion relating to custody, access, child protection, adoption or child support.

(4) Case Conference for Every Motion — A case conference shall be held for every motion.

(4.1) No Motion before a Case Conference — No notice of motion or supporting evidence may be served and no motion may be heard before the case conference is held.

(4.2) Urgency, Hardship Etc. — Subrules (4) and (4.1) do not apply if the court is of the opinion that there is a situation of urgency or hardship or that a case conference is not required for some other reason in the interest of justice.

(5) Motion to Change Final Order — Despite subrule (4), a party may serve a notice of motion and supporting evidence for an order to change a final order or agreement under rule 15 before a case conference has been held, but the motion may not be heard before a case conference has been held.

(6) Other Motions — Subrule (4) does not apply to a motion,

(a) to change a temporary order under subrule 15(14) (fraud, mistake, lack of notice);

(b) for a contempt order under rule 31 or an order striking out a document under subrule (22);

(c) for summary judgment under rule 16;

(d) to require the Director of the Family Responsibility Office to refrain from suspending a licence;

(e) to limit or suspend a support deduction order;

(e.1) in a child protection case;

(f) for an oral hearing under subrule 37(8) or 37.1(8); or

(g) to set aside the registration of an interjurisdictional support order made outside Canada.

(7) Motion Involving Complicated Matters — The judge who hears a motion involving complicated matters may,

(a) order that the motion or any part of it be heard as a trial; and

(b) give any directions that are necessary.

(8) Motion by Telephone or Video Conference — A party who wants a motion to be heard by telephone or video conference shall,

(a) obtain an appointment from the clerk for the hearing of the motion;

(b) make the necessary arrangements;

(c) serve a notice of the appointment and arrangements on all other parties, and file it; and

(d) participate in the motion as the notice specifies.

(9) Documents for a Motion — A motion, whether made with or without notice,

(a) requires a notice of motion (Form 14) and an affidavit (Form 14A); and

(b) may be supported by additional evidence.

(10) Procedural, Uncomplicated or Unopposed Matters — Motion Form — If a motion is limited to procedural, uncomplicated or unopposed matters, the party making the motion may use a motion form (Form 14B) instead of a notice of motion and affidavit.

(11) Motion with Notice — A party making a motion with notice shall,

(a) serve the documents mentioned in subrule (9) or (10) on all other parties, not later than four days before the motion date;

(b) file the documents as soon as possible after service, but not later than two days before the motion date; and

(c) file a confirmation (Form 14C) not later than 2 p.m. two days before the motion date.

(11.1) No Late Documents — No documents for use on the motion may be served or filed after 2 p.m. two days before the motion date.

(12) Motion Without Notice — A motion may be made without notice if,

(a) the nature or circumstances of the motion make notice unnecessary or not reasonably possible;

(b) there is an immediate danger of a child's removal from Ontario, and the delay involved in serving a notice of motion would probably have serious consequences;

(c) there is an immediate danger to the health or safety of a child or of the party making the motion, and the delay involved in serving a notice of motion would probably have serious consequences; or

(d) service of a notice of motion would probably have serious consequences.

(13) Filing for Motion Without Notice — The documents for use on a motion without notice shall be filed on or before the motion date, unless the court orders otherwise.

(14) Order Made on Motion Without Notice — An order made on motion without notice (Form 14D) shall require the matter to come back to the court and, if possible, to the same judge, within 14 days or on a date chosen by the court.

(15) Service of Order Made Without Notice — An order made on motion without notice shall be served immediately on all parties affected, together with all documents used on the motion, unless the court orders otherwise.

(16) Withdrawing a Motion — A party making a motion may withdraw it in the same way as an application or answer is withdrawn under rule 12.

(17) Evidence on a Motion — Evidence on a motion may be given by any one or more of the following methods:

1. An affidavit or other admissible evidence in writing.

2. A transcript of the questions and answers on a questioning under rule 20.

3. With the court's permission, oral evidence.

(18) Affidavit Based on Personal Knowledge — An affidavit for use on a motion shall, as much as possible, contain only information within the personal knowledge of the person signing the affidavit.

(19) Affidavit Based on Other Information — The affidavit may also contain information that the person learned from someone else, but only if,

(a) the source of the information is identified by name and the affidavit states that the person signing it believes the information is true; and

(b) in addition, if the motion is a contempt motion under rule 31, the information is not likely to be disputed.

(20) Restrictions on Evidence — The following restrictions apply to evidence for use on a motion, unless the court orders otherwise:

1. The party making the motion shall serve all the evidence in support of the motion with the notice of motion.

2. The party responding to the motion shall then serve all the evidence in response.

3. The party making the motion may then serve evidence replying to any new matters raised by the evidence served by the party responding to the motion.

4. No other evidence may be used.

(21) No Motions Without Court's Permission — If a party tries to delay the case or add to its costs or in any other way to abuse the court's process by making numerous motions without merit, the court may order the party not to make any other motions in the case without the court's permission.

(22) Motion to Strike Out Document — The court may, on motion, strike out all or part of any document that may delay or make it difficult to have a fair trial or that is inflammatory, a waste of time, a nuisance or an abuse of the court process.

(23) Failure to Obey Order Made on Motion — A party who does not obey an order that was made on motion is not entitled to any further order from the court unless the court orders that this subrule does not apply, and the court may on motion, in addition to any other remedy allowed under these rules,

(a) dismiss the party's case or strike out the party's answer or any other document filed by the party;

(b) postpone the trial;

(c) make any other order that is appropriate, including an order for costs.

O. Reg. 544/99, s. 6; 202/01, s. 4; 56/03, s. 2; 91/03, s. 4

Rule 15 — Motions to Change an Order or Agreement

15. (0.1) Status Review Applications — This rule does not apply to a final order in a child protection case that is reviewable under section 64 of the *Child and Family Services Act*.

(1) Special Service, Minimum Notice Period — Motion to Change Final Order or Agreement — Notice of a motion to change a final order or agreement and the supporting evidence shall be served by special service (subrule 6(3)), and not by regular service,

(a) not later than 30 days before the motion is to be heard, if the party to be served resides in Canada or the United States of America;

(b) not later than 60 days before the motion is to be heard, if the party to be served resides elsewhere.

(2) Regular Service on Officials, Agencies, etc. — Despite subrule (1), the notice of motion and evidence may be served on the persons mentioned in subrule 8(6) (officials, agencies, etc.) by regular service.

(3) Place for Motion to Change Order or Agreement — Rule 5 (where a case starts) applies to a motion to change an order or agreement as if the motion were a new case.

(4) Change of Support — Service on Assignee of Support — In a motion to change a support order or agreement that has been assigned to a person or agency, as the *Divorce Act* (Canada) and the *Family Law Act* permit, the parties shall serve their documents on the assignee as if the assignee were also a party.

(5) Assignee May Become Party — On serving and filing a notice claiming a financial interest in the motion, the assignee becomes a respondent to the extent of the financial interest.

(6) Sanctions if Assignee not Served — If the assignee is not served as subrule (4) requires,

(a) the court may at any time, on motion by the assignee with notice to the other parties, set aside the changed order to the extent that it affects the assignee's financial interest;

(b) the party who asked for the change has the burden of proving that the changed order should not be set aside; and

(c) if the changed order is set aside, the assignee is entitled to full recovery of its costs of the motion to set aside, unless the court orders otherwise.

(7) Contents of Affidavit — An affidavit for use on a motion to change an order or agreement shall set out,

(a) the place where the parties and the children ordinarily reside;

(b) the name and birth date of each child to whom a proposed change relates;

(c) whether a party has married or begun living with another person;

(d) details of current custody and access arrangements;

(e) details of current support arrangements, including details of any unpaid support;

(f) details of the change asked for and of the changed circumstances that are grounds for a change in the order or agreement;

(g) details of any efforts made to mediate or settle the issues and of any assessment report on custody or access;

(h) in a motion to change a support order or agreement, whether the support was assigned and any details of the assignment known to the party asking for the change;

(i) in a motion to change a child support order or agreement, income and financial information required by section 21 of the applicable child support guidelines; and

(j) in a motion to change a child support order or agreement to an amount different from the amount in the table of the applicable child support guidelines, evidence to satisfy the court that it should make the order asked for.

(8) Exhibit to Affidavit — In addition, a copy of any existing order or agreement that deals with custody, access or support shall be attached as an exhibit to the affidavit, unless a copy is already in the continuing record, and then the affidavit shall indicate its location in the record.

(9) Child Support Change on Consent — Subrule (10) applies instead of subrule (7) if the parties have agreed to an order,

(a) that changes only a child support order or agreement; and

(b) the only terms of which are one or more of the following:

1. Payment of child support, whether in accordance with the applicable child support guidelines or not, or ending child support.

2. Suspension, reduction or cancellation of unpaid child support.

3. Payment of unpaid child support in accordance with a payment schedule.

4. Payment of costs.

(10) Child Support Change on Consent — Material to be Filed — In a case described in subrule (9), instead of serving and filing a notice of motion and the affidavit described in subrule (7), the parties shall file,

(a) a change information form (Form 15) with all required attachments;

(b) a consent (Form 15A);

(c) five copies of a draft order;

(d) a stamped envelope addressed to each party;

(e) a support deduction order information form prescribed under the *Family Responsibility and Support Arrears Enforcement Act, 1996*; and

(f) a draft support deduction order.

(11) Consent Motion — Parties Not to Come to Court — If the parties have filed the material described in subrule (10),

(a) they shall not come to court, but the clerk shall present the material to a judge; and

(b) the judge may make the order asked for, or require one or both parties to file further material or come to court.

(12) Contested Child Support Change — Material to be Served — If a motion to change a child support order or agreement is not proceeding with the other party's consent,

(a) the party asking for the change may serve and file a change information form (Form 15) with all required attachments, instead of an affidavit;

(b) the party responding to the motion shall serve and file an affidavit that sets out any disagreement with the evidence of the party asking for the change; and

(c) if a party claims that an order should not be made in accordance with the tables in the applicable child support guidelines, the support recipient and the support payor shall each serve and file an affidavit containing the evidence required by the following sections of the applicable child support guidelines, or the evidence that is otherwise necessary to satisfy the court that it should make the order asked for:

> Section 4 (income over $150,000)
> Section 5 (step-parent)
> Section 7 (special expenses)
> Section 8 (split custody)
> Section 9 (shared custody)
> Section 10 (undue hardship)
> Section 21 (income and financial information)

(13) Powers of Court — If the court is of the opinion that a motion, whether made on consent or not, can not be properly dealt with because of the material filed, because of the matters in dispute or for any other reason, the court may give directions, including directions for a trial.

(14) Changing Order — Fraud, Mistake, Lack of Notice — The court may, on motion, change an order that,

(a) was obtained by fraud;

(b) contains a mistake;

(c) needs to be changed to deal with a matter that was before the court but that it did not decide;

(d) was made on a motion without notice; or

(e) was made on a motion with notice, if through accident or inadequate notice an affected party did not appear on the motion.

(15) [Revoked O. Reg. 544/99, s. 7(2).]

O. Reg. 544/99, s. 7

Rule 16 — Summary Judgment

16. (1) When Available — After the respondent has served an answer or after the time for serving an answer has expired, a party may make a motion for summary judgment for a final order without a trial on all or part of any claim made or any defence presented in the case.

(2) Available in Any Case Except Divorce — A motion for summary judgment under subrule (1) may be made in any case (including a child protection case) that does not include a divorce claim.

(3) Divorce Claim — In a case that includes a divorce claim, the procedure provided in rule 36 (divorce) for an uncontested divorce may be used, or the divorce claim may be split from the rest of the case under subrule 12(6).

(4) Evidence Required — The party making the motion shall serve an affidavit or other evidence that sets out specific facts showing that there is no genuine issue requiring a trial.

(4.1) Evidence of Responding Party — In response to the affidavit or other evidence served by the party making the motion, the party responding to the motion may not rest on mere allegations or denials but shall set out, in an affidavit or other evidence, specific facts showing that there is a genuine issue for trial.

(5) Evidence not from Personal Knowledge — If a party's evidence is not from a person who has personal knowledge of the facts in dispute, the court may draw conclusions unfavourable to the party.

(6) No Issue for Trial — If there is no genuine issue requiring a trial of a claim or defence, the court shall make a final order accordingly.

(7) Only Issue Amount of Entitlement — If the only genuine issue is the amount to which a party is entitled, the court shall order a trial to decide the amount.

(8) Only Issue Question of Law — If the only genuine issue is a question of law, the court shall decide the issue and make a final order accordingly.

(9) Order Giving Directions — If the court does not make a final order, or makes an order for a trial of an issue, the court may also,

(a) specify what facts are not in dispute, state the issues and give directions about how and when the case will go to trial (in which case the order governs how the trial proceeds, unless the trial judge orders otherwise to prevent injustice);

(b) give directions; and

(c) impose conditions (for example, require a party to pay money into court as security, or limit a party's pretrial disclosure).

(10) Costs of Unsuccessful Motion — If the party who made the motion has no success on the motion, the court shall decide the amount of the other party's costs of the motion on a full recovery basis and order the party who made the motion to pay them immediately, unless the motion was justified, although unsuccessful.

(11) Costs — Bad Faith — If a party has acted in bad faith, the court shall decide the costs of the motion on a full recovery basis and shall order the party to pay them immediately.

(12) Motion for Summary Decision on Legal Issue — The court may, on motion,

(a) decide a question of law before trial, if the decision may dispose of all or part of the case, substantially shorten the trial or save substantial costs;

(b) strike out an application, answer or reply because it sets out no reasonable claim or defence in law; or

(c) dismiss or suspend a case because,

    (i) the court has no jurisdiction over it,

    (ii) a party has no legal capacity to carry on the case,

    (iii) there is another case going on between the same parties about the same matter, or

    (iv) the case is a waste of time, a nuisance or an abuse of the court process.

(13) Evidence on Motion for Summary Decision of Legal Issue — On a motion under subrule (12), evidence is admissible only if the parties consent or the court gives permission.

                                              O. Reg. 91/03, s. 5

Rule 17 — Conferences

17. (1) Conferences in Defended Cases — In each case in which an answer is filed,

    (a) a judge shall conduct at least one case conference, except as subrule (1.1) provides; and

    (b) a judge may conduct a settlement conference, a trial management conference or both.

(1.1) Exception, Case Conference Optional in Child Protection Case — In a child protection case, a case conference may be conducted if,

    (a) a party requests it; or

    (b) the court considers it appropriate.

(2) Undefended Cases — If no answer is filed,

    (a) the clerk shall, on request, schedule a case conference or set a date for an uncontested trial or, in an uncontested divorce case, prepare the documents for a judge; and

    (b) settlement conference or trial management conference shall be conducted only if the court orders it.

(3) Motions to Change Order or Agreement — Subrule (1) applies, with necessary changes, to a motion to change a final order or agreement under rule 15 in which an affidavit is served in response to the motion.

(4) Purposes of Case Conference — The purposes of a case conference include,

    (a) exploring the chances of settling the case;

    (b) identifying the issues that are in dispute and those that are not in dispute;

    (c) exploring ways to resolve the issues that are in dispute;

    (d) ensuring disclosure of the relevant evidence;

    (e) noting admissions that may simplify the case;

    (f) setting the date for the next step in the case;

    (g) if possible, having the parties agree to a specific timetable for the steps to be taken in the case before it comes to trial; and

    (h) organizing a settlement conference, or holding one if appropriate.

(4.1) A party who asks for a case conference shall serve and file a case conference notice (Form 17).

(5) Purposes of Settlement Conference — The purposes of a settlement conference include,

    (a) exploring the chances of settling the case;

    (b) settling or narrowing the issues in dispute;

    (c) ensuring disclosure of the relevant evidence;

    (d) noting admissions that may simplify the case;

    (e) if possible, obtaining a view of how the court might decide the case;

    (f) considering any other matter that may help in a quick and just conclusion of the case;

    (g) if the case is not settled, identifying the witnesses and other evidence to be presented at trial, estimating the time needed for trial and scheduling the case for trial; and

    (h) organizing a trial management conference, or holding one if appropriate.

(6) Purposes of Trial Management Conference — The purposes of a trial management conference include,

    (a) exploring the chances of settling the case;

    (b) arranging to receive evidence by a written report, an agreed statement of facts, an affidavit or another method, if appropriate;

    (c) deciding how the trial will proceed;

    (d) ensuring that the parties know what witnesses will testify and what other evidence will be presented at trial;

    (e) estimating the time needed for trial; and

    (f) setting the trial date, if this has not already been done.

(7) Combined Conference — On the consent of the judge and the parties, part or all of a case conference, settlement conference and trial management conference may be combined.

(8) Orders at Conference — At a case conference, settlement conference or trial management conference the judge may, if it is appropriate to do so,

    (a) make an order for document disclosure (rule 19) or questioning (rule 20), set the times for events in the case or give directions for the next step or steps in the case;

    (a.1) order that the evidence of a witness at trial be given by affidavit;

    (b) if notice has been served, make a temporary or final order;

    (c) make an unopposed order or an order on consent; and

    (d) on consent, refer any issue for alternative dispute resolution.

(9) Conferences with a Non-Judge — A case conference or settlement conference may be conducted by a person who has been named by the appropriate senior judge, unless a party requests a conference with a judge.

(10) Settlement Conference with Judge Before Case Set for Trial — A case shall not be scheduled for trial unless,

    (a) a judge has conducted a settlement conference; or

    (b) a judge has ordered that the case be scheduled for trial.

(11) Case Conference — Motion to Change Final Order or Agreement — Except in a child protection case, a motion for an order to change a final order or agreement under rule 15 shall not be heard before a case conference has been held.

(12) Enforcement — Conferences Optional — In an enforcement, a case conference, settlement conference or trial management conference may be held at a party's request or on a judge's direction.

(13) Parties to Serve Briefs — For each conference, each party shall serve and file a case conference brief (Form 17A or Form 17B), settlement conference brief (Form 17C or Form 17D) or trial management conference brief (Form 17E), as appropriate.

(13.0.1) Case Conference Brief in Child Protection Case — In a child protection case, a case conference brief shall be served and filed only if a case conference is being held under subrule (1.1).

(13.1) Time for Service of Briefs — The party requesting the conference (or, if the conference is not requested by a party, the applicant) shall serve and file a brief not later than seven days before the date scheduled for the conference and the other party shall do so not later than four days before that date.

(14) Parties to Confirm Attendance — Not later than 2 p.m. two days before the date scheduled for the conference, each party shall file a confirmation (Form 14C).

(14.1) No Late Briefs — No brief or other document for use at the conference may be served or filed after 2 p.m. two days before the date scheduled for the conference.

(15) Parties and Lawyers to Come to Conference — The following shall come to each conference:

1. The parties, unless the court orders otherwise.

2. For each represented party, the lawyer with full knowledge of and authority in the case.

(16) Participation by Telephone or Video Conference — With permission obtained in advance from the judge who is to conduct a conference, a party or lawyer may participate in the conference by telephone or video conference.

(17) Setting Up Telephone or Video Conference — A party or lawyer who has permission to participate by telephone or video conference shall,

(a) make the necessary arrangements;

(b) serve a notice of the arrangements on all other parties and file it; and

(c) participate in the conference as the notice specifies.

(18) Costs of Adjourned Conference — If a conference is adjourned because a party is not prepared, has not served the required brief, has not made the required disclosure or has otherwise not followed these rules, the judge shall,

(a) order the party to pay the costs of the conference immediately;

(b) decide the amount of the costs; and

(c) give any directions that are needed.

(19) Conference Agreement — No agreement reached at a conference is effective until it is signed by the parties, witnessed and, in a case involving a special party, approved by the court.

(20) Agreement Filed in Continuing Record — The agreement shall be filed as part of the continuing record, unless the court orders otherwise.

(21) Continuing Record, Case Conference Brief and Trial Management Conference Brief — Case conference briefs and trial management conference briefs form part of the continuing record.

(22) Continuing Record, Settlement Conference Briefs — A settlement conference brief does not form part of the continuing record unless the court orders otherwise at the settlement conference.

(22.1) Settlement Conference Brief to Be Returned or Destroyed — A settlement conference brief that does not form part of the continuing record shall be returned, at the end of the conference, to the party who filed it, or shall be destroyed by the court staff immediately after the conference.

(22.2) Offers to Settle — An offer to settle shall not be filed in the court file or continuing record except,

(a) as part of a settlement conference brief; or

(b) as directed by the court.

(23) Confidentiality of Settlement Conference — No brief or evidence prepared for a settlement conference and no statement made at a settlement conference shall be disclosed to any other judge, except in,

(a) an agreement reached at a settlement conference; or

(b) an order.

(24) Settlement Conference Judge Cannot Hear Issue — A judge who conducts a settlement conference about an issue shall not hear the issue, except as subrule (25) provides.

(25) Exception, Child Protection Case — In a child protection case, if a finding that the child is in need of protection is made without a trial and a trial is needed to determine which order should be made under section 57 of the *Child and Family Services Act*, any judge who has not conducted a settlement conference on that issue may conduct the trial.

O. Reg. 544/99, s. 8; 202/01, s. 5; 91/03, s. 6

Rule 18 — Offers to Settle

18. (1) Definition — In this rule,

"offer" means an offer to settle one or more claims in a case, motion, appeal or enforcement, and includes a counter-offer.

(2) Application — This rule applies to an offer made at any time, even before the case is started.

(3) Making an Offer — A party may serve an offer on any other party.

(4) Offer to be Signed by Party and Lawyer — An offer shall be signed personally by the party making it and also by the party's lawyer, if any.

(5) Withdrawing an Offer — A party who made an offer may withdraw it by serving a notice of withdrawal, at any time before the offer is accepted.

(6) Time-Limited Offer — An offer that is not accepted within the time set out in the offer is considered to have been withdrawn.

(7) Offer Expires When Court Begins to Give Decision — An offer may not be accepted after the court begins to give a decision that disposes of a claim dealt with in the offer.

(8) Confidentiality of Offer — The terms of an offer,

(a) shall not be mentioned in any document filed in the continuing record; and

(b) shall not be mentioned to the judge hearing the claim dealt with in the offer, until the judge has dealt with all the issues in dispute except costs.

(9) Accepting an Offer — The only valid way of accepting an offer is by serving an acceptance on the party who made the offer, at any time before,

(a) the offer is withdrawn; or

(b) the court begins to give a decision that disposes of a claim dealt with in the offer.

(10) Offer Remains Open Despite Rejection or Counter-Offer — A party may accept an offer in accordance with subrule (9) even if the party has previously rejected the offer or made a counter-offer.

(11) Costs not Dealt with in Offer — If an accepted offer does not deal with costs, either party is entitled to ask the court for costs.

(12) Court Approval, Offer Involving Special Party — A special party may make, withdraw and accept an offer, but another party's acceptance of a special party's offer and a special party's acceptance of another party's offer are not binding on the special party until the court approves.

(13) Failure to Carry Out Terms of Accepted Offer — If a party to an accepted offer does not carry out the terms of the offer, the other party may,

(a) make a motion to turn the parts of the offer within the court's jurisdiction into an order; or

(b) continue the case as if the offer had never been accepted.

(14) Costs Consequences of Failure to Accept Offer — A party who makes an offer is, unless the court orders otherwise, entitled to costs to the date the offer was served and full recovery of costs from that date, if the following conditions are met:

1. If the offer relates to a motion, it is made at least one day before the motion date.

2. If the offer relates to a trial or the hearing of a step other than a motion, it is made at least seven days before the trial or hearing date.

3. The offer does not expire and is not withdrawn before the hearing starts.

4. The offer is not accepted.

5. The party who made the offer obtains an order that is as favourable as or more favourable than the offer.

(15) Costs Consequences — Burden of Proof — The burden of proving that the order is as favourable as or more favourable than the offer to settle is on the party who claims the benefit of subrule (14).

(16) Costs — Discretion of Court — When the court exercises its discretion over costs, it may take into account any written offer to settle, the date it was made and its terms, even if subrule (14) does not apply.

Rule 19 — Document Disclosure

19. (1) Affidavit Listing Documents — Every party shall, within 10 days after another party's request, give the other party an affidavit listing every document that is,

(a) relevant to any issue in the case; and

(b) in the party's control, or available to the party on request.

(2) Access to Listed Documents — The other party is entitled, on request,

(a) to examine any document listed in the affidavit, unless it is protected by a legal privilege; and

(b) to receive, at the party's own expense at the legal aid rate, a copy of any document that the party is entitled to examine under clause (a).

(3) Access to Documents Mentioned in Court Papers — Subrule (2) also applies, with necessary changes, to a document mentioned in a party's application, answer, reply, notice of motion, affidavit, financial statement or net family property statement.

(4) Documents Protected by Legal Privilege — If a party claims that a document is protected by a legal privilege, the court may, on motion, examine it and decide the issue.

(5) Use of Privileged Documents — A party who claims that a document is protected by a legal privilege may use it at trial only,

(a) if the other party has been allowed to examine the document and been supplied with a copy, free of charge, at least 30 days before the settlement conference; or

(b) on the conditions the trial judge considers appropriate, including an adjournment if necessary.

(6) Documents of Subsidiary or Affiliated Corporation — The court may, on motion, order a party to give another party an affidavit listing the documents that are,

(a) relevant to any issue in the case; and

(b) in the control of, or available on request to a corporation that is controlled, directly or indirectly, by the party or by another corporation that the party controls directly or indirectly.

(7) Access to Listed Documents — Subrule (2) also applies, with necessary changes, to any document listed in an affidavit ordered under subrule (6).

(8) Documents Omitted from Affidavit or Found Later — A party who, after serving an affidavit required under subrule (1) or (6), finds a document that should have been listed in it, or finds that the list is not correct or not complete, shall immediately serve on the other party a new affidavit listing the correct information.

(9) Access to Additional Documents — The other party is entitled, on request,

(a) to examine any document listed in an affidavit served under subrule (8), unless it is protected by a legal privilege; and

(b) to receive, free of charge, a copy of any document that the party is entitled to examine under clause (a).

(10) Failure to Follow Rule or Obey Order — If a party does not follow this rule or obey an order made under this rule, the court may, on motion, do one or more of the following:

1. Order the party to give another party an affidavit, let the other party examine a document or supply the other party with a copy free of charge.

2. Order that a document favourable to the party's case may not be used except with the court's permission.

3. Order that the party is not entitled to obtain disclosure under these rules until the party follows the rule or obeys the order.

4. Dismiss the party's case or strike out the party's answer.

5. Order the party to pay the other party's costs for the steps taken under this rule, and decide the amount of the costs.

6. Make a contempt order against the party.

7. Make any other order that is appropriate.

(11) Document in Non-Party's Control — If a document is in a non-party's control, or is available only to the non-party, and is not protected by a legal privilege, and it would be unfair to a party to go on with the case without the document, the court may, on motion with notice served on every party and served on the non-party by special service,

(a) order the non-party to let the party examine the document and to supply the party with a copy at the legal aid rate; and

(b) order that a copy be prepared and used for all purposes of the case instead of the original.

Rule 20 — Questioning a Witness and Disclosure

20. (1) Questioning — Procedure — Questioning under this rule shall take place orally under oath or affirmation.

(2) Cross-Examination — The right to question a person includes the right to cross-examine.

(3) Child Protection Case — Available as of Right — In a child protection case, a party is entitled to obtain information from another party about any issue in the case,

(a) by questioning the other party, in which case the party shall serve the other party with a summons to witness (Form 23) by a method of special service set out in clause 6(3)(a); or

(b) by affidavit or by another method, in which case the party shall serve the other party with a request for information (Form 20).

(4) Other Cases — Consent or Order — In a case other than a child protection case, a party is entitled to obtain information from another party about any issue in the case,

(a) with the other party's consent; or

(b) by an order under subrule (5).

(5) Order for Questioning or Disclosure — The court may, on motion, order that a person (whether a party or not) be questioned by a party or disclose information by affidavit or by another method about any issue in the case, if the following conditions are met:

1. It would be unfair to the party who wants the questioning or disclosure to carry on with the case without it.

2. The information is not easily available by any other method.

3. The questioning or disclosure will not cause unacceptable delay or undue expense.

(6) Questioning Special Party — If a person to be questioned is a special party, the court may, on motion, order that someone else be questioned in addition to or in place of the person.

(7) Questioning About Affidavit or Net Family Property Statement — The court may make an order under subrule (5) that a person be questioned or disclose details about information in an affidavit or net family property statement.

(8) Questioning or Disclosure — Preconditions — A party who wants to question a person or obtain information by affidavit or by another method may do so only if the party,

(a) has served and filed any answer, financial statement or net family property statement that these rules require; and

(b) promises in writing not to serve or file any further material for the next step in the case, except in reply to the answers or information obtained.

(9) Notice and Summons to Non-Party — The court may make an order under this rule affecting a non-party only if the non-party has been served with the notice of motion, a summons to witness (Form 23) and the witness fee required by subrule 23(4), all by special service (subrule 6(3)).

(10) Penalty for Failure to Obey Summons — Subrule 23(7) (failure to obey summons to witness) applies, with necessary changes, if a person summoned under subrule (9) fails to obey the summons.

(11) Place of Questioning — The questioning shall take place in the municipality in which the person to be questioned lives, unless that person and the party who wants to do the questioning agree to hold it in another municipality.

(12) Other Arrangements for Questioning — If the person to be questioned and the party who wants to do the questioning do not agree on one or more of the following matters, the court shall, on motion, make an order to decide the matter:

1. The date and time for the questioning.

2. The person responsible for recording the questioning.

3. The method for recording the questioning.

4. Payment of the expenses of the person to be questioned, if a non-party.

(13) Notice to Parties — The parties shall, not later than three days before the questioning, be served with notice of the name of the person to be questioned and the address, date and time of the questioning.

(14) Questioning Person Outside Ontario — If a person to be questioned lives outside Ontario and will not come to Ontario for questioning, the court may decide,

(a) the date, time and place for the questioning;

(b) how much notice the person should be given;

(c) the person before whom the questioning will be held;

(d) the amount of the witness fee to be paid to the person to be questioned;

(e) the method for recording the questioning;

(f) where necessary, that the clerk shall issue,

(i) an authorization to a commissioner (Form 20A) who is to supervise the questioning outside Ontario, and

(ii) a letter of request (Form 20B) to the appropriate court or authorities outside Ontario, asking for their assistance in getting the person to be questioned to come before the commissioner; and

(g) any other related matter.

(15) Commissioner's Duties — A commissioner authorized under subrule (14) shall,

(a) supervise the questioning according to the terms of the court's authorization, these rules and Ontario's law of evidence, unless the law of the place where the questioning is to be held requires some other manner of questioning;

(b) make and keep a copy of the record of the questioning and, if possible, of the exhibits, if any;

(c) deliver the original record, any exhibits and the authorization to the clerk who issued it; and

(d) notify the party who asked for the questioning that the record has been delivered to the clerk.

(16) Order to Bring Documents or Things — An order for questioning and a summons to witness may also require the person to bring any document or thing that is,

(a) relevant to any issue in the case; and

(b) in the person's control or available to the person on request.

(17) Other Rules Apply — Subrules 19(2), (4) and (5) (right to examine document and obtain copy, documents protected by legal privilege, use of privileged documents) apply, with necessary changes, to the documents mentioned in the order.

(18) Scope of Questions — A person to be questioned may be asked about,

(a) the names of persons who might reasonably be expected to know about the claims in the case and, with the court's permission, their addresses;

(b) the names of the witnesses whom a party intends to call at trial and, with the court's permission, their addresses;

(c) the names, addresses, findings, conclusions and opinions of expert witnesses whom a party intends to call or on whose reports the party intends to rely at trial;

(d) if it is relevant to the case, the existence and details of any insurance policy under which the insurance company may be required to pay all or part of an order for the payment of money in the case or to pay back to a party money that the party has paid under an order; and

(e) any other matter in dispute in the case.

(19) Refusal to Answer Question — If a person being questioned refuses to answer a question,

(a) the court may, on motion,

(i) decide whether the question is proper,

(ii) give directions for the person's return to the questioning, and

(iii) make a contempt order against the person; and

(b) if the person is a party or is questioned on behalf or in place of a party, the party shall not use the information that was refused as evidence in the case, unless the court gives permission under subrule (20).

(20) Court's Permission — The court shall give permission unless the use of the information would cause harm to another party or an unacceptable delay in the trial, and may impose any appropriate conditions on the permission, including an adjournment if necessary.

(21) Duty to Correct or Update Answers — A person who has been questioned or who has provided information in writing by affidavit or by another method and who finds that an answer or information given was incorrect or incomplete, or is no longer correct or complete, shall immediately provide the correct and complete information in writing to all parties.

(22) Lawyer Answering — If there is no objection, questions may be answered by the lawyer for a person being questioned, and the answer shall be taken as the person's own answer unless the person corrects or changes it before the questioning ends.

(23) Method for Recording Questioning — All the questions and answers at a questioning shall be recorded electronically or manually.

(24) Obligation to Keep Information Confidential — When a party obtains evidence under this rule, rule 13 (financial statements) or rule 19 (document disclosure), the party and the party's lawyer may use the evidence and any information obtained from it only for the purposes of the case in which the evidence was obtained, subject to the exceptions in subrule (25).

(25) Use of Information Permitted — Evidence and any information obtained from it may be used for other purposes,

(a) if the person who gave the evidence consents;

(b) if the evidence is filed with the court, given at a hearing or referred to at a hearing;

(c) to impeach the testimony of a witness in another case; or

(d) in a later case between the same parties or their successors, if the case in which the evidence was obtained was withdrawn or dismissed.

(26) Court May Lift Obligation of Confidentiality — The court may, on motion, give a party permission to disclose evidence or information obtained from it if the interests of justice outweigh any harm that would result to the party who provided the evidence.

Rule 21 — Report of Children's Lawyer

21. Report of Children's Lawyer — When the Children's Lawyer investigates and reports on custody of or access to a child under section 112 of the *Courts of Justice Act*,

(a) the Children's Lawyer shall first serve notice on the parties and file it;

(b) the parties shall, from the time they are served with the notice, serve the Children's Lawyer with every document in the case that involves the child's custody, access, support, health or education, as if the Children's Lawyer were a party in the case;

(c) the Children's Lawyer has the same rights as a party to document disclosure (rule 19) and questioning witnesses (rule 20) about any matter involving the child's custody, access, support, health or education;

(d) within 90 days after serving the notice under clause (a), the Children's Lawyer shall serve a report on the parties and file it;

(e) within 30 days after being served with the report, a party may serve and file a statement disputing anything in it; and

(f) the trial shall not be held and the court shall not make a final order in the case until the 30 days referred to in clause (e) expire or the parties file a statement giving up their right to that time.

Rule 22 — Admission of Facts

22. (1) Meaning of Admission that Document Genuine — An admission that a document is genuine is an admission,

(a) if the document is said to be an original, that it was written, signed or sealed as it appears to have been;

(b) if it is said to be a copy, that it is a complete and accurate copy; and

(c) if it is said to be a copy of a document that is ordinarily sent from one person to another (for example, a letter, fax or electronic message), that it was sent as it appears to have been sent and was received by the person to whom it is addressed.

(2) Request to Admit — At any time, by serving a request to admit (Form 22) on another party, a party may ask the other party to admit, for purposes of the case only, that a fact is true or that a document is genuine.

(3) Copy of Document to be Attached — A copy of any document mentioned in the request to admit shall be attached to it, unless the other party already has a copy or it is impractical to attach a copy.

(4) Response Required within 20 Days — The party on whom the request to admit is served is considered to have admitted, for purposes of the case only, that the fact is true or that the document is genuine, unless the party serves a response (Form 22A) within 20 days,

(a) denying that a particular fact mentioned in the request is true or that a particular document mentioned in the request is genuine; or

(b) refusing to admit that a particular fact mentioned in the request is true or that a particular document mentioned in the request is genuine, and giving the reasons for each refusal.

(5) Withdrawing Admission — An admission that a fact is true or that a document is genuine (whether contained in a document served in the case or resulting from subrule (4)), may be withdrawn only with the other party's consent or with the court's permission.

Rule 23 — Evidence and Trial

23. (1) Trial Record — At least 30 days before the start of the trial, the applicant shall serve and file a trial record containing a table of contents and the following documents:

1. The application, answer and reply, if any.

2. Any agreed statement of facts.

3. If relevant to an issue at trial, financial statements and net family property statements by all parties, completed not more than 30 days before the record is served.

4. Any assessment report ordered by the court or obtained by consent of the parties.

5. Any temporary order relating to a matter still in dispute.

6. Any order relating to the trial.

7. The relevant parts of any transcript on which the party intends to rely at trial.

8. Any expert report on which the party intends to rely at trial.

(2) Respondent May Add to Trial Record — Not later than seven days before the start of the trial, a respondent may serve, file and add to the trial record any document referred to in subrule (1) that is not already in the trial record.

(3) Summons to Witness — A party who wants a witness to give evidence in court or to be questioned and to bring documents or other things shall serve on the witness a summons to witness (Form 23), together with the witness fee set out in subrule (4).

(4) Witness Fee — A person summoned as a witness shall be paid, for each day that the person is needed in court or to be questioned,

(a) $50 for coming to court or to be questioned;

(b) travel money in the amount of,

(i) $5, if the person lives in the city or town where the person gives evidence,

(ii) 30 cents per kilometre each way, if the person lives elsewhere but within 300 kilometres of the court or place of questioning,

(iii) the cheapest available air fare plus $10 a day for airport parking and 30 cents per kilometre each way from the person's home to the airport and from the airport to the court or place of questioning, if the person lives 300 or more kilometres from the court or place of questioning; and

(c) $100 per night for meals and overnight stay, if the person does not live in the city or town where the trial is held and needs to stay overnight.

(4.1) Meaning of "City or Town" — For the purposes for subrule (4), a municipality shall be considered a city or town if it was a city or town on December 31, 2002.

(5) Continuing Effect of Summons — A summons to witness remains in effect until it is no longer necessary to have the witness present.

(6) Summons for Original Document — If a document can be proved by a certified copy, a party who wants a witness to bring the original shall not serve a summons on the witness for that purpose without the court's permission.

(7) Failure to Obey Summons — The court may issue a warrant for arrest (Form 32B) to bring a witness before the court if,

    (a) the witness has been served as subrule (3) requires, but has not obeyed the summons; and

    (b) it is necessary to have the witness present in court or at a questioning.

(8) Interprovincial Summons to Witness — A summons to a witness outside Ontario under the *Interprovincial Summonses Act* shall be in Form 23A.

(9) Setting Aside Summons to Witness — The court may, on motion, order that a summons to witness be set aside.

(10) Attendance of a Prisoner — If it is necessary to have a prisoner come to court or to be questioned, the court may order (Form 23B) the prisoner's custodian to deliver the prisoner on payment of the fee set out in the regulations under the *Administration of Justice Act*.

(11) Calling Opposing Party as Witness — A party may call the opposing party as a witness and may cross-examine the opposing party.

(11.1) Attendance of Opposing Party — A party who wishes to call an opposing party as a witness may have the opposing party attend,

    (a) by serving a summons under subrule (3) on the opposing party; or

    (b) by serving on the opposing party's lawyer, at least 10 days before the start of the trial, a notice of intention to call the opposing party as a witness.

(12) Opposing Party Disobeying Summons — When an opposing party has been served with a summons under subrule (3), the court may make a final order in favour of the party calling the witness, adjourn the case or make any other appropriate order, including a contempt order, if the opposing party,

    (a) does not come to or remain in court as required by the summons; or

    (b) refuses to be sworn or to affirm, to answer any proper question or to bring any document or thing named in the summons.

(13) Reading Opposing Party's Answers into Evidence — An answer or information given under rule 20 (questioning) by an opposing party may be read into evidence at trial if it is otherwise proper evidence, even if the opposing party has already testified at trial.

(14) Reading Other Person's Answers into Evidence — Subrule (13) also applies, with necessary changes, to an answer or information given by a person questioned on behalf of or in place of an opposing party, unless the trial judge orders otherwise.

(15) Using Answers — Special Circumstances — Subrule (13) is subject to the following:

    1. If the answer or information is being read into evidence to show that a witness's testimony at trial is not to be believed, answers or information given by the witness earlier must be put to the witness as sections 20 and 21 of the *Evidence Act* require.

2. At the request of an opposing party, the trial judge may direct the party reading the answer or information into evidence to read in, as well, any other answer or information that qualifies or explains what the party has read into evidence.

3. A special party's answer or information may be read into evidence only with the trial judge's permission.

(16) Rebutting Answers — A party who has read answers or information into evidence at trial may introduce other evidence to rebut the answers or information.

(17) Using Answers of Witness not Available for Trial — The trial judge may give a party permission to read into evidence all or part of the answers or information given under rule 20 (questioning) by a person who is unable or unwilling to testify at the trial, but before doing so the judge shall consider,

    (a) the importance of the evidence;

    (b) the general principle that trial evidence should be given orally in court;

    (c) the extent to which the person was cross-examined; and

    (d) any other relevant factor.

(18) Taking Evidence Before Trial — The court may order that a witness whose evidence is necessary at trial may give evidence before trial at a place and before a person named in the order, and then may accept the transcript as evidence.

(19) Taking Evidence Before Trial Outside Ontario — If a witness whose evidence is necessary at trial lives outside Ontario, subrules 20(14) and (15) (questioning person outside Ontario, commissioner's duties) apply, with necessary changes.

(20) Evidence by Affidavit or Electronic Recording — The court may allow a witness to give evidence at trial by affidavit or electronic recording if,

    (a) the parties consent;

    (b) the witness is ill or unavailable to come to court for some other good reason;

    (c) the evidence concerns minor or uncontroversial issues; or

    (d) it is in the interests of justice to do so.

(20.1) Direction, Evidence by Affidavit — A direction made at a conference that the evidence of a witness be given by affidavit shall be followed at trial unless the trial judge orders otherwise.

(21) Conditions for Use of Affidavit or Electronic Recording — Evidence at trial by affidavit or electronic recording may be used only if,

    (a) the use is in accordance with an order under subrule (20);

    (b) the evidence is served at least 30 days before the start of the trial; and

    (c) the evidence would have been admissible if given by the witness in court.

(22) Affidavit Evidence at Uncontested Trial — At an uncontested trial, evidence by affidavit in Form 14A or Form 23C may be used without an order under subrule (20), unless the court directs that oral evidence must be given.

(23) Expert Witness Report Served Before Trial — A party who wants to call an expert witness at trial shall, at least 14 days before the start of the trial, serve on all other parties and file a report that,

    (a) is signed by the expert;

    (b) sets out the expert's name, address and qualifications; and

    (c) summarizes the expert's proposed evidence.

(24) Failure to Serve Expert Witness Report — A party who has not followed subrule (23) may not call the expert witness unless the trial judge allows otherwise.

O. Reg. 544/99, s. 9; 202/01, s. 6; 92/03, s. 2

Rule 24 — Costs

24. (1) Successful Party Presumed Entitled to Costs — There is a presumption that a successful party is entitled to the costs of a motion, enforcement, case or appeal.

(2) No Presumption in Child Protection Case or if Party is Government Agency — The presumption does not apply in a child protection case or to a party that is a government agency.

(3) Court's Discretion — Costs for or Against Government Agency — The court has discretion to award costs to or against a party that is a government agency, whether it is successful or unsuccessful.

(4) Successful Party Who has Behaved Unreasonably — Despite subrule (1), a successful party who has behaved unreasonably during a case may be deprived of all or part of the party's own costs or ordered to pay all or part of the unsuccessful party's costs.

(5) Decision on Reasonableness — In deciding whether a party has behaved reasonably or unreasonably, the court shall examine,

    (a) the party's behaviour in relation to the issues from the time they arose, including whether the party made an offer to settle;

    (b) the reasonableness of any offer the party made; and

    (c) any offer the party withdrew or failed to accept.

(6) Divided Success — If success in a step in a case is divided, the court may apportion costs as appropriate.

(7) Absent or Unprepared Party — If a party does not appear at a step in the case, or appears but is not properly prepared to deal with the issues at that step, the court shall award costs against the party unless the court orders otherwise in the interests of justice.

(8) Bad Faith — If a party has acted in bad faith, the court shall decide costs on a full recovery basis and shall order the party to pay them immediately.

(9) Costs Caused by Fault of Lawyer or Agent — If a party's lawyer or agent has run up costs without reasonable cause or has wasted costs, the court may, on motion or on its own initiative, after giving the lawyer or agent an opportunity to be heard,

    (a) order that the lawyer or agent shall not charge the client fees or disbursements for work specified in the order, and order the lawyer or agent to repay money that the client has already paid toward costs;

(b) order the lawyer or agent to repay the client any costs that the client has been ordered to pay another party;

(c) order the lawyer or agent personally to pay the costs of any party; and

(d) order that a copy of an order under this subrule be given to the client.

(10) Costs to be Decided at Each Step — Promptly after each step in the case, the judge or other person who dealt with that step shall decide in a summary manner who, if anyone, is entitled to costs, and set the amount of costs.

(11) Factors in Costs — A person setting the amount of costs shall consider,

(a) the importance, complexity or difficulty of the issues;

(b) the reasonableness or unreasonableness of each party's behaviour in the case;

(c) the lawyer's rates;

(d) the time properly spent on the case, including conversations between the lawyer and the party or witnesses, drafting documents and correspondence, attempts to settle, preparation, hearing, argument, and preparation and signature of the order;

(e) expenses properly paid or payable; and

(f) any other relevant matter.

(12) Payment of Expenses — The court may make an order that a party pay an amount of money to another party to cover part or all of the expenses of carrying on the case, including a lawyer's fees.

(13) Order for Security for Costs — A judge may, on motion, make an order for security for costs that is just, based on one or more of the following factors:

1. A party ordinarily resides outside Ontario.

2. A party has an order against the other party for costs that remains unpaid, in the same case or another case.

3. A party is a corporation and there is good reason to believe it does not have enough assets in Ontario to pay costs.

4. There is good reason to believe that the case is a waste of time or a nuisance and that the party does not have enough assets in Ontario to pay costs.

5. A statute entitles the party to security for costs.

(14) Amount and Form of Security — The judge shall determine the amount of the security, its form and the method of giving it.

(15) Effect of Order for Security — Until the security has been given, a party against whom there is an order for security for costs may not take any step in the case, except to appeal from the order, unless a judge orders otherwise.

(16) Failure to Give Security — If the party does not give the security as ordered, a judge may, on motion, dismiss the party's case or strike out the party's answer or any other document filed by the party, and then subrule (15) no longer applies.

(17) Security may be Changed — The amount of the security, its form and the method of giving it may be changed by order at any time.

O. Reg 544/99, s. 10

Rule 25 — Orders

25. (1) Consent Order — If the parties agree, the court may make an order under these rules or an Act without having the parties or their lawyers come to court.

(2) Successful Party Prepares Draft Order — The party in whose favour an order is made shall prepare a draft of the order (Form 25, 25A, 25B, 25C or 25D), unless the court orders otherwise.

(3) Other Party may Prepare Draft Order — If the party in whose favour an order is made does not have a lawyer or does not prepare a draft order within 10 days after the order is made, any other party may prepare the draft order, unless the court orders otherwise.

(4) Approval of Draft Order — A party who prepares an order shall serve a draft, for approval of its form and content, on every other party who was in court or was represented when the order was made (including a child who has a lawyer).

(5) Settling Contents of Disputed Order — Unless the court orders otherwise, a party who disagrees with the form or content of a draft order shall serve, on every party who was served under subrule (4) and on the party who served the draft order,

    (a) a notice disputing approval (Form 25E);

    (b) a copy of the order, redrafted as proposed; and

    (c) notice of a time and date at which the clerk will settle the order by telephone conference.

(6) Time and Date — The time and date shall be set by the clerk and shall be within five days after service of the notice disputing approval.

(7) Disputed Order — Settlement by Judge — If unable to settle the order at the telephone conference, the clerk shall, as soon as possible, refer the order to the judge who made it, to be settled at a further telephone conference, unless the judge orders the parties to come to court for settlement of the order.

(8) No Approval Required if no Response from Other Party — If no approval or notice disputing approval (Form 25E) is served within 10 days after the draft order is served for approval, it may be signed without approval.

(9) No Approval Required for Certain Orders — If an order dismisses a motion, case or appeal, without costs, or is prepared by the clerk under subrule (11), it may be signed without approval.

(10) No Approval Required in Emergencies — If the delay involved in getting an order approved would have serious consequences, the judge who made it may sign it without approval.

(11) When Clerk Prepares Order — The clerk shall prepare the order for signature,

    (a) within 10 days after it is made, if no party has a lawyer;

    (b) as soon as it is made,

        (i) if it is a support deduction order under the *Family Responsibility and Support Arrears Enforcement Act, 1996* or an order under the *Interjurisdictional Support Orders Act, 2002,* or

        (ii) if the judge directs the clerk to do so.

(12) Who Signs Order — An order may be signed by the judge who made it or by the clerk.

(13) Service of Order — Unless the court orders otherwise, the person who prepared an order shall serve it, by regular service (subrule 6(2)) or by mail, fax or electronic mail to the person's last known address,

(a) on every other party, including a respondent to whom subrule 10(5) (no notice to respondent) applies;

(b) if a child involved in the case has a lawyer, on the lawyer; and

(c) on any other person named by the court.

(14) Support Deduction Order Not Served — A support deduction order under the *Family Responsibility and Support Arrears Enforcement Act, 1996* does not have to be served.

(15) Service of Crown Wardship Order — An order for Crown wardship under Part III of the *Child and Family Services Act* shall be served on the following persons, in addition to the ones mentioned in subrule (13):

1. The child, if that Act requires notice to the child.

2. Any foster parent or other person who is entitled to notice under subsection 39(3) of that Act.

3. A Director appointed under that Act.

(16) Service of Secure Treatment Order — An order for secure treatment under Part VI of the *Child and Family Services Act* shall be served on the administrator of the secure treatment program, in addition to the persons mentioned in subrule (13).

(17) Service of Adoption Order — An adoption order shall be served on the following persons, in addition to the ones mentioned in subrule (13):

1. The adopted child, if the child gave consent under subsection 137(6) of the *Child and Family Services Act.*

2. The persons mentioned in subsection 162(3) of that Act.

(18) Effective Date — An order is effective from the date on which it is made, unless it states otherwise.

O. Reg. 56/03, s. 3

Rule 26 — Enforcement of Orders

26. (1) Where to Enforce an Order — The place for enforcement of an order is governed by subrules 5(5) and (6) (place for starting enforcement).

(2) How to Enforce an Order — An order that has not been obeyed may, in addition to any other method of enforcement provided by law, be enforced as provided by subrules (3) and (4).

(3) Payment Orders — A payment order may be enforced by,

(a) a request for a financial statement (subrule 27(1));

(b) a request for disclosure from an income source (subrule 27(7));

(c) a financial examination (subrule 27(11));

(d) seizure and sale (rule 28);

(e) garnishment (rule 29);

(f) a default hearing (rule 30), if the order is a support order;

(g) the appointment of a receiver under section 101 of the *Courts of Justice Act*; and

(h) registration under section 42 of the *Family Responsibility and Support Arrears Enforcement Act, 1996*.

(4) Other Orders — An order other than a payment order may be enforced by,

(a) a writ of temporary seizure of property (subrule 28(10));

(b) a contempt order (rule 31); and

(c) the appointment of a receiver under section 101 of the *Courts of Justice Act*.

(5) Statement of Money Owed — A statement of money owed shall be in Form 26, with a copy of the order that is in default attached.

(6) Special Forms for Statement of Money Owed — Despite subrule (5),

(a) if the *Family Responsibility and Support Arrears Enforcement Act, 1996* applies, a statement of arrears in the form used by the Director may be used instead of Form 26;

(b) if the *Interjurisdictional Support Orders Act, 2002* applies, a document receivable under subsection 49 of that Act may be used instead of Form 26.

(7) Recipient's or Director's Entitlement to Costs — Unless the court orders otherwise, the recipient or the Director is entitled to the costs,

(a) of carrying out a financial examination; and

(b) of issuing, serving, filing and enforcing a writ of seizure and sale, a writ of temporary seizure and a notice of garnishment and of changing them by statutory declaration.

(8) Enforcement of Administrative Costs — For the purpose of subrule (7), the recipient or the Director may collect under a writ of seizure and sale, a notice of garnishment or a statutory declaration changing either of them,

(a) the amounts set out in the regulations under the *Administration of Justice Act* and awarded under rule 24 (costs) for filing and renewing with the sheriff a writ of seizure and sale or a writ of temporary seizure;

(b) payments made to a sheriff, clerk, official examiner, court reporter or other public officer in accordance with the regulations under the *Administration of Justice Act* and awarded under rule 24 (costs), on filing with the sheriff or clerk a copy of a receipt for each payment or an affidavit setting out the payments made; and

(c) the actual expense for carrying out a financial examination, or any other costs to which the recipient or the Director is entitled under subrule (7), on filing with the sheriff or clerk an affidavit (Form 26A) setting out the items of expense in detail.

(9) Affidavit for Filing Domestic Contract or Paternity Agreement — An affidavit for filing a domestic contract or paternity agreement under subsection 35(1) of the *Family Law Act* shall be in Form 26B.

(10) Director's Status — If the Director enforces an order under the *Family Responsibility and Support Arrears Enforcement Act, 1996*, anything in these rules relating to enforcement by the person in whose favour the order was made applies to the Director.

(11) Filing and Refiling with the Director — A person who files or refiles a support order in the Director's office shall immediately send notice of the filing, by mail, fax or electronic mail to the clerk at any court office where the recipient is enforcing the order.

(12) Transferring Enforcement from Recipient to Director — A recipient who files a support order in the Director's office shall, on the Director's request, assign to the Director any enforcement that the recipient has started, and then the Director may continue with the enforcement as if the Director had started it.

(13) Transferring Enforcement from Director to Recipient — If the parties withdraw a support order from the Director's office, the Director shall, on the recipient's request, given to the Director at the same time as the notice of withdrawal, assign to the recipient any enforcement that the Director has started, and then the recipient may continue with the enforcement as if the recipient had started it.

(14) Notice of Transfer of Enforcement — A person who continues an enforcement under subrule (12) or (13) shall immediately send a notice of transfer of enforcement (Form 26C), by mail, fax or electronic mail to,

(a) all parties to the enforcement;

(b) the clerk at every court office where the enforcement is being carried on; and

(c) every sheriff who is involved with the enforcement at the time of transfer.

O. Reg. 544/99, s. 11; 56/03, s. 4

Rule 27 — Requiring Financial Information

27. (1) Request for Financial Statement — If a payment order is in default, a recipient may serve a request for a financial statement (Form 27) on the payor.

(2) Effect of Request for Financial Statement — Within 15 days after being served with the request, the payor shall send a completed financial statement (Form 13) to the recipient by mail, fax or electronic mail.

(3) Frequency of Requests for Financial Statements — A recipient may request a financial statement only once in a six-month period, unless the court gives the recipient permission to do so more often.

(4) Application of Rule 13 — If a party is required under this rule to give a financial statement, the following subrules apply with necessary changes:

13(6) (full disclosure)

13(7) (income tax documents)

13(11) (additional information)

13(12) (updating financial statement)

13(15) (correcting and updating)

13(16) (order to file statement)

13(17) (failure to file).

(5) Order for Financial Statement — The court may, on motion, order a payor to serve and file a financial statement.

(6) Failure to Obey Order — If the payor does not serve and file a financial statement within 10 days after being served with the order, the court may, on motion with special service (subrule 6(3)), order that the payor be imprisoned continuously or intermittently for not more than 40 days.

(7) Request for Statement of Income from Income Source — If a payment order is in default, the recipient may serve a request for a statement of income (Form 27A) on an income source of the payor, requiring the income source to prepare and send to the recipient, by mail, fax or electronic mail a statement of income (Form 27B).

(8) Frequency of Requests for Statement of Income — A recipient may request a statement of income from an income source only once in a six-month period, unless the court gives the recipient permission to do so more often.

(9) Order for Statement of Income — The court may, on the recipient's motion, order an income source to serve and file a statement of income.

(10) Income Source's Failure to Obey Order — If the income source does not serve and file a statement of income within 10 days after being served with the order, the court may, on the recipient's motion, order the income source to post a bond (Form 32).

(11) Appointment for Financial Examination — If a payment order is in default, the recipient may serve on the payor, by special service (subrule 6(3)), an appointment for a financial examination (Form 27C), requiring the payor to,

    (a) come to a financial examination;

    (b) bring to the examination any document or thing named in the appointment that is in the payor's control or available to the payor on request, relevant to the enforcement of the order, and not protected by a legal privilege; and

    (c) serve a financial statement (Form 13) on the recipient, not later than seven days before the date of the examination.

(12) Financial Examination of Person Other than Payor — If a payment order is in default and a person other than the payor may know about the matters listed in subrule (17), the recipient may require that person to come to a financial examination by serving a summons to witness (Form 23) and the witness fee (subrule 23(4)) on the person by special service (subrule 6(3)).

(13) Place Where Financial Examination Held — A financial examination shall be held,

    (a) in a place where the parties and the person to be examined agree;

    (b) where the person to be examined lives in Ontario, in the municipality where the person lives; or

    (c) in a place chosen by the court.

(14) Other Rules Apply — Subrules 19(4), (5) and (8) (documents protected by legal privilege, use of privileged documents, documents omitted from affidavit) and 23(7) (failure to obey summons) apply to a financial examination, with necessary changes.

(15) Notice of Time and Place of Examination — A payor who is served with an appointment or a person who is served with a summons for a financial examination shall have at least 10 days' notice of the time and place of the examination.

(16) Before Whom Examination is Held, Method of Recording — A financial examination shall be held under oath or affirmation, before a person chosen by agreement of the

Family Rules

payor and recipient or in accordance with subrule 20(12) (other arrangements for questioning), and shall be recorded by a method chosen in the same way.

(17) Scope of Examination — On a financial examination, the payor or other person may be questioned about,

(a) the reason for the payor's default;

(b) the payor's income and property;

(c) the debts owed to and by the payor;

(d) the disposal of any property by the payor either before or after the making of the order that is in default;

(e) the payor's past, present and future ability to pay under the order;

(f) whether the payor intends to obey the order, and any reason for not doing so; and

(g) any other matter relevant to the enforcement of the order.

(18) Resistance to Examination — Subrule (19) applies if a payor who is served with an appointment or a person who is served with a summons for a financial examination,

(a) does not come to the examination as required by the appointment or summons;

(b) does not serve on the recipient a financial statement as required by the appointment;

(c) comes to the examination, but does not bring a document or thing named in the appointment or summons; or

(d) comes to the examination, but refuses to take an oath or affirm or to answer a question.

(19) Order for Another Examination — The court may, on motion, make an order and give directions for another financial examination of the payor or other person and may in addition require the payor or person to post a bond (Form 32).

(20) Imprisonment — If a payor or other person, without sufficient excuse, fails to obey an order or direction made under subrule (19), the court may, on motion with special service (subrule 6(3)), order that the payor or person be imprisoned continuously or intermittently for not more than 40 days.

(21) Imprisonment Power is Additional — The court may exercise its power under subrule (20) in addition to or instead of its power of forfeiture under rule 32 (bonds, recognizances and warrants).

(22) Frequency of Examinations — A recipient may conduct only one financial examination of a payor and one financial examination of any other person in a six-month period, or more often with the court's permission.

O. Reg. 544/99, s. 12

Rule 28 — Seizure and Sale

28. (1) Issue of Writ of Seizure and Sale — The clerk shall issue a writ of seizure and sale (Form 28) if a recipient files,

(a) a request for a writ of seizure and sale (Form 28A); and

(b) a statement of money owed (subrules 26(5) and (6)).

(2) Statutory Declaration to Change Amount Owed — The statutory declaration to sheriff mentioned in section 44 of the *Family Responsibility and Support Arrears Enforcement Act, 1996* shall be in Form 28B.

(3) Statutory Declaration if Order Changed — If a court changes a payment order that is being enforced by a writ of seizure and sale, a statutory declaration to sheriff (Form 28B) may be filed with the sheriff and once filed, it has the same effect as a declaration mentioned in subrule (2).

(4) Duration of Writ — A writ of seizure and sale continues in effect until,

(a) the recipient withdraws it under subrule (7); or

(b) the court orders otherwise under subrule (8).

(5) Writ Issued Under Former Rules — A writ directing the sheriff to seize and sell a payor's property that was issued by the court under the rules that applied before these rules take effect has the same legal effect as a writ of seizure and sale issued under these rules, and does not expire except as subrule (4) provides.

(6) Notifying Sheriff of Payment Received — If a writ of seizure and sale has been filed with a sheriff,

(a) the recipient shall, on the sheriff's request, provide a statutory declaration setting out details of all payments received by or on behalf of the recipient; and

(b) the sheriff shall update the writ accordingly.

(7) Withdrawing Writ — The person who obtained a writ to enforce an order shall immediately withdraw it from every sheriff's office where it has been filed if,

(a) the person no longer wants to enforce the order by a writ;

(b) in the case of a payment order, the payor's obligation to make periodic payments under the order has ended and all other amounts owing under it have been paid; or

(c) in the case of any other order, the person against whom the writ was issued has obeyed the order.

(8) Order Changing, Withdrawing or Suspending Writ — The court may, on motion, make an order changing the terms of a writ, withdrawing it or temporarily suspending it, even if the writ was issued by another court in Ontario.

(9) Service of Order — The person making the motion, or another person named by the court, shall serve a copy of the order on,

(a) every sheriff in whose office the writ has been filed; and

(b) if the writ was issued by the court in another place, or by another court, on the clerk of the court in the other place or the clerk of the other court.

(10) Writ of Temporary Seizure of Property — The court may, on motion with special service (subrule 6(3)), give permission to issue a writ of temporary seizure (Form 28C) directing the sheriff to take possession of and hold all or part of the land and other property of a person against whom an order has been made and to hold any income from the property until the person obeys the order.

O. Reg. 544/99, s. 13

Rule 29 — Garnishment

29. (1) Issue of Notice or Notices of Garnishment — The clerk shall issue as many notices of garnishment (Form 29A or 29B) as a recipient requests if the recipient files,

(a) a request for garnishment (Form 29) or an extra-provincial garnishment process referred to in section 50 of the *Family Responsibility and Support Arrears Enforcement Act, 1996*; and

(b) a statement of money owed (subrules 26(5) and (6)).

(2) One Recipient and One Garnishee per Notice — Each notice of garnishment shall name only one recipient and one garnishee.

(3) Service on Payor and Garnishee — The notice of garnishment shall be served on the payor and on the garnishee but the payor shall, in addition, be served with the documents filed under subrule (1).

(4) Effect of Notice of Garnishment — A notice of garnishment attaches,

(a) every debt that is payable by the garnishee to the payor at the time the notice is served; and

(b) every debt that is payable by the garnishee to the payor,

(i) after the notice is served, or

(ii) on the fulfilment of a condition after the notice is served.

(5) Duration — The notice of garnishment continues in effect from the time of service on the garnishee until it is withdrawn or stopped under this rule or until the court orders otherwise under this rule.

(6) Financial Institution — If the garnishee is a financial institution, the notice of garnishment and all further notices required to be served under this rule shall be served at the branch of the institution where the debt to the payor is payable, unless subrule (6.1) applies.

(6.1) Federally Regulated Financial Institution — Garnishment Re Support — If the garnishee is a financial institution to which the Bank Act (Canada), the *Cooperative Credit Associations Act* (Canada) or the *Trust and Loan Companies Act* (Canada) applies and the garnishment enforces a support order, the notice of garnishment and all further notices required to be served under this rule,

(a) shall be served at the designated office of the institution established for this purpose; and

(b) shall be accompanied by a statement to garnishee financial institution re support (Form 29J).

(6.2) New Accounts — Subrules (4) and (5) do not apply to money in an account opened after a notice of garnishment is served as described in subrule (6) or (6.1).

(7) Joint Debts Garnishable — Subrules (4) and (5) also apply to debts owed to the payor and another person jointly.

(8) Procedure When Joint Debt Garnished — If a garnishee has been served with a notice of garnishment and the garnishee owes a debt to which subrules (4) and (5) apply to the payor and another person jointly,

> (a) the garnishee shall pay, in accordance with subrule (11), half of the debt, or the larger or smaller amount that the court orders;

> (b) the garnishee shall immediately send the other person a notice to co-owner of debt (Form 29C) by mail, fax or electronic mail, to the person's address in the garnishee's records; and

> (c) the garnishee shall immediately serve the notice to co-owner of debt on the recipient or the Director, depending on who is enforcing the order, and on the sheriff or clerk if the sheriff or clerk is to receive the money under subrule (11) or (12).

(9) Joint Debt — Money to be Held — Despite subrule (12), if served with notice under clause (8)(c), the sheriff, clerk or Director shall hold the money received for 30 days, and may pay it out when the 30 days expire, unless the other person serves and files a dispute within the 30 days.

(10) Payment of Arrears Does not End Garnishment — A notice of garnishment continues to attach future periodic payments even though the total amount owed when it was served is fully paid up.

(11) Persons to Whom Garnishee Makes Payments — A garnishee who has been served with a notice of garnishment shall make the required payments to,

> (a) the Director, if the notice of garnishment relates to an order being enforced by the Director;

> (b) the clerk, if the notice of garnishment does not relate to an order being enforced by the Director.

(12) Clerk or Director to Pay Out Money — On receiving money under a notice of garnishment, the Director or clerk shall, even if a dispute has been filed, but subject to subrules (9) and (13), immediately pay,

> (a) to the recipient, any part of the money that comes within the priority created by subsection 4(1) of the *Creditors' Relief Act;* and

> (b) to the sheriff, any part of the money that exceeds that priority.

(13) Order that Subrule (12) Does not Apply — The court may, at a garnishment hearing or on a motion to change the garnishment under this rule, order that subrule (12) does not apply.

(14) Change in Garnishment, Indexed Support — If a notice of garnishment enforces a support order that indexes periodic payments for inflation, the recipient may serve on the garnishee and on the payor a statutory declaration of indexed support (Form 29D) setting out the new amount to be paid under the order, and file the declaration with the court.

(15) Effect of Statutory Declaration of Indexed Support — A statutory declaration of indexed support requires the garnishee to pay the new amount set out in the declaration from the time it is served on the garnishee.

(16) Garnishment Dispute — Within 10 days after being served with a notice of garnishment or a statutory declaration of indexed support, a payor, garnishee or co-owner of a debt may serve on the other parties and file a dispute (Form 29E, 29F or 29G).

Family Rules

(17) Notice of Garnishment Hearing — The clerk shall, on request, issue a notice of garnishment hearing (Form 29H),

(a) within 10 days after a dispute is served and filed; or

(b) if the recipient says that the garnishee has not paid any money or has not paid enough money.

(18) Service of Notice — The clerk shall serve and file the notice not later than 10 days before the hearing.

(19) Garnishment Hearing — At a garnishment hearing, the court may make one or more of the following temporary or final orders:

1. An order dismissing the dispute.

2. An order that changes how much is being garnished on account of a periodic payment order. The court may make an order under this paragraph even if it does not have the authority to change the payment order itself.

2.1 An order that changes how much is being garnished on account of a periodic payment order and that, at the same time, changes the payment order itself. The court may make an order under this paragraph only if,

i. the payment order is one that the court has the authority to change, and

ii. the parties to the payment order agree to the change, or one of those parties has served and filed notice of a motion to have the change made.

3. An order changing how much is being garnished on account of a non-periodic payment order.

4. An order suspending the garnishment or any term of it, while the hearing is adjourned or until the court orders otherwise.

5. An order setting aside the notice of garnishment or any statutory declaration of indexed support.

6. An order that garnished money held or received by the clerk, Director or sheriff be held in court.

7. An order that garnished money that has been paid out in error to the recipient be paid into and held in court, returned to the garnishee or sent to the payor or to the co-owner of the debt.

8. An order that garnished money held in court be returned to the garnishee or be sent to the payor, the co-owner of the debt, the sheriff, the clerk or the Director.

9. An order deciding how much remains owing under a payment order that is being enforced by garnishment against the payor or garnishee.

10. If the garnishee has not paid what was required by the notice of garnishment or statutory declaration of indexed support, an order that the garnishee pay all or part of what was required.

11. An order deciding who is entitled to the costs of the garnishment hearing and setting the amount of the costs.

(20) Changing Garnishment at Other Times — The court may also use the powers listed in subrule (19), on motion or on its own initiative, even if the notice of garnishment was issued by another court,

(a) on a motion under section 7 of the *Wages Act;*

(b) if the court replaces a temporary payment order with a final payment order;

(c) if the court indexes or changes a payment order; or

(d) if the court allows an appeal.

(21) Changing Garnishment When Ability to Pay Changes — If there has been a material change in the payor's circumstances affecting the payor's ability to pay, the court may, on motion, use the powers listed in subrule (19).

(22) Garnishee's Payment Pays Debt — Payment of a debt by a garnishee under a notice of garnishment or statutory declaration of indexed support pays off the debt between the garnishee and the payor to the extent of the payment.

(23) Notice by Garnishee — Payor not Working or Receiving Money — Within 10 days after a payor stops working for or is no longer receiving any money from a garnishee, the garnishee shall send a notice as subrule (27) requires,

(a) saying that the payor is no longer working for or is no longer receiving any money from the garnishee;

(b) giving the date on which the payor stopped working for or receiving money from the garnishee and the date of the last payment to the payor from the garnishee; and

(c) giving the name and address of any other income source of the payor, if known.

(24) Notice by Garnishee — Payor Working or Receiving Money Again — Within 10 days after the payor returns to work for or starts to receive money again from the garnishee, the garnishee shall send another notice as subrule (27) requires, saying that the payor has returned to work for or started to receive money again from the garnishee.

(25) Notice by Payor — Working or Receiving Money Again — Within 10 days after returning to work for or starting to receive money again from the garnishee, the payor shall send a notice as subrule (27) requires, saying that the payor has returned to work for or started to receive money again from the garnishee.

(26) Notice by Payor — New Income Source — Within 10 days after starting to work for or receive money from a new income source, the payor shall send a notice as subrule (27) requires, saying that the payor has started to work for or to receive money from the new income source.

(27) Notice Sent to Clerk and Recipient or Director — A notice referred to in subrule (23), (24), (25) or (26) shall be sent to the clerk, and to the recipient or the Director (depending on who is enforcing the order), by mail, fax or electronic mail.

(28) Notice by Clerk — When the clerk receives a notice under subrule (26), the clerk shall immediately notify the recipient or the Director (depending on who is enforcing the order) by mail, fax or electronic mail.

(29) New Notice of Garnishment — If no written objection is received within 10 days, the clerk shall,

(a) issue a new notice of garnishment directed to the new garnishee, requiring the same deductions as were required to be made, under the previous notice of garnishment or statutory declaration of indexed support, on the day that the notice under subrule (26) was received; and

(b) send a copy of the new notice of garnishment to the payor and the new garnishee, by mail, fax or electronic mail.

(30) Effect of New Notice of Garnishment — Issuing a new notice of garnishment under clause (29)(a) does not cancel any previous notice of garnishment or statutory declaration of indexed support.

(31) Notice to Stop Garnishment — The recipient shall immediately send a notice to stop garnishment (Form 29I), by mail, fax or electronic mail to the garnishee and payor and file it with the clerk if,

(a) the recipient no longer wants to enforce the order by garnishment; or

(b) the requirement to make periodic payments under the order has ended and all other amounts owing under the order have been paid.

(32) Old Orders — This rule applies, with necessary changes, to,

(a) an attachment order made under section 30 of the *Family Law Reform Act* (chapter 152 of the Revised Statutes of Ontario, 1980); and

(b) a garnishment order issued by the court under the rules that were in effect before January 1, 1985.

O. Reg. 544/99, s. 14; 56/03, s. 5

Rule 30 — Default Hearing

30. (1) Issuing Notice of Default Hearing — The clerk shall issue a notice of default hearing (Form 30),

(a) if the support order is being enforced by the recipient, when the recipient files a request for a default hearing (Form 30A) and a statement of money owed (subrule 26(5));

(b) if it is being enforced by the Director, when the Director files a statement of money owed.

(2) Serving Notice of Default Hearing — The notice of default hearing shall be served on the payor by special service (subrule 6(3)) and filed.

(3) Payor's Dispute — Within 10 days after being served with the notice, the payor shall serve on the recipient and file,

(a) a financial statement (Form 13); and

(b) a default dispute (Form 30B).

(4) Updating Statement of Money Owed — The recipient shall serve and file a new statement of money owed (subrule 26(5)) not more than seven days before the default hearing.

(5) When Director to Update Statement — Despite subrule 26(10), subrule (4) applies to the Director only if,

(a) the amount the Director is asking the court to enforce is greater than the amount shown in the notice of default hearing; or

(b) the court directs it.

(6) Statement of Money Owed Presumed Correct — The payor is presumed to admit that the recipient's statement of money owed is correct, unless the payor has filed a default dispute stating that the statement of money owed is not correct and giving detailed reasons.

(7) Arrears Enforceable to Date of Hearing — At the default hearing, the court may decide and enforce the amount owing as of the date of the hearing.

(8) Conditional Imprisonment — The court may make an order under clause 41(9)(g) or (h) of the *Family Responsibility and Support Arrears Enforcement Act, 1996*, suspending the payor's imprisonment on appropriate conditions.

(9) Issuing Warrant of Committal — If the recipient, on a motion with special service (subrule 6(3)) on the payor, states by affidavit (or by oral evidence, with the court's permission) that the payor has not obeyed a condition that was imposed under subrule (8), the court may issue a warrant of committal against the payor, subject to subsection 41(13) (variation of order) of the *Family Responsibility and Support Arrears Enforcement Act, 1996*.

Rule 31 — Contempt of Court

31. (1) When Contempt Motion Available — An order, other than a payment order, may be enforced by a contempt motion made in the case in which the order was made, even if another penalty is available.

(2) Notice of Contempt Motion — The notice of contempt motion (Form 31) shall be served together with a supporting affidavit, by special service as provided in clause 6(3)(a), unless the court orders otherwise.

(3) Affidavit for Contempt Motion — The supporting affidavit may contain statements of information that the person signing the affidavit learned from someone else, but only if the requirements of subrule 14(19) are satisfied.

(4) Warrant to Bring to Court — To bring before the court a person against whom a contempt motion is made, the court may issue a warrant for the person's arrest if,

    (a) the person's attendance is necessary in the interest of justice; and

    (b) the person is not likely to attend voluntarily.

(5) Contempt Orders — If the court finds a person in contempt of the court, it may order that the person,

    (a) be imprisoned for any period and on any conditions that are just;

    (b) pay a fine in any amount that is appropriate;

    (c) pay an amount to a party as a penalty;

    (d) do anything else that the court decides is appropriate;

    (e) not do what the court forbids;

    (f) pay costs in an amount decided by the court; and

    (g) obey any other order.

(6) Writ of Temporary Seizure — The court may also give permission to issue a writ of temporary seizure (Form 28C) against the person's property.

Family Rules

(7) Limited Imprisonment or Fine — In a contempt order under one of the following provisions, the period of imprisonment and the amount of a fine may not be greater than the relevant Act allows:

1. Section 38 of the *Children's Law Reform Act*.

2. Section 49 of the *Family Law Act*.

3. Section 53 of the *Family Responsibility and Support Arrears Enforcement Act, 1996*.

(8) Conditional Imprisonment or Fine — A contempt order for imprisonment or for the payment of a fine may be suspended on appropriate conditions.

(9) Issuing Warrant of Committal — If a party, on a motion with special service (subrule 6(3)) on the person in contempt, states by an affidavit in Form 32C (or by oral evidence, with the court's permission) that the person has not obeyed a condition imposed under subrule (8), the court may issue a warrant of committal against the person.

(10) Payment of Fine — A contempt order for the payment of a fine shall require the person in contempt to pay the fine,

(a) in a single payment, immediately or before a date that the court chooses; or

(b) in instalments, over a period of time that the court considers appropriate.

(11) Corporation in Contempt — If a corporation is found in contempt, the court may also make an order under subrule (5), (6) or (7) against any officer or director of the corporation.

(12) Change in Contempt Order — The court may, on motion, change an order under this rule, give directions and make any other order that is just.

Rule 32 — Bonds, Recognizances and Warrants

32. (1) Warrant to Bring a Person to Court — If a person does not come to court after being served with notice of a case, enforcement or motion that may result in an order requiring the person to post a bond,

(a) the court may issue a warrant for the person's arrest, to bring the person before the court, and adjourn the case to await the person's arrival; or

(b) the court may,

(i) hear and decide the case in the person's absence and, if appropriate, make an order requiring the person to post a bond, and

(ii) if the person has been served with the order and does not post the bond by the date set out in the order, issue a warrant for the person's arrest, on motion without notice, to bring the person before the court.

(2) Form of Bond and Other Requirements — A bond shall be in Form 32, does not need a seal, and shall,

(a) have at least one surety, unless the court orders otherwise;

(b) list the conditions that the court considers appropriate;

(c) set out an amount of money to be forfeited if the conditions are not obeyed;

(d) shall require the person posting the bond to deposit the money with the clerk immediately, unless the court orders otherwise; and

(e) name the person to whom any forfeited money is to be paid out.

(3) Person Before Whom Recognizance to be Entered into — A recognizance shall be entered into before a judge, a justice of the peace or the clerk.

(4) Change of Conditions in a Bond — The court may, on motion, change any condition in a bond if there has been a material change in a party's circumstances since the date of the order for posting the bond or the date of an order under this subrule, whichever is more recent.

(5) Change in Bond under Children's Law Reform Act — In the case of a bond under the *Children's Law Reform Act*, subrule (4) also applies to a material change in circumstances that affects or is likely to affect the best interests of the child.

(6) Removal or Replacement of Surety — The court may, on motion, order that a surety be removed or be replaced by another person as surety, in which case as soon as the order is made, the surety who is removed or replaced is free from any obligation under the bond.

(7) Motion to Enforce Bond — A person requesting the court's permission to enforce a bond under subsection 143(1) (enforcement of recognizance or bond) of the *Courts of Justice Act* shall serve a notice of forfeiture motion (Form 32A), with a copy of the bond attached, on the person said to have broken the bond and on each surety.

(8) Forfeiture if no Deposit Made — If an order of forfeiture of a bond is made and no deposit was required, or a deposit was required but was not made, the order shall require the payor or surety to pay the required amount to the person to whom the bond is payable,

(a) in a single payment, immediately or before a date that the court chooses; or

(b) in instalments, over a period of time that the court considers appropriate.

(9) Change in Payment Schedule — If time is allowed for payment under subrule (8), the court may, on a later motion by the payor or a surety, allow further time for payment.

(10) Order for Forfeiture of Deposit — If an order of forfeiture of a bond is made and a deposit was required and was made, the order shall direct the clerk to pay the required amount immediately to the person to whom the bond is made payable.

(11) Cancelling Bond — The court may, on motion, make an order under subrule (4), or an order cancelling the bond and directing a refund of all or part of the deposit, if,

(a) a payor or surety made a deposit under the bond;

(b) the conditions of the bond have not been broken; and

(c) the conditions have expired or, although they have not expired or do not have an expiry date, the payor or surety has good reasons for getting the conditions of the bond changed.

(12) Form of Warrant for Arrest — A warrant for arrest issued against any of the following shall be in Form 32B:

1. A payor who does not file a financial statement ordered under subsection 40(4) of the *Family Responsibility and Support Arrears Enforcement Act, 1996* or under these rules.

461

2. A payor who does not come to a default hearing under section 41 of the *Family Responsibility and Support Arrears Enforcement Act, 1996.*

3. An absconding respondent under subsection 43(1) or 59(2) of the *Family Law Act.*

4. An absconding payor under subsection 49(1) of the *Family Responsibility and Support Arrears Enforcement Act, 1996.*

5. A witness who does not come to court or remain in attendance as required by a summons to witness.

6. A person who does not come to court in a case that may result in an order requiring the person to post a bond under these rules.

7. A person who does not obey an order requiring the person to post a bond under these rules.

8. A person against whom a contempt motion is made.

9. Any other person liable to arrest under an order.

10. Any other person liable to arrest for committing an offence.

(13) Bail on Arrest — Section 150 (interim release by justice of the peace) of the *Provincial Offences Act* applies, with necessary changes, to an arrest made under a warrant mentioned in paragraph 1, 2, 3 or 4 of subrule (12).

(14) Affidavit for Warrant of Committal — An affidavit in support of a motion for a warrant of committal shall be in Form 32C.

(15) Form of Warrant of Committal — A warrant of committal issued to enforce an order of imprisonment shall be in Form 32D.

Rule 33 — Child Protection

33. (1) Timetable — Every child protection case, including a status review application, is governed by the following timetable:

Step in the case	Maximum time for completion, from start of case
First hearing, if child has been apprehended	5 days
Service and filing of answers and plans of care	30 days
Temporary care and custody hearing	35 days
Settlement conference	80 days
Hearing	120 days

(2) Case Management Judge — Wherever possible, at the start of the case a judge shall be assigned to manage it and monitor its progress.

(3) Court may Lengthen Times Only in Best Interests of Child — The court may lengthen a time shown in the timetable only if the best interests of the child require it.

(4) Parties may not Lengthen Times — The parties may not lengthen a time shown in the timetable by consent under subrule 3(6).

(5) Plan of Care or Supervision to be Served — A party who wants the court to consider a plan of care or supervision shall serve it on the other parties and file it not later than seven days before the case conference, even if that is sooner than the timetable would require.

(6) Temporary Care and Custody Hearing — Affidavit Evidence — The evidence at a temporary care and custody hearing shall be given by affidavit, unless the court orders otherwise.

(6.1) Status Review — A status review application under clause 64(2)(a) or (b) of the *Child and Family Services Act* shall be served at least 30 days before the date the order for society supervision or society wardship expires.

(7) Forms for Child Protection Cases — In a child protection case,

    (a) an information for a warrant to apprehend a child shall be in Form 33;

    (b) a warrant to apprehend a child shall be in Form 33A;

    (c) an applicant's plan of care for a child shall be,

        (i) if the applicant is a children's aid society, in Form 33B, and

        (ii) if the applicant is not a children's aid society, in Form 33B.1;

    (c.1) a respondent's answer and plan of care for a child shall be,

        (i) if the respondent is not a children's aid society, in From 33B.1,

        (ii) if the respondent is a children's aid society, in Form 10 and Form 33B;

    (d) an agreed statement of facts in a child protection case shall be in Form 33C; and

    (e) an agreed statement of facts in a status review application shall be in Form 33D.

(8) Forms for Secure Treatment Cases — In an application under Part VI (secure treatment) of the *Child and Family Services Act*, a consent signed by the child shall be in Form 33E and a consent signed by any other person shall be in Form 33F.

O. Reg. 91/03, s. 7

Rule 34 — Adoption

34. (1) CFSA Definitions Apply — The definitions in the *Child and Family Services Act* apply to this rule and, in particular,

"Director" means a Director within the meaning of the Act.

(2) Meaning of "Act" — In this rule,

"Act" means the *Child and Family Services Act*.

(2.1) Use of Initials in Documents — An applicant or respondent may be referred to by only the first letter of his or her surname in any document in the case, except that,

    (a) the applicant's full names shall appear in the adoption order; and

    (b) the child's full names shall appear in the adoption order, unless the court orders that the child's first name and the first letter of his or her surname be used.

(3) Certified Copy of Order from Outside Ontario — When this rule requires a copy of an order to be filed and the order in question was made outside Ontario, it shall be a copy that is certified by an official of the court or other authority that made it.

(4) Material to be Filed with Adoption Applications — The following shall be filed with every application for an adoption:

1. A certified copy of the statement of live birth of the child, or an equivalent that satisfies the court.

2. If required, the child's consent to adoption (Form 34) or a notice of motion and supporting affidavit for an order under subsection 137(9) of the Act dispensing with the child's consent.

3. If the child is not a Crown ward, an affidavit of parentage (Form 34A) or any other evidence about parentage that the court requires from the child's parent, or a person named by the court.

4. If the applicant has a spouse who has not joined in the application, a consent to the child's adoption by the spouse (Form 34B).

5. If required by the Act or by an order, a Director's or local director's statement on adoption (Form 34C) under subsection 149(1) or (6) of the Act.

6. An affidavit signed by the applicant (Form 34D) that includes details about the applicant's education, employment, health, background and ability to support and care for the child, a history of the relationship between the parent and the child and any other evidence relating to the best interests of the child, and states whether the child is an Indian or a native person.

(5) Report of Child's Adjustment — A report under subsection 149(5) or (6) of the Act of the child's adjustment in the applicant's home shall also be filed with the application if the child is under 16 years of age, or is 16 years of age or older but has not withdrawn from parental control and has not married.

(6) Additional Material — Crown Ward — If the child is a Crown ward, the following shall also be filed with the application:

1. A Director's consent to adoption (Form 34E).

2. A copy of any order under subsection 58(1) of the Act ending access to the child.

3. A copy of the order of Crown wardship.

4. Proof of service of the orders referred to in paragraphs 2 and 3, or a copy of any order dispensing with service.

5. An affidavit, signed by a person delegated by the local director of the children's aid society that has placed the child for adoption, stating that there is no appeal in progress from an order referred to in paragraph 2 or 3, or that the appeal period has expired without an appeal being filed, or that an appeal was filed but has been withdrawn or finally dismissed.

6. If the child is an Indian or native person, proof of 30 days written notice to the child's band or native community of the intention to place the child for adoption.

(7) Additional Material — Child not Crown Ward — If the child is not a Crown ward and is placed for adoption by a licensee or children's aid society, the following shall also be filed with the application:

1. A copy of any custody or access order that is in force and is known to the person placing the child, or to an applicant.

2. [Revoked O. Reg. 337/02, s. 3(4).]

3. A consent to adoption (Form 34F) under section 137 of the Act from every parent, other than the applicant, of whom the person placing the child or an applicant is aware. An order under section 138 of the Act dispensing with a parent's consent may be filed instead of the consent.

4. An affidavit (Form 34G) signed by the licensee or by an authorized employee of the children's aid society (depending on who is placing the child).

5. If the child is placed by a licensee, a copy of the licensee's licence to make the placement at the time of placing the child for adoption.

6. If the child is an Indian or native person, proof of 30 days written notice to the child's band or native community of the intention to place the child for adoption.

(8) Additional Material — Relative or Step-parent — If the applicant is the child's relative or the spouse of the child's parent, an affidavit from each applicant (Form 34H) shall also be filed with the application.

(9) Application By Step-Parent or Relative — An application by a relative of the child or the spouse of the child's parent,

(a) shall not be commenced until the 21-day period referred to in subsection 137(8) of the Act has expired; and

(b) shall be accompanied by the applicant's affidavit confirming that he or she did not receive a withdrawal of consent during the 21-day period.

(10) Step-Parent Adoption, Parent's Consent — An application by the spouse of the child's parent shall be accompanied by the parent's consent (Form 34I).

(11) Independent Legal Advice, Child's Consent — The consent of a child to be adopted (Form 34) shall be witnessed by a representative of the Children's Lawyer, who shall complete the affidavit of execution and independent legal advice contained in the form.

(11.1) Independent Legal Advice, Consent of Parent Under 18 — The consent of a person under the age of 18 years who is a parent of the child to be adopted (Form 34F) shall be witnessed by a representative of the Children's Lawyer, who shall complete an affidavit of execution and independent legal advice (Form 34J).

(12) Independent Legal Advice, Adult Parent's Consent — The consent of an adult parent of the child to be adopted shall be witnessed by an independent lawyer, who shall complete the affidavit of execution and independent legal advice.

(13) Copy of Consent for Person Signing — A person who signs a consent to an adoption shall be given a copy of the consent and of the affidavit of execution and independent legal advice.

(13.1) Withdrawal of Consent by Parent — A parent who has given consent to an adoption under subsection 137(2) of the Act may withdraw the consent under subsection 137(8) of the Act in accordance with the following:

1. If the child is placed for adoption by a children's aid society, the parent who wishes to withdraw the consent shall ensure that the children's aid society receives the written withdrawal within 21 days after the consent was given.

2. If the child is placed for adoption by a licensee, the parent who wishes to withdraw the consent shall ensure that the licensee receives the written withdrawal within 21 days after the consent was given.

3. If a relative of the child or a spouse of a parent proposes to apply to adopt the child, the parent who wishes to withdraw the consent shall ensure that the relative or spouse receives the written withdrawal within 21 days after the consent was given.

(13.2) Withdrawal of Consent by Child Aged Seven or Older — A child who has given consent to an adoption under subsection 137(6) of the Act may withdraw the consent under subsection 137(8) of the Act in accordance with the following:

1. The withdrawal shall be signed within 21 days after the consent was given, and witnessed by the person who witnesses the consent under subrule (11) or by another representative of the Children's Lawyer.

2. The person who witness the withdrawal shall give the original withdrawal document to the child and promptly serve a copy on the children's aid society, licensee, relative or spouse, as the case may be, by regular service.

(14) Motion to Withdraw Consent — Despite subrule 5(4) (place for steps other than enforcement), a motion to withdraw a consent to an adoption under subsection 139(1) of the Act shall be made in,

(a) the municipality where the person who gave the consent lives; or

(b) in any other place that the court decides.

(15) Clerk to Check Adoption Application — Before the application is presented to a judge, the clerk shall,

(a) review the application and other documents filed to see whether they are in order; and

(b) prepare a certificate (Form 34K).

(16) Dispensing With Consent Before Placement — In an application to dispense with a parent's consent before placement for adoption,

(a) the applicant may be the licensee, a parent, the children's aid society or the person who wants to adopt;

(b) the respondent is the person who has not given consent;

(c) if an order that service is not required is sought, the request shall be made in the application and not by motion;

(d) if the application is being served, the applicant shall serve and file with it an affidavit (Form 14A) setting out the facts of the case;

(e) if the application is not being served, the applicant shall file with it an affidavit (Form 14A) setting out the facts of the case, and the clerk shall send the case to a judge for a decision on the basis of affidavit evidence.

(17) Transitional Provision — Consent, Evidence of Parentage — If a consent to adoption was validly given before November 15, 1999,

(a) it remains valid under these rules; and

(b) the evidence of parentage is acceptable if it was acceptable under the rules in effect when the consent was given.

(18) Revocation — Subrule (17) is revoked on December 31, 2004.

O. Reg. 337/02, s. 3

Rule 35 — Change of Name

35. (1) Time for Application — An application under subsection 7(3) (application to court for change of name) of the *Change of Name Act* shall be made within 30 days after the applicant is notified that the Registrar General has refused to make the requested change of name.

(2) Service on the Registrar General — The applicant shall serve the application and any supporting material on the Registrar General by delivering or mailing a copy of the documents to the Deputy Registrar General.

(3) Registrar General's Reasons for Refusal — Within 15 days after being served under subrule (2), the Registrar General may file reasons for refusing to make the requested change of name.

Rule 36 — Divorce

36. (1) Application for Divorce — Either spouse may start a divorce case by,

(a) filing an application naming the other spouse as a respondent; or

(b) filing a joint application with no respondent.

(2) Joint Application — In a joint application, the divorce and any other order sought shall be made only with the consent of both spouses.

(3) Allegation of Adultery — In an application for divorce claiming that the other spouse committed adultery with another person, that person does not need to be named, but if named, shall be served with the application and has all the rights of a respondent in the case.

(4) Marriage Certificate and Central Divorce Registry Certificate — The court shall not grant a divorce until the following have been filed:

1. A marriage certificate or marriage registration certificate, unless the application states that it is impractical to obtain a certificate and explains why.

2. A report on earlier divorce cases started by either spouse, issued under the *Central Registry of Divorce Proceedings Regulations* (Canada).

(5) Divorce Based on Affidavit Evidence — If the respondent files no answer, or files one and later withdraws it, the applicant shall file an affidavit (Form 36) that,

(a) confirms that all the information in the application is correct, except as stated in the affidavit;

(b) if no marriage certificate or marriage registration certificate has been filed, provides sufficient information to prove the marriage;

467

(c) contains proof of any previous divorce or the death of a party's previous spouse, unless the marriage took place in Canada;

(d) contains the information about arrangements for support of any children of the marriage required by paragraph 11(1)(b) of the *Divorce Act* (Canada), and attaches as exhibits the income and financial information required by section 21 of the child support guidelines; and

(e) contains any other information necessary for the court to grant the divorce.

(6) Draft Divorce Order — The applicant shall file with the affidavit,

(a) three copies of a draft divorce order (Form 25A);

(b) a stamped envelope addressed to each party; and

(c) if the divorce order is to contain a support order,

(i) an extra copy of the draft divorce order for the clerk to file with the Director of the Family Responsibility Office, and

(ii) two copies of a draft support deduction order.

(7) Clerk to Present Papers to Judge — When the documents mentioned in subrules (4) to (6) have been filed, the clerk shall prepare a certificate (Form 36A) and present the documents to a judge, who may,

(a) grant the divorce as set out in the draft order;

(b) have the clerk return the documents to the applicant to make any needed corrections; or

(c) grant the divorce but make changes to the draft order, or refuse to grant the divorce, after giving the applicant a chance to file an additional affidavit or come to court to explain why the order should be made without change.

(8) Divorce Certificate — When a divorce takes effect, the clerk shall, on either party's request,

(a) check the continuing record to verify that,

(i) no appeal has been taken from the divorce order, or any appeal from it has been disposed of, and

(ii) no order has been made extending the time for an appeal, or any extended time has expired without an appeal; and

(b) if satisfied of those matters, issue a divorce certificate (Form 36B) and mail it to the parties, unless the court orders otherwise.

(9) Registration of Orders Made Outside Ontario — If a court outside Ontario has made an order for support, custody or access under the *Divorce Act* (Canada), a person who wants it registered for enforcement in Ontario under paragraph 20(3)(a) of that Act shall mail a certified copy of the order to the clerk at the office of the Superior Court of Justice in a municipality where the order may be enforced under subrule 5(6).

Rule 37 — Interjurisdictional Support Orders Act, 2002

37. (1) Application — This rule applies to cases under the Act.

(2) Definitions — In this rule,

"Act" means the *Interjurisdictional Support Orders Act, 2002*; *("Loi")*

"appropriate authority" has the same meaning as in the Act; *("autorité compétente")*

"designated authority" has the same meaning as in the Act; *("autorité désignée")*

"general regulation" means Ontario Regulation 55/03; *("règlement général")*

"send", when used in reference to a person, means to,

> (a) mail to the person's lawyer or, if none, to the person,

> (b) send by courier to the person's lawyer or, if none, to the person,

> (c) deposit at a document exchange to which the person's lawyer belongs, or

> (d) fax to the person's lawyer or, if none, to the person.

("envoyer")

(3) Notice of Hearing — When the court receives a support application or a support variation application the clerk shall, under section 10 or 33 of the Act,

> (a) serve on the respondent, by special service,

>> (i) the notice of hearing mentioned in clause 10(b) or 33(b) of the Act (Form 37),

>> (ii) a copy of the documents sent by the designated authority, and

>> (iii) blank response forms; and

> (b) send to the designated authority a copy of the notice of hearing and an information sheet (Form 37A).

(4) Information And Documents To Be Provided By Respondent — The respondent shall file, within 30 days after service of the notice of hearing,

> (a) an answer in Form N under the general regulation,

>> (i) identifying any issues the respondent intends to raise with respect to the support application, and

>> (ii) containing the financial information referred to in subsection 21(1) of Ontario Regulation 391/97 (Child Support Guidelines), if the support application includes a claim for child support;

> (b) an affidavit (Form 14A) setting out the evidence on which the respondent relies; and

> (c) a financial statement in Form K under the general regulation.

(5) Respondent's Financial Statement — The respondent is required to file a financial statement whether he or she intends to dispute the claim or not.

(6) Applicant's Financial Statement — The fact that the applicant has provided financial information in a form different than that required by these rules does not affect the case.

(7) Written Hearing — Unless the court orders otherwise under subrule (9), the application shall be dealt with on the basis of written documents without the parties or their lawyers needing to come to court.

(8) Request For Oral Hearing — The respondent may request an oral hearing by filing a motion (Form 14B) within 30 days after being served with the notice of hearing.

(9) Order For Oral Hearing — The court may order an oral hearing, on the respondent's motion or on its own initiative, if it is satisfied that an oral hearing is necessary to deal with the case justly.

Family Rules

(10) Direction to Request Further Information or Documents — A direction to request further information or documents under clause 11(2)(a) or 34(2)(a) of the Act shall be in Form 37B, and a statement of the court's reasons for requesting further evidence shall be attached to the direction.

(11) Direction to be Sent to Respondent — When a direction is sent to the designated authority under clause 11(2)(a) of the Act, the clerk shall also send a copy to the respondent.

(12) Adjournment — When the court adjourns the hearing under clause 11(2)(b) or 34(2)(b) of the Act, it shall specify the date on which the hearing is to continue.

(13) Copies of Further Information or Documents — When the court receives the further information or documents, the clerk shall promptly prepare a notice of continuation of hearing (Form 37C) and send it, with copies of the information or documents, to the respondent and to the designated authority.

(14) Respondent's Affidavit — If the respondent wishes to respond to the further information or documents, he or she shall file an affidavit (Form 14A) containing the response with the court, within 30 days after receiving the notice of continuation of hearing.

(15) Preparation of Order — The clerk shall prepare the order for signature as soon as it is made, in accordance with subrule 25(11).

(16) Sending Copies of Order to Respondent and Designated Authority — The court shall send,

(a) a copy of the order to the respondent, addressed to the respondent's last known address if sent by mail; and

(b) a certified copy of the order to the designated authority.

(17) Sending Copy of Order to Appropriate Authority — The designated authority shall send the certified copy of the order to the appropriate authority.

(18) Notice of Registration, Order Made Outside Canada — For the purpose of subsection 20(1) of the Act, the clerk of the Ontario court shall give notice of the registration of an order made outside Canada by providing a notice in Form 37D, as described in subrule (19), to any party to the order who is believed to ordinarily reside in Ontario.

(19) Sending or Special Service — If the party to whom notice is to be provided applied for the order in Ontario, the clerk shall send the notice to the party, but in any other case, the clerk shall serve the notice on the party by special service.

(20) Motion to Set Aside Registration — For the purpose of subsection 20(3) of the Act, a party shall give notice of a motion to set aside the registration of an order made outside Canada by,

(a) filing in the Ontario court a notice of motion (Form 14) setting out the grounds for the motion;

(b) sending the notice of motion and supporting documents to the claimant at the address shown in the order; and

(c) serving the notice of motion and supporting documents on the designated authority by regular service at least 10 days before the motion hearing date.

(21) Designated Authority Need Not Appear On Motion — The designated authority is not required to appear on the motion to set aside registration.

(22) Notice of Decision or Order — When the court makes a decision or order under section 20 of the Act, the clerk shall send copies of the order, with the court's reasons, if any,

(a) to each party, addressed to the party's last known address if sent by mail; and

(b) to the designated authority.

(23) Party in Reciprocating Jurisdiction — If a party ordinarily resides in a reciprocating jurisdiction and the order was originally sent to Ontario for registration by the appropriate authority there, the clerk may send it to that appropriate authority rather than sending it to the party as set out in clause (22)(a).

(24) Provisional Orders — When the court makes a provisional order under section 7 or 30 of the Act, the clerk shall send the following to the designated authority, to be sent to the reciprocating jurisdiction:

1. One copy of,

    i. the application (Form A under the general regulation),

    ii. the applicant's financial statement (Form K under the general regulation), and

    iii. a statement giving any information about the respondent's identification, whereabouts, income, assets and liabilities.

2. Three certified copies of,

    i. the applicant's evidence and, if reasonably possible, the exhibits, and

    ii. the provisional order.

(25) Further Evidence — When the court that made a provisional order receives a request for further evidence from the confirming court under subsection 7(4) or 30(4) of the Act, the clerk shall send to the applicant a notice for taking further evidence (Form 37E) and a copy of the documents sent by the confirming court.

O. Reg. 56/03, s. 6

Rule 37.1 — Provisional Orders and Confirmation of Provisional Orders — Divorce Act, Family Law Act

37.1 (1) Application — This rule applies to orders made under sections 18 and 19 of the *Divorce Act* (Canada) and under section 44 of the *Family Law Act*.

(2) Definitions — In this rule,

"confirming court" means,

(a) in the case of an order under section 19 of the *Divorce Act* (Canada), the court in Ontario or another province or territory of Canada that has jurisdiction to confirm a provisional variation of the order, or

(b) for the purpose of section 44 of the *Family Law Act*,

(i) the Ontario Court of Justice sitting in the municipality where the respondent resides, or

(ii) the Family Court of the Superior Court of Justice, if the respondent resides in an area where that court has jurisdiction;

("tribunal d'homologation")

"originating court" means,

> (a) in the case of an order under section 18 of the *Divorce Act* (Canada), the court in Ontario or another province or territory of Canada that has jurisdiction under section 5 of that Act to deal with an application for a provisional variation of the order, or

> (b) for the purpose of section 44 of the *Family Law Act*,

>> (i) the Ontario Court of Justice sitting in the municipality where the provisional order is made, or

>> (ii) the Family Court of the Superior Court of Justice when it makes the provisional order;

("tribunal d'origine")

"send" , when used in reference to a person, means to,

> (a) mail to the person's lawyer or, if none, to the person,

> (b) send by courier to the person's lawyer or, if none, to the person,

> (c) deposit at a document exchange to which the person's lawyer belongs, or

> (d) fax to the person's lawyer or, if none, to the person.

("envoyer")

(3) Documents To Be Sent To Confirming Court — When the court makes a provisional order under section 18 of the *Divorce Act* (Canada) or section 44 of the *Family Law Act*, the clerk shall send the following to the confirming court (if it is in Ontario) or to the Attorney General to be sent to the confirming court (if it is outside Ontario):

> 1. One copy of,

>> i. the application (Form 8),

>> ii. the applicant's financial statement (Form 13),

>> iii. a statement giving any information about the respondent's identification, whereabouts, income, assets and liabilities, and

>> iv. if the confirming court is in another municipality in Ontario, proof that the application was served on the respondent.

> 2. Three certified copies of,

>> i. the applicant's evidence and, if reasonably possible, the exhibits, and

>> ii. the provisional order.

(4) No Financial Statement From Foreign Applicant — When a confirming court in Ontario receives a provisional order made outside Ontario, the applicant does not have to file a financial statement.

(5) Notice of Confirmation Hearing — A clerk of a confirming court in Ontario who receives a provisional order shall,

> (a) serve on the respondent, by special service (subrule 6 (3)),

>> (i) a notice of hearing (Form 37),

>> (ii) a copy of the documents sent by the originating court, and

>> (iii) blank response forms; and

> (b) send a notice of hearing and an information sheet (Form 37A) to,

>> (i) the applicant,

(ii) the clerk of the originating court, and

(iii) the Attorney General, if the provisional order was made outside Ontario.

(6) Respondent's Financial Statement — A respondent at a confirmation hearing under section 19 of the *Divorce Act* (Canada) shall serve and file a financial statement (Form 13) within 30 days after service of the notice of confirmation hearing.

(7) Written Hearing — Unless the court orders otherwise under subrule (9), the application shall be dealt with on the basis of written documents without the parties or their lawyers needing to come to court.

(8) Request For Oral Hearing — The respondent may request an oral hearing by filing a motion (Form 14B) within 30 days after being served with the notice of hearing.

(9) Order For Oral Hearing — The court may order an oral hearing, on the applicant's motion or on its own initiative, if it is satisfied that an oral hearing is necessary to deal with the case justly.

(10) Court Receives Request For Further Evidence — When an originating court in Ontario receives a request for further evidence from the confirming court, the clerk shall send to the applicant a notice for taking further evidence (Form 37E) and a copy of the documents sent by the confirming court.

(11) Court Sends Request For Further Evidence — When a confirming court in Ontario requests further evidence from the originating court,

(a) the confirming court shall adjourn the confirmation hearing to a new date; and

(b) the clerk shall send to the originating court two certified copies of the evidence taken in the confirming court.

(12) Continuing The Confirmation Hearing — When a confirming court in Ontario receives further evidence from the originating court, the clerk shall promptly prepare a notice of continuation of hearing (Form 37C) and send it, with copies of the evidence, to the respondent and, if the provisional order was made outside Ontario, to the Attorney General.

(13) Respondent's Affidavit — If the respondent wishes to respond to the further evidence, he or she shall file an affidavit containing the response with the court, within 30 days after receiving the notice of continuation of hearing.

O. Reg. 56/03, s. 6

Rule 38 — Appeals

38. (1) Appeals Governed by this Rule — This rule applies to appeals under the following:

Section 48 of the *Family Law Act*

Section 73 of the *Children's Law Reform Act*

Section 69 or 156 of the *Child and Family Services Act*

Section 11 of the *Change of Name Act*

Section 40 of the *Courts of Justice Act*

(2) Appeal to Superior Court of Justice — Time, Service and Filing of Notice —
To start an appeal from the Ontario Court of Justice to the Superior Court of Justice under
any of the provisions listed in subrule (1), a party shall,

> (a) within 30 days after the date of the order being appealed, serve a notice of appeal
> (Form 38), by regular service (subrule 6(2)), on,
>
>> (i) every other party affected by the appeal or entitled to appeal,
>>
>> (ii) the clerk of the court in the place where the order was made, and
>>
>> (iii) in an appeal under section 69 of the *Child and Family Services Act*, every
>> other person entitled to notice under subsection 39(3) of that Act who appeared at
>> the hearing; and
>
> (b) within 10 days after serving the notice under clause (a), file it.

(3) Name of Case Unchanged — The name of a case in an appeal shall be the same as
the name of the case in the order being appealed, and shall also identify the parties as appellant and respondent.

(4) Grounds Stated in Notice of Appeal — The notice of appeal shall state the order
that the appellant wants the appeal court to make and the legal grounds for the appeal.

(5) Other Grounds — At the hearing of the appeal, no grounds other than the ones stated
in the notice of appeal may be argued unless the court gives permission.

(6) Appeal Record and Appellant's Factum — The appellant shall, not later than 10
days before the hearing of the appeal, serve on the respondent and file an appeal record
(subrule (7)) and an appellant's factum (subrule (8)).

(7) Contents of Appeal Record — The appeal record shall contain a copy of the following documents, in the following order:

> 1. A table of contents describing each document, including each exhibit, by its na-
> ture and date and, for an exhibit, by exhibit number or letter.
>
> 2. The notice of appeal.
>
> 3. The order being appealed, as signed, and any reasons given by the court appealed
> from, as well as a further printed copy of the reasons if they are handwritten.
>
> 4. A transcript of the oral evidence (which the parties to the appeal may agree to
> limit to the portions necessary for the appeal).
>
> 5. Any other material that was before the court appealed from and that is necessary
> for the appeal.

(8) Contents of Appellant's Factum — The appellant's factum shall be not more than
30 pages long, shall be signed by the appellant's lawyer or, if none, by the appellant and
shall consist of the following parts, containing paragraphs numbered consecutively from the
beginning to the end of the factum:

> 1. Part 1: Identification. A statement identifying the appellant and respondent and
> the court appealed from, and stating the result in that court.
>
> 2. Part 2: Overview. A brief overview of the case and the issues on the appeal.
>
> 3. Part 3: Facts. A brief summary of the facts relevant to the appeal, with reference
> to the evidence by page and line as necessary.

4. Part 4: Issues. A brief statement of each issue, followed by a brief argument referring to the law relating to that issue.

5. Part 5: Order. A precise statement of the order the appeal court is asked to make, including any order for costs.

6. Part 6: Time estimate. An estimate of how much time will be needed for the appellant's oral argument, not including reply to the respondent's argument.

7. Part 7: List of authorities. A list of all statutes, regulations, rules, cases and other authorities referred to in the factum.

8. Part 8: Legislation. A copy of all relevant provisions of statutes, regulations and rules.

(9) Respondent's Factum and Appeal Record — The respondent shall, not later than three days before the hearing of the appeal, serve on every other party to the appeal and file,

(a) a respondent's factum (subrule (10)); and

(b) if applicable, a respondent's appeal record containing a copy of any material that was before the court appealed from and is necessary for the appeal but is not included in the appellant's appeal record.

(10) Contents of Respondent's Factum — The respondent's factum shall be not more than 30 pages long, shall be signed by the respondent's lawyer or, if none, by the respondent and shall consist of the following parts, containing paragraphs numbered consecutively from the beginning to the end of the factum:

1. Part 1: Overview. A brief overview of the case and the issues on the appeal.

2. Part 2: Facts. A brief statement of the facts in the appellant's factum that the respondent accepts as correct and the facts that the respondent says are incorrect, and a brief summary of any additional facts relied on by the respondent, with reference to the evidence by page and line as necessary.

3. Part 3: Issues. A statement of the respondent's position on each issue raised by the appellant, followed by a brief argument referring to the law relating to that issue.

4. Part 4: Additional issues. A brief statement of each additional issue raised by the respondent, followed by a brief argument referring to the law relating to that issue.

5. Part 5: Order. A precise statement of the order the appeal court is asked to make, including any order for costs.

6. Part 6: Time estimate. An estimate of how much time will be needed for the respondent's oral argument.

7. Part 7: List of authorities. A list of all statutes, regulations, rules, cases and other authorities referred to in the factum.

8. Part 8: Legislation. A copy of all relevant provisions of statutes, regulations and rules not included in the appellant's factum.

(11) Prompt Hearing of CFSA Appeals — An appeal under the *Child and Family Services Act* shall be heard within 30 days after the appellant's factum and appeal record are filed.

(12) Appeals under CFSA from Family Court to Divisional Court — Subrules (2) to (11) apply, with necessary changes, to an appeal under the *Child and Family Services Act* from the Family Court of the Superior Court of Justice to the Divisional Court.

(13) Motion for Permission to Appeal Temporary Order to Divisional Court — On a motion for permission to appeal a temporary order to the Divisional Court under clause 19(1)(b) of the *Courts of Justice Act*, the following apply:

1. A motion made in Toronto shall be heard by a judge of the Divisional Court (other than the one who made the order to be appealed). A motion made anywhere else may be heard by any judge other than the one who made the order to be appealed.

2. The notice of motion shall be served and filed within 30 days after the date of the order to be appealed.

3. Permission to appeal shall not be given unless,

i. there is a conflicting decision by another judge or court in Ontario or elsewhere on the matter involved in the proposed appeal, or there appears to the judge hearing the motion good reason to doubt the correctness of the order in question, and

ii. in the judge's opinion, permission to appeal should be granted.

4. The party asking for permission to appeal shall, when filing the notice of motion, request that the continuing record be sent to the judge hearing the motion.

5. Each party shall serve a factum as described in subrule (8) (appellant's factum) and file it not later than 2 p.m. on the day before the motion is heard.

6. The party asking for permission to appeal shall file a confirmation form (Form 14C) not later than 2 p.m. on the day before the motion is heard.

7. The judge shall give brief written reasons if permission to appeal is given.

8. The appellant shall serve and file the notice of appeal within seven days after permission is given.

9. The appeal is governed by the Rules of Civil Procedure and these rules do not apply.

Rule 39 — Case Management in Family Court of Superior Court of Justice

39. (1) Case Management in Certain Areas Only — This rule applies only to cases in the Family Court of the Superior Court of Justice, which has jurisdiction in the municipalities listed in subrule 1(3).

(2) Excluded Cases — This rule does not apply to,

(a) enforcements;

(b) child protection cases; or

(c) cases under rule 37 or 37.1.

(3) Parties May not Lengthen Times — A time set out in this rule may be lengthened only by order of the case management judge and not by the parties' consent under subrule 3(6).

(4) Fast Track — Applications to which this rule applies, except the ones mentioned in subrule (7), and motions to change a final order or agreement are fast track cases (subrules (5) and (6)).

(5) Fast Track — First Court Date — In a fast track case the clerk shall, on or before the first court date,

(a) confirm that all necessary documents have been served and filed;

(b) refer the parties to sources of information about the court process, alternatives to court (including mediation), the effects of separation and divorce on children and community resources that may help the parties and their children;

(c) if no answer has been filed in response to an application, or if no affidavit has been filed in response to a motion to change a final order or agreement, send the case to a judge for a decision on the basis of affidavit evidence or, on request, schedule a case conference; and

(d) if an answer has been filed in response to an application, or if an affidavit has been filed in response to a motion to change a final order or agreement, confirm that the case is ready for a hearing, case conference or settlement conference and schedule it accordingly.

(6) Fast Track — Case Management Judge Assigned at Start — In a fast track case, a case management judge shall be assigned by the first time the case comes before a judge.

(7) Standard Track — Applications in which the applicant makes a claim for a divorce or a property claim are standard track cases (subrule (8)).

(8) Features of Standard Track — In a standard track case,

(a) the clerk shall not set a court date when the application is filed;

(b) a case management judge shall be assigned when a case conference is scheduled or when a notice of motion is served before a case conference has been held (subrule 14(4), (5) or (6)), whichever comes first; and

(c) the clerk shall schedule a case conference on any party's request.

(9) Functions of Case Management Judge — The case management judge assigned to a case,

(a) shall generally supervise its progress;

(b) shall conduct the case conference and the settlement conference;

(c) may schedule a case conference or settlement conference at any time, on the judge's own initiative;

(d) shall hear motions in the case, when available to hear motions; and

(e) may, on motion, set aside an order of the clerk under subrule (12).

(10) Substitute Case Management Judge — If the case management judge is, for any reason, unavailable to continue as the case management judge, another case management judge may be assigned for part or all of the case.

(11) Notice, Case not Scheduled for Trial After 200 Days — If a case has not been scheduled for trial within 200 days after it was started, the clerk shall serve a notice (Form 39) on the parties by mail, fax or electronic mail saying that the case will be dismissed without further notice unless one of the parties, within 30 days after the notice is served,

   (a) files an agreement signed by all parties and their lawyers, if any, for a final order disposing of all issues in the case, and a notice of motion for an order carrying out the agreement; or

   (b) arranges a case conference or settlement conference for the first available date.

(12) Dismissal After Notice — If the clerk serves a notice under subrule (11) and no party takes any of the steps set out in clauses (11)(a) and (b) within 30 days after the notice is served, the clerk shall prepare and sign an order dismissing the case, with no costs payable by any party.

(13) Service of Dismissal Order by Clerk — The clerk shall serve the order on each party by mail, fax or electronic mail.

(14) Service of Dismissal Order by Lawyer on Client — A lawyer who is served with a dismissal order on behalf of a client shall serve it on the client by mail, fax or electronic mail and file proof of service of the order.

(15) Transitional Provision — If a case was started before these rules come into effect, but a party serves and files a document or requests a case conference after they come into effect,

   (a) the clerk shall serve the notice (Form 39) mentioned in subrule (11) if the case has not been scheduled for trial within 200 days after it was started or within 90 days after the party files the document or requests the case conference, whichever comes later; and

   (b) once the notice is served, this rule applies with necessary changes.

O. Reg. 202/01, s. 7; 56/03, s. 7

Rule 40 — Case Management in Ontario Court of Justice

40. (1) Case Management in Certain Areas Only — This rule applies only to cases in the Ontario Court of Justice.

(2) Excluded Cases — This rule does not apply to,

   (a) enforcements;

   (b) child protection cases; or

   (c) cases under rule 37 or 37.1.

(3) Parties may not Lengthen Times — A time set out in this rule may be lengthened only by order and not by the parties' consent under subrule 3(6).

(4) First Court Date — The clerk shall, on or before the first court date,

   (a) confirm that all necessary documents have been served and filed;

   (b) refer the parties to sources of information about the court process, alternatives to court (including mediation), the effects of separation and divorce on children and community resources that may help the parties and their children;

(c) if no answer has been filed in response to an application, or if no affidavit has been filed in response to a motion to change a final order or agreement, send the case to a judge for a decision on the basis of affidavit evidence or, on request, schedule a case conference; and

(d) if an answer has been filed in response to an application, or if an affidavit has been filed in response to a motion to change a final order or agreement, confirm that the case is ready for a hearing, case conference or settlement conference and schedule it accordingly.

(5) Notice, Case not Scheduled for Trial After 200 Days — If a case has not been scheduled for trial within 200 days after it was started, the clerk shall serve a notice (Form 39) on the parties by mail, fax or electronic mail saying that the case will be dismissed without further notice unless one of the parties, within 30 days after the notice is served,

(a) files an agreement signed by all parties and their lawyers, if any, for a final order disposing of all issues in the case, and a notice of motion for an order carrying out the agreement; or

(b) arranges a case conference or settlement conference for the first available date.

(6) Dismissal After Notice — If the clerk serves a notice under subrule (5) and no party takes any of the steps set out in clauses (5)(a) and (b) within 30 days after the notice is served, the clerk shall prepare and sign an order dismissing the case, with no costs payable by any party.

(7) Service of Dismissal Order by Clerk — The clerk shall serve the order on each party by mail, fax or electronic mail.

(8) Service of Dismissal Order by Lawyer on Client — A lawyer who is served with a dismissal order on behalf of a client shall serve it on the client by mail, fax or electronic mail and file proof of service of the order.

(9) Judge May Set Clerk's Order Aside — A judge may, on motion, set aside an order of the clerk under subrule (6).

(10) Transitional Provision — If a case was started before these rules come into effect, but a party serves and files a document or requests a case conference after they come into effect,

(a) the clerk shall serve the notice (Form 39) mentioned in subrule (5) if the case has not been scheduled for trial within 200 days after it was started or within 90 days after the party files the document or requests the case conference, whichever comes later; and

(b) once the notice is served, subrules (5) to (9) apply with necessary changes.

O. Reg. 202/01, s. 8; 56/03, s. 7

41. (1) Regulation 202 of the Revised Regulations of Ontario, 1990 and Ontario Regulations 72/92, 468/93, 282/95, 429/97, 215/98 and 294/98 are revoked.

(2) Despite subrule (1), Regulation 202, as it read on the day before Ontario Regulation 441/99 comes into force, continues in force in the Family Court of the Superior Court of Justice up to and including November 14, 1999 except in the County of Middlesex.

O. Reg. 441/99, s. 2

42. (1) Regulation 199 of the Revised Regulations of Ontario, 1990 and Ontario Regulations 705/91, 71/92, 467/93, 428/97, 216/98 and 293/98 are revoked.

(2) Despite subrule (1), Regulation 199, as it read on the day before Ontario Regulatin 441/99 comes into force, continues in force up to and including November 14, 1999 in the Ontario Court of Justice in the following municipalities:

Regional Municipality of Durham
County of Haliburton
County of Lanark
United Counties of Leeds and Grenville
Territorial District of Muskoka
The part of The Regional Municipality of Niagara that was the County of Lincoln as it existed on December 31, 1969
County of Northumberland
Regional Municipality of Ottawa–Carleton
County of Peterborough
United Counties of Prescott and Russell
United Counties of Stormont, Dundas and Glengarry
County of Victoria
Regional Municipality of York

O. Reg. 441/99, s. 2

43. *This Regulation comes into force on September 15, 1999.*

TABLE OF FORMS

Form number	Title	Rule creating form
4	Notice of change in representation	4(10)
6	Acknowledgment of service (prepaid return postcard)	6(3)
6A	Advertisement	6(17)
6B	Affidavit of service	6(19)
8	Application (general)	8(1)
8A	Application (divorce)	8(1)
8B	Application (child protection and status review)	8(1)
8C	Application (secure treatment)	8(1)
8D	Application (adoption)	8(1)
8E	Summary of court cases	8(1)
10	Answer	10(1)
10A	Reply	10(6)
12	Notice of withdrawal	12(1)
13	Financial statement	13(1)
13.1	Financial statement	13(1)
13A	Direction to Department of National Revenue, Taxation	13(7)
13B	Net family property statement	13(14)
14	Notice of motion	14(9)

TABLE OF FORMS

Form number	Title	Rule creating form
14A	Affidavit	14(9)
14B	Motion form	14(10)
14C	Confirmation	14(11)
14D	Order on motion without notice	14(14)
15	Change information form (motion to change child support)	15(10)
15A	Consent (motion to change child support)	15(10)
17	Case conference brief	17(13)
17A	Settlement conference brief	17(13)
17B	Trial management conference brief	17(13)
20	Request for information	20(3)
20A	Authorization to commissioner	20(14)
20B	Letter of request	20(14)
22	Request to admit	22(2)
22A	Response to request to admit	22(4)
23	Summons to witness	23(3)
23A	Summons to witness outside Ontario	23(8)
23B	Order for prisoner's attendance	23(10)
23C	Affidavit for uncontested trial	23(22)
25	Order (general)	25(2)
25A	Divorce order	25(2)
25B	Secure treatment order	25(2)
25C	Adoption order	25(2)
25D	Order (uncontested trial)	25(2)
25E	Notice disputing approval of order	25(5)
26	Statement of money owed	26(5)
26A	Affidavit of enforcement expenses	26(8)
26B	Affidavit for filing domestic contract or paternity agreement	26(9)
26C	Notice of transfer of enforcement	26(14)
27	Request for financial statement	27(1)
27A	Request for statement of income	27(7)
27B	Statement of income	27(7)
27C	Appointment for financial examination	27(11)
28	Writ of seizure and sale	28(1)
28A	Request for writ of seizure and sale	28(1)
28B	Statutory declaration to sheriff	28(2)
28C	Writ of temporary seizure	28(10)
29	Request for garnishment	29(1)
29A	Notice of garnishment (lump sum debt)	29(1)

Family Rules

TABLE OF FORMS

Form number	Title	Rule creating form
29B	Notice of garnishment (periodic debt)	29(1)
29C	Notice to co-owner of debt	29(8)
29D	Statutory declaration of indexed support	29(14)
29E	Dispute (payor)	29(16)
29F	Dispute (garnishee)	29(16)
29G	Dispute (co-owner of debt)	29(16)
29H	Notice of garnishment hearing	29(17)
29I	Notice to stop garnishment	29(31)
29J	Statement to garnishee financial institution re support	29(6.1)
30	Notice of default hearing	30(1)
30A	Request for default hearing	30(1)
30B	Default dispute	30(3)
31	Notice of contempt motion	31(2)
32	Bond (recognizance)	32(2)
32A	Notice of forfeiture motion	32(7)
32B	Warrant for arrest	32(12)
32C	Affidavit for warrant of committal	32(14)
32D	Warrant of committal	32(15)
33	Information for warrant to apprehend child	33(7)
33A	Warrant to apprehend child	33(7)
33B	Plan of care for child(ren)	33(7)
33B.1	Answer and Plan of Care	33(7)
33C	Statement of agreed facts (child protection)	33(7)
33D	Statement of agreed facts (status review)	33(7)
33E	Child's consent to secure treatment	33(8)
33F	Consent to secure treatment (person other than child)	33(8)
34	Child's consent to adoption	34(4)
34A	Affidavit of parentage	34(4)
34B	Non-parent's consent to adoption by spouse	34(4)
34C	Director's or local director's statement on adoption	34(4)
34D	Affidavit of adoption applicant(s)	34(4)
34E	Director's consent to adoption	34(6)
34F	Parent's or custodian's consent to adoption	34(7)
34G	Affidavit of adoption licensee or society employee	34(7)
34H	Affidavit of adopting relative or step-parent	34(8)

TABLE OF FORMS

Form number	Title	Rule creating form
34I	Parent's consent to adoption by spouse	34(9)
34J	Affidavit of execution and independent legal advice (Children's Lawyer)	34(10)
34K	Certificate of clerk (adoption)	34(15)
36	Affidavit for divorce	36(5)
36A	Certificate of clerk (divorce)	36(7)
36B	Divorce certificate	36(8)
37	Notice of confirmation hearing	37(4)
37A	Information sheet	37(3), 37.1(5)
37B	Direction to request further information	37(10)
37C	Notice of continuation of hearing	37(13), 37.1(12)
37D	Notice of registration of order	37(18)
37E	Notice for taking further evidence	37(25), 37.1(10)
38	Notice of appeal	38(2)
39	Notice of Approaching Dismissal	39(11)

Family Rules

FAMILY ORDERS AND AGREEMENTS ENFORCEMENT ASSISTANCE ACT

An Act to provide for the release of information that may assist in locating persons in default and other persons and to permit, for the enforcement of support orders and support provisions, the garnishment and attachment of certain moneys payable by Her Majesty in right of Canada

R.S.C. 1985, c. 4 (2nd Supp.), as am. S.C. 1992, c. 1, s. 66; 1993, c. 8, ss. 6–18; 1996, c. 11, ss. 95, 97, 99; 1997, c. 1, ss. 16–23; SOR/98-511; 1999, c. 17, s. 158; 1999, c. 31, s. 91 (Fr.); 2000, c. 12, s. 115; 2001, c. 4, s. 81.

Short Title

1. Short title — This Act may be cited as the *Family Orders and Agreements Enforcement Assistance Act*.

PART I — RELEASE OF INFORMATION

Interpretation

2. Definitions — In this Part,

"access right" means a right, granted in an order or agreement, of access to or visitation of a child;

"court" means a court having jurisdiction with respect to the enforcement of family provisions;

"custody provision" means a provision of an order or agreement awarding custody of a child;

"family provision" means a support provision, a custody provision or an access right;

"information bank director" means

(a) with respect to any of the information banks controlled by the Department of Human Resources Development that may be searched under this Part, the Minister of Human Resources Development,

(b) with respect to any of the information banks controlled by the Canada Employment and Immigration Commission that may be searched under this Part, the Chairman of the Canada Employment Insurance Commission, and

(c) with respect to any of the information banks controlled by the Canada Customs and Revenue Agency that may be searched under this Part, the Minister of National Revenue;

485

"Minister" means the Minister of Justice;

"order" means any order or judgment, or interim order or judgment, relating to family support, custody or access that is enforceable in a province;

"provincial enforcement service" means any service, agency or body designated in an agreement with a province under section 3 that is entitled under the laws of the province to enforce family provisions;

"provincial information bank" means a source of information designated in an agreement made under section 3;

"support provision" means a provision of an order or agreement for maintenance, alimony or family financial support and includes any order for arrears of payments thereof.

1996, c. 11, ss. 95, 97, 99; 1997, c. 1, s. 16; 1999, c. 17, s. 158

Federal-Provincial Agreements

3. Agreements with provinces for application of Part — With the approval of the Governor in Council, the Minister may, on behalf of the Government of Canada, enter into agreements with each of the provinces concerning the searching for and the release of information under this Part.

4. Contents of agreements — Every agreement with a province under section 3 must provide for

(a) the establishment of safeguards in the province for the protection of information released under this Part; and

(b) the designation of the provincial information bank or banks that, subject to this Part, must be searched before information may be released under this Part.

5. Designation of provincial enforcement services — The Minister and a province may designate in an agreement made under section 3 one or more provincial enforcement services for the purposes of this Part.

6. Agreements regarding comprehensive pension plans — With the approval of the Governor in Council, the Minister of Human Resources Development may, on behalf of the Government of Canada, enter into an agreement with each province providing a comprehensive pension plan, as defined under the *Canada Pension Plan*, for the purpose of obtaining the approval of that province for

(a) the creation, for the purposes of this Act, of an information bank to be controlled by the Department of Human Resources Development in respect of contributors to and beneficiaries under that comprehensive pension plan; and

(b) the release of information under this Part from the information bank referred to in paragraph (a) and from any other information bank controlled by the Department of Human Resources Development that contains information in respect of contributors to and beneficiaries under that comprehensive pension plan.

1996, c. 11, ss. 95, 97

Applications to Court

7. Applications to court — Any person, service, agency or body entitled to have a family provision enforced may, by *ex parte* application, request that the court apply for the release to the court of information under this Part.

1993, c. 8, s. 6

8. (1) Applications in relation to family provisions — An application under section 7 in relation to a family provision must be accompanied by

(a) a certified copy of the order, or a copy of the agreement, containing the support provision, custody provision or access right to which the application relates;

(b) an affidavit in accordance with section 9; and

(c) subject to subsection (2), proof, as supplied by the province where the court seized of the application has jurisdiction, that the provincial information banks designated with respect to that province have been searched for information helpful in locating, as the case may be, the person who is in arrears under the support provision or the child or children who is or are the object of the custody provision or access right.

(2) Where proof not necessary — The proof referred to in paragraph (1)(c) is not necessary where the affidavit in support of the application discloses that there are reasonable grounds to believe that the person, child or children referred to in that paragraph has or have left the province of the court seized of the application.

9. Contents of affidavit — An affidavit in support of an application under section 7 in relation to a family provision must

(a) allege a breach of the family provision;

(b) set out particulars of the breach and identify the person who

(i) where the family provision is a support provision, is in arrears, or

(ii) where the family provision is a custody provision or access right, is believed to have possession of the child or children who is or are the object of the custody provision or access right;

(c) disclose that reasonable steps have been taken to locate the person who is in arrears or the child or children who is or are the object of the custody provision or access right and that the person, child or children have not been located;

(d) set out particulars of the reasonable steps referred to in paragraph (c); and

(e) where the affidavit is not accompanied by the proof referred to in paragraph 8(1)(c), disclose that there are reasonable grounds to believe that the person, child or children referred to in paragraph (c) has or have left the province of the court seized of the application to which the affidavit relates and set out information in support of that belief.

10. [Repealed 1993, c. 8, s. 7.]

11. [Repealed 1993, c. 8, s. 7.]

487

12. Court shall grant authorization — A court seized of a valid application under section 7 shall, if it is satisfied

(a) that reasonable steps have been taken to locate the person, child or children to whom the application relates, and

(b) where it is alleged that the person, child or children to whom the application relates has or have left the province of the court, that the allegation is based on reasonable grounds,

grant an authorization in writing authorizing any judge of that court or any officer thereof, as the case may be, to apply for the release of information under this Part.

1993, c. 8, s. 8

Applications for the Release of Information

13. Applications for the release of information — Subject to this Part, the following, namely,

(a) a judge of a court or any officer thereof, if authorized to do so under section 12,

(b) a provincial enforcement service, or

(c) a peace officer investigating a child abduction pursuant to section 282 or 283 of the *Criminal Code*,

may apply to the Minister, in the manner prescribed by the regulations, to have the information banks referred to in section 15 searched for the information referred to in section 16 and to have any such information found in those information banks released on a confidential basis.

1993, c. 8, s. 9; 1997, c. 1, s. 17

14. (1) Form of application — An application under section 13 for the release of information must contain the information and be in the form prescribed by the regulations.

(2) Supporting documents — Where an application under section 13 is made by a person referred to in paragraph 13(a), the application must be accompanied by

(a) a copy of the family provision to which the application relates;

(b) the applicant's authorization under section 12;

(c) a copy of the affidavit submitted in support of the application for the authorization; and

(d) where the applicant's affidavit does not contain the allegation referred to in paragraph 9(e), proof, as supplied by the province where the court that granted the authorization has jurisdiction, that the provincial information banks designated with respect to that province have been searched for information helpful in locating the person, child or children to whom the application relates.

(3) Supporting documents for provincial enforcement service — Where an application under section 13 is made by a provincial enforcement service, the application must be accompanied by an affidavit submitted by an officer of the provincial enforcement service in accordance with subsection (4).

(3.1) Supporting documents for peace officer — Where an application under section 13 is made by a peace officer investigating a child abduction pursuant to section 282 or 283 of the *Criminal Code*, the application must be accompanies by

(a) a copy of the information to which the application relates; and

(b) an affidavit, submitted by the peace officer in accordance with subsection (5).

(4) Contents of affidavit — An affidavit submitted by an officer of a provincial enforcement service must

(a) allege a breach of the family provision;

(b) set out particulars of the breach and identify the person who

(i) where the family provision is a support provision, is in arrears, or

(ii) where the family provision is a custody provision or an access right, is believed to have possession of the child or children who is or are the object of the custody provision or access right;

(c) disclose that reasonable steps have been taken to locate the person who is in arrears or the child or children who is or are the object of the custody provision or access right and that the person, child or children has or have not been located;

(d) set out particulars of the reasonable steps referred to in paragraph (c); and

(e) disclose

(i) that the provincial information banks designated with respect to the province of the provincial enforcement service have been searched for information helpful in locating the person who is in arrears or the child or children who is or are the object of the custody provision or access right, or

(ii) that there are reasonable grounds to believe that the person, child or children referred to in subparagraph (i) has or have left the province of the provincial enforcement service, and set out information in support of that belief.

(5) Idem — An affidavit submitted by a peace officer must

(a) disclose that reasonable steps have been taken to locate the person against whom the information was laid and the child or children alleged to have been abducted and that the person, child or children has or have not been located;

(b) set out particulars of the reasonable steps referred to in paragraph (a); and

(c) disclose

(i) that the provincial information banks designated with respect to the province where the information was laid have been searched for information helpful in locating the person, child or children referred to in paragraph (a), or

(ii) that there are reasonable grounds to believe that the person, child or children referred to in paragraph (a) has or have left the province where the information was laid, and set out information in support of that belief.

1993, c. 8, s. 10; 1997, c. 1, s. 18

15. Information banks that may be searched — The information banks that may be searched under this Part are the information banks designated by the regulations from among the information banks controlled by the Department of Human Resources Development, the Department of National Revenue and the Canada Employment Insurance Commission.

1996, c. 11, ss. 97, 99; 1997, c. 1, s. 19

16. Information that may be released — The information that may be searched for and released under this Part is

(a) the address of the person who, as the case may be,

(i) is in arrears under the support provision to which the application relates,

(ii) is believed to have possession of the child or children who is or are the object of the custody provision or access right to which the application relates, or

(iii) is believed to have possession of the child or children who is or are the object of the investigation pursuant to section 282 or 283 of the *Criminal Code* to which the application relates;

(b) the name and address of the employer of the person referred to in paragraph (a);

(c) the address of the child or children to whom the application relates; and

(d) the name and address of the employer of every child to whom the application relates.

17. Request to information bank directors — Forthwith on the receipt of an application under section 13, the Minister shall transmit a search request to the information bank directors who shall, in accordance with the regulations, cause their designated information banks to be searched forthwith and periodically during the twelve month period immediately following the receipt by the Minister of the application.

1993, c. 8, s. 11

18. Transfer of information between information banks — Subject to the regulations, information in any information banks that may be searched under this Part may be released by one information bank director to the other information bank director to assist that other director in conducting a search under this Part.

19. Transmission of information to Minister — Where information requested in an application under section 13 is found in an information bank that may be searched under this Part, the information bank director of that information bank shall cause to be transmitted to the Minister, in accordance with the regulations, all information obtained during any search conducted pursuant to section 17.

1993, c. 8, s. 12

19.1 New information — Where new information is obtained during a periodic search, the Minister shall not release the information to an applicant under section 13 unless the Minister is satisfied that the applicant still requires the information for the reasons set out in the application.

1993, c. 8, s. 12

20. Release of information to applicant — The Minister shall release information under this Part to an applicant under section 13 only if the Minister is satisfied that the safeguards established by the agreement under section 3 with the province of that applicant are in place.

21. Exception for security name changes — No information may be released under this Part in respect of any person whose identity has been changed for security or law enforcement purposes.

Regulations

22. Regulations by Governor in Council — The Governor in Council may make regulations

(a) prescribing the form of an application for the release of information under this Part and the information that must be contained therein;

(a.1) prescribing the manner in which an application for the searching of information banks and the release of information under this Part may be made;

(b) designating, for the purposes of section 15, the information banks that may be searched under this Part;

(c) setting out the manner in which searches for information under this Part are to be conducted;

(d) prescribing the conditions under which information may be released under section 18 by one information bank director to the other information bank director;

(e) establishing the procedures to be followed for the transmission to the Minister of information found in any information bank searched under this Part; and

(f) generally, for carrying out the purposes and provisions of this Part.

1997, c. 1, s. 20

PART II — GARNISHMENT OF FEDERAL MONEYS TO SATISFY SUPPORT ORDERS AND SUPPORT PROVISIONS

Interpretation

23. (1) Definitions — In this Part,

"garnishable moneys" means moneys authorized to be paid by Her Majesty by or under such Acts of Parliament or provisions thereof or programs thereunder as are designated by the regulations;

"garnishee summons" includes any document or court order of similar nature;

"garnishment" includes attachment;

"Her Majesty" means Her Majesty in right of Canada;

"judgment debtor" means a person named in a garnishee summons in respect of whom garnishable moneys are sought to be garnisheed under this Part;

"Minister" means the Minister of Justice;

"provincial garnishment law" means the law of a province relating to garnishment as it applies to the enforcement of support orders and support provisions;

"support order" means an order or judgment for maintenance, alimony or family financial support that is enforceable in any province;

"support provision" means a provision in an agreement relating to the payment of maintenance or family financial support that is enforceable by a garnishee summons under provincial garnishment law.

(2) Notwithstanding the acquisition by a discounter from a client of a right to a refund of tax for the purposes of the *Tax Rebate Discounting Act*, the refund of tax remains, for the purposes of this Part, payable to the client and not the discounter.

1992, c. 1, s. 66

Garnishment of Her Majesty

24. Her Majesty may be garnisheed — Notwithstanding any other Act of Parliament preventing the garnishment of Her Majesty, Her Majesty may, for the enforcement of support orders and support provisions, be garnisheed in accordance with this Part in respect of all garnishable moneys.

25. Provincial garnishment law applies — Subject to section 26 and any regulations made under this Part, garnishment under this Part shall be in accordance with provincial garnishment law.

1993, c. 8, s. 14

26. Inconsistencies with provincial garnishment law — In the event of any inconsistency between this Part or a regulation made under this Part and provincial garnishment law, the provincial garnishment law is overridden to the extent of the inconsistency.

27. Location of garnishable moneys — For the purposes of this Part, garnishable moneys are deemed to be located in the jurisdiction of every court requested to issue a garnishee summons in respect thereof.

Garnishee Summons

28. Service binds Her Majesty for five years — Subject to this Part and the regulations, service of the following documents on the Minister, namely,

    (a) a garnishee summons, and

    (b) [Repealed 1997, c. 1, s. 21.]

    (c) an application in the form prescribed by the regulations,

binds Her Majesty for five years in respect of all garnishable moneys payable to the judgment debtor named in the garnishee summons.

1993, c. 8, s. 15; 1997, c. 1, s. 21

29. Calculation of five year period — For the purposes of section 28, the five year period referred to in that section commences on the expiration of the period prescribed by the regulations that immediately follows the service of the garnishee summons on the Minister.

1993, c. 8, s. 15

Garnishee Summons of Continuing Effect

30. Garnishee summons of continuing effect — Subject to section 31, where a garnishee summons of continuing effect is served on the Minister under this Part and garnishable moneys become payable to the judgment debtor in the five year period during which Her Majesty is bound by the garnishee summons, Her Majesty shall, at the expiration of that period, continue to be bound in accordance with the garnishee summons in respect of all subsequent payments of garnishable moneys to the judgment debtor that are authorized by the same Act of Parliament, provision thereof or program thereunder that authorized the payments of the garnishable moneys to the judgment debtor in the period during which Her Majesty was originally bound by the garnishee summons.

1993, c. 8, s. 15

Note: S.C. 1993, c. 8, s. 19(4), provides that:

> *(4) Sections 28–30 of the Family Orders and Agreements Enforcement Assistance Act, as enacted by section 15 of this Act, apply only to garnishee summonses served after the coming into force of that section [February 2, 1994].*

31. Limitation — Her Majesty shall cease to be bound under section 30 in respect of any garnishable moneys authorized by any particular Act of Parliament, provision thereof or program thereunder if no such moneys become payable to the judgment debtor for any period of one hundred and eighty consecutive days.

Service of Documents

32. Time of service — A garnishee summons served on the Minister has effect only if it is served on the Minister in the first thirty days following the first day on which it could have been validly served on the Minister.

33. Place of service — Service of documents on the Minister in connection with garnishment proceedings permitted by this Part must be effected at the place specified in the regulations.

34. Method of service — In addition to any method of service permitted in accordance with provincial garnishment law, service of documents on the Minister under this Part may be effected by registered mail or by any other method prescribed in the regulations.

35. Service by registered mail — Where service of a document on the Minister under this Part is effected by registered mail, the document shall be deemed to be served on the day of its receipt by the Minister.

Administrative Procedures

36. Notice to ministers — Forthwith after receipt of the documents referred to in section 28, the Minister shall notify every minister responsible for garnishable moneys of the service thereof and provide each such minister with such information as may be necessary to assist that other minister in determining whether any garnishable moneys are payable to the judgment debtor.

1993, c. 8, s. 16

37. Initial report by ministers — Forthwith after being notified pursuant to section 36, each minister responsible for garnishable moneys shall report to the Minister on whether such moneys are payable or are foreseeably payable to the judgment debtor.

38. Obligation to monitor and report back — In addition to reporting under section 37, each minister responsible for garnishable moneys shall continue to monitor the payments of those moneys the entire time during which Her Majesty is bound in respect of payments thereof and report to the Minister whenever any payments to the judgment debtor become payable or foreseeably payable.

39. Additional information with every report — When reporting that garnishable moneys are payable or are foreseeably payable to the judgment debtor, each minister shall also inform the Minister of the amounts payable and the times when those moneys became, or will become, payable.

40. Right to search information banks — Subject to the regulations, every minister responsible for garnishable moneys is entitled to have any of the information banks that may be searched under Part I searched for any information that minister deems necessary to confirm the identity of any judgment debtor.

Response to Garnishee Summons

41. Response time — The Minister, on behalf of Her Majesty, shall respond to every garnishee summons within the time prescribed by the regulations.

42. Methods of response to garnishee summons — In addition to any method of responding to a garnishee summons permitted by provincial garnishment law, the Minister may respond to a garnishee summons by registered mail or by any other method prescribed by the regulations.

43. Response by registered mail — Where the Minister responds to a garnishee summons by registered mail, the receipt issued in accordance with regulations relating to registered mail made under the *Canada Post Corporation Act* shall be received in evidence and is, unless the contrary is shown, proof that the Minister has responded to the garnishee summons.

Discharge of Liability

44. (1) Effect of payment into court — A payment into court by the Minister is, to the extent of the payment, a good and sufficient discharge of Her Majesty's liability under this Part and under the legislation governing the garnishable moneys.

(2) Effect of payment to provincial enforcement service — Where a payment to a provincial enforcement service as defined in section 2 is permitted under the provincial garnishment law of the province of a provincial enforcement service, a payment to the provincial enforcement service by the Minister is, to the extent of the payment, a good and sufficient discharge of Her Majesty's liability under this Part and under the legislation governing the garnishable moneys.

Notice to Judgment Debtor

45. Notice to judgment debtor — Where a garnishee summons is served on the Minister under this Part, the Minister shall, in the form, within the time and in the manner prescribed by the regulations, notify the judgment debtor named in the garnishee summons of that service.

1993, c. 8, s. 17

Delay of Payments

46. [Repealed 1993, c. 8, s. 17.]

47. [Repealed 1993, c. 8, s. 17.]

48. [Repealed 1993, c. 8, s. 17.]

Recovery of Payments

49. Payments to judgment debtor — Where a judgment debtor is paid any garnishable moneys to which he is not entitled by reason of garnishment proceedings permitted under this Part, the amount thereof is a debt due to Her Majesty by the judgment debtor and may be recovered as such in accordance with the *Financial Administration Act* or the legislation governing the particular garnishable moneys paid to the judgment debtor.

50. Payments to party that instituted proceedings — Subject to section 51, where garnishable moneys are paid under this Part to or for the benefit of a party that instituted garnishment proceedings permitted under this Part in excess of the amount that should be paid to or for the benefit of that party, the amount thereof is a debt due to Her Majesty by that party and may be recovered as such in accordance with the *Financial Administration Act* or by deduction or set-off against any garnishable moneys payable to or for the benefit of that party under this Part.

51. Exception — Where it is determined that the reason for the payment of excess moneys referred to in section 50 is that the judgment debtor was not entitled to the garnishable moneys garnisheed under this Part, the amount of the excess is a debt due to Her Majesty by the judgment debtor and may be recovered as such in accordance with the *Financial Administration Act* or the legislation governing the garnishable moneys garnisheed under this Part.

General

52. Ranking of Her Majesty — When a judgment debtor is indebted to

(a) Her Majesty, or

(b) Her Majesty in right of a province on account of taxes payable to any province, and an agreement exists between Canada and the province under which Canada is authorized to collect the tax on behalf of the province,

Her Majesty ranks in priority over the party that instituted the garnishment proceedings permitted under this Part with respect to any garnishable moneys that are payable to the judgment debtor notwithstanding that a garnishee summons in respect of those moneys has been served on the Minister, and the amount of indebtedness may be recovered or retained in any manner authorized by law.

2001, c. 4, s. 81

53. Multiple garnishee summonses — Where more than one garnishee summons is served on the Minister under this Part in respect of the same judgment debtor and the garnishable moneys payable to the judgment debtor are insufficient to satisfy all the garnishee summonses, payment shall be made on a proportional basis.

54. No execution against Her Majesty — No execution shall issue on a judgment given against Her Majesty in garnishment proceedings permitted by this Part.

Garnishment, Attachment and Pension Diversion Act

55. Garnishment, Attachment and Pension Diversion Act — In the event that a garnishee summons that binds Her Majesty may be honoured under this Part or the *Garnishment, Attachment and Pension Diversion Act*, the garnishee summons shall be honoured first under the *Garnishment, Attachment and Pension Diversion Act* and secondly under this Part.

Prohibitions

56. Prohibition on disentitlement — No person may be disentitled or disqualified in respect of any payment or future payment of garnishable moneys solely on the ground that garnishment proceedings permitted by this Part may be or have been taken in respect of that person.

57. Prohibition on dismissal — No person may be dismissed, suspended or laid off solely on the ground that garnishment proceedings permitted by this Part may be or have been taken in respect of that person.

Fee

58. Fee — A fee in the amount prescribed by the regulations is chargeable in respect of the processing of every garnishee summons served on the Minister.

59. Chargeable against judgment debtor — Subject to any regulations respecting the remittance thereof, the fee referred to in section 58 is a debt due to Her Majesty by the judgment debtor and may, subject to section 60, be recovered by deduction or set-off against any garnishable moneys payable to the judgment debtor.

60. Restriction — The fee referred to in section 58 may not be recovered out of any garnishable moneys to be used to honour a garnishee summons.

Regulations

61. Regulations — The Governor in Council may make regulations

(a) designating Acts of Parliament, provisions thereof and programs thereunder for the purposes of the definition "garnishable moneys";

(a.1) prescribing the percentage of the amount of garnishable moneys, in relation to the Act of Parliament or provision thereof or program thereunder by or under which the garnishable moneys are authorized to be paid, that is to be exempt from the enforcement of support orders and support provisions;

(b) prescribing the form of the application referred to in paragraph 28(c);

(c) prescribing the period of time before which Her Majesty becomes bound by the service of the documents referred to in section 28;

(d) specifying the place where service of documents on the Minister must be effected in connection with garnishment proceedings permitted under this Part;

(e) prescribing the methods in which service of documents in connection with garnishment proceedings permitted under this Part may be effected on the Minister;

(f) respecting the conducting of searches for the purposes of this Part of the information banks that may be searched under Part I;

(g) prescribing the time within which and the methods by which the Minister must respond to garnishee summonses;

(h) prescribing the form of the notification referred to in section 45 and the time within which and the manner in which it must be sent;

(i) prescribing a fee in respect of the processing of garnishee summonses and the manner of collecting the fee;

(j) respecting the remission, in whole or in part, of the fee referred to in section 58; and

(k) generally, for carrying out the purposes and provisions of this Part.

1993, c. 8, s. 18

PART III — LICENCE DENIAL

Interpretation

62. Definitions — The definitions in this section apply in this Part.

"appropriate Minister" means a minister of the Crown in right of Canada who is responsible for the issuance of any type or class of licence set out in the schedule.

"debtor" means a person who is in arrears under a support order or a support provision.

"licence" means a licence, a permit, a certificate or an authorization of any kind, and includes a passport within the meaning of section 2 of the *Canadian Passport Order*.

"licence denial application" means an application made under section 67.

"Minister" means the Minister of Justice.

"persistent arrears", in respect of a support order or support provision, means

(a) arrears in any amount where the arrears are due to the failure to make in full the payments required in respect of any three payment periods, within the meaning of the support order or the support provision, or

(b) accumulated arrears of $3000 or more.

"prescribed" means prescribed by the regulations.

"provincial enforcement service" has the meaning assigned by section 2.

"schedule licence" means a licence of a type or class set out in the schedule.

"support order" has the meaning assigned by subsection 23(1).

497

"support provision" means a provision in an agreement relating to the payment of maintenance or family financial support that is enforceable under provincial law

1997, c. 1, s. 22

63. Amendments to schedule — The Governor in Council may, by order, add to or delete from the schedule any type or class of licence that may be issued to an individual under an Act of Parliament or under an order made pursuant to a prerogative of the Crown.

1997, c. 1, s. 22

Purpose of Part

64. Purpose of Part — The purpose of this Part is to help provincial enforcement services enforce support orders and support provisions by providing for the denial of certain licences to debtors who are in persistent arrears.

1997, c. 1, s. 22

Application of Part

65. Application of Part — This Part applies notwithstanding the provisions of any other Act of Parliament, of any regulation or order made under any other Act of Parliament or of any order made pursuant to a prerogative of the Crown respecting the issuance, renewal or suspension of licences.

1997, c. 1, s. 22

66. Royal prerogative — Nothing in this Part in any manner limits or affects Her Majesty's royal prerogative with respect to passports.

1997, c. 1, s. 22

Licence Denial Application

67. (1) Application — Where a debtor is in persistent arrears under a support order or a support provision, a provincial enforcement service may apply to the Minister that the following actions be taken against the debtor:

    (a) that no new schedule licences be issued to the debtor;

    (b) that all schedule licences held by the debtor be suspended; and

    (c) that schedule licences held by the debtor not be renewed.

(2) Contents of application — An application must be in the prescribed form and must contain the prescribed information concerning

    (a) the identity of the debtor; and

    (b) the support order or support provision.

(3) Contents of supporting affidavit — An application must be accompanied by an affidavit in the prescribed form. The affidavit must be submitted by an officer of the provincial enforcement service and must contain the following statements:

    (a) that the provincial enforcement service is satisfied that the debtor is in persistent arrears under the support order or the support provision;

(b) that the provincial enforcement service has made reasonable attempts to enforce the support order or the support provision before making the licence denial application; and

(c) that the provincial enforcement service has sent a notice to the debtor at the debtor's last known address,

(i) stating that the provincial enforcement service has reasonable grounds to believe that the debtor is in persistent arrears under the support order or support provision,

(ii) stating that the provincial enforcement service intends to make a licence denial application in relation to the debtor,

(iii) informing the debtor of the consequences to the debtor of a licence denial application, and

(iv) advising the debtor that a licence denial application will not be made if the debtor enters into a payment plan that is acceptable to the provincial enforcement service or satisfies the provincial enforcement service that the debtor is unable to pay the amount in arrears and that the making of the application is not reasonable in the circumstances.

(4) Time for making application — An application may be made only after thirty days have expired after the notice referred to in subsection (3) was received by the debtor.

(5) Deemed receipt — A notice referred to in subsection (3) is deemed to have been received by a debtor ten days after it is sent to the debtor.

1997, c. 1, s. 22

Processing of Licence Denial Applications

68. Informing appropriate Ministers — Immediately on the receipt of a licence denial application and the affidavit referred to in subsection 67(3), the Minister shall inform each appropriate Minister of the receipt of the application, and shall provide the appropriate Minister with such information as may be necessary to help the appropriate Minister determine whether the debtor to whom the application relates is the holder of a schedule licence.

1997, c. 1, s. 22

Obligations of Appropriate Ministers

69. (1) Determination — does debtor hold schedule licence — On being informed of a licence denial application in respect of a debtor, an appropriate Minister shall immediately determine whether the debtor is the holder of a schedule licence issued by the appropriate Minister.

(2) Suspension and non-renewal of schedule licences — If an appropriate Minister determines that a debtor is the holder of a schedule licence, the appropriate Minister shall suspend the schedule licence and, where applicable, refuse to renew the schedule licence.

(3) Notice to debtor — An appropriate Minister who takes any action under subsection (2) against a debtor shall send the debtor a notice in writing informing the debtor that the action has been taken.

1997, c. 1, s. 22

70. Refusal to issue schedule licence — An appropriate Minister who is informed of a licence denial application in respect of a debtor shall refuse to issue a schedule licence to the debtor.

1997, c. 1, s. 22

No Appeal

71. No appeal — Notwithstanding the provisions of any other Act of Parliament, of any regulation or order made under any other Act of Parliament or of any order made pursuant to a prerogative of the Crown, no appeal lies from any action taken under this Part.

1997, c. 1, s. 22

Request to Terminate Application of Part

72. (1) Request to terminate application of Part — A provincial enforcement service shall immediately request that all actions taken under this Part in respect of a debtor be terminated where

(a) the provincial enforcement service is satisfied that the debtor

(i) is no longer in arrears under all support orders and support provisions against the debtor that have been enforced by a licence denial application,

(ii) is complying, in respect of all support orders and support provisions against the debtor that have been enforced by a licence denial application, with a payment plan that the provincial enforcement service considers reasonable, or

(iii) is unable to pay the amount in arrears and that the application of this Part against the debtor is not reasonable in the circumstances; or

(b) the provincial enforcement service ceases to enforce all support orders and support provisions against the debtor that have been enforced by a licence denial application.

(2) Prescribed manner — A request under subsection (1) must be made to the Minister in the prescribed manner.

1997, c. 1, s. 22

73. Informing appropriate Ministers — Where the Minister receives a request under section 72, the Minister shall immediately inform each appropriate Minister of the receipt of the request.

1997, c. 1, s. 22

74. Obligation of appropriate Ministers — Immediately on being informed under section 73, each appropriate Minister shall

(a) cancel the suspension of every schedule licence suspended by that appropriate Minister and inform the licence holder that the suspension has been cancelled;

(b) stop refusing to renew schedule licences of the debtor solely on the basis of this Part, and

(c) stop refusing to issue schedule licences to the debtor solely on the basis of this Part.

1997, c. 1, s. 22

75. When licence not revived — The cancellation of the suspension of a schedule licence pursuant to section 74 does not operate to revive the licence if the term of the licence expired while the suspension was in force.

1997, c. 1, s. 22

Offence

76. Offence — Every person who is notified that a passport issued to the person has been suspended under this Part and who fails to return the passport forthwith to a Passport Office, as defined in section 2 of the *Canadian Passport Order*, or who subsequently uses the passport after being so notified, is guilty of an offence punishable on summary conviction and liable to a fine not exceeding $5,000 or to imprisonment for a term not exceeding six months or to both.

1997, c. 1, s. 22

No Liability

77. No liability — No action lies against Her Majesty in right of Canada, any Minister of the Crown in right of Canada or any officer or employee of Her Majesty in right of Canada for anything done or omitted to be done, in good faith in the administration of this Part or the discharge of any obligation, power or duty under this Part.

1997, c. 1, s. 22

Regulations

78. Regulations — The Governor in Council may make regulations prescribing anything that by this Part is to be or may be prescribed.

1997, c. 1, s. 22

PART IV — RELEASE AUTHORIZATION AND CONFIDENTIALITY

Release Authorization

79. Release authorization — Notwithstanding any provision in any other Act of Parliament that prohibits or restricts the release of information, the following information may be released for the purposes of this Act:

(a) information in any information bank that may be searched under Part I,

(b) information that is necessarily incidental to the garnishment of moneys under Part II, and

(c) information that is necessarily incidental to the administration of Part III.

1997, c. 1, s. 22

Prohibition, Offence and Punishment

80. Prohibition — No officer or employee of Her Majesty, and no person who is hired on a contractual basis by Her Majesty to assist in the administration of this Act, who obtains any information pursuant to this Act shall, except as provided in this Act, knowingly communicate or knowingly allow the information to be communicated to any person, or knowingly allow any person to inspect or have access to any statement or other writing containing the information.

1997, c. 1, s. 22

81. Offence and punishment — Every person who contravenes section 80 is guilty of an offence, and is liable on summary conviction to imprisonment for a term not exceeding six months or to a fine not exceeding $1,000, or to both.

1997, c. 1, s. 22

82. Limitation period — Any proceedings under section 81 may be instituted at any time within but not later than three years after the time when the subject-matter of the proceedings arose.

1997, c. 1, s. 22

SCHEDULE [1]
(Sections 62 and 63)
Number in brackets editorially added by Carswell.

Licences

Canadian Passport Order

Passport
> *Passeport*

Aeronautics Act

Air traffic controller licence
> *Licence de contrôleur de la circulation aérienne*

Aircraft maintenance engineer licence
> *Licence de technicien d'entretien d'aéronef*

Airline transport pilot licence — aeroplane
> *Licence de pilote de ligne — avion*

Airline transport pilot licence — helicopter
> *Licence de pilote de ligne — hélicoptère*

Balloon pilot licence
> *Licence de pilote de ballon*

Commercial pilot licence — aeroplane
> *Licence de pilote professionnel — avion*

Commercial pilot licence — helicopter
> *Licence de pilote professionnel — hélicoptère*

Flight engineer licence
> *Licence de mécanicien navigant*

Foreign licence validation certificate
Certificat de validation de licence étrangère
Glider pilot licence
Licence de pilote de planeur
Medical certificate
Certificat médical
Pilot permit — gyroplane
Permis de pilote — autogire
Pilot permit — recreational — aeroplane
Permis de pilote de loisir — avion
Pilot permit — recreational — helicopter
Permis de pilote de loisir — hélicoptère
Pilot permit — ultra-light aeroplane
Permis de pilote — avion ultra-léger
Private pilot licence — aeroplane
Licence de pilote privé — avion
Private pilot licence — helicopter
Licence de pilote privé — hélicoptère

Family Orders

Canada Shipping Act

Able seaman certificate
Certificat de matelot qualifié
Barge supervisor, MODU/inland certificate
Certificat de surveillant de chaland, UMFM/eaux internes
Barge supervisor, MODU/self-elevating certificate
Certificat de surveillant de chaland, UMFM/auto élévatrice
Barge supervisor, MODU/surface certificate
Certificat de surveillant de chaland, UMFM/surface
Bridge watchman certificate
Certificat d'homme de quart à la passerelle
Certificate of qualification efficient deck hand
Certificat de capacité d'homme de pont compétent
Certificate of service as master of a fishing vessel of not more than 100 tons, gross tonnage
Brevet de service de capitaine de bateau de pêche d'au plus 100 tonneaux de jauge brute
Certificate of service as master of a ship of not more than 1600 tons, gross tonnage
Brevet de service de capitaine de navire d'au plus 1600 tonneaux de jauge brute
Chemical tanker, level 1 certificate
Certificat de transporteur de produits chimiques, niveau 1

Chemical tanker, level 2 certificate

Certificat de transporteur de produits chimiques, niveau 2

Chief engineer, motor ship certificate

Certificat d'officier mécanicien en chef, navire à moteur

Chief engineer, motor-driven fishing vessel certificate

Certificat d'officier mécanicien en chef, bateau de pêche à moteur

Chief engineer, steamship certificate

Certificat d'officier mécanicien en chef, navire à vapeur

Continued proficiency certificate

Certificat de maintien des compétences

Deep sea fishing

Pêche en haute mer

Electrician certificate

Certificat d'électricien

Engine-room assistant certificate

Certificat d'adjoint de la salle des machines

Engine-room rating certificate

Certificat de matelot de la salle des machines

First mate, intermediate voyage certificate

Certificat de premier officier de pont, voyage intermédiaire

First mate, limited certificate

Certificat de premier officier de pont avec restrictions

First mate, local voyage certificate

Certificat de premier officier de pont, voyage local

First Mate of a Ferry Steamship, Intermediate Run

Premier lieutenant d'un bac ou transbordeur à vapeur à trajet intermédiaire

First Mate of a Ferry Steamship, Long Run

Premier lieutenant d'un bac ou transbordeur à vapeur à trajet long

First Mate of a Ferry Steamship, Short Run

Premier lieutenant d'un bac ou transbordeur à vapeur à trajet court

First Mate of a Foreign-going Steamship

Premier lieutenant d'un navire à vapeur au long cours

First Mate of Home-trade Steamship

Premier lieutenant de navire à vapeur de cabotage

First Mate of a Home-Trade Steamship, Second Mate of a Foreign-going Steamship

Premier lieutenant d'un navire à vapeur de cabotage, Deuxième lieutenant d'un navire à vapeur au long cours

First Mate of a Minor Waters Steamship

Premier lieutenant d'un navire à vapeur d'eaux secondaires

First Mate of an Inland Waters Steamship
  Premier lieutenant d'un navire à vapeur d'eaux intérieures
First-class engineer, motor ship certificate
  Certificat d'officier mécanicien de première classe, navire à moteur
First-class engineer, steamship certificate
  Certificat d'officier mécanicien de première classe, navire à vapeur
Fishing master, first-class certificate
  Certificat de capitaine de pêche, première classe
Fishing master, fourth-class certificate
  Certificat de capitaine de pêche, quatrième classe
Fishing master, second-class certificate
  Certificat de capitaine de pêche, deuxième classe
Fishing master, third-class certificate
  Certificat de capitaine de pêche, troisième classe
Fourth-class engineer, motor ship certificate
  Certificat d'officier mécanicien de quatrième classe, navire à moteur
Fourth-class engineer, steamship certificate
  Certificat d'officier mécanicien de quatrième classe, navire à vapeur
Great Lakes navigation certificate
  Brevet de navigation sur les Grands Lacs
Lifeboat Man (Proficiency in Survival Craft), in accordance with STCW 1978 Regulation VI/1
  Canotier (aptitude à l'exploitation des embarcations et radeaux de sauvetage), conformément à la Convention STCW 1978, Règlement VI/1
Lifeboat Man Qualified in Marine Emergency Duties in accordance with STCW 1978, Regulation VI/1
  Canotier qualifié dans les fonctions d'urgence en mer conformément à la Convention STCW 1978, Règlement VI/1
Liquefied gas tanker, level 1 certificate
  Certificat de transporteur de gaz liquéfié, niveau 1
Liquefied gas tanker, level 2 certificate
  Certificat de transporteur de gaz liquéfié, niveau 2
Maintenance supervisor, MODU/self-elevating certificate
  Certificat de surveillant de la maintenance, UMFM/auto élévatrice
Maintenance supervisor, MODU/surface certificate
  Certificat de surveillant de la maintenance, UMFM/surface
Master, intermediate voyage certificate
  Certificat de capitaine, voyage intermédiaire
Master, limited certificate
  Certificat de capitaine avec restrictions

Master, local voyage certificate

Certificat de capitaine, voyage local

Master, Minor Waters Tug

Capitaine, remorqueur aux eaux secondaires

Master, steamship of not more than 350 tons, gross tonnage or tug, local voyage

Certificat de capitaine, navire à vapeur d'au plus 350 tonneaux de jauge brute ou remorqueur, voyage local

Master Home-trade tug

Capitaine d'un navire à vapeur au cabotage, remorqueur

Master Inland Waters Steamship 350

Capitaine d'un navire à vapeur d'eaux intérieures 350

Master mariner certificate

Certificat de capitaine au long cours

Master of a Dynamically Supported Craft, Class 1

Capitaine d'un engin à portance dynamique, classe 1

Master of a Dynamically Supported Craft, Class 2

Capitaine d'un engin à portance dynamique, classe 2

Master of a Dynamically Supported Craft, Class 3

Capitaine d'un engin à portance dynamique, classe 3

Master of a Dynamically Supported Craft, Class 4

Capitaine d'un engin à portance dynamique, classe 4

Master of a Dynamically Supported Craft, restricted

Capitaine d'un engin à portance dynamique, restreint

Master of a Ferry Steamship, Intermediate Run

Capitaine d'un bac ou transbordeur à vapeur à trajet intermédiaire

Master of a Ferry Steamship, Long Run

Capitaine d'un bac ou transbordeur à vapeur à trajet long

Master of a Ferry Steamship, Short Run

Capitaine d'un bac ou transbordeur à vapeur à trajet court

Master of a fishing vessel

Capitaine d'un bateau de pêche

Master of a fishing vessel under 150 gross tons

Capitaine d'un bateau de pêche de moins de 150 tonneaux

Master of a Home-trade Steamship

Capitaine d'un navire à vapeur de cabotage

Master of a Home-trade Steamship, First Mate of a Foreign-going Steamship

Capitaine d'un navire à vapeur de cabotage, Premier lieutenant d'un navire à vapeur au long cours

Master of a Home-trade Steamship of under 350 Tons Gross Tonnage or a Home-trade Tug

> *Capitaine d'un navire à vapeur au cabotage d'une jauge brute inférieure à 350 tonneaux ou capitaine d'un remorqueur au cabotage*

Master of an Inland Waters Steamship

> *Capitaine d'un navire à vapeur d'eaux intérieures*

Master of a Minor Waters Steamship

> *Capitaine de navire à vapeur d'eaux secondaires*

Master of a Passenger Steamship certified to carry not more than forty passengers or of a Steamship other than a Passenger Steamship of not more than forty tons gross tonnage

> *Capitaine d'un navire à vapeur à passagers autorisé à transporter au plus quarante passagers ou d'un navire à vapeur autre qu'un navire à vapeur à passagers ne dépassant quarante tonneaux de jauge brute*

Master of a Passenger Vessel not exceeding sixty-five feet in length

> *Capitaine d'un bâtiment à passagers dont la longueur ne dépasse pas soixante-cinq pieds*

Master of a vessel carrying more than forty passengers

> *Capitaine d'un bâtiment de plus de quarante passagers*

Mate of a Fishing Vessel

> *Lieutenant d'un bateau de pêche*

MODU certificate

> *Certificat UMFM*

Offshore installation manager, MODU/inland certificate

> *Certificat de directeur d'installation extracôtière, UMFM/eaux internes*

Offshore installation manager, MODU/self-elevating certificate

> *Certificat de directeur d'installation extracôtière, UMFM/auto élévatrice*

Offshore installation manager, MODU/surface certificate

> *Certificat de directeur d'installation extracôtière, UMFM/surface*

Oil tanker, level 1 certificate

> *Certificat de pétroliers, niveau 1*

Oil tanker, level 2 certificate

> *Certificat de pétroliers, niveau 2*

Proficiency in chemical tankers certificate

> *Certificat de compétence en transporteurs de produits chimiques*

Proficiency in compass deviation certificate

> *Certificat de compétence en dérive magnétique*

Proficiency in liquefied gas tankers certificate

> *Certificat de compétence en transporteurs de gaz liquéfié*

Proficiency in oil tankers certificate

> *Certificat de compétence en pétroliers*

Family Orders

Proficiency in survival craft certificate
> *Certificat de compétence en embarcations de sauvetage*

Rating, Chemical Tanker
> *Matelot, navire-citerne de produits chimiques*

Rating, Liquified Gas Tanker
> *Matelot, navire-citerne de gas liquifié*

Rating, Oil Tanker
> *Matelot, Pétrolier*

Restricted engineer, motor ship certificate
> *Certificat d'officier mécanicien avec restrictions, navire à moteur*

Restricted Lifeboat Man
> *Canotier avec restrictions*

Restricted proficiency in survival craft certificate
> *Certificat de compétence en embarcations de sauvetage avec restrictions*

Restricted watchkeeping mate, ship certificate
> *Certificat d'officier de pont de quart de navire avec restrictions*

Second engineer, motor ship certificate
> *Certificat d'officier mécanicien en second, navire à moteur*

Second engineer, steamship certificate
> *Certificat d'officier mécanicien en second, navire à vapeur*

Second Mate of a Foreign-going Steamship
> *Deuxième lieutenant d'un navire à vapeur au long cours*

Second Mate of a Home-trade Steamship
> *Deuxième lieutenant d'un navire à vapeur au cabotage*

Second Mate of Home-Trade Steamship, Watchkeeping Mate of a Foreign-going Steamship
> *Deuxième lieutenant d'un navire à vapeur au cabotage, Lieutenant de quart d'un navire à vapeur au long cours*

Second Mate of an Inland Waters Steamship
> *Deuxième lieutenant d'un navire à vapeur d'eaux intérieures*

Second-class engineer, motor ship certificate
> *Certificat d'officier mécanicien de deuxième classe, navire à moteur*

Second-class engineer, steamship certificate
> *Certificat d'officier mécanicien de deuxième classe, navire à vapeur*

Service as Master of a Fishing Vessel
> *Service de capitaine d'un bateau de pêche*

Service as Master of a Foreign-going Steamship
> *Service de capitaine d'un navire à vapeur au long cours*

Service as a Master of a Steamship Not Exceeding 350 tons Gross Tonnage, Not Carrying Passengers, and Not Being a Tug

Service de capitaine d'un navire à vapeur d'une jauge brute inférieure à 350 tonneaux, ne transportant pas de passagers, et n'étant pas un remorqueur

Service as Mate of a fishing vessel

Service de lieutenant d'un bateau de pêche

Ship's cook certificate

Certificat de cuisinier de navire

Supervisor of a chemical transfer operation certificate

Certificat de surveillant d'opérations de transbordement de produits chimiques

Supervisor of a liquefid gas transfer operation certificate

Certificat de surveillant d'opérations de transbordement de gaz liquéfié

Supervisor of an oil transfer operation certificate

Certificat de surveillant d'opérations de transbordement de pétrole

Supervisor of an oil transfer operation in Arctic waters (north of 60°00'N) certificate

Certificat de surveillant d'opérations de transbordement de pétrole, eaux de l'Artique (au nord de 60°00'N.)

Temporary Engineer

Mécanicien temporaire

Third-class engineer, motor ship certificate

Certificat d'officier mécanicien de troisième classe, navire à moteur

Third-class engineer, steamship certificate

Certificat d'officier mécanicien de troisième classe, navire à vapeur

Watchkeeping engineer, motor-driven fishing vessel certificate

Certificat d'officier mécanicien de quart, bateau de pêche à moteur

Watchkeeping mate, MODU/inland certificate

Certificat d'officier de pont de quart, UMFM/eaux internes

Watchkeeping mate, MODU/self-elevating certificate

Certificat d'officier de pont de quart, UMFM/auto élévatrice

Watchkeeping mate, MODU/surface certificate

Certificat d'officier de pont de quart, UMFM/surface

Watchkeeping mate, ship certificate

Certificat d'officier de pont de quart de navire

SOR/98-511

CAN. REG. 87-315 — RELEASE OF INFORMATION FOR FAMILY ORDERS AND AGREEMENTS ENFORCEMENT REGULATIONS

made under The *Family Orders and Agreements Enforcement Assistance Act*

SOR/87-315, as am. SOR/97-178; SOR/2002-278, ss. 1, 2.

[Note: The long title of this regulation was changed from "Regulations Respecting the Release of Information that may Assist in Locating Defaulting Spouses and Other Persons" to "Release of Information for Family Orders and Agreements Enforcement Regulations" by SOR/2002-278, s. 1.]

1. [Repealed SOR/2002-278, s. 2.]

2. Interpretation — In these Regulations, **"Act"** means the *Family Orders and Agreements Enforcement Assistance Act. (Loi)*

3. Designated Information Banks — For the purposes of section 15 of the Act, the following information banks are designated as information banks that may be searched under Part I of the Act:

(a) information banks controlled by the Department of Human Resources Development, namely,

(i) Canada Pension Plan Record of Earnings (HRDC/PPU-140),

(ii) Canada Pension Plan Retirement and Survivors' Benefits (Individual) (HRDC/PPU-146), and

(iii) International Social Security — Domestic and Foreign Benefits — Computer Master Benefit Data (HRDC/PPU-175);

(b) information banks controlled by the Canada Employment Insurance Commission, namely,

(i) Record of Employment (Third Copy) (HRDC/PPU-385),

(ii) Benefit and Overpayment Master File (HRDC/PPU-180),

(iii) Social Insurance Number Registration (HRDC/PPU-390).

(c) information banks controlled by the Department of National Revenue, namely,

(i) Taxation Taxpayer Master File (RC/PPU-040), and

(ii) Information Returns (INFODEC) Data Bank (RC/PPU-150).

SOR/97-178.

4. Application Form and Affidavit — **(1)** An application under section 13 of the Act for the release of information shall be

(a) in the form set out in Schedule I;

511

(b) accompanied by an affidavit in the form set out in Schedule II and the supporting documentation required under section 14 of the Act; and

(c) mailed to

The Minister of Justice,
Department of Justice,
Family Orders and Agreements Enforcement Assistance Unit,
Ottawa, Ontario
K1A 0H8.

(2) For the purposes of subsection 14(3) of the Act, where an application under section 13 of the Act is made by a provincial enforcement service, the application and accompanying affidavit may also be sent by the means of electronic communication that has been agreed upon by the provincial enforcement service and the Department of Justice.

SOR/97-178.

5. Search Request — The Minister shall, on receiving an application referred to in section 4 together with the supporting documents required under section 14 of theAct, request that the Chairman of the Canada Employment Insurance Commission provide or verify the social insurance number of the person who is the subject of that application, and shall

(a) where he receives the social insurance number or verification thereof, transmit a search request in respect of that person to the information bank directors; or

(b) where he is informed by the Chairman of the Canada Employment Insurance Commission that the social insurance number cannot be provided or verified, inform the applicant that the search cannot be carried out.

SOR/97-178.

6. Search of Designated Information Banks — For the purpose of section 17 of the Act and subject to section 7 of these Regulations, an information bank director shall, on receiving a search request from the Minister, search the designated information banks under the control of the information bank director for such information concerning the person who is the subject of the search request as may be released under section 16 of the Act.

7. (1) Release of Information Between Information Bank Directors — An information bank director who receives a search request from the Minister may, before or while carrying out the search referred to in section 6, make a request to the other information bank director for such additional information as may be necessary in order to conduct that search.

(2) An information bank director who receives a request referred to in subsection (1) for additional information shall search the designated information banks under his control and shall

(a) if the additional information requested is found, communicate the information to the requesting director; or

(b) if the additional information requested is not found, report that result to the requesting director.

8. Release of Information to the Minister — An information bank director shall transmit to the Minister

(a) the information referred to in section 6; or

(b) where the information referred to in section 6 has not been found, a report of that result.

SCHEDULE 1

(Paragraph 4(1)(a))

Form T01 — Application: Release of Information Under Part I of the *Family Orders and Agreements Enforcement Assistance Act*. Page 1

Department of Justice   Ministère de la Justice
Canada   Canada

Protected when received by the Department of Justice
Protégé dès réception par le ministère de la Justice

SCHEDULE I / ANNEXE I
(Paragraph 4(1)(a) / alinéa 4(1)a))

**T01
APPLICATION: RELEASE OF INFORMATION UNDER PART I OF THE *FAMILY ORDERS AND AGREEMENTS ENFORCEMENT ASSISTANCE ACT***

**T01
DEMANDE DE COMMUNICATION DE RENSEIGNEMENTS EN VERTU DE LA PARTIE I DE LA *LOI D'AIDE À L'EXÉCUTION DES ORDONNANCES ET DES ENTENTES FAMILIALES***

**PART 1
APPLICANT IDENTIFICATION**

**PARTIE 1
RENSEIGNEMENTS SUR LE DEMANDEUR**

Court, peace officer or provincial enforcement service name
Nom du tribunal, de l'agent de la paix ou de l'autorité provinciale   01

Application reference code no.
N° de code de la demande   02

Court, peace officer or provincial enforcement service reference no.
N° de référence du tribunal, de l'agent de la paix ou de l'autorité provinciale   03

**PART 2
INFORMATION ON PERSON TO BE LOCATED**

**PARTIE 2
RENSEIGNEMENTS SUR LA PERSONNE RECHERCHÉE**

The name of the person to be located must correspond with the name on the affidavit in support of this application.

Le nom de la personne recherchée doit correspondre au nom inscrit sur l'affidavit à l'appui de la présente demande.

Surname
Nom de famille   04

First name
Prénom   05

Second name
Second prénom   06

Date of birth
Date de naissance   07   Day/Jour   Month/Mois   Year/Année   08 Sex (M or F)
Sexe (M ou F)

Social Insurance Number
Numéro d'assurance sociale   09

Mother's name at her birth
Nom de la mère à sa naissance   10   Surname Only / Nom de famille seulement

JUS 527 (97-01)

Canada

Form T01 — Application: Release of Information Under Part I of the *Family Orders and Agreements Enforcement Assistance Act*. P. 2

PART 3
PERSON TO BE LOCATED CODE

PARTIE 3
CODE POUR LA PERSONNE RECHERCHÉE

A - A person in default of the support provision

11 ☐

A - Personne ne s'étant pas conformée à la disposition alimentaire

B - A person believed to have a child or children in contravention of the custody provision

12 ☐

B - Personne soupçonnée de détenir un enfant en violation de la disposition de garde

C - A person charged with an offence under section 282 or 283 of the *Criminal Code*

13 ☐

C - Personne accusée d'une infraction aux articles 282 ou 283 du *Code criminel*

D - A missing child

14 ☐

D - Enfant porté disparu

E - A person believed to have a child or children in contravention of the access right

15 ☐

E - Personne soupçonnée de détenir un enfant en violation du droit d'accès

---

PART 4
DOCUMENTS

All applications must be accompanied by the following documents:

a) where the application is made by a judge of a court or any officer thereof,
(i) a copy of the family provision to which the application relates,
(ii) the court's authorization obtained under section 12 of the Act, and
(iii) a copy of the affidavit submitted in support of the application for the court's authorization;

b) where the application is made by a provincial enforcement service, an affidavit in support of the application in accordance with subsection 14(4) of the Act;

c) where the application is made by a peace officer investigating a child abduction pursuant to section 282 or 283 of the *Criminal Code*,
(i) a copy of the *Criminal Code* information, and
(ii) an affidavit in support of the application in accordance with subsection 14(5) of the Act.

PARTIE 4
DOCUMENTS

Les documents suivants doivent être joints au présent formulaire :

a) dans le cas où la demande est présentée par un juge ou un fonctionnaire d'un tribunal :
(i) une copie de la disposition familiale en cause,
(ii) l'autorisation du tribunal accordée au titre de l'article 12 de la Loi,
(iii) une copie de l'affidavit à l'appui de la demande d'autorisation du tribunal;

b) dans le cas où la demande est présentée par l'autorité provinciale, un affidavit à l'appui de la demande en conformité avec le paragraphe 14(4) de la Loi;

c) dans le cas où la demande est présentée par un agent de la paix enquêtant sur un enlèvement d'enfant au sens des articles 282 ou 283 du *Code criminel* :
(i) une copie de la dénonciation en vertu du *Code criminel*,
(ii) un affidavit à l'appui de la demande en conformité avec le paragraphe 14(5) de la Loi.

PART 5
DECLARATION

I declare that the information given in this application is true and is for the purpose of applying for the release of information to assist in locating a person in accordance with the *Family Orders and Agreements Enforcement Assistance Act*.

PARTIE 5
ATTESTATION

J'atteste que les renseignements donnés dans la présente demande sont vrais et sont fournis aux fins de la demande de communication de renseignements pouvant aider à retrouver une personne en conformité avec la *Loi d'aide à l'exécution des ordonnances et des ententes familiales*.

Date D-J M Y-A

_____
Name of declarant (print)
Nom de l'attestataire (en caractères d'imprimerie)

JUS 527 (97-01)

_____
Signature of declarant
Signature de l'attestataire

SCHEDULE II

(Paragraph 4(1)(b))

Form II — Affidavit in Support Of An Application Under Part I Of the *Family Orders And Agreements Enforcement Assistance Act.* **P. 1**

I✦I Department of Justice Ministère de la Justice Canada Canada		SCHEDULE II / ANNEXE II *(Paragraph 4(1)(b) / alinéa 4(1)b))*

Protected by the Department of Justice under the provisions of the *Privacy Act*
Protégé par le ministère de la Justice en vertu de la *Loi sur la protection des renseignements personnels*

TO2
AFFIDAVIT IN SUPPORT OF AN APPLICATION UNDER PART I OF THE *FAMILY ORDERS AND AGREEMENTS ENFORCEMENT ASSISTANCE ACT*

TO2
AFFIDAVIT À L'APPUI D'UNE DEMANDE PRÉSENTÉE SOUS LE RÉGIME DE LA PARTIE I DE LA *LOI D'AIDE À L'EXÉCUTION DES ORDONNANCES ET DES ENTENTES FAMILIALES*

In the _____
(province or territory)

Dans _____
(province ou territoire)

BETWEEN:

entre

-and-

- et -

AFFIDAVIT

AFFIDAVIT

I, _____ , make
oath and say as follows: (Full name of applicant)

Je soussigné(e), _____ ,
(nom complet du demandeur)
déclare sous serment ce qui suit :

1. The following person to be located, _____
(Full name of person)
_____

1. La personne suivante, _____
(nom complet)
_____ , est à retrouver; elle :

Check and fill in either A or B   A. ( ) is in breach of the family provision identified as
_____ , and the
(identification of family provision)
particulars of the said breach are as follows: _____
_____
_____

Cocher et remplir A ou B   A. ( ) a violé la disposition familiale suivante :
_____ , de la façon
(préciser la nature de la disposition familiale)
décrite ci-après (donner des précisions) : _____
_____
_____

B. ( ) has had laid against him or her an information pursuant to
section _____ of the *Criminal Code.*
(indicate either section 282 or 283)

B. ( ) fait l'objet d'une dénonciation en vertu de l'article
_____ du *Code criminel.*
(préciser article 197 ou 283)

2. ( ) The full name(s) of the missing child(ren) is (are):

Check and fill in if applicable
_____
_____

2. ( ) Nom complet de l'enfant (des enfants) porté(s) disparu(s) :

Cocher et remplir s'il y a lieu
_____
_____

3.   A. ( ) One or more provincial or territorial information bank(s)

Check and fill in A and/or B if applicable   (i) that is (are) identified as: _____
(name(s) of information bank(s))
or

3.   A. ( ) Le (les) fichier(s) provincial(aux) ou territorial(aux) :

Cocher et remplir A ou B ou les deux s'il y a lieu   (i) appelé(s) _____
(préciser le nom du (des) fichier(s))
ou

JUS 528 (97-01)

Canada

515

Form II — Affidavit In Support Of An Application Under Part I Of the *Family Orders And Agreements Enforcement Assistance Act*, P. 2

(ii) that may be searched pursuant to _____

_____
(name(s) of provincial statute(s))

has (have) been searched for information helpful in locating

_____

_____

_____
(name of the person to be located and/or name(s) of missing child(ren))

B. ( ) There are reasonable grounds to believe that the following

person(s) has (have) left the province or territory:

_____

_____

_____
(name of the person to be located and/or name(s) of missing child(ren))

The reasonable grounds are: _____

_____

_____

_____

SWORN (or AFFIRMED) before me at the _____

_____ of _____

in the _____

of _____

on_____, _____

_____
(Commissioner of oaths, justice of the peace, notary public, etc.)

_____
(Signature)

_____
(Type or print name)

(ii) qui peut (peuvent) être consulté(s) en vertu de _____

_____
(titre de la (des) loi(s) provinciale(s))

a (ont) été consulté(s) pour qu'on y trouve des renseignements

susceptibles d'aider à retrouver :_____

_____

_____
(nom de la personne à retrouver ou de l'enfant (des enfants) porté(s) disparu(s))

B. ( ) Il y a des motifs raisonnables de croire que la (les)

personnes(s) suivante(s) a(ont) quitté la province ou le territoire :

_____

_____

_____
(nom de la personne à retrouver ou de l'enfant (des enfants) porté(s) disparu(s))

Ces motifs raisonnables sont les suivants : _____

_____

_____

_____

Déclaré sous serment (ou affirmé solennellement) devant moi au

_____

de_____

de _____

le_____

_____
(commissaire aux serments, juge de paix, notaire, etc.)

_____
(signature)

_____
(nom en caractères d'imprimerie)

JUS 626 (97-01)

CAN. REG. 97-180 — DENIAL OF LICENCES FOR FAMILY ORDERS AND AGREEMENTS ENFORCEMENT REGULATIONS

made under the *Family Orders and Agreements Enforcement Assistance Act*

SOR/97-180

Interpretation

1. In these Regulations, **"Act"** means the *Family Orders and Agreements Enforcement Assistance Act.*

Application for Licence Denial

2. For the purpose of subsection 67(2) of the Act, an application for licence denial shall be made in the form set out in Schedule I and contain the following information:

(a) in respect of a debtor, the debtor's

   (i) surname and given names,

   (ii) latest known address,

   (iii) date of birth,

   (iv) sex,

   (v) social insurance number, if known,

   (vi) mother's surname at her birth,

   (vii) city and country of birth, if known,

   (viii) height, if known,

   (ix) eye colour, if known,

   (x) employer's name, if known, and

   (xi) employer's address, if known; and

(b) in respect of the support order or support provision,

   (i) the name of the court that issued the support order,

   (ii) the date of the support order or support provision,

   (iii) the names of the parties set out in the support order or support provision, and

   (iv) amount in arrears or payment periods in arrears.

3. An application referred to in section 2 shall be acccompanied by an affidavit in the form set out in Schedule II.

Request to Terminate an Application

4. For the purpose of section 72 of the Act, a request for the termination of a licence denial application shall be made in the form set out in Schedule III and shall be made to the Minister of Justice.

Documentation

5. Any document to be given to the Minister of Justice under section 3 or 4 can be sent to the Department of Justice, Family Orders and Agreements Enforcement Assistance Unit, Ottawa, Ontario, K1A 0H8, by mail or by the means of electronic communication that has been agreed upon by the provincial enforcement service and the Department of Justice.

Coming Into Force

6. These Regulations come into force on May 1, 1997.

SCHEDULE I, PAGE 1 [1]

(Section 2/article 2)

Schedule I — Application: Licence Denial Under Part III of the Family Orders and Agreements Enforcement Assistance Act, P. 1

Department of Justice   Ministère de la Justice
Canada   Canada

SCHEDULE I / ANNEXE I
(Section 2 / article 2)

Protected by the Department of Justice under the provisions of the *Privacy Act*
Protégé par le ministère de la Justice en vertu de la *Loi sur la protection des renseignements personnels*

L01
APPLICATION: LICENCE DENIAL UNDER PART III OF THE *FAMILY ORDERS AND AGREEMENTS ENFORCEMENT ASSISTANCE ACT*

L01
DEMANDE DE REFUS D'AUTORISATION EN VERTU DE LA PARTIE III DE LA *LOI D'AIDE À L'EXÉCUTION DES ORDONNANCES ET DES ENTENTES FAMILIALES*

PART 1
APPLICANT IDENTIFICATION

PARTIE 1
RENSEIGNEMENTS SUR LE DEMANDEUR

Provincial enforcement service name
Nom de l'autorité provinciale   01

Application reference code no.
N° de code de la demande   02

Enforcement service reference no.
N° de référence de l'autorité provinciale   03

Date notice sent to debtor
Date d'envoi de l'avis au débiteur   04
Day/Jour Month/Mois Year/Année

PART 2
DEBTOR INFORMATION

PARTIE 2
RENSEIGNEMENTS SUR LE DÉBITEUR

Surname
Nom de famille   05

First name
Prénom   06

Second name
Second prénom   07

Date of birth
Date de naissance   08
Day/Jour Month/Mois Year/Année   09 Sex (M or F) / Sexe (M ou F)

Social Insurance Number
Numéro d'assurance sociale   10

Mother's name at her birth
Nom de la mère à la naissance   11
Surname Only - Nom de famille seulement

Height
Taille   12
(If known/S'il est connu)   ► Metric (M) or Imperial (I) / Métrique (M) ou Impérial (I)

Colour of eyes
Couleur des yeux   13
(If known/S'il est connu)

City and country of birth
Ville et pays de naissance   14
City - Ville   (If known/S'il est connu)

15
Country - Pays   (If known/S'il est connu)

Latest known address
Dernière adresse connue   16

City/Province
Ville/Province   17

Postal code
Code postal   18   19 Country / Pays

JUS 342 (97-01)

Canada

519

SCHEDULE I, PAGE 2 [2]

Schedule I — Application: Licence Denial Under Part III of the Family Orders and Agreements Enforcement Assistance Act, P. 2

Employer name
Nom de l'employeur   20

(If known/Si elle est connue)   (If known/Si elle est connue)
Employer address   21
Adresse de l'employeur

City/Province   22
Ville/Province

Postal code   23   24 Country
Code postal   Pays

PART 3	PARTIE 3
ORDER OR PROVISION IN DEFAULT	**ORDONNANCE OU DISPOSITION NON RESPECTÉE**
The debtor is in default of the following order or support provision:	Le débiteur ne s'est pas conformé à l'ordonnance ou à la disposition alimentaire suivante :

Date of support order or provision
Date de l'ordonnance ou de la disposition alimentaire   25

Day/Jour   Month/Mois   Year/Année

Name of court
Nom du tribunal   26

Surname of parties
Nom de famille des parties en cause   27

VS./C.

                                                         28

Number of payments in default
Nombre de paiements dus   29

Payment period code
Code de la période de paiement   30

Amount of arrears
Montant des arriérés   31 $

PART 4	PARTIE 4
DOCUMENTS	**DOCUMENTS**
This application must be accompanied by a Licence Denial Affidavit (L02).	La présente demande doit être accompagnée d'un affidavit relatif au refus d'autorisation (L02).

PART 5	PARTIE 5
DECLARATION	**ATTESTATION**
I declare that the information given in this application is true and is for the purpose of applying for licence denial in accordance with the *Family Orders and Agreements Enforcement Assistance Act.*	J'atteste que les renseignements donnés dans la présente demande sont vrais et sont fournis aux fins de la demande de refus d'autorisation en conformité avec la *Loi d'aide à l'exécution des ordonnances et des ententes familiales.*

D-J   M   Y-A

Date

_____   _____
Name of declarant (print)   Signature of declarant
Nom de l'attestataire (en caractères d'imprimerie) Signature de l'attestataire

JUS 342 (97-01)

520

SCHEDULE II, PAGE 1 [3]

(Paragraph 3(a)/alinéa 3a))

Schedule II — Affidavit in Support of an Application Under Part III of the Family Orders and Agreements Enforcement Assistance Act. P. 1

⬛◆⬛ Department of Justice   Ministère de la Justice
Canada   Canada

SCHEDULE II / ANNEXE II
(Paragraph 3(a) / alinéa 3a))

Protected by the Department of Justice under the provisions of the Privacy Act
Protégé par le ministère de la Justice en vertu de la *Loi sur la protection des renseignements personnels*

LO2

AFFIDAVIT IN SUPPORT OF AN APPLICATION UNDER PART III OF *THE FAMILY ORDERS AND AGREEMENTS ENFORCEMENT ASSISTANCE ACT*

In the _____
            (province or territory)

BETWEEN

- and-

AFFIDAVIT

I, _____
   (full name and title of provincial enforcement service officer)

_____, make

oath and say as follows:

1. The following support debtor,_____
                                    (full name of debtor)

_____,

is in persistent arrears under the support order or the support provision.

2. Reasonable attempts to enforce the support order or the support provision have been made by the provincial enforcement service prior to the making of the licence denial application.

3. A notice was sent to the debtor, at the debtor's last known address, on _____:
                                    (date)

(i) stating that the provincial enforcement service has reasonable grounds to believe that the debtor is in persistent arrears under the support order or support provision,

(ii) stating that the provincial enforcement service intends to make a licence denial application in relation to the debtor,

(iii) informing the debtor of the consequences to the debtor of a licence denial application, and

(iv) advising the debtor that a licence denial application will not be made if the debtor enters into a payment plan that is acceptable to the provincial enforcement service or satisfies the provincial enforcement service that the debtor is unable to pay the amount in arrears and that the making of the application is not reasonable in the circumstances.

LO2

AFFIDAVIT À L'APPUI D'UNE DEMANDE PRÉSENTÉE SOUS LE RÉGIME DE LA PARTIE III DE LA *LOI D'AIDE À L'EXÉCUTION DES ORDONNANCES ET DES ENTENTES FAMILIALES*

Dans_____
            (province ou territoire)

entre

- et -

AFFIDAVIT

Je soussigné(e),_____
                  (nom et titre du fonctionnaire de l'autorité provinciale)

_____.

déclare sous serment ce qui suit :

1. Le débiteur suivant, _____
                          (nom complet)

_____

est en défaut de façon répétée au titre de l'ordonnance ou de la disposition alimentaire.

2. L'autorité provinciale a pris, avant de présenter la demande de refus d'autorisation, des mesures raisonnables en vue d'exécuter l'ordonnance alimentaire ou la disposition alimentaire.

3. Un avis a été envoyé au débiteur, à sa dernière adresse connue, le _____:
                                    (date)

(i) précisant que l'autorité provinciale a des motifs raisonnables de croire qu'il est en défaut de façon répétée au titre de l'ordonnance ou de la disposition alimentaire,

(ii) précisant que l'autorité provinciale a l'intention de présenter une demande de refus d'autorisation le visant,

(iii) l'informant des conséquences découlant d'une telle demande,

(iv) l'informant qu'une telle demande ne sera pas présentée s'il conclut un accord en matière de paiement que l'autorité provinciale juge acceptable ou s'il la convainc qu'il ne peut acquitter les arriérés et qu'il n'est pas raisonnable de présenter une telle demande en l'espèce.

Family Orders Regs

JUS 340 (97-01)

Canadä

SCHEDULE II, PAGE 2 [4]

Schedule II — Affidavit in Support of an Application Under Part III of the Family Orders and Agreements Enforcement Assistance Act, P. 2

SWORN (or AFFIRMED) before me at the _____

_____ of _____

in the _____

of _____

on _____._____

(Commissioner of oaths, justice of the peace, notary public, etc.)

_____

Signature

_____

(Type or print name)

Déclaré sous serment (ou affirmé solennellement) devant moi au

_____

de _____

de _____

le _____

(commissaire aux serments, juge de paix, notaire, etc.)

_____

Signature

_____

(nom en caractères d'imprimerie)

SCHEDULE III [5]

(Section 4/article 4)

Schedule III — Request for Termination of a Licence Denial Application

Department of Justice / **Ministère de la Justice** / SCHEDULE III / ANNEXE III / Protected when received by the Department of Justice
Canada / Canada / (Section 4 / article 4) / Protégé dès réception par le ministère de la Justice

L03	L03
REQUEST FOR TERMINATION OF A LICENCE DENIAL APPLICATION	**DEMANDE DE CESSATION D'EFFET DE LA DEMANDE DE REFUS D'AUTORISATION**
Please be advised that all actions taken under the following licence denial application under Part III of the *Family Orders and Agreements Enforcement Assistance Act* should be terminated as soon as possible after receipt of this request.	Soyez avisé que les mesures prises en vertu de la demande de refus d'autorisation au titre de la partie III de la *Loi d'aide à l'exécution des ordonnances et des ententes familiales* devraient cesser aussitôt que possible après réception de la présente demande.

PART 1	**PARTIE 1**
APPLICANT IDENTIFICATION	**RENSEIGNEMENTS SUR LE DEMANDEUR**

Provincial enforcement service name
Nom de l'autorité provinciale   01

Application reference code no.
N° de code de la demande   02

Enforcement service reference no.
N° de référence de l'autorité provinciale   03

Date of the request
Date de la demande   04   Day/Jour   Month/Mois   Year/Année

PART 2	**PARTIE 2**
DEBTOR INFORMATION	**RENSEIGNEMENTS SUR LE DÉBITEUR**

Surname
Nom de famille   05

First name
Prénom   06

Second name
Second prénom   07

Social Insurance Number
Numéro d'assurance sociale   08

PART 3 - REASON FOR TERMINATION	**PARTIE 3 - RAISON POUR LA CESSATION**
This termination request is being issued for the following reason:	**Cette demande de cessation d'effet est présentée pour la raison suivante :**
the provincial enforcement service is satisfied that the debtor is no longer in arrears under all support orders and support provisions against the debtor that have been enforced by a licence denial application; **09**	l'autorité provinciale est convaincue que le débiteur n'est plus en défaut en ce qui concerne toutes les ordonnances alimentaires et les dispositions alimentaires visées par toute demande de refus d'autorisation le touchant ;
the provincial enforcement service is satisfied that the debtor is complying, in respect of all support orders and support provisions against the debtor that have been enforced by a licence denial application, with a payment plan that the provincial enforcement service considers reasonable; **10**	l'autorité provinciale est convaincue que le débiteur se conforme, à l'égard de ces ordonnances et ces dispositions, à l'accord en matière de paiement qu'elle juge acceptable ;
the provincial enforcement service is satisfied that the debtor is unable to pay the amount in arrears and the application of Part III of the Act against the debtor is not reasonable in the circumstances; **11**	l'autorité provinciale est convaincue que le débiteur ne peut acquitter les arriérés et qu'il n'est pas raisonnable dans les circonstances de mettre en application la partie III ;
the provincial enforcement service has ceased to enforce all support orders and support provisions against the debtor that have been enforced by the licence denial application. **12**	l'autorité provinciale n'exécute plus ces ordonnances et ces dispositions contre le débiteur.

PART 4 - DECLARATION	**PARTIE 4 - ATTESTATION**
I declare that the information given in this request is true and is for the purpose of the request for termination of a licence denial application in accordance with the *Family Orders and Agreements Enforcement Assistance Act.*	J'atteste que les renseignements donnés dans la présente demande sont vrais et sont fournis aux fins de la demande de cessation d'effet de la demande de refus d'autorisation en conformité avec la *Loi d'aide à l'exécution des ordonnances et des ententes familiales.*

JUS 343   Name of declarant (print) / Nom de l'attestataire (en caractères d'imprimerie)   Signature of declarant / Signature de l'attestataire   **Canada**

FAMILY RESPONSIBILITY AND SUPPORT ARREARS ENFORCEMENT ACT, 1996

S.O. 1996, c. 31, [ss. 6(5), 23(2), (4), 64, 71 not in force at date of publication]; as am. S.O. 1997, c. 16, s. 18, item 10; 1997, c. 25, Sched., s. 2; 1999, c. 6, s. 26; 1999, c.12, Sched. B, s. 8; 2001, c. 9, Sched. C, s. 1; 2002, c. 8, Sched. I, s. 11 [Not in force at date of publication.]; 2002, c. 13, s. 57; 2002, c. 17, Sched. F, s. 1.

PART I — INTERPRETATION

1. (1) Definitions — In this Act,

"Director" means the Director of the Family Responsibility Office; ("directeur")

"income source" means an individual, corporation or other entity that owes or makes any payment, whether periodically or in a lump sum, to or on behalf of a payor of,

(a) wages, wage supplements or salary, or draws or advances on them,

(b) a commission, bonus, piece-work allowance or similar payment,

(c) a payment made under a contract for service,

(d) a benefit under an accident, disability or sickness plan,

(e) a disability, retirement or other pension,

(f) an annuity,

(g) vacation pay, termination pay and severance pay,

(h) an employee loan,

(i) a shareholder loan or dividends on shares, if the corporation that issued the shares is effectively controlled by the payor or the payor and the payor's parent, spouse, child, other relative or same-sex partner or a body corporate which the payor and his or her parent, spouse, child, other relative or same-sex partner effectively control, directly or indirectly,

(j) refunds under the *Income Tax Act* (Canada),

(k) lump sum payments under the *Family Orders and Agreements Enforcement Assistance Act* (Canada),

(l) income of a type described in the regulations; ("source de revenu")

"payor" means a person who is required to pay support under a support order; ("payeur")

"provisional order" means an order that has no effect until it is confirmed by another court and includes orders made under subsection 18(2) of the *Divorce Act* (Canada), sections 7 and 30 of the *Interjurisdictional Support Orders Act, 2002* and section 44 of the *Family Law Act*; ("ordonnance conditionnelle")

"recipient" means a person entitled to support under a support order or the parent, other than the payor, of a child entitled to support under a support order; ("bénéficiaire")

"regulations" means the regulations made under this Act; ("règlements")

"same-sex partner" means either of two persons of the same sex who live together in a conjugal relationship outside marriage; ("partenaire de même sexe")

"spouse" means,

(a) a spouse as defined in section 1 of the *Family Law Act*, or

(b) either of two persons of the opposite sex who live together in a conjugal relationship outside marriage. ("conjoint")

"support deduction order" means a support deduction order made or deemed to have been made under this Act or its predecessor; ("ordonnance de retenue des aliments")

"support order" means a provision in an order made in or outside Ontario and enforceable in Ontario for the payment of money as support or maintenance, and includes a provision for,

(a) the payment of an amount periodically, whether annually or otherwise and whether for an indefinite or limited period, or until the happening of a specified event,

(b) a lump sum to be paid or held in trust,

(c) payment of support or maintenance in respect of a period before the date of the order,

(d) payment to an agency of an amount in reimbursement for a benefit or assistance provided to a party under a statute, including a benefit or assistance provided before the date of the order,

(e) payment of expenses in respect of a child's prenatal care and birth,

(f) the irrevocable designation, by a spouse or same-sex partner who has a policy of life insurance or an interest in a benefit plan, of the other spouse or same-sex partner or a child as the beneficiary, or

(g) interest or the payment of legal fees or other expenses arising in relation to support or maintenance,

and includes such a provision in a domestic contract or paternity agreement that is enforceable under section 35 of the *Family Law Act*. ("ordonnance alimentaire")

(2) Interpretation — income source — An individual, corporation or other entity continues to be an income source despite temporary interruptions in the payments owed to a payor.

(3) Same — related orders — A support deduction order is related to the support order on which it is based and a support order is related to the support deduction order that is based on it.

1999, c. 6, s. 26; 2002, c. 13, s. 57(1)

PART II — DIRECTOR OF THE FAMILY RESPONSIBILITY OFFICE

2. Director of Family Responsibility Office — There shall be a Director of the Family Responsibility Office who shall be appointed by the Lieutenant Governor in Council.

3. (1) Enforcement officers — The Director may appoint employees of the Director's office as enforcement officers for the purposes of this Act.

(2) Powers — An enforcement officer may act for the Director and in his or her name.

4. (1) Assignment of Director's powers, etc. — The Attorney General may, subject to the approval of the Lieutenant Governor in Council, assign to any person, agency or body, or class thereof, any of the powers, duties or functions of the Director under this Act, subject to the limitations, conditions and requirements set out in the assignment.

(2) Same — An assignment may include powers, duties or functions that are not purely administrative in nature, including statutory powers of decision and discretionary powers given to the Director under this Act, and may provide that an assignee may be a party in any action or proceeding instead of the Director.

(3) Fees, etc. — An assignment may, subject to any regulation made under clause 63(1), set out the fees, costs, disbursements, surcharges and other charges that the assignee may charge to the payor, or a method for determining them, how and when they may be collected, and may exempt the assignee from clause 22(a) of the *Collection Agencies Act*.

(4) Same — An assignee may charge fees, costs, disbursements, surcharges and other charges as set out in the assignment and such fees, costs, disbursements, surcharges and other charges may,

(a) be in respect of services for which the Director may not charge anything;

(b) be higher than a fee, cost, disbursement, surcharge or other charge that the Director is permitted to charge for the same service; and

(c) be applied in a manner other than that provided in section 57.

(5) Same — Any fees, costs, disbursements, surcharges or other charges charged by an assignee must be charged to the payor and may be added to the amount of arrears owing by the payor and may be collected in like manner as arrears.

(6) Interest — For the purposes of subsections (3), (4) and (5),

"other charges" includes interest at a rate prescribed by regulation.

(7) Use of information restricted — An assignee shall not use or disclose the information it has collected in carrying out any power, duty or function assigned to the assignee under subsection (1) except for the purposes of this Act.

5. (1) Duty of Director — It is the duty of the Director to enforce support orders where the support order and the related support deduction order, if any, are filed in the Director's office and to pay the amounts collected to the person to whom they are owed.

(2) Transition — Subject to subsection (4), a support order or support deduction order that is filed in the office of the Director of the Family Support Plan immediately before the day this section comes into force shall be deemed to be filed in the Director's office on the day this section comes into force.

(3) Same — If a support deduction order is filed in the office of the Director of the Family Support Plan immediately before the day this section comes into force and the related support order was never filed in his or her office before that day, it is the duty of the Director to enforce the support deduction order so long as it is filed in the Director's office.

(4) Same — If a support deduction order is filed in the office of the Director of the Family Support Plan immediately before the day this section comes into force and the related support order was withdrawn from his or her office before that day, either when the support order was made or later, the support deduction order shall be deemed to be withdrawn from the Director's office on the day this section comes into force.

6. (1) Powers — The Director shall carry out his or her duties in the manner, if any, that appears practical to the Director and, for the purpose, may commence and conduct a proceeding and take any steps in the Director's name for the benefit of recipients, including,

  (a) enforcing support deduction orders that are filed in the Director's office, as provided by this Act;

  (b) employing any other enforcement mechanisms expressly provided for in this Act;

  (c) employing any other enforcement mechanisms not expressly provided for in this Act.

(2) Transition — The Director may enforce the payment of arrears of support under a support order although they were incurred before the order was filed in the Director's office or before July 2, 1987.

(3) Same — The Director may enforce the payment of the arrears of support owed on the day this section comes into force under an order that,

  (a) is not a support order as defined in subsection 1(1) but was a support order within the meaning of the *Family Support Plan Act*, as it read immediately before its repeal by this Act; and

  (b) is filed in the office of the Director of the Family Support Plan immediately before such repeal.

(4) Same — For the purpose of subsection (3), an order described in that subsection shall be deemed to be a support order as defined in subsection 1(1).

Unproclaimed Text — 6(5)

(5) Same — The Director shall not enforce custody orders made by a Canadian court, even if they were filed with the Director before this section comes into force.

(6) Enforcement alternatives — Enforcement of a support order or support deduction order by one means does not prevent enforcement by other means at the same time or different times.

(7) Enforcement by Director exclusive — Subject to section 4, no person other than the Director shall enforce a support order that is filed in the Director's office.

(8) Same — Subject to section 4, no person other than the Director shall enforce a support deduction order, whether the order is filed in the Director's office or not.

7. (1) Director may refuse to enforce — Despite section 5, the Director may at any time refuse to enforce a support order or support deduction order that is filed in the Director's office if, in his or her opinion,

  (a) the amount of the support is nominal;

(b) the amount of the support cannot be determined from the face of the order because it is expressed as a percentage of the payor's income or it is dependent on another variable that does not appear on the order;

(c) the meaning of the order is unclear or ambiguous;

(d) the recipient has not complied with reasonable requests to provide the Director with accurate or sufficient information as may be needed in order to enforce the order or respecting the amount of arrears owed under the order;

(e) the whereabouts of the recipient cannot be determined after reasonable efforts have been made;

(f) the payor is in prison serving a sentence of five years or longer and has no assets or income available to satisfy the support order and any arrears under the order;

(g) the payor is receiving benefits under the *Family Benefits Act*, assistance under the *General Welfare Assistance Act* or the *Ontario Works Act, 1997* or income support under the *Ontario Disability Support Program Act, 1997* and has no assets or income available to satisfy the support order and any arrears under the order.

(h) the recipient repeatedly accepts payment of support directly from the payor;

(i) the recipient consents to a limitation of enforcement of the support order by the Director;

(j) enforcement of the support order has been stayed by a court; or

(k) enforcement of the order is otherwise unreasonable or impractical.

(2) Policies and procedures — The Attorney General may establish policies and procedures respecting subsection (1) and the Director shall consider them in exercising his or her discretion under that subsection.

(3) Order deemed withdrawn — If the Director refuses to enforce an order under subsection (1), the Director shall notify the payor and the recipient and the support order and the related support deduction order, if any, shall be deemed to be withdrawn from the Director's office on the date set out in the notice.

(4) Cost of living clauses — The Director shall not enforce a cost of living clause in a support order or support deduction order made in Ontario unless it is calculated in accordance with subsection 34(5) of the *Family Law Act* or in a manner prescribed by regulation.

(5) Same — The Director shall not enforce a cost of living clause in a support order or a support deduction order if the support order was made outside Ontario unless it is calculated in a manner that the Director considers similar to that provided in subsection 34(5) of the *Family Law Act* or in a manner prescribed by regulation.

(6) Same — Where the cost of living clause in an order is not calculated in accordance with subsection 34(5) of the *Family Law Act* or in a manner prescribed by regulation or, if the order was made outside Ontario, in a manner that the Director considers similar, the Director shall, subject to subsection (1), enforce the order as if it contained no cost of living clause.

(7) Transition — Despite subsections (5) and (6), if an order contains a cost of living clause that is not calculated in accordance with subsection 34(5) of the *Family Law Act* or in a manner prescribed by regulation or, if the order was made outside Ontario, in a manner that the Director considers similar, which became effective before this section came into force,

> (a) the Director shall continue to enforce the order and the cost of living clause at the same amount at which the Director of the Family Support Plan was enforcing them immediately before this section came into force; and

> (b) the Director shall not make any further adjustments under the cost of living clause after this section comes into force.

(8) Same — This section applies even if the order was filed in the Director's office before this section comes into force.

1997, c. 25, Sched. E, s. 2(2).

8. (1) Director to cease enforcement — The Director shall cease enforcement of a support obligation provided for in a support order or support deduction order filed in the Director's office if the support obligation has terminated; however, if the support order has been assigned to an agency described in subsection 33(3) of the *Family Law Act*, the Director shall not cease enforcement of the support obligation without the agency's consent.

(2) Same — The Director shall not enforce a support order or support deduction order against the estate of a payor after he or she is notified, in accordance with the regulations, of the payor's death.

(3) Date of termination — For the purpose of subsection (1), the termination of a support obligation shall be determined in one of the following ways:

> 1. If the parties to the support order or support deduction order agree in the manner prescribed by the regulations that the support obligation has terminated.

> 2. If the support obligation is stated in the support order or support deduction order to terminate on a set calendar date.

> 3. If a court orders that the obligation has terminated.

(4) Notice to Director — Each of the parties to a support order, if the support order or related support deduction order is filed in the Director's office, shall give to the Director notice of the termination of a support obligation under the order, in the manner and at such time as may be prescribed by the regulations.

(5) Disputes — If the parties to the order do not agree or if the agency referred to in subsection (1) does not consent, the court that made the support order shall, on the motion of a party to the order or of the agency, decide if the support obligation has terminated and shall make an order to that effect.

(6) Same — If the support order was not made by a court, the order described in subsection (5) shall be made by the Ontario Court (Provincial Division) or the Family Court.

(7) Order to repay — A court that finds that a support obligation has terminated may order repayment in whole or in part from a person who received support after the obligation was terminated if the court is of the opinion that the person ought to have notified the Director that the support obligation had terminated.

(8) Same — In determining whether to make an order under subsection (7), the court shall consider the circumstances of each of the parties to the support order.

(9) Continued enforcement — The Director shall continue to enforce the support obligation until he or she receives a copy of the court's order terminating the support obligation.

(10) Same — Despite the termination of a support obligation, the Director shall continue to enforce the support obligation in respect of any arrears which have accrued.

(11) Director not a party — The Director is not a party to any proceeding to determine the entitlement of any person to support under a support order or to a motion to decide whether a support obligation has terminated.

PART III — SUPPORT ORDERS AND SUPPORT DEDUCTION ORDERS — MAKING AND FILING

9. (1) Contents of support order — Every support order made by an Ontario court, other than a provisional order, shall state in its operative part that unless the order is withdrawn from the Director's office, it shall be enforced by the Director and that amounts owing under the order shall be paid to the Director, who shall pay them to the person to whom they are owed.

(2) Court may require that order may not be withdrawn — If the court considers it appropriate to do so, it may state in the operative part of the order, instead of the wording prescribed by subsection (1), that the order and the related support deduction order shall be enforced by the Director and that they cannot be withdrawn from the Director's office.

(3) Director retains discretion to not enforce orders — Section 7 applies to every support order worded as provided in subsection (1) or (2), whether the order was made before or after this section comes into force and despite the wording of an order made under subsection (2).

10. (1) Support deduction orders to be made — An Ontario court that makes a support order, as defined in subsection 1(1), shall also make a support deduction order.

(2) New orders to be made — When a support order is varied, and the varied order is a support order as defined in subsection 1(1), the court shall also make a support deduction order to reflect the variation.

(3) Transition — When a support order, within the meaning of the *Family Support Plan Act* as it read immediately before its repeal by this Act, is varied such that the new order is a support order as defined in subsection 1(1), the court shall also make a support deduction order to reflect the variation.

(4) Order mandatory — A support deduction order shall be made even though the court cannot identify an income source in respect of the payor at the time the support order is made.

(5) Exception — A support deduction order shall not be made in respect of a provisional order.

11. (1) Form of support deduction order — A support deduction order shall be in the form prescribed by the regulations.

(2) Information re payor, income source — Before making a support deduction order, the court shall make such inquiries of the parties as it considers necessary to determine the names and addresses of each income source of the payor and the amounts paid to the payor by each income source and shall make such other inquiries to obtain information as may be prescribed by the regulations.

(3) Same — If the support order is sought on consent or by way of motion for judgment or if the making of the support order is uncontested, the parties shall give the court the particulars described in subsection (2) and such other information as may be prescribed by the regulations.

(4) Completion of form, etc. — The support deduction order shall be completed and signed by the court, or by the clerk or registrar of the court, at the time the support order is made and shall be entered in the court records promptly after it is signed, even if the support order may not have been settled or signed at that time.

12. (1) Court to file support orders — The clerk or registrar of the court that makes a support order shall file it with the Director's office promptly after it is signed.

(2) Court to file support deduction orders — The clerk or registrar of the court that makes a support deduction order shall file it with the Director's office promptly after it is signed, even if the related support order may not have been settled or signed at the time.

13. (1) Orders of other jurisdictions — When a support order made by a court outside Ontario is registered under subsection 19(1) of the *Interjurisdictional Support Orders Act, 2002*, the clerk who registers the order shall promptly file it with the Director's office, unless the order is accompanied by a notice signed by the person seeking enforcement stating that he or she does not want the order enforceed by the Director.

(2) Same — *Divorce Act* (Canada) orders — A support order made by a court outside Ontario under the *Divorce Act* (Canada) may be filed in the Director's office by the recipient under the order and, for the purpose of subsection 20(3) of the *Divorce Act* (Canada), the order becomes enforceable by the Director upon its filing in the Director's office without it having been registered in a court in Ontario.

2002, c. 13, s. 57(2)

14. (1) Minister may file orders — If a recipient has applied and is eligible for, or has received, a benefit under the *Family Benefits Act* or assistance under the *General Welfare Assistance Act* or the *Ontario Works Act, 1997* or income support under the *Ontario Disability Support Program Act, 1997*, a support order may be filed in the Director's office, whether or not the payor and recipient have given a notice to withdraw under subsection 16(1) by the following:

1. The Ministry of Community and Social Services in the name of the Minister.

2. A municipality, excluding a lower-tier municipality in a regional municipality.

3. A district social services administration board under the *District Social Services Administration Boards Act*.

4. A band approved under section 15 of the *General Welfare Assistance Act*.

5. A delivery agent under the *Ontario Works Act, 1997*.

(2) Same — If a support order is filed under subsection (1), the related support deduction order, if any, shall be deemed to be filed in the Director's office ant the same time.

1997, c. 25, Sched. E, s. 2; 2002, c. 17, Sched. F, s. 1

15. Payors, recipients may file support orders — Subject to sections 12, 13 and 14, a support order may be filed in the Director's office only by the payor or recipient under the order.

16. (1) Withdrawal of orders — A support order or support deduction order filed in the office of the Director may be withdrawn at any time by a written notice signed by the payor and the recipient unless the support order states that it and the related support deduction order cannot be withdrawn from the Director's office.

(2) Consent of agency filing order — A support order and related support deduction order, if any, that have been assigned to an agency referred to in subsection 14(1) may not be withdrawn under subsection (1) except by the agency or with the consent of the agency so long as the orders are under assignment.

(3) Effect of withdrawal — The Director shall cease enforcement of an order upon its withdrawal from the Director's office.

(4) Same — If there are arrears owing to an agency referred to in subsection 14(1) from a past assignment, the Director may continue to enforce the support order and related support deduction order, if any, to collect the arrears owed to the agency, even if the payor and recipient have withdrawn the orders under this section.

(5) Support and support deduction order must be withdrawn together — A support order cannot be withdrawn under subsection (1) unless the related support deduction order, if any, is also withdrawn and a support deduction order cannot be withdrawn under subsection (1) unless the related support order, if any, is also withdrawn.

(6) Filing after withdrawal — A support order or support deduction order that has been withdrawn under subsection (1) or that has been deemed to have been withdrawn under subsection 7(3) may be filed in the office of the Director at any time by a written notice signed by either the payor or the recipient.

(7) Effect — Filing under subsection (6) has the same effect for all purposes, including the purposes of subsection 6(2), as filing under sections 12 to 15.

(7.1) Application — Subsection (7) applies whether the order was filed under subsection (6) before or after the day the *Government Efficiency Act, 2001* receives Royal Assent.

(7.2) Support and support deduction orders, filing together after withdrawal — A support order cannot be filed under subsection (6) unless the related support deduction order, if any, is also filed and a support deduction order cannot be filed under subsection (6) unless the related support order is also filed.

(8) Transition — Despite subsection 6(4), subsection (7) does not apply to an order that is not a support order as defined in subsection 1(1), but was a support order within the meaning of the *Family Support Plan Act*, as it read immediately before its repeal by this Act, and was filed in the office of the Director of the Family Support Plan immediately before this section came into force.

1997, c. 25, Sched. E, s. 2; 2001, c. 9, Sched. C, s. 1

17. Notice of filings and withdrawals — The Director shall give notice of the filing or withdrawal of a support order or support deduction order to all the parties to the order, and at the request of any agency referred to in subsection 14(1), to the agency.

1997, c. 25, Sched. E, s. 2

18. Duty to advise re unfiled support orders — Where a support deduction order that was made before this section came into force is filed in the Director's office but the related support order was never filed in the Director's office, the recipient shall inform the Director in writing of,

(a) the amount of money received on account of the support order other than through the support deduction order; and

(b) any changes in the amount to be paid under the support order.

19. Payor's and recipient's duty to advise of address change — If a payor or recipient under a support order or support deduction order filed in the Director's office changes address, he or she shall advise the Director of the new address within 10 days of the change.

Part IV — Support Deduction Orders — Enforcement

20. (1) Director to enforce support deduction orders — The Director shall enforce a support deduction order that is filed in the Director's office, subject to section 7 and to any suspension or variation of the support deduction order, until the related support order is terminated or withdrawn and there are no arrears owing or until the support deduction order is withdrawn.

(2) Notice of support deduction order to income sources — The Director may serve a notice of a support deduction order to each income source from whom the Director is seeking payment, and may serve new notices when the amount to be paid under a support order changes or arrears are owing.

(3) Contents of notice — The notice shall set out the amount of support owed by the payor under the support order and may also set out any amount in arrears under the support order and the amount required to be paid by the income source to the Director.

(4) Notice to payor — The Director shall send to the payor a copy of every notice sent under subsection (2).

(5) Notice deemed garnishment for Family Orders and Agreements Enforcement Assistance Act (Canada) — A notice of a support deduction order shall be deemed to be a notice of garnishment made under provincial garnishment law for the purposes of the *Family Orders and Agreements Enforcement Assistance Act* (Canada).

(6) Support deduction order not affected by stay of enforcement of support order — The operation or enforcement of a support deduction order is not affected by an order staying the enforcement of the related support order unless the support order is also stayed.

21. (1) Support deduction order deemed to be made — A support deduction order shall be deemed to have been made in respect of a support order described in subsection (8) if,

(a) the recipient requests that the Director enforce the support order under this Part and the Director considers it practical to do so; or

(b) the Director considers it advisable to enforce the support order under this Part.

(2) Notice to payor — The Director shall give notice to the payor of the Director's intention to enforce the support order under this Part.

(3) When and by what court deemed order is made — The support deduction order shall, 30 days after the notice is served on the payor, be deemed to have been made by the court that made the support order or,

    (a) if the support order was made under the *Divorce Act* (Canada) by a court outside Ontario, by the Ontario Court (General Division) or, where applicable, the Family Court;

    (b) if the support order (other than an order under the *Divorce Act* (Canada)) was made by a court outside Ontario, by a court in Ontario that is the same level as the court that has the jurisdiction to make the order enforceable in Ontario;

    (c) if the support order is a domestic contract or paternity agreement, by the Ontario Court (Provincial Division) or the Family Court.

(4) Suspension — The payor may, within 30 days after being served with the notice under subsection (2), commence a motion under section 28 in the court that is deemed to have made the support deduction order for its suspension.

(5) Delay of effective date — If a motion is brought under subsection (4), a deemed support deduction order does not come into force until the motion is determined.

(6) Withdrawal of support deduction order — Section 16 applies to a deemed support deduction order.

(7) No form required — Subsection 11(1) does not apply to a deemed support deduction order.

(8) Application of this section — This section applies only to support orders filed in the Director's office that are,

    (a) support orders made by an Ontario court before March 1, 1992;

    (b) domestic contracts or paternity agreements that are enforceable under section 35 of the *Family Law Act*;

    (c) support orders made by a court outside Ontario that are enforceable in Ontario.

22. (1) Duty of income source — An income source that receives notice of a support deduction order, whether or not the income source is named in the order, shall, subject to section 23, deduct from the money the income source owes to the payor the amount of the support owed by the payor, or such other amount that is set out in the notice, and shall pay that amount to the Director.

(2) First payment — The income source shall begin making payments to the Director not later than the day the first payment is to be paid to the payor that falls at least 14 days after the day on which the income source is served with the notice.

(3) Payor's duty to pay — Until an income source begins deducting support payments in respect of a support deduction order or if payments by an income source are interrupted or terminated, the payor shall pay the amounts owing under the support order to the Director, if the support order is filed in the Director's office, or to the recipient, if the support order is not filed in the Director's office.

Family
Responsibility

23. (1) Maximum deduction by income source — The total amount deducted by an income source and paid to the Director under a support deduction order shall not exceed 50 per cent of the net amount owed by the income source to the payor.

Unproclaimed Text — 23(2)

(2) Deduction must equal ongoing support — Despite subsection (1), the total amount deducted by an income source and paid to the Director under a support deduction order made or deemed to have been made after this section comes into force shall not be less than the amount of ongoing support specified in the support order, even if that amount is greater than 50 per cent of the net income owed by the income source to the payor, unless the court orders otherwise when it makes the support order.

(3) Exception for certain federal payments — Despite subsection (1), up to 100 per cent of a payor's income tax refund or other lump sum payment that is attachable under the *Family Orders and Agreements Enforcement Assistance Act* (Canada) may be deducted and paid to the Director under a support deduction order.

Unproclaimed Text — 23(4)

(4) Transition — The Director may, on notice to the payor, bring a motion to the court that made or is deemed to have made a support deduction order before this section comes into force, to increase the amount required to be deducted and paid to the Director up to the amount of the ongoing support specified in the support order, even if that amount is greater than 50 per cent of the net income owed by the income source to the payor.

(5) Interpretation — net amount — For the purposes of this section,

"net amount" means the total amount owed by the income source to the payor at the time payment is to be made to the Director, less the total of the following deductions:

1. Income Tax.
2. Canada Pension Plan.
3. Employment Insurance.
4. Union dues.
5. Such other deductions as may be prescribed by the regulations.

(6) Same — Despite any other provision of this Act, no deduction shall be made under a support deduction order in respect of amounts owing to a payor as reimbursement for expenses covered by a medical, health, dental or hospital insurance contract or plan.

24. (1) Crown bound by support deduction order — A support deduction order is effective against the Crown only in respect of amounts payable on behalf of the administrative unit served with notice of the support deduction order to the payor named in the notice.

(2) Social assistance benefits — Despite subsection (1), no amounts shall be deducted from any amount payable to a payor as a benefit under the *Family Benefits Act* or as assistance under the *General Welfare Assistance Act* or the *Ontario Works Act, 1997* or as income support under the *Ontario Disability Support Program Act, 1997*, in order to comply with a support deduction order unless authorized under the *Ontario Works Act, 1997* or the *Ontario Disability Support Program Act, 1997*.

(3) Definition — In subsection (1),

"administrative unit" means a ministry of the Government of Ontario, a Crown agency within the meaning of the *Crown Agency Act* or the Office of the Assembly.

1997, c. 25, Sched. E, s. 2

25. (1) Duty to inform re payment interruption — Within 10 days after the termination or beginning of an interruption of payments by an income source to a payor, both the income source and the payor shall give written notice of the termination or interruption to the Director, together with such other information as may be required by the regulations.

(2) Same — If notice has been or should have been given under subsection (1),

(a) the payor and the income source, within 10 days after the resumption of payments that have been interrupted, shall give written notice to the Director of the resumption;

(b) the payor, within 10 days of beginning employment with another income source or of becoming entitled to payments from another income source, shall give written notice to the Director of the new employment or entitlement and of the name and address of the income source.

26. (1) Disputes re income source — If an individual, corporation or other entity served with notice of a support deduction order is not an income source of the payor named in the notice, the individual, corporation or other entity shall give written notice in the prescribed form of that fact to the Director within 10 days after the service of the notice.

(2) Same — The Director or an individual, corporation or other entity who has notified the Director under subsection (1) may, on notice to each other, bring a motion to the court that made or is deemed to have made the support deduction order to determine whether the individual, corporation or other entity is an income source.

(3) Same — The Director or an income source may, on notice to each other, bring a motion to the court that made or is deemed to have made the support deduction order to determine,

(a) whether the income source has failed to comply with the order; or

(b) whether the amount the income source is deducting and paying to the Director under the order is correct.

(4) Determination by court — In a motion under subsection (2) or (3), the court shall determine the issue in a summary manner and make such order as it considers appropriate in the circumstances.

(5) Limitation — A motion shall not be brought under subsection (2) by an individual (other than the Director), corporation or other entity until at least 14 days after the individual, corporation or other entity gave written notice to the Director as required by subsection (1).

(6) Same — A motion shall not be brought by an income source under subsection (3) unless the income source has given written particulars of the proposed motion to the Director at least 14 days before serving the Director with notice of the motion.

(7) Liability — An income source is liable to pay to the Director any amount that it failed without proper reason to deduct and pay to the Director after receiving notice of a support deduction order and, in a motion under subsection (3), the court may order the income source to pay the amount that it ought to have deducted and paid to the Director.

(8) Other enforcement — In addition to any other method available to enforce an order in a civil proceeding, any order made under subsection (4) or (7) may be enforced under this Act in the same manner and with the same remedies as a support order.

27. (1) Disputes, etc., by payor — A payor, on motion in the court that made or is deemed to have made the support deduction order,

> (a) may dispute the amount being deducted by an income source under a support deduction order if he or she is of the opinion that because of a mistake of fact more is being deducted than is required under this Act;

> (b) may dispute whether he or she has defaulted in paying support after a suspension order has been made under section 28;

> (c) may seek relief regarding the amount that is being deducted by an income source under a support deduction order for arrears under a support order.

(2) Motion to increase deductions for arrears — If an order has been made on a motion under clause (1)(c), the Director may, on motion in the court that made the order, request that the amount to be deducted by an income source be increased if there has been an improvement in the payor's financial circumstances.

(3) Dispute over entitlement — On a motion under subsection (1) or (2), the payor shall not dispute the entitlement of a person to support under a support order.

(4) Necessary party — The Director is a necessary party to a motion under subsection (1) and the payor is a necessary party to a motion under subsection (2).

(5) Determination by court — The court shall determine the issue in a motion under subsection (1) or (2) in a summary manner and make such order as it considers appropriate in the circumstances.

(6) Same — On a motion under clause (1)(c), the payor shall be presumed to have the ability to pay the amount being deducted for arrears and the court may vary the amount being deducted only if it is satisfied that the payor is unable for valid reasons to pay that amount, but this does not affect the accruing of arrears.

(7) Variation of support deduction order — A court shall not vary the amount to be paid under a support deduction order except under subsection (5) or 23(4) or if the related support order is varied.

28. (1) Suspension of support deduction order — A court that makes a support deduction order may make an order to suspend its operation at the same time as it makes the order, or, on motion, subsequently.

(2) Same — A court that is deemed to have made a support deduction order may, on a motion made under subsection 21(4), make an order suspending its operation.

(3) Criteria for suspension — The court may suspend a support deduction order under subsection (1) or (2) only if,

> (a) it finds that it would be unconscionable, having regard to all of the circumstances, to require the payor to make support payments through a support deduction order; or

> (b) the parties to the support order agree that they do not want support payments collected through a support deduction order and the court requires the payor to post such security as it considers adequate and in accordance with the regulations.

(4) Agency's consent required — If the support order has been assigned to an agency described in subsection 33(3) of the *Family Law Act* or if there are arrears owing to the agency from a past assignment, the court shall not suspend the support deduction order in the circumstances described in clause (3)(b) without the agency's consent.

(5) Unconscionable, determination — The following shall not be considered by a court in determining whether it would be unconscionable to require a payor to make support payments through a support deduction order:

1. The fact that the payor has demonstrated a good payment history in respect of his or her debts, including support obligations.

2. The fact that the payor has had no opportunity to demonstrate voluntary compliance in respect of support obligations.

3. The fact that the parties have agreed to the suspension of the support deduction order.

4. The fact that there are grounds upon which a court might find that the amount payable under the support order should be varied.

(6) Security — For the purposes of clause (3)(b), security shall be in a minimum amount equal to the support payable for four months and the security shall be in money or in such other form as may be prescribed in the regulations.

(7) When Director is a party — The Director is not a party to a motion brought to suspend the operation of a support deduction order; however, if the payor brings a motion with respect to a support deduction order deemed to have been made under section 21, the Director must also be served with notice of the motion and may be added as a party.

(8) When agency is a party — An agency that has filed the related support order in the Director's office under subsection 14(1) and an agency referred to in subsection 14(1) to which a related support order has been assigned must also be served with notice of the motion and may be added as a party.

(9) Completion of form, etc. — A suspension order shall be completed and signed by the court or by the clerk or registrar of the court at the time it is made and shall be entered in the court records promptly after it is signed.

(10) Prompt filing — The clerk or registrar of the court that makes a suspension order shall file it in the Director's office promptly after it is made.

(11) Form and effective date — A suspension order shall be in the form prescribed by the regulations and takes effect only when it is filed in the Director's office and every income source affected by the order has received notice of the suspension.

(12) Termination of suspension order — A suspension order is automatically terminated if the payor fails to post security of the type or within the time period set out in the suspension order or if the payor fails to comply with the support order.

(13) Effect of termination — When a suspension order is terminated under subsection (12), the support deduction order is reinstated and the Director may immediately realize on any security that was posted.

(14) Effect of withdrawal of support deduction order — If the support deduction order is withdrawn from the Director's office while a suspension order is in effect, the suspension order is terminated and the Director shall repay to the payor any security that was posted.

(15) Support order not affected by suspension order — A suspension order under this section does not affect the payor's obligations under the support order nor does it affect any other means of enforcing the support order.

1997, c. 25, Sched. E, s. 2

29. Income source to keep information confidential — Information about a payor obtained as a result of the application of this Part by an income source or an individual, corporation or other entity believed to be an income source shall not be disclosed by the income source or the individual, corporation or other entity, as the case may be, or any director, officer, employee or agent thereof, except for the purposes of complying with a support deduction order or this Act.

30. (1) Priority of support deduction orders — Despite any other Act, a support deduction order has the same priority over other judgment debts as a support order has under the *Creditors' Relief Act* and all support orders and support deduction orders rank equally with each other.

(2) Same — If an income source is required to make payments to the Director under a support deduction order and the income source receives a garnishment notice related to the same support obligation, the income source shall make full payment under the support deduction order and the garnishment shall be of no effect until the income source has received notice from the Director that the support deduction order is suspended, terminated or withdrawn from the Director's office.

31. Anti-avoidance — An agreement by the parties to a support order to vary enforcement of a support deduction order that is filed in the Director's office and any agreement or arrangement to avoid or prevent enforcement of a support deduction order that is filed in the Director's office are of no effect.

32. Conflict with other Acts — A support deduction order may be enforced despite any provision in any other Act protecting any payment owed by an income source to a payor from attachment or other process for the enforcement of a judgment debt.

PART V — SUSPENSION OF DRIVERS' LICENCES

33. Definition — In this Part,

"driver's licence" has the same meaning as in subsection 1(1) of the *Highway Traffic Act*.

34. First notice — When a support order that is filed in the Director's office is in default, the Director may serve a first notice on the payor, informing the payor that his or her driver's licence may be suspended unless, within 30 days after the day the first notice is served,

(a) the payor makes an arrangement satisfactory to the Director for complying with the support order and for paying the arrears owing under the support order;

(b) the payor obtains an order to refrain under subsection 35(1) and files the order in the Director's office; or

(c) the payor pays all arrears owing under the support order.

35. (1) Order to refrain — A payor who receives a first notice may, on notice to the Director, in an application to vary the support order, make a motion for an order that the Director refrain from directing the suspension of the payor's driver's licence under subsection 37(1), on the terms that the court considers just.

(2) Exception — Despite subsection (1), a motion for an order that the Director refrain from directing the suspension of the payor's driver's licence may be made before the commencement of an application to vary the support order on the undertaking of the payor or the payor's solicitor to commence the proceeding forthwith.

(3) Time limits and variation — A court shall not make an order to refrain after the 30-day period referred to in the first notice, but an order to refrain may be varied, on motion by the payor or the Director, at any time before the application to vary support is determined if there is a material change in the payor's circumstances.

(4) Same — A court may make an order to refrain only within the 30-day period referred to in the first notice and may make only one order to refrain in respect of any first notice.

(5) Order re arrears — When determining the variation application, a court that makes an order to refrain,

(a) shall state the amount of the arrears owing, after any variation; and

(b) may make an order respecting payment of the arrears.

(6) Same — For the purpose of clause (5)(b), the court may make any order that may be made under clause 41(9)(a), (b), (c), (d), (g) or (h) or subsection 41(16) and, in the case of an order provided by clause 41(9)(g) or (h), imprisonment does not discharge arrears under the support order.

(7) When Director is a party — The Director is not a party to an application to vary a support order referred to in subsection (1), but the Director and the payor are the only parties to a motion under subsection (1) for an order to refrain.

(8) Filing with Director's office — The court shall file a copy of the order in the Director's office promptly after the order is signed.

(9) Form and effective date — An order to refrain shall be in the form prescribed by the regulations and takes effect only when it is filed in the Director's office.

(10) Duration of order — An order to refrain terminates on the earliest of the day the application to vary is determined, the day the support order is withdrawn from the Director's office and the day that is six months after the order to refrain is made.

(11) Exception — Despite subsection (10), an order to refrain made before the commencement of an application to vary the support order is automatically terminated if the payor does not commence the application within 20 days of the date of the order to refrain.

(12) Extension of order — The court that makes an order to refrain may, on a motion by the payor before the order terminates and with notice to the Director, extend the order for one further period of three months.

(13) Application of order — An order to refrain is applicable only to the notice in respect of which the motion was made under subsection (1).

36. (1) Second notice — The Director may serve a second notice on the payor if, at any time in the 24 months after the payor made an arrangement under clause 34(a) or obtained an order under subsection 35(1) or clause 35(5)(b), the payor fails to comply with,

(a) the terms of the arrangement made with the Director in response to the first notice;

(b) the terms of an order to refrain under subsection 35(1); or

(c) the terms of the varied support order and an order respecting payment of arrears under clause 35(5)(b).

(2) Contents — The second notice shall inform the payor that his or her driver's licence may be suspended,

(a) unless, within 15 days after the day the second notice is served,

(i) the payor complies with clause (1)(a), (b) or (c), or

(ii) the payor pays all arrears owing under the support order; or

(b) if, within 24 months after the payor makes an arrangement under clause (1)(a) or obtains an order under subsection 35(1) or clause 35(5)(b), the payor fails to comply with the arrangement or order.

(3) Interpretation: arrangement in response to notice — For the purposes of this section, an arrangement is made in response to a first notice if it is made within the time referred to in the first notice.

(4) Same — An arrangement that is made in response to a first notice and is then amended by agreement in writing remains an arrangement made in response to the first notice.

37. (1) Direction to suspend — after first notice — The Director may direct the Registrar of Motor Vehicles to suspend a payor's driver's licence if, within the 30-day period referred to in the first notice, the payor does not,

(a) make an arrangement satisfactory to the Director for complying with the support order;

(b) obtain an order to refrain under subsection 35(1) and file the order in the Director's office; or

(c) pay all arrears owing under the support order.

(2) Same — after second notice — The Director may direct the Registrar of Motor Vehicles to suspend a payor's driver's licence if, within the 15-day period referred to in the second notice or at any time in the 24-month period referred to in the second notice, the payor does not,

(a) comply with clause 36(1)(a), (b) or (c); or

(b) pay all arrears owing under the support order.

(3) Form of direction — A direction under this section shall be in a form approved by the Director and the Registrar of Motor Vehicles.

38. (1) Direction to reinstate — The Director shall direct the Registrar of Motor Vehicles to reinstate a driver's licence suspended as a result of a direction under section 37 if,

(a) the payor pays all the arrears owing under the support order;

(b) the payor is complying with the terms of the arrangement made with the Director in response to the first notice;

(c) the payor is complying with the terms of the support order as well as the terms of any order under section 35 or 41 that relates to the support order;

(d) the payor makes an arrangement satisfactory to the Director for complying with the support order; or

(e) the support order is withdrawn under section 16.

(2) Notice revived if payor breaches arrangement or order — If the Director directs the Registrar of Motor Vehicles to reinstate a driver's licence under clause (1)(b), (c) or (d) and the payor subsequently defaults within 24 months from the date of reinstatement or if the payor subsequently defaults within 24 months after the payor entered into an arrangement under clause 34(a) or obtained an order under clause 35(5)(b), the Director may proceed to act in accordance with the last notice that was served on the payor under this Part.

(3) Where more than one order in default — Where the payor is in default on one or more other support orders, the Director shall not direct the Registrar of Motor Vehicles to reinstate the driver's licence unless all arrears under all the support orders are,

(a) paid;

(b) arranged to be paid on terms satisfactory to the Director and the payor is in compliance with such arrangement or arrangements; or

(c) the subject of a court order or orders for payment and the payor is in compliance with such court order or orders.

(4) Discretion to reinstate — The Director may direct the Registrar of Motor Vehicles to reinstate a driver's licence suspended as a result of a direction under section 37 if, in the opinion of the Director, it would be unconscionable not to do so.

(5) Form of direction — A direction under this section shall be in a form approved by the Director and the Registrar of Motor Vehicles.

39. Anti-avoidance — An agreement by the parties to a support order to avoid or prevent its enforcement under this Part is of no effect.

PART VI — OTHER ENFORCEMENT MECHANISMS

40. (1) Financial statements — The Director may request that a payor who is in default under a support order, where the support order or related support deduction order is filed in the Director's office, complete and deliver to the Director a financial statement in the form prescribed by the regulations together with such proof of income as may be required by the regulations.

Family
Responsibility

(2) Same — The payor shall deliver the completed financial statement to the Director within 15 days after he or she was served with the request to complete the form.

(3) Changes in information — If a payor discovers that any information was incomplete or wrong at the time he or she completed the financial statement, he or she shall, within 10 days of the discovery, deliver the corrected information to the Director.

(4) Failure to comply — The Ontario Court (Provincial Division) or the Family Court, on the motion of the Director, may order a payor to comply with a request under subsection (1) and subsections 41(6) and (7) apply with necessary modifications.

(5) Limitation — The Director may request a financial statement under this section once in any six-month period but this does not restrict the Director's right to obtain a financial statement under section 41.

41. (1) Default hearing — When a support order that is filed in the Director's office is in default, the Director may prepare a statement of the arrears and, by notice served on the payor together with the statement of arrears, may require the payor to deliver to the Director a financial statement and such proof of income as may be required by the regulations and to appear before the court to explain the default.

(2) Same — When a support order that is not filed in the Director's office is in default, the recipient may file a request with the court, together with a statement of arrears, and, on such filing, the clerk of the court shall, by notice served on the payor together with the statement of arrears, require the payor to file a financial statement and appear before the court to explain the default.

(3) Persons financially connected to payor — The Director or the recipient may, at any time during a default proceeding under subsection (1) or (2), as the case may be, request that the court order a person who is financially connected to the payor to file a financial statement and any other relevant documents with the court or add such person as a party to the hearing.

(4) Same — If the court is satisfied that there is some evidence that a person who is financially connected to the payor has sheltered assets or income of the payor such that enforcement of the support order against the payor may be frustrated, the court may, by order, having regard to all the circumstances, including the purpose and effect of the dealings and the benefit or expected benefit therefrom to the payor,

   (a) add the person as a party to the hearing;

   (b) require the person, whether or not such person has been added as a party under clause (a), to file a financial statement and any other relevant documents with the court.

(5) Form of statements — A financial statement and statement of arrears required by subsection (2) shall be in the form prescribed by the rules of the court and a financial statement required by subsection (1) or (4) shall be in the form prescribed by the regulations.

(6) Arrest of payor — Where the payor fails to file the financial statement or to appear as the notice under subsection (1) or (2) requires, the court may issue a warrant for the payor's arrest for the purpose of bringing him or her before the court.

(7) Bail — Section 150 (interim release by justice of the peace) of the *Provincial Offences Act* applies with necessary modifications to an arrest under the warrant.

(8) Presumptions at hearing — At the default hearing, unless the contrary is shown, the payor shall be presumed to have the ability to pay the arrears and to make subsequent payments under the order, and the statement of arrears prepared and served by the Director shall be presumed to be correct as to arrears accruing while the order is filed in the Director's office.

(9) Powers of court — The court may, unless it is satisfied that the payor is unable for valid reasons to pay the arrears or to make subsequent payments under the order, order that the payor,

   (a) pay all or part of the arrears by such periodic payments as the court considers just, but an order for partial payment does not discharge any unpaid arrears;

(b) discharge the arrears in full by a specified date;

(c) comply with the order to the extent of the payor's ability to pay, but an order under this clause does not affect the accruing of arrears;

(d) provide security in such form as the court directs for the arrears and subsequent payment;

(e) report periodically to the court, the Director or a person specified in the order;

(f) provide to the court, the Director or a person specified in the order particulars of any future change of address or employment as soon as they occur;

(g) be imprisoned continuously or intermittently for not more than 90 days unless the arrears are sooner paid; and

(h) be imprisoned continuously or intermittently for not more than 90 days on default in any payment ordered under this subsection.

(10) Order against person financially connected to payor — If the court is satisfied that a person who was made a party to the hearing under clause (4)(a) sheltered assets or income of the payor such that enforcement of the support order against the payor has been frustrated, the court may, having regard to all the circumstances, including the purpose and effect of the dealings and the benefit or expected benefit therefrom to the payor, make any order against the person that it may make against the payor under clauses (9)(a) to (f) to the extent of the value of the sheltered assets or income and, for the purpose, in clause (9)(c), "payor's" shall be read as "person's".

(11) Same — Subsections (6) and (7) apply with necessary modifications to a person with respect to whom an order is made under clause (4)(a) or (b).

(12) Interim orders — The court may make an i nterim order against the payor, or a person who was made a party to the hearing under clause (4)(a), that includes any order that may be made under subsection (9) or (10), as the case may be.

(13) Power to vary order — The court that made an order under subsection (9) or (10) may vary the order on motion if there is a material change in the payor's or other person's circumstances, as the case may be.

(14) Enforcement of order — The Director may enforce an order against a person made under subsection (10), (12) or (13) in the same manner he or she may enforce an order against the payor.

(15) Imprisonment does not discharge arrears — Imprisonment of a payor under clause (9)(g) or (h) does not discharge arrears under an order.

(16) Realizing on security — An order for security under clause (9)(d) or a subsequent order of the court may provide for the realization of the security by seizure, sale or other means, as the court directs.

(17) Proof of service not necessary — Proof of service of a support order on the payor is not necessary for the purpose of a default hearing.

(18) Joinder of default and variation hearings — A default hearing under this section and a hearing on an application for variation of the support order in default may be held together or separately.

(19) Spouses compellable witnesses — Spouses are competent and compellable witnesses against each other on a default hearing.

(20) Records sealed — A financial statement or other document filed under subsection (4) shall be sealed in the court file and shall not be disclosed except as permitted by the order or a subsequent order or as necessary to enforce an order made under subsection (10) or (12) against a person other than the payor.

(21) Interpretation — In this section,

"court" means the Ontario Court (Provincial Division) or the Family Court.

42. (1) Registration against land — A support order may be registered in the proper land registry office against the payor's land and on registration the obligation under the order becomes a charge on the property.

(2) Sale of property — A charge created by subsection (1) may be enforced by sale of the property against which it is registered in the same manner as a sale to realize on a mortgage.

(3) Discharge or postponement of charge — A court may order the discharge, in whole or in part, or the postponement, of a charge created by subsection (1), on such terms as to security or other matters as the court considers just.

(4) Director to be served — An order under subsection (3) may be made only after notice to the Director.

43. (1) Registration under the Personal Property Security Act — Arrears owing from time to time under a support order are, upon registration by the Director or the recipient with the registrar under the *Personal Property Security Act* of a notice claiming a lien and charge under this section, a lien and charge on any interest in all the personal property in Ontario owned or held at the time of registration or acquired afterwards by the payor.

(2) Amounts included and priority — The lien and charge is in respect of the arrears owed by the payor under a support order at the time of registration of the notice and the arrears owed by the payor under the support order which accrue afterwards while the notice remains registered and, upon registration of a notice of lien and charge, the lien and charge has priority over,

  (a) any perfected security interest registered after the notice is registered;

  (b) any security interest perfected by possession after the notice is registered; and

  (c) any encumbrance or other claim that is registered against or that otherwise arises and affects the payor's property after the notice is registered.

(3) Exception — For the purpose of subsection (2), the notice of lien and charge does not have priority over a perfected purchase money security interest in collateral or its proceeds and shall be deemed to be a security interest perfected by registration for the purpose of the priority rules under section 28 of the *Personal Property Security Act.*

(4) Effective period — The notice of lien and charge is effective from the time assigned to its registration by the registrar or branch registrar until its discharge or expiry.

(5) Secured party — In addition to any other rights and remedies, if any arrears under a support order remain unpaid, the Director or recipient, as the case may be, has, in respect of the lien and charge,

  (a) all the rights, remedies and duties of a secured party under sections 17, 59, 61, 62, 63 and 64, subsections 65(4), (5), (6) and (7) and section 66 of the *Personal Property Security Act;*

(b) a security interest in the collateral for the purpose of clause 63(4)(c) of that Act; and

(c) a security interest in the personal property for the purposes of sections 15 and 16 of the *Repair and Storage Liens Act*, if it is an article as defined in that Act.

(6) Registration of documents — The notice of lien and charge shall be in the form of a financing statement as prescribed by regulation under the *Personal Property Security Act* and may be tendered for registration at a branch office as provided in Part IV of that Act.

(7) Errors in documents — The notice of lien and charge is not invalidated nor its effect impaired by reason only of an error or omission in the notice or in its execution or registration, unless a reasonable person is likely to be materially misled by the error or omission.

(8) Bankruptcy and Insolvency Act (Canada) unaffected — Subject to Crown rights provided under section 87 of the *Bankruptcy and Insolvency Act* (Canada), nothing in this section affects or purports to affect the rights and obligations of any person under that Act.

44. (1) Writs of seizure and sale — amending amounts owing — If a writ of seizure and sale is filed with a sheriff in respect of a support order, the person who filed the writ may at any time file with the sheriff a statutory declaration specifying the amount currently owing under the order.

(2) Same — When a statutory declaration is filed under subsection (1), the writ of seizure and sale shall be deemed to be amended to specify the amount owing in accordance with the statutory declaration.

(3) Notice from sheriff of opportunity to amend writ — A sheriff who comes into possession of money to be paid out under a writ of seizure and sale in respect of a support order shall, not later than seven days after making the entry required by subsection 5(1) of the *Creditors' Relief Act*, give notice to the person who filed the writ of the opportunity to file a statutory declaration under subsection (1).

(4) Same — A sheriff who receives a request for information about the amount owing under a writ of seizure and sale in respect of a support order from a person seeking to have the writ removed from the sheriff's file shall promptly give notice to the person who filed the writ of the opportunity to file a statutory declaration under subsection (1).

(5) Removal of writ from sheriff's file — A sheriff shall not remove a writ of seizure and sale in respect of a support order from his or her file unless,

(a) the writ has expired and has not been renewed;

(b) the sheriff receives written notice from the person who filed the writ to the effect that the writ should be withdrawn;

(c) notice is given under subsection (3) or (4), a statutory declaration is subsequently filed under subsection (1) and the writ, as deemed to be amended under subsection (2), has been fully satisfied; or

(d) notice is given under subsection (3) or (4), 10 days have elapsed since the notice was given, no statutory declaration has been filed under subsection (1) since the giving of the notice and the writ has been fully satisfied.

(6) Delivery of statutory declaration to land registrar — If a copy of a writ of seizure and sale has been delivered by the sheriff to a land registrar under section 136 of the *Land Titles Act* and a statutory declaration is filed under subsection (1) in respect of the writ, the sheriff shall promptly deliver a copy of the statutory declaration to the land registrar and the

Family
Responsibility

amendment deemed to be made to the writ under subsection (2) does not bind land registered under the *Land Titles Act* until a copy of the statutory declaration has been received and recorded by the land registrar.

45. (1) Garnishment of joint accounts — Upon being served on a financial institution, a notice of garnishment issued by the Director to enforce a support order against a payor attaches 50 per cent of the money credited to a deposit account held in the financial institution in the name of the payor together with one or more other persons as joint or joint and several deposit account holders, and the financial institution shall pay up to 50 per cent of the money credited to the deposit account to the Director in accordance with the notice of garnishment.

(2) Duties of financial institution — The financial institution shall, within 10 days of being served with the notice of garnishment,

> (a) pay the money to the Director and, at the same time, notify the Director if the account is held jointly or jointly and severally in the name of two or more persons; and

> (b) notify the co-holders of the account who are not named in the notice of garnishment of the garnishment.

(3) Dispute by co-holder — Within 30 days after the financial institution notified the Director under clause (2)(a), a co-holder of the deposit account may file a dispute to the garnishment in the Ontario Court (Provincial Division) or the Family Court claiming ownership of all or part of the money that the financial institution paid to the Director.

(4) Director to hold money for 30 days — If the financial institution notifies the Director under clause (2)(a), the Director shall not release the money received under subsection (1) until 30 days after the financial institution so notified the Director, and the Director may release the money after the 30 days unless a co-holder of the deposit account first serves on the Director a copy of the dispute to the garnishment that the co-holder filed under subsection (3).

(5) Determination by court — In a hearing to determine the dispute to the garnishment, the money paid to the Director shall be presumed to be owned by the payor and the court shall order,

> (a) that the garnishment be limited to the payor's interest in the money that was paid to the Director; and

> (b) that all or part of the money that was paid to the Director be returned to the co-holder only if it is satisfied that the co-holder owns that money.

(6) Payment by Director — Upon receipt of a copy of the court's order, the Director shall return to the co-holder any money determined by the court to belong to the co-holder and may release any remaining money, if any, to the recipient.

(7) Action by joint account co-holder against payor — A co-holder may bring an action against the payor in a court of competent jurisdiction,

> (a) to recover any money owned by the co-holder that was paid to the Director under subsection (1);

> (b) to recover any interest that the coholder would have earned on the money owned by the co-holder that was paid to the Director under subsection (1).

(8) Director and recipient are not parties — The Director and the recipient are not parties to an action under subsection (7).

(9) Definition — In this section,

"deposit account" includes a deposit as defined in the *Deposits Regulation Act* and a demand account, time account, savings account, passbook account, checking account, current account and other similar accounts in,

    (a) a bank listed in Schedule I or II to the *Bank Act* (Canada),

    (b) a loan corporation or trust corporation as defined in the *Loan and Trust Corporations Act*,

    (c) a credit union as defined in the *Credit Unions and Caisses Populaires Act, 1994*,

    (d) the Province of Ontario Savings Office, or

    (e) a similar institution.

Proposed Amendment — 45(9) "deposit account"

"deposit account" includes a deposit as defined in the *Deposits Regulation Act* and a demand account, time account, savings account, passbook account, checking account, current account and other similar accounts in,

    (a) a bank listed in Schedule I or II to the *Bank Act* (Canada),

    (b) a loan corporation or trust corporation as defined in the *Loan and Trust Corporations Act*,

    (c) a credit union as defined in the *Credit Unions and Caisses Populaires Act, 1994*, or

    (d) a similar institution.

    (e) [Repealed 2002, c. 8, Sched. I, s. 11. Not in force at date of publication.]

          2002, c. 8, Sched. I, s. 11 [Not in force at date of publication.]

46. (1) Definitions — In this section,

"Corporation" means the Ontario Lottery Corporation; ("Société")

"lottery" means a lottery scheme, as defined in section 1 of the *Ontario Lottery Corporation Act*, that is conducted by the Corporation in Ontario and involves the issuance and sale of tickets; ("loterie")

"prize" means a prize in a lottery. ("prix")

(2) Deduction of arrears from prize — If a payor who owes arrears under a support order that is filed in the Director's office is entitled to a single monetary prize of $1,000 or more from the Corporation, the Corporation shall,

    (a) deduct from the prize the amount of the arrears or the amount of the prize, whichever is less;

    (b) pay the amount deducted to the Director; and

    (c) pay any balance to the payor.

(3) Non-monetary prize — If a payor who owes arrears under a support order that is filed in the Director's office is entitled to a non-monetary prize from the Corporation that the

Family
Responsibility

Corporation values at $1,000 or more, the Corporation shall promptly disclose to the Director,

(a) any identifying information about the payor from the Corporation's records, including his or her name and address; and

(b) a complete description of the prize.

(4) Exchange of information — For the purposes of subsections (2) and (3),

(a) the Director shall disclose to the Corporation any identifying information about payors from the Director's records, including their names and addresses and the status and particulars of their support obligations; and

(b) the Corporation shall disclose to the Director any identifying information about prize winners from its records, including their names and addresses.

1999, c.12, Sched. B, s. 8

47. Defaulters reported to consumer reporting agencies — The Director may disclose to a consumer reporting agency registered under the *Consumer Reporting Act*,

(a) the name of a payor who is in default on a support order filed in the Director's office;

(b) the date of the support order;

(c) the amount and frequency of the payor's support obligation under the support order;

(d) the amount of the arrears owing under the support order at the time of the disclosure; and

(e) such other information as may be prescribed.

48. Restraining order — A court, including the Ontario Court (Provincial Division), may make an order restraining the disposition or wasting of assets that may hinder or defeat the enforcement of a support order or support deduction order.

49. (1) Arrest of absconding payor — The Ontario Court (Provincial Division) or the Family Court may issue a warrant for a payor's arrest for the purpose of bringing him or her before the court if the court is satisfied that the payor is about to leave Ontario and that there are reasonable grounds for believing that the payor intends to evade his or her obligations under the support order.

(2) Bail — Section 150 (interim release by justice of the peace) of the *Provincial Offences Act* applies with necessary modifications to an arrest under the warrant.

(3) Powers of court — When the payor is brought before the court, it may make any order provided for in subsection 41 (9).

50. (1) Recognition of extraprovincial garnishments — On the filing of a garnishment process that,

(a) is issued outside Ontario and is directed to a garnishee in Ontario;

(b) states that it is issued in respect of support or maintenance; and

(c) is written in or accompanied by a sworn or certified translation into English or French, the clerk of the Ontario Court (Provincial Division) or Family Court shall issue a notice of garnishment to enforce the support or maintenance obligation.

(2) Foreign currencies — If the garnishment process refers to an obligation in a foreign currency, section 44 of the *Interjurisdictional Support Orders Act, 2002* applies with necessary modifications.

2002, c. 13, s. 57(3)

PART VII — OFFENCES AND PENALTIES

51. (1) Offences — payors — A payor who knowingly contravenes or knowingly fails to comply with section 19 or subsection 25(1) or (2) or 40(2) or (3) is guilty of an offence and on conviction is liable to a fine of not more than $10,000.

(2) Same — income sources — An income source who knowingly contravenes or knowingly fails to comply with subsection 22(2) or 25(1) or (2) or section 29 is guilty of an offence and on conviction is liable to a fine of not more than $10,000.

(3) Same — individuals, etc., believed to be an income source — An individual, corporation or other entity that knowingly contravenes or knowingly fails to comply with subsection 26(1) or section 29 is guilty of an offence and on conviction is liable to a fine of not more than $10,000.

52. (1) Offences — assignees — An assignee under section 4 who knowingly contravenes or knowingly fails to comply with this Act or its regulations or the limitations, conditions or requirements set out in the assignment is guilty of an offence and on conviction is liable to a fine of not more than $10,000.

(2) Same — directors, officers, employees, agents — A director, officer, employee or agent of an assignee who commits an offence described in subsection (1) on conviction is liable to a fine of not more than $10,000.

(3) Same — directors, officers — A director or officer of an assignee is guilty of an offence if he or she,

(a) knowingly causes, authorizes, permits or participates in the commission of an offence described in subsection (1); or

(b) fails to take reasonable care to prevent the commission of an offence described in subsection (1).

(4) Penalty — A person who is convicted of an offence under subsection (3) is liable to a fine of not more than $10,000.

53. (1) Contempt — In addition to its powers in respect of contempt, a court, including the Ontario Court (Provincial Division), may punish by fine or imprisonment, or by both, any wilful contempt of, or resistance to, its process, rules or orders under this Act, but the fine shall not exceed $10,000 nor shall the imprisonment exceed 90 days.

(2) Conditions of imprisonment — An order for imprisonment under subsection (1) may be conditional upon default in the performance of a condition set out in the order and may provide for the imprisonment to be served intermittently.

PART VIII — MISCELLANEOUS

54. (1) Director's access to information — The Director may, for the purpose of enforcing a support order or support deduction order filed in the Director's office or for the purpose of assisting an office or person in another jurisdiction performing similar functions to those performed by the Director,

(a) demand from any person or public body information from a record in the person's or public body's possession or control that indicates the employer, place of employment, wages, salary, other income, assets, liabilities, address or location of a payor or payors;

(b) subject to subsections (2), (3) and (4), have access to all records that may indicate the employer, place of employment, wages, salary, other income, assets, liabilities, address or location of a payor or payors and that are in the possession or control of any ministry, agency, board or commission of the Government of Ontario in order to search for and obtain such information from those records;

(c) enter into an agreement with any person or public body, including the Government of Canada, a Crown corporation, the government of another province or territory or any agency, board or commission of such government, to permit the Director to have access to a record in the person's or public body's possession or control that may indicate the employer, place of employment, wages, salary, other income, assets, liabilities, address or location of a payor or payors in order to search for and obtain such information from the record; and

(d) disclose information obtained under clause (a), (b) or (c) to a person performing similar functions to the Director in another jurisdiction.

(2) Access to part of records — Where the record referred to in clause (1)(b) is part of a larger record, the Director,

(a) may have access to that part of the record that may indicate the employer, place of employment, wages, salary, other income, assets, liabilities, address or location of a payor or payors; and

(b) may have incidental access to any other information contained in the part of the record referred to in clause (a) but may not use or disclose such information.

(3) Same — For the purposes of subsection (2), "larger record" and "part of the record" shall be defined by regulation.

(4) Restriction on access to health information — Despite subsection (2), if a record described in clause (1)(b) contains health information, as defined in the regulations, the Director shall not have access to the health information but shall have access only to the part of the record that may indicate the employer, place of employment, wages, salary, other income, assets, liabilities, address or location of a payor or payors.

(5) Information confidential — Information obtained under subsection (1) shall not be disclosed except,

(a) to the extent necessary for the enforcement of the support order or support deduction order;

(b) as provided in clause (1)(d); or

(c) to a police officer who needs the information for a criminal investigation that is likely to assist the enforcement of the support order or support deduction order.

(6) Order of court for access to information — If, on motion to a court, it appears that,

(a) the Director has been refused information after making a demand under clause (1)(a);

(b) the Director has been refused access to a record under clause (1)(b); or

(c) a person needs an order under this subsection for the enforcement of a support order that is not filed in the Director's office,

the court may order any person or public body to provide the court or the person whom the court names with any information that is shown on a record in the possession or control of the person or public body and indicates the employer, place of employment, wages, salary, other income, assets, liabilities, address or location of the payor.

(7) Costs — If the Director obtains an order under clause (6)(a) or (b), the court shall award the costs of the motion to the Director.

(8) Information confidential — Information obtained under an order under clause (6)(c) shall be sealed in the court file and shall not be disclosed except,

(a) as permitted by the order or a subsequent order;

(b) to the extent necessary for the enforcement of the support order or support deduction order;

(c) as provided in clause (1)(d); or

(d) to a police officer who needs the information for a criminal investigation that is likely to assist the enforcement of the support order or support deduction order.

(9) Section governs — This section applies despite any other Act or regulation and despite any common law rule of confidentiality.

55. (1) Federal — provincial agreement — The Attorney General may, on behalf of the Government of Ontario, enter into an agreement with the Government of Canada concerning the searching for and the release of information under Part I of the *Family Orders and Agreements Enforcement Assistance Act* (Canada).

(2) Information obtained from federal government — The Director shall not disclose information obtained under the *Family Orders and Agreements Enforcement Assistance Act* (Canada) for the enforcement of a support order, except,

(a) to the extent necessary for the enforcement of the order; or

(b) as permitted by the *Freedom of Information and Protection of Privacy Act*.

56. (1) Payments pending court decisions — The Director shall pay any money he or she receives in respect of a support order or a support deduction order to the recipient despite the commencement of any court proceeding in respect of the support obligation or its enforcement, in the absence of a court order to the contrary.

(2) Exception — If a court orders the Director to hold any of the money received in respect of a support order or a support deduction order pending the disposition of the proceeding, the Director shall, upon receipt of a copy of the order, hold any money he or she receives to the extent required by the court.

57. (1) Application of payments — Money paid to the Director on account of a support order or support deduction order shall be credited as prescribed by the regulations.

(2) Same — Despite anything in this Act, the payor shall not be credited with making a payment until the money for that payment is received by the Director and if a payment is made but not honoured, the amount of the payment shall be added to the support arrears owed by the payor.

58. (1) Fees — The Director shall not charge any fee to any person for his or her services except as provided by regulation.

(2) Enforcement of orders to collect fees, etc. — The Director may continue to enforce a support order or support deduction order to collect fees, costs ordered by a court to the Director and any amount owed to the Director as reimbursement for money paid to a recipient, even if the support order or support deduction order with respect to which the fees, costs or other debt were incurred has been withdrawn from the Director's office or if the arrears of support under such order have been ordered rescinded or if the support obligation has terminated.

59. (1) Protection from personal liability — No action or other proceeding for damages shall be instituted against the Director or any employee of the Director's office for any act done in good faith in the execution or intended execution of any duty or authority under this Act or for any alleged neglect or default in the execution in good faith of any duty or authority under this Act.

(2) Crown not relieved of liability — Despite subsections 5(2) and (4) of the *Proceedings Against the Crown Act*, subsection (1) does not relieve the Crown of liability in respect of a tort committed by a person mentioned in subsection (1) to which it would otherwise be subject.

60. Acting by solicitor — Anything that this Act requires to be signed or done by a person, or that is referred to in this Act as signed or done by a person, may be signed or done by a lawyer acting on the person's behalf.

61. (1) Disclosure of personal information — The Director shall collect, disclose and use personal information about an identifiable individual for the purpose of enforcing a support order or a support deduction order under this Act.

(2) Same — Any person, agency, board, commission or body that is referred to in section 54 shall disclose personal information about an identifiable individual to the Director for the purpose of that section.

(3) Notice to individual not required — Subsection 39(2) of the *Freedom of Information and Protection of Privacy Act* does not apply to the collection of personal information about an identifiable individual under this Act.

(4) Act prevails over confidentiality provisions — This Act prevails over a confidentiality provision in another Act that would, if not for this Act, prohibit the disclosure of information to the Director.

62. Act binds Crown — This Act binds the Crown.

63. Regulations — The Lieutenant Governor in Council may make regulations,

 (a) prescribing forms and providing for their use;

(b) prescribing types of income for the purposes of clause (1) of the definition of "income source" in subsection 1(1);

(c) prescribing the manner of calculating a cost of living clause for the purposes of subsections 7(4), (5), (6) and (7);

(d) prescribing classes of persons and information to be supplied to the court and the manner in which information is to be supplied for the purposes of subsections 11(2) and (3);

(e) prescribing practices and procedures related to the filing and withdrawal of support orders and support deduction orders and to the enforcement, suspension and termination of such orders filed in the Director's office;

(f) prescribing deductions for the purposes of subsection 23(5);

(g) prescribing information that shall be supplied under subsection 25(1);

(h) governing the form and posting of security by a payor under section 28 and the realization thereon;

(i) respecting proof of income for the purposes of sections 40 and 41;

(j) prescribing other information that may be disclosed by the Director to a consumer reporting agency under section 47;

(k) prescribing fees to be charged by the Director for administrative services, including preparing and photocopying documents on request, prescribing fees for repeated filings of a support order or support deduction order, as specified in the regulations, and prescribing fees for any steps taken by the Director to enforce a support order in response to the persistent or wilful default by a payor;

(l) prescribing the maximum fees, costs, disbursements, surcharges and other charges, or a method for determining the maximum fees, costs, disbursements, surcharges and other charges, that an assignee under section 4 may charge a payor, including fees, costs, disbursements, surcharges and other charges for services for which the Director is not permitted to charge and including fees, costs, disbursements, surcharges or other charges that are higher than the fees, costs, disbursements, surcharges and other charges that the Director may charge for the same service, prescribing how and when such fees, costs, disbursements, surcharges and other charges may be collected, prescribing the manner in which they may be applied and prescribing the rate of interest to be charged on any of them;

(m) prescribing methods of and rules respecting service, filing and notice for the purposes of this Act, including different methods and rules for different provisions and different methods and rules for service on or notice to the Crown;

(n) providing that a support deduction order is not effective against the Crown unless a statement of particulars in the prescribed form is served with the notice of the order;

(o) defining "larger record" and "part of the record" for the purpose of subsection 54(2) and defining "health information" for the purpose of subsection 54(4);

(p) prescribing the manner in which payments received by the Director are to be credited;

(q) prescribing anything that is required or authorized by this Act to be prescribed.

64. On a day to be named by proclamation of the Lieutenant Governor, Part V of this Act is repealed and the following substituted:

PART V — SUSPENSION OF DRIVERS' LICENCES AND VEHICLE PERMITS

33. Definitions — In this Part,

"driver's licence" has the same meaning as in subsection 1(1) of the *Highway Traffic Act*; ("permis de conduire")

"permit" means a permit, or a portion of a permit, issued exclusively in the name of an individual under subsection 7(7) of the *Highway Traffic Act*, but does not include a permit issued in respect of a commercial motor vehicle, as defined in subsection 16(1) of that Act, or in respect of a trailer. ("certificat d'immatriculation")

34. First notice — When a support order that is filed in the Director's office is in default, the Director may serve a first notice on the payor, informing the payor that his or her driver's licence and permit may be suspended and his or her permit may not be validated and he or she may be refused issuance of a new permit unless, within 30 days after the day the first notice is served,

   (a) the payor makes an arrangement satisfactory to the Director for complying with the support order and for paying the arrears owing under the support order;

   (b) the payor obtains an order to refrain under subsection 35(1) and files the order in the Director's office; or

   (c) the payor pays all arrears owing under the support order.

35. (1) Order to refrain — A payor who receives a first notice may, on notice to the Director, in an application to vary the support order, make a motion for an order that the Director refrain from making a direction under subsection 37(1) on the terms that the court considers just.

(2) Exception — Despite subsection (1), a motion for an order that the Director refrain from directing the suspension of the payor's driver's licence may be made before the commencement of an application to vary the support order on the undertaking of the payor or the payor's solicitor to commence the proceeding forthwith.

(3) Time limits and variation — A court shall not make an order to refrain after the 30-day period referred to in the first notice, but an order to refrain may be varied, on motion by the payor or the Director, at any time before the application to vary support is determined if there is a material change in the payor's circumstances.

(4) Same — A court may make an order to refrain only within the 30-day period referred to in the first notice and may make only one order to refrain in respect of any first notice.

(5) Order re arrears — When determining the variation application, a court that makes an order to refrain,

> (a) shall state the amount of the arrears owing, after any variation; and

> (b) may make an order respecting payment of the arrears.

(6) Same — For the purpose of clause (5)(b), the court may make any order that may be made under clause 41(9)(a), (b), (c), (d), (g) or (h) or subsection 41(16) and, in the case of an order provided for in clause 41(9)(g) or (h), imprisonment does not discharge arrears under the support order.

(7) When Director is a party — The Director is not a party to an application to vary a support order referred to in subsection (1), but the Director and the payor are the only parties to a motion under subsection (1) for an order to refrain.

(8) Filing with Director's office — The court shall file a copy of the order in the Director's office promptly after the order is signed.

(9) Form and effective date — An order to refrain shall be in the form prescribed by the regulations and takes effect only when it is filed in the Director's office.

(10) Duration of order — An order to refrain terminates on the earliest of the day the application to vary is determined, the day the support order is withdrawn from the Director's office and the day that is six months after the order to refrain is made.

(11) Exception — Despite subsection (10), an order to refrain made before the commencement of an application to vary the support order is automatically terminated if the payor does not commence the application within 20 days of the date of the order to refrain.

(12) Extension of order — The court that makes an order to refrain may, on a motion by the payor before the order terminates and with notice to the Director, extend the order for one further period of three months.

(13) Application of order — An order to refrain is applicable only to the notice in respect of which the motion was made under subsection (1).

36. (1) Second notice — The Director may serve a second notice on the payor if, at any time in the 24 months after the payor made an arrangement under clause 34(a) or obtained an order under subsection 35(1) or clause 35(5)(b), the payor fails to comply with,

> (a) the terms of the arrangement made with the Director in response to the first notice;

> (b) the terms of an order to refrain under subsection 35(1); or

> (c) the terms of the varied support order and an order respecting payment of arrears under clause 35(5)(b).

(2) Contents — The second notice shall inform the payor that his or her driver's licence and permit may be suspended, his or her permit may not be validated and he or she may be refused issuance of a new permit,

> (a) unless, within 15 days after the day the second notice is served,

> > (i) the payor complies with clause (1)(a), (b) or (c), or

> > (ii) the payor pays all arrears owing under the support order; or

(b) if, within 24 months after the payor makes an arrangement under clause (1)(a) or obtains an order under subsection 35(1) or clause 35(5)(b), the payor fails to comply with the arrangement or order.

(3) **Interpretation: arrangement in response to notice** — For the purposes of this section, an arrangement is made in response to a first notice if it is made within the time referred to in the first notice.

(4) **Same** — An arrangement that is made in response to a first notice and is then amended by agreement in writing remains an arrangement made in response to the first notice.

37. (1) **Direction to suspend, etc. — after first notice** — The Director may direct the Registrar of Motor Vehicles to suspend a payor's driver's licence and permit or to refuse to validate his or her permit or to refuse to issue a new permit to the payor if, within the 30-day period referred to in the first notice, the payor does not,

(a) make an arrangement satisfactory to the Director for complying with the support order;

(b) obtain an order to refrain under subsection 35(1) and file the order in the Director's office; or

(c) pay all arrears owing under the support order.

(2) **Same — after second notice** — The Director may direct the Registrar of Motor Vehicles to suspend a payor's driver's licence and permit or to refuse to validate his or her permit or to refuse to issue a new permit to the payor if, within the 15-day period referred to in the second notice or at any time in the 24-month period referred to in the second notice, the payor does not,

(a) comply with clause 36(1)(a), (b) or (c); or

(b) pay all arrears owing under the support order.

(3) **Form of direction** — A direction under this section shall be in a form approved by the Director and the Registrar of Motor Vehicles and may contain any one or more of the directions that the Director is permitted to make under this section.

38. (1) **Direction to reinstate** — The Director shall direct the Registrar of Motor Vehicles to reinstate a driver's licence and permit suspended as a result of a direction under section 37 and to rescind a direction under section 37 to refuse to validate a permit or to refuse to issue a new permit to the payor if,

(a) the payor pays all the arrears owing under the support order;

(b) the payor is complying with the terms of the arrangement made with the Director in response to the first notice;

(c) the payor is complying with the terms of the support order as well as the terms of any order under section 35 or 41 that relates to the support order;

(d) the payor makes an arrangement satisfactory to the Director for complying with the support order;

(e) the support order is withdrawn under section 16; or

(f) in the case of a permit issued in respect of a vehicle that is registered as a security interest under the *Personal Property Security Act*, the secured party enforces on the security interest and requests that the Director direct the reinstatement of the permit for that purpose.

(2) **Notice revived if payor breaches arrangement or order** — If the Director directs the Registrar of Motor Vehicles under clause (1)(b), (c) or (d) and the payor subsequently defaults within 24 months from the date of reinstatement or if the payor subsequently defaults within 24 months after the payor entered into an arrangement under clause 34(a) or obtained an order under clause 35(5)(b), the Director may proceed to act in accordance with the last notice that was served on the payor under this Part.

(3) **Where more than one order in default** — Where the payor is in default on one or more other support orders, the Director shall not direct the Registrar of Motor Vehicles to reinstate a driver's licence or permit or to validate a permit or issue a new permit unless all arrears under all the support orders are,

(a) paid;

(b) arranged to be paid on terms satisfactory to the Director and the payor is in compliance with such arrangement or arrangements; or

(c) the subject of a court order or orders for payment and the payor is in compliance with such court order or orders.

(4) **Discretion to reinstate** — The Director may direct the Registrar of Motor Vehicles to reinstate a driver's licence or permit suspended as a result of a direction under section 37 or to validate a permit or issue a new permit if the validation or issuance was refused as a result of a direction under section 37 if, in the opinion of the Director, it would be unconscionable not to do so.

(5) **Form of direction** — A direction under this section shall be in a form approved by the Director and the Registrar of Motor Vehicles and may contain one or more of the directions that the Director is permitted to make under this section.

39. **Anti-avoidance** — An agreement by the parties to a support order to avoid or prevent its enforcement under this Part is of no effect.

PART IX — COMPLEMENTARY AMENDMENTS TO OTHER ACTS

Courts of Justice Act

65. Paragraph 1 of the Schedule to section 21.8 of the *Courts of Justice Act*, as enacted by the Statutes of Ontario, 1994, chapter 12, section 8, is amended by striking out "*Family Support Plan Act*" and substituting "*Family Responsibility and Support Arrears Enforcement Act, 1996*".

66. Clause 21.12(2)(b) of the Act, as enacted by the Statutes of Ontario, 1994, chapter 12, section 8, is amended by striking out "the *Family Support Plan Act*" in the sixth and seventh lines and substituting "the *Family Responsibility and Support Arrears Enforcement Act, 1996*".

Creditors' Relief Act

67. Clause 4(1)(a) of the *Creditors' Relief Act* is repealed and the following substituted:

(a) if the order is for periodic payments, in the amount of the arrears owing under the order at the time of seizure or attachment.

Highway Traffic Act

68. The heading to Part XIII of the Act is repealed and the following substituted:

Suspension for Failure to Pay Judgments or Meet Support Obligations

69. Section 197 of the Act, as amended by the Statutes of Ontario, 1996, chapter 20, section 30, is repealed.

70. Part XIII of the Act is amended by adding the following sections:

198.1 (1) **Licence suspension on direction of Director of Family Responsibility Office** — On receiving a direction under section 37 of the *Family Responsibility and Support Arrears Enforcement Act, 1996* to suspend the driver's licence of a person, the Registrar shall suspend the person's driver's licence, if it is not already under suspension under this section.

(2) **Reinstatement** — On receiving a direction under section 38 of the *Family Responsibility and Support Arrears Enforcement Act, 1996* to reinstate the driver's licence of a person, the Registrar shall reinstate the licence unless,

(a) the licence is otherwise under suspension;

(b) interest charged or a penalty imposed under subsection 5(2) has not been paid; or

(c) an applicable prescribed administrative fee for handling a dishonoured payment has not been paid.

198.2 **Personal information** — The Registrar shall, for purposes related to section 198.1, collect, use and disclose personal information about an identifiable individual disclosed in a direction from the Director of the Family Responsibility Office.

198.3 (1) **Protection from personal liability** — No action or other proceeding for damages shall be instituted against the Registrar or any employee of the Ministry for acting in good faith in the execution or intended execution of a duty under this Part.

(2) **Crown not relieved of liability** — Despite subsections 5(2) and (4) of the *Proceedings Against the Crown Act*, subsection (1) does not relieve the Crown of liability in respect of a tort committed by a person mentioned in subsection (1) to which it would otherwise be subject.

Unproclaimed Text — 71

71. On a day to be named by proclamation of the Lieutenant Governor, Part XIII of the Act is amended by adding the following section:

198.4 (1) **Definition** — In this section,

"permit" means a permit, or a portion of a permit, issued exclusively in the name of an individual under subsection 7(7), but does not include a permit issued in respect of a commercial motor vehicle, as defined in subsection 16(1), or in respect of a trailer.

(2) **Notice of suspension** — On receiving a direction under section 37 of the *Family Responsibility and Support Arrears Enforcement Act, 1996* to suspend an individual's permit, the Registrar shall give the individual in whose name the permit is held notice in writing that the permit shall be suspended on the day that is 15 days after the day the Registrar received the direction.

(3) **When notice given** — Notice under subsection (2) is sufficiently given if delivered personally or sent by registered mail addressed to the person to whom the permit was issued at the latest address of the person appearing on the records of the Ministry and where notice is given by registered mail it shall be deemed to have been given on the fifth day after the mailing unless the person to whom the notice is given establishes that he or she did not, acting in good faith through absence, accident, illness or other cause beyond his or her control, receive the notice.

(4) **Permits suspended** — On the day that is 15 days after the day the Registrar received the direction to suspend a permit under section 37 of the *Family Responsibility and Support Arrears Enforcement Act, 1996*, he or she shall suspend all permits issued to the individual, if they are not already under suspension under this section.

(5) **Effect of direction to suspend permit** — Effective the day the Registrar receives a notice under section 37 of the *Family Responsibility and Support Arrears Enforcement Act, 1996*, the individual in whose name the permit is held is not entitled to have any permit validated in his or her name, is not entitled to have any other permit issued, either individually or jointly, is not entitled to renew any permit held individually and is not entitled to transfer the permit to any other person's name.

(6) **Notice of reinstatement** — On receiving a direction under section 38 of the *Family Responsibility and Support Arrears Enforcement Act, 1996* to reinstate an individual's permit, the Registrar shall give the individual in whose name the permit was held notice in writing that the permit may be reinstated.

(7) **Conditions for reinstatement** — Where notice has been given under subsection (6), the permit shall be reinstated upon the application by the individual to the Ministry and upon the individual's meeting the requirements of subsection 7(7).

(8) **Copies of notices to other holders affected** — If a permit consists of two portions, only one of which is to be or has been suspended under this section the Registrar shall give a copy of the notice given under subsection (2) or (6) to the holder or holders of the other portion of the permit.

(9) **When notice given** — Notice under subsection (6) or (8) is sufficiently given if sent by regular mail addressed to the person to whom the permit was issued at the latest address of the person appearing on the records of the Ministry.

(10) **Offence** — Every individual whose permit is suspended under this section and who applies for the issuance of or procures a permit or has possession of the suspended permit issued to him or her for a vehicle is guilty of an offence and on conviction is liable to a fine of not less than $200 and not more than $2,000.

Family
Responsibility

(11) **Same** — Every individual whose vehicle portion of a permit is suspended under this section is guilty of an offence if the vehicle for which the permit is issued is driven on a highway while the permit is under suspension, unless the vehicle was in the possession of a person other than the holder of the suspended permit without the holder's consent, and on conviction is liable to a fine of not less than $200 and not more than $2,000.

(12) **Same** — Every individual whose plate portion of a permit is suspended under this section is guilty of an offence if a vehicle is driven on a highway with the number plates attached thereto bearing the number of the permit that is under suspension, unless the vehicle was in the possession of a person other than the holder of the suspended permit without the holder's consent, and on conviction is liable to a fine of not less than $200 and not more than $2,000.

(13) **Same** — Every individual who, after having received a notice from the Registrar under subsection (2), sells, transfers, encumbers or otherwise alienates a vehicle that is registered exclusively to him or her is guilty of an offence and on conviction is liable to a fine of not less than $500 and not more than $5,000 or imprisonment for a term of not more than six months, or to both.

(14) **Same** — Every individual who, after having received a notice from the Registrar under subsection (2), applies for the validation, renewal or issuance of a permit or procures a permit is guilty of an offence and on conviction is liable to a fine of not less than $500 and not more than $5,000 or imprisonment for a term of not more than six months, or to both.

(15) **When suspension does not apply to new owner** — Where the vehicle portion of a permit has been suspended under this section and a person who became the new owner of the vehicle before the effective date of the suspension applies for a new permit for the vehicle, the Director of the Family Responsibility Office shall be deemed to have directed the Registrar to reinstate the permit under section 38 of the *Family Responsibility and Support Arrears Enforcement Act, 1996*.

(16) **Section 51 does not apply** — Section 51 does not apply to a suspension under this section.

(17) **Refusal to validate** — On receiving a direction under section 37 of the *Family Responsibility and Support Arrears Enforcement Act, 1996* to refuse to validate an individual's permit, the Registrar shall refuse to validate the plate portion of the permit or to issue a new permit until the Registrar receives a subsequent direction under section 38 of that Act in respect of the permit.

(18) **Refusal to issue** — On receiving a direction under section 37 of the *Family Responsibility and Support Arrears Enforcement Act, 1996* to refuse to issue a new permit to an individual, the Registrar shall refuse to issue a new permit to the individual until the Registrar receives a subsequent direction under section 38 of that Act in respect of the individual.

Workers' Compensation Act

72. [Repealed 1997, c. 16, s. 18, item 10.]

PART X — REPEALS, COMMENCEMENT AND SHORT TITLE

73. (1) Repeals — The *Family Support Plan Act* and the *Family Support Plan Amendment Act, 1991* are repealed.

(2) Transition — Despite subsection (1), any document and any court order that refers to the Family Support Plan or the Director of the Family Support Plan or the *Family Support Plan Act* is valid and shall be read as if it referred, respectively, to the Family Responsibility Office, the Director of the Family Responsibility Office or the *Family Responsibility and Support Arrears Enforcement Act, 1996*.

(3) Same — Despite subsection (1), any action taken in the name of the Director of the Family Support Plan or taken by or against the Director of the Family Support Plan before subsection (1) comes into force may be continued by, against or on behalf of the Director of the Family Responsibility Office and subsection (2) applies in respect of such action.

(4) Same — Despite subsection (1), the Director of the Family Responsibility Office may continue to use the title Director of the Family Support Plan for a period of one year after subsection (1) comes into force and may, during that time, take any action and create and issue any documents in the name of the Director of the Family Support Plan and subsection (2) applies to any document created or issued or court order made in that period.

(5) Same — Despite subsection (1), the regulations made under the *Family Support Plan Act* and in force immediately before subsection (1) comes into force continue in force, with necessary modifications, as if they had been made under this Act and they may be amended or revoked under this Act by the Lieutenant Governor in Council.

74. Commencement — This Act comes into force on a day to be named by proclamation of the Lieutenant Governor.

75. Short title — The short title of this Act is the *Family Responsibility and Support Arrears Enforcement Act, 1996*.

Family
Responsibility

ONT. REG. 176/98 — COST OF LIVING ADJUSTMENTS — METHODS OF CALCULATION

made under the *Family Responsibility and Support Arrears Enforcement Act, 1996*

O. Reg. 176/98

1. The following manners of calculating cost of living adjustments required by a support order or a support deduction order are prescribed for the purposes of subsections 7(4) to (7) of the Act:

1. A calculation made by applying cost of living adjustment factors derived from any part of the Consumer Price Index.

2. A calculation made by applying either the greater or the lesser of,

   i. a percentage change in the payor's or recipient's income and

   ii. a percentage change in the Consumer Price Index,

as specified in the support order or support deduction order.

3. A calculation made by applying a rate of increase or decrease specified in the support order or support deduction order.

4. A calculation made in accordance with the methods specified in Quebec legislation dealing with cost of living adjustments to support orders.

Family Respons. Regs

ONT. REG. 167/97 — FAMILY RESPONSIBILITY AND SUPPORT ARREARS ENFORCEMENT REGULATION

made under the *Family Responsibility and Support Arrears Enforcement Act, 1996*

O. Reg. 167/97, as am. O. Reg. 359/97.

General

Termination of Support Obligation

1. (1) For the purposes of subsection 8(2) of the Act (notice of payor's death), notice of the payor's death must be given in writing and be accompanied by a copy of the death certificate, a funeral notice, a copy of the certificate of appointment of estate trustee or a letter from the solicitor for the payor's estate.

(2) The notice and accompanying information must be sufficient to identify the deceased person as the payor.

O. Reg. 359/97.

1.1 For the purposes of paragraph 1 of subsection 8(3) of the Act (agreement re termination), the matters agreed upon by the recipient and payor must be set out in writing and the agreement must be signed by the recipient and payor.

O. Reg. 359/97.

2. (1) For the purposes of subsection 8(4) of the Act, notice that a support obligation under a support order or support deduction order is terminated must be in writing and must contain the following information:

1. The case number assigned to the support order by the Director's office.

2. The payor's full name.

3. The recipient's full name.

4. The telephone number of the party submitting the notice.

5. Information sufficient to identify the specific support obligation that is terminated including the date of the support order to which the support obligation relates.

6. The reason for the termination.

7. The date of the termination.

(2) The notice must be given as soon as possible after the support obligation is terminated and may be given before the support obligation is terminated.

3. (1) The Director shall notify the recipient when the Director receives notice from the payor that a support obligation is terminated and shall request that the recipient confirm the notice.

(2) The Director is not required to request confirmation of the notice if the support obligation terminates on a calendar date specified in the support order.

(3) A recipient who agrees with the notice shall give the Director confirmation in writing.

4. (1) Until the Director receives confirmation of the notice, the support recipient and support payor under the support order or support deduction order are considered not to agree that the support obligation is terminated as set out in the notice.

(2) If the recipient confirms part, but not all, of the notice, the parties are considered to have agreed that the support obligation is terminated to the extent of the confirmation.

5. (1) The Director shall notify the payor when the Director receives notice or confirmation from the recipient that a support obligation is terminated.

(2) The Director is not required to notify the payor if the support obligation terminates on a calendar date specified in the support order.

6. If a payor's or recipient's most recent address as it is shown in the records in the Director's office is outside Ontario, the Director may send the notice referred to in subsection 3(1) or 5(1) to an office or person in the other jurisdiction performing similar functions to those of the Director.

Support Deduction Orders

7. (1) A support deduction order shall be in Form 1.

(2) A support deduction order information form shall be in Form 2.

(3) The payor and the recipient shall complete Parts A and B of Form 2 before the support deduction order is made.

(4) Despite subsection (3), if the payor has not responded to the motion, application or petition, the recipient alone shall complete Parts A and B of Form 2.

(5) The clerk or registrar of the court shall ensure that Parts A and B of Form 2 are completed before the support deduction order is made.

(6) The clerk or registrar shall complete Part C of Form 2 after the support deduction order is made.

8. For the purposes of subsections 11(2) and (3) of the Act (information re payor, income source), the prescribed information is all the information in Part A of the Support Deduction Order Information Form.

Income Sources

9. The following information is prescribed for the purposes of subsection 25(1) of the Act (duty to inform re payment interruption):

    1. The case number assigned to the support deduction order by the Director's office.

    2. The payor's full name.

    3. The name and address of the income source.

    4. The name and telephone number of a contact person for the income source.

    5. A statement indicating whether the payments are terminated or interrupted and the date of the termination or interruption.

    6. The reason for the termination or interruption.

    7. If the payments are interrupted, the date on which the payments are expected to resume, if the income source knows the date.

    8. The name and address of any other income sources for the payor, if the income source knows of any.

10. A notice under subsection 26(1) of the Act that an individual, corporation or other entity is not an income source shall be in Form 5.

Suspension Orders

11. An order to suspend the operation of a support deduction order shall be in Form 3.

12. (1) If a court requires a payor to post security under clause 28(3)(b) of the Act, the payor shall post the security with the Director by the earlier of,

    (a) the day on which the first support payment under the support order is due after the suspension order is made; or

    (b) 10 days after the suspension order is made.

(2) The following forms of security are prescribed for the purposes of subsection 28(6) of the Act:

    1. A money order payable to the Director.

    2. A bank draft or certified cheque, payable to the Director and drawn on a bank listed in Schedule I or II to the *Bank Act* (Canada), the Province of Ontario Savings Office, a loan or trust corporation registered under the *Loan and Trust Corporations Act* or a credit union as defined in section 1 of the *Credit Unions and Caisses Populaires Act, 1994*.

    3. A cheque payable to the Director and drawn on a lawyer's trust account.

(3) The payor shall give the Director the following information and documents when posting the security:

    1. The payor's full name, address and telephone number.

    2. The recipient's full name and, if known by the payor, the recipient's address.

    3. A copy of the suspension order or the court endorsement on the record setting out the terms of the order.

4. The date on which the suspension order was made.

5. The case number assigned to the support deduction order by the Director's office, if known by the payor.

13. (1) The Director shall use security that is realized under subsection 28(13) of the Act to make payments to the recipient until regular payments in compliance with the support order are established to the satisfaction of the Director.

(2) The Director shall pay to the payor as soon as is practical the amount of any security that remains when the regular payments are established to the satisfaction of the Director. The payment shall be made at the most recent address of the payor as shown on the records in the Director's office.

Suspension of Drivers' Licences

13.1 An order that the Director refrain from directing the suspension of a payor's driver's licence shall be in Form 6.

O. Reg. 359/97.

Financial Statement and Proof of Income

14. A financial statement under subsection 40(1) or 41(1) of the Act shall be in Form 4.

15. The following types of proof of income are prescribed for the purposes of subsections 40(1) and 41(1) of the Act:

1. Either,

   i. a copy of the payor's income tax returns that were filed with the Department of National Revenue for the past three taxation years, together with a copy of all material filed with the returns and a copy of any notices of assessment or re-assessment received from the Department for those years, or

   ii. a statement from the Department of National Revenue that the payor has not filed any income tax returns for the past three taxation years.

2. Copies of pay cheques, pay stubs or other pay statements for the three consecutive pay periods immediately preceding the date of the financial statement.

3. A copy of the financial statements for any business in which the payor has held an interest during the 12 months immediately preceding the date of the financial statement.

4. Letters from the payor's sources of income verifying the payor's income for the three consecutive payments made to the payor immediately before the date of the financial statement. For the purposes of this paragraph, a source of income may be a person who is not an income source within the meaning of the Act.

5. Such other documents as may be necessary to verify the information set out in the financial statement.

Service and Delivery of Documents

16. (1) Service on the Director of a document under the Act may be made by personal delivery, by ordinary mail or by telephone facsimile.

(2) Anything required to be given to the Director in writing under the Act must be delivered by personal delivery, by ordinary mail or by telephone facsimile.

(3) Service on the Director of a document under the Act shall be deemed to have been made five days after the date of service as determined in accordance with the Rules of Civil Procedure made under the *Courts of Justice Act*.

17. (1) Service of a document by the Director under the Act may be made,

(a) by personal service, by ordinary mail, by telephone facsimile or by another form of electronic transmission addressed to the person at the person's most recent address as shown in the records in the Director's office;

(b) by service on the person's solicitor of record; or

(c) by depositing a copy of the document at a document exchange in which the person or the solicitor is a member or subscriber.

(2) Documents that must or may be given to a payor, recipient or income source by the Director under the Act must be delivered,

(a) by personal delivery, by ordinary mail, by telephone facsimile or by another form of electronic transmission addressed to the payor, recipient or income source at the most recent address as shown in the records in the Director's office;

(b) by delivery to the solicitor of record for the payor, recipient or income source; or

(c) by depositing a copy of the document at a document exchange in which the payor, recipient, income source or solicitor is a member or subscriber.

(3) Service by ordinary mail on a payor, recipient or income source shall be deemed to have been made five days after the date of service as determined under the Rules of Civil Procedure made under the *Courts of Justice Act*.

(4) If there is a conflict between this section and the rules of court, the rules of court prevail.

17.1 Service of a notice under Part V of the Act on a payor must be made by ordinary mail,

(a) addressed to the payor at his or her most recent address as shown in the records in the Director's office; and

(b) addressed to the payor at his or her most recent address as shown in the records of the Registrar of Motor Vehicles, if this address is different than the address described in clause (a).

O. Reg. 359/97.

18. (1) Service on the Crown of a notice of a support deduction order or a notice of garnishment must be made,

(a) by personal service on the chief financial officer of the applicable administrative unit of the Crown or with an employee of the chief financial officer; or

(b) by ordinary mail, by telephone facsimile or by another form of electronic transmission addressed to the chief financial officer at the head office of the applicable administrative unit of the Crown.

(2) Notice of a support deduction order shall be deemed to have been served on the Crown on the day that is 30 days after the actual date of service.

Application of Payments

19. Money paid on account of a support order and support deduction order shall be credited in the following order:

    1. To the principal of the most recent support accrual due and then to any interest owing on that principal.

    2. To the principal balance outstanding and then to any interest owing on that principal in the manner set out in paragraph 1.

Consumer Reporting Information

20. The following information may be disclosed by the Director to a consumer reporting agency:

    1. Current address of payor as shown in the records in the Director's office.

    2. The payor's date of birth.

    3. The Family Responsibility Office case number.

Repeal and Commencement

21. (1) Ontario Regulations 765/91 and 475/93 are repealed.

(2) Despite subsection (1), the forms to Ontario Regulation 765/91 may continue to be used, where appropriate, instead of the forms to this Regulation until January 31, 1998.

22. This Regulation comes into force on the day section 63 of the *Family Responsibility and Support Arrears Enforcement Act, 1996* is proclaimed in force.

SCHEDULE [1]

Name of Court/*Nom du tribunal*....................................

REFRAINING ORDER/*ORDONNANCE RESTRICTIVE*

Location/Lieu....................................

Family Responsibility and Support Arrears Enforcement Act/*Loi sur les obligations familiales et l'exécution des arriérés d'aliments*

Court file no./*No de dossier du tribunal*

Form/*Formule 6*

Judge/*Juge*..

Date..

Between:/*Entre:*

Applicant/Petitioner/Plaintiff *Requérant/Demandeur*

and/*et*

Respondent/Defendant *Intimé/Défendeur*

Refraining Order/*Ordonnance Restrictive*

1. THIS COURT ORDERS that the Family Responsibility Office shall refrain from directing the Registrar of Motor Vehicles to suspend the driver's licence of

name of payor/*nom du payeur*...

1. LE PRÉSENT TRIBUNAL ORDONNE que le Bureau des obligations familiales s'abstienne d'ordonner au registrateur des véhicules automobiles de suspendre le permis de conduire de

Conditional on the payor complying with the following terms:

si le payeur se conforme aux conditions suivantes:

- Commence an Application to Vary within 20 days from the date of this order/*Introduction d'une requête en modification dans les 20 jours qui suivent la date de la présente ordonnance.*
- Payment of ongoing support of $ .... /*Versement des obligations alimentaires courantes de*.......... $/per/*par* timeperiod/*période*..........
- Payment of $ .... *Versement, au titre des arriérés, de* .... $/on account of arrears per/*par* timeperiod/*période*..........
- Lump sum payment(s) of $ .... /*Versement(s) d'une (de) somme(s) forfaitaire(s) de*..........$/and $ .... /*et de* .... $ by/*par* .... date .... and/*et* .... date ....
- Other/*Autre* ....

2. THIS COURT ORDERS that this order shall automatically terminate six months from the date of this order.

2. LE PRÉSENT TRIBUNAL ORDONNE que la présente ordonnance prend fin automatiquement dans six mois à compter de la date de la présente ordonnance.

Signature of Judge, Registrar or Clerk of the Court/*Signature de juge ou du greffier du tribunal*...

Note:

1. If an Application to Vary is not commenced within 20 days from the date of this order, the order automatically terminates.

2. If you do not comply with all the terms of the refraining order, a second notice to suspend your driver's licence may be issued.

3. This order may be extended for a further three months period upon motion to the court that made this order on notice to the Family Responsibility Office.

Remarque:

1. Si une requête en modification n'est pas introduite dans les 20 jours qui suivent la date de la présente ordonnance, l'ordonnance prend fin automatiquement.

2. Si vous ne vous conformez pas à toutes les conditions de l'ordonnance restrictive, un deuxième avis de suspension de votre permis de conduire peut être délivré.

3. La présente ordonnance peut être prorogée d'une période supplémentaire de trois mois sur motion présentée devant le tribunal qui a rendu la présente ordonnance et sur avis donné au Bureau des obligations familiiales.

O. Reg. 359/97, s. 3.

ONT. REG 160/00 — FEES CHARGED BY DIRECTOR

made under the *Family Responsibility and Support Arrears Enforcement Act, 1996*

O. Reg. 160/00

1. In this Regulation,

"confirmation of identity letter" means a letter issued by the Director stating that a named person is not the same person as another named person against whom the Director has caused a writ of seizure and sale to be issued and filed with a sheriff; (« lettre de confirmation d'identité »)

"Director statement of arrears" means the Director's statutory declaration setting out the amount of support arrears owed by a payor that have accrued while the support order (including any related support deduction order) is filed in the Director's office; (« état de l'arriéré dressé par le directeur »)

"direct payment" means a payment that is made by the payor directly to the recipient without passing through or being recorded by the Family Responsibility Office. (« versement direct »)

2. (1) Fees charged by the Director are payable as shown in the following Table, subject to section 3:

TABLE

Action Taken or Service Provided	Fee
Issuing Director's statement of arrears	$ 25.00
Processing post-dated cheque	10.00
Issuing confirmation of identity letter	150.00
Adjusting arrears records as a result of a direct payment	100.00
Step taken by Director to enforce a support order (including any related support deduction order) in response to persistent or wilful default: — under section 37 of Act — under section 41 of Act — under section 42 of Act — under section 45 of Act — under Rule 29 of *Family Law Rules* — under Part III of *Family Orders and Agreements Enforcement Assistance Act* (Canada)	400.00

(2) If the Director takes more than one step during a nine-month period to enforce a support order (including any related support deduction order) in response to persistent or wilful default, the total fee for those steps shall not exceed $400.

3. (1) No fee is payable for issuing the first Director's statement of arrears in respect of a support order (including any related support deduction order) that is requested by any of the following:

> 1. The payor or a lawyer or other person authorized by the payor to act on the payor's behalf.

> 2. The recipient or a lawyer or other person authorized by the recipient to act on the recipient's behalf.

> 3. A person or body listed in subsection 14(1) of the Act.

(2) No fee is payable for issuing a Director's statement of arrears that is requested by a support enforcement agency in a reciprocating state under the *Reciprocal Enforcement of Support Orders Act*.

(3) No fee is payable for adjusting an arrears record as a result of a direct payment that is made before the Director first registers the support order or within three months after the Director first registers it.

4. *This Regulation comes into force on April 1, 2000.*

GARNISHMENT, ATTACHMENT AND PENSION DIVERSION ACT

An Act to provide for the garnishment or attachment of Her Majesty in right of Canada and for the diversion of pension benefits payable by Her Majesty in right of Canada under certain enactments

R.S.C. 1985, c. G-2, as am. R.S.C. 1985, c. 3 (2nd Supp.), s. 29; S.C. 1992, c. 1, s. 141 (Sched. IV, item 1); 1997, c. 1, ss. 24-40; 2000, c. 12, ss. 120, 121.

Short Title

1. Short title — This Act may be cited as the *Garnishment, Attachment and Pension Diversion Act*.

PART I — GARNISHMENT AND ATTACHMENT PROCEEDINGS

Interpretation

2. Definitions — In this Part,

"debtor", in respect of a garnishee summons, means the person whose salary or remuneration is sought to be garnisheed; ("débiteur")

"garnishment" includes attachment; (Version anglaise seulement)

"Her Majesty" means Her Majesty in right of Canada; ("Sa Majesté ")

"Minister", in relation to any provision of this Part, means the member or members of the Queen's Privy Council for Canada designated by the Governor in Council as the Minister or Ministers for the purposes of that provision; ("ministre")

"provincial garnishment law" means the law of general application of a province relating to garnishment that is in force at the time in question. ("droit ...")

1997, c. 1, s. 24.

Garnishment of Her Majesty

3. Her Majesty in right of Canada may be garnisheed — Notwithstanding any provision of any other Act of Parliament preventing the garnishment of Her Majesty, Her Majesty may be garnisheed, subject to and in accordance with this Part and any regulation made thereunder.

DIVISION I — DEPARTMENTS AND CERTAIN CROWN CORPORATIONS

4. Definitions — In this Division,

"department" has the meaning assigned by paragraphs (*a*), (*a*.1), (*b*) and (*d*) of the definition "department" in section 2 of the *Financial Administration Act*; ("ministère")

"garnishee summons" includes any document or court order of like import; ("bref ...")

"pay period" means, in respect of any particular person, the period commencing on the day following the day that that person's salary cheque is normally dated and ending on the day that his next salary cheque is normally dated; ("période ...")

"prescribed" means prescribed by regulations made under this Division; ("prescrit")

"salary" means

    (a) in the case of a judge to whom the *Judges Act* applies, the salary payable under that Act, or

    (b) in the case of any other person,

        (i) the basic pay payable to that person for the performance of the regular duties of a position or office, and

        (ii) any amount payable as allowances, special remuneration, payment for overtime or other compensation or as a gratuity,

    excluding any amount deemed to be or to have been excluded from that person's salary pursuant to regulations made under paragraph 12(*b*). ("traitement")

1992, c. 1, s. 141, Sched. IV, item 1.

5. Garnishment of salaries, remuneration — Her Majesty is, subject to this Division and any regulation made thereunder, bound by provincial garnishment law in respect of

    (a) salaries, and

    (b) remuneration as fees, honoraria or other payments of like import, in respect of any office or position or in respect of the performance of any services

payable to judges to whom the *Judges Act* applies, or payable to any other person, excluding corporations, on behalf of a department or by a Crown corporation prescribed under paragraph 12(*c*) for the purposes of this Division.

6. (1) Service binds Her Majesty — Subject to this Division, service on Her Majesty of a garnishee summons, together with a copy of the judgment or order against the debtor and an application in the prescribed form, binds Her Majesty fifteen days after the day on which those documents are served.

(2) When service is effective — A garnishee summons served on Her Majesty is of no effect unless it is served on Her Majesty in the first thirty days following the first day on which it could have been validly served on Her Majesty.

1997, c. 1, s. 25.

7. (1) Where documents must be served on Her Majesty — Service of documents on Her Majesty in connection with garnishment proceedings permitted by this Division must be effected at the place specified in the regulations.

(2) Method of service on Her Majesty — In addition to any method of service permitted by the law of a province, service of documents on Her Majesty under subsection (1) may be effected by registered mail, whether within or outside the province, or by any other method prescribed.

(3) Where service by registered mail — Where service of a document on Her Majesty is effected by registered mail, the document shall be deemed to be served on the day of its receipt by Her Majesty.

8. Moneys bound by service of garnishee summons — For the purposes of garnishment proceedings permitted by this Division, service of a garnishee summons binds Her Majesty in respect of the following money to be paid by Her Majesty to the debtor named in the garnishee summons:

    (a) in the case of a salary,

        (i) the salary to be paid on the last day of the second pay period next following the pay period in which Her Majesty is bound by the garnishee summons, and

        (ii) where the garnishee summons has continuing effect under the law of the province, the salary to be paid on the last day of each subsequent pay period; or

    (b) in the case of remuneration described in paragraph 5(*b*),

        (i) the remuneration payable, in respect of the department or Crown corporation named in the application referred to in section 6, on the fifteenth day following the day on which Her Majesty is bound by the garnishee summons, and

        (ii) either

           (A) any remuneration becoming payable in respect of that department or Crown corporation in the thirty days following the fifteenth day after the day on which Her Majesty is bound by the garnishee summons that is owing on that fifteenth day or that becomes owing in the fourteen days following that fifteenth day, or

           (B) where the garnishee summons has continuing effect under the law of the province, any remuneration becoming payable in respect of that department or Crown corporation subsequent to the fifteenth day after the day on which Her Majesty is bound by the garnishee summons.

1997, c. 1, s. 26.

9. [Repealed 1997, c. 1, s. 26.]

10. Time period for Her Majesty's response to a garnishee summons — Her Majesty has the following time period within which to respond to a garnishee summons:

    (a) in the case of a salary, fifteen days, or such lesser number of days as is prescribed, after the last day of the second pay period next following the pay period in which Her Majesty is bound by the garnishee summons; or

    (b) in the case of remuneration described in paragraph 5(*b*), fifteen days, or such lesser number of days as is prescribed, after the day on which the remuneration is garnisheed.

1997, c. 1, s. 27.

11. (1) Method of response to garnishee summons — In addition to any method of responding to a garnishee summons permitted by provincial garnishment law, Her Majesty may respond to a garnishee summons by registered mail or by any other method prescribed.

(2) Where response is by registered mail — Where Her Majesty responds to a garnishee summons by registered mail, the receipt issued in accordance with regulations relating to registered mail made under the *Canada Post Corporation Act* shall be received in evidence and is, unless the contrary is shown, proof that Her Majesty has responded to the garnishee summons.

(3) Effect of payment into court — A payment into court by Her Majesty under this section is a good and sufficient discharge of liability, to the extent of the payment.

(4) Recovery of overpayment to debtor — Where, in honouring a garnishee summons, Her Majesty, through error, pays to a debtor by way of salary or remuneration an amount in excess of the amount that Her Majesty should have paid to that debtor, the excess becomes a debt due to Her Majesty by that debtor and may be recovered from the debtor at any time by set-off against future moneys payable to the debtor as salary or remuneration.

1997, c. 1, s. 28.

12. Regulations — The Governor in Council may, on the recommendation of the Minister, make regulations

    (a) specifying the place where service of documents on Her Majesty must be effected in connection with garnishment proceedings permitted by this Division;

    (b) deeming, for the purposes of the definition "salary" in section 4, any amount to be or to have been excluded from a person's salary;

    (c) prescribing Crown corporations for the purposes of this Division; and

    (d) prescribing any other matters that are by this Division to be prescribed.

13. Information to be made available to public — The Minister shall cause information on the manner of commencing garnishment proceedings permitted by this Division to be made available throughout Canada in such a manner that the public will have reasonable access thereto.

DIVISION II — CROWN CORPORATIONS NOT COVERED BY DIVISION I

14. (1) Crown corporations — Subject to subsection (2), in respect of moneys payable by Crown corporations not prescribed under paragraph 12(c) for the purposes of Division I, Her Majesty is bound by provincial garnishment law.

(2) Idem — In respect of Crown corporations to which subsection (1) applies that are prescribed under subsection (3) for the purposes of this subsection, Her Majesty is not bound by provincial garnishment law in relation to a "pension benefit" as defined in Part II.

(3) Regulations — The Governor in Council may, on the recommendation of the Minister, make regulations prescribing Crown corporations for the purposes of subsection (2).

DIVISION III — CANADIAN FORCES

15. Canadian Forces — In respect of pay and allowances payable to members of the Canadian Forces, Her Majesty is bound by provincial garnishment law to the extent, in the manner, and subject to the terms and conditions that may be provided by or under regulations made by the Governor in Council pursuant to the *National Defence Act*.

DIVISION IV — SENATE, HOUSE OF COMMONS AND LIBRARY OF PARLIAMENT

16. Definitions — In this Division,

"garnishee summons" includes any document or court order of like import; ("bref ...")

"pay period" means, in respect of any particular person, the period commencing on the day following the day that that person's salary cheque is normally dated and ending on the day that his next salary cheque is normally dated; ("période ...")

"prescribed" means prescribed by regulations made under this Division; ("prescrit ...")

"salary" means

(a) in the case of a member of the Senate or House of Commons, all moneys payable under the *Parliament of Canada Act*, the *Salaries Act* and any appropriation Act, other than moneys not included in computing the member's income for the purposes of Part I of the *Income Tax Act*, or

(b) in the case of the staff of the Senate, House of Commons or Library of Parliament or the staff of members of the Senate or House of Commons, or in the case of any other person paid out of moneys appropriated by Parliament for use by the Senate, House of Commons or Library of Parliament,

(i) the basic pay payable to a person for the performance of the regular duties of a position or office, and

(ii) any amount payable as allowances, special remuneration, payment for overtime or other compensation or as a gratuity,

excluding any amount deemed to be or to have been excluded from that person's salary pursuant to regulations made under paragraph 24(*b*). ("traitement")

17. Garnishment of salaries, remuneration — The Senate, House of Commons and Library of Parliament are, subject to this Division and any regulation made thereunder, bound by provincial garnishment law in respect of

(a) salaries; and

(b) remuneration to persons, excluding corporations, as fees, honoraria or other payments of like import, in respect of any office or position or in respect of the performance of any services.

18. (1) Service binds the Senate, House of Commons or Library of Parliament — Subject to this Division, service on the Senate, House of Commons or Library of Parliament of a garnishee summons, together with a copy of the judgment or order against the debtor and an application in the prescribed form, binds the Senate, House of Commons or Library of Parliament, as the case may be, fifteen days after the day on which those documents are served.

(2) When service is effective — A garnishee summons served on the Senate, House of Commons or Library of Parliament is of no effect unless it is served on the Senate, House of Commons or Library of Parliament, as the case may be, in the first thirty days following the first day on which it could have been validly served on the Senate, House of Commons or Library of Parliament, as the case may be.

1997, c. 1, s. 29.

19. (1) Place of service — Service of documents on the Senate, House of Commons or Library of Parliament in connection with garnishment proceedings permitted by this Division must be effected at the place specified in the regulations.

(2) Method of service — In addition to any method of service permitted by the law of a province, service of documents on the Senate, House of Commons or Library of Parliament under subsection (1) may be effected by registered mail, whether within or outside the province, or by any other method prescribed.

(3) Where service by registered mail — Where service of a document on the Senate, House of Commons or Library of Parliament is effected by registered mail, the document shall be deemed to be served on the day of its receipt by the Senate, House of Commons or Library of Parliament, as the case may be.

20. [Repealed 1997, c. 1, s. 30.]

21. Moneys bound by service of garnishee summons — For the purposes of garnishment proceedings permitted by this Division, service of a garnishee summons is binding in respect of the following money to be paid to the debtor named in the garnishee summons:

(a) in the case of a salary,

(i) the salary to be paid on the last day of the second pay period next following the pay period in which the Senate, House of Commons or Library of Parliament, as the case may be, is bound by the garnishee summons, and

(ii) where the garnishee summons has continuing effect under the law of the province, the salary to be paid on the last day of each subsequent pay period; or

(b) in the case of remuneration described in paragraph 17(*b*),

(i) the remuneration payable on the fifteenth day following the day on which the Senate, House of Commons or Library of Parliament, as the case may be, is bound by the garnishee summons, and

(ii) either

(A) any remuneration becoming payable in the thirty days following the fifteenth day after the day on which the Senate, House of Commons or Library of Parliament, as the case may be, is bound by the garnishee summons that is owing on that fifteenth day or that becomes owing in the fourteen days following that fifteenth day, or

(B) where the garnishee summons has continuing effect under the law of the province, any remuneration becoming payable subsequent to the fifteenth day after the day on which the Senate, House of Commons or Library of Parliament, as the case may be, is bound by the garnishee summons.

1997, c. 1, s. 30.

22. Time period to respond to a garnishee summons — The Senate, House of Commons or Library of Parliament has the following time period within which to respond to a garnishee summons:

(a) in the case of a salary, fifteen days, or such lesser number of days as is prescribed, after the last day of the second pay period next following the pay period in which the Senate, House of Commons or Library of Parliament is bound by the garnishee summons; or

(b) in the case of remuneration described in paragraph 17(b), fifteen days, or such lesser number of days as is prescribed, after the day on which the remuneration is garnisheed.

1997, c. 1, s. 30.

23. (1) Method of response — In addition to any method of responding to a garnishee summons permitted by provincial garnishment law, the Senate, House of Commons or Library of Parliament may respond to a garnishee summons by registered mail or by any other method prescribed.

(2) Where response is by registered mail — Where the Senate, House of Commons or Library of Parliament responds to a garnishee summons by registered mail, the receipt issued in accordance with regulations relating to registered mail made under the *Canada Post Corporation Act* shall be received in evidence and is, unless the contrary is shown, proof that the Senate, House of Commons or Library of Parliament, as the case may be, has responded to the garnishee summons.

(3) Effect of payment into court — A payment into court by the Senate, House of Commons or Library of Parliament under this section is a good and sufficient discharge of liability, to the extent of the payment.

(4) Recovery of overpayment to debtor — Where, in honouring a garnishee summons, the Senate, House of Commons or Library of Parliament, through error, pays to a debtor by way of salary or remuneration an amount in excess of the amount that it should have paid to that debtor, the excess becomes a debt due to the Senate, House of Commons or Library of Parliament, as the case may be, by that debtor and may be recovered from the debtor at any time by set-off against future moneys payable to the debtor as salary or remuneration.

1997, c. 1, s. 31.

24. Regulations — The Governor in Council may, on the recommendation of the Minister, made after consultation between the Minister and the Speaker of the Senate and the Speaker of the House of Commons, make regulations

(a) specifying the place where service of documents on the Senate, House of Commons or Library of Parliament must be effected in connection with garnishment proceedings permitted by this Division;

(b) deeming, for the purposes of the definition "salary" in section 16, any amount to be or to have been excluded from a person's salary; and

(c) prescribing any other matters that are by this Division to be prescribed.

25. Information to be made available to public — The Speaker of the Senate and the Speaker of the House of Commons shall cause information on the manner of commencing garnishment proceedings permitted by this Division to be made available throughout Canada in such a manner that the public will have reasonable access thereto.

26. No execution — No execution shall issue on a judgment given against the Senate, House of Commons or Library of Parliament in garnishment proceedings permitted by this Part.

DIVISION V — GENERAL

27. Inconsistency between federal and provincial law — In the event of any inconsistency between this Part, any other Act of Parliament or a regulation made under this Part or under any other Act of Parliament, and the provincial garnishment law, the provincial garnishment law is overridden to the extent of the inconsistency.

28. No execution against Her Majesty — No execution shall issue on a judgment given against Her Majesty in garnishment proceedings permitted by this Part.

29. Regulations — The Governor in Council may,

    (a) on the recommendation of the Minister, make regulations generally for carrying out the purposes and provisions of Divisions I, II and III; and

    (b) on the recommendation of the Minister, made after consultation between the Minister and the Speaker of the Senate and the Speaker of the House of Commons, make regulations generally for carrying out the purposes and provisions of Division IV.

30. Prohibition — No employee may be dismissed, suspended or laid off solely on the ground that garnishment proceedings permitted by this Part may be or have been taken with respect to him.

PART II — DIVERSION OF PENSION BENEFITS TO SATISFY FINANCIAL SUPPORT ORDERS

Application of Part

31. Application of Part — This Part applies only in respect of the enforcement of financial support orders against pension benefits payable pursuant to the superannuation Acts and like enactments referred to in the schedule.

Interpretation

32. (1) Definitions — In this Part,

"applicant" means a person by or on behalf of whom an application is made to the Minister for a diversion of a pension benefit under this Part; ("requérant")

"application" means, except in subsection 35.1(2), sections 35.3 and 35.4, subsection 41(2) and paragraph 46(c), a request in writing to the Minister for a diversion of a pension benefit under this Part, containing the prescribed information, accompanied by a certified copy of the financial support order on which the application is based and any prescribed additional documentation; ("requête")

"financial support order" means, subject to subsection (2), an order or judgment for maintenance, alimony or support, including an order or judgment for arrears of payments, made pursuant to the *Divorce Act*, chapter D-8 of the Revised Statutes of Canada, 1970, or the *Divorce Act* or pursuant to the laws of a province relating to family financial support or the enforcement of family financial support; ("ordonnance de soutien financier")

"Minister", in relation to any provision of this Part and items 12 and 16 of the schedule, means the member or members of the Queen's Privy Council for Canada designated by the Governor in Council as the Minister or Ministers for the purposes of that provision or those items; ("ministre")

"net pension benefit" means a pension benefit minus the prescribed deductions; ("prestation nette ...")

"pension benefit" means any

(a) pension,

(b) annual allowance,

(c) annuity,

(d) lump sum return of pension contributions, including interest, if any,

(e) gratuity,

(f) cash termination allowance,

(g) withdrawal allowance, including interest, if any, or

(h) transfer value

payable pursuant to an enactment referred to in the schedule, and includes any benefit payable under the *Supplementary Retirement Benefits Act* or the *Public Service Pension Adjustment Act*, chapter P-33 of the Revised Statutes of Canada, 1970, in respect of that pension, annual allowance or annuity; ("prestation de ...")

"prescribed" means prescribed by regulation made under this Part; ("prescrit" ...)

"recipient" means

(a) in respect of a pension benefit referred to in any of paragraphs (*a*) to (*g*) of the definition **"pension benefit"**, a child or other person to whom the pension benefit is immediately payable, but does not include a child or other person whose entitlement to the pension benefit is based on his or her status as a survivor of the person who was originally entitled to the pension benefit or would have been entitled to it had death not intervened, or

(b) in respect of a pension benefit referred to in paragraph (*h*) of the definition **"pension benefit"**, a person who is entitled to the pension benefit. ("prestataire")

(2) Financial support order — For the purposes of this Part, the Minister shall disregard a component of a financial support order the dollar value of which cannot be readily ascertained from the financial support order itself or from the Minister's records relating to the recipient's pension benefit.

(3) Interpretation of the provincial law — With respect to the expression "the law of that province" in paragraphs 36(*c*) and (*e*), where the law of the province refers to the percentage or the maximum percentage of a pension that is to be or may be garnisheed, attached or diverted, the reference to "pension", or equivalent expression, in the law of the province shall be construed, for the purpose of this Part, to mean "net pension benefit" as defined in this section.

(4) Interpretation of financial support orders — Where a financial support order is expressed in terms of a percentage of a recipient's pension, the reference to "pension", or equivalent expression, in the financial support order shall be construed, for the purpose of this Part, to mean "net pension benefit" as defined in this section.

R.S.C. 1985, c. 3 (2nd Supp.), s. 29; 1997, c. 1, s. 32; 2000, c. 12, s. 120

Conditions for Diversion of Pension Benefits

33. (1) Application for diversion — Subject to this Part and the regulations, where

(a) any court in Canada of competent jurisdiction has, either before or after January 1, 1984,

(i) made a financial support order requiring a person to pay an amount to a child or other person, or

(ii) made an order permitting the enforcement of a financial support order described in subparagraph (i),

and the order referred to in subparagraph (i) or (ii) is valid and subsisting, and

(b) the person against whom the financial support order has been made is a recipient,

a person named in the financial support order may make an application to the Minister for diversion of a pension benefit payable to the recipient.

(2) Idem — An application may be made by a person on behalf of another person in accordance with regulations made under paragraph 46(a).

(3) Diversion of pension benefits — When an application made under this section has been duly completed, the Minister shall, not later than the first day of the fourth month following the month in which the application was duly completed, divert an amount or amounts computed in accordance with sections 36 to 40 and the regulations from any net pension benefit that is payable to the recipient named in the application, and any amount so diverted shall be paid, subject to subsection (4), to the applicant or to such other person as is designated in the financial support order.

(4) Where applicant under 18 years of age — Where, pursuant to this section, a diverted amount is to be paid to an applicant who is under eighteen years of age, payment thereof shall instead be made to the person having the custody and control of that applicant or, where there is no person having custody and control of the applicant, to such person as the Minister may direct.

2000, c. 12, s. 121

34. (1) Minister to notify recipient where a diversion is to be made — Forthwith after receiving a duly completed application, the Minister shall cause a written notification, containing the prescribed information, to be sent in prescribed manner to the recipient named in the application, at the recipient's latest known address, advising that an application for diversion of the recipient's pension benefit has been received and that a diversion will be made in accordance with this Part.

(2) Recipient deemed to have received notification — The notification required under subsection (1) shall be deemed to have been received by the recipient one month after it has been sent to the recipient.

35. Conditions for diversion of pension benefits — No diversion of pension benefits under this Part shall be made unless the amount to be diverted is at least

(a) twenty-five dollars per annum, in the case of periodic diversion payments; or

(b) twenty-five dollars, in the case of a lump sum diversion payment.

1997, c. 1, s. 33.

35.1 (1) Where pension benefit not immediately payable — *Public Service Superannuation Act* — Where a person against whom there is a valid and subsisting financial support order

(a) has ceased to be employed in the Public Service,

(b) is not a recipient but has exercised an option for a deferred annuity under section 12 or 13 of the *Public Service Superannuation Act* or is entitled to exercise an option for a deferred annuity under either of those sections, and

(c) has reached 50 years of age but has not yet reached 60 years of age,

a person entitled to support under the financial support order may apply for an order under subsection (2) to any court in Canada that has jurisdiction to make a financial support order.

(2) Order — A court to whom an application is made under subsection (1) may make an order deeming the person against whom there is a valid and subsisting financial support order to have exercised an option under section 12 or 13 of the *Public Service Superannuation Act* in favour of an annual allowance payable as of the date of the making of the order under this subsection if the court is satisfied that

(a) there is an extended pattern of non-payment of the financial support order; and

(b) the person making the application has taken reasonable steps to enforce the financial support order through other means.

1997, c. 1, s. 33.

35.2 Effect of order — An order made under subsection 35.1(2) shall be deemed for all purposes to have the same effect as if the person to whom the order relates had exercised the option referred to in the order.

1997, c. 1, s. 33.

35.3 Provision of information — On application by a person entitled to support under a valid and subsisting financial support order, the Minister shall, in accordance with the regulations, provide the person with the prescribed information concerning any matter related to the making of an application under subsection 35.1(1).

1997, c. 1, s. 33.

35.4 Application may be made by provincial enforcement service — An application under subsection 35.1(1) or section 35.3 may be made on behalf of a person by any other person or by a provincial enforcement service, within the meaning of section 2 of the *Family Orders and Agreements Enforcement Assistance Act*.

1997, c. 1, s. 33.

Amount of Diversion

36. Rules governing amount of diversion — Where

(a) a financial support order provides only for periodic payments and the recipient's pension benefit consists only of periodic payments, or

(b) a financial support order provides only for a lump sum payment and the recipient's pension benefit consists only of a lump sum payment,

the amount to be diverted from the recipient's net pension benefit shall be governed by the following rules:

(c) where the recipient is domiciled in Canada and ordinarily resident in a province in which there is in force a law of general application permitting garnishment, attachment or diversion of pensions for the enforcement of financial support orders, the amount to be diverted shall be determined in accordance with the law of that province in force at the time of the diversion payment,

(d) where the recipient is domiciled in Canada and ordinarily resident elsewhere than in a province described in paragraph (c), the amount to be diverted shall be the amount required to satisfy the financial support order, up to a maximum of fifty per cent of the recipient's net pension benefit,

(e) where the recipient is domiciled outside Canada and the applicant is ordinarily resident in a province described in paragraph (c), the amount to be diverted shall be determined in accordance with the law of that province in force at the time of the diversion payment,

(f) where the recipient is domiciled outside Canada and the applicant is ordinarily resident in a province other than one described in paragraph (c), the amount to be diverted shall be the amount required to satisfy the financial support order, up to a maximum of fifty per cent of the recipient's net pension benefit, or

(g) where the recipient and the applicant are domiciled outside Canada and are ordinarily resident outside Canada, the amount to be diverted shall be the amount required to satisfy the financial support order, up to a maximum of fifty per cent of the recipient's net pension benefit.

1997, c. 1, s. 34.

37. (1) Lump sum financial support order vs. periodic pension benefit — Where a financial support order provides only for a lump sum payment and the recipient's pension benefit consists only of periodic payments, no diversion shall be made, except as provided in subsection (2).

(2) Circumstances in which diversion shall be made — Where the Minister is of the opinion that it is impossible or impracticable for a financial support order described in subsection (1) to be varied to stipulate periodic payments and the Minister has so notified the applicant and the recipient, a diversion shall be made in the amount of fifty per cent of the recipient's monthly net pension benefit, subject to subsection (3), until

(a) the financial support order has been satisfied in full by the diversion; or

(b) the Minister is satisfied, on receipt of evidence submitted by the applicant or recipient, that the financial support order has been satisfied in full by other means or is no longer valid and subsisting.

(3) Filing of annual statement — Where a diversion described in subsection (2) is made, the applicant must file annually with the Minister, within the prescribed time, a written statement respecting the applicant's continued entitlement to the diversion, containing the prescribed information, signed by the applicant and witnessed by a person of a prescribed category.

(4) Where subsection (3) not complied with — Where subsection (3) is not complied with, the diversion shall be terminated as of the first day of the month following the expiration of the time prescribed under subsection (3), without prejudice to the applicant's right to re-apply under this Part.

38. Financial support order providing for lump sum and periodic payments vs. periodic pension benefit — Where a financial support order provides for a lump sum payment and for periodic payments and the recipient's pension benefit consists only of periodic payments, the two components of the financial support order shall be treated as follows:

(a) the periodic component of the financial support order shall be dealt with in accordance with the rules in paragraphs 36(c) to (g); and

(b) where

(i) the amount diverted pursuant to paragraph (a) is less than fifty per cent of the recipient's net pension benefit, and

(ii) the maximum that could be diverted pursuant to paragraph (a) as a result of the application of the rules in paragraphs 36(c) to (g) exceeds the amount actually diverted pursuant to paragraph (a),

then, in respect of the excess referred to in subparagraph (ii), section 37 applies, with such modifications as the circumstances require, to the lump sum component of the financial support order, but the application of that section may not raise the total diversion under this Part to more than fifty per cent of the recipient's net pension benefit.

1997, c. 1, s. 35.

39. (1) Periodic financial support order vs. lump sum pension benefit — Where a financial support order provides only for periodic payments and the recipient's pension benefit consists only of a lump sum, the Minister shall, forthwith after receiving a duly completed application,

(a) take all reasonable steps to cause payment to the recipient of any portion of the recipient's pension benefit that could be subject to diversion as a result of the application of the rules in paragraphs 36(c) to (g) to be delayed, in accordance with this section; and

(b) cause the applicant to be notified by registered mail that, unless the financial support order is varied in accordance with this section, it will be treated as a financial support order for a lump sum payment of an amount equal to one periodic payment under the original financial support order.

(2) Applicant must seek variation of financial support order — Where, within thirty days of receipt by the applicant of the notification referred to in paragraph (1)(b), the Minister is satisfied, on receipt of evidence submitted by the applicant, that the applicant has applied to court for variation of the financial support order to one providing in whole or in part for a lump sum payment, the Minister shall cause payment of the pension benefit to the recipient to be further delayed for a further period not exceeding ninety days.

(3) When notification deemed to be received by applicant — For purposes of subsection (2), the date set out in an acknowledgment of receipt issued in accordance with regulations relating to registered mail made under the *Canada Post Corporation Act* shall be deemed to be the date of receipt by the applicant of the notification to which that acknowledgment of receipt relates.

(4) Where condition not satisfied — Where the evidence referred to in subsection (2) is not received by the Minister within the period mentioned in that subsection, the Minister shall forthwith treat the application for diversion as an application based on a financial support order for the payment of a lump sum equal to the amount of one periodic payment under the original financial support order.

(5) Applicant must submit varied financial support order to Minister — Where, within ninety days after receiving the evidence referred to in subsection (2), the Minister receives a certified copy of a varied financial support order providing in whole or in part for a lump sum payment, the Minister shall proceed with the application for diversion in accordance with this Part.

(6) Where condition not satisfied — Where a certified copy of the varied financial support order referred to in subsection (5) is not received by the Minister within the period mentioned in that subsection, the Minister shall forthwith treat the application for diversion as an application based on a financial support order for the payment of a lump sum equal to the amount of one periodic payment under the original financial support order.

1997, c. 1, s. 36.

40. Financial support order for lump sum and periodic payments vs. lump sum pension benefit — Where a financial support order provides for a lump sum payment and periodic payments and the recipient's pension benefit consists only of a lump sum, the two components of the financial support order shall be treated as follows:

(a) the lump sum component of the financial support order shall be dealt with in accordance with the rules in paragraphs 36(c) to (g); and

(b) where the maximum that could be diverted pursuant to paragraph (a) as a result of the application of the rules in paragraphs 36(c) to (g) exceeds the amount actually diverted pursuant to paragraph (a), then, in respect of that excess, section 39 applies, with such modifications as the circumstances require, to the periodic component of the financial support order.

1997, c. 1, s. 37.

40.1 Arrears of payment of support — Notwithstanding paragraph 36(d), (f) or (g), subsection 37(2) or section 38, 39 or 40, where the financial support order is an order or judgment for arrears of payments, the amount to be diverted may exceed fifty per cent of the recipient's net pension benefit.

1997, c. 1, s. 38.

General

41. (1) Application for change in amount being diverted or for termination of diversion — Where a diversion is being carried out, either the applicant or the recipient may at any time apply to the Minister, in accordance with the regulations made under paragraph 46(c), for a variation in the amount being diverted or for termination of the diversion.

(2) When variation or termination effective — Notwithstanding a recipient's entitlement under an enactment referred to in the schedule, a variation or termination of a diversion pursuant to an application under subsection (1) is effective only as of the first day of the month following the month in which the Minister receives the duly completed application for variation or termination, as the case may be.

42. (1) Errors in amounts paid — Where a diversion payment made to an applicant is less than the amount that should have been paid to the applicant pursuant to this Part, the amount of the deficiency

(a) to the extent that it was in error paid to the recipient, becomes a debt due to Her Majesty by the recipient, and may be recovered from the recipient at any time by set-off against future pension benefits to be paid to the recipient; and

(b) to the extent that it was in error retained by Her Majesty, becomes a debt due to the applicant by Her Majesty.

(2) Idem — Where a diversion payment made to an applicant is greater than the amount that should have been paid to the applicant pursuant to this Part, the amount of the excess becomes a debt due to Her Majesty by the applicant, and may be recovered from the applicant at any time by set-off against future diversion payments to be paid to the applicant under this Part.

43. Where diversion is less than $10 per month — Where periodic diversion payments under this Part are less than ten dollars per month, the Minister may direct that they be paid in arrears, in equal instalments, either quarterly, semi-annually or annually.

44. Death of recipient — Periodic diversion payments shall terminate at the end of the month in which the recipient dies.

45. Offence — Every person who makes a false or misleading representation to the Minister in any application or other proceeding under this Part is guilty of an offence punishable on summary conviction.

46. Regulations — The Governor in Council may, on the recommendation of the Minister, make regulations

(a) respecting the making of applications by one person on behalf of another, and respecting the payment of diverted amounts to one person for the benefit of another;

(b) respecting the amount or amounts to be diverted from a recipient's net pension benefit and the procedure to be followed in any situation not dealt with in sections 36 to 40;

(b.1) respecting the provision of information for the purposes of section 35.3;

(c) respecting the grounds for, and the procedure relating to applications for, variations in the amount being diverted or for termination of a diversion;

(d) prescribing anything that by this Part is to be prescribed; and

(e) generally for carrying out the purposes and provisions of this Part.

1997, c. 1, s. 39.

47. Information to be made available to the public — The Minister shall cause information on the manner of applying for a diversion under this Part to be made available throughout Canada in such a manner that the public will have reasonable access thereto.

SCHEDULE [1]

The number in square brackets has been editorially added by Carswell.

(Sections 31, 32 and 41)

1.   *Governor General's Act.*

2.   *Lieutenant Governors' Superannuation Act.*

3.   *Members of Parliament Retiring Allowances Act.*

4.   *Judges Act.*

5.   *Diplomatic Service (Special) Superannuation Act.*

6.   *Public Service Superannuation Act.*

7.   *Civil Service Superannuation Act.*

8.   *Canadian Forces Superannuation Act.*

9.   *Defence Services Pension Continuation Act*, R.S.C. 1970, c. D-3.

10. *Royal Canadian Mounted Police Superannuation Act*, Part I.

11. *Royal Canadian Mounted Police Pension Continuation Act*, R.S.C. 1970, c. R-10, Parts II and III.

12. Regulations made by the Governor in Council or the Treasury Board that, in the opinion of the Minister, provide for the payment out of the Consolidated Revenue Fund of a pension to be charged to the Public Service Superannuation Account that is calculated on the basis of length of service of the person to or in respect of whom it was granted or is payable.

13. *Currency, Mint and Exchange Fund Act*, R.S.C. 1952, c. 315, subsection 15(2).

14. *War Veterans Allowance Act*, subsection 28(10).

15. Regulations made under Vote 181 of *Appropriation Act No. 5, 1961.*

16. An appropriation Act of Parliament that, in the opinion of the Minister, provides for the payment of a pension calculated on the basis of length of service of the person to or in respect of whom it was granted or is payable.

17. *Tax Court of Canada Act.*

18. *Special Retirement Arrangements Act.*

1997, c. 1, s. 40.

INCOME TAX ACT

An Act Respecting Income Taxes

REVISED STATUTES OF CANADA 1985, c. 1 (5TH SUPPLEMENT), AS
AMENDED BY 1994, cc. 7, 8, 13, 21, 28, 29, 38, 41; 1995, cc. 1, 3, 11, 17, 18,
21, 38, 46; 1996, cc. 6, 11, 21, 23; 1997, cc. 10, 12, 25, 26; 1998, cc. 19, 21, 34;
1999, cc. 10, 17, 22, 26, 31; 2000, cc. 9, 12, 14, 19, 30; 2001, cc. 16, 17, 27, 41;
2002, cc. 8 [not yet in force], 9.

*[Note: only sections 56(1)(b), 56(1)(c.2), 56(1)(l), 56(1)(l.1), 56.1(1)–(4), 60(b), 60(c.2),
60(o), 60(o.1), 60.1 and 63(1)–(4) are reproduced here.]*

. . . . .

PART I — INCOME TAX

DIVISION B — COMPUTATION OF INCOME

Subdivision d — Other Sources of Income

56. (1) Amounts to be included in income for year — Without restricting the generality of section 3, there shall be included in computing the income of a taxpayer for a taxation year,

. . . . .

(b) **[spousal or child] support** — the total of all amounts each of which is an amount determined by the formula

$$A - (B + C)$$

where

A   is the total of all amounts each of which is a support amount received after 1996 and before the end of the year by the taxpayer from a particular person where the taxpayer and the particular person were living separate and apart at the time the amount was received,

B   is the total of all amounts each of which is a child support amount that became receivable by the taxpayer from the particular person under an agreement or order on or after its commencement day and before the end of the year in respect of a period that began on or after its commencement day, and

C   is the total of all amounts each of which is a support amount received after 1996 by the taxpayer from the particular person and included in the taxpayer's income for a preceding taxation year;

(c), (c.1) [Repealed]

(c.2) **reimbursement of support payments** — an amount received by the taxpayer in the year under a decree, order or judgment of a competent tribunal as a reimbursement of an amount deducted under paragraph 60(b) or (c), or under paragraph 60(c.1) as it applies, in computing the taxpayer's income for the year or a preceding taxation year to decrees, orders and judgments made before 1993;

. . . . .

(l) **legal expenses [awarded or reimbursed]** — amounts received by the taxpayer in the year as

(i) legal costs awarded to the taxpayer by a court on an appeal in relation to an assessment of any tax, interest or penalties referred to in paragraph 60(o),

(ii) reimbursement of costs incurred in relation to a decision of the Canada Employment and Immigration Commission, the Canada Employment and Insurance Commission, a board of referees or an umpire under the *Unemployment Insurance Act* or the *Employment Insurance Act*, or

(iii) reimbursement of costs incurred in relation to an assessment or a decision under the *Canada Pension Plan* or a provincial pension plan as defined in section 3 of that Act,

if with respect to that assessment or decision, as the case may be, an amount has been deducted or may be deductible under paragraph 60(o) in computing the taxpayer's income;

(l.1) **idem** — amounts received by the taxpayer in the year as an award or a reimbursement in respect of legal expenses (other than those relating to a division or settlement of property arising out of, or on a breakdown of, a marriage or common-law partnership) paid to collect or establish a right to a retiring allowance or a benefit under a pension fund or plan (other than a benefit under the *Canada Pension Plan* or a provincial pension plan as defined in section 3 of that Act) in respect of employment;

. . . . .

56.1 (1) Support — For the purposes of paragraph 56(1)(b) and subsection 118(5), where an order or agreement, or any variation thereof, provides for the payment of an amount to a taxpayer or for the benefit of the taxpayer, children in the taxpayer's custody or both the taxpayer and those children, the amount or any part thereof

(a) when payable, is deemed to be payable to and receivable by the taxpayer; and

(b) when paid, is deemed to have been paid to and received by the taxpayer.

(2) Agreement — For the purposes of section 56, this section and subsection 118(5), the amount determined by the formula

$$A - B$$

where

A   is the total of all amounts each of which is an amount (other than an amount that is otherwise a support amount) that became payable by a person in a taxation year, under an order of a competent tribunal or under a written agreement, in respect of an expense (other than an expenditure in respect of a self-contained domestic establishment in which the person resides or an expenditure for the acquisition of tangible property that is not an expenditure on account of a medical or education expense or in respect of the acquisition, improvement or maintenance of a self-contained domestic establishment in which the taxpayer described in paragraph (a) or (b) resides) incurred in the year or the preceding taxation year for the maintenance of a taxpayer, children in the taxpayer's custody or both the taxpayer and those children, where the taxpayer is

(a) the person's spouse or common-law partner or former spouse or common-law partner, or

(b) where the amount became payable under an order made by a competent tribunal in accordance with the laws of a province, an individual who is the parent of a child of whom the person is a natural parent,

and

B   is the amount, if any, by which

(a) the total of all amounts each of which is an amount included in the total determined for A in respect of the acquisition or improvement of a self-contained domestic establishment in which the taxpayer resides, including any payment of principal or interest in respect of a loan made or indebtedness incurred to finance, in any manner whatever, such acquisition or improvement

exceeds

(b) the total of all amounts each of which is an amount equal to $\frac{1}{5}$ of the original principal amount of a loan or indebtedness described in paragraph (a),

is, where the order or written agreement, as the case may be, provides that this subsection and subsection 60.1(2) shall apply to any amount paid or payable thereunder, deemed to be an amount payable to and receivable by the taxpayer as an allowance on a periodic basis, and the taxpayer is deemed to have discretion as to the use of that amount.

(3) Prior payments — For the purposes of this section and section 56, where a written agreement or order of a competent tribunal made at any time in a taxation year provides that an amount received before that time and in the year or the preceding taxation year is to be considered to have been paid and received thereunder,

(a) the amount is deemed to have been received thereunder; and

(b) the agreement or order is deemed, except for the purpose of this subsection, to have been made on the day on which the first such amount was received, except that, where the agreement or order is made after April 1997 and varies a child support amount payable to the recipient from the last such amount received by the recipient before May 1997, each varied amount of child support received under the agreement or order is deemed to have been receivable under an agreement or order the commencement day of which is the day on which the first payment of the varied amount is required to be made.

(4) Definitions — The definitions in this subsection apply in this section and section 56.

"child support amount" means any support amount that is not identified in the agreement or order under which it is receivable as being solely for the support of a recipient who is a spouse or common-law partner or former spouse or common-law partner of the payer or who is a parent of a child of whom the payer is a natural parent.

"commencement day" at any time of an agreement or order means

(a) where the agreement or order is made after April 1997, the day it is made; and

(b) where the agreement or order is made before May 1997, the day, if any, that is after April 1997 and is the earliest of

(i) the day specified as the commencement day of the agreement or order by the payer and recipient under the agreement or order in a joint election filed with the Minister in prescribed form and manner,

(ii) where the agreement or order is varied after April 1997 to change the child support amounts payable to the recipient, the day on which the first payment of the varied amount is required to be made,

(iii) where a subsequent agreement or order is made after April 1997, the effect of which is to change the total child support amounts payable to the recipient by the payer, the commencement day of the first such subsequent agreement or order, and

(iv) the day specified in the agreement or order, or any variation thereof, as the commencement day of the agreement or order for the purposes of this Act.

"support amount" means an amount payable or receivable as an allowance on a periodic basis for the maintenance of the recipient, children of the recipient or both the recipient and children of the recipient, if the recipient has discretion as to the use of the amount, and

(a) the recipient is the spouse or common-law partner or former spouse or common-law partner of the payer, the recipient and payer are living separate and apart because of the breakdown of their marriage or common-law partnership and the amount is receivable under an order of a competent tribunal or under a written agreement; or

(b) the payer is a natural parent of a child of the recipient and the amount is receivable under an order made by a competent tribunal in accordance with the laws of a province.

Subdivision e — Deductions in Computing Income

60. Other deductions — There may be deducted in computing a taxpayer's income for a taxation year such of the following amounts as are applicable:

. . . . .

(b) **[spousal or child] support** — the total of all amounts each of which is an amount determined by the formula

$$A - (B + C)$$

where

A   is the total of all amounts each of which is a support amount paid after 1996 and before the end of the year by the taxpayer to a particular person, where the taxpayer and the particular person were living separate and apart at the time the amount was paid,

B   is the total of all amounts each of which is a child support amount that became payable by the taxpayer to the particular person under an agreement or order on or after its commencement day and before the end of the year in respect of a period that began on or after its commencement day, and

C   is the total of all amounts each of which is a support amount paid by the taxpayer to the particular person after 1996 and deductible in computing the taxpayer's income for a preceding taxation year;

(c), (c.1) [Repealed]

(c.2) **repayment of support payments** — an amount paid by the taxpayer in the year or one of the 2 preceding taxation years under a decree, order or judgment of a competent tribunal as a repayment of an amount included under paragraph 56(1)(b) or (c), or under paragraph 56(1)(c.1) (as it applies, in computing the taxpayer's income for the year or a preceding taxation year, to decrees, orders and judgments made before 1993) to the extent that it was not so deducted for a preceding taxation year;

. . . . .

(o) **legal [or other] expenses [of objection or appeal]** — amounts paid by the taxpayer in the year in respect of fees or expenses incurred in preparing, instituting or prosecuting an objection to, or an appeal in relation to,

(i) an assessment of tax, interest or penalties under this Act or an Act of a province that imposes a tax similar to the tax imposed under this Act,

(ii) a decision of the Canada Employment and Immigration Commission, the Canada Employment and Insurance Commission, a board of referees or an umpire under the *Unemployment Insurance Act* or the *Employment Insurance Act*,

(iii) an assessment of any income tax deductible by the taxpayer under section 126 or any interest or penalty with respect thereto, or

(iv) an assessment or a decision made under the *Canada Pension Plan* or a provincial pension plan as defined in section 3 of that Act;

(o.1) **legal expenses** — the amount, if any, by which the lesser of

(i) the total of all legal expenses (other than those relating to a division or settlement of property arising out of, or on a breakdown of, a marriage or common-law partnership) paid by the taxpayer in the year or in any of the 7 preceding taxation years to collect or establish a right to an amount of

(A) a benefit under a pension fund or plan (other than a benefit under the *Canada Pension Plan* or a provincial pension plan as defined in section 3 of that Act) in respect of the employment of the taxpayer or a deceased individual of whom the taxpayer was a dependant, relation or legal representative, or

(B) a retiring allowance of the taxpayer or a deceased individual of whom the taxpayer was a dependant, relation or legal representative, and

(ii) the amount, if any, by which the total of all amounts each of which is

(A) an amount described in clause (i)(A) or (B)

(I) that is received after 1985,

(II) in respect of which legal expenses described in subparagraph (i) were paid, and

(III) that is included in computing the income of the taxpayer for the year or a preceding taxation year, or

(B) an amount included in computing the income of the taxpayer under paragraph 56(1)(l.1) for the year or a preceding taxation year,

exceeds the total of all amounts each of which is an amount deducted under paragraph (j), (j.01), (j.1) or (j.2) in computing the income of the taxpayer for the year or a preceding taxation year, to the extent that the amount may reasonably be considered to have been deductible as a consequence of the receipt of an amount referred to in clause (A), exceeds

> (iii) the portion of the total described in subparagraph (i) in respect of the taxpayer that may reasonably be considered to have been deductible under this paragraph in computing the income of the taxpayer for a preceding taxation year;

· · · · ·

60.1 (1) Support — For the purposes of paragraph 60(b) and subsection 118(5), where an order or agreement, or any variation thereof, provides for the payment of an amount by a taxpayer to a person or for the benefit of the person, children in the person's custody or both the person and those children, the amount or any part thereof

> (a) when payable, is deemed to be payable to and receivable by that person; and

> (b) when paid, is deemed to have been paid to and received by that person.

(2) Agreement — For the purposes of section 60, this section and subsection 118(5), the amount determined by the formula

$$A - B$$

where

A   is the total of all amounts each of which is an amount (other than an amount that is otherwise a support amount) that became payable by a taxpayer in a taxation year, under an order of a competent tribunal or under a written agreement, in respect of an expense (other than an expenditure in respect of a self-contained domestic establishment in which the taxpayer resides or an expenditure for the acquisition of tangible property that is not an expenditure on account of a medical or education expense or in respect of the acquisition, improvement or maintenance of a self-contained domestic establishment in which the person described in paragraph (a) or (b) resides) incurred in the year or the preceding taxation year for the maintenance of a person, children in the person's custody or both the person and those children, where the person is

> (a) the taxpayer's spouse or common-law partner or former spouse or common-law partner, or

> (b) where the amount became payable under an order made by a competent tribunal in accordance with the laws of a province, an individual who is a parent of a child of whom the taxpayer is a natural parent,

and

B   is the amount, if any, by which

> (a) the total of all amounts each of which is an amount included in the total determined for A in respect of the acquisition or improvement of a self-contained domestic establishment in which that person resides, including any payment of principal or interest in respect of a loan made or indebtedness incurred to finance, in any manner whatever, such acquisition or improvement

exceeds

> (b) the total of all amounts each of which is an amount equal to $1/5$ of the original principal amount of a loan or indebtedness described in paragraph (a),

is, where the order or written agreement, as the case may be, provides that this subsection and subsection 56.1(2) shall apply to any amount paid or payable thereunder, deemed to be an amount payable by the taxpayer to that person and receivable by that person as an allowance on a periodic basis, and that person is deemed to have discretion as to the use of that amount.

(3) Prior payments — For the purposes of this section and section 60, where a written agreement or order of a competent tribunal made at any time in a taxation year provides that an amount paid before that time and in the year or the preceding taxation year is to be considered to have been paid and received thereunder,

(a) the amount is deemed to have been paid thereunder; and

(b) the agreement or order is deemed, except for the purpose of this subsection, to have been made on the day on which the first such amount was paid, except that, where the agreement or order is made after April 1997 and varies a child support amount payable to the recipient from the last such amount paid to the recipient before May 1997, each varied amount of child support paid under the agreement or order is deemed to have been payable under an agreement or order the commencement day of which is the day on which the first payment of the varied amount is required to be made.

(4) Definitions — The definitions in subsection 56.1(4) apply in this section and section 60.

. . . . .

63. (1) Child care expenses — Subject to subsection (2), where a prescribed form containing prescribed information is filed with a taxpayer's return of income (other than a return filed under subsection 70(2) or 104(23), paragraph 128(2)(e) or subsection 150(4)) under this Part for a taxation year, there may be deducted in computing the taxpayer's income for the year such amount as the taxpayer claims not exceeding the total of all amounts each of which is an amount paid, as or on account of child care expenses incurred for services rendered in the year in respect of an eligible child of the taxpayer,

(a) by the taxpayer, where the taxpayer is described in subsection (2) and the supporting person of the child for the year is a person described in clause (i)(D) of the description of C in the formula in that subsection, or

(b) by the taxpayer or a supporting person of the child for the year, in any other case,

to the extent that

(c) the amount is not included in computing the amount deductible under this subsection by an individual (other than the taxpayer), and

(d) the amount is not an amount (other than an amount that is included in computing the taxpayer's income and that is not deductible in computing the taxpayer's taxable income) in respect of which any taxpayer is or was entitled to a reimbursement or any other form of assistance,

and the payment of which is proven by filing with the Minister one or more receipts each of which was issued by the payee and contains, where the payee is an individual, that individual's Social Insurance Number, but not exceeding the amount, if any, by which

(e) the lesser of

(i) $\frac{2}{3}$ of the taxpayer's earned income for the year, and

(ii) the total of all amounts each of which is the annual child care expense amount in respect of an eligible child of the taxpayer for the year exceeds

> (f) the total of all amounts each of which is an amount that is deducted, in respect of the taxpayer's eligible children for the year, under this section in computing the income for the year of an individual (other than the taxpayer) to whom subsection (2) applies for the year.

(2) Income exceeding income of supporting person — Where the income for a taxation year of a taxpayer who has an eligible child for the year exceeds the income for that year of a supporting person of that child (on the assumption that both incomes are computed without reference to this section and paragraphs 60(v.1) and (w)), the amount that may be deducted by the taxpayer under subsection (1) for the year as or on account of child care expenses shall not exceed the lesser of

> (a) the amount that would, but for this subsection, be deductible by the taxpayer for the year under subsection (1); and

> (b) the amount determined by the formula

$$A \times C$$

where

A   is the total of all amounts each of which is the periodic child care expense amount in respect of an eligible child of the taxpayer for the year, and

C   is the total of

> > (i) the number of weeks in the year during which the child care expenses were incurred and throughout which the supporting person was

> > > (A) a student in attendance at a designated educational institution or a secondary school and enrolled in a program of the institution or school of not less than 3 consecutive weeks duration that provides that each student in the program spend not less than 10 hours per week on courses or work in the program,

> > > (B) a person certified by a medical doctor to be a person who

Proposed Amendment — 63(2)(b)C(B) opening words

(B) a person certified in writing by a medical doctor to be a person who

> > > > (I) was incapable of caring for children because of the person's mental or physical infirmity and confinement throughout a period of not less than 2 weeks in the year to bed, to a wheelchair or as a patient in a hospital, an asylum or other similar institution, or

> > > > (II) was in the year, and is likely to be for a long, continuous and indefinite period, incapable of caring for children, because of the person's mental or physical infirmity,

> > > (C) a person confined to a prison or similar institution throughout a period of not less than 2 weeks in the year, or

> > > (D) a person who, because of a breakdown of the person's marriage or common-law partnership, was living separate and apart from the taxpayer at the end of the year and for a period of at least 90 days that began in the year, and

(ii) the number of months in the year (other than a month that includes all or part of a week included in the number of weeks referred to in subparagraph (i)), each of which is a month during which the child care expenses were incurred and the supporting person was a student in attendance at a designated educational institution or a secondary school and enrolled in a program of the institution or school that is not less than 3 consecutive weeks duration and that provides that each student in the program spend not less than 12 hours in the month on courses in the program.

(2.1) Taxpayer and supporting person with equal incomes — For the purposes of this section, where in any taxation year the income of a taxpayer who has an eligible child for the year and the income of a supporting person of the child are equal (on the assumption that both incomes are computed without reference to this section and paragraphs 60(v.1) and (w)), no deduction shall be allowed under this section to the taxpayer and the supporting person in respect of the child unless they jointly elect to treat the income of one of them as exceeding the income of the other for the year.

(2.2) Expenses while at school — There may be deducted in computing a taxpayer's income for a taxation year such part of the amount determined under subsection (2.3) as the taxpayer claims, where

(a) the taxpayer is, at any time in the year, a student in attendance at a designated educational institution or a secondary school and enrolled in a program of the institution or school of not less than 3 consecutive weeks duration that provides that each student in the program spend not less than

(i) 10 hours per week on courses or work in the program, or

(ii) 12 hours per month on courses in the program;

(b) there is no supporting person of an eligible child of the taxpayer for the year or the income of the taxpayer for the year exceeds the income for the year of a supporting person of the child (on the assumption that both incomes are computed without reference to this section and paragraphs 60(v.1) and (w)); and

(c) a prescribed form containing prescribed information is filed with the taxpayer's return of income (other than a return filed under subsection 70(2) or 104(23), paragraph 128(2)(e) or subsection 150(4)) for the year.

(2.3) Amount deductible [while at school] — For the purpose of subsection (2.2), the amount determined in respect of a taxpayer for a taxation year is the least of

(a) the amount by which the total of all amounts, each of which is an amount paid as or on account of child care expenses incurred for services rendered in the year in respect of an eligible child of the taxpayer, exceeds the amount that is deductible under subsection (1) in computing the taxpayer's income for the year,

(b) $\frac{2}{3}$ of the taxpayer's income for the year computed without reference to this section and paragraphs 60(v.1) and (w),

(c) the amount determined by the formula

$$A \times C$$

where

A   is the total of all amounts each of which is the periodic child care expense amount in respect of an eligible child of the taxpayer for the year, and

C   is

> (i) if there is a supporting person of an eligible child of the taxpayer for the year,
>
>> (A) the number of weeks, in the year, in which both the taxpayer and the supporting person were students who would be described in paragraph (2.2)(a) if that paragraph were read without reference to subparagraph (ii), and
>>
>> (B) the number of months in the year (other than a month that includes all or part of a week included in the number of weeks referred to in clause (A)), in which both the taxpayer and the supporting person were students described in paragraph (2.2)(a), and
>
> (ii) in any other case,
>
>> (A) the number of weeks, in the year, in which the taxpayer was a student who would be described in paragraph (2.2)(a) if that paragraph were read without reference to subparagraph (ii), and
>>
>> (B) the number of months in the year (other than a month that includes all or part of a week included in the number of weeks referred to in clause (A)), in which the taxpayer was a student described in paragraph (2.2)(a),

(d) the amount by which the total calculated under subparagraph (1)(e)(ii) in respect of eligible children of the taxpayer for the year exceeds the amount that is deductible under subsection (1) in computing the taxpayer's income for the year, and

(e) where there is a supporting person of an eligible child of the taxpayer for the year, the amount by which the amount calculated under paragraph (2)(b) for the year in respect of the taxpayer exceeds ⅔ of the taxpayer's earned income for the year.

(3) Definitions — In this section,

"annual child care expense amount", in respect of an eligible child of a taxpayer for a taxation year, means

(a) $10,000, where the child is a person in respect of whom an amount may be deducted under section 118.3 in computing a taxpayer's tax payable under this Part for the year, and

(b) where the child is not a person referred to in paragraph (a),

> (i) $7,000, where the child is under 7 years of age at the end of the year, and
>
> (ii) $4,000, in any other case;

"child care expense" means an expense incurred in a taxation year for the purpose of providing in Canada, for an eligible child of a taxpayer, child care services including baby sitting services, day nursery services or services provided at a boarding school or camp if the services were provided

(a) to enable the taxpayer, or the supporting person of the child for the year, who resided with the child at the time the expense was incurred,

> (i) to perform the duties of an office or employment,
>
> (ii) to carry on a business either alone or as a partner actively engaged in the business,
>
> (iii) [Repealed]

(iv) to carry on research or any similar work in respect of which the taxpayer or supporting person received a grant, or

(v) to attend a designated educational institution or a secondary school, where the taxpayer is enrolled in a program of the institution or school of not less than three consecutive weeks duration that provides that each student in the program spend not less than

(A) 10 hours per week on courses or work in the program, or

(B) 12 hours per month on courses in the program, and

(b) by a resident of Canada other than a person

(i) who is the father or the mother of the child,

(ii) who is a supporting person of the child or is under 18 years of age and related to the taxpayer, or

(iii) in respect of whom an amount is deducted under section 118 in computing the tax payable under this Part for the year by the taxpayer or by a supporting person of the child,

except that

(c) any such expenses paid in the year for a child's attendance at a boarding school or camp to the extent that the total of those expenses exceeds the product obtained when the periodic child care expense amount in respect of the child for the year is multiplied by the number of weeks in the year during which the child attended the school or camp, and

(d) for greater certainty, any expenses described in subsection 118.2(2) and any other expenses that are paid for medical or hospital care, clothing, transportation or education or for board and lodging, except as otherwise expressly provided in this definition,

are not child care expenses;

"earned income" of a taxpayer means the total of

(a) all salaries, wages and other remuneration, including gratuities, received by the taxpayer in respect of, in the course of, or because of, offices and employments,

(b) all amounts that are included, or that would, but for paragraph 81(1)(a) or subsection 81(4), be included, because of section 6 or 7 or paragraph 56(1)(n), (o) or (r), in computing the taxpayer's income,

(c) all the taxpayer's incomes or the amounts that would, but for paragraph 81(1)(a), be the taxpayer's incomes from all businesses carried on either alone or as a partner actively engaged in the business, and

(d) all amounts received by the taxpayer as, on account of, in lieu of payment of or in satisfaction of, a disability pension under the *Canada Pension Plan* or a provincial pension plan as defined in section 3 of that Act;

"eligible child" of a taxpayer for a taxation year means

(a) a child of the taxpayer or of the taxpayer's spouse or common-law partner, or

(b) a child dependent on the taxpayer or the taxpayer's spouse or common-law partner for support and whose income for the year does not exceed the amount used under paragraph (c) of the description of B in subsection 118(1) for the year

if, at any time during the year, the child

(c) is under 16 years of age, or

(d) is dependent on the taxpayer or on the taxpayer's spouse or common-law partner and has a mental or physical infirmity;

"periodic child care expense amount", in respect of an eligible child of a taxpayer for a taxation year, means $1/40$ of the annual child care expense amount in respect of the child for the year;

"supporting person" of an eligible child of a taxpayer for a taxation year means a person, other than the taxpayer, who is

(a) a parent of the child,

(b) the taxpayer's spouse or common-law partner, or

(c) an individual who deducted an amount under section 118 for the year in respect of the child,

if the parent, spouse or common-law partner or individual, as the case may be, resided with the taxpayer at any time during the year and at any time within 60 days after the end of the year.

(4) Commuter's child care expense — Where in a taxation year a person resides in Canada near the boundary between Canada and the United States and while so resident incurs expenses for child care services that would be child care expenses if

(a) the definition "child care expense" in subsection (3) were read without reference to the words "in Canada", and

(b) the reference in paragraph (b) of the definition "child care expense" in subsection (3) to "resident of Canada" were read as "person",

those expenses (other than expenses paid for a child's attendance at a boarding school or camp outside Canada) shall be deemed to be child care expenses for the purpose of this section if the child care services are provided at a place that is closer to the person's principal place of residence by a reasonably accessible route, having regard to the circumstances, than any place in Canada where such child care services are available and, in respect of those expenses, subsection (1) shall be read without reference to the words "and contains, where the payee is an individual, that individual's Social Insurance Number".

. . . . .

INTERCOUNTRY ADOPTION ACT, 1998

S.O. 1998, c. 29, as am. S.O. 1999, c. 12, Sched. G, s. 25.

INTERPRETATION

1. (1) Definitions — In this Act,

"Board" means the Child and Family Services Review Board; *("Commission")*

"child" means a person under the age of 18 years; *("enfant")*

"Convention" means the Convention on Protection of Children and Co-operation in respect of Intercountry Adoption set out in the Schedule; *("Convention")*

"Director" means a person or member of a class of persons designated by the regulations; *("directeur")*

"intercountry adoption" means,

    (a) an adoption to which the Convention applies, or

    (b) any other adoption of a child who is habitually resident outside Canada, by an Ontario resident,

        (i) that is intended to create a permanent parent-child relationship, and

        (ii) that is finalized in the child's country of origin;

("adoption internationale")

"licence" means a licence to facilitate intercountry adoptions issued under section 8, and **"licensee"** and **"licensed"** have corresponding meanings; *("permis"), ("titulaire de permis"), ("autoris en vertu d'un permis")*

"Minister" means the Minister of Community and Social Services; *("ministre")*

"regulations" means the regulations made under this Act. *("règlements")*

"Tribunal" means the Licence Appeal Tribunal. *("Tribunal")*

(2) Words and expressions in Convention — Words and expressions used in this Act have the same meaning as the corresponding words and expressions in the Convention.

1999, c. 12, Sched. G, s. 25(1)

IMPLEMENTATION OF CONVENTION

2. (1) Request for Convention — The Minister shall request that the Government of Canada declare, in accordance with Article 45 of the Convention, that the Convention extends to Ontario.

(2) Publication — The Minister shall publish in *The Ontario Gazette* notice of the date the Convention enters into force in Ontario.

3. (1) Convention is law — On and after the date the Convention enters into force in respect of Ontario, as determined by Article 46 of the Convention, it has the force of law in Ontario.

(2) Conflict — The law of Ontario also applies to adoptions to which the Convention applies, but if there is a conflict between the law of Ontario and the Convention, the Convention prevails.

4. Central Authority — For the purposes of the Convention's application in Ontario, the Central Authority is the person designated by the regulations.

INTERCOUNTRY ADOPTION REQUIREMENTS

5. (1) Application, homestudy and approval required — No person who is habitually resident in Ontario shall leave Ontario for the purpose of an intercountry adoption or finalize an intercountry adoption without first,

(a) making an application to a licensee;

(b) obtaining an adoption homestudy to assess the person's eligibility and suitability to adopt, and submitting a report of the adoption homestudy to a Director; and

(c) obtaining the Director's approval, on the basis of the adoption homestudy.

(2) Director — The application may be made to a Director rather than to a licensee, in which case the report of the adoption homestudy shall be submitted to the same Director.

(3) Who may make adoption homestudy — The report of the adoption homestudy shall be prepared by a person who, in the Director's opinion, is qualified to make an adoption homestudy.

(4) Review by Director — The Director shall review the report of the adoption homestudy promptly and,

(a) approve the person unconditionally;

(b) approve the person subject to any conditions the Director considers appropriate; or

(c) refuse to approve the person.

(5) Notice — The Director shall promptly give notice of the approval, the approval subject to conditions or the refusal, as the case may be,

(a) to the person who is the subject of the adoption homestudy;

(b) to the licensee, if any; and

(c) to the authority responsible for adoption matters in the child's country of origin.

(6) Right to hearing — When a Director gives notice of a refusal or of an approval subject to conditions, the person is entitled to a hearing before the Board.

(7) Application of other sections — Sections 11, 13, 15 and 16 (hearing, appeal) apply to the hearing with necessary modifications and for that purpose references to the Tribunal shall be deemed to be references to the Board.

1999, c. 12, Sched. G, s. 25(2)

6. (1) Request of foreign authority — When an intercountry adoption by an Ontario resident is proposed, the authority responsible for adoption matters in the child's country of origin may request that a Director review the proposed adoption.

(2) Review by Director — The Director shall promptly review the proposed adoption and,

    (a) approve it unconditionally;

    (b) approve it subject to any conditions the Director considers appropriate; or

    (c) refuse to approve it.

(3) Notice — The Director shall promptly give notice of the approval, the approval subject to conditions or the refusal, as the case may be,

    (a) to the Ontario resident;

    (b) to the licensee, if any; and

    (c) to the foreign authority.

(4) Right to hearing — When a Director gives notice of a refusal or of an approval subject to conditions, the Ontario resident is entitled to a hearing before the Board.

(5) Application of other sections — Sections 11, 13 15 and 16 (hearing, appeal) apply to the hearing with necessary modifications and for that purpose references to the Tribunal shall be deemed to be references to the Board.

1999, c. 12, Sched. G, s. 25(3)

7. Sharing information — If a Director is aware of an application under section 5, has reviewed the report of an adoption homestudy under section 5 or a proposed adoption under section 6, or is otherwise aware that an Ontario resident is pursuing an intercountry adoption, the Director may share relevant information with,

    (a) the authorities responsible for adoption matters, child welfare, the administration of justice and law enforcement in the child's country of origin;

    (b) the Government of Canada and its agencies;

    (c) the governments of other provinces and territories of Canada and their agencies; and

    (d) a prescribed person or body.

LICENSING AND HEARINGS

8. (1) Only Directors and licensees may facilitate intercountry adoptions — No person except a Director or a licensee shall facilitate an intercountry adoption.

(2) Issuing licence — Subject to subsection (4), a person who applies for a licence in accordance with the regulations and pays the prescribed fee is entitled to be issued a licence by a Director, subject to any conditions imposed by the Director.

(3) Renewal — Subject to subsection (4), a licensee who applies for renewal of the licence in accordance with the regulations and pays the prescribed fee is entitled to have the licence renewed by a Director, subject to any conditions imposed by the Director.

(4) Provisional licence or renewal — If an applicant for a licence or renewal does not meet all the requirements for the issuing or renewal of the licence and requires time to meet them, a Director may issue a provisional licence for the period the Director considers necessary to give the applicant time to meet the requirements, and may impose conditions on the provisional licence.

(5) Non-transferable — A licence is not transferable.

9. Refusal to issue licence — A Director may refuse to issue a licence if, in his or her opinion,

(a) the applicant, an employee of the applicant or, if the applicant is a corporation, an officer or director of the applicant is not competent to facilitate intercountry adoptions in a responsible manner in accordance with this Act and the regulations; or

(b) the past conduct of the applicant, an employee of the applicant or, if the applicant is a corporation, an officer or director of the applicant affords reasonable grounds for belief that intercountry adoptions will not be facilitated in a responsible manner in accordance with this Act and the regulations.

10. Refusal to renew, revocation — A Director may refuse to renew or may revoke a licence if, in his or her opinion,

(a) the licensee, an employee of the licensee or, if the licensee is a corporation, an officer or director of the licensee has contravened or has knowingly permitted a person under his or her control or direction or associated with him or her to contravene,

(i) this Act or the regulations,

(ii) another Act, or the regulations made under another Act, that applies to adoptions, or

(iii) a condition of the licence;

(b) intercountry adoptions are being facilitated in a manner that is prejudicial to the health, safety or welfare of children;

(c) a person has made a false statement in the application for the licence or for its renewal, or in a report or document required to be furnished by this Act or the regulations, or by another Act or the regulations made under another Act that applies to adoptions; or

(d) a change has occurred in the employees, officers or directors of the applicant that would, if the applicant were applying for the licence in the first instance, afford grounds for refusal under clause 9(b).

11. (1) Notice of proposal — If a Director proposes to refuse to issue a licence under section 9 or to revoke or refuse to renew a licence under section 10, he or she shall cause notice of the proposal, together with written reasons, to be served on the applicant or licensee.

(2) Right to hearing — The applicant or licensee is entitled to a hearing by the Tribunal if the applicant or licensee mails or delivers to the Director and to the Tribunal, within 10 days after the notice is served, a written request for a hearing, and the notice shall so inform the applicant or licensee.

(3) Carrying out proposal if no hearing required — If no hearing is requested, the Director may carry out the proposal.

(4) Powers of Tribunal if hearing required — If a hearing is requested, the Tribunal shall set a time for and hold a hearing and may, on hearing the matter,

(a) order the Director to carry out the proposal; or

(b) order the Director to take any other action that the Tribunal considers appropriate, in accordance with this Act and the regulations.

(5) Same — The Tribunal may substitute its opinion for that of the Director.

1999, c. 12, Sched. G, s. 25(4)

12. (1) Tribunal review of licence conditions — A licensee who is dissatisfied with a condition imposed by a Director under subsection 8(2), (3) or (4) is entitled to a hearing by the Tribunal if the licensee mails or delivers to the Director and to the Tribunal, within 15 days after receiving the licence, a written request for a hearing.

(2) Powers of Tribunal — If a hearing is requested, the Tribunal shall set a time for and hold a hearing and may, on hearing the matter,

(a) confirm any or all of the conditions;

(b) strike out any or all of the conditions; or

(c) impose any other conditions that the Tribunal considers appropriate.

(3) Time of receipt — For the purposes of subsection (1), a licensee shall be deemed to receive the licence on the 10th day after the day it is mailed, unless it is established that the licensee did not receive it or did not, through absence, accident, illness or another cause beyond the licensee's control, acting in good faith, receive the licence until a later date.

1999, c. 12, Sched. G, s. 25(4)

13. (1) Extension of time — The Board may extend the time fixed for requesting a hearing under subsection 5(6) or 6(4), either before or after its expiration, if,

(a) it appears to the Board that there are reasonable grounds for granting relief to the applicant or licensee; and

(b) the Board is satisfied that the applicant or licensee has reasonable grounds to seek an extension.

(2) Directions — The Board may give such directions as it considers proper in connection with an extension.

(3) Continuation of licence pending renewal — Subject to section 14, if a licensee has applied for renewal of the licence and paid the prescribed fee within the prescribed time or, if no time is prescribed, before the licence expires, the licence is deemed to continue,

(a) until the renewal is granted; or

(b) if the licensee is served with notice that the Director proposes to refuse to grant the renewal, until the time for requesting a hearing has expired and, if a hearing is requested, until the Tribunal has made its decision.

1999, c. 12, Sched. G, s. 25(6), (7)

14. (1) Provisional suspension of licence — A Director may, by causing notice to be served on a licensee, suspend the licence provisionally and without a hearing, if in his or her opinion the manner in which intercountry adoptions are being facilitated is an immediate threat to the health, safety or welfare of children.

(2) Contents of notice — The notice shall contain a statement of the grounds for suspension.

(3) When suspension takes effect — The provisional suspension takes effect on the day the licensee receives the notice.

(4) Application of s. 11(2–5) — Subsections 11(2), (3), (4) and (5) apply, with necessary modifications.

15. (1) Parties — The Director, the applicant or licensee who requests the hearing and any other persons that the Tribunal specifies are parties to the proceeding.

(2) Prior involvement — A member of the Tribunal who has taken part before a hearing in any investigation or consideration of its subject matter shall not take part in the hearing.

(3) Discussion of subject matter of hearing — A member of the Tribunal who takes part in a hearing shall not communicate about the subject matter of the hearing with any person (except another member, a lawyer who does not represent any party, or an employee of the Tribunal) unless all parties are notified and given an opportunity to participate.

(4) Independent legal advice — The Tribunal may seek independent legal advice about the subject matter of a hearing and, if it does so, shall disclose the nature of the advice to the parties to enable them to respond.

(5) Examination of documentary evidence and reports — Every party shall be given an opportunity, before the hearing, to examine any documentary evidence that will be produced and any report whose contents will be given in evidence at the hearing.

(6) Recording of evidence — The evidence taken before the Board at a hearing under subsection 5(6) or 6(4) shall be recorded.

(7) Only members present throughout hearing to participate in decision — No member of the Tribunal shall participate in a decision of the Tribunal unless he or she was present throughout the hearing and heard the evidence and argument of the parties.

(8) All members present at hearing to participate in decision — Unless the parties consent, the Tribunal shall not make a decision unless all the members who were present at the hearing participate in the decision.

(9) Time for final decision — Despite section 21 of the *Statutory Powers Procedure Act* (adjournments), the Tribunal shall make a final decision and notify the parties of it within 90 days after the day the Tribunal receives the request for a hearing.

1999, c. 12, Sched. G, s. 25(7)–(9)

16. (1) Appeal —

[Editor's Note: Section 25(5) of the Red Tape Reduction Act, 1999, S.O. 1999, c. 12, Schedule G. provides that despite the replacement of the Child and Family Services Review Board (the "Board") with the Licence Appeal Tribunal (the "Tribunal"), members of the Board immediately before subsection 16(4) comes into force shall be members of the Tribunal for the purpose of performing the duties of the Tribunal with respect to proceedings before the Board that were commenced before that subsection comes into force.]

An appeal lies to the Divisional Court from the Tribunal's decision.

(2) Record to be filed — When notice of an appeal is filed, the Tribunal shall promptly file with the court the record of the proceeding in which the decision appealed from was made.

(3) Minister — The Minister is entitled to be heard, by counsel or otherwise, on the argument of the appeal.

1999, c. 12, Sched. G, s. 25(9)

17. (1) Powers of inspection — For the purpose of ensuring compliance with this Act, the regulations and any conditions imposed on licences, a Director or a person who has a Director's written authorization may, at all reasonable times, upon producing proper identification,

(a) enter the premises of a licensee;

(b) inspect the premises and any financial or other records there dealing with activities in connection with intercountry adoptions; and

(c) make copies of the records or remove them from the premises to copy them as may be reasonably required.

(2) Offence — No person shall,

(a) hinder, obstruct or attempt to hinder or obstruct a Director or other person in the exercise of the power conferred by subsection (1);

(b) knowingly give false information about a licensee's activities in connection with intercountry adoptions; or

(c) refuse to give a Director or other person access to the records referred to in clause (1)(b) or refuse to give him or her information about the premises or about the licensee's activities in connection with intercountry adoptions that the Director or other person reasonably requires.

(3) Regulations — The power conferred by subsection (1) shall be exercised in accordance with the regulations.

18. Delivery of licence and records — A licensee whose licence is revoked or who ceases to facilitate intercountry adoptions shall deliver up to a Director or to the Minister the licence and all the records in the licensee's possession or control that relate to intercountry adoptions.

Offences

19. No payments for intercountry adoption — No person shall give, receive or agree to give or receive a payment or reward of any kind in connection with an intercountry adoption or proposed intercountry adoption, except for,

(a) the expenses of a licensee that belong to a prescribed class, or such other expenses as are approved by a Director;

(b) the expenses of a person referred to in subsection 5(3) that belong to a prescribed class;

(c) the expenses of a Director that belong to a prescribed class; and

(d) proper legal fees and disbursements.

20. (1) Offence, penalty — A person who contravenes subsection 5(1) (application, homestudy and approval required) is guilty of an offence and on conviction is liable to a fine of not more than $2,000 or to imprisonment for not more than two years, or to both.

(2) Same — A person who contravenes subsection 8(1) (facilitating intercountry adoptions without licence), and a director, officer or employee of a corporation who authorizes, permits or concurs in such a contravention by the corporation, is guilty of an offence and on conviction is liable to a fine of not more than $1,000 for each day on which the offence continues or to imprisonment for not more than one year, or to both.

(3) Same — Every person who knowingly furnishes false information in an application under subsection 8(2) or (3) (licence, renewal) or in a statement, report or return required to be furnished under the regulations, and a director, officer or employee of a corporation who authorizes, permits or concurs in such a contravention by the corporation, is guilty of an offence and on conviction is liable to a fine of not more than $2,000.

(4) Same — Every person who knowingly contravenes subsection 17(2) (obstruction), and a director, officer or employee of a corporation who authorizes, permits or concurs in such a contravention by the corporation, is guilty of an offence and on conviction is liable to a fine of not more than $2,000.

(5) Same — A person who contravenes section 19, and a director, officer or employee of a corporation who authorizes, permits or concurs in such a contravention by the corporation, is guilty of an offence and on conviction is liable to a fine of not more than $25,000 or to imprisonment for not more than three years, or to both.

(6) Limitation — A proceeding under subsection (1), (2) or (5) shall not be commenced more than two years after the date on which the offence is alleged to have been committed.

General

21. Non-application of FIPPA and MFIPPA — The *Freedom of Information and Protection of Privacy Act* and the *Municipal Freedom of Information and Protection of Privacy Act* do not apply to information that relates to an intercountry adoption or proposed intercountry adoption.

22. Child and Family Services Act, ss. 165, 170 — Directors and licensees under this Act are deemed to be licensees for the purposes of sections 165 and 170 of the *Child and Family Services Act* (confidentiality of adoption records, persons adopted outside Ontario).

23. Conflict — If there is a conflict between this Act and any other Act, this Act prevails.

Regulations

24. Regulations — The Lieutenant Governor in Council may make regulations,

(a) designating the Central Authority in accordance with Article 6 of the Convention;

(b) assigning functions of the Central Authority to public authorities, accredited bodies or other bodies or persons in accordance with Article 22 of the Convention;

(c) defining words and expressions used but not defined in the Convention;

(d) further defining "intercountry adoption" for the purpose of this Act;

(e) exempting from this Act, a provision of this Act, the regulations or a provision of the regulations,

    (i) a class or classes of intercountry adoptions, or

    (ii) a class or classes of persons;

(f) prescribing persons and classes of persons and bodies and classes of bodies for the purpose of clause 7(d);

(g) defining "facilitate" for the purpose of subsection 8(1);

(h) governing the issuing, renewal and expiry of licences and prescribing fees payable by an applicant for a licence or its renewal;

(i) prescribing the records to be kept by licensees;

(j) requiring licensees to provide the prescribed information and reports and prescribing the information and reports;

(k) requiring applications, reports and other documents to be prepared in a form approved or provided by the Minister;

(l) governing the qualifications of persons or classes of persons employed by licensees;

(m) governing the exercise of the power of entry set out in subsection 17(1);

(n) designating persons or classes of persons as Directors for the purposes of this Act;

(o) prescribing classes of expenses for the purposes of clauses 19(a), (b) and (c) and prescribing the conditions under which such classes of expenses may be charged.

Transition

25. (1) Transition — This Act does not apply to an intercountry adoption if,

    (a) before the effective date,

        (i) an application to adopt the child has been made to an authority responsible for adoption matters in the child's country of origin, or has been received by the Ministry of Community and Social Services or the National Adoption Desk of Human Resources Development (Canada),

        (ii) the child has been placed with the proposed adoptive parent, or

        (iii) the consents and approvals necessary for the adoption have been given; and

    (b) the adoption is finalized within 24 months after the effective date.

(2) Same — A report of an adoption homestudy that was prepared before the effective date may be used for the purposes of subsection 5(1) if the person who prepared it is a person referred to in subsection 5(3).

(3) Definition — In subsections (1) and (2),

"effective date" means the day on which subsection 5(1) comes into force.

26. Commencement — This Act comes into force on a day to be named by proclamation of the Lieutenant Governor.

27. Short title — The short title of this Act is the *Intercountry Adoption Act, 1998.*

SCHEDULE

[CONVENTION] — CONVENTION ON PROTECTION OF CHILDREN AND CO-OPERATION IN RESPECT OF INTERCOUNTRY ADOPTION

The text in square brackets has been editorially added by Carswell and does not form part of the text of the legislation.

The States signatory to the present Convention,

Recognizing that the child, for the full and harmonious development of his or her personality, should grow up in a family environment, in an atmosphere of happiness, love and understanding,

Recalling that each State should take, as a matter of priority, appropriate measures to enable the child to remain in the care of his or her family of origin,

Recognizing that intercountry adoption may offer the advantage of a permanent family to a child for whom a suitable family cannot be found in his or her State of origin,

Convinced of the necessity to take measures to ensure that intercountry adoptions are made in the best interests of the child and with respect for his or her fundamental rights, and to prevent the abduction, the sale of, or traffic in children,

Desiring to establish common provisions to this effect, taking into account the principles set forth in international instruments, in particular the *United Nations Convention on the Rights of the Child*, of November 20, 1989, and the United Nations Declaration on Social and Legal Principles relating to the Protection and Welfare of Children, with Special Reference to Foster Placement and Adoption Nationally and Internationally (General Assembly Resolution 41/85, of 3 December 1986),

Have agreed upon the following provisions,

Chapter 1 — Scope of the Convention

Article 1

The objects of the present Convention are,

(a) to establish safeguards to ensure that intercountry adoptions take place in the best interests of the child and with respect for his or her fundamental rights as recognized in international law;

(b) to establish a system of co-operation amongst Contracting States to ensure that those safeguards are respected and thereby prevent the abduction, the sale of, or traffic in children;

(c) to secure the recognition in Contracting States of adoptions made in accordance with the Convention.

Article 2

1. The Convention shall apply where a child habitually resident in one Contracting State ('the State of origin') has been, is being, or is to be moved to another Contracting State ('the receiving State') either after his or her adoption in the State of origin by spouses or a person habitually resident in the receiving State, or for the purposes of such an adoption in the receiving State or in the State of origin.

2. The Convention covers only adoptions which create a permanent parent-child relationship.

Article 3

The Convention ceases to apply if the agreements mentioned in Article 17, subparagraph (c), have not been given before the child attains the age of 18 years.

Chapter II — Requirements for Intercountry Adoptions

Article 4

An adoption within the scope of the Convention shall take place only if the competent authorities of the State of origin,

(a) have established that the child is adoptable;

(b) have determined, after possibilities for placement of the child within the State of origin have been given due consideration, that an intercountry adoption is in the child's best interests;

(c) have ensured that,

(1) the persons, institutions and authorities whose consent is necessary for adoption, have been counselled as may be necessary and duly informed of the effects of their consent, in particular whether or not an adoption will result in the termination of the legal relationship between the child and his or her family of origin,

(2) such persons, institutions and authorities have given their consent freely, in the required legal form, and expressed or evidenced in writing,

(3) the consents have not been induced by payment or compensation of any kind and have not been withdrawn, and

(4) the consent of the mother, where required, has been given only after the birth of the child; and

(d) have ensured, having regard to the age and degree of maturity of the child, that,

(1) he or she has been counselled and duly informed of the effects of the adoption and of his or her consent to the adoption, where such consent is required,

(2) consideration has been given to the child's wishes and opinions,

(3) the child's consent to the adoption, where such consent is required, has been given freely, in the required legal form, and expressed or evidenced in writing, and

(4) such consent has not been induced by payment or compensation of any kind.

Article 5

An adoption within the scope of the Convention shall take place only if the competent authorities of the receiving State,

(a) have determined that the prospective adoptive parents are eligible and suited to adopt;

(b) have ensured that the prospective adoptive parents have been counselled as may be necessary; and

(c) have determined that the child is or will be authorized to enter and reside permanently in that State.

Chapter III — Central Authorities and Accredited Bodies

Article 6

1. A Contracting State shall designate a Central Authority to discharge the duties which are imposed by the Convention upon such authorities.

2. Federal States, States with more than one system of law or States having autonomous territorial units shall be free to appoint more than one Central Authority and to specify the territorial or personal extent of their functions. Where a State has appointed more than one Central Authority, it shall designate the Central Authority to which any communication may be addressed for transmission to the appropriate Central Authority within that State.

Article 7

1. Central Authorities shall co-operate with each other and promote co-operation amongst the competent authorities in their States to protect children and to achieve the other objects of the Convention.

2. They shall take directly all appropriate measures to,

(a) provide information as to the laws of their States concerning adoption and other general information, such as statistics and standard forms;

(b) keep one another informed about the operation of the Convention and, as far as possible, eliminate any obstacles to its application.

Article 8

Central Authorities shall take, directly or through public authorities, all appropriate measures to prevent improper financial or other gain in connection with an adoption and to deter all practices contrary to the objects of the Convention.

Article 9

Central Authorities shall take, directly or through public authorities or other bodies duly accredited in their State, all appropriate measures, in particular to,

(a) collect, preserve and exchange information about the situation of the child and the prospective adoptive parents, so far as is necessary to complete the adoption;

(b) facilitate, follow and expedite proceedings with a view to obtaining the adoption;

(c) promote the development of adoption counselling and post-adoption services in their States;

(d) provide each other with general evaluation reports about experience with intercountry adoption;

(e) reply, in so far as is permitted by the law of their State, to justified requests from other Central Authorities or public authorities for information about a particular adoption situation.

Article 10

Accreditation shall only be granted to and maintained by bodies demonstrating their competence to carry out properly the tasks with which they may be entrusted.

Article 11

An accredited body shall,

(a) pursue only non-profit objectives according to such conditions and within such limits as may be established by the competent authorities of the State of accreditation;

(b) be directed and staffed by persons qualified by their ethical standards and by training or experience to work in the field of intercountry adoption; and

(c) be subject to supervision by competent authorities of that State as to its composition, operation and financial situation.

Article 12

A body accredited in one Contracting State may act in another Contracting State only if the competent authorities of both States have authorized it to do so.

Article 13

The designation of the Central Authorities and, where appropriate, the extent of their functions, as well as the names and addresses of the accredited bodies shall be communicated by each Contracting State to the Permanent Bureau of the Hague Conference on Private International Law.

Chapter IV — Procedural Requirements in Intercountry Adoption

Article 14

Persons habitually resident in a Contracting State, who wish to adopt a child habitually resident in another Contracting State, shall apply to the Central Authority in the State of their habitual residence.

Article 15

1. If the Central Authority of the receiving State is satisfied that the applicants are eligible and suited to adopt, it shall prepare a report including information about their identity, eligibility and suitability to adopt, background, family and medical history, social environment, reasons for adoption, ability to undertake an intercountry adoption, as well as the characteristics of the children for whom they would be qualified to care.

2. It shall transmit the report to the Central Authority of the State of origin.

Article 16

1. If the Central Authority of the State of origin is satisfied that the child is adoptable, it shall,

(a) prepare a report including information about his or her identity, adoptablity, background, social environment, family history, medical history including that of the child's family, and any special needs of the child;

(b) give due consideration to the child's upbringing and to his or her ethnic, religious and cultural background;

(c) ensure that consents have been obtained in accordance with Article 4; and

(d) determine, on the basis in particular of the reports relating to the child and the prospective adoptive parents, whether the envisaged placement is in the best interests of the child.

2. It shall transmit to the Central Authority of the receiving State its report on the child, proof that the necessary consents have been obtained and the reasons for its determination on the placement, taking care not to reveal the identity of the mother and the father if, in the State of origin, these identities may not be disclosed.

Article 17

Any decision in the State of origin that a child should be entrusted to prospective adoptive parents may only be made if,

(a) the Central Authority of that State has ensured that the prospective adoptive parents agree;

(b) the Central Authority of the receiving State has approved such decision, where such approval is required by the law of that State or by the Central Authority of the State of origin;

(c) the Central Authorities of both States have agreed that the adoption may proceed; and

(d) it has been determined, in accordance with Article 5, that the prospective adoptive parents are eligible and suited to adopt and that the child is or will be authorized to enter and reside permanently in the receiving State.

Article 18

The Central Authorities of both States shall take all necessary steps to obtain permission for the child to leave the State of origin and to enter and reside permanently in the receiving State.

Article 19

1. The transfer of the child to the receiving State may only be carried out if the requirements of Article 17 have been satisfied.

2. The Central Authorities of both States shall ensure that this transfer takes place in secure and appropriate circumstances and, if possible, in the company of the adoptive or prospective adoptive parent.

3. If the transfer of the child does not take place, the report referred to in Articles 15 and 16 are to be sent back to the authorities who forwarded them.

Article 20

The Central Authorities shall keep each other informed about the adoption process and the measures taken to complete it, as well as about the progress of the placement if a probationary period is required.

Article 21

1. Where the adoption is to take place after the transfer of the child to the receiving State and it appears to the Central Authority of that State that the continued placement of the child with the prospective adoptive parents is not in the child's best interests, such Central Authority shall take the measures necessary to protect the child, in particular,

(a) to cause the child to be withdrawn from the prospective adoptive parents and to arrange temporary care;

(b) in consultation with the Central Authority of the State of origin, to arrange without delay a new placement of the child with a view to adoption or, if this is not appropriate, to arrange alternative long-term care; an adoption shall not take place until the Central Authority of the State of origin has been duly informed concerning the new prospective adoptive parents;

(c) as a last resort, to arrange the return of the child, if his or her interests so require.

2. Having regard in particular to the age and degree of maturity of the child, he or she shall be consulted and, where appropriate, his or her consent obtained in relation to measures to be taken under this Article.

Article 22

1. The functions of a Central Authority under this Chapter may be performed by public authorities or by bodies accredited under Chapter III, to the extent permitted by the law of its State.

2. Any Contracting State may declare to the depositary of the Convention that the functions of the Central Authority under Articles 15 to 21 may be performed in that State, to the extent permitted by the law and subject to the supervision of the competent authorities of that State, also by bodies or persons who,

> (a) meet the requirements of integrity, professional competence, experience and accountability of that State; and

> (b) are qualified by their ethical standards and by training or experience to work in the field of intercountry adoption.

3. A Contracting State which makes the declaration provided for in paragraph 2 shall keep the Permanent Bureau of the Hague Conference on Private International Law informed of the names and addresses of these bodies and persons.

4. Any Contracting State may declare to the depositary of the Convention that adoptions of children habitually resident in its territory may only take place if the functions of the Central Authorities are performed in accordance with paragraph 1.

5. Notwithstanding any declaration made under paragraph 2, the reports provided for in Articles 15 and 16 shall, in every case, be prepared under the responsibility of the Central Authority or other authorities or bodies in accordance with paragraph 1.

Chapter V — Recognition and Effects of the Adoption

Article 23

1. An adoption certified by the competent authority of the State of the adoption as having been made in accordance with the Convention shall be recognized by operation of law in the other Contracting States. The certificate shall specify when and by whom the agreements under Article 17, subparagraph (c), were given.

2. Each Contracting State shall, at the time of signature, ratification, acceptance, approval or accession, notify the depositary of the Convention of the identity and the functions of the authority or the authorities which, in that State, are competent to make the certification. It shall also notify the depositary of any modification in the designation of these authorities.

Article 24

The recognition of an adoption may be refused in a Contracting State only if the adoption is manifestly contrary to its public policy, taking into account the best interests of the child.

Article 25

Any Contracting State may declare to the depositary of the Convention that it will not be bound under this Convention to recognize adoptions made in accordance with an agreement concluded by application of Article 39, paragraph 2.

Article 26

1. The recognition of an adoption includes recognition of,

(a) the legal parent-child relationship between the child and his or her adoptive parents;

(b) parental responsibility of the adoptive parents for the child;

(c) the termination of a pre-existing legal relationship between the child and his or her mother and father, if the adoption has this effect in the Contracting State where it was made.

2. In the case of an adoption having the effect of terminating a pre-existing legal parent-child relationship, the child shall enjoy in the receiving State, and in any other Contracting State where the adoption is recognized, rights equivalent to those resulting from adoptions having this effect in each such State.

3. The preceding paragraphs shall not prejudice the application of any provision more favourable for the child, in force in the Contracting State which recognizes the adoption.

Article 27

1. Where an adoption granted in the State of origin does not have the effect of terminating a pre-existing legal parent-child relationship, it may, in the receiving State which recognizes the adoption under the Convention, be converted into an adoption having such an effect,

(a) if the law of the receiving State so permits; and

(b) if the consents referred to in Article 4, subparagraphs (c) and (d), have been or are given for the purpose of such an adoption.

2. Article 23 applies to the decision converting the adoption.

Chapter VI — General Provisions

Article 28

The Convention does not affect any law of a State of origin which requires that the adoption of a child habitually resident within that State take place in that State or which prohibits the child's placement in, or transfer to, the receiving State prior to adoption.

Article 29

There shall be no contact between the prospective adoptive parents and the child's parents or any other person who has care of the child until the requirements of Article 4, subparagraphs (a) to (c), and Article 5, subparagraph (a), have been met, unless the adoption takes place within the family or unless the contact is in compliance with the conditions established by the competent authority of the State of origin.

Intercountry Adoption

Article 30

1. The competent authorities of a Contracting State shall ensure that information held by them concerning the child's origin, in particular information concerning the identity of his or her parents, as well as the medical history, is preserved.

2. They shall ensure that the child or his or her representative has access to such information, under appropriate guidance, in so far as is permitted by the law of that State.

Article 31

Without prejudice to Article 30, personal data gathered or transmitted under the Convention, especially data referred to in Articles 15 and 16, shall be used only for the purposes for which they were gathered or transmitted.

Article 32

1. No one shall derive improper financial or other gain from an activity related to an intercountry adoption.

2. Only costs and expenses, including reasonable professional fees of persons involved in the adoption, may be charged or paid.

3. The directors, administrators and employees of bodies involved in an adoption shall not receive remuneration which is unreasonably high in relation to services rendered.

Article 33

A competent authority which finds that any provision of the Convention has not been respected or that there is a serious risk that it may not be respected, shall immediately inform the Central Authority of its State. This Central Authority shall be responsible for ensuring that appropriate measures are taken.

Article 34

If the competent authority of the State of destination of a document so requests, a translation certified as being in conformity with the original must be furnished. Unless otherwise provided, the costs of such translation are to be borne by the prospective adoptive parents.

Article 35

The competent authorities of the Contracting States shall act expeditiously in the process of adoption.

Article 36

In relation to a State which has two or more systems of law with regard to adoption applicable in different territorial units,

(a) any reference to habitual residence in that State shall be construed as referring to habitual residence in a territorial unit of that State;

(b) any reference to the law of that State shall be construed as referring to the law in force in the relevant territorial unit;

(c) any reference to the competent authorities or to the public authorities of that State shall be construed as referring to those authorized to act in the relevant territorial unit;

(d) any reference to the accredited bodies of that State shall be construed as referring to bodies accredited in the relevant territorial unit.

Article 37

In relation to a State which with regard to adoption has two or more systems of law applicable to different categories of persons, any reference to the law of that State shall be construed as referring to the legal system specified by the law of that State.

Article 38

A State within which different territorial units have their own rules of law in respect of adoption shall not be bound to apply the Convention where a State with a unified system of law would not be bound to do so.

Article 39

1. The Convention does not affect any international instrument to which Contracting States are Parties and which contains provisions on matters governed by the Convention, unless a contrary declaration is made by the States Parties to such instrument.

2. Any Contracting State may enter into agreements with one or more other Contracting States, with a view to improving the application of the Convention in their mutual relations. These agreements may derogate only from the provisions of Articles 14 to 16 and 18 to 21. The States which have concluded such an agreement shall transmit a copy to the depositary of the Convention.

Article 40

No reservation to the Convention shall be permitted.

Article 41

The Convention shall apply in every case where an application pursuant to Article 14 has been received after the Convention has entered into force in the receiving State and the State of origin.

Article 42

The Secretary General of the Hague Conference on Private International Law shall at regular intervals convene a Special Commission in order to review the practical operation of the Convention.

Chapter VII — Final Clauses

Article 43

1. The Convention shall be opened for signature by the States which were Members of the Hague Conference on Private International Law at the time of its Seventeenth Session and by the other States which participated in that Session.

2. It shall be ratified, accepted or approved and the instruments of ratification, acceptance or approval shall be deposited with the Ministry of Foreign Affairs of the Kingdom of the Netherlands, depositary of the Convention.

Article 44

1. Any other State may accede to the Convention after it has entered into force in accordance with Article 46, paragraph 1.

2. The instrument of accession shall be deposited with the depositary.

3. Such accession shall have effect only as regards the relations between the acceding State and those Contracting States which have not raised an objection to its accession in the six months after the receipt of the notification referred to in subparagraph (b) of Article 48. Such an objection may also be raised by States at the time when they ratify, accept or approve the Convention after an accession. Any such objection shall be notified to the depositary.

Article 45

1. If a State has two or more territorial units in which different systems of law are applicable in relation to matters dealt with in the Convention, it may at the time of signature, ratification, acceptance, approval or accession declare that this Convention shall extend to all its territorial units or only to one or more of them and may modify this declaration by submitting another declaration at any time.

2. Any such declaration shall be notified to the depositary and shall state expressly the territorial units to which the Convention applies.

3. If a State makes no declaration under this Article, the Convention is to extend to all territorial units of the State.

Article 46

1. The Convention shall enter into force on the first day of the month following the expiration of three months after the deposit of the third instrument of ratification, acceptance or approval referred to in Article 43.

2. Thereafter the Convention shall enter into force,

(a) for each State ratifying, accepting or approving it subsequently, or acceding to it, on the first day of the month following the expiration of three months after the deposit of its instrument of ratification, acceptance, approval or accession;

(b) for a territorial unit to which the Convention has been extended in conformity with Article 45, on the first day of the month following the expiration of three months after the notification referred to in that Article.

Article 47

1. A State Party to the Convention may denounce it by a notification in writing addressed to the depositary.

2. The denunciation takes effect on the first day of the month following the expiration of 12 months after the notification is received by the depositary. Where a longer period for the denunciation to take effect is specified in the notification, the denunciation takes effect upon the expiration of such longer period after the notification is received by the depositary.

Article 48

The depositary shall notify the States Members of the Hague Conference on Private International Law, the other States which participated in the Seventeenth Session and the States which have acceded in accordance with Article 44, of the following,

(a) the signatures, ratifications, acceptances and approvals referred to in Article 43;

(b) the accessions and objections raised to accessions referred to in Article 44;

(c) the date on which the Convention enters into force in accordance with Article 46;

(d) the declarations and designations referred to in Articles 22, 23, 25 and 45;

(e) the agreements referred to in Article 39;

(f) the denunciation referred to in Article 47.

Applicable Provision

— 1999, c. 12, Sched. G, s. 25(5):

(5) Despite subsection (4), members of the Child and Family Services Review Board immediately before that subsection comes into force shall be members of the Licence Appeal Tribunal for the purpose of performing the duties of the Tribunal with respect to proceedings before the Board that were commenced before that subsection comes into force.

ONT. REG. 200/99 — GENERAL REGULATION

made under the *Intercountry Adoption Act, 1998*

O. Reg. 200/99, as am. O. Reg. 135/00.

CENTRAL AUTHORITY AND DIRECTORS

1. For the purpose of Article 6 of the Convention, the Central Authority for Ontario is the Ministry of Community and Social Services.

2. The following persons are Directors for the purposes of the Act:

1. The Manager, Central Services Unit, Ministry of Community and Social Services.

2. The Coordinator of Private and International Adoption, Ministry of Community and Social Services.

ASSIGNMENT OF FUNCTIONS OF CENTRAL AUTHORITY

3. If a licensee meets the qualifications for an accredited body under Article 11 of the Convention, the licensee may perform the following functions of the Central Authority:

1. Receive applications from persons wishing to adopt a child from another country, as provided for in Article 14.

2. Ensure that prospective adoptive parents have agreed to the proposed adoption of a child from another country, as provided for in Article 17 (a).

3. Take all necessary steps to obtain permission for the child to leave the State of origin and to enter and reside permanently in the receiving State, as provided for in Article 18.

4. Ensure that the transfer of the child takes place in secure and appropriate circumstances and, if possible, in the company of the adoptive or prospective adoptive parents, as provided for in Article 19 (2).

5. Provide progress reports to the Central Authority of a child's State of origin or to a Director about the adoption process and measures taken to complete it, as well as the progress of the placement if a probationary period is required, as provided for in Article 20.

6. Take the measures necessary to protect a child during a probationary period in accordance with Article 21.

PRESCRIBED PERSONS AND BODIES

4. The following are prescribed persons and bodies for the purposes of clause 7 (d) of the Act:

1. Children's aid societies in Ontario.

2. Ministries and agencies of the Government of Ontario.

3. The authorities responsible for law enforcement in Ontario.

DEFINITION OF FACILITATE

5. For the purpose of subsection 8 (1) of the Act,

"facilitate", with respect to an adoption, means any of the following:

1. Receive an application under section 5 of the Act.

2. Submit a report of an adoption homestudy to a Director.

3. Present a proposal to adopt a particular child to an applicant whose eligibility and suitability to adopt has been approved by a Director.

4. Submit an applicant's consent or refusal to adopt a particular child to the Central authority of a child's State of origin, the authority responsible for adoption in the child's State of origin or a Director.

5. Submit to the Central authority of a child's State of origin, the authority responsible for adoption in the child's State of origin or a Director a progress report concerning a child who has been placed for adoption but whose adoption has not been finalized when such a report is requested by the state of origin.

EXPENSES FOR WHICH FEES MAY BE CHARGED

6. The following are prescribed as classes of expenses incurred by a licensee for the purposes of clause 19 (a) of the Act:

1. Expenses incurred in receiving and processing applications for intercountry adoptions from prospective adoptive parents.

2. Expenses incurred with respect to the provision of adoption orientation and preparation to applicants for intercountry adoptions.

3. Expenses incurred with respect to an adoption homestudy.

4. Expenses incurred with respect to proposals to adopt particular children presented to applicants whose eligibility and suitability to adopt has been approved by a Director.

5. Expenses incurred in submitting applicants' consents or refusals to adopt particular children to the Central authority of a child's State of origin, the authority responsible for adoption in the child's State of origin or a Director.

6. Expenses incurred in obtaining permission for a child to leave his or her State of origin and enter and reside permanently in Ontario.

7. Expenses incurred in making arrangements for the secure and appropriate transfer of a child from the State of origin to Ontario.

8. If an adoption placement requires a probationary period before finalization, expenses incurred in making arrangements for supervising the placement.

9. Expenses incurred in making progress reports and follow up reports.

10. Any expenses the licensee incurs with respect to services related to the adoption provided in the child's State of origin in accordance with the laws of that State.

11. Expenses with respect to the administration of an intercountry adoption.

7. The following is prescribed as a class of expenses incurred by a person authorized to make a home study under subsection 5 (3) of the Act for the purposes of clause 19 (b) of the Act:

1. Expenses incurred by the person in preparing a home study to assess the prospective adoptive parent's eligibility and suitability to adopt.

8. The following is prescribed as a class of expenses incurred by a Director for the purposes of clause 19 (c) of the Act:

1. Expenses incurred by the Director in processing an adoptive parent's or prospective adoptive parent's intercountry adoption file.

2. Expenses with respect to the administration of an adoptive parent's or prospective adoptive parent's intercountry adoption file.

LICENCES

9. (1) An application under section 8 of the Act for a licence or for renewal of a licence shall be in the form approved by the Minister.

(2) The application shall contain the following information:

1. The name, address, telephone number and other relevant identifying information concerning the applicant.

2. Information concerning the applicant's knowledge of the legislation of Canada, Ontario and foreign jurisdictions relevant to intercountry adoption.

3. Information concerning the applicant's training, experience and expertise with respect to intercountry adoption.

4. Information concerning the applicant's ability to provide services and carry out administrative procedures in accordance with the Act.

(3) The fee payable on an application for a licence or for renewal of a licence is $1,800.

(4) A licence expires one year after it is issued.

RECORDS AND REPORTS

10. (1) Every licensee shall open and keep up to date a separate file with respect to each prospective adoptive parent.

(2) If a child who is the subject of an adoption proposal is not transferred to Ontario from his or her State of origin, the licensee with respect to that child shall return to a Director all copies of the adoption proposal with respect to that child.

(3) Subject to subsection (2) and section 18 of the Act, every licensee shall permanently retain each file referred to in subsection (1).

11. (1) Every licensee shall keep a record of all expenditures made and money received with respect to the licensee's facilitation of intercountry adoptions.

(2) Every licensee shall keep a separate book of account showing, for each prospective adoptive parent with respect to whom the licensee makes a deposit or withdrawal of money, the name of the adoptive parent from whom the deposit or withdrawal is made and the date of that deposit or withdrawal.

(3) Every licensee shall, when required by a Director, prepare and submit financial reports, including reports by a public accountant licensed under the *Public Accountancy Act*, with respect to the licensee's facilitation of intercountry adoptions.

12. A corporate licensee shall notify a Director in writing within 15 days after any change in the officers or directors of the corporation.

POWER OF ENTRY

13. A person entering premises under section 17 of the Act shall produce identification, including evidence of appointment, on the request of the occupier.

EXEMPTION

13.1 The Act and the regulations do not apply to an adoption to which the Convention applies if the adoption will be finalized in an Ontario court.

O. Reg. 135/00, s. 1

TABLE OF CONCORDANCE

Marriage

MARRIAGE ACT

R.S.O. 1990, c. M.3, as am. O. Reg. 726/91, s. 1; S.O. 1993, c. 27, Sched.; 1994, c. 27, s. 89; 1998, c. 18, Sched. E, ss. 179–182 [ss. 180–182 not in force at date of publication.]; 1999, c. 12, Sched. F, ss. 30–32 [Not in force at date of publication.]; 2001, c. 9, Sched. D, s. 10 [s. 10(4) not in force at date of publication.]; 2001, c. 13, s. 20 (Fr.); 2002, c. 14, Sched., s. 11; 2002, c. 17, Sched. F, s. 1; 2002, c. 25 [Not in force at date of publication.].

1. (1) Definitions — In this Act,

"band" means a band as defined in the *Indian Act* (Canada); ("bande")

"church" includes chapel, meeting-house or place set aside for religious worship; ("église")

"Indian" means a person who is registered as an Indian or entitled to be registered as an Indian under the *Indian Act* (Canada); ("Indien")

"issuer" means a person authorized under this Act to issue marriage licences; ("délivreur de licences")

"judge" means a provincial judge or a judge of the Superior Court of Justice; ("juge")

"licence" means a marriage licence issued under this Act; ("licence")

"Minister" means the Minister of Consumer and Business Services; ("ministre")

"prescribed" means prescribed by the regulations; ("prescrit")

"regulations" means the regulations made under this Act; ("règlements")

"reserve" means a reserve as defined in the *Indian Act* (Canada). ("réserve")

(2) Application of Act to subsequent ceremonies — This Act does not apply in respect of any ceremony or form of marriage gone through by two persons who are married to each other by a marriage previously solemnized in accordance with this Act or recognized as valid in Ontario.

2001, c. 9, Sched. D, s. 10(1), (2)

2. Administration — The administration of this Act is under the direction of the Minister.

3. (1) Delegation of powers and duties — The Minister may delegate any of his or her powers or duties under this Act to the Deputy Minister of Consumer and Business Services or to any persons employed in the Ministry of Consumer and Business Services.

(2) Same — The delegation shall be in writing and may be made subject to such conditions as are set out in it.

1994, c. 27, s. 89(1); 2001, c. 9, Sched. D, s. 10(2)

4. Authority to marry — No marriage may be solemnized except under the authority of a licence issued in accordance with this Act or the publication of banns.

5. (1) Who may marry — Any person who is of the age of majority may obtain a licence or be married under the authority of the publication of banns, provided no lawful cause exists to hinder the solemnization.

(2) Idem — No person shall issue a licence to a minor, or solemnize the marriage of a minor under the authority of the publication of banns, except where the minor is of the age of sixteen years or more and has the consent in writing of both parents in the form prescribed by the regulations.

(3) Giving of consent — The consent referred to in subsection (2) is not required in respect of a person who is a widow, a widower or divorced.

(4) Idem — Where one of the parents of a minor is dead or both parents are living apart, the consent required by subsection (2) may be given by the parent having actual or legal custody of the minor.

(5) Idem — Where both parents of a minor are dead or are voluntary or involuntary patients in a psychiatric facility, or are residents of a facility under the *Developmental Services Act*, the consent required by subsection (2) may be given by a lawfully appointed guardian or an acknowledged guardian who has brought up or who for the three years immediately preceding the intended marriage has supported the minor.

(6) Idem — Where a minor is made a ward of someone other than a parent by order of a court or under any Act, the consent required by subsection (2) may be given by the lawful guardian of the minor or person responsible for exercising the rights and duties of a guardian of the minor.

6. (1) Application to dispense with consent — Where a person whose consent is required by section 5 is not available or unreasonably or arbitrarily withholds consent, the person in respect of whose marriage the consent is required may apply to a judge without the intervention of a litigation guardian for an order dispensing with the consent.

(2) Powers of judge — The judge shall hear the application in a summary manner and may, in his or her discretion, make an order dispensing with the consent required by section 5.

7. Persons mentally ill or under influence — No person shall issue a licence to or solemnize the marriage of any person whom he or she knows or has reasonable grounds to believe lacks capacity to marry by reason of being mentally ill or mentally defective or under the influence of intoxicating liquor or drugs.

8. (1) Where dissolution of former marriage recognized in Ontario — An applicant for a licence who has been previously married is entitled to be issued a licence if such marriage has been dissolved or annulled and such dissolution or annulment is recognized under the law of Ontario and the applicant otherwise complies with the requirements of this Act.

(2) Proof of divorce, etc. — Subject to subsection (6), an issuer shall not issue a licence to a person whose previous marriage has been dissolved or annulled in Canada unless the person produces for inspection by the issuer,

  (a) the final decree or judgment dissolving or annulling the previous marriage;

  (b) a copy of the final decree, judgment or Act dissolving or annulling the previous marriage certified by the proper officer; or

(c) a certificate of divorce issued by the registrar under the Rules of Civil Procedure.

(2.1) Same — Before issuing a licence, an issuer may require a person to whom subsection (2) applies to deposit with the issuer such material as the issuer considers relevant to the proof of the divorce or annulment.

(3) Where dissolution, etc., outside Canada — Subject to subsection (6), no issuer shall issue a licence to a person whose previous marriage has been dissolved or annulled elsewhere than in Canada, unless the authorization in writing of the Minister is obtained upon the deposit of such material as the Minister may require.

(4) Review of refusal to issue licence — Where an issuer refuses to issue a licence, or the Minister refuses to issue an authorization under subsection (3), the applicant may apply to the Divisional Court for judicial review under the *Judicial Review Procedure Act* and for an order directing that a licence be issued to the applicant and if the court finds that the applicant is so entitled it may make such an order.

(5) Parties — The applicant, the Minister and such other persons as the court may order are parties to an application under subsection (4).

(6) Issue of licence under court order — Where an applicant for a licence files with an issuer, together with his or her application, an order of the Divisional Court made on an application under subsection (4) directing that a licence be issued to the applicant, the issuer shall issue the licence.

1993, c. 27, Sched.; 1994, c. 27, s. 89(2)

9. (1) Order under *Declarations of Death Act, 2002* — If an order has been made under the *Declarations of Death Act, 2002* declaring that a married person's spouse has died, the married person may, subject to the provisions of this Act, obtain a licence or be married under the authority of the publication of banns upon depositing a certified copy of the order with the person issuing the licence or solemnizing the marriage together with an affidavit in the required form.

(2) Exception — Subsection (1) does not apply if the order is limited, under subsection 2(6) of the *Declarations of Death Act, 2002*, to specified purposes other than remarriage.

2001, c. 9, Sched. D, s. 10(3); 2002, c. 14, Sched., s. 11

10. Discretionary power of Minister — Despite anything in this Act, if the Minister considers that circumstances justify the issue of a licence in any particular case, the Minister may, in his or her absolute discretion, authorize the issue of the licence.

11. (1) Issuers — Marriage licenses may be issued by the clerk of every local municipality except a township.

(1.1) Interpretation — In subsection (1) and clause (2)(a), **"township"** means a local municipality that had the status of a township on December 31, 2002 and, but for the enactment of the *Municipal Act, 2001*, would have had the status of a township on January 1, 2003.

(2) Same — If the Minister considers it expedient for the public convenience, the Minister may in writing appoint as an issuer,

    (a) the clerk of a township, or a resident of a county or township adjacent thereto;

    (b) a resident of a territorial district; or

    (c) a member of a band, on the band council's recommendation.

(3) Deputy issuers — An issuer may, with the approval in writing of the Minister or of the head of the council of the local municipality of which he or she is clerk, appoint in writing one or more deputies to act for him or her, and any such deputy while so acting has the power of the issuer appointing him or her.

(4) Notice of appointment of deputy — The issuer shall, upon appointing a deputy, forthwith transmit to the Minister a notice of the appointment, and of the name and official position of the person by whom the appointment has been approved, and the Minister may at any time cancel the appointment.

(5) Signature of licences by deputy — The deputy shall sign each licence that he or she issues with the issuer's name as well as the deputy's name, using the words "AB, Issuer of Marriage Licences, per CD, Deputy Issuer" or "Le délivreur de licences AB, par son adjoint CD".

Proposed Repeal — 11(5)

(5) [Repealed 1999, c. 12, Sched. F, s. 30. Not in force at date of publication.]

1994, c. 27, s. 89(3); 2002, c. 17, Sched. F, s. 1

12. (1) Evidence on applications — An issuer or the Minister may require evidence to identify any applicant or to establish his or her status and may examine, under oath if required, any applicant or other person as to any matter pertaining to the issue of a licence.

(2) Untrue information — Where an issuer has reason to believe that any information set out in an application for a licence is untrue, he or she shall not issue the licence unless, on the production of such further evidence as the issuer may require, he or she is satisfied as to the truth of the information.

13. (1) Record of licences — Every issuer shall keep in his or her office a record of the serial number and the date of issue of every licence issued by him or her, and the names and addresses of the parties to the intended marriage.

(2) Searches — Any person is entitled, upon application, to have a search made respecting any licence issued within three months immediately preceding the date of application.

Proposed Addition — 13(3)

(3) Information disclosed — The search shall not disclose any information other than whether or not a licence has been issued and, if so, the date of issue of the licence.

1999, c. 12, Sched. F, s. 31 [Not in force at date of publication.]

14. Material to be forwarded to Registrar General — Every issuer immediately upon issuing a licence and every person registered as authorized to solemnize marriage upon publishing banns shall forward to the Registrar General,

(a) any consent under section 5;

(b) any judge's order under section 6;

(c) any affidavit or judge's order under section 9;

(d) any documentary or other material filed on the application for a licence under section 8;

(e) any affidavit as to age;

(f) any documentary material obtained under section 12.

15. Oaths — Issuers may administer reoaths for the purposes of this Act.

16. Indians — Where both parties to an intended marriage are Indians ordinarily resident on a reserve in Ontario or on Crown lands in Ontario, no fee shall be charged for the licence.

17. (1) Publication of banns — Where a marriage is to be solemnized under the authority of the publication of banns, the intention to marry shall be proclaimed openly in an audible voice during divine service,

(a) where the parties are in the habit of attending worship at the same church, being within Canada, at that church; or

(b) where the parties are in the habit of attending worship in different churches, being within Canada, in each such church.

(2) Method and time of publication — The banns shall be published according to the usage of the denomination, faith or creed of the church in which they are published and during divine Sunday service.

(3) Exception — Where the usage of any denomination, faith or creed substitutes any other day as the usual and principal day of the week for the celebration of divine service, the banns shall be published on such other day.

(4) Proof — The person or persons who publish banns shall certify proof thereof in the prescribed form.

18. Where banns not to be published — Banns shall not be published where either of the parties to the intended marriage has been married and the marriage has been dissolved or annulled.

19. Prohibited degrees to be endorsed — The Form to this Act respecting the prohibited degrees of affinity and consanguinity shall be endorsed on the licence and on the proof of publication of banns.

Proposed Amendment — 19

19. Prohibited degrees — If the regulations prescribe a form setting out the relationships by consanguinity or adoption that, under the *Marriage (Prohibited Degrees) Act* (Canada), bar the lawful solemnization of marriage, the form shall be endorsed on the licence and on the proof of publication of banns.

1998, c. 18, Sched. E, s. 180 [Not in force at date of publication.]

20. (1) Who may solemnize marriage — No person shall solemnize a marriage unless he or she is authorized by or under section 24 or is registered under this section as a person authorized to solemnize marriage.

(2) Application for registration — Upon application the Minister may, subject to subsection (3), register any person as a person authorized to solemnize marriage.

(3) Who may be registered — No person shall be registered unless it appears to the Minister,

> (a) that the person has been ordained or appointed according to the rites and usages of the religious body to which he or she belongs, or is, by the rules of that religious body, deemed ordained or appointed;

> (b) that the person is duly recognized by the religious body to which he or she belongs as entitled to solemnize marriage according to its rites and usages;

> (c) that the religious body to which the person belongs is permanently established both as to the continuity of its existence and as to its rites and ceremonies; and

> (d) that the person is resident in Ontario or has his or her parish or pastoral charge in whole or in part in Ontario; provided that in the case of a person who is in Ontario temporarily and who, if resident in Ontario, might be registered under this section, the Minister may register him or her as authorized to solemnize marriage during a period to be fixed by the Minister.

(4) Where no person authorized to solemnize marriage — Despite subsection (1), where it appears to the Minister that the doctrines of a religious body described in clause (3)(c) do not recognize any person as authorized to solemnize marriage, the Minister may register a person duly designated by the the the governing authority of the religious body who shall, in respect of marriages performed according to the rites, usages and customs of the religious body, perform all the duties imposed by this Act upon a person solemnizing a marriage, other than solemnizing the marriage.

(5) Idem — Where a person registered under subsection (4) performs the duties imposed by subsection (4), every marriage solemnized according to the rites, usages and customs of the religious body is valid.

21. (1) Register — The Minister shall keep a register of the name of every person registered as a person authorized to solemnize marriage, the date of such registration, and such other particulars as the Minister considers advisable.

(2) Certificate of registration — The Minister may issue a certificate of registration under this section in the prescribed form.

22. (1) Cancellation of registration — Where it appears to the Minister that any person registered as authorized to solemnize marriage has ceased to possess the qualifications entitling him or her to be so registered, or for any other cause, the Minister may cancel the registration.

(2) Notice of change — Every religious body, members of which are registered under this Act, shall notify the Minister of the name of every such member so registered who has died or has ceased to reside in Ontario or has ceased to be associated with such religious body.

23. Publication of registration and cancellation — When a person is registered under this Act as authorized to solemnize marriage, and when any such registration is cancelled, the Minister shall publish notice thereof in *The Ontario Gazette*.

24. (1) Civil marriage — A judge, a justice of the peace or any other person of a class designated by the regulations may solemnize marriages under the authority of a licence.

Proposed Amendment — 24(1)

(1) Civil marriage — A judge, a justice of the peace, a marriage commissioner or any other person of a class designated by the regulations may solemnize marriages under the authority of a licence.

2002, c. 25, s. 1 [Not in force at date of publication.]

(2) Time and place — The solemnization of a marriage by a judge shall take place in the judge's office and shall be performed between the hours of 9 o'clock in the morning and 5 o'clock in the afternoon.

Proposed Amendment — 24(2)

(2) Regulations, marriage commissioners — The Lieutenant Governor in Council may make regulations,

(a) authorizing the person or body specified in the regulations to appoint persons or classes of persons as marriage commissioners;

(b) respecting any matter pertaining to the governance of marriage commissioners, including their appointment, their training, their registration, the standards required for the performance of their powers and duties, their remuneration, their disciplining and their dismissal.

2002, c. 25, s. 1 [Not in force at date of publication.]

Proposed Addition — 24(2.1), (2.2)

(2.1) General or specific application — A regulation made under subsection (2) may be of general application or specific to any person or persons or class or classes in its application.

(2.2) Classes — A class described in the regulations made under subsection (2) or under clause 34(g) may be described according to any characteristic or combination of characteristics and may be described to include or exclude any specified member, whether or not with the same characteristics.

2002, c. 25, s. 1 [Not in force at date of publication.]

(3) Form of ceremony — No particular form of ceremony is required except that in some part of the ceremony, in the presence of the person solemnizing the marriage and witnesses, each of the parties shall declare:

I do solemnly declare that I do not know of any lawful impediment why I, AB, may not be joined in matrimony to CD,

Je déclare solennellement que moi, AB, je ne connais aucun empêchement légal à mon mariage avec CD,

and each of the parties shall say to the other:

I call upon these persons here present to witness that I, AB, do take you, CD, to be my lawful wedded wife (*or husband*),

Je demande aux personnes qui sont ici présentes d'être témoins que moi, AB, je prends CD comme légitime époux (*épouse*),

after which the person solemnizing the marriage shall say:

I, EF, by virtue of the powers vested in me by the *Marriage Act*, do hereby pronounce you AB and CD to be husband and wife,

En vertu des pouvoirs qui me sont conférés par la *Loi sur le mariage,* moi, EF, je vous déclare mari et femme, AB et CD.

(4) Language — For the purposes of subsection (3), it is sufficient to use only the English or only the French language.

25. Attendance of parties and witnesses — Every marriage shall be solemnized in the presence of the parties and at least two witnesses who shall affix their names as witnesses to the entry in the register made under section 28.

26. Proof of publication — No marriage shall be solemnized under the authority of the publication of banns unless proof of publication by the person or persons publishing the banns has been deposited with the person solemnizing the marriage.

27. (1) [Repealed 1994, c. 27, s. 89(4).]

(2) Idem: under banns — A marriage shall not be solemnized under the authority of the publication of banns, earlier than the fifth day after the date of the publication of banns.

(3) Time within which marriage to be solemnized — A marriage shall be solemnized only within the three months immediately following the issue of the licence or the publication of banns, as the case may be.

28. (1) Entry in marriage register — Every person shall immediately after he or she has solemnized a marriage,

    (a) where the marriage was solemnized in a church, enter in the church register kept for the purpose; or

    (b) where the marriage was solemnized elsewhere than in the church, enter in a register kept by him or her for the purpose,

the particulars prescribed by the regulations, and the entry shall be authenticated by his or her signature and those of the parties and witnesses.

(2) Marriage certificate — Every person who solemnizes a marriage shall, at the time of the marriage, if required by either of the parties thereto, give a certificate of the marriage specifying the names of the parties, the date of the marriage, the names of the witnesses, and whether the marriage was solemnized under the authority of a licence or publication of banns.

Proposed Amendment — 28(2)

(2) Record of marriage — Every person who solemnizes a marriage shall, at the time of the marriage, if required by either of the parties, give a record of solemnization of the marriage specifying the names of the parties, the date of the marriage, the names of the witnesses, and whether the marriage was solemnized under the authority of a licence or publication of banns.

1999, c. 12, Sched. F, s. 32 [Not in force at date of publication.]; 2001, c. 9, Sched. D, s. 10(4)
[Not in force at date of publication.]

---

29. (1) Supply of marriage registers — Every person or religious body authorized to solemnize marriages may apply to the Minister for a marriage register, and the Minister shall thereupon supply the register.

(2) Property of Crown — Every register supplied by the Minister is the property of the Crown.

30. Protection of persons solemnizing marriage in good faith — No person who solemnizes or purports to solemnize a marriage is subject to any action or liability by reason of there having been any legal impediment to the marriage unless, at the time the person performed the ceremony, he or she was aware of the impediment.

31. Marriages solemnized in good faith — If the parties to a marriage solemnized in good faith and intended to be in compliance with this Act are not under a legal disqualification to contract such marriage and after such solemnization have lived together and cohabited as man and wife, such marriage shall be deemed a valid marriage, although the person who solemnized the marriage was not authorized to solemnize marriage, and despite the absence of or any irregularity or insufficiency in the publication of banns or the issue of the licence.

32. (1) Breach of promise of marriage abolished — No action shall be brought for a breach of a promise to marry or for any damages resulting therefrom.

(2) Application of subs. (1) — Subsection (1) does not apply in respect of actions for breach of promise to marry or damages resulting therefrom commenced before the 1st day of August, 1978.

33. Recovery of gifts made in contemplation of marriage — Where one person makes a gift to another in contemplation of or conditional upon their marriage to each other and the marriage fails to take place or is abandoned, the question of whether or not the failure or abandonment was caused by or was the fault of the donor shall not be considered in determining the right of the donor to recover the gift.

34. Regulations — The Lieutenant Governor in Council may make regulations,

(a) prescribing forms for the purposes of this Act and providing for their use, and requiring any matter therein to be verified by affidavit;

(b) prescribing any matter required by this Act to be prescribed by the regulations;

(c) requiring the payment of fees in respect of any matter required or authorized to be done under this Act, and providing for the retention of fees or any portion thereof by issuers and persons solemnizing marriages or any class of them and for the commutation of such fees;

(d) prescribing the duties of issuers;

(e) requiring persons authorized to solemnize marriages to furnish such information and returns as are prescribed;

(f) amending the Form to this Act to make it conform to the law for the time being;

Proposed Amendment — 34(f)

(f) prescribing a form setting out the relationships by consanguinity or adoption that, under the *Marriage (Prohibited Degrees) Act* (Canada), bar the lawful solemnization of marriage.

1998, c. 18, Sched. E, s. 181 [Not in force at date of publication.]

(g) designating classes of persons authorized to solemnize marriages under section 24.

35. (1) Penalty: false statements — Every person who knowingly makes any false statement in any document required under this Act, in addition to any other penalty or punishment to which the person may be liable, is guilty of an offence and on conviction is liable to a fine of not more than $1,000 or to imprisonment for a term of not more than one year, or to both.

(2) Idem: general — Every person who contravenes any provision of this Act for which no other penalty is provided is guilty of an offence and on conviction is liable to a fine of not more than $500.

Form [1]

Number in brackets editorially added by Carswell.

(Section 19)

Degrees of consanguinity which, under the *Marriage (Prohibited Degrees) Act* (Canada), bar the lawful solemnization of marriage.

A man may not marry his	**A woman may not marry her**
1. Grandmother	1. Grandfather
2. Mother	2. Father
3. Daughter	3. Son
4. Sister	4. Brother
5. Granddaughter	5. Grandson

The relationships set forth in this table include all such relationships, whether by the whole or half blood or by order of adoption.

Proposed Repeal — Form

[Repealed 1998, c. 18, Sched. E, s. 182. Not in force at date of publication.]

O. Reg. 726/91, s. 1

ONT. REG. 738 — GENERAL

made under the *Marriage Act*

R.R.O. 1990, Reg. 738, as am. O. Reg. 327/91; 726/91; 352/95; 418/96; 170/97; 441/98, s. 2.

1. (1) Where there is an application for a licence in Form 2,

(a) both applicants for the licence shall complete Form 3 and Form 4; or

(b) both applicants for the licence shall complete Form 3 and one of the applicants shall complete Form 4, and

(i) produce to the issuer the birth certificate of the other applicant, or

(ii) deposit with the issuer Form 5 completed by the other applicant.

(2) Form 6 is the consent prescribed for the purposes of subsection 5(2) of the Act.

(3) Subject to section 16 of the Act, an applicant for a licence shall pay a fee of $75 on the issue of the licence.

O. Reg. 327/91, s. 1; 418/96, s. 1.

(4) Where both applicants for a licence are Indians to whom section 16 of the Act applies, one of the applicants shall complete Form 8.

2. (1) The parties to the marriage shall complete the particulars in Form 7 and leave it with the person who will solemnize the marriage or who will perform the duties imposed by the Act in accordance with subsection 20(4) of the Act.

(2) Form 7 and Form 9 shall be completed by,

(a) the parties to a marriage;

(b) two witnesses to the marriage; and

(c) the person who solemnized the marriage or who performed the duties imposed by the Act in accordance with subsection 20(4) of the Act.

(3) Every person who solemnizes a marriage or who performs the duties imposed by the Act in accordance with subsection 20(4) of the Act shall forward Form 7 duly completed in accordance with subsections (1) and (2) to the Registrar General within two days following the day of the marriage.

3. (1) A fee of $75 is payable for the solemnization of a marriage by a judge or a justice of the peace.

(2) The judge or justice of the peace who receives the fee shall remit it to the Minister of Finance.

327/91, s. 2; 418/96, s. 2.

3.1 [Revoked O. Reg. 441/98, s. 2.]

4. The duties of an issuer of licences are,

> (a) to requisition from the Minister and maintain on hand sufficient supplies of licences and other forms prescribed by the regulations; and

> (b) to ensure that every applicant for a licence is aware of the prohibited degrees of affinity and consanguinity set out in the Form to the Act.

5. (1) For each licence issued, the issuer of the licence shall remit $48 to the Minister of Finance and retain $27.

O. Reg. 327/91, s. 3; 418/96, s. 3.

(2) Where the issuer is the clerk of a municipality, the council of the municipality may commute the issuer's fees provided for in subsection (1) for a fixed sum payable annually by the municipality to the issuer, in which case the fees that would otherwise be retained by the issuer shall belong to the municipality.

(3) Where the council and the issuer do not agree upon the amount of the commutation, the amount may be fixed by a judge.

6. The Form set out in the Act is amended to read as follows:

SCHEDULE [FORMS]

The text in square brackets has been editorially added by Carswell and does not form part of the text of the legislation.

Form 1

(Section 19)

Degrees of consanguinity which, under the *Marriage, Prohibited Degrees) Act* (Canada), bar the lawful solemnization of marriage.

A man may not marry his

1. Grandmother
2. Mother
3. Daughter
4. Sister
5. Granddaughter

A woman may not marry her

1. Grandfather
2. Father
3. Son
4. Brother
5. Grandson

The relationships set forth in this table include all such relationships, whether by whole or half blood or by order of adoption.

(O. Reg. 726/91)

Form 2

Marriage Act

— Minister of Consumer and Commercial Relations and Registrar General

I do hereby authorize and grant this licence for the solemnization of marriage between

I, ... (name in full)

of .... (address)

and .... (name in full)

of.. (address)

Provided always that, by reason of affinity, consanguinity, prior marriage, or other lawful cause there is no legal impediment in this behalf; but if otherwise, this licence is null and void to all intents and purposes whatsoever.

Dated at the City of Toronto in the Province of Ontario this .... day of .... 19..........

....
Deputy Registrar General

Issued this .... day of ...., 19..........

....
(signature or name of Issuer, as required)

Issuer of marriage licences at ....

R.R.O. 1980, Reg. 606, Form 2

Form 3 — Marriage Act — Marriage Licence Application

Form 3 — Marriage Licence Application

Form 3

Marriage Act

Licence No.

MARRIAGE LICENCE APPLICATION

BRIDEGROOM						BRIDE				
					Surname or Last Name					
					Given or First Names					
					Occupation					
Age	Date of Birth	Day	Month	Year	**Age and Date of Birth**	Age	Date of Birth	Day	Month	Year
☐ Bachelor ☐ Widower ☐ Divorced					**Marital Status**	☐ Spinster ☐ Widow ☐ Divorced				
Former Marriage to					**Details if an Applicant is Divorced**	Former Marriage to				
Annulled /Dissolved by the				Court		Annulled /Dissolved by the				Court
Of						Of				
On						On				
					Religious Denomination					
Street and Number					**Present Residence or Postal Address**	Street and Number				
Municipality			Postal Code			Municipality			Postal Code	
			Postal Code		**Permanent Home Address if Different to Above**				Postal Code	
Municipality and Country						Municipality and Country				
Intended Place of Marriage	City, Town, Village				**Place of Birth** (Regional municipality, county or district)			Intended Date of Marriage		
					Father's Name					
					Father's Address					
					Mother's Maiden Name					
					Mother's Address if Different to Father's					
I declare that the above information is correct: Bridegroom's Signature						*I declare that the above information is correct:* Bride's Signature				
Date						Date				

R.R.O. 1980, Reg. 606, Form 3.

Form 4 — Marriage Act — Affidavit

Form 4 — Affidavit

Form 4

Marriage Act

AFFIDAVIT

I, ... and
(name in full of deponent)

I, ... make oath and say as follows:
(name in full of other deponent if both parties attend before the Issuer)

That I believe there is no affinity, consanguinity, prior marriage or other lawful cause or legal impediment to bar or hinder the solemnization of the marriage, and

That the contents set forth herein are to the best of .... knowledge, information and belief,
(my or our)

true in every particular:

Names in full		Age		Age
Occupation				
Condition In Life	Bachelor, Widower or Divorcee		Spinster, Widow or Divorcee	
Religious Denomination				
Residence				
Place of Birth				
Intended Place of Marriage	.... of .... in the County, District or Regional Municipality of			

SWORN (or affirmed) before me at the ....

of .... in the County, District or Regional

Municipality of .... this ....
(write date in words not numerals)
(signature of deponent or deponents, as case may be)

day of ...., 19......

.... Issuer of Marriage Licences at ....
(signature of Issuer or Deputy Issuer, as case may be)

R.R.O. 1980, Reg. 606, Form 4.

Marriage Regs

Form 5 — Marriage Act — Affidavit of Age

Form 5 — Affidavit of Age

Form 5

Marriage Act

AFFIDAVIT OF AGE

IN THE MATTER OF AN APPLICATION FOR A LICENCE
UNDER THE *MARRIAGE ACT* FOR THE MARRIAGE OF

CANADA,
PROVINCE
OF ONTARIO
TO WIT:

Name in Full	Address—Giving Street and Number
	OF

AND

Name in Full	
	OF

I, | Name in Full | of | Status of Municipality   Name of Municipality |

the | | OF |

in the | (Write Regional Municipality, County or District) | in the | (Write Province or State) |

OF | | OF |

make oath and say that according to the best of my knowledge, information and belief, I, one of the parties aforesaid am

| Age (in words) | | Status of Municipality   Name of Municipality |

YEARS OF AGE AND WAS BORN IN THE | OF |

in the | (Write Regional Municipality, County or District) | in the | (Write Province or State) |

OF | | OF |

the | Age (in words) | day of | Month | , ONE THOUSAND NINE HUNDRED AND |

I believe there is no affinity, consanguinity, prior marriage or other lawful cause or legal impediment to bar or hinder the solemnization of the said marriage.

SWORN (OR AFFIRMED) BEFORE ME AT THE

Status of Municipality	Name of Municipality
	OF

In the | (Write County or District) |

| | OF |

in the | (Write Province or State) |

| | OF |

dated this | day of | , 19 |

....
Signature of Deponent

A Commissioner, etc.

R.R.O. 1980, Reg. 606, Form 4.

Form 6 — Marriage Act — Consent of Parent or Guardian to Marriage

Form 6 — Consent of Parent or Guardian to Marriage

Form 6

Marriage Act

CONSENT OF PARENT OR GUARDIAN TO MARRIAGE

A | PROVINCE OF ONTARIO

IN THE MATTER OF the proposed marriage of

.... of ....
(Name in Full)   (Address—Giving Street and Number)

.... of ....
(Name in Full)   (Address—Giving Street and Number)

B | I, ... hereby swear
(Name in Full)

That I am the .... of the said ....
("Father" "Mother" or "Guardian")

I, ... hereby swear
(Name in Full)

That I am the .... of the said ....
("Father" "Mother" or "Guardian")

NOTE: The signature of both parents is required except where Section "C" is applicable

C | COMPLETE SECTION APPLICABLE

1. That the .... is/are deceased.
(Mother, Father, Both Parents)

2. That the .... is/are a patient in a psychiatric facility or
(Mother, Father, Both Parents)
resident in a facility under *The Developmental Services Act* (strike out condition not applicable).

3. That I am living apart from the child's .... and have custody of the
(Mother or Father)

said ....

D | That .... is under the age of eighteen and was born on the ....
(He or She)

day of .... 19.....;

That I/we hereby give my/our consent to the said marriage.

SWORN (OR AFFIRMED) BEFORE ME AT THE

Status of Municipality	Name of Municipality
	OF
In the (Write Regional Municipality, County or District)	OF
in the (Write Province or State)	OF
dated this	day of 19

....
(Signature of Parent or Guardian)

....
(Signature of Parent or Guardian)

A Commissioner, etc.

R.R.O. 1980, Reg. 606, Form 6.

Marriage Regs

649

Form 7 — Marriage Act — Statement of Marriage

Form 7 — Statement of Marriage

Form 7

Marriage Act

STATEMENT OF MARRIAGE

(For use of Registrar General only)

1. Place of Marriage: The .... of .... in the .... of ....
   (City, Town, Village or Township)   (Regional municipality, county or district)

2. Date of Marriage: ....   3. Licence ☐   Banns ☐
   (Month by Name)   (Day)   (Year)   (Place X in Proper Square)

Bridegroom   **Bride**

Bridegroom		Bride
4. (Surname) (Given Names)	Names	16. (Surname) (Given Names)
5. The .... of .... in the .... of .... (city, town, village or township) (county, district or regional municipality)	Residence	17. The .... of .... in the .... of .... (city, town, village or township) (county, district or regional municipality)
6. (Bachelor, Widower, Divorcee)	Marital Status	18. (Spinster, Widow, Divorcee)
7.	Religious Denomination	19.
8. Age .... 9. Citizenship .... (in years)	Age Citizenship	20. Age .... 21. Citizenship .... (in years)
10. (If in Canada, state Province; if foreign born, state country)	Place of Birth	22. (If in Canada, state Province; if foreign born, state country)
11.	Occupation	23.
12. (Surname) (Given Names)	Name of Father	24. (Surname) (Given Names)
13. (Maiden Surname) (Given Names)	Maiden Name of Mother	25. (Maiden Surname) (Given Names)
14. (Province or Country)	Birthplace of Father	26. (Province or Country)
15. (Province or Country)	Birthplace of Mother	27. (Province or Country)

....
(Signature of Bridegroom)   (Signature of Bride)

....
(Signature of Witness)   (Signature of Witness)

....
(Address of Witness)   (Address of Witness)

I CERTIFY that the marriage of the parties named in Items 4 and 16 was solemnized on the date and at the place set out above. (indicate status)

☐ Clergy   ☐ Judge   ☐ Justice of the Peace   ☐ Other (Specify) ....

Date ....   Registration No. ....
                                            (Signature of person solemnizing the marriage)

Postal Code

Religious Denomination ....
(Clergy only)   (Post Office Address)

R.R.O. 1980, Reg. 606, Form 7.

Form 8 — Marriage Act — Affidavit by Indian

Form 8 — Affidavit by Indian
Form 8

Marriage Act

AFFIDAVIT BY INDIAN

CANADA,
PROVINCE
OF ONTARIO,

IN THE MATTER OF an application for a Licence under the *Marriage Act* for the marriage of

TO WIT:

.... of ....
(Name in Full)   (Address—Giving Street and Number)

.... of ....
(Name in Full)   (Address—Giving Street and Number)

I, ...,
(Name in Full)

of the .... of ....
(City, Town, Village or Township)

in the .... in the ....
(Regional Municipality, County or District)   (Province)

of .... MAKE OATH AND SAY THAT:
(Occupation)

1. I am one of the parties aforesaid.

2. According to the best of my knowledge, information and belief, both the parties aforesaid are Indians ordinarily resident on a reserve in Ontario (or on Crown lands in Ontario, as the case may be).

SWORN (OR AFFIRMED) before me at the .... of ....

in the .... of .... in the Province of ....
(Signature of Deponent)

Ontario, this .... day of ...., 19......

....

....

This Affidavit May Be Taken in Ontario by the Marriage Licence Issuer,
Commissioner for Taking Affidavits or Notary Public

.... 19....   ....
(No. of Marriage Licence)   (Date of Issue)   (Place of Issue)   (Signature of Issuer)

R.R.O. 1980, Reg. 606, Form 10.

Form 9

Marriage Act

PARTICULARS OF MARRIAGE

BRIDEGROOM

Surname		Given Names		Age	
Occupation		Date of Birth			Bachelor
					Widower
Religious Denomination		Place of Birth			Divorced
Residence at Time of Marriage					
Father's Name		Mother's Name			

Form 9 — Marriage Act — Particulars of Marriage

Form 9 — Particulars of Marriage

BRIDE

Surname	Given Names	Age	
Occupation	Date of Birth		Spinster
Religious Denomination	Place of Birth		Widow
			Divorced
Residence at Time of Marriage			
Father's Name	Mother's Name		

	Married By	Licence	Banns

SIGNATURES

Bridegroom	Bride
Witness	Witness
Residence	Residence

Place of Marriage	I certify that the above named parties were married by me at the place and on the date shown at left.	Signature
Regional municipality, county or district		Address
Date		

Marriage Licence or Banns Serial No.	Date of Issue (Licence Only)	Place of Issue (Licence Only)

R.R.O. 1980, Reg. 606, Form 12.

MARRIAGE (PROHIBITED DEGREES) ACT

S.C. 1990, c. 46

1. Short title — This Act may be cited as the *Marriage (Prohibited Degrees) Act*.

2. (1) No prohibition — Subject to subsection (2), persons related by consanguinity, affinity or adoption are not prohibited from marrying each other by reason only of their relationship.

(2) Prohibition — No person shall marry another person if they are related

(a) lineally by consanguinity or adoption;

(b) as brother and sister by consanguinity, whether by the whole blood or by the half-blood; or

(c) as brother and sister by adoption.

3. (1) Marriage not invalid — Subject to subsection (2), a marriage between persons related by consanguinity, affinity or adoption is not invalid by reason only of their relationship.

(2) Marriage void — A marriage between persons who are related in the manner described in paragraph 2(2)(a), (b) or (c) is void.

4. Complete code — This Act contains all of the prohibitions in law in Canada against marriage by reason of the parties being related.

5. Repeal of R.S., c. M-2 — The *Marriage Act* is repealed.

6. Commencement — This Act shall come into force on the day that is one year after the date it is assented to, or on such earlier day in any province as may be fixed by order of the Governor in Council at the request of that province.

PARENTAL RESPONSIBILITY ACT, 2000

An Act to make parents responsible for wrongful acts intentionally committed by their children

S.O. 2000, c. 4

Her Majesty, by and with the advice and consent of the Legislative Assembly of the Province of Ontario, enacts as follows:

1. Definitions — In this Act, except as otherwise provided in section 10,

"child" means a person who is under the age of 18 years; *("enfant")*

"parent" means,

(a) a biological parent of a child, unless section 158 of the *Child and Family Services Act* applies to the child,

(b) an adoptive parent of a child,

(c) an individual declared to be a parent of a child under the *Children's Law Reform Act*,

(d) an individual who has lawful custody of a child, and

(e) an individual who has a lawful right of access to a child. *("père ou mère")*

2. (1) Parents' liability — Where a child takes, damages or destroys property, an owner or a person entitled to possession of the property may bring an action in the Small Claims Court against a parent of the child to recover damages, not in excess of the monetary jurisdiction of the Small Claims Court,

(a) for loss of or damage to the property suffered as a result of the activity of the child; and

(b) for economic loss suffered as a consequence of that loss of or damage to property.

(2) Same — The parent is liable for the damages unless the parent satisfies the court that,

(a) he or she was exercising reasonable supervision over the child at the time the child engaged in the activity that caused the loss or damage and made reasonable efforts to prevent or discourage the child from engaging in the kind of activity that resulted in the loss or damage; or

(b) the activity that caused the loss or damage was not intentional.

(3) Factors — For the purposes of clause (2)(a), in determining whether a parent exercised reasonable supervision over a child or made reasonable efforts to prevent or discourage the child from engaging in the kind of activity that resulted in the loss or damage, the court may consider,

(a) the age of the child;

(b) the prior conduct of the child;

655

(c) the potential danger of the activity;

(d) the physical or mental capacity of the child;

(e) any psychological or other medical disorders of the child;

(f) whether the child was under the direct supervision of the parent at the time when the child was engaged in the activity;

(g) if the child was not under the direct supervision of the parent when the child engaged in the activity, whether the parent acted unreasonably in failing to make reasonable arrangements for the supervision of the child;

(h) whether the parent has sought to improve his or her parenting skills by attending parenting courses or otherwise;

(i) whether the parent has sought professional assistance for the child designed to discourage activity of the kind that resulted in the loss or damage; and

(j) any other matter that the court considers relevant.

3. (1) Definition — In this section,

"offence" has the same meaning as in the *Young Offenders Act* (Canada).

(2) Proof of conviction — In an action brought under this Act, proof that a child has been found guilty under the *Young Offenders Act* (Canada) of an offence is proof, in the absence of evidence to the contrary, that the offence was committed by the child, if,

(a) no appeal of the finding of guilt was taken and the time for an appeal has expired; or

(b) an appeal of the finding of guilt was taken but was dismissed or abandoned and no further appeal is available.

(3) Same — For the purposes of subsection (2), a copy of an order of disposition under the *Young Offenders Act* (Canada) showing that the original order appeared to be signed by the officer having custody of the records of the court that made the order is, on proof of the identity of the child named as guilty of the offence in the order, sufficient evidence that the child was found guilty of the offence, without proof of the signature or of the official character of the person appearing to have signed the order.

(4) Notice re evidence obtained under Young Offenders Act (Canada) — A person who presents evidence obtained under the *Young Offenders Act* (Canada) in an action brought under this Act shall first give the court notice, in the prescribed form.

(5) Record sealed — When evidence obtained under the *Young Offenders Act* (Canada) is presented in an action brought under this Act,

(a) the court file shall not be disclosed to any person except,

(i) the court and authorized court employees,

(ii) the claimant and the claimant's lawyer or agent, and

(iii) the child, his or her parents and their lawyers or agents; and

(b) once the action has been finally disposed of, the court file shall be sealed up and shall not be disclosed to any person, except one mentioned in clause (a).

4. Young Offenders Act (Canada) — For greater certainty, when information from records under the *Young Offenders Act* (Canada) is made available for the purposes of an action brought under this Act or presented as evidence in such an action, nothing in this Act affects any provision of the *Young Offenders Act* limiting disclosure or publication of the information.

5. Restitution — In determining the amount of damages in an action brought under this Act, the court may take into account any amount ordered by a court as restitution or paid voluntarily as restitution.

6. Joint and several liability — Where more than one parent is liable in an action brought under this Act for a child's activity, their liability is joint and several.

7. (1) Method of payment — In awarding damages in an action brought under this Act, the court may order payment of the damages,

(a) to be made in full on or before a fixed date; or

(b) to be made in instalments on or before fixed dates, if the court considers that a lump sum payment is beyond the financial resources of the parent or will otherwise impose an unreasonable financial burden on the parent.

(2) Security — The court may order security to be provided by the parent in any form that the court considers appropriate.

8. Insurers subrogated — An insurer who has paid an amount as compensation to a person in connection with the loss or damage is subrogated to the rights of the person under this Act to the extent of the amount.

9. Other remedies — Nothing in this Act shall be interpreted to limit remedies otherwise available under existing law or to preclude the development of remedies under the law.

10. (1) Parents' onus of proof in actions not under this Act — This section applies to any action brought otherwise than under this Act.

(2) Same — In an action against a parent for damage to property or for personal injury or death caused by the fault or neglect of a child who is a minor, the onus of establishing that the parent exercised reasonable supervision and control over the child rests with the parent.

(3) Same — In subsection (2),

"**child**" and "**parent**" have the same meaning as in the *Family Law Act*.

11. Regulations — The Lieutenant Governor in Council may, by regulation,

(a) prescribe forms to be used for requests under paragraph 44.1(1)(h) of the *Young Offenders Act* (Canada);

(b) prescribe a form for the purpose of subsection 3(4) (notice re evidence).

12. Repeal — Section 68 of the *Family Law Act* is repealed.

13. Commencement — This Act comes into force on a day to be named by proclamation of the Lieutenant Governor.

14. Short title — The short title of this Act is the *Parental Responsibility Act, 2000.*

ONT. REG. 402/00 — GENERAL

made under the *Parental Responsibility Act, 2000*
O. Reg. 402/00

1. Form 1 is prescribed as the form to be used for requests under paragraph 44.1(1)(h) of the *Young Offenders Act* (Canada).

2. Form 2 is prescribed as the form to be used for the purpose of subsection 3(4) of the Act.

Form 1 — Parental Responsibility Act, 2000

Request for a Copy of a Young Offenders Act (Canada) Order of Disposition

(Check as applicable)

❏ *Individual (Victim or Litigation Guardian)*

    I, *(insert full name)* of the *(City, etc.)* of

❏ *Corporation*

    I, *(insert name and title of representative)* for the *(name of corporation)*, of the *(City, etc.)* of in the *(County, etc.)* of

❏ *Insurer*

    I, *(insert name and title of representative)* for the *(name of insurer)*, of the *(City, etc.)* of in the *(County, etc.)* of

    MAKE OATH AND SAY (OR AFFIRM) as follows:

❏ I am a victim of the offence(s) described below.

❏ I am the litigation guardian for a victim of the offence(s) described below.

❏ I am a representative of a corporation that is a victim of the offence(s) described below.

❏ I am a representative of an insurer of property affected by the offence(s) described below.

❏ I have *(or the corporation has or the insurer has)* commenced an action under the *Parental Responsibility Act, 2000* at *(location) Small Claims Court.*

I believe that *(name, address and date of birth of alleged young offender)* was charged with the following offence(s) *(brief description of incident)*:

I believe that the person named above was found guilty by the *(name of court)* at *(location)*

I am entitled under paragraph 44.1(1)(h) of the *Young Offenders Act* (Canada) and Ontario Order-in-Council No. 1509/00 to obtain a copy of the Order of Disposition.

I would like a copy of the Order of Disposition to be mailed to me at the following address:

(complete mailing address)

NOTE: The document requested can be provided only if a complete mailing address is provided.

Sworn (*or* affirmed) before me at   *(Signature of deponent)*

on

Signature

A Commissioner for Taking Affidavits

THIS SPACE TO BE COMPLETED BY COURT STAFF

Copy of Order of Disposition *(case or file number)* was mailed to above address

on

by   *(Signature of Clerk)*

WARNINGS

1. The information in the Order of Disposition is subject to the publication prohibitions and disclosure provisions of the *Young Offenders Act* (Canada). It is an offence punishable by up to two years' imprisonment to publish, disclose or use the information contained in the Order of Disposition in any way that contravenes the *Young Offenders Act*.

2. You may use a copy of the Order of Disposition as evidence in a claim under the *Parental Responsibility Act, 2000*.

3. It is a criminal offence knowingly to swear a false affidavit.

Form 2 — Parental Responsibility Act, 2000

Notice About Evidence Obtained Under the Young Offenders Act (Canada)

To the Small Claims Court at

Name

Title (if applicable):

Name of Corporation or insurer (if applicable)

Litigation guardian for (if applicable)

Address

Small Claims Court file number

This is to notify you that I will be presenting in an action under the *Parental Responsibility Act, 2000* the following evidence, obtained under the *Young Offenders Act* (Canada):

(List evidence)

(Signature) *(Date)*

TABLE OF CONCORDANCE

Former Act	Revised Act
Partition Act	**Partition Act**
R.S.O. 1980, c. 369	**R.S.O. 1990, c. P-4**
1	1
2	2
3(1)	3(1)
3(2)	3(2)
4(1)	4(1)
4(2)	4(2)
4(3)	4(3)
5(1)	5(1)
5(2,3)	5(2,3)
6	6
7(1)	—
7(2)	—
8	7

PARTITION ACT

R.S.O. 1990, c. P.4

1. Definitions — In this Act,

"court" means the Ontario Court (General Division); ("tribunal")

"land" includes lands, tenements, and hereditaments, and all estate and interests therein. ("bien-fonds")

2. Who may be compelled to make partition or sale — All joint tenants, tenants in common, and coparceners, all doweresses, and parties entitled to dower, tenants by the curtesy, mortgagees or other creditors having liens on, and all parties interested in, to or out of, any land in Ontario, may be compelled to make or suffer partition or sale of the land, or any part thereof, whether the estate is legal and equitable or equitable only.

3. (1) Who may bring action or make application for partition — Any person interested in land in Ontario, or the guardian of a minor entitled to the immediate possession of an estate therein, may bring an action or make an application for the partition of such land or for the sale thereof under the directions of the court if such sale is considered by the court to be more advantageous to the parties interested.

(2) When proceedings may be commenced — Where the land is held in joint tenancy or tenancy in common or coparcenary by reason of a devise or an intestacy, no proceeding shall be taken until one year after the decease of the testator or person dying intestate in whom the land was vested.

4. (1) Appointment of guardian to estate of person unheard of for three years — Where a person interested in the land has not been heard of for three years or upwards and it is uncertain whether such person is living or dead, the court upon the application of any one interested in the land may appoint a guardian to take charge of the interest of such person and of those who, in the event of his or her being dead, are entitled to his or her share or interest in the land.

(2) Powers of such guardian — The guardian shall, in the proceeding, represent the absent person and those who, if he or she is dead, are entitled to his or her share or interest in the land, and whether they or any of them are minors or otherwise under disability, and his or her acts in relation to such share or interest are binding on the absent person and all others claiming or entitled to claim under or through him, and are as valid as if done by him or her or them.

(3) Power of the court to deal with the estate — The court upon proof of such absence of such person as affords reasonable ground for believing such person to be dead, upon the application of the guardian, or any one interested in the estate represented by the guardian, may deal with the estate or interest of such person, or the proceeds thereof, and may order payment of the proceeds, or the income or produce thereof, to the person who, in the event of the absent person being dead, appears to be entitled to the same.

5. (1) Sales including estates in dower or by the curtesy or for life — In a proceeding for partition or administration, or in a proceeding in which a sale of land in lieu of partition is ordered, and in which the estate of a tenant in dower or tenant by the curtesy or for life is established, if the person entitled to the estate is a party, the court shall determine whether the estate ought to be exempted from the sale or whether it should be sold, and in making such determination regard shall be had to the interests of all the parties.

(2) What to pass to purchaser — If a sale is ordered including such estate, all the estate and interest of every such tenant passes thereby, and no conveyance or release to the purchaser shall be required from such tenant, and the purchaser, the purchaser's heirs and assigns, hold the premises freed and discharged from all claims by virtue of the estate or interest of any such tenant, whether the same be to any undivided share or to the whole or any part of the premises sold.

(3) Compensation to owners of particular estates — The court may direct the payment of such sum in gross out of the purchase money to the person entitled to dower or estate by the curtesy or for life, as is considered, upon the principles applicable to life annuities, a reasonable satisfaction for such estate, or may direct the payment to the person entitled of an annual sum or of the income or interest to be derived from the purchase money or any part thereof, as seems just, and for that purpose may make such order for the investment or other disposition of the purchase money or any part thereof as is necessary.

6. Effect upon persons under a disability — A partition or sale made by the court is as effectual for the apportioning or conveying away of the estate or interest of a minor or mentally incompetent person, party to the proceedings by which the sale or partition is made or declared, as of a person who is competent to act.

7. Appeal — An appeal lies to the Divisional Court from any order made under this Act.

PENSION BENEFITS ACT

R.S.O. 1990, c. P.8, as am. S.O. 1997, c. 28, ss. 190–224; 1998, c. 34, ss. 91, 92;
1999, c. 6, s. 53; 1999, c. 15, ss. 1–19; 2002, c. 18, Sched. H, s. 5.

[Note: only sections 1–5, and 35–54 are reproduced here.]

1. Definitions — In this Act,

"additional voluntary contribution" means a contribution to the pension fund by a member of the pension plan beyond any amount that the member is required to contribute, but does not include a contribution in relation to which the employer is required to make a concurrent additional contribution to the pension fund; ("cotisation faculative supplémentaire")

"administrator" means the person or persons that administer the pension plan; ("administrateur")

"assets", in relation to an employer, means assets that in the ordinary course of business would be entered in books of account, whether or not a particular asset is entered in the books of account of the employer; ("actif")

"bridging benefit" means a periodic payment provided under a pension plan to a former member of the pension plan for a temporary period of time after retirement for the purpose of supplementing the former member's pension benefit until the former member is eligible to receive benefits under the *Old Age Security Act* (Canada) or is either eligible for or commences to receive retirement benefits under the *Canada Pension Plan* or the *Quebec Pension Plan*; ("prestation de raccordement")

"certified copy" means a copy certified to be a true copy; ("copie certifiée conforme")

"collective agreement" has the same meaning as in the *Labour Relations Act*; ("convention collective")

"Commission" means the Financial Services Commission of Ontario established under the *Financial Services Commission of Ontario Act, 1997*; ("Commission")

"commuted value" means the value calculated in the prescribed manner and as of a fixed date of a pension, a deferred pension, a pension benefit or an ancillary benefit; ("valeur de rachat")

"continuous", in relation to employment, membership or service, means without regard to periods of temporary suspension of the employment, membership or service and without regard to periods of lay-off from employment; ("continu")

"contributory benefit" means a pension benefit or part of a pension benefit to which a member is required to make contributions under the terms of the pension plan; ("prestation contributive")

"deferred pension" means a pension benefit, payment of which is deferred until the person entitled to the pension benefit reaches the normal retirement date under the pension plan; ("pension différée")

"defined benefit" means a pension benefit other than a defined contribution benefit; ("prestation déterminée")

"defined contribution benefit" means a pension benefit determined with reference to and provided by contributions, and the interest on the contributions, paid by or for the credit of a member and determined on an individual account basis; ("prestation à cotisation déterminée")

"designated province" means a province or territory of Canada that is prescribed by the regulations as a province or territory in which there is in force legislation substantially similar to this Act; ("province désignée")

"employee" means a natural person who is employed by an employer; ("employé")

"employer" in relation to a member or a former member of a pension plan, means the person or persons from whom or the organization from which the member or former member receives or received remuneration to which the pension plan is related, and "employed" and "employment" have a corresponding meaning; ("employeur", "employé", "emploi")

"file" means file with the Superintendent; ("déposer")

"former member" means a person who has terminated employment or membership in a pension plan, and,

(a) is entitled to a deferred pension payable from the pension fund,

(b) is in receipt of a pension payable from the pension fund,

(c) is entitled to commence receiving payment of pension benefits from the pension fund within one year after termination of employment or membership, or

(d) is entitled to receive any other payment from the pension fund; ("ancien participant")

"Guarantee Fund" means the Pension Benefits Guarantee Fund continued by this Act; ("Fonds de garantie")

"insurance company" means a corporation authorized to undertake life insurance in Canada; ("compagnie d'assurance")

"joint and survivor pension" means a pension payable during the joint lives of the person entitled to the pension and his or her spouse or same-sex partner and thereafter during the life of the survivor of them; ("pension réversible")

"member" means a member of the pension plan; ("participant")

"Minister" means a member of the Executive Council designated by the Lieutenant Governor in Council for the purposes of this Act; ("ministre")

"multi-employer pension plan" means a pension plan established and maintained for employees of two or more employers who contribute or on whose behalf contributions are made to a pension fund by reason of agreement, statute or municipal by-law to provide a pension benefit that is determined by service with one or more of the employers, but does not include a pension plan where all the employers are affiliates within the meaning of the *Business Corporations Act*; ("régime de retraite interenterprises")

"normal retirement date" means the date or age specified in the pension plan as the normal retirement date of members; ("date normale de retraite")

"partial wind up" means the termination of part of a pension plan and the distribution of the assets of the pension fund related to that part of the pension plan; ("liquidation partielle")

"participating employer" in relation to a multi-employer pension plan, means an employer required to make contributions to the multi-employer pension plan; ("employeur participant")

"pension" means a pension benefit that is in payment; ("pension")

"pension benefit" means the aggregate monthly, annual or other periodic amounts payable to a member or former member during the lifetime of the member or former member, to which the member or former member will become entitled under the pension plan or to which any other person is entitled upon the death of a member or former member; ("prestation de retraite")

"pension committee" means a committee that is the administrator of a pension plan; ("comité de retraite")

"pension fund" means the fund maintained to provide benefits under or related to the pension plan; ("caisse de retraite")

"pension plan" means a plan organized and administered to provide pensions for employees, but does not include,

(a) an employee's profit sharing plan or a deferred profit sharing plan as defined in sections 144 and 147 of the *Income Tax Act* (Canada),

(b) a plan to provide a retiring allowance as defined in subsection 248(1) of the *Income Tax Act* (Canada),

(c) a plan under which all pension benefits are provided by contributions made by members, or

(d) any other prescribed type of plan; ("régime de retraite")

"prescribed" means prescribed by the regulations; ("prescrit")

"qualification date" means, in respect of Ontario, the 1st day of January, 1965, and, in respect of a designated province, the date on which under the law of the designated province a pension plan must be registered by the proper authority in the designated province; ("date d'habilitation")

"reciprocal transfer agreement" means an agreement related to two or more pension plans that provides for the transfer of money or credits for employment or both in respect of individual members; ("accord réciproque de transfert")

"registration" means registration under this Act; ("enregistrement")

"regulations" means regulations made under this Act; ("règlements")

"same-sex partner" means either of two persons of the same sex who are living together in a conjugal relationship,

(a) continuously for a period of not less than three years, or

(b) in a relationship of some permanence, if they are the natural or adoptive parents of a child, both as defined in the *Family Law Act*. ("partenaire de même sexe")

"spouse" means either of a man and woman who,

(a) are married to each other, or

(b) are not married to each other and are living together in a conjugal relationship,

    (i) continuously for a period of not less than three years, or

    (ii) in a relationship of some permanence, if they are the natural or adoptive parents of a child, both as defined in the *Family Law Act*; ("conjoint")

"Superintendent" means the Superintendent of Financial Services appointed under the *Financial Services Commission of Ontario Act, 1997.* ("surintendant")

"surplus" means the excess of the value of the assets of a pension fund related to a pension plan over the value of the liabilities under the pension plan, both calculated in the prescribed manner; ("excédent")

"termination" in relation to employment, includes retirement and death; ("cessation")

"trade union" has the same meaning as in the *Labour Relations Act*; ("syndicat")

"Tribunal" means the Financial Services Tribunal established under the *Financial Services Commission of Ontario Act, 1997.* ("Tribunal")

"wind up" means the termination of a pension plan and the distribution of the assets of the pension fund; ("liquidation")

"Year's Maximum Pensionable Earnings" has the same meaning as in the *Canada Pension Plan.* ("maximum des gains annuels ouvrant droit à pension")

1997, c. 28, s. 190; 1999, c. 6, s. 53(1), (2)

Application

2. Crown bound — This Act binds the Crown.

3. Employees in Ontario — This Act applies to every pension plan that is provided for persons employed in Ontario.

4. (1) Place of employment — For the purposes of this Act, a person shall be deemed to be employed in the province in which the establishment of his or her employer is located and to which the person is required to report for work.

(2) Idem — A person who is not required to report for work at an establishment of his or her employer shall be deemed to be employed in the province in which is located the establishment of his or her employer from which the person's remuneration is paid.

5. Greater pension benefits — The requirements of this Act and the regulations shall not be construed to prevent the registration or administration of a pension plan and related pension fund that provide pension benefits or ancillary benefits more advantageous to members than those required by this Act and the regulations.

. . . . .

Retirement and Vesting

35. (1) Normal retirement date — The normal retirement date under a pension plan submitted for registration after the 1st day of January, 1988 shall not be later than one year after the attainment of sixty-five years of age.

(2) Transitional — Every pension plan registered or submitted for registration before the 1st day of January, 1988 shall be deemed to specify a normal retirement date in respect of pension benefits that accrue after the 1st day of January, 1988, that is not later than one year after attainment of sixty-five years of age, unless the pension plan specifies an earlier retirement date.

(3) Right to pension — A member of a pension plan who continues employment and membership in the pension plan after attaining the age that is the normal retirement date under the pension plan is entitled on retirement from employment to payment of the pension benefits to which the member would have been entitled had the member retired from employment or terminated membership in the pension plan on attaining the normal retirement date and any additional pension benefits accrued under the pension plan that result from the member's employment after the normal retirement date.

(4) Continuation after normal retirement date — A member of a pension plan who continues employment after attaining the age that is the normal retirement date under the pension plan and who is not receiving a pension under the pension plan is entitled to continue membership in the pension plan and has the right to continue to accrue pension benefits under the pension plan subject to any terms of the pension plan,

    (a) fixing a maximum number of years of employment or membership that can be taken into account for purposes of determining a pension benefit; or

    (b) fixing a maximum amount of the pension benefit.

36. (1) Deferred pension for past service — A member of a pension plan who meets the qualifications in subsection (2) is entitled to the benefit mentioned in subsection (3).

(2) Qualifications — The qualifications are,

    (a) that the member must have been employed by the employer, or have been a member of the pension plan, for a continuous period of at least ten years;

    (b) that the member must have reached the age of forty-five years; and

    (c) that the member must terminate his or her employment with the employer before reaching the normal retirement date under the pension plan.

(3) Amount — The benefit is a deferred pension equal to the pension benefit provided under the pension plan as it existed on the 31st day of December, 1986 in respect of employment before the 1st day of January, 1987 in Ontario or in a designated province,

    (a) under the terms of the pension plan, with respect to employment on or after the qualification date;

    (b) by an amendment to the pension plan made on or after the qualification date; and

    (c) by the creation of a new pension plan on or after the qualification date.

(4) Application of subss. (1–3) — Subsections (1) to (3) do not apply in respect of benefits that result from additional voluntary contributions.

37. (1) Deferred pension — A member of a pension plan who meets the qualifications in subsection (2) is entitled to the benefit mentioned in subsection (3).

(2) Qualifications — The qualifications are,

    (a) that the member must be a member on or after the 1st day of January, 1988;

(b) that the member must be a member for a continuous period of at least twenty-four months; and

(c) that the member must terminate his or her employment with the employer before reaching the normal retirement date under the pension plan.

(3) Amount — The benefit is a deferred pension equal to the pension benefit provided in respect of employment in Ontario or in a designated province,

(a) under the pension plan in respect of employment by the employer after the later of the 31st day of December, 1986 or the qualification date;

(b) under any amendment made to the pension plan after the 31st day of December, 1986; and

(c) under any new pension plan established after the 31st day of December, 1986 for members of the pension plan.

(4) Application of subss. (1–3) — Subsections (1) to (3) do not apply in respect of benefits that result from additional voluntary contributions.

38. (1) Termination by member — A person who is,

(a) a member of a multi-employer pension plan;

(b) a member of a pension plan who is employed by the employer on a less than full-time basis; or

(c) a member of a pension plan who has been laid off from employment by the employer,

is entitled to terminate his or her membership in the pension plan if no contributions are paid or are required to be paid to the pension fund by or on behalf of the member for twenty-four consecutive months or for such shorter period of time as is specified in the pension plan.

(2) Effect of termination — For the purpose of determining benefits under this Act, a person mentioned in subsection (1) who terminates his or her membership in a pension plan shall be deemed to have terminated his or her employment.

(3) Application of subss. (1, 2) — Subsections (1) and (2) do not apply if contributions are not paid or are not required to be paid because the person has become a member of another pension plan and there is a reciprocal transfer agreement respecting the two pension plans.

(4) Determination of entitlement — For the purpose of determining entitlement to a deferred pension, a member of a multi-employer pension plan who terminates employment with a participating employer or an employer on whose behalf contributions are made under the pension plan shall be deemed not to have terminated employment until the member terminates membership in the pension plan.

(5) Certification of new bargaining agent — Where a member of a multi-employer pension plan is represented by a trade union, which, in accordance with section 57 of the *Labour Relations Act*, ceases to represent the member, and the member joins a different pension plan, the member is entitled to terminate membership in the first plan.

(6) Application of subs. (5) — Subsection (5) does not apply where there is a reciprocal agreement respecting the two pension plans.

Benefits

39. (1) Value of deferred pension — If the commuted value of a former member's pension or deferred pension accrued in respect of employment before the 1st day of January, 1987 is less than the value of the contributions the former member was required to make under the pension plan before that date plus interest credited to the contributions, the former member is entitled to have the commuted value of the pension or deferred pension increased so that the commuted value is equal to the value of the contributions plus interest.

(2) Effect of amendment — An increase in the value of the pension or deferred pension in respect of employment before the 1st day of January, 1987 that results from an amendment to the pension plan made on or after that date may be included in calculating the commuted value of the pension or deferred pension for the purposes of subsection (1).

(3) 50 per cent rule — A former member's contributions to a pension plan made on or after the 1st day of January, 1987 and the interest on the contributions shall not be used to provide more than 50 per cent of the commuted value of a pension or deferred pension in respect of contributory benefits accrued after that date to which the member is entitled under the pension plan on termination of membership or employment.

(4) Entitlement to excess amount — A former member who is entitled to a pension or deferred pension on termination of employment or membership is entitled to payment from the pension fund of a lump sum payment equal to the amount by which the former member's contributions under the pension plan made on or after the 1st day of January, 1987 and the interest on the contributions exceed one-half of the commuted value of the former member's pension or deferred pension in respect of the contributory benefit accrued after that date.

(5) Exclusions — The following may be excluded in determining that part of the commuted value of a pension or deferred pension to which subsections (3) and (4) apply:

1. Defined contribution benefits.

2. Benefits that result from additional voluntary contributions.

2.1 Benefits that result from voluntary contributions for past service, as defined in the regulations.

3. In the case of a multi-employer pension plan that permits a member who has not accrued maximum pension benefits permitted under the plan in a fiscal year of the plan to make contributions to increase the member's pension benefit to the maximum permitted for the fiscal year, benefits resulting from such contributions.

4. Any other benefits prescribed for the purposes of this subsection.

(6) Matters that may be included — The following may be included by the administrator of the pension plan in calculating a member's contributory benefit for the purposes of subsection (3):

1. Ancillary benefits related to employment on or after the 1st day of January, 1987.

2. Increases to pension benefits and ancillary benefits related to employment before the date of the amendment resulting from an amendment to the pension plan made on or after the 1st day of January, 1987 but that are not included in calculating commuted value under subsection (2).

3. Pension benefits and ancillary benefits related to employment before the date of the establishment of the pension plan, in the case of a pension plan established on or after the 1st day of January, 1987.

1999, c. 15, s. 5

40. (1) Ancillary benefits — A pension plan may provide the following ancillary benefits:

1. Disability benefits.

2. Death benefits in excess of those provided in section 48 (pre-retirement death benefit).

3. Bridging benefits.

4. Supplemental benefits, other than bridging benefits, payable for a temporary period of time.

5. Early retirement options and benefits in excess of those provided by section 41 (early retirement option).

6. Postponed retirement options and benefits in excess of those referred to in subsection 35(4).

7. Any prescribed ancillary benefit.

(2) Use in calculating pension benefit — An ancillary benefit for which a member has met all eligibility requirements under the pension plan necessary to exercise the right to receive payment of the benefit shall be included in calculating the member's pension benefit or the commuted value of the pension benefit.

(3) Consent of employer — For the purposes of subsection (2) and clause 14(1)(c), where the consent of an employer is an eligibility requirement for entitlement to receive an ancillary benefit and a member or former member has met all other eligibility requirements, the employer shall be deemed to have given the consent to the member or former member.

41. (1) Early retirement option — A former member is entitled to elect to receive an early retirement pension under the pension plan if he or she,

(a) terminated employment on or after the 1st day of January, 1988;

(b) is entitled to a deferred pension under this Act; and

(c) is within ten years of attaining the normal retirement date.

(2) Idem — A member who is within ten years of attaining the normal retirement date and who would be entitled to a deferred pension on termination of employment with the employer is entitled upon termination of the employment or on the wind up of the pension plan in whole or in part to receive an early retirement pension under the pension plan.

(3) Commuted value — The commuted value of a member's early retirement pension must be not less than the commuted value of the member's pension benefit under the pension plan.

(4) Idem, former member — The commuted value of a former member's early retirement pension must be not less than the commuted value of the former member's deferred pension benefit under the pension plan.

(5) Payment — The member or former member is entitled to require the commencement of payment of the early retirement pension at any time within the ten year period mentioned in subsection (1) or (2).

(6) Election — An election under subsection (1) or (2) shall be made in writing, signed by the member or former member and delivered to the administrator of the pension plan.

42. (1) Transfer — A former member of a pension plan who, on or after the 1st day of January, 1988, terminates employment or ceases to be a member of the pension plan and who is entitled to a deferred pension is entitled to require the administrator to pay an amount equal to the commuted value of the deferred pension,

(a) to the pension fund related to another pension plan, if the administrator of the other pension plan agrees to accept the payment;

(b) into a prescribed retirement savings arrangement; or

(c) for the purchase for the former member of a life annuity that will not commence before the earliest date on which the former member would have been entitled to receive payment of pension benefits under the pension plan.

(2) Limitation — The entitlement under subsection (1) is subject to the prescribed limitations in respect of the transfer of funds from pension funds.

(3) Application of subs. (1) — Subsection (1) does not apply to a former member whose employment is terminated and who is entitled to immediate payment of a pension benefit under the pension plan or under section 41, unless the pension plan provides such an entitlement.

(4) Direction — A former member may exercise his or her entitlement under subsection (1) by delivering to the administrator within the prescribed period of time a direction in a form approved by the Superintendent.

(5) Compliance with direction — Subject to compliance with the requirements of this section and the regulations, the administrator shall comply with the direction within the prescribed period of time after delivery of the direction.

(6) Terms of arrangement or deferred annuity — The administrator shall not make payment,

(a) under clause (1)(b) unless the retirement savings arrangement meets the requirements prescribed by the regulations; or

(b) under clause (1)(c) unless the contract to purchase the deferred life annuity meets the prescribed requirements.

(6.1) Lump sum payment — If the amount of the commuted value of the deferred pension of the former member to be paid into a prescribed retirement savings arrangement under clause (1)(b) is greater than the amount prescribed under the *Income Tax Act* (Canada) for such a transfer, the administrator shall pay the portion that exceeds the prescribed amount as a lump sum to the former member.

(7) Approval — If a payment under subsection (1) does not meet the limitations prescribed in relation to transfers of funds from pension funds, the administrator shall not make the payment without the approval of the Superintendent.

(8) Terms and conditions — The Superintendent may approve the payment subject to such terms and conditions as the Superintendent considers appropriate in the circumstances.

(9) Order for repayment — If a payment that does not meet the limitations prescribed in relation to transfers of funds from pension funds is made without the approval of the Superintendent or there is failure to comply with a term or condition attached to the approval, the

Superintendent by order, subject to section 89 (hearing and appeal), may require any person to whom payment under subsection (1) has been made to repay an amount not greater than the amount of the payment together with interest thereon.

(10) Enforcement — Subject to section 89 (hearing and appeal), an order for payment under subsection (9), exclusive of the reasons therefor, may be filed in the Ontario Court (General Division) and is thereupon enforceable as an order of that court.

(11) Discharge of administrator — The administrator is discharged on making the payment or transfer in accordance with the direction of the former member if the payment or transfer complies with this Act and the regulations.

1997, c. 28, s. 197; 1999, c. 15, s. 6

43. (1) Purchase of pension — The administrator of a pension plan who is required by the pension plan to provide a pension, a deferred pension or an ancillary benefit may purchase the pension, deferred pension or ancillary benefit from an insurance company.

(2) Limitations — The authority of the administrator under subsection (1) is subject to the entitlement of a member under section 42 and to the limitations prescribed in relation to transfers of funds from pension funds.

(3) Approval by Superintendent — If a purchase under subsection (1) does not meet the limitations prescribed in relation to transfers of funds from pension funds, the administrator shall not make the purchase without the prior approval of the Superintendent.

(4) Idem — The Superintendent may approve a purchase mentioned in subsection (3) subject to such terms and conditions as the Superintendent considers appropriate in the circumstances.

(5) Order for repayment — If a purchase that does not meet the limitations prescribed in relation to transfers of funds from pension funds is made without the approval of the Superintendent or there is a failure to comply with a term or condition attached to the approval, the Superintendent, subject to section 89 (hearing and appeal), by order may require any person to whom payment under subsection (1) has been made to repay an amount not greater than the amount of the payment together with interest thereon.

(6) Enforcement — Subject to section 89 (hearing and appeal), an order for payment under subsection (5), exclusive of the reasons therefor, may be filed in the Ontario Court (General Division) and is thereupon enforceable as an order of that court.

44. (1) Joint and survivor pension benefits — Every pension paid under a pension plan to a former member who has a spouse or same-sex partner on the date that the payment of the first instalment of the pension is due shall be a joint and survivor pension.

(2) Commuted value — The commuted value of a joint and survivor pension under subsection (1) shall not be less than the commuted value of the pension that would be payable under the pension plan to the former member.

(3) Amount of survivor benefit — The amount of the pension payable to the survivor of the former member and the spouse or same-sex partner of the former member shall not be less than 60 per cent of the pension paid to the former member during the joint lives of the former member and his or her spouse or same-sex partner.

(4) Application of subss. (1–3) — Subsections (1) to (3) do not apply,

(a) in respect of a pension benefit if payment of the pension has commenced before the 1st day of January, 1988; or

(b) in respect of a former member who is living separate and apart from his or her spouse or same-sex partner on the date that payment of the first instalment of the pension is due.

(5) Deferred life annuity — Where,

(a) prior to the 1st day of January, 1988, a deferred life annuity has been purchased from an insurance company for a person entitled to a deferred pension under the *Pension Benefits Act*, being chapter 373 of the Revised Statutes of Ontario, 1980;

(b) payments have not commenced under the annuity on the 1st day of January, 1988; and

(c) the recipient of the payments has a spouse or same-sex partner on the date payments commence,

the annuity shall be paid as a joint and survivor pension in accordance with the requirements of this section and the insurance company shall make payments accordingly.

(6) Application of ss. 45, 46 — For the purposes of subsection (5), the insurance company shall be deemed to be the administrator under sections 45 and 46.

1999, c. 6, s. 53(5)–(8)

45. (1) Information for payment — Before commencing payment of a pension or pension benefit, the administrator of a pension plan shall require the person entitled to the payment to provide to the administrator the information needed to calculate and pay the pension or pension benefit.

(2) Person to provide information — The person entitled to the payment shall provide the information to the administrator.

(3) Discharge of administrator — In the absence of actual notice to the contrary, the administrator is discharged on paying the pension or pension benefit in accordance with the information provided by the person in accordance with subsection (2) or, if the person does not provide the information, in accordance with the latest information in the records of the administrator.

46. (1) Waiver of joint and survivor pension benefit — The persons entitled to a joint and survivor pension benefit may waive the entitlement to receive payment of pension benefits in the form of a joint and survivor pension by delivering to the administrator of the pension plan or, in the case of a deferred life annuity, to the insurance company a written waiver in the form approved by the Superintendent or a certified copy of a domestic contract, as defined in Part IV of the *Family Law Act*, containing the waiver.

(2) Time — The waiver is not effective unless the form or the certified copy of the domestic contract is delivered to the administrator or the insurance company, as the case may be, within the 12 months preceding the commencement of payment of the pension benefit.

(3) Cancellation of waiver — Persons who have delivered a waiver may jointly cancel it by delivering a written and signed notice of cancellation to the administrator or the insurance company, as the case may be, before the commencement of payment of the pension benefit.

1997, c. 28, s. 198; 1999, c. 15, s. 7

47. Remarriage of spouse — The spouse or same-sex partner of a deceased former member of a pension plan who is receiving a pension under the pension plan is not disentitled to payment of the pension by reason only of becoming the spouse or same-sex partner of another person after the death of the former member.

1999, c. 6, s. 53(9)

48. (1) Pre-retirement death benefit — If a member or former member of a pension plan who is entitled under the pension plan to a deferred pension described in section 37 (entitlement to deferred pension) dies before commencement of payment of the deferred pension, the person who is the spouse or same-sex partner of the member or former member on the date of death is entitled,

  (a) to receive a lump sum payment equal to the commuted value of the deferred pension; or

  (b) to an immediate or deferred pension the commuted value of which is at least equal to the commuted value of the deferred pension.

(2) Idem — If a member of a pension plan continues in employment after the normal retirement date under the pension plan and dies before commencement of payment of pension benefits referred to in section 37, the person who is the spouse or same-sex partner of the member or former member on the date of death is entitled,

  (a) to receive a lump sum payment equal to the commuted value of the pension benefit; or

  (b) to an immediate or deferred pension the commuted value of which is at least equal to the commuted value of the pension benefit.

(3) Application of subss. (1, 2) — Subsections (1) and (2) do not apply where the member or former member and his or her spouse or same-sex partner are living separate and apart on the date of the death of the member or former member.

(4) Election — A spouse or same-sex partner who has an entitlement under subsection (1) or (2) shall elect within the prescribed period of time to receive payment under clause (a) or (b) of the subsection and if the spouse or same-sex partner does not make an election, the spouse or same-sex partner shall be deemed to have elected to receive an immediate pension.

(5) Calculation of benefit — For the purposes of this section, the deferred pension or pension benefits to which a member is entitled if the member dies while employed shall be calculated as if the member's employment were terminated immediately before the member's death.

(6) Designated beneficiary — A member or former member of a pension plan may designate a beneficiary and the beneficiary is entitled to be paid an amount equal to the commuted value of the deferred pension mentioned in subsection (1) or (2) if,

  (a) the member or former member does not have a spouse or same-sex partner on the date of death; or

  (b) the member or former member is living separate and apart from his or her spouse or same-sex partner on that date.

(7) Estate entitlement — The personal representative of the member or former member is entitled to receive payment of the commuted value mentioned in subsection (1) or (2) as the property of the member or former member, if the member or former member has not designated a beneficiary under subsection (6) and,

(a) does not have a spouse or same-sex partner on the date of the member or former member's death; or

(b) is living separate and apart from his or her spouse or same-sex partner on that date.

(8) Dependent children — If the pension plan provides for payment of pension benefits to or for a dependent child or dependent children of the member or former member upon the death of the member or former member, the commuted value of the payments may be deducted from the entitlement of a beneficiary designated under subsection (6) or of a personal representative under subsection (7).

(9) Information — It is the responsibility of the person entitled to the payment to provide to the administrator the information needed to make the payment.

(10) Discharge of administrator — In the absence of actual notice to the contrary, the administrator is discharged on making payment in accordance with the information provided by the person.

(11) Offset — A pension plan may provide for reduction of an amount to which a person is entitled under this section to offset any part of a prescribed additional benefit that is attributable to an amount paid by an employer, subject to the following:

1. The reduction shall be calculated in the prescribed manner.

2. The reduction shall not exceed the prescribed limits.

(12) Discharge of entitlement — Payment in accordance with this section replaces the entitlement of a member or former member in respect of a deferred pension mentioned in section 37.

(13) Order or domestic contract — An entitlement to a benefit under this section is subject to any right to or interest in the benefit set out in a domestic contract or an order referred to in section 51 (payment on marriage breakdown).

(14) Waiver — The spouse or same-sex partner of a member or former member may waive the spouse's or partner's entitlement under subsection (1) or (2) by delivering a written waiver, in the form approved by the Superintendent, to the administrator of the pension plan.

(14.1) Cancellation of waiver — A spouse or same-sex partner who has delivered a waiver may cancel it by delivering a written and signed notice of cancellation to the administrator before the date of death of the member or former member.

(14.2) Effect of waiver — If a waiver is in effect on the date of death of the member or former member, subsections (6) and (7) apply as if the member or former member does not have a spouse or same-sex partner, as the case may be, on the date of death.

(15) Definition — In this section, "personal representative" has the same meaning as in the *Estates Administration Act*.

1997, c. 28, s. 198; 1999, c. 6, s. 53(10)–(16); 1999, c. 15, s. 8

49. (1) Variation of payment to disabled person — A pension plan may permit variation in the terms of payment of a pension or deferred pension by reason of the mental or physical disability of a member or former member that is likely to shorten considerably the life expectancy of the member or former member.

(2) Shortened life expectancy — A pension plan shall be deemed to permit variation in the terms of payment of a pension or deferred pension in such circumstances of shortened life expectancy as may be prescribed, if the prescribed conditions are satisfied.

1999, c. 15, s. 9

50. (1) Commuted value — A pension plan may provide for payment to a former member of the commuted value of a benefit if the annual benefit payable at the normal retirement date is not more than 2 per cent of the Year's Maximum Pensionable Earnings in the year that the former member terminated employment.

(2) Idem — A pension plan registered before the 1st day of January, 1988 may provide that upon termination of employment a person entitled to a deferred pension under section 36 (deferred pension) is entitled to payment of an amount not greater than 25 per cent of the commuted value of the deferred pension.

51. (1) Payment on marriage breakdown — A domestic contract as defined in Part IV of the *Family Law Act*, or an order under Part I of that Act is not effective to require payment of a pension benefit before the earlier of,

(a) the date on which payment of the pension benefit commences; or

(b) the normal retirement date of the relevant member or former member.

(2) Maximum percentage — A domestic contract or an order mentioned in subsection (1) is not effective to cause a party to the domestic contract or order to become entitled to more than 50 per cent of the pension benefits, calculated in the prescribed manner, accrued by a member or former member during the period when the party and the member or former member were spouses or same-sex partners.

(3) Discharge of administrator — If payment of a pension or a deferred pension is divided between spouses or same-sex partners by a domestic contract or an order mentioned in subsection (1), the administrator is discharged on making payment in accordance with the domestic contract or order.

(4) Revaluation of joint and survivor pension — If a domestic contract or an order mentioned in subsection (1) affects a pension, the administrator of the pension plan shall revalue the pension in the prescribed manner.

(5) Transfer — A spouse or same-sex partner on whose behalf a certified copy of a domestic contract or order mentioned in subsection (1) is given to the administrator of a pension plan has the same entitlement, on termination of employment by the member or former member, to any option available in respect of the spouse's or same-sex partner's interest in the pension benefits as the member or former member named in the domestic contract or order has in respect of his or her pension benefits.

1999, c. 6, s. 53(17)–(19)

52. (1) Discrimination on basis of sex — The sex of a member, former member or other beneficiary under a pension plan shall not be taken into account in,

(a) determining the amount of contributions required to be made by a member of the plan;

(b) determining the pension benefits or the commuted value of pension benefits that a member, former member or other beneficiary is or may become entitled to;

(c) the provision of eligibility conditions for membership; and

(d) the provision of ancillary benefits.

(2) **Administration** — In order to comply with subsection (1), the administrator may,

(a) use annuity factors that do not differentiate as to sex;

(b) provide for employer contributions that vary according to the sex of the employee; or

(c) use any prescribed method of calculation or valuation.

(3) **Application** — This section applies in respect of contributions, benefits and conditions in relation to,

(a) employment after the 31st day of December, 1986;

(b) employment before the 1st day of January, 1987, in so far as it is dealt with in an amendment made to the pension plan after the 31st day of December, 1986; and

(c) employment before the 1st day of January, 1987, in so far as it is dealt with in a pension plan established after the 31st day of December, 1986.

53. (1) Inflation protection — Pension benefits, pensions or deferred pensions shall be adjusted in accordance with the established formula or formulas and in the prescribed manner to provide inflation-related increases.

(2) **Idem** — Any formula or formulas for any inflation related adjustments to pension benefits, pensions or deferred pensions shall be established only by amendment to this Act.

54. (1) C.P.P./Q.P.P. offsets — The reduction of a pension benefit that may be required by a pension plan in relation to payments under the *Canada Pension Plan*, the *Quebec Pension Plan* or the *Old Age Security Act* (Canada) shall not exceed the reduction calculated in accordance with the prescribed formula applied in the prescribed manner.

(2) **Idem** — The amount of the reduction of a member's pension benefit required under the pension plan in relation to payments mentioned in subsection (1) shall not be increased by reason of an increase in the payments after the date on which the member's employment is terminated.

(3) **Reduction re Old Age Security Act (Canada)** — A pension plan for registration of which application is made on or after the 1st day of January, 1988 shall not permit the reduction of a pension benefit based on a person's entitlement under the *Old Age Security Act* (Canada).

(4) **Application of subs. (3)** — Subsection (3) does not apply to a pension plan that is a successor of a pension plan registered under the *Pension Benefits Act*, being chapter 373 of the Revised Statutes of Ontario, 1980, that permitted such a reduction.

(5) **Idem** — A pension plan shall not permit reduction of a pension benefit based on a person's entitlement under the *Old Age Security Act* (Canada) in respect of a benefit accrued on or after the 1st day of January, 1987.

. . . . .

INTERJURISDICTIONAL SUPPORT ORDERS ACT, 2002

An Act to facilitate the making, recognition and variation of interjurisdicational support orders

S.O. 2002, c. 13

PART I — GENERAL

1. Definitions — In this Act,

"appropriate authority", when used in reference to a reciprocating jurisdiction, means the person or persons in that jurisdiction who correspond to the designated authority in Ontario; *("autorité compétente")*

"certified" when used to refer to a copy of an order or reasons, means certified by the court that made the order or gave the reasons; *("certifiée conforme")*

"child" has the same meaning as in the *Family Law Act*; *("enfant")*

"claimant" means a person who applies under this Act for support; *("requérant")*

"clerk" means a person who has the authority of a clerk or registrar of the court; *("greffier")*

"delivery agent" means a delivery agent under the *Ontario Works Act, 1997*; *("agent de prestation des services")*

"designated authority" means the person appointed under subsection 41(1), and includes a person to whom a power or duty is delegated under subsection 41(2); *(autorité désignée")*

"former Act" means the *Reciprocal Enforcement of Support Orders Act*; *("ancienne loi")*

"Ontario court" means a court designated under section 2; *("tribunal de l'Ontario")*

"prescribed" means prescribed by the regulations, if any, or by the rules of court; *(prescrit")*

"provisional order" means,

(a) a support order of an Ontario court that has no effect until confirmed by a court in a reciprocating jurisdiction, or

(b) a similar order made in a reciprocating jurisdiction and received for confirmation in Ontario; *("ordonnance conditionnelle")*

"provisional variation order" means,

(a) an order of an Ontario court that varies a support order and that has no effect until confirmed by a court in a reciprocating jurisdiction, or

(b) a similar order made in a reciprocating jurisdiction and received for confirmation in Ontario; *("ordonnance modificative conditionnelle")*

"reciprocating jurisdiction" means a jurisdiction prescribed as such in the regulations made under subsection 52(1); *("autorité pratiquant la réciprocité")*

"regulations" means the regulations made under this Act; *("règlements")*

"support" includes maintenance and alimony; *("aliments")*

"support order" means an order requiring the payment of support that is made by a court or by an administrative body, and includes the provisions of a written agreement requiring the payment of support if they are enforceable in the jurisdiction in which the agreement was made as if they were contained in an order of a court of that jurisdiction. *("ordonnance alimentaire")*

2. Designation of court — The Attorney General may designate a court or courts in Ontario for the purpose of proceedings under this Act.

PART II — NEW ORDERS

3. Definition — In this Part,

"respondent" means the person against whom support is sought.

4. Application of Part — This Part applies only if there is no support order in effect requiring the respondent to pay support for the claimant, for any children or for both.

Claimant in Ontario

5. (1) Support application — A claimant who ordinarily resides in Ontario and believes that the respondent ordinarily resides in a reciprocating jurisdiction may start a proceeding in Ontario that could result in a support order being made in the reciprocating jurisdiction.

(2) Same — To start the proceeding, the claimant shall complete a support application that includes,

(a) the claimant's name and address for service;

(b) a copy of the specific statutory or other legal authority on which the application is based, unless he claimant is relying on the law of the jurisdiction where the respondent ordinarily resides;

(c) particulars of the support claimed;

(d) the affidavit described in subsection (3); and

(e) any other prescribed documents.

(3) Affidavit — The affidavit shall set out,

(a) the respondent's name and any other information known to the claimant that can be used to locate or identify the respondent

(b) the respondent's financial circumstances, to the extent known by the claimant;

(c) the name of each person for whom support is claimed and the date of birth of any child for whom support is claimed;

(d) the evidence in support of the application that is relevant to establishing entitlement to or the amount of support, including,

    (i) if support is claimed for a child, details of the child's parentage and information about his or her financial and other circumstances, and

    (ii) if support is claimed for the claimant, information about the claimant's financial and other circumstances and his or her relationship with the respondent; and

(e) any other prescribed information.

(4) No notice to respondent required — The claimant is not required to notify the respondent that a proceeding has been started under this section.

6. (1) Submission of application to designated authority — The claimant shall submit the support application to the designated authority in Ontario.

(2) Duty of designated authority — On receiving a support application, the designated authority shall promptly,

(a) review the application to ensure that it is complete; and

(b) send a copy of the completed application to the appropriate authority in the reciprocating jurisdiction in which the claimant believes the respondent ordinarily resides.

(3) Further information or documents — On receiving a request for further information or documents from a reciprocating jurisdiction under an enactment in that jurisdiction that corresponds to clause 11(2)(a), the claimant or the designated authority shall provide the further information or documents, within the time referred to in the request and in accordance with the regulations.

(4) Copy of order and reasons — On receiving a certified copy of an order and reasons, if any, from a reciprocating jurisdiction under an enactment in that jurisdiction that corresponds to section 16, the designated authority shall provide a copy of the order and reasons, if any, to the claimant, in accordance with the regulations.

7. (1) Provisional order — If the claimant reasonably believes that the respondent ordinarily resides in a reciprocating jurisdiction that requires a provisional order, the Ontario court may, on the claimant's application and without notice to the respondent, make a provisional order taking into account the legal authority on which the claimant's application for support is based.

(2) Evidence — Evidence in an application under subsection (1) may be given orally, in writing or in any other prescribed manner.

(3) Material to be sent to reciprocating jurisdiction — If a provisional order is made, the court shall send it to the designated authority, which shall send to the reciprocating jurisdiction,

(a) three certified copies of the provisional order; and

(b) a support application referred to in subsection 5(2).

(4) Further evidence — If, in considering whether to confirm a provisional order, a court in a reciprocating jurisdiction sends a matter back for further evidence to the Ontario court that made the provisional order, the Ontario court shall, after giving notice to the claimant, receive further evidence.

(5) Transcript of further evidence, copies of modified order — If evidence is received under subsection (4), the clerk of the Ontario court shall send to the court in the reciprocating jurisdiction,

> (a) a certified transcript of the evidence; and

> (b) if the Ontario court considers it appropriate to modify its provisional order, three certified copies of the order as modified.

(6) New provisional order — If a provisional order made under this section comes before a court in a reciprocating jurisdiction and confirmation is denied in respect of one or more persons for whom support is sought, the Ontario court that made the provisional order may, on motion within six months after the denial of confirmation, reopen the matter, receive further evidence and make a new provisional order for a person in respect of whom confirmation was denied.

Claimant Outside Ontario

8. (1) Application of ss. 9 to 16 — Sections 9 to 16 apply in respect of,

> (a) provisional orders referred to in clause (b) of the definition of "provisional order" in section 1; and

> (b) documents from reciprocating jurisdictions corresponding to a support application described in subsection 5(2).

(2) Meaning of "support application" — In sections 9 to 16, "support application" refers to the orders and documents described in subsection (1).

9. Steps taken by designated authority — If the designated authority receives a support application from an appropriate authority in a reciprocating jurisdiction, with information that the respondent ordinarily resides in Ontario, it shall take the following steps:

1. Verify the information about the respondent's ordinary residence.

2. If the information is confirmed, send the support application to the Ontario court.

3. If the information is not confirmed and the designated authority knows or believes that the respondent ordinarily resides in another reciprocating jurisdiction in Canada,

> i. send the support application to the appropriate authority in that other reciprocating jurisdiction, and

> ii. notify the appropriate authority in the originating reciprocating jurisdiction that it has done so.

4. If the information is not confirmed and the designated authority has no information about the respondent's ordinary residence, return the support application to the appropriate authority in the originating reciprocating jurisdiction.

5. If the information is not confirmed and the designated authority knows or believes that the respondent ordinarily resides in a jurisdiction outside Canada, return the support application to the appropriate authority in the originating reciprocating jurisdiction with any available information about the respondent's location and circumstances.

10. Notice of hearing — When the Ontario court receives a support application under paragraph 2 of section 9, the clerk shall serve on the respondent, in accordance with the regulations,

(a) a copy of the support application; and

(b) a notice requiring the respondent to appear at a place and time set out in the notice and to provide the prescribed information or documents.

11. (1) Information to be considered — In dealing with a support application, the Ontario court shall consider,

(a) the evidence provided to the Ontario court; and

(b) the documents sent from the reciprocating jurisdiction.

(2) If further information or documents needed — If the Ontario court needs further information or documents from the claimant to consider making a support order, the Ontario court shall,

(a) send the designated authority a direction to request the information or documents from the claimant or the appropriate authority in the reciprocating jurisdiction; and

(b) adjourn the hearing.

(3) Temporary order — When the Ontario court acts under subsection (2), it may also make a temporary support order.

(4) 18-month delay — If the Ontario court does not receive the information or documents requested under subsection (2) within 18 months after the request is made, it may dismiss the support application and terminate any temporary support order made under subsection (3).

(5) New application — The dismissal of the application under subsection (4) does not preclude the claimant from commencing a new support application.

12. (1) Parentage — If a child's parentage is in issue and has not previously been determined by a court of competent jurisdiction, the Ontario court may determine the matter.

(2) Restriction — A determination of parentage under this section has effect only for the purposes of proceedings relating to support for the child.

13. Choice of law rules — The following rules apply with respect to determining entitlement to support and the amount of support:

1. In determining a child's entitlement to support, the Ontario court shall first apply the law of the jurisdiction in which the child ordinarily resides, but if the child is not entitled to support under that law, the Ontario court shall apply Ontario law.

2. In determining the claimant's entitlement to support, the Ontario court shall first apply Ontario law, but if the claimant is not entitled to support under Ontario law, the Ontario court shall apply the law of the jurisdiction in which the claimant and the respondent last maintained a common habitual residence.

3. In determining the amount of support for a child or for the claimant, the Ontario court shall apply Ontario law.

14. (1) Order — On the conclusion of a hearing, the Ontario court may, in respect of a claimant, a child or both,

    (a) make a support order;

    (b) make a temporary support order and adjourn the hearing to a specified date;

    (c) adjourn the hearing to a specified date without making a temporary support order; or

    (d) refuse to make a support order.

(2) Retroactivity — The Ontario court may make a retroactive support order.

(3) Periodic payments or lump sum — A support order may require support to be paid in periodic payments, as a lump sum, or both.

(4) Reasons for refusal — If the Ontario court refuses to make a support order, it shall give written reasons for its decision and send them to the designated authority.

15. (1) Order if notice not complied with — If the respondent does not appear as required in the notice or does not provide the information or documents required under clause 10(b), the Ontario court may make an order in the absence of the respondent or of the information or documents and in making the order may draw any inference it considers appropriate.

(2) Copies of order — If the Ontario court makes an order under subsection (1), it shall send copies of the order to the designated authority and to the respondent, in accordance with the regulations.

16. Sending order to reciprocating jurisdiction — When it receives an order that is made under section 14 or 15, the designated authority shall promptly send a certified copy of it, with reasons, if any, to the appropriate authority in the reciprocating jurisdiction that sent the claimant's support application.

PART III — REGISTRATION AND ENFORCEMENT OF ORDERS MADE OUTSIDE ONTARIO

17. Application of Part — This Part applies in respect of support orders, temporary support orders and orders varying support orders made in reciprocating jurisdictions in and outside Canada, but not in respect of provisional orders or provisional variation orders.

18. (1) Receipt of order in Ontario — To enforce an order to which this Part applies, the claimant or the appropriate authority of the reciprocating jurisdiction shall send a certified copy of it to the designated authority, together with information about the location and circumstances of any party who is believed to ordinarily reside in Ontario.

(2) Sending to court — On receiving the certified copy, the designated authority shall send it, in accordance with the regulations, to the clerk of the Ontario court sitting nearest the place where the party is believed to reside.

19. (1) Registration — On receiving the order under subsection 18(2), the clerk of the Ontario court shall register it as an order of the court.

(2) Effect of registration — From the date of registration, the order has the same effect as a support order made by an Ontario court.

(3) Notice — If the order was made outside Canada, notice of its registration shall be given in accordance with section 20, but there is no requirement to give notice of the registration of an order made in Canada.

(4) Same — The registered order may be enforced or varied under this Act with respect to arrears accrued before registration as well as with respect to obligations accruing after registration.

(5) Same — Subsections (2), (3) and (4) apply whether the registered order is made before, on or after the day on which this Act comes into force.

(6) Copies of registered order — When an order has been registered under subsection (1), the clerk of the Ontario court shall,

    (a) file a copy with the Director of the Family Responsibility Office under the Family Responsibility and *Support Arrears Enforcement Act, 1996*, unless the order is accompanied by a notice signed by the person seeking enforcement stating that he or she does not want the order enforced by the Director; and

    (b) send a copy to the designated authority.

(7) 30-day delay, order made outside Canada — Despite subsection (6), if the registered order was made outside Canada, copies shall not be filed with the Director of the Family Responsibility Office or sent to the designated authority until,

    (a) the 30-day period described in subsection 20(2) has expired without a motion being made to set aside the registration; or

    (b) if such a motion is made during the 30-day period, the motion has been finally disposed of.

20. (1) Notice of registration, order made outside Canada — After the registration of an order made in a reciprocating jurisdiction outside Canada, the clerk of the Ontario court shall, in accordance with the regulations, give notice of the registration of the order to any party to the order who is believed to ordinarily reside in Ontario.

(2) Motion to set registration aside — Within 30 days after receiving notice of the registration of the order, a party to the order may make a motion to the Ontario court to set aside the registration.

(3) Notice of motion — A party who makes a motion under subsection (2) shall give notice of it to the designated authority and to the claimant in accordance with the regulations.

(4) Power of court — On a motion under subsection (2), the Ontario court may,

    (a) confirm the registration; or

    (b) set aside the registration if the Ontario court determines that,

        (i) in the proceeding in which the order was made, a party to the order did not have proper notice or a reasonable opportunity to be heard,

        (ii) the order is contrary to public policy in Ontario, or

        (iii) the court that made the order did not have jurisdiction to make it.

(5) Reasons for setting aside — If the Ontario court sets aside the registration, it shall give written reasons for its decision and send them to the designated authority.

(6) Jurisdiction — For the purposes of subclause (4)(b)(iii), a court has jurisdiction,

(a) if both parties to the order ordinarily reside in the reciprocating jurisdiction outside Canada; or

(b) if a party does not ordinarily reside in the reciprocating jurisdiction outside Canada but is subject to the jurisdiction of the court that made the order.

(7) Notice — The clerk of the Ontario court shall give notice of a decision or order of that court to the parties and the designated authority, in accordance with the regulations.

(8) Proof of notice — In a proceeding to enforce a registered order made in a reciprocating jurisdiction outside Canada, it is not necessary to prove that the respondent received notice under subsection (1) or (7).

21. (1) Effect of setting aside — If the registration of an order made in a reciprocating jurisdiction outside Canada is set aside under section 20, the order shall be dealt with under this Act as if it were a document corresponding to a support application received under paragraph 2 of section 9 or a support variation application received under paragraph 2 of section 32.

(2) Request for information and documents — If the order does not contain the necessary information or documents required for a support application or support variation application, the designated authority shall request them from the claimant or from the appropriate authority of the reciprocating jurisdiction in which the order was made, and no further steps shall be taken in the proceeding until the designated authority has received the required material.

PART IV — VARIATION OF ORDERS

22. Definitions — In this Part,

"applicant" means the party applying to vary a support order; *("requérant")*

"respondent" means the party who is the respondent in a support variation application. *("intimé")*

23. Application of Part — This Part applies in respect of support orders that are made in Ontario or made in a reciprocating jurisdiction and registered in an Ontario court under Part III or the former Act, but not in respect of provisional orders or provisional variation orders.

24. Variation of registered order — It is not necessary to reregister an order that is registered under Part III and subsequently varied under this Part.

25. Variation in reciprocating jurisdiction — If a support order originally made in Ontario is varied in a reciprocating jurisdiction under provisions that correspond to sections 32 to 38, it shall be deemed to be so varied in Ontario.

26. (1) Restrictions — Nothing in this Part,

(a) authorizes a judge of the Ontario Court of Justice to vary a support order made in Canada by a federally appointed judge; or

(b) allows a support order originally made under the *Divorce Act* (Canada) to be varied except as authorized by federal enactment.

(2) Powers of provincially appointed judge — Despite subsection (1), a judge of the Ontario Court of Justice may make a provisional order to vary a support order made in Canada under a provincial enactment by a federally appointed judge.

Applicant in Ontario

27. (1) Support variation application — An applicant who ordinarily resides in Ontario and believes that the respondent ordinarily resides in a reciprocating jurisdiction may start a proceeding in Ontario that could result in a variation order being made in the reciprocating jurisdiction.

(2) Same — To start the proceeding, the applicant shall complete a support variation application that includes,

(a) the applicant's name and address for service;

(b) a copy of the support order;

(c) a copy of the specific statutory or other legal authority on which the application is based, unless the applicant is relying on the law of the jurisdiction where the respondent ordinarily resides;

(d) details of the variation applied for, which may include a termination of the support order; and

(e) the affidavit described in subsection (3).

(3) Affidavit — The affidavit shall set out,

(a) the respondent's name and any information known to the applicant that can be used to locate or identify the respondent;

(b) the respondent's financial circumstances, to the extent known by the applicant, including whether the respondent is receiving social assistance;

(c) whether the support order was assigned, and any details of the assignment known to the applicant;

(d) the name of each person, to the extent known by the applicant, for whom support is payable or who would be affected by the variation;

(e) the evidence in support of the application, including,

(i) if support to the applicant or respondent is an issue, information about their relationship, and

(ii) if the variation would affect support for a child, information about the child's financial and other circumstances, including any extraordinary expenses;

(f) the prescribed information about the applicant's financial circumstances; and

(g) any other prescribed information.

(4) No notice to respondent required — The applicant is not required to notify the respondent that a proceeding has been started under this section.

28. (1) Submission of application to designated authority — The applicant shall submit the support variation application to the designated authority in Ontario.

(2) Duty of designated authority — On receiving a support variation application, the designated authority shall promptly,

(a) review the application to ensure that it is complete; and

(b) send a copy of the completed application to the appropriate authority in the reciprocating jurisdiction in which the applicant believes the respondent ordinarily resides.

(3) Further information or documents — On receiving a request for further information or documents from a reciprocating jurisdiction under an enactment in that jurisdiction that corresponds to clause 34(2)(a), the applicant or the designated authority shall provide the further information or documents, within the time referred to in the request and in accordance with the regulations.

(4) Copy of order and reasons — On receiving a certified copy of an order and reasons, if any, from a reciprocating jurisdiction under an enactment in that jurisdiction that corresponds to section 38, the designated authority shall provide a copy of the order and reasons, if any, to the applicant, in accordance with the regulations.

29. Variation if respondent no longer resident in reciprocating jurisdiction — If the applicant ordinarily resides in Ontario and the respondent no longer ordinarily resides in a reciprocating jurisdiction, the applicant may apply directly to the Ontario court to vary the support order, and the court may make a variation order if the respondent has been given notice of the proceeding.

30. (1) Provisional variation order — If the applicant reasonably believes that the respondent ordinarily resides in a reciprocating jurisdiction that requires a provisional variation order, the Ontario court may, on the applicant's motion and without notice to the respondent, make a provisional variation order taking into account the legal authority on which the applicant's application for variation is based.

(2) Evidence — Evidence on a motion under subsection (1) may be given orally, in writing or in any other prescribed manner.

(3) Material to be sent to reciprocating jurisdiction — If a provisional variation order is made, the court shall send it to the designated authority, which shall send to the reciprocating jurisdiction,

(a) three certified copies of the provisional variation order; and

(b) a support variation application referred to in subsection 27(2).

(4) Further evidence — If, in considering whether to confirm a provisional variation order, a court in a reciprocating jurisdiction sends a matter back for further evidence to the Ontario court that made the provisional variation order, the Ontario court shall, after giving notice to the applicant, receive further evidence.

(5) Transcript of further evidence, copy of modified order — If evidence is received under subsection (4), the clerk of the Ontario court shall send to the court in the reciprocating jurisdiction,

(a) a certified transcript of the evidence; and

(b) if the Ontario court considers it appropriate to modify its provisional variation order, three certified copies of the order as modified.

(6) New provisional variation order — If a provisional variation order made under this section comes before a court in a reciprocating jurisdiction and confirmation is denied in respect of one or more persons for whom support is payable, the Ontario court that made the provisional variation order may, on motion within six months after the denial of confirmation, reopen the matter, receive further evidence and make a new provisional variation order for a person in respect of whom confirmation was denied.

Applicant Outside Ontario

31. (1) Application of ss. 32 to 38 — Sections 32 to 38 apply in respect of,

(a) provisional variation orders referred to in clause (b) of the definition of "provisional variation order" in section 1; and

(b) documents from reciprocating jurisdictions corresponding to a support variation application described in subsection 27(2).

(2) Meaning of "support variation application" — In sections 32 to 38, "support variation application" refers to the orders and documents described in subsection (1).

32. Steps taken by designated authority — If the designated authority receives a support variation application from an appropriate authority in a reciprocating jurisdiction, with information that the respondent ordinarily resides in Ontario, it shall take the following steps:

1. Verify the information about the respondent's ordinary residence.

2. If the information is confirmed, send the support variation application to the Ontario court.

3. If the information is not confirmed and the designated authority knows or believes that the respondent ordinarily resides in another reciprocating jurisdiction in Canada,

    i. send the support variation application to the appropriate authority in that other reciprocating jurisdiction, and

    ii. notify the appropriate authority in the originating reciprocating jurisdiction that it has done so.

4. If the information is not confirmed and the designated authority has no information about the respondent's ordinary residence, return the support variation application to the appropriate authority in the originating reciprocating jurisdiction.

5. If the information is not confirmed and the designated authority knows or believes that the respondent ordinarily resides in a jurisdiction outside Canada, return the support variation application to the appropriate authority in the originating reciprocating jurisdiction with any available information about the respondent's location and circumstances.

33. Notice of hearing — When the Ontario court receives a support variation application under paragraph 2 of section 32, the clerk shall serve on the respondent, in accordance with the regulations,

(a) a copy of the support variation application; and

(b) a notice requiring the respondent to appear at a place and time set out in the notice and to provide the prescribed information or documents.

34. (1) Information to be considered — In dealing with a support variation application, the Ontario court shall consider,

(a) the evidence provided to the Ontario court; and

(b) the documents sent from the reciprocating jurisdiction.

(2) If further information or documents needed — If the Ontario court needs further information or documents from the applicant to consider making a support variation order, the Ontario court shall,

(a) send the designated authority a direction to request the information or documents from the applicant or the appropriate authority in the reciprocating jurisdiction; and

(b) adjourn the hearing.

(3) Temporary order — When the Ontario court acts under subsection (2), it may also make a temporary support variation order.

(4) 18-month delay — If the Ontario court does not receive the information or documents requested under subsection (2) within 18 months after the request is made, it may dismiss the support variation application and terminate any temporary support variation order made under subsection (3).

(5) New application — The dismissal of the application under subsection (4) does not preclude the applicant from commencing a new support variation application.

35. Choice of law rules — The following rules apply with respect to determining entitlement to receive or to continue to receive support and the amount of support:

1. In determining a child's entitlement to receive or to continue to receive support, the Ontario court shall first apply the law of the jurisdiction in which the child ordinarily resides, but if the child is not entitled to support under that law, the Ontario court shall apply Ontario law.

2. In determining the amount of support for a child, the Ontario court shall apply the law of the jurisdiction where the person liable to pay the support ordinarily resides.

3. In determining the entitlement of the applicant to receive or to continue to receive support, the Ontario court shall first apply Ontario law, but if the applicant is not entitled to support under Ontario law, the Ontario court shall apply,

i. the law of the jurisdiction in which the applicant ordinarily resides, or

ii. if the applicant is not entitled to support under the law of the jurisdiction in which he or she ordinarily resides, the law of the jurisdiction in which the parties last maintained a common habitual residence.

4. In determining the amount of support for the applicant, the Ontario court shall apply Ontario law.

36. (1) Order — On the conclusion of a hearing, the Ontario court may, in respect of the applicant, a child or both,

(a) make a support variation order;

(b) make a temporary support variation order and adjourn the hearing to a specified date;

(c) adjourn the hearing to a specified date without making a temporary support variation order; or

(d) refuse to make a support variation order.

(2) Retroactivity — The Ontario court may make a retroactive support variation order.

(3) Periodic payments or lump sum — A support variation order may require support to be paid in periodic payments, as a lump sum or both.

(4) Reasons for refusal — If the Ontario court refuses to make a support variation order, it shall give written reasons for its decision and send them to the designated authority.

37. (1) Order if notice not complied with — If the respondent does not appear as required in the notice or does not provide the information or documents required under clause 33(b), the Ontario court may make an order in the absence of the respondent or of the information or documents and in making the order may draw any inference it considers appropriate.

(2) Copies of order — If the Ontario court makes an order under subsection (1), it shall send copies of the order to the designated authority and to the respondent, in accordance with the regulations.

38. Sending order to reciprocating jurisdiction — When it receives an order that is made under section 36 or 37, the designated authority shall promptly send a certified copy of it, with reasons, if any, to the appropriate authority in the reciprocating jurisdiction in which the applicant ordinarily resides and if the support order was originally made in another reciprocating jurisdiction, to the appropriate authority in that jurisdiction.

Variation of Registered Orders

39. (1) Jurisdiction — The Ontario court may, on a party's motion, after taking into account any right of a government or delivery agent under section 45, vary a support order registered in Ontario under Part III or the former Act,

(a) if both the applicant and respondent accept the Ontario court's jurisdiction;

(b) if both the applicant and respondent ordinarily reside in Ontario; or

(c) if the respondent ordinarily resides in Ontario and the support order was registered by the applicant under Part III or the former Act

(2) Application of Family Law Act — The *Family Law Act* applies for the purposes of varying a support order under the circumstances referred to in subsection (1), as if the order being varied were an order for support under that Act.

PART VI — APPEALS AND MISCELLANEOUS

40. (1) Appeals — Subject to subsections (2) and (4), a claimant, applicant or respondent or the designated authority may appeal any decision of the Ontario court under this Act to the proper appellate court as determined under the *Courts of Justice Act.*

(2) Appeal period — An appeal shall be commenced within 90 days after the date the Ontario court's decision is entered as a judgment.

(3) Same — Despite subsection (2), the appellate court may extend the appeal period, even after it has expired.

(4) Same — A person responding to an appeal under subsection (2) may appeal a decision in the same proceeding within 30 days after receiving notice of the appeal.

(5) Order in force pending determination of appeal — An order under appeal remains in force pending the determination of the appeal unless the court that made the order or the appellate court orders otherwise.

(6) Notice of decision on appeal — The registrar of the appellate court shall send a copy of that court's decision on the appeal to the designated authority, which shall notify the appropriate authority in the reciprocating jurisdiction of the decision on the appeal.

41. (1) Appointment of designated authority — The Attorney General may appoint a person to act as the designated authority in Ontario for the purposes of this Act.

(2) Delegation — The person appointed under subsection (1) may, in writing, delegate any power or duty under this Act to any other person or persons.

(3) Protection from personal liability — No proceeding for damages shall be commenced against the designated authority or any employee of the designated authority's office for any act done in good faith in the execution or intended execution of any duty or authority under this Act or for any alleged neglect or default in the execution in good faith of any duty or authority under this Act.

(4) Crown not relieved of liability — Despite subsections 5(2) and (4) of the *Proceedings Against the Crown Act*, subsection (3) does not relieve the Crown of liability in respect of a tort committed by a person mentioned in subsection (3) to which it would otherwise be subject.

42. Sending documents — On receipt of an order or document to be sent under this Act to a reciprocating jurisdiction, the designated authority shall send the order or document to the appropriate authority of the reciprocating jurisdiction.

43. (1) Translation — An order or other document that is to be sent to a reciprocating jurisdiction that requires it to be translated into a language other than English or French shall be accompanied by a certified translation into that language.

(2) Same — An order or other document from a reciprocating jurisdiction that is written in a language other than English or French shall be accompanied by a certified translation into English or French.

44. Order or application expressed in foreign currency — If a support order or an application made in a reciprocating jurisdiction outside Canada and received by the Ontario court under this Act refers to an amount of support that is not expressed in Canadian currency, the clerk shall convert the amount into Canadian currency in accordance with the regulations.

45. (1) Right of subrogation — Any government or delivery agent that is providing or has provided social assistance to or on behalf of a person who is entitled to make a claim for support has the rights of a claimant or applicant under this Act for the following purposes:

(a) Obtaining support or a variation of support in the name of the government or delivery agent.

(b) Obtaining reimbursement of the social assistance provided to or on behalf of that person by the government or delivery agent.

(c) Assigning a support order made or registered under this Act.

(d) Sending an order to the designated authority for registration.

(2) Same — Where a person who is required to pay support makes an application for a variation under Part IV, a government or delivery agent has the rights of the respondent with respect to the application for the following purposes if the government or delivery agent is providing or has provided social assistance to or on behalf of the respondent:

1. To respond to the application for variation of the support order for that person.

2. To obtain reimbursement of the social assistance provided to or on behalf of that person by the government or delivery agent.

(3) Same — Subsections (1) and (2) also apply, with necessary modifications, if the government or delivery agent has received an application for social assistance but has not yet provided it.

(4) Definition — In this section,

"social assistance" means a benefit, assistance or income support under the *Family Benefits Act*, the *General Welfare Assistance Act*, the *Ontario Disability Support Program Act, 1997* or the *Ontario Works Act, 1997*.

46. Terminology — If, in a proceeding under this Act, a document from a court in a reciprocating jurisdiction contains terminology different from the terminology in this Act or contains terminology or is in a form different than that customarily in use in the Ontario court, the Ontario court shall give a broad and liberal interpretation to the terminology or form so as to give effect to the document.

47. (1) Judicial notice of law of reciprocating jurisdiction — In a proceeding under this Act, the Ontario court shall take judicial notice of the law of a reciprocating jurisdiction and, where required, apply it.

(2) Proof of enactment — An enactment of a reciprocating jurisdiction may be pleaded and proved for the purposes of this Act by producing a copy of the enactment received from the reciprocating jurisdiction.

48. Proof of appointment — In a proceeding under this Act, a document purporting to be signed by a judge, officer of a court or public officer in a reciprocating jurisdiction is, unless the contrary is proved, proof of the appointment, signature and authority of the person who signed it.

49. (1) Receipt in evidence — Statements in writing sworn to by the maker, depositions or transcripts of evidence taken in a reciprocating jurisdiction may be received in evidence by an Ontario court under this Act.

(2) Same, proof of default — Default in paying support or arrears of support may be proved by a sworn document made by a person who declares that he or she has knowledge of, or information and belief concerning, the default or arrears.

50. Spouses as witnesses — Spouses are competent and compellable witnesses against each other in proceedings under this Act.

51. Other remedies — This Act does not impair any other remedy available to a person, the Province of Ontario, a province or territory of Canada, a jurisdiction outside Canada or a political subdivision or official agency of the Province of Ontario, of a province or territory of Canada or of a jurisdiction outside Canada.

52. (1) Regulations re reciprocating jurisdictions — If the Lieutenant Governor in Council is satisfied that laws are or will be in effect in a jurisdiction for the reciprocal enforcement of support orders made in Ontario on a basis substantially similar to this Act, the Lieutenant Governor in Council may make regulations declaring that jurisdiction to be a reciprocating jurisdiction.

(2) Conditions — In declaring a jurisdiction to be a reciprocating jurisdiction under subsection (1), the Lieutenant Governor in Council may impose any conditions with respect to the enforcement and recognition of support orders made or registered in that jurisdiction.

(3) Revocation — The Lieutenant Governor in Council may, by regulation, revoke a declaration made under subsection (1), and the jurisdiction to which the revocation relates ceases to be a reciprocating jurisdiction for the purposes of this Act.

53. Other regulations — The Lieutenant Governor in Council may make regulations,

    (a) respecting notices, information and documents required by this Act;

    (b) respecting the serving or giving of notices, information and documents under this Act;

    (c) respecting proceedings under this Act;

    (d) respecting conversion into Canadian currency for the purposes of section 44;

    (e) prescribing forms for the purposes of this Act;

    (f) prescribing anything that is referred to in this Act as being prescribed.

54. (1) Transition — An order that was made or registered under the former Act remains effective and may be varied, enforced or otherwise dealt with as if it had been made or registered under this Act.

(2) Same — If the respondent received notice of a hearing to consider a provisional order or a provisional variation order or notice of registration of a final order under the former Act before the commencement date, the matter shall be dealt with in accordance with the former Act as if it had not been repealed.

(3) Same — If a person who ordinarily resides in Ontario applied for a provisional order or a provisional variation order under the former Act before the commencement date, the application continues under the former Act as if it had not been repealed.

(4) Same — If a final order was received for registration under the former Act before the commencement date but, on that day, has not yet been registered, the order shall be dealt with in accordance with this Act as if it had been received under Part III.

(5) Same — If a provisional order or a provisional variation order was received under the former Act before the commencement date but, on that day, the respondent had not received notice of the hearing to consider the order, the order shall be dealt with in accordance with this Act as if it had been received under Part III or Part IV, as the case may be.

(6) Definition — In this section,

"commencement date" means the day this Act comes into force.

55. Repeal — The *Reciprocal Enforcement of Support Orders Act*, as amended by the Statutes of Ontario, 1993, chapter 27, Schedule and 1997, chapter 25, Schedule E, section 10, is repealed.

56. Paragraph 1 of the Schedule to section 21.8 of the *Courts of Justice Act*, as enacted by the Statutes of Ontario, 1994, chapter 12, section 8 and amended by 1996, chapter 31, section 65 and 2000, chapter 33, section 20, is amended by striking out *"Reciprocal Enforcement of Support Orders Act"* and substituting *"Interjurisdictional Support Orders Act, 2002"*.

57. (1) The definition of "provisional order" in subsection 1(1) of the *Family Responsibility and Support Arrears Enforcement Act, 1996* is amended by striking out "sections 3 and 7 of the *Reciprocal Enforcement of Support Orders Act*" and substituting "sections 7 and 30 of the *Interjurisdictional Support Orders Act, 2002"*.

(2) Subsection 13(1) of the Act is repealed and the following substituted:

> **(1) Orders of other jurisdictions** — When a support order made by a court outside Ontario is registered under subsection 19(1) of the *Interjurisdictional Support Orders Act, 2002*, the clerk who registers the order shall promptly file it with the Director's office, unless the order is accompanied by a notice signed by the person seeking enforcement stating that he or she does not want the order enforced by the Director.

(3) Subsection 50(2) of the Act is amended by striking out "section 14 of the *Reciprocal Enforcement of Support Orders Act*" and substituting "section 44 of the *Interjurisdictional Support Orders Act, 2002"*.

58. Commencement — This Act comes into force on a day to be named by proclamation of the Lieutenant Governor.

59. Short Title — The short title of this Act is the *Interjurisdictional Support Orders Act, 2002*.

TABLE OF CONCORDANCE

Reciprocal Enforcement of Maintenance Orders Act, 1982	Reciprocal Enforcement of Support Orders Act
S.O. 1982, c. 9	R.S.O. 1990, c. R-7
1–21	1–21
22–24	—

RECIPROCAL ENFORCEMENT OF SUPPORT ORDERS ACT
[REPEALED]

R.S.O. 1990, c. R.7, as am. 1993, c. 27, Sched.; 1997, c. 25, s. 3, Sched. E, s. 10; 2002, c. 13, s. 55; 2002, c. 17, Sched. C, s. 25.

[Editor's Note: Reciprocal Enforcement of Support Orders Act *(the 'former Act') has been repealed by Statutes of Ontario, 2002, c. 13, s. 55 and replaced with the new* Interjurisdictional Support Orders Act, *S.O. 2002, c. 13 (the 'new Act'). S. 54 of the new Act provides transitional provisions pursuant to the former Act.]*

1. Definitions — In this Act,

"Attorney General" includes a person authorized by the Attorney General to act for him or her in the performance of a power or duty under this Act;

"certified copy" means, in relation to a document of a court, the original or a copy of the document certified by the original or facsimile signature of a proper officer of the court to be a true copy;

"claimant" means a person who has or is alleged to have a right to support;

"confirmation order" means a confirmation order made under this Act or under the corresponding enactment of a reciprocating state;

"court" means an authority having jurisdiction to make an order;

"final order" means an order made in a proceeding of which the claimant and respondent had proper notice and in which they had an opportunity to be present or represented and includes,

(a) the support provisions in a written agreement between a claimant and a respondent where those provisions are enforceable in the state in which the agreement was made as if contained in an order of a court of that state, and

(b) a confirmation order made in a reciprocating state;

"order" means an order or determination of a court providing for the payment of money as support by the respondent named in the order for the benefit of the claimant named in the order, or the support provisions of an order or determination that includes other matters;

"provisional order" means an order of a court in Ontario that has no force or effect in Ontario until confirmed by a court in a reciprocating state or a corresponding order made in a reciprocating state for confirmation in Ontario;

"reciprocating state" means a state declared under section 19 to be a reciprocating state and includes a province or territory of Canada;

"registered order" means,

(a) a final order made in a reciprocating state and filed under this Act with a court in Ontario,

(b) a final order deemed under subsection 2(3) to be a registered order, or

(c) a confirmation order that is filed under subsection 5(8);

"registration court" means the court in Ontario,

(a) in which the registered order is filed under this Act, or

(b) that deemed a final order to be a registered order under this Act;

"respondent" means a person in Ontario or in a reciprocating state who has or is alleged to have an obligation to pay support for the benefit of a claimant, or against whom a proceeding under this Act, or a corresponding enactment of a reciprocating state, is commenced;

"state" includes a political subdivision of a state and an official agency of a state;

"support" includes maintenance or alimony.

1993, c. 27, Sched.

2. (1) Final orders of reciprocating state — Where the Attorney General receives a certified copy of a final order made in a reciprocating state with information that the respondent is in Ontario, the Attorney General shall designate a court in Ontario for the purposes of the registration and enforcement of the order and forward the order and supporting material to that court.

(2) Filing for registration — On receipt of a final order transmitted to a court under subsection (1) or under a provision in a reciprocating state corresponding to clause 5(8)(a), the proper officer of the court shall file the order with the court and give notice of the registration of the order to the respondent.

(3) Claimant leaving Ontario after final order made in Ontario — Where a final order is made in Ontario and the claimant subsequently leaves Ontario and is apparently resident in a reciprocating state, the court that made the order shall, on the written request of the claimant, the respondent or the Attorney General, deem the order to be a registered order.

(4) Variation of registered order — A registered order varied in a manner consistent with this Act continues to be a registered order.

(5) Setting aside a registered order — A respondent may, within one month after receiving notice of the registration of a registered order, apply to the registration court to set the registration aside.

(6) Grounds — On application under subsection (5), the registration court shall set aside the registration if it determines that the order was obtained by fraud or error or was not a final order.

(7) Disposition — An order determined not to be a final order and set aside under subsection (6) may be dealt with by the registration court under section 5 as a provisional order.

(8) Invalid final order treated as provisional — Where an order purporting to be a final order is made by a court in a reciprocating state and the order is not enforceable in Ontario under the conflict of laws rules of Ontario, the court in Ontario may, in its discretion, deem the order to be provisional order and deal with it under section 5.

[Editor's Note: Reciprocal Enforcement of Support Orders Act (the 'former Act') has been repealed by Statutes of Ontario, 2002, c. 13, s. 55 and replaced with the new Interjurisdictional Support Orders Act, S.O. 2002, c. 13 (the 'new Act'). S. 54(1) of the new Act provides that an order made or registered under the former Act remains effective and may be varied, enforced or otherwise dealt with as if it had been made or registered under the new Act.

Furthermore, s. 54(2) provides that if the respondent received notice of a hearing to consider a provisional order or a provisional variation order or notice of registration of a final order under the former Act before the commencement date, the matter shall be dealt with in accordance with the former Act as if it had not been repealed.

Furthermore, s. 54(4) provides that if a final order was received for registration under the former Act before the new Act comes into force but, on that day, has not yet been registered, the order shall be dealt with in accordance with this Act as if it had been received under Part III of the new Act.]

3. (1) Making of provisional orders — On application by a claimant, a court may, without notice to and in the absence of a respondent, make a provisional order against the respondent.

(2) Support provisions in provisional orders — An order under subsection (1) may only include the support provisions the court could have included in a final order in a proceeding of which the respondent had notice in Ontario but in which the respondent failed to appear.

(3) Transmission of provisional orders — Where a provisional order is made, a proper officer of the court shall send to the Attorney General for transmission to a reciprocating state,

(a) three certified copies of the provisional order;

(b) a certified or sworn document setting out or summarizing the evidence given in the proceeding;

(c) a copy of the enactments under which the respondent is alleged to have an obligation to support the claimant; and

(d) a statement giving available information respecting identification, location, income and assets of the respondent.

(4) Further evidence — Where, during a proceeding for a confirmation order, a court in a reciprocating state remits the matter back for further evidence to the court in Ontario that made the provisional order, the court in Ontario shall, after giving notice to the claimant, receive further evidence.

(5) Evidence and recommendations — Where evidence is received under subsection (4), a proper officer of the court shall forward to the court in the reciprocating state a certified or sworn document setting out or summarizing the evidence with such recommendations as the court in Ontario considers appropriate.

(6) New provisional orders — Where a provisional order made under this section comes before a court in a reciprocating state and confirmation is denied in respect of one or more claimants, the court in Ontario that made the provisional order may, on application within six months from the denial of confirmation, reopen the matter and receive further evidence and make a new provisional order for a claimant in respect of whom confirmation was denied.

[Editor's Note: Reciprocal Enforcement of Support Orders Act (the 'former Act') has been repealed by Statutes of Ontario, 2002, c. 13, s. 55 and replaced with the new Interjurisdictional Support Orders Act, S.O. 2002, c. 13 (the 'new Act'). S. 54(1) of the new Act provides that an order made or registered under the former Act remains effective and may be varied, enforced or otherwise dealt with as if it had been made or registered under the new Act.

Furthermore, s. 54(2) provides that if the respondent received notice of a hearing to consider a provisional order or a provisional variation order or notice of registration of a final order under the former Act before the new Act comes into force, the matter shall be dealt with in accordance with the former Act as if it had not been repealed.

Furthermore, s. 54(3) provides that if a person who ordinarily resides in Ontario applied for a provisional order or a provisional variation order under the former Act before the commencement date, the application continues under the former Act as if it had not been repealed.

Furthermore, s. 54(5) provides that if a provisional order or a provisional variation order was received under the former Act before the new Act comes into force but, on that day, the respondent had not received notice of the hearing to consider the order, the order shall be dealt with in accordance with the new Act as if it had been received under Part III or Part IV, as the case may be, of the new Act.]

4. (1) Parentage — Where the parentage of a child is in issue and has not previously been determined by a court of competent jurisdiction, the parentage may be determined as part of a support proceeding under this Act.

(2) Determination of parentage in confirmation proceeding — If the respondent disputes parentage in the course of a proceeding to confirm a provisional order for support, the matter of parentage may be determined even though the provisional order makes no reference to parentage.

5. (1) Making of confirmation orders — Where the Attorney General receives from a reciprocating state documents corresponding to those described in subsection 3(3) with the information that the respondent is in Ontario, the Attorney General shall designate a court in Ontario for the purpose of proceedings under this section and forward the documents to that court.

(2) Procedure — On receipt of the documents referred to in subsection (1), the court shall serve or cause to be served upon the respondent a copy of the documents together with a notice of the confirmation hearing containing a notice to file a statement of financial affairs in the same manner as in a proceeding under the *Family Law Act*, and shall proceed with the hearing taking into consideration the certified or sworn document setting out or summarizing the evidence given in the proceeding in the reciprocating state.

(3) Report to Attorney General — Where the respondent apparently is outside the territorial jurisdiction of the court and will not return, a proper officer of the court, on receipt of documents under subsection (1), shall return the documents to the Attorney General with available information respecting the whereabouts and circumstances of the respondent.

(4) Orders of confirmation or refusal — At the conclusion of a proceeding under this section, the court may make a confirmation order in the amount it considers appropriate or make an order refusing support to any claimant.

(5) Commencement of payments — Where the court makes a confirmation order for periodic support payments, the court may direct that the payments begin from a date not earlier than the date of the provisional order.

(6) Further evidence — The court, before making a confirmation order in a reduced amount or before denying support, shall decide whether to remit the matter back for further evidence to the court that made the provisional order.

(7) Interim order — Where a court remits a matter under subsection (6), it may make an interim order for support against the respondent.

(8) Report and filing — At the conclusion of a proceeding under this section, the court, or a proper officer of the court, shall,

  (a) forward a certified copy of the order to the court that made the provisional order and to the Attorney General;

  (b) file the confirmation order, where one is made; and

  (c) where an order is made refusing or reducing support, give written reasons to the court that made the provisional order and to the Attorney General.

[Editor's Note: Reciprocal Enforcement of Support Orders Act (the 'former Act') has been repealed by Statutes of Ontario, 2002, c. 13, s. 55 and replaced with the new Interjurisdictional Support Orders Act, *S.O. 2002, c. 13 (the 'new Act'). S. 54(1) of the new Act provides that an order made or registered under the former Act remains effective and may be varied, enforced or otherwise dealt with as if it had been made or registered under the new Act.]*

6. (1) Choice of law — Where the law of the reciprocating state is pleaded to establish the obligation of the respondent to maintain a claimant resident in that state, the court in Ontario shall take judicial notice of that law and apply it.

(2) Proof of foreign enactment — An enactment of a reciprocating state may be pleaded and proved for the purposes of this section by producing a copy of the enactment received from the reciprocating state.

(3) Adjournment — Where the law of the reciprocating state is not pleaded under subsection (1), the court in Ontario shall,

  (a) make an interim order for support against the respondent where appropriate;

  (b) adjourn the proceeding for a period not exceeding ninety days; and

  (c) request the Attorney General to notify the appropriate officer of the reciprocating state of the requirement to plead and prove the applicable law of that state if that law is to be applied.

(4) Application of local law — Where the law of the reciprocating state is not pleaded after an adjournment under subsection (3), the court shall apply the law of Ontario.

(5) Statement of local law — Where the law of a reciprocating state requires the court in Ontario to provide the court in the reciprocating state with a statement of the grounds on which the making of the confirmation order might have been opposed if the respondent were served and had appeared at the hearing of the court in Ontario, the Attorney General shall be deemed to be the proper officer of the court for the purpose of making and providing the statement of the grounds.

[Editor's Note: Reciprocal Enforcement of Support Orders Act (the 'former Act') has been repealed by Statutes of Ontario, 2002, c. 13, s. 55 and replaced with the new Interjurisdictional Support Orders Act, *S.O. 2002, c. 13 (the 'new Act'). S. 54(3) of the new Act provides that if a person who ordinarily resides in Ontario applied for a provisional order or a provisional variation order under the former Act before the new Act comes into force, the application continues under the former Act as if it had not been repealed.]*

7. (1) Variation or rescission of registered orders — The provisions of this Act respecting the procedure for making provisional orders and confirmation orders apply with necessary modifications to a proceeding, except under subsection (5), for the variation or rescission of registered orders.

(2) Restricted jurisdiction — This section does not,

(a) authorize a provincially appointed judge to vary or rescind a registered order made in Canada by a federally appointed judge; or

(b) allow a registered order originally made under a federal enactment to be varied or rescinded except as authorized by federal enactment.

(3) Powers of provincially appointed judge — Despite subsection (2), a provincially appointed judge may make a provisional order to vary or rescind a registered order made in Canada under a provincial enactment by a federally appointed judge.

(4) Acceptance of jurisdiction — Subject to subsections (2) and (3), a registration court has jurisdiction to vary or rescind a registered order where both claimant and respondent accept its jurisdiction.

(5) Variation and rescission where respondent resides in Ontario — Where the respondent is ordinarily resident in Ontario, a registration court may, on application by the claimant, vary or rescind a registered order.

(6) Confirmation of provisional orders of variation and rescission — A registration court may make a confirmation order for the variation or rescission of a registered order where,

(a) the respondent is ordinarily resident in Ontario;

(b) the claimant is ordinarily resident in a reciprocating state;

(c) a certified copy of a provisional order of variation or rescission made by a court in a reciprocating state is received by the registration court through the Attorney General; and

(d) the respondent is given notice of the proceeding and an opportunity to appear.

(7) Application by respondent residing in Ontario — A registration court may, on application by the respondent, make a provisional order varying or rescinding a registered order where,

(a) the respondent is ordinarily resident in Ontario; and

(b) the claimant is ordinarily resident in the reciprocating state in which the order was first made,

and section 3 applies with necessary modifications to the proceeding.

(8) Idem — A registration court may, on application by the respondent, vary or rescind a registered order where,

(a) the respondent is ordinarily resident in Ontario;

(b) the claimant is ordinarily resident in a reciprocating state other than the state in which the order was first made; and

(c) the registration court, in the course of the proceeding, remits the matter to the court nearest to the place where the claimant lives or works for the purpose of obtaining evidence on behalf of the claimant,

or where

(d) the respondent is ordinarily resident in Ontario;

(e) the claimant is not ordinarily resident in a reciprocating state; and

(f) the claimant is given notice of the proceeding.

(9) Application by claimant resident in Ontario — Where a claimant ordinarily resident in Ontario applies for a variation or rescission of a final order and the respondent is apparently ordinarily resident in a reciprocating state, the court may make a provisional order of variation or rescission and section 3 applies with necessary modifications to the proceeding.

8. Effect of variation or rescission of orders of Ontario by courts in reciprocating states — Where an order originally made in Ontario is varied or rescinded in a reciprocating state under the law in that state corresponding to section 7, the order shall be deemed to be so varied or rescinded in Ontario.

9. (1) Enforcement — The registration court has jurisdiction to enforce a registered order even though the order,

(a) was made in a proceeding in respect of which the registration court would have had no jurisdiction; or

(b) is of a kind that the registration court has no jurisdiction to make.

(2) Procedure — The provisions of the *Family Law Act* for the enforcement of support orders apply with necessary modifications to registered orders and interim orders made under this Act.

(3) Effect of registered order — A registered order has, from the date it is filed or deemed to be registered, the same effect as if it had been a final order originally made by the registration court and may, both with respect to arrears accrued before registration, and with respect to obligations accruing after registration, be enforced, varied or rescinded as provided in this Act.

(4) Status of order — A registered order may be registered with another court in Ontario and enforced as if it were an order of that court.

(5) Service not necessary — Where a proceeding is brought to enforce a registered order, it is not necessary to prove that the respondent was served with the order.

(6) Recording variations — Where a registered order is being enforced and the registration court finds that the order has been varied by a court subsequent to the date of registration, the registration court shall record the fact of the variation and enforce the order as varied.

10. Social assistance agency as claimant — A proceeding under this Act may be brought by,

(a) the Ministry of Community and Social Services in the name of the Minister;

(b) a municipality, excluding a lower-tier municipality in a regional municipality;

(c) a district social services administration board under the *District Social Services Administration Boards Act*;

(d) a band approved under section 15 of the *General Welfare Assistance Act*; or

(e) a delivery agent under the *Ontario Works Act, 1997*,

as claimant if the agency is providing or has provided a benefit under the *Family Benefits Act*, assistance under the *General Welfare Assistance Act* or the *Ontario Works Act, 1997* or income support under the *Ontario Disability Support Program Act, 1997* in respect of the dependant's support or if an application for such a benefit, assistance or income support has been made to the agency by or on behalf of the dependant.

1997, c. 25, Sched. E, s. 10.; 2002, c. 17, Sched. C, s. 25

11. (1) Duties of the Attorney General — The Attorney General shall, on request in writing by a claimant or an officer or court of a reciprocating state, take all reasonable measures to enforce an order made or registered under this Act.

(2) Transmission of documents — On receipt of a document for transmission under this Act to a reciprocating state, the Attorney General shall transmit the document to the proper officer of the reciprocating state.

(3) Delegation — The Attorney General may in writing authorize a person to perform or exercise a power or duty given to the Attorney General under this Act.

12. (1) Documents from reciprocating states — Where a document in the nature of an order or a certified copy of the document is received by a court in Ontario through the Attorney General, the court in Ontario shall characterise the document as a provisional order or a final order, according to the tenor of the document, and proceed accordingly.

(2) Terminology — Where, in a proceeding under this Act, a document from a court in the reciprocating state contains terminology different from the terminology of this Act or customarily in use in the court in Ontario, the court in Ontario shall give a broad and liberal interpretation to the terminology so as to given effect to the document.

13. Presumption of regularity — For the purposes of this Act, is shall be presumed, unless the contrary is established, that procedures taken in a reciprocating state have been regular and complete and that the court making an order in a reciprocating state had jurisdiction to do so and that the jurisdiction is recognized under the conflict of laws rules of Ontario.

14. (1) Conversion to Canadian currency — Where confirmation of a provisional order or registration of a final order is sought and the documents received by a court refer to amounts of support or arrears not expressed in Canadian currency, a proper officer of the court shall first obtain from a bank a quotation for the equivalent amounts in Canadian currency at a rate of exchange applicable on the day the order was made or last varied.

(2) Certification — The amounts in Canadian currency certified on the order by the proper officer of the court under subsection (1) shall be deemed to be the amounts of the order.

(3) Translation — Where an order or other document received by a court is not in English or French, the order or other document shall have attached to it from the other jurisdiction a translation in English or French approved by the court and the order or other document shall be deemed to be in English or French for the purposes of this Act.

15. (1) Appeals — Subject to subsection (2) and (3), a claimant, respondent or the Attorney General may appeal any ruling, decision or order of a court in Ontario under this Act and the *Family Law Act* applies with necessary modifications to the appeal.

(2) Time for appeal by appellant — A person resident in the reciprocating state and entitled to appear in the court in the reciprocating state in the proceeding being appealed from, or the Attorney General on that person's behalf, may appeal within seventy-five days after the making of the ruling, decision or order of the court in Ontario appealed from.

(3) Time for appeal by persons responding to appeal — A person responding to an appeal under subsection (2) may appeal a ruling, decision or order in the same proceeding within fifteen days after receipt of notice of the appeal.

(4) Order in force pending appeal — An order under appeal remains in force pending the determination of the appeal, unless the court appealed to otherwise orders.

16. (1) Evidentiary matters — In a proceeding under this Act, spouses are competent and compellable witnesses against each other.

(2) Proof of documents — In a proceeding under this Act, a document purporting to be signed by a judge, officer of a court or public officer in a reciprocating state shall, unless the contrary is proved, be proof of the appointment, signature and authority of the person who signed it.

(3) Sworn documents and transcripts — Statements in writing sworn by the maker, depositions or transcripts of evidence taken in a reciprocating state may be received in evidence by a court in Ontario under this Act.

(4) Proof of default — For the purposes of proving default or arrears under this Act, a court may receive in evidence a sworn document made by any person deposing to have knowledge of, or information and belief concerning, the fact.

17. Statement of payments — A registration court or a proper officer of it shall, on reasonable request of a claimant, respondent, the Attorney General, a proper officer of a reciprocating state or a court of the state, furnish a sworn itemized statement showing with respect to support under an order,

(a) all amounts that became due and owing by the respondent during the twenty-four months preceding the date of the statement; and

(b) all payments made through the court by or on behalf of the respondent during that period.

1993, c. 27, Sched.

18. Transmission of documents by court where respondent leaves Ontario — Where a proper officer of a court in Ontario believes that a respondent under a registered order has ceased to reside in Ontario and is resident in or proceeding to another province or state, the officer shall inform the Attorney General and the court that made the order of any information the officer has respecting the whereabouts and circumstances of the respondent and, on request by the Attorney General, a proper officer of the court that made the order or the claimant, shall send to the court or person indicated in the request,

(a) three certified copies of the order as filed with the court in Ontario; and

(b) a sworn certificate of arrears.

19. Regulations — The Lieutenant Governor in Council may, where satisfied that laws are or will be in effect in a state for the reciprocal enforcement of orders made in Ontario on a basis substantially similar to this Act, by regulation, designate that state to be a reciprocating state.

20. Saving — This Act does not impair any other remedy available to a claimant or another person, Ontario, a province, a state or a political subdivision or official agency of Ontario, a province or a state.

21. Application to past orders — This Act applies to orders, whether provisional, confirmation, final or registered, even though they were made or registered before this Act comes into force.

[Editor's Note: Reciprocal Enforcement of Support Orders Act *(the 'former Act') has been repealed by Statutes of Ontario, 2002, c. 13, s. 55 and replaced with the new* Interjurisdictional Support Orders Act, *S.O. 2002, c. 13 (the 'new Act'). S. 54(1) of the new Act provides that an order made or registered under the former Act remains effective and may be varied, enforced or otherwise dealt with as if it had been made or registered under the new Act.]*

ONT. REG. 140/94 — RECIPROCATING STATES [REVOKED]

made under the *Reciprocal Enforcement of Support Orders Act*

O. Reg. 140/94, as am. O. Reg. 461/98; 313/00; 207/02; 53/03, s. 2.

[Note: Reciprocating States *revoked by O. Reg. 53/03, s. 2.]*

Reciprocating States

1. The states named in the Schedule are declared to be reciprocating states for the purposes of the Act.

Schedule

1. All provinces and territories of Canada apart from Ontario.

2. The United States of America, including the 50 states, American Samoa, District of Columbia, Guam, Puerto Rico, United States Virgin Islands and any other jurisdiction of the United States participating in Title IV-D of the *Social Security Act* (U.S.A.).

3. The Commonwealth of Australia and the following States and Territories of Australia:

    Capital Territory of Australia

    New South Wales

    Northern Territory of Australia

    Queensland

    South Australia

    Tasmania

    Victoria

    Western Australia

4. The following jurisdictions:

    Federal Republic of Germany

    Fiji

    Finland

    Gibraltar

    Guernsey, Alderney and Sark

    Hong Kong

    Isle of Man

    Malta and its Dependencies

    New Zealand and the Cook Islands

    Papua New Guinea

Republic of Austria
Republic of Ghana
Republic of Poland
Republic of South Africa

States of Jersey

United Kingdom

Zimbabwe

O. Reg. 461/98, s. 1; 313/00, s. 1; 207/02, s. 1

2. Regulation 988 of the Revised Regulations of Ontario, 1990 and Ontario Regulations 174/91 and 363/93 are revoked.

ONT. REG. 194 — RULES OF CIVIL PROCEDURE

made under the *Courts of Justice Act*

R.R.O. 1990, Reg. 194, as am. O. Reg. 219/91; 396/91; 73/92; 175/92; 535/92; 770/92; 212/93; 465/93; 466/93; 766/93; 351/94; 484/94; 739/94; 740/94; 69/95; 70/95; 377/95; 533/95; 534/95; 60/96; 61/96; 175/96; 332/96; 333/96; 536/96; 554/96; 555/96; 118/97; 348/97; 427/97; 442/97; 171/98; 214/98; 217/98; 292/98; 452/98 ; 453/98 [s. 2(2) revoked O. Reg. 244/01, s. 7.]; 570/98; 627/98; 288/99; 290/99; 292/99; 484/99; 488/99; 583/99; 24/00; 25/00; 504/00; 652/00; 653/00; 654/00; 113/01; 243/01; 244/01; 284/01; 427/01 [ss. 1(2), 4(2), 5(2), 6(2), (5) not in force at date of publication. Revoked O. Reg. 308/02, ss. 1(2), 2(2), 3(2), 4(3), (5).]; 447/01; 457/01; 206/02; 308/02; 336/02; 19/03 [To come into force June 30, 2003.]; 54/03.

[Note: only Rules 14.04 and 69–71 are reproduced here.]

. . . . .

COMMENCEMENT OF PROCEEDINGS

Rule 14 — Originating Process

. . . . .

14.04 Divorce Actions — By Petition — The originating process for the commencement of a divorce action is a petition for divorce (Form 69A or 69B), except as provided by sub-rule 69.09(6) (counterpetition against person not already a party (Form 69G)).

. . . . .

PARTICULAR PROCEEDINGS

. . . . .

Rule 69 — Divorce Actions

69.01 Application Of Rules Of Civil Procedure — **(1)** All the Rules of Civil Procedure that apply in an action apply in a divorce action, with necessary modifications, except where rules 69.03 to 69.27 provide otherwise.

(2) They do not apply to proceedings in the Family Court of the Superior Court of Justice, which are governed by Ontario Regulation 114/99 (Family Law Rules), except as provided by those rules.

O. Reg. 73/92, s. 2; 288/99, s. 23

69.02 Definitions — In rules 69.02 to 69.26,

"Act" means the *Divorce Act* (Canada);

715

"child of the marriage" has the same meaning as in section 2 of the Act.

69.03 Petition —

General

(1) The originating process for the commencement of a divorce action is a petition for divorce (Form 69A or 69B), except as provided by subrule 69.09(6) (counterpetition against person not already a party (Form 69G)).

(2) A certificate of the marriage or of the registration of the marriage shall be filed before a petition is issued, unless the petition states that it is impossible to obtain the certificate, or that the certificate will be filed before the action is set down for trial or a motion is made for judgment.

(3) The party commencing the action is called the petitioner and the opposite party is called the respondent.

Person Alleged to Have Been Involved in Adultery

(4) In a petition in which it is alleged that the respondent spouse has committed adultery, it is not necessary to set out the name of the other person alleged to have been involved.

Joint Petition for Divorce

(5) Spouses may commence a divorce action jointly without a respondent.

(6) A joint petition for divorce shall not contain a claim for any relief other than a divorce and, if applicable, an order on consent.

Claim for Relief

(7) A petition that contains a claim for support or division of property shall set out the nature and amount of relief claimed and, if support is claimed, the amount for each dependant.

69.04 Service of petition —

Manner of Service

(1) A petition shall be served on the respondent personally or in accordance with subrules 16.03(2) to (4) (acceptance of service by solicitor, service by mail with acknowledgment of receipt card), unless the court makes an order under rule 16.04 for substituted service or dispensing with service.

(2) A person who effects personal service of a petition shall ask the respondent to complete and sign the acknowledgment of service on the back of the petition and shall sign as witness to the respondent's signature, or record the fact that the respondent declined to sign the acknowledgment of service, as the case may be.

Person Alleged to Have Been Involved in Adultery

(3) If a petition sets out the name of a person alleged to have been involved in adultery with the respondent, it shall be served on the person, unless the court orders otherwise, by any method authorized by Rule 16 for service of an originating process, or by mailing a copy of the petition to the person at his or her last known address.

Petitioner not to Effect Personal Service

(4) A petition that is served personally shall be served by someone other than the petitioner.

Service Outside Ontario

(5) A petition may be served outside Ontario without a court order.

Substituted Service by Advertisement

(6) Where substituted service of a petition by advertisement in a newspaper is ordered by the court, the advertisement shall be in Form 69C.

69.05 Time For Service Of Petition — A petition shall be served within six months after it is issued.

69.05.1 Mandatory Information Program —

Application of rule

(1) This rule applies to a divorce action commenced at Toronto after July 1, 1998 in which any relief, other than a divorce, costs and the incorporation of the terms of a separation agreement or prior court order, is sought.

Contents of Program

(2) The program referred to in this rule shall provide parties to divorce proceedings with information about separation and the legal process, and may include information on topics such as,

    (a) the options available for resolving differences, including alternatives to a court proceeding;

    (b) the impact the separation of parents has on children; and

    (c) resources available to deal with problems arising from separation.

Attendance Compulsory

(3) Each party to a proceeding described in subrule (1) shall attend the program no later than 45 days after the proceeding is commenced.

Appointments to Attend

(4) The petitioner shall arrange his or her own appointment to attend the program, obtain an appointment for the respondent from the person who conducts the program, and serve notice of the respondent's appointment with the petition.

Certificate

(5) The person who conducts the program shall provide for each party who attends a certificate of attendance, which shall be filed as soon as possible, and in any event not later than the time set out in subrule (10).

No Other Steps

(6) A party shall not take any step in the proceeding before his or her certificate of attendance is filed, except that a respondent may serve and file an answer and a party may make an appointment for a case conference under subrule (8).

Exception

(7) The court may, on a party's motion, order that any or all of subrules (3) to (6) and (8) do not apply to the party, because of urgency or hardship or for some other reason in the interest of justice.

Case Conference

(8) Before any motion for interlocutory relief is heard, the parties shall attend a case conference with a judge.

(9) The purposes of the case conference include,

(a) identifying the issues that are in dispute and those that are not in dispute;

(b) exploring ways to resolve the issues that are in dispute, including alternatives to a court proceeding;

(c) if possible, obtaining the parties' agreement to a specific timetable for the steps to be taken in the case before it comes to trial; and

(d) organizing or, if appropriate, holding a settlement conference.

Steps Required Before Case Conference

(10) The parties shall take the following steps by 2 p.m. on the second day before the day of the case conference:

1. Each party shall file a confirmation of his or her intention to attend.

2. The petitioner shall serve, and file with proof of service, a case conference brief.

3. The respondent shall serve, and file with proof of service,

i. a case conference brief, or

ii. a brief stating any points of difference from the petitioner's case conference brief.

Revocation

(11) This rule is revoked on December 31, 2003.

O. Reg. 214/98, s. 1; 484/99, s. 1; 583/99, s. 1; 654/00, s. 1; 447/01, s. 1; 336/02, s. 1

69.06 Pleadings — **(1)** In a divorce action, pleadings shall consist of the petition (Form 69A or 69B), answer (Form 69D) and reply (Form 69E), if any.

(2) In a counterpetition, pleadings shall consist of the counterpetition (Form 69F or 69G), answer to counterpetition (Form 69H) and reply to answer to counterpetition (Form 69I), if any.

69.07 Answer —

Time for Delivery of Answer

(1) Except as provided in subrule (3), 19.01(5) (late delivery of defence) or 69.10(2) (counterpetition against petitioner and non-party), a respondent who wishes to oppose a claim made in the petition shall deliver an answer,

(a) within twenty days after service of the petition, where the respondent is served in Ontario;

(b) within forty days after service of the petition, where the respondent is served elsewhere in Canada or in the United States of America; or

(c) within sixty days after service of the petition, where the respondent is served anywhere else.

Notice of Intent to Defend

(2) A respondent served with a petition who intends to defend the action may deliver a notice of intent to defend (Form 69J) within the time prescribed for delivery of the answer.

(3) A respondent who delivers a notice of intent to defend within the prescribed time is entitled to ten days, in addition to the time prescribed by subrule (1), within which to deliver an answer.

69.08 Reply — A reply, if any, shall be delivered within ten days after service of the answer.

69.09 Counterpetition —

Where Available

(1) A respondent who claims any relief against the petitioner, other than dismissal of the action and costs, shall do so by way of counterpetition.

(2) A respondent who counterpetitions against the petitioner may join as a respondent to the counterpetition any other person, whether a party to the main action or not, who is a necessary or proper party to the counterpetition.

Person Alleged to Have Been Involved in Adultery

(3) Subrules 69.03(4) and 69.04(3) (naming and service of person alleged to have been involved in adultery) apply, with necessary modifications, to a counterpetition.

Counterpetition to be in Same Document as Answer

(4) A respondent shall include the counterpetition (Form 69F or 69G) and the answer in a single document entitled an answer and counterpetition.

Claim for Relief

(5) A counterpetition that contains a claim for support or division of property shall set out the nature and amount of relief claimed and, if support is claimed, the amount for each dependant.

Counterpetition to be Issued where Respondent to Counterpetition not Already Party to Main Action

(6) Where a person who is not already a party to the main action is made a respondent to the counterpetition, the answer and counterpetition,

　　(a) shall be issued,

　　　　(i) within the time prescribed by rule 69.07 for the delivery of an answer in the main action, or at any time before the respondent is noted in default, or

　　　　(ii) subsequently with leave of the court; and

　　(b) shall contain a second title of proceeding showing who is petitioner by counterpetition and who are respondents to the counterpetition.

Service Outside Ontario

(7) A counterpetition may be served outside Ontario without a court order.

69.10 Time For Delivery Or Service Of Answer And Counterpetition —

Where all Parties are Parties to the Main Action

(1) Where a counterpetition is only against the petitioner, or only against the petitioner and another person who is already a party to the main action, the answer and counterpetition shall be delivered within the time prescribed by rule 69.07 for the delivery of the answer in the main action, or at any time before the respondent has been noted in default.

Where New Party is Brought In

(2) Where a counterpetition is against the petitioner and a respondent to the counterpetition who is not already a party to the main action, the answer and counterpetition shall be served, after it has been issued, on the parties to the main action and, together with all the pleadings previously delivered in the main action, on the respondent to the counterpetition who is not already a party to the main action, and shall be filed with proof of service,

> (a) within thirty days after the answer and counterpetition is issued or at any time before the respondent is noted in default; or

> (b) subsequently with leave of the court.

(3) An answer and counterpetition need not be served personally on any person who is a party to the main action, except where a respondent to the counterpetition is also a respondent in the main action and has failed to deliver a notice of intent to defend or an answer in the main action, in which case the respondent shall be served in the manner prescribed by subrule 69.04(1), whether or not the respondent has been noted in default in the main action.

69.11 Amending Answer To Add Counterpetition — **(1)** A respondent who has delivered an answer that does not contain a counterpetition and who wishes to counterpetition only against the petitioner, or only against the petitioner and another person who is already a party to the main action, may amend the answer in accordance with rules 26.02 and 26.03 in order to add the counterpetition, and rule 26.05 (responding to amended pleading) applies to the amended answer and counterpetition.

(2) A respondent referred to in subrule (1) who wishes to counterpetition against the petitioner and another person who is not already a party to the main action may, with leave of the court, have the registrar issue an amended answer and counterpetition, and rule 26.05 (responding to amended pleading) applies to the amended answer and counterpetition.

69.12 Answer To Counterpetition —

By Petitioner and Other Party to Main Action

(1) The petitioner and any other respondent to a counterpetition who is already a party to the main action shall deliver an answer to counterpetition (Form 69H) within twenty days after service of the counterpetition.

(2) Where the petitioner delivers a reply in the main action, the answer to counterpetition and the reply shall be included in a single document entitled a reply and answer to counterpetition.

By Respondent added by Counterpetition

(3) Except as provided in subrule (5) or 19.01(5) (late delivery of defence), a respondent to a counterpetition who is not already a party to the main action shall deliver an answer to counterpetition (Form 69H),

> (a) within twenty days after service of the answer and counterpetition, where the respondent to the counterpetition is served in Ontario;

(b) within forty days after service of the answer and counterpetition, where the respondent to the counterpetition is served elsewhere in Canada or in the United States of America; or

(c) within sixty days after service of the answer and counterpetition, where the respondent to the counterpetition is served anywhere else.

(4) Where a respondent to a counterpetition who is not already a party to the main action is served with a counterpetition and intends to defend the action, he or she may deliver a notice of intent to defend (Form 69J) within the time prescribed for delivery of the answer to counterpetition.

(5) A respondent to a counterpetition who delivers a notice of intent to defend within the prescribed time is entitled to ten days, in addition to the time prescribed by subrule (3), within which to deliver an answer to counterpetition.

69.13 Reply To Answer To Counterpetition — A reply to answer to counterpetition (Form 69I), if any, shall be delivered within ten days after service of the answer to counterpetition.

69.14 Financial Statements —

Where Required

(1) Where a petition contains a claim for support or division of property, the petitioner shall file and serve a financial statement (Form 69K) with the petition and the respondent spouse shall deliver a financial statement with the answer.

(2) Where no claim for support or division of property is made in the petition, but such a claim is made in the counterpetition, the respondent spouse shall deliver a financial statement with the answer and counterpetition and the petitioner shall deliver a financial statement with the answer to counterpetition.

Waiver of Financial Statements

(3) Subrules (1) and (2) do not apply in respect of a claim for support under the Act if both spouses have filed a waiver of financial statements (Form 69L), but the spouses may not waive the obligation to deliver financial statements in respect of a claim under the *Family Law Act*.

Registrar to Refuse Documents Unless Accompanied by Financial Statements

(4) Where a financial statement is required to be filed or delivered with a petition or counterpetition, or an answer to it, the registrar shall not accept the petition, counterpetition or answer for issuing or filing without the financial statement.

Respondent must File Even When Not Defending

(5) A respondent spouse who does not intend to defend a claim for support or division of property shall nevertheless deliver a financial statement within the time prescribed for delivery of an answer or answer to counterpetition, but the failure of the respondent spouse to do so does not prevent the petitioner from setting the action down for trial or moving for judgment.

Order to Require Delivery

(6) Where a respondent spouse fails to deliver a financial statement within the time prescribed for delivery of the answer or answer to counterpetition, the court may, on motion without notice, make an order requiring the delivery of a financial statement within a specified time.

(7) If a claim is made in the action for custody of a child, the court may order the parties to deliver financial statements (short form) (Form 69M) within a specified time.

Particulars of Financial Statement

(8) Where a financial statement lacks particularity, a spouse may demand particulars and if the other spouse fails to supply them within seven days the court may, on such terms as are just,

>   (a) order particulars to be delivered within a specified time; or

>   (b) strike out the financial statement and order that a new financial statement be delivered within a specified time.

Sanctions for Failure to Deliver Financial Statement or to Give Particulars

(9) Where a spouse fails to comply with an order to deliver a financial statement, a new financial statement or particulars,

>   (a) the court may dismiss the spouse's action or strike out his or her answer; and

>   (b) a judge may make a contempt order against the spouse.

Cross-examination on Financial Statement

(10) A spouse may cross-examine the other spouse on his or her financial statement.

(11) A cross-examination on a financial statement may be used,

>   (a) on a motion for interim relief; and

>   (b) at trial, in the same manner as an examination for discovery.

(12) A spouse who has set the action down for trial or who has consented to the action being placed on a trial list may not cross-examine before trial on the other spouse's financial statement without leave of the court, but is not relieved of the obligation imposed by subrules (13) to (15).

Duty to Correct Financial Statement and Answers on Cross-examination

(13) A spouse who has delivered a financial statement and subsequently discovers,

>   (a) that any information in the financial statement or answer on cross-examination on it was incorrect or incomplete when made; or

>   (b) that there has been a material change in any information contained in it,

shall forthwith provide information concerning the change or correction in writing to the other spouse, and subrules 31.09(2) and (3) (correcting answers and sanctions for failure to correct) apply, with necessary modifications.

(14) A spouse who has delivered a financial statement shall deliver a fresh financial statement at least seven days before the commencement of the trial of the action, but may not be cross-examined before trial on the fresh financial statement except with leave of the court.

Net Family Property Statement

(15) In an action in which a claim is made for a division of property, each spouse shall deliver a net family property statement (Form 69N) at least seven days before each of the following:

>   1. A pre-trial conference.

2. A motion for judgment.

3. The trial.

69.15 Interim Relief —

Notice of Motion

(1) A notice of motion for interim relief shall set out the precise relief sought, including the amount of support claimed for each dependant.

Pre-motion Conference

(2) At the hearing of the motion, the court may direct a pre-motion conference to consider the possibility of settling any or all the issues raised by the motion or the action.

(3) The costs of a pre-motion conference shall be assessed as part of the costs of the action, unless a judge or master who conducts the conference orders otherwise.

(4) A judge or officer who conducts a pre-motion conference under subrule (2) shall not preside at a motion for interim relief, the trial, a reference in the action or a motion for judgment, except that where the pre-trial conference has resolved all the issues in the action, a judge who conducted it may preside at a motion for judgment on consent of the parties.

Written Proposal for Settlement and Costs of Interim Motion

(5) In exercising his or her discretion concerning costs, the judge or officer who hears a motion for interim relief shall take into account any written proposal for settlement of the motion or the failure to make such a proposal.

Failure to Comply with Interim Order

(6) Where a party fails to comply with an order for interim relief and the court is satisfied that the party is able to comply with the order, the court may postpone the trial of the action or strike out any pleading or affidavit of the party in default.

69.16 Children's Lawyer's Report —

Notice of Intention to Investigate and Report

(1) Where the Children's Lawyer intends to investigate and report to the court concerning custody of or access to a child, he or she shall serve notice of that intention (Form 69O) on the parties and shall file a copy of the notice with proof of service.

(2) Service of the notice on a party who has been noted in default shall be effected by mail addressed to the party at his or her last known address, unless the court orders otherwise.

Service of Documents on Children's Laywer

(3) Where the Children's Lawyer has served notice, a party who subsequently serves an answer, reply or notice of motion or any other document that relates to custody of or access to the child or relates to the child's support or education shall also serve it on the Children's Lawyer within the time prescribed for service on the parties.

Discovery by Children's Lawyer

(4) Where the Children's Lawyer has served notice, he or she has the right to discovery in respect of any matter that relates to custody of or access to the child or relates to the child's support or education.

Rules of
Procedure

Service of Report

(5) The Children's Lawyer shall serve his or her report on the parties interested in custody of or access to the child or in the child's support or education, within sixty days after serving notice under subrule (1), and shall then forthwith file a copy of the report and supporting affidavit, if any, with proof of service.

(6) Subrule (2) applies, with necessary modifications, to service of the report.

Dispute of Report

(7) A party on whom the report is served may dispute a statement in it or in any supporting affidavit by serving a concise statement of the nature of the dispute on every other party interested in custody of or access to the child or in the child's support or education, and on the Children's Lawyer, and filing the statement, with proof of service, within fifteen days after service of the report.

(8) Where the Children's Lawyer has served notice under subrule (1), the action shall not be tried and no motion for judgment shall be heard until,

(a) all disputes have been filed or the time for filing disputes has expired; or

(b) every party interested in custody of or access to the child or in the child's support or education has filed a waiver (Form 69P) of the right to dispute the report.

Application of Former Rule

(9) Rule 70.16 as it read on February 2, 1987 continues to apply to divorce actions commenced on or before that date.

O. Reg. 69/95, s. 19

69.17 Naming Place Of Trial And Trial Judge —

Place of Trial

(1) The petitioner shall name in the petition as the place of trial a place where the court normally sits in the county in which the petitioner proposes that the action be tried.

(2) A petitioner who makes a claim for custody of or access to a child who ordinarily resides in Ontario shall name in the petition as the place of trial a place where the court normally sits in the county in which the child ordinarily resides.

(3) The trial shall be held at the place named in the petition unless an order is made to change the place of trial under rule 46.03.

69.18 Marriage Certificate And Certificate Respecting Prior Pending Proceedings — No divorce action shall be tried and no motion for judgment in a divorce action shall be heard until the registrar has received and attached to the trial or motion record,

(a) a certificate of the marriage or of the registration of the marriage, unless the petition states that it is impossible to obtain a certificate; and

(b) a certificate or report with respect to prior pending proceedings commenced by either spouse, issued under the Divorce Regulations (Canada) after the petition was filed.

69.19 Motion For Judgment —

Requisition and Notice of Motion

(1) A requisition to note the respondent in default and a notice of motion for judgment in a divorce action under subrule 19.05(1) (motion for default judgment) shall be combined in Form 69Q.

Petitioner's Affidavit

(2) The affidavit of the petitioner in support of the motion (Form 69R) shall,

(a) contain sufficient information for the court to satisfy itself that there is no possibility of the reconciliation of the spouses, or that the circumstances of the case are of such a nature that it would clearly not be appropriate to do so;

(b) confirm that all the information in the petition is correct, except as specified in the affidavit;

(c) if the certificate of marriage or of registration of marriage filed in the action is not signed and sealed by the Registrar General of Ontario, refer to the certificate by its title, date and place of issue and the name and office of the person who issued it and state that it contains the correct particulars of the marriage;

(d) if no certificate of marriage or of registration of marriage has been filed in the action, state,

    (i) what efforts have been made to obtain a certificate and why it is impossible to obtain one,

    (ii) the date and place of marriage, and

    (iii) sufficient particulars to prove the marriage;

(e) set out particulars of the grounds for divorce;

(f) state that there has been no agreement, conspiracy, understanding or arrangement to which the petitioner is either directly or indirectly a party for the purpose of subverting the administration of justice, fabricating or suppressing evidence or deceiving the court;

(g) if the petitioner is relying on the respondent's adultery or cruelty, state that the petitioner has not condoned or connived at the act or conduct complained of, or if there has been condonation or connivance, set out the circumstances that indicate that the public interest would be better served by granting the divorce;

(h) provide particulars of the present and proposed custody and access arrangements in respect of each child of the marriage, if different from those set out in the petition;

(i) if the petitioner claims support, provide particulars of his or her and the children's needs and of the respondent's means, with reference to the financial statements filed in the action, and set out particulars of any change in circumstances since the financial statements were filed;

(j) if the petitioner does not claim a division of property, confirm that he or she does not wish to claim a division of property at this time and state that he or she is aware that a claim for a division of property may be barred after the divorce;

(k) if the petitioner wishes to include in the judgment provisions of a consent, settlement, separation agreement or previous court order, refer to the document as an exhibit and refer to the specific provisions to be included;

(l) if the petitioner claims costs, set out sufficient facts to enable the court to determine whether costs should be awarded;

(m) if the petitioner seeks to have the divorce take effect earlier than thirty-one days after it is granted, set out the special circumstances that justify the earlier effective date, state that the spouses have agreed that no appeal will be taken from the judgment and refer to the agreement as an exhibit; and

(n) provide the respondent spouse's last known address and state the means by which the address is known.

Respondent's Affidavit

(3) An affidavit made by a respondent spouse in support of the motion (Form 69S) shall,

(a) state that the respondent is the petitioner's spouse;

(b) provide the respondent's address for service of the judgment;

(c) if the petitioner is relying on the respondent's adultery and the respondent is prepared to admit the adultery, state that the respondent is aware that he or she is not obliged to give evidence that he or she has committed adultery, but that he or she is willing to give that evidence;

(d) contain the matters referred to in clauses (2)(a), (b), (f), (g), (h) and (i); and

(e) if the respondent does not claim a division of property, confirm that he or she does not wish to claim a division of property at this time and state that he or she is aware that a claim for a division of property may be barred after the divorce.

Where Counterpetitioner Moves for Judgment

(4) If the motion for judgment is made by the counterpetitioner, subrules (2) and (3) (petitioner's and respondent's affidavits) apply and references to the petition and petitioner shall be deemed to be references to the counterpetition and counterpetitioner.

Affidavit of Person Involved in Adultery

(5) Where a person with whom a respondent spouse is alleged to have committed adultery is prepared to admit the adultery and files an affidavit in support of the motion, the affidavit shall state that the person is aware that he or she is not obliged to give evidence that the respondent spouse committed adultery with him or her, but that he or she is willing to give that evidence.

Oral Evidence at Hearing of Motion

(6) Instead of or in addition to filing an affidavit in support of the motion, the petitioner or counterpetitioner may examine witnesses at the hearing of the motion and subrule 39.03(4) (leave to examine witness at hearing) does not apply.

Draft Judgment

(7) The moving party shall file with the notice of motion four copies of the draft divorce judgment (Form 69T), a stamped envelope addressed to each of the parties and, where the Children's Lawyer has prepared a report in the action, a stamped envelope addressed to the Children's Lawyer.

(8) If a draft judgment provides for the payment of support, the moving party shall file with the notice of motion a fifth copy for filing by the registrar in the office of the Director of the Family Responsibility Office.

Registrar to Present Motion to Judge

(9) The registrar shall present the notice of motion and the evidence filed in support to a judge.

(10) Before presenting the motion to a judge, the registrar shall examine the notice of motion, the evidence filed in support and the draft divorce judgment and shall complete a registrar's certificate (Form 69U).

Judgment

(11) If judgment is granted on the motion in accordance with the draft filed, the registrar shall forthwith sign and enter judgment and mail a copy of it in each envelope provided under subrule (7).

(12) If judgment is to be granted on the motion, but not in accordance with the draft filed, the judge shall hear submissions on behalf of the moving party or adjourn the motion for that purpose.

O. Reg. 351/94, s. 7; 69/95, s. 19; 292/98, s. 3

69.20 Adjournment Of Trial —

Resumption after Adjournment

(1) Where a jude grants an adjournment of the trial under subsection 10(2) of the Act before hearing any evidence, a motion for resumption of the trial under subsection 10(3) of the Act may be made to any judge.

(2) Where a judge grants an adjournment of the trial under subsection 10(2) of the Act after commencing the hearing of evidence, a motion for resumption of the trial under subsection 10(3) of the Act may be made only to the same judge.

Notice to Attorney General

(3) The judge trying a divorce action may adjourn the trial for any reason to such time and place as are just and, in a proper case, may direct that the registrar forthwith give notice to the Attorney General of the proceeding, its state and the reasons of the judge for directing that notice be given.

(4) Where notice is given, the Attorney General may appear by counsel on the adjourned trial and make submissions and otherwise participate in the proceeding to the extent that the judge allows.

69.21 [Revoked O. Reg. 288/99, s. 24.]

69.22 Certificate Of Divorce — The registrar in the office where a divorce action was commenced shall issue a certificate of divorce (Form 69V) when,

(a) the divorce has taken effect;

(b) a requisition has been filed with the registrar, accompanied by an affidavit sworn after the divorce took effect and stating that,

(i) no appeal from the divorce is pending, or any such appeal has been abandoned or dismissed, and

(ii) no order has been made extending the time for appealing from the divorce, or if any such order has been made, the extended time has expired without an appeal being taken; and

(c) the registrar has searched the court records and ascertained that there is no indication that the affidavit is incorrect.

69.23 Registrar To Notify Local Registrar Of Appeal — On the filing of a notice of appeal from a divorce or the making of an order extending the time for such an appeal, the Registrar of the Court of Appeal shall forthwith notify the registrar in the office where the action was commenced.

69.24 Variation Of Final Order For Corollary Relief —

By Application

(1) A person who wishes to vary, suspend or rescind a final order for support, custody or access under section 17 of the Act or to obtain such an order after a divorce shall do so by notice of application.

Filing of Financial Statement

(2) If an application under subrule (1) is in respect of support, the applicant shall file and serve a financial statement (short form) (Form 69M) and a notice to file financial statement (Form 69W) with the notice of application, and the respondent shall deliver a financial statement (short form) (Form 69M) with the notice of appearance.

(3) A respondent who does not intend to defend the application shall nevertheless deliver a financial statement (short form) (Form 69M) within the time prescribed for delivery of a notice of appearance, but a respondent's failure to do so does not prevent the applicant from bringing the application on for hearing.

(4) Where a respondent fails to comply with a notice to file financial statement, the applicant may move without notice for an order requiring the delivery of a financial statement within a specified time.

(5) Where a financial statement is required to be filed or delivered under subrule (2) or (3), the registrar shall not accept the notice of application or notice of appearance for issuing or filing without the financial statement.

(6) In an application in which a claim is made in relation to custody of a child, the court may order the parties to deliver financial statements within a specified time.

Assigned Support Order

(6.1) In an application under subrule (1) in respect of a support order that has at any time been assigned in accordance with subsection 20.1(1) or its predecessor of the Act,

(a) the applicant shall also serve the assignee of the support order with the applicant's notice of application, affidavit in support and financial statement; and

(b) the respondent shall also serve the assignee with the respondent's notice of appearance, responding affidavit and financial statement.

(6.2) On delivering a notice of appearance, the assignee becomes a respondent to the extent of its financial interest.

(6.3) The assignee is not required to serve a financial statement.

(6.4) If the applicant does not serve the assignee as required by subrule (6.1), the court may at any time, on motion by the assignee on notice to the parties to the application, set aside an order made in the application so far as it deals with an issue in which the assignee has a financial interest.

(6.5) On a motion referred to in subrule (6.4), the burden of proving that the order should not be set aside is on the party who asked for the variation order.

(6.6) If the order made in the application is set aside, the assignee of the support order is entitled to substantial indemnity costs of the motion to set aside, unless the court orders otherwise.

Contents of Affidavit in Support

(7) An affidavit in support of the application shall set out,

    (a) the place of ordinary residence of the parties and the children of the marriage;

    (b) the current marital status of the parties;

    (c) particulars of the change in circumstances relied on;

    (d) particulars of current custody and access arrangements and of any proposed change;

    (e) particulars of current support arrangements and any proposed change;

    (f) particulars of any arrears of support under an order or agreement;

    (f.1) in an application to vary a support order, whether the support order was assigned and any particulars of the assignment known to the applicant; and

    (g) particulars of any efforts made to mediate the matters in issue or of any assessment made in relation to custody or access.

Interprovincial Variation

(8) Evidence given by a person in Ontario in an application referred to in subsection 18(2) of the Act (provisional order) shall be given by affidavit, unless the court orders otherwise.

(9) The registrar shall serve a notice of confirmation hearing (Form 69X) under subsection 19(2) of the Act and the other documents referred to in that subsection,

    (a) on the respondent, in the same manner as an originating process; and

    (b) on the applicant, by mail.

(10) A respondent in an application referred to in subsection 18(2) of the Act shall serve and file a financial statement (short form) (Form 69M) within ten days after service of the notice of confirmation hearing.

(11) Where a court outside Ontario remits a variation proceeding to a court in Ontario for further evidence, the registrar shall serve a notice requiring further evidence (Form 69Y) on the parties by mail.

(12) Where a court in Ontario receives further evidence from a court outside Ontario under subsection 18(6) or 19(6) of the Act, the registrar shall serve a notice of resumption of hearing (Form 69Z) on the parties by mail.

(13) The registrar shall perform the duties imposed on the court or an officer of the court by subsections 18(3) and (6) and 19(3) and (12) of the Act (transmission and filing of documents).

O. Reg. 427/97, s. 1; 284/01, s. 24

69.24.1 Motion to Vary Child Support Order —

Rules of Procedure

Where Available

(1) This rule applies where a person asks to vary only a provision of an interim or final order that deals with child support and asks only for one or more of the following in the variation order:

    1. An order that child support be paid, whether in accordance with the Child Support Guidelines or not, or an order that child support be terminated.

    2. An order suspending, reducing or rescinding child support arrears.

    3. An order setting a payment schedule for child support arrears.

    4. Costs.

Procedure by Motion

(2) Despite subrule 69.24(1) (variation by application), a person who asks for a variation order described in subrule (1) shall do so by motion.

(3) Subrules 69.24(6.1) to (6.6) (assigned orders), (8), (9) and (11) to (13) (interprovincial variations) apply, with necessary modifications, to motions under this rule.

Place for Motion

(4) Despite rule 37.03 (place of hearing for motions), the notice of motion and other material required by this rule shall be filed and the motion shall be heard,

    (a) in the county where any party resides; or

    (b) in a county chosen by all parties, but only with the court's permission given in advance in that county.

Service

(5) The notice of motion and other material required by this rule shall be served in accordance with Rule 16 as if the notice of motion were an originating process.

Financial Statements

(6) The party asking for the variation order shall serve and file, with proof of service, a financial statement (short form) (Form 69M) and a notice to file financial statement (Form 69W) with the notice of motion.

(7) The other party shall serve and file, with proof of service, a financial statement (short form) within the time for serving and filing responding material, whether or not the other party intends to defend the motion.

(8) Where the other party does not comply with a notice to file financial statement, the party asking for the variation order may make a motion without notice for an order requiring the other party to serve and file a financial statement within a specified time.

(9) Where a financial statement is required to be served and filed under subrules (6) to (8), the registrar shall not accept the notice of motion or the responding material for filing without the financial statement.

(10) Despite subrules (6) to (9), the parties do not have to serve or file financial statements where they file an agreement in writing that financial statements are not required.

Consent Variation — Materials to be Filed

(11) Where the parties have agreed on the terms of a variation order and the terms include only the matters referred to in subrule (1), they shall file a variation information form (Form

69Z.1), a consent (Form 69Z.2), five copies of a draft variation order, a stamped envelope addressed to each of the parties, a support deduction order information form prescribed by the regulations under the *Family Responsibility and Support Arrears Enforcement Act, 1996* and a draft support deduction order, but the parties do not need to serve or file a notice of motion.

(12) The variation information form shall have attached to it as exhibits,

(a) a copy of any existing interim or final order or agreement that deals with child support;

(b) a copy of every personal income tax return filed by the payor for the three most recent taxation years and every notice of assessment or reassessment of the returns;

(c) where the payor is an employee, proof of the current year's earnings from the payor's employer as provided in clause 21(1)(c) of the Child Support Guidelines; and

(d) where the payor is self-employed, is a partner in a partnership, controls a corporation or is a beneficiary under a trust, the material referred to in clauses 21(1)(d) to (g) of the Child Support Guidelines.

(13) Where,

(a) the variation order asked for is for an amount other than only the table amount under the Child Support Guidelines;

(b) the variation order asked for relates to a child over the age of 18 years, a child for whom the payor stands in the place of a parent or a child in respect of whom the payor has access or physical custody not less than 40 per cent of the time over the course of a year;

(c) each party has custody of one or more children; or

(d) the payor's annual income as determined under the Child Support Guidelines is greater than $150,000;

the variation information form shall also have attached to it as exhibits the following documents:

1. A copy of every personal income tax return filed by the recipient for the three most recent taxation years and every notice of assessment or reassessment of the returns.

2. Where the recipient is an employee, proof of the current year's earnings from the recipient's employer as provided in clause 21(1)(c) of the Child Support Guidelines.

3. Any other material referred to in clauses 21(1)(d) to (g) of the Child Support Guidelines.

(14) Where the parties agree that the court should make an order not in accordance with the Child Support Guidelines because special provisions in an order or agreement directly or indirectly benefit a child or because reasonable arrangements have been made on consent for child support, the parties shall provide evidence to satisfy the court that it should make the order asked for.

Consent Variation — Parties not to Appear

(15) Where the parties file the material required by subrules (11) to (14), they shall not appear in court and the registrar shall present the material to a judge.

(16) The judge may grant the order sought or may require one or both of the parties to file further material or to appear in court.

Variation not on Consent — Minimum Notice Period

(17) Where the parties have not agreed on the terms of a variation order, notice of a variation motion shall be served, despite subrule 37.07(6) (minimum notice period),

> (a) at least 30 days before the date on which the motion is to be heard, where the responding party resides in Canada or the United States of America; or

> (b) at least 60 days before the date on which the motion is to be heard, where the responding party resides elsewhere.

Variation not on Consent — Materials to be Served

(18) Where the parties have not agreed on the terms of a variation order, the party asking for the variation order shall serve and file, with proof of service, a notice of motion and either a variation information form or an affidavit that sets out,

> (a) the municipality and province where the parties and the children for whom support is payable or for whom support is asked ordinarily reside;

> (b) the name and birth date of each child for whom support is payable or is asked;

> (c) the current marital status of the parties;

> (d) particulars of current custody and access arrangements;

> (e) particulars of current child and spousal support arrangements, and a copy of any existing final order or agreement that deals with child support shall be attached as an exhibit to the affidavit;

> (f) particulars of any arrears of child or spousal support under an order or agreement;

> (g) whether the support order was assigned in accordance with subsection 20.1(1) or its predecessor of the Act, and any particulars of the assignment known to the party asking for the variation order;

> (h) particulars of the change asked for in child support, including any special or extraordinary expenses and where applicable, any contribution that the support recipient or the child could make;

> (i) particulars of the change in circumstances relied on and the reason for the change asked for in child support;

> (j) particulars of the support payor's annual income and the Child Support Guidelines table amount for that income;

> (k) particulars of the support recipient's annual income where,

>> (i) the variation order asked for is for an amount other than only the table amount under the Child Support Guidelines,

>> (ii) the variation order asked for relates to a child over the age of 18 years,

>> (iii) the variation order asked for relates to a child for whom the payor stands in the place of a parent,

>> (iv) the variation order asked for relates to a child in respect of whom the payor has access or physical custody not less than 40 per cent of the time over the course of a year,

>> (v) each party has custody of one or more children, or

>> (vi) the party claims that support in accordance with the Child Support Guidelines would cause undue hardship;

(l) where the party claims that support in accordance with the Child Support Guidelines would cause undue hardship, the evidence required under subsection 10(3) of the Child Support Guidelines; and

(m) where the party claims that the court should make an order for support not in accordance with the Child Support Guidelines because of special provisions in an order or agreement that directly or indirectly benefit a child, the evidence necessary to satisfy the court that it should make the order asked for.

(19) The party responding to the motion shall serve and file, with proof of service, an affidavit that,

(a) sets out any disagreement with the contents of the variation information form or affidavit served under subrule (18) and corrects any errors in it;

(b) where the party claims that support in accordance with the Child Support Guidelines would cause undue hardship, sets out the evidence required under subsection 10(3) of the Child Support Guidelines; and

(c) where the party claims that the court should make an order for support not in accordance with the Child Support Guidelines because of special provisions in an order or agreement that directly or indirectly benefit a child, the evidence necessary to satisfy the court that it should make the order asked for.

(20) The payor shall attach as exhibits to the variation information form or affidavit required by subrule (18) or (19),

(a) a copy of every personal income tax return filed by the payor for the three most recent taxation years and every notice of assessment or reassessment of the returns;

(b) where the payor is an employee, proof of the current year's earnings from the payor's employer as provided in clause 21(1)(c) of the Child Support Guidelines; and

(c) where the payor is self-employed, is a partner in a partnership, controls a corporation or is a beneficiary under a trust, the material referred to in clauses 21(1)(d) to (g) of the Child Support Guidelines.

(21) Where,

(a) the variation order asked for is for an amount other than only the table amount under the Child Support Guidelines;

(b) the variation order asked for relates to a child over the age of 18 years;

(c) the variation order asked for relates to a child for whom the payor stands in the place of a parent;

(d) the variation order asked for relates to a child in respect of whom the payor has access or physical custody not less than 40 per cent of the time over the course of a year;

(e) each party has custody of one or more children; or

(f) either party claims that support in accordance with the Child Support Guidelines would cause undue hardship,

the recipient shall attach the following documents as exhibits to the variation information form or affidavit required by subrule (18) or (19):

1. A copy of every personal income tax return filed by the recipient for the three most recent taxation years and every notice of assessment or reassessment of the returns.

Rules of Procedure

2. Where the recipient is an employee, proof of the current year's earnings from the recipient's employer as provided in clause 21(1)(c) of the Child Support Guidelines.

3. Any other material referred to in clauses 21(1)(d) to (g) of the Child Support Guidelines.

Powers of Court

(22) Where the court is of the opinion that a variation motion, whether or not on consent, can not be properly determined because of the material filed, because of the matters in dispute between the parties or for any other reason, the court may give directions accordingly, including an order under clause 37.13(2)(b) (trial of issue).

O. Reg. 217/98, s. 1

69.25 Registration Of Orders For Corollary Relief From Other Provinces — (1) An order under section 15, 16 or 17 of the Act that was made by a court outside Ontario may be registered under paragraph 20(3)(a) of the Act by filing a certified copy with the local registrar at Toronto, and the order shall then be entered as an order of the Court.

(2) The certified copy of the order may be filed with the local registrar at Toronto by forwarding it to him or her by ordinary mail, accompanied by a written request that it be registered under paragraph 20(3)(a) of the Act.

O. Reg. 73/92, s. 3

69.26 Costs — The costs of a divorce action shall be assessed in accordance with Tariff B, unless a judge orders otherwise.

69.27 Support Order Enforcement — Rule 70.10.1 (support order enforcement) applies, with necessary modifications, to a divorce action and to a support order made in a divorce action.

O. Reg. 73/92, s. 4

Rule 70 — Family Law Proceedings

70.01 Application Of The Rule — **(1)** Rules 70.02 to 70.14 apply to proceedings under,

(a) Parts I, II and III of the *Family Law Act*;

(b) Part III of the *Children's Law Reform Act*;

(c) the *Interjurisdictional Support Orders Act, 2002*;

(d) section 11 of the *Change of Name Act*; and

(e) the *Family Responsibility and Support Arrears Enforcement Act, 1996*.

(2) They do not apply to proceedings in the Family Court of the Superior Court of Justice, which are governed by Ontario Regulation 114/99 (Family Law Rules), except as provided by those rules.

O. Reg. 73/92, s. 5; 292/98, s. 4; 288/99, s. 25; 54/03, s. 2

70.02 Definitions — In rules 70.03 to 70.14,

"applicant" includes a plaintiff;

"respondent" includes a defendant; and

"responding document" means a statement of defence, defence to counterclaim or affidavit in opposition to an application.

70.03 Originating Process —

Claim for Relief

(1) An originating process that contains a claim for support or division of property shall set out the nature and amount of relief claimed and, if support is claimed, the amount for each dependant.

Application by Government Agency

(2) Where the Ministry of Community and Social Services, a municipality, a district welfare administration board or a band is an applicant for an order for the support of a dependant under subsection 33(3) of the *Family Law Act*, it shall serve the originating process on the dependant.

70.03.1 Mandatory Information Program —

Application of rule 69.05.1

(1) Rule 69.05.1 applies, with necessary modifications, to proceedings governed by this Rule that are commenced at Toronto after July 1, 1998 and in which any relief, other than costs, the incorporation of the terms of a separation agreement or prior court order and variation of the terms of a final order, is sought.

Exceptions

(2) Despite subrule (1), rule 69.05.1 does not apply to proceedings under,

    (a) the *Change of Name Act*;

    (b) the *Family Responsibility and Support Arrears Enforcement Act, 1996*; or

    (c) the *Interjurisdictional Support Orders Act, 2002*.

Exception

(3) Subrules 69.05.1 (3) to (6) do not apply to,

    (a) a person or agency referred to in subsection 33(3) of the *Family Law Act*;

    (b) the Director of the Family Responsibility Office.

Revocation

(4) This rule is revoked on December 31, 2003.
O. Reg. 214/98, s. 2; 484/99, s. 2; 583/99, s. 2; 654/00, s. 2; 447/01, s. 2; 336/02, s. 2; 54/03, s. 3

70.04 Financial Statements —

Applicant's Financial Statement

(1) Where an order is sought under section 7 (division of property), 33 (support) or 37 (variation of support) of the *Family Law Act*, a financial statement (Form 69K) shall be filed and served with the originating process, together with a notice to file financial statement (Form 69W).

(2) Where the originating process is a notice of action, the financial statement shall be delivered with the statement of claim.

Respondent's Financial Statement

(3) A respondent served with the applicant's financial statement shall deliver a financial statement with his or her responding document.

(4) A respondent who does not intend to defend the proceeding shall nevertheless deliver a financial statement within the time prescribed for the delivery of his or her responding document, but a respondent's failure to do so does not prevent the applicant from bringing the proceeding on for hearing or moving for judgment.

Registrar to Refuse Documents Unless Accompanied by Financial Statements

(5) Where a financial statement is required to be filed or delivered with an originating process, statement of claim or responding document, the registrar shall not accept the originating process, statement of claim or responding document for issuing or filing without the financial statement.

Order for Delivery

(6) Where a respondent fails to comply with a notice to file financial statement, the applicant may move without notice for an order requiring the delivery of a financial statement within a specified time.

(7) In a proceeding in which a claim is made for custody of a child, the court may order the parties to deliver financial statements (short form) (Form 69M) within a specified time.

Subrules 69.14(8) to (14) Apply

(8) Subrules 69.14(8) to (14) (particulars, failure to deliver, cross-examination, duty to correct) apply, with necessary modifications, to financial statements referred to in subrules (1) to (7).

Net Family Property Statement

(9) In a proceeding in which a claim is made for a division of property, each spouse shall deliver a net family property statement (Form 69N) at least seven days before each of the following:

    1. A pre-trial conference.

    2. A motion for judgment.

    3. The hearing.

Divorce Action

(10) Where a claim under the *Family Law Act* or the *Children's Law Reform Act* is made in a divorce action, the obligations of the spouses respecting financial statements are governed by rule 69.14.

70.05 Place Of Hearing — **(1)** An applicant who makes a claim for custody of or access to a child who ordinarily resides in Ontario shall name in the originating process as the place of hearing a place where the court normally sits in the county in which the child ordinarily resides.

(2) Where a claim referred to in subrule (1) is made in a divorce action, the place of trial is governed by rule 69.17.

(3) The hearing shall be held at the place named in the originating process unless an order is made under rule 46.03 to change the place of hearing, and for the purpose of changing the place of hearing an application shall be treated as an action.

70.06 Children's Lawyer's Report — Subrules 69.16(1) to (8) (Children's Lawyer's report) apply, with necessary modifications, to proceedings under Part III of the *Children's Law Reform Act.*

O. Reg. 69/95, s. 19

70.07 [Revoked O. Reg. 288/99, s. 26.]

70.08 Interim Relief — Rule 69.15 (interim relief) applies, with necessary modifications, to a motion for interim relief in a proceeding under the *Family Law Act* or the *Children's Law Reform Act.*

70.08.1 Variation Application — **(1)** Rule 69.24 (variation of final order) applies, with necessary modifications, in respect of a support order made under the *Family Law Act* or a custody or access order made under the *Children's Law Reform Act.*

(2) Rule 37 of the Family Law Rules (Ontario Regulation 114/99) applies, with necessary modifications, to a support order made under the *Interjurisdictional Support Orders Act, 2002.*

O. Reg. 427/97, s. 2; 54/03, s. 4

70.08.2 Motion to Vary Child Support Order — **(1)** Rule 69.24.1 (motion to vary child support) applies, with necessary modifications, in respect of a support order made under the *Family Law Act.*

(2) Rule 37 of the Family Law Rules (Ontario Regulation 114/99) applies, with necessary modifications, to a support order made under the *Interjurisdictional Support Orders Act, 2002.*

O. Reg. 217/98, s. 2; 54/03, s. 4

70.09 Proceeding Transferred from Ontario Court of Justice — **(1)** Where a proceeding is transferred from the Ontario Court of Justice to the Superior Court of Justice under subsection 2(2) of the *Family Law Act* or section 66 of the *Children's Law Reform Act,* the proceeding shall continue without duplication of any steps taken before the transfer unless the court to which the proceeding is transferred directs otherwise.

(2) The court to which a proceeding is transferred may, on motion, give directions for the conduct of the proceeding.

O. Reg. 292/99, ss. 1(2), 7

70.10 [Revoked O. Reg. 288/99, s. 26.]

70.10.1 Support Order Enforcement —

Support deduction information form

(1) In a proceeding where support or a variation of support is claimed, the parties shall file with the court, with the material for the hearing of a motion for judgment or for interim support and with the material for the trial or the hearing of the application, the support deduction order information form prescribed by the regulations under the *Family Responsibility and Support Arrears Enforcement Act, 1996.*

(2) The court may proceed in the absence of complete information on the information form about the payor's address or income sources.

Form of support deduction order or suspension order

(3) Subrule 59.03(1) (approval of draft order) does not apply to a support deduction order or suspension order under the *Family Responsibility and Support Arrears Enforcement Act, 1996.*

Terminology in enforcement

(4) In any document in relation to the enforcement of a support order, "recipient" shall be used instead of "creditor" and "payor" shall be used instead of "debtor".

(5) Despite subrule (4), a document served, filed or issued before the 1st day of January, 1993 is not incorrect for the reason that it uses "creditor" or "debtor".

Place of hearing

(6) A hearing in relation to the enforcement of a support order, including the hearing of a motion for a suspension order, shall be held, despite subrule 37.03(2) (place of hearing of motion made on notice),

(a) in the county where the recipient under the order resides;

(b) where the recipient does not reside in Ontario, in the county where the support order is filed for enforcement with a sheriff or with the Director of the Family Responsibility Office;

(c) on consent of the person enforcing the order, in the county where the payor under the order resides; or

(d) in the case of a motion made under subsection 26(2) or (3) of the *Family Responsibility and Support Arrears Enforcement Act, 1996*, in the county where the income source resides.

Garnishment by Director

(7) A notice of garnishment issued on requisition by the Director of the Family Responsibility Office shall be in Form 70A.2, and subrules 60.08(11) to (19) (liability, payment, dispute, enforcement) apply, with necessary modifications, as if the Director were a sheriff.

Statutory declaration indexing garnishment

(8) Subrules (9) and (10) apply where a notice of garnishment is issued to enforce a support order, domestic contract or paternity agreement that provides for indexation of periodic payments to account for inflation.

(9) The person enforcing the order, contract or agreement may serve on the garnishee and the payor, by ordinary mail, personal service or an alternative to personal service under rule 16.03, a statutory declaration (Form 70A.3) setting out the new amount to be paid under the order, contract or agreement as a result of indexation, and may file the declaration with the court with proof of service.

(10) The garnishee is liable from the date of service on the garnishee to pay the new amount set out in the declaration as if that amount were set out in the notice of garnishment, and subrules 60.08(15) to (19) (dispute, enforcement, payment) apply, with necessary modifications.

O. Reg. 73/92, s. 6; 292/98, s. 5

70.11 Warrant For Arrest — A warrant for the arrest of a debtor or respondent referred to in section 43 of the *Family Law Act* or section 49 of the *Family Responsibility and Support Arrears Enforcement Act, 1996* shall be in Form 70B.

O. Reg. 351/94, s. 8; 292/98, s. 6

70.12 Recognizance — A recognizance required by an order made under subsection 46(1) of the *Family Law Act* or section 35 of the *Children's Law Reform Act* shall be in Form 70C and shall be entered into before the registrar or such other officer as a judge directs.

70.13 [Revoked O. Reg. 54/03, s. 5.]

70.14 Request By Extra-Provincial Tribunal For Evidence In Custody Cases —

Issuing Summons to Give Evidence

(1) Where the Attorney General refers a request of an extra-provincial tribunal to the court under section 33 of the *Children's Law Reform Act*, the registrar shall issue a summons in Form 70D requiring the person named in the request to produce or give evidence in accordance with the request.

Service of Summons

(2) The summons and a copy of the request of the extra-provincial tribunal and any supporting material that accompanied the request shall be served on the person named in the request, personally and not by an alternative to personal service, at least five days before he or she is required to produce or give evidence.

(3) Where the person named in the request is not a party to the proceeding before the extra-provincial tribunal and the summons requires the person to give oral evidence, attendance money calculated in accordance with Tariff A shall be paid or tendered to the person when the summons is served.

(4) A copy of the summons shall be served on the Attorney General within the time prescribed by subrule (2).

Affidavit Evidence

(5) Where the summons does not require the person to give oral evidence, the person may file with the registrar the evidence required, verified by the person's affidavit.

Oral Evidence

(6) Where the summons requires the person to give oral evidence, the person shall attend before a judge or officer of the court, as set out in the summons, to be examined in accordance with the summons.

Evidence to be Sent to Extra-Provincial Tribunal

(7) The registrar shall send to the extra-provincial tribunal a certified copy of evidence produced or given under this rule.

Sanctions for Disobeying Summons

Rules of Procedure

(8) Subrules 53.04(7) and (8) apply, with necessary modifications, to a person who after having been served in accordance with subrules (2) and (3) fails to comply with the summons.

Rule 71 — Child And Family Services Act Appeals

71.01 [Revoked O. Reg. 288/99, s. 26.]

. . . . .

SUCCESSION LAW REFORM ACT

R.S.O. 1990, c. S.26, as am. S.O. 1994, c. 27, s. 63; 1997, c. 25, Sched. E, s. 12; 1999, c. 6, s. 61; 1999, c. 12, Sched. B, s. 17; 2001, c. 13, s. 31 (Fr.); 2002, c. 17, Sched. F, s. 1.

1. (1) Definitions — In this Act,

"child" includes a child conceived before and born alive after the parent's death;

"grandchild" means the child of a child;

"issue" includes a descendant conceived before and born alive after the person's death;

"parent" means the father or mother of a child;

"personal representative" means an executor, an administrator or an administrator with will annexed;

"spouse" means either of a man and woman who,

    (a) are married to each other, or

    (b) have together entered into a marriage that is voidable or void, in good faith on the part of the person asserting a right under this Act;

"will" includes,

    (a) a testament,

    (b) a codicil,

    (c) an appointment by will or by writing in the nature of a will in exercise of a power, and

    (d) any other testamentary disposition.

(2) Polygamous marriages — In the definition of "spouse", a reference to marriage includes a marriage that is actually or potentially polygamous, if it was celebrated in a jurisdiction whose system of law recognizes it as valid.

(3) Relationship of persons born outside marriage — In this Act, and in any will unless a contrary intention is shown in the will, a reference to a person in terms of a relationship to another person determined by blood or marriage shall be deemed to include a person who comes within the description despite the fact that he or she or any other person through whom the relationship is traced was born outside marriage.

(4) Application of subs. (3) — Subsection (3) applies in respect of wills made on or after 31st day of March, 1978.

PART I — TESTATE SUCCESSION

General

2. Power to dispose of property by will — A person may by will devise, bequeath or dispose of all property (whether acquired before or after making his or her will) to which at the time of his or her death he or she is entitled either at law or in equity, including,

(a) estates for another's life, whether there is or is not a special occupant and whether they are corporeal or incorporeal hereditaments;

(b) contingent, executory or other future interests in property, whether the testator is or is not ascertained as the person or one of the persons in whom those interests may respectively become vested, and whether he or she is entitled to them under the instrument by which they were respectively created or under a disposition of them by deed or will; and

(c) rights of entry, whether for conditions broken or otherwise.

3. Will to be in writing — A will is valid only when it is in writing.

4. (1) Execution — Subject to sections 5 and 6, a will is not valid unless,

(a) at its end it is signed by the testator or by some other person in his or her presence and by his or her direction;

(b) the testator makes or acknowledges the signature in the presence of two or more attesting witnesses present at the same time; and

(c) two or more of the attesting witnesses subscribe the will in the presence of the testator.

(2) Idem — Where witnesses are required by this section, no form of attestation is necessary.

5. (1) Will of member of forces on active service — A person who is,

(a) a member of the Canadian Forces placed on active service under the *National Defence Act* (Canada);

(b) a member of any other naval, land or air force while on active service; or

(c) a sailor when at sea or in the course of a voyage,

may make a will by a writing signed by him or her or by some other person in his or her presence and by his or her direction without any further formality or any requirement of the presence of or attestation or signature by a witness.

(2) Certificate of active service — For the purposes of this section, a certificate purporting to be signed by or on behalf of an officer having custody of the records certifying that he or she has custody of the records of the force in which a person was serving at the time the will was made, setting out that the person was on active service at that time, is proof, in the absence of evidence to the contrary, of that fact.

(3) Where certificate not available — For the purposes of this section, if a certificate under subsection (2) is not available, a member of a naval, land or air force is deemed to be on active service after he or she has taken steps under the orders of a superior officer preparatory to serving with or being attached to or seconded to a component of such a force that has been placed on active service.

6. Holograph wills — A testator may make a valid will wholly by his or her own handwriting and signature, without formality, and without the presence, attestation or signature of a witness.

7. (1) Position of signature — In so far as the position of the signature is concerned, a will, whether holograph or not, is valid if the signature of the testator made either by him or her or the person signing for him or her is placed at, after, following, under or beside or opposite to the end of the will so that it is apparent on the face of the will that the testator intended to give effect by the signature to the writing signed as his or her will.

(2) Idem — A will is not rendered invalid by the circumstance that,

(a) the signature does not follow or is not immediately after the end of the will;

(b) a blank space intervenes between the concluding words of the will and the signature;

(c) the signature,

(i) is placed among the words of a testimonium clause or of a clause of attestation,

(ii) follows or is after or under a clause of attestation either with or without a blank space intervening, or

(iii) follows or is after, under or beside the name of a subscribing witness;

(d) the signature is on a side, page or other portion of the paper or papers containing the will on which no clause, paragraph or disposing part of the will is written above the signature; or

(e) there appears to be sufficient space on or at the bottom of the preceding side, page or other portion of the same paper on which the will is written to contain the signature.

(3) Idem — The generality of subsection (1) is not restricted by the enumeration of circumstances set out in subsection (2), but a signature in conformity with section 4, 5 or 6 or this section does not give effect to,

(a) a disposition or direction that is underneath the signature or that follows the signature; or

(b) a disposition or direction inserted after the signature was made.

8. (1) Wills by minors — A will made by a person who is under the age of eighteen years is not valid unless at the time of making the will the person,

(a) is or has been married;

(b) is contemplating marriage and the will states that it is made in contemplation of marriage to a named person except that such a will is not valid unless and until the marriage to the named person takes place;

(c) is a member of a component of the Canadian Forces,

(i) that is referred to in the *National Defence Act* (Canada) as a regular force, or

(ii) while placed on active service under the *National Defence Act* (Canada); or

(d) is a sailor and at sea or in the course of a voyage.

(2) Certificate of active service — A certificate purporting to be signed by or on behalf of an officer having custody of the records certifying that he or she has custody of the records of the force in which a person was serving at the time the will was made, setting out that the person was at that time a member of a regular force or was on active service within clause (1)(c), is proof, in the absence of evidence to the contrary, of that fact.

(3) Revocation — A person who has made a will under subsection (1) may, while under the age of eighteen years, revoke the will.

9. Exercise of appointments by will — No appointment made by will in exercise of any power is valid unless the appointment is executed in the manner hereinbefore required, and every will executed in the manner hereinbefore required is, so far as respects the execution and attestation thereof, a valid execution of a power of appointment by will, despite the fact that it has been expressly required that a will made in exercise of such power shall be executed with some additional or other form of execution or solemnity.

10. Publication unnecessary — A will made in accordance with this Part is valid without other publication.

11. Effect of incompetency of witness — Where a person who attested a will was at the time of its execution or afterward has become incompetent as a witness to prove its execution, the will is not on that account invalid.

12. (1) Bequests to witness void — Where a will is attested by a person to whom or to whose then spouse a beneficial devise, bequest or other disposition or appointment of or affecting property, except charges and directions for payment of debts, is thereby given or made, the devise, bequest or other disposition or appointment is void so far only as it concerns,

(a) the person so attesting;

(b) the spouse; or

(c) a person claiming under either of them,

but the person so attesting is a competent witness to prove the execution of the will or its validity or invalidity.

(2) Where will signed for testator by another person — Where a will is signed for the testator by another person in accordance with section 4, to whom or to whose then spouse a beneficial devise, bequest or other disposition or appointment of or affecting property, except charges and directions for payment of debts, is thereby given or made, the devise, bequest, or other disposition is void so far only as it concerns,

(a) the person so signing;

(b) the spouse; or

(c) a person claiming under either of them,

but the will is not invalid for that reason.

(3) Where no undue influence — Despite anything in this section, where the Ontario Court (General Division) is satisfied that neither the person so attesting or signing for the testator nor the spouse exercised any improper or undue influence upon the testator, the devise, bequest or other disposition or appointment is not void.

(4) Exception — Where a will is attested by at least two persons who are not within subsection (1) or where no attestation is necessary, the devise, bequest or other disposition or appointment is not void under that subsection.

13. Creditor as witness — Where property is charged by a will with a debt and a creditor or the spouse of a creditor whose debt is so charged attests a will, the person so attesting, despite the charge, is a competent witness to prove the execution of the will or its validity or invalidity.

14. Executor as witness — A person is not incompetent as a witness to prove the execution of a will or its validity or invalidity solely because he or she is an executor.

15. Revocation — A will or part of a will is revoked only by,

(a) marriage, subject to section 16;

(b) another will made in accordance with the provisions of this Part;

(c) a writing,

(i) declaring an intention to revoke, and

(ii) made in accordance with the provisions of this Part governing making of a will; or

(d) burning, tearing or otherwise destroying it by the testator or by some person in his or her presence and by his or her direction with the intention of revoking it.

16. Revocation by marriage — A will is revoked by the marriage of the testator except where,

(a) there is a declaration in the will that it is made in contemplation of the marriage;

(b) the spouse of the testator elects to take under the will, by an instrument in writing signed by the spouse and filed within one year after the testator's death in the office of the Estate Registrar for Ontario; or

(c) the will is made in exercise of a power of appointment of property which would not in default of the appointment pass to the heir, executor or administrator of the testator or to the persons entitled to the estate of the testator if he or she died intestate.

17. (1) Change in circumstances — Subject to subsection (2), a will is not revoked by presumption of an intention to revoke it on the ground of a change in circumstances.

(2) Exception on termination of marriage — Except when a contrary intention appears by the will, where, after the testator makes a will, his or her marriage is terminated by a judgment absolute of divorce or is declared a nullity,

(a) a devise or bequest of a beneficial interest in property to his or her former spouse;

(b) an appointment of his or her former spouse as executor or trustee; and

(c) the conferring of a general or special power of appointment on his or her former spouse,

are revoked and the will shall be construed as if the former spouse had predeceased the testator.

SLRA

18. (1) Alterations in will — Subject to subsection (2), unless an alteration that is made in a will after the will has been made is made in accordance with the provisions of this Part governing making of the will, the alteration has no effect except to invalidate words or the effect of the will that it renders no longer apparent.

(2) How validly made — An alteration that is made in a will after the will has been made is validly made when the signature of the testator and subscription of witnesses to the signature of the testator to the alteration, or, in the case of a will that was made under section 5 or 6, the signature of the testator, are or is made,

(a) in the margin or in some other part of the will opposite or near to the alteration; or

(b) at the end of or opposite to a memorandum referring to the alteration and written in some part of the will.

19. (1) Revival — A will or part of a will that has been in any manner revoked is revived only,

(a) by a will made in accordance with the provisions of this Part; or

(b) by a codicil that has been made in accordance with the provisions of this Part,

that shows an intention to give effect to the will or part that was revoked, or,

(c) by re-execution thereof with the required formalities, if any.

(2) As to part formerly revoked — Except when a contrary intention is shown, when a will which has been partly revoked and afterward wholly revoked is revived, the revival does not extend to the part that was revoked before the revocation of the whole.

20. (1) Operation of will as to interest left in testator — A conveyance of or other act relating to property that is the subject of a devise, bequest or other disposition, made or done after the making of a will, does not prevent operation of the will with respect to any estate or interest in the property that the testator had power to dispose of by will at the time of his or her death.

(2) Rights in place of property devised — Except when a contrary intention appears by the will, where a testator at the time of his or her death,

(a) has a right, chose in action or equitable estate or interest that was created by a contract respecting a conveyance of, or other act relating to, property that was the subject of a devise or bequest, made before or after the making of a will;

(b) has a right to receive the proceeds of a policy of insurance covering loss of or damage to property that was the subject of a devise or bequest, whether the loss or damage occurred before or after the making of the will;

(c) has a right to receive compensation for the expropriation of property that was the subject of a devise or bequest, whether the expropriation occurred before or after the making of the will; or

(d) has a mortgage, charge or other security interest in property that was the subject of a devise or bequest, taken by the testator on the sale of such property, whether such mortgage, charge or other security interest was taken before or after the making of the will,

the devisee or donee of that property takes the right, chose in action, equitable estate or interest, right to insurance proceeds or compensation, or mortgage, charge or other security interest of the testator.

21. When revived will deemed made — When a will has been revived in the manner described in section 19, the will shall be deemed to have been made at the time at which it was so revived.

22. Will to speak from death — Except when a contrary intention appears by the will, a will speaks and takes effect as if it had been made immediately before the death of the testator with respect to,

(a) the property of the testator; and

(b) the right, chose in action, equitable estate or interest, right to insurance proceeds or compensation, or mortgage, charge or other security interest of the testator under sub-section 20(2).

23. Disposition of property in void devise — Except when a contrary intention appears by the will, property or an interest therein that is comprised or intended to be comprised in a devise or bequest that fails or becomes void by reason of,

(a) the death of the devisee or donee in the lifetime of the testator; or

(b) the devise or bequest being disclaimed or being contrary to law or otherwise incapable of taking effect,

is included in the residuary devise or bequest, if any, contained in the will.

24. Leasehold estates under devise of real property — Except when a contrary intention appears by the will, where a testator devises,

(a) his or her real property;

(b) his or her real property in a place mentioned in the will, or in the occupation of a person mentioned in the will;

(c) real property described in a general manner; or

(d) real property described in a manner that would include a leasehold estate if the testator had no freehold estate which could be described in the manner used,

the devise includes the leasehold estates of the testator or any of them to which the description extends, as well as freehold estates.

25. (1) Disposition of real property over which testator has power of appointment under devise — Except when a contrary intention appears by the will, a general devise of,

(a) the real property of the testator;

(b) the real property of the testator,

(i) in a place mentioned in the will, or

(ii) in the occupation of a person mentioned in the will; or

(c) real property described in a general manner,

includes any real property, or any real property to which the description extends, which he or she has power to appoint in any manner he or she thinks proper and operates as an execution of the power.

(2) Disposition of personal property over which testator has power of appointment under bequest — Except when a contrary intention appears by the will, a bequest of,

(a) the personal property of the testator; or

(b) personal property described in a general manner,

includes any personal property, or any personal property to which the description extends, which he or she has power to appoint in any manner he or she thinks proper and operates as an execution of the power.

26. Real property passing under devise without words of limitation — Except when a contrary intention appears by the will, where real property is devised to a person without words of limitation, the devise passes the fee simple or the whole of any other estate or interest that the testator had power to dispose of by will in the real property.

27. Meaning of "heir" in devise of property — Except when a contrary intention appears by the will, where property is devised or bequeathed to the **"heir" or "heirs"** of the testator or of another person, the words **"heir" or "heirs"** mean the person to whom the beneficial interest in the property would have gone under the law of Ontario if the testator or the other person died intestate.

28. (1) Import of words "die without issue", etc. — Subject to subsection (2), in a devise or bequest of property,

(a) the words,

    (i) "die without issue",

    (ii) "die without leaving issue", or

    (iii) "have no issue"; or

(b) other words importing either a want or failure of issue of a person in his or her lifetime or at the time of his or her death or an indefinite failure of his or her issue,

mean a want or failure of issue in the lifetime or at the time of death of that person, and do not mean an indefinite failure of his or her issue unless contrary intention appears by the will.

(2) Cases to which Part not to extend — This Part does not extend to cases where the words defined in subsection (1) import,

(a) if no issue described in a preceding gift be born; or

(b) if there be no issue who live to attain the age or otherwise answer the description required for obtaining a vested estate by a preceding gift to that issue.

29. Devise to trustee or executor — Except when there is devised to a trustee expressly or by implication an estate for a definite term of years absolute or determinable or an estate of freehold, a devise of real property to a trustee or executor passes the fee simple or the whole of any other estate or interest that the testator had power to dispose of by will in the real property.

30. When devise to trustee to pass whole estate beyond what is requisite for trust — Where real property is devised to a trustee without express limitation of the estate to be taken by the trustee and the beneficial interest in the real property or in the surplus rents and profits,

(a) is not given to a person for life; or

(b) is given to a person for life but the purpose of the trust may continue beyond his or her life,

the devise vests in the trustee the fee simple or the whole of any other legal estate that the testator had power to dispose of by will in the real property and not an estate determinable when the purposes of the trust are satisfied.

31. Substitutional gifts — Except when a contrary intention appears by the will, where a devise or bequest is made to a child, grandchild, brother or sister of the testator who dies before the testator, either before or after the testator makes his or her will, and leaves a spouse or issue surviving the testator, the devise or bequest does not lapse but takes effect as if it had been made directly to the persons among whom and in the shares in which the estate of that person would have been divisible,

(a) if that person had died immediately after the death of the testator;

(b) if that person had died intestate;

(c) if that person had died without debts; and

(d) if section 45 had not been passed.

32. (1) Primary liability of real property to satisfy mortgage — Where a person dies possessed of, or entitled to, or under a general power of appointment by his or her will disposes of, an interest in freehold or leasehold property which, at the time of his or her death, is subject to a mortgage, and the deceased has not, by will, deed or other document, signified a contrary or other intention,

(a) the interest is, as between the different persons claiming through the deceased, primarily liable for the payment or satisfaction of the mortgage debt; and

(b) every part of the interest, according to its value, bears a proportionate part of the mortgage debt on the whole interest.

(2) Consequence of general direction to pay debts out of personalty or residue — A testator does not signify a contrary or other intention within subsection (1) by,

(a) a general direction for the payment of debts or of all the debts of the testator out of his or her personal estate, his or her residuary real or personal estate or his or her residuary real estate; or

(b) a charge of debts upon that estate,

unless he or she further signifies that intention by words expressly or by necessary implication referring to all or some part of the mortgage debt.

(3) Saving of mortgagee's rights — Nothing in this section affects a right of a person entitled to the mortgage debt to obtain payment or satisfaction either out of the other assets of the deceased or otherwise.

(4) Definitions — In this section,

"mortgage" includes an equitable mortgage, and any charge whatsoever, whether equitable, statutory or of other nature, including a lien or claim upon freehold or leasehold property for unpaid purchase money, and **"mortgage debt"** has a meaning similarly extended.

SLRA

33. (1) Undisposed of residue — Where a person dies having by will appointed a person executor, the executor is a trustee of any residue not expressly disposed of, for the person or persons, if any, who would be entitled to that residue in the event of intestacy in respect of it, unless it appears by the will that the person so appointed executor was intended to take the residue beneficially.

(2) Where no person entitled to residue — Nothing in this section prejudices any right in respect of any residue not expressly disposed of to which, if this Part had not been passed, an executor would have been entitled where there is not any person who would be entitled to the testator's estate under Part II in case of an intestacy.

Conflict of Laws

34. Interpretation — In sections 36 to 41,

(a) an interest in land includes a leasehold estate as well as a freehold estate in land, and any other estate or interest in land whether the estate or interest is real property or is personal property;

(b) an interest in movables includes an interest in a tangible or intangible thing other than land, and includes personal property other than an estate or interest in land;

(c) "internal law" in relation to any place excludes the choice of law rules of that place.

35. Wills made in or out of Ontario — Sections 36 to 41 apply to a will made either in or out of Ontario.

36. (1) Formalities, re interests in land — The manner and formalities of making a will, and its essential validity and effect, so far as it relates to an interest in land, are governed by the internal law of the place where the land is situated.

(2) Re interests in movables — Subject to other provisions of this Part, the manner and formalities of making a will, and its essential validity and effect, so far as it relates to an interest in movables, are governed by the internal law of the place where the testator was domiciled at the time of his or her death.

37. (1) Formalities re interests in movables or in land — As regards the manner and formalities of making a will of an interest in movables or in land, a will is valid and admissible to probate if at the time of its making it complied with the internal law of the place where,

(a) the will was made;

(b) the testator was then domiciled;

(c) the testator then had his or her habitual residence; or

(d) the testator then was a national if there was in that place one body of law governing the wills of nationals.

(2) Idem — As regards the manner and formalities of making a will of an interest in movables or in land, the following are properly made,

(a) a will made on board a vessel or aircraft of any description, if the making of the will conformed to the internal law in force in the place with which, having regard to its registration, if any, and other relevant circumstances, the vessel or aircraft may be taken to have been most closely connected;

(b) a will so far as it revokes a will which under sections 34 to 42 would be treated as properly made or revokes a provision which under those sections would be treated as comprised in a properly made will, if the making of the later will conformed to any law by reference to which the revoked will or provision would be treated as properly made; and

(c) a will so far as it exercises a power of appointment, if the making of the will conforms to the law governing the essential validity of the power.

38. Change of domicile — A change of domicile of the testator occurring after a will is made does not render it invalid as regards the manner and formalities of its making or alter its construction.

39. Construction of will — Nothing in sections 34 to 42 precludes resort to the law of the place where the testator was domiciled at the time of making a will in aid of its construction as regards an interest in land or an interest in movables.

40. Movables used in relation to land — Where the value of a thing that is movable consists mainly or entirely in its use in connection with a particular parcel of land by the owner or occupier of the land, succession to an interest in the thing under a will is governed by the law that governs succession to the interest in the land.

41. (1) Where law outside Ontario to be applied to will — Where, whether under sections 34 to 42 or not, a law in force outside Ontario is to be applied in relation to a will, any requirement of that law that,

(a) special formalities are to be observed by testators answering a particular description; or

(b) witnesses to the making of a will are to possess certain qualifications,

shall be treated, despite any rule of that law to the contrary, as a formal requirement only.

(2) Formal requirements of law — In determining for the purposes of sections 34 to 40 whether or not the making of a will conforms to a particular law, regard shall be had to the formal requirements of that law at the time the will was made, but account shall be taken of an alteration of law affecting wills made at that time if the alteration enables the will to be treated as properly made.

International Wills

42. (1) Convention on form of international will — In this section,

"convention" means the convention providing a uniform law on the form of international will, a copy of which is set out in the Schedule to this section.

(2) Effective date — The convention is in force in Ontario and applies to wills as law of Ontario and the rules regarding an international will set out in the Annex to the convention are law in Ontario.

(3) Persons authorized under convention — All members of the Law Society of Upper Canada, other than student members, are designated as persons authorized to act in connection with international wills.

(4) Validity of wills under other laws — Nothing in this section detracts from or affects the validity of a will that is valid under the laws in force in Ontario other than this section.

Schedule

CONVENTION PROVIDING A UNIFORM LAW ON THE FORM OF AN INTERNATIONAL WILL

The States signatory to the present Convention,

DESIRING to provide to a greater extent for the respecting of last wills by establishing an additional form of will hereinafter to be called an "international will" which, if employed, would dispense to some extent with the search for the applicable law;

HAVE RESOLVED to conclude a Convention for this purpose and have agreed upon the following provisions:

Article I

1. Each Contracting Party undertakes that not later than six months after the date of entry into force of this Convention in respect of that Party it shall introduce into its law the rules regarding an international will set out in the Annex to this Convention.

2. Each Contracting Party may introduce the provisions of the Annex into its law either by reproducing the actual text, or by translating it into its official language or languages.

3. Each Contracting Party may introduce into its law such further provisions as are necessary to give the provisions of the Annex full effect in its territory.

4. Each Contracting Party shall submit to the Depositary Government the text of the rules introduced into its national law in order to implement the provisions of this Convention.

Article II

1. Each Contracting Party shall implement the provisions of the Annex in its law, within the period provided for in the preceding article, by designating the persons who, in its territory, shall be authorized to act in connection with international wills. It may also designate as a person authorized to act with regard to its nationals its diplomatic or consular agents abroad in so far as the local law does not prohibit it.

2. The Party shall notify such designation, as well as any modifications thereof, to the Depositary Government.

Article III

The capacity of the authorized person to act in connection with an international will, if conferred in accordance with the law of a Contracting Party, shall be recognized in the territory of the other Contracting Parties.

Article IV

The effectiveness of the certificate provided for in Article 10 of the Annex shall be recognized in the territories of all Contracting Parties.

Article V

1. The conditions requisite to acting as a witness of an international will shall be governed by the law under which the authorized person was designated. The same rule shall apply as regards an interpreter who is called upon to act.

2. Nonetheless no one shall be disqualified to act as a witness of an international will solely because he is an alien.

Article VI

1. The signature of the testator, of the authorized person, and of the witnesses to an international will, whether on the will or on the certificate, shall be exempt from any legalization or like formality.

2. Nonetheless, the competent authorities of any Contracting Party may, if necessary, satisfy themselves as to the authenticity of the signature of the authorized person.

Article VII

The safekeeping of an international will shall be governed by the law under which the authorized person was designated.

Article VIII

No reservation shall be admitted to this Convention or to its Annex.

Article IX

1. The present Convention shall be open for signature at Washington from October 26, 1973, until December 31, 1974.

2. The Convention shall be subject to ratification.

3. Instruments of ratification shall be deposited with the Government of the United States of America, which shall be the Depositary Government.

Article X

1. The Convention shall be open indefinitely for accession.

2. Instruments of accession shall be deposited with the Depositary Government.

Article XI

1. The present Convention shall enter into force six months after the date of deposit of the fifth instrument of ratification or accession with the Depositary Government.

2. In the case of each State which ratifies this Convention or accedes to it after the fifth instrument of ratification or accession has been deposited, this Convention shall enter into force six months after the deposit of its own instrument of ratification or accession.

Article XII

1. Any Contracting Party may denounce this Convention by written notification to the Depositary Government.

2. Such denunciation shall take effect twelve months from the date on which the Depositary Government has received the notification, but such denunciation shall not affect the validity of any will made during the period that the Convention was in effect for the denouncing State.

753

Article XIII

1. Any State may, when it deposits its instrument of ratification or accession or at any time thereafter, declare, by a notice addressed to the Depositary Government, that this Convention shall apply to all or part of the territories for the international relations of which it is responsible.

2. Such declaration shall have effect six months after the date on which the Depositary Government shall have received notice thereof or, if at the end of such period the Convention has not yet come into force, from the date of its entry into force.

3. Each Contracting Party which has made a declaration in accordance with paragraph 1 of this Article may, in accordance with Article XII, denounce this Convention in relation to all or part of the territories concerned.

Article XIV

1. If a State has two or more territorial units in which different systems of law apply in relation to matters respecting the form of wills, it may at the time of signature, ratification, or accession, declare that this Convention shall extend to all its territorial units or only to one or more of them, and may modify its declaration by submitting another declaration at any time.

2. These declarations shall be notified to the Depositary Government and shall state expressly the territorial units to which the Convention applies.

Article XV

If a Contracting Party has two or more territorial units in which different systems of law apply in relation to matters respecting the form of wills, any reference to the internal law of the place where the will is made or to the law under which the authorized person has been appointed to act in connection with international wills shall be construed in accordance with the constitutional system of the Party concerned.

Article XVI

1. The original of the present Convention, in the English, French, Russian and Spanish languages, each version being equally authentic, shall be deposited with the Government of the United States of America, which shall transmit certified copies thereof to each of the signatory and acceding States and to the International Institute for the Unification of Private Law.

2. The Depositary Government shall give notice to the signatory and acceding States, and to the International Institute for the Unification of Private Law, of:

(a) any signature;

(b) the deposit of any instrument of ratification or accession;

(c) any date on which this Convention enters into force in accordance with Article XI;

(d) any communication received in accordance with Article I, paragraph 4;

(e) any notice received in accordance with Article II, paragraph 2;

(f) any declaration received in accordance with Article XIII, paragraph 2, and the date on which such declaration takes effect;

(g) any denunciation received in accordance with Article XII, paragraph 1, or Article XIII, paragraph 3, and the date on which the denunciation takes effect;

(h) any declaration received in accordance with Article XIV, paragraph 2, and the date on which the declaration takes effect.

IN WITNESS WHEREOF, the undersigned Plenipotentiaries, being duly authorized to that effect, have signed the present Convention.

DONE at Washington this twenty-sixth day of October, one thousand nine hundred and seventy-three.

Annex

UNIFORM LAW ON THE FORM OF AN INTERNATIONAL WILL

Article 1

1. A will shall be valid as regards form, irrespective particularly of the place where it is made, of the location of the assets and of the nationality, domicile or residence of the testator, if it is made in the form of an international will complying with the provisions set out in Articles 2 to 5 hereinafter.

2. The invalidity of the will as an international will shall not affect its formal validity as a will of another kind.

Article 2

This law shall not apply to the form of testamentary dispositions made by two or more persons in one instrument.

Article 3

1. The will shall be made in writing.

2. It need not be written by the testator himself.

3. It may be written in any language, by hand or by any other means.

Article 4

1. The testator shall declare in the presence of two witnesses and of a person authorized to act in connection with international wills that the document is his will and that he knows the contents thereof.

2. The testator need not inform the witnesses, or the authorized person, of the contents of the will.

Article 5

1. In the presence of the witnesses and of the authorized person, the testator shall sign the will or, if he has previously signed it, shall acknowledge his signature.

2. When the testator is unable to sign, he shall indicate the reason therefor to the authorized person who shall make note of this on the will. Moreover, the testator may be authorized by the law under which the authorized person was designated to direct another person to sign on his behalf.

3. The witnesses and the authorized person shall there and then attest the will by signing in the presence of the testator.

Article 6

1. The signatures shall be placed at the end of the will.

SLRA

2. If the will consists of several sheets, each sheet shall be signed by the testator or, if he is unable to sign, by the person signing on his behalf or, if there is no such person, by the authorized person. In addition, each sheet shall be numbered.

Article 7

1. This date of the will shall be the date of its signature by the authorized person.

2. This date shall be noted at the end of the will by the authorized person.

Article 8

In the absence of any mandatory rule pertaining to the safekeeping of the will, the authorized person shall ask the testator whether he wishes to make a declaration concerning the safekeeping of his will. If so and at the express request of the testator the place where he intends to have his will kept shall be mentioned in the certificate provided for in Article 9.

Article 9

The authorized person shall attach to the will a certificate in the form prescribed in Article 10 establishing that the obligations of this law have been complied with.

Article 10

The certificate drawn up by the authorized person shall be in the following form or in a substantially similar form:

Certificate (Convention of October 26, 1973)

1. I, ..., (name, address and capacity), a person authorized to act in connection with international wills

2. Certify   that   on   .... (date)   at .... (place)

3. (testator) .... (name, address, date and place of birth) in my presence and that of the witnesses

4.(a) .... (name, address, date and place of birth),

4.(b) .... (name, address, date and place of birth) has declared that the attached document is his will and that he knows the contents thereof.

5. I furthermore certify that:

6.(a) in my presence and in that of the witnesses

(1) the testator has signed the will or has acknowledged his signature previously affixed.

*(2) following a declaration of the testator stating that he was unable to sign his will for the following reason ....

*   — I have mentioned this declaration on the will

*   — the signature has been affixed by .... (name, address)

7.(b) the witnesses and I have signed the will;

8.*(c) each page of the will has been signed by .... and numbered;

9.(d) I have satisfied myself as to the identity of the testator and of the witnesses as designated above;

10.(e) the witnesses met the conditions requisite to act as such according to the law under which I am acting;

11.*(f) the testator has requested me to include the following statement concerning the safekeeping of his will:

12.   PLACE

13.   DATE

14.   SIGNATURE and, if necessary, SEAL

*To be completed if appropriate.

Article 11

The authorized person shall keep a copy of the certificate and deliver another to the testator.

Article 12

In the absence of evidence to the contrary, the certificate of the authorized person shall be conclusive of the formal validity of the instrument as a will under this Law.

Article 13

The absence or irregularity of a certificate shall not affect the formal validity of a will under this Law.

Article 14

The international will shall be subject to the ordinary rules of revocation of wills.

Article 15

In interpreting and applying the provisions of this law, regard shall be had to its international origin and to the need for uniformity in its interpretation.

43. Application of Part — This Part applies to wills made before, on or after the 31st day of March, 1978 where the testator has not died before that date.

PART II — INTESTATE SUCCESSION

44. Intestacy where spouse and no issue — Where a person dies intestate in respect of property and is survived by a spouse and not survived by issue, the spouse is entitled to the property absolutely.

45. (1) Preferential share of spouse — Subject to subsection (3), where a person dies intestate in respect of property having a net value of not more than the preferential share and is survived by a spouse and issue, the spouse is entitled to the property absolutely.

(2) Same — Subject to subsection (3), where a person dies intestate in respect of property having a net value of more than the preferential share and is survived by a spouse and issue, the spouse is entitled to the preferential share absolutely.

(3) Same — Despite subsection (1), where a person dies testate as to some property and intestate as to other property and is survived by a spouse and issue, and,

(a) where the spouse is entitled under the will to nothing or to property having a net value of less than the preferential share, the spouse is entitled out of the intestate property to the amount by which the preferential share exceeds the net value of the property, if any, to which the spouse is entitled under the will;

757

(b) where the spouse is entitled under the will to property having a net value of more than the preferential share, subsections (1) and (2) do not apply.

(4) Definition — In this section,

"net value" means the value of the property after payment of the charges thereon and the debts, funeral expenses and expenses of administration, including succession duty.

(5) Preferential share — The preferential share is the amount prescribed by a regulation made under subsection (6).

(6) Regulation — The Lieutenant Governor in Council may, by regulation, prescribe the amount of the preferential share.

1994, c. 27, s. 63

[Editor's Note: Section 45 of the Succession Law Reform Act, *which deals with the preferential share of a spouse in intestate estates, was amended by 1994, c. 27, s. 63(1) and (2). This amendment is applicable to the estate of persons who died on or after April 1, 1995, the date on which the amendments came into force.*

The estates of persons, who died before April 1995, are governed by s. 45 as it read immediately before the amendments came into force.]

46. (1) Residue: spouse and one child — Where a person dies intestate in respect of property and leaves a spouse and one child, the spouse is entitled to one-half of the residue of the property after payment under section 45, if any.

(2) Idem: spouse and two or more children — Where a person dies intestate in respect of property and leaves a spouse and more than one child, the spouse is entitled to one-third of the residue of the property after payment under section 45, if any.

(3) Idem: issue of predeceased children — Where a child has died leaving issue living at the date of the intestate's death, the spouse's share shall be the same as if the child had been living at that date.

47. (1) Issue — Subject to subsection (2), where a person dies intestate in respect of property and leaves issue surviving him or her, the property shall be distributed, subject to the rights of the spouse, if any, equally among his or her issue who are of the nearest degree in which there are issue surviving him or her.

(2) Share of predeceasing issue — Where any issue of the degree entitled under subsection (1) has predeceased the intestate, the share of such issue shall be distributed among his or her issue in the manner set out in subsection (1) and the share devolving upon any issue of that and subsequent degrees who predecease the intestate shall be similarly distributed.

(3) Parents — Where a person dies intestate in respect of property and leaves no spouse or issue, the property shall be distributed between the parents of the deceased equally or, where there is only one parent surviving the deceased, to that parent absolutely.

(4) Brothers and sisters — Where a person dies intestate in respect of property and there is no surviving spouse, issue or parent, the property shall be distributed among the surviving brothers and sisters of the intestate equally, and if any brother or sister predeceases the intestate, the share of the deceased brother or sister shall be distributed among his or her children equally.

(5) Nephews and nieces — Where a person dies intestate in respect of property and there is no surviving spouse, issue, parent, brother or sister, the property shall be distributed among the nephews and nieces of the intestate equally without representation.

(6) Next of kin — Where a person dies intestate in respect of property and there is no surviving spouse, issue, parent, brother, sister, nephew or niece, the property shall be distributed among the next of kin of equal degree of consanguinity to the intestate equally without representation.

(7) Escheat — Where a person dies intestate in respect of property and there is no surviving spouse, issue, parent, brother, sister, nephew, niece or next of kin, the property becomes the property of the Crown, and the *Escheats Act* applies.

(8) Degrees of kindred — For the purposes of subsection (6), degrees of kindred shall be computed by counting upward from the deceased to the nearest common ancestor and then downward to the relative, and the kindred of the half-blood shall inherit equally with those of the whole-blood in the same degree.

(9) Descendants conceived but unborn — For the purposes of this section, descendants and relatives of the deceased conceived before and born alive after the death of the deceased shall inherit as if they had been born in the lifetime of the deceased and had survived him or her.

48. Abolition of curtesy — The common law right of a widower to curtesy is abolished.

49. Application — This Part applies to an intestacy upon a death occurring on or after the 31st day of March, 1978.

PART III — DESIGNATION OF BENEFICIARIES OF INTEREST IN FUNDS OR PLANS

50. Definitions — In this Part,

"participant" means a person who is entitled to designate another person to receive a benefit payable under a plan on the participant's death; (« participant »)

"plan" means,

(a) a pension, retirement, welfare or profit-sharing fund, trust, scheme, contract or arrangement or a fund, trust, scheme, contract or arrangement for other benefits for employees, former employees, directors, former directors, agents or former agents of an employer or their dependants or beneficiaries,

(b) a fund, trust, scheme, contract, or arrangement for the payment of a periodic sum for life or for a fixed or variable term, or

(c) a fund, trust, scheme, contract or arrangement of a class that is prescribed for the purposes of this Part by a regulation made under section 53.1,

and includes a retirement savings plan, a retirement income fund and a home ownership savings plan as defined in the *Income Tax Act* (Canada) and an Ontario home ownership savings plan under the *Ontario Home Ownership Savings Plan Act*. (« régime »)

1994, c. 27, s. 63(4)

51. (1) Designation of beneficiaries — A participant may designate a person to receive a benefit payable under a plan on the participant's death,

    (a) by an instrument signed by him or her or signed on his or her behalf by another person in his or her presence and by his or her direction; or

    (b) by will,

and may revoke the designation by either of those methods.

(2) Idem — A designation in a will is effective only if it relates expressly to a plan, either generally or specifically.

52. (1) Revocation of designation — A revocation in a will is effective to revoke a designation made by instrument only if the revocation relates expressly to the designation, either generally or specifically.

(2) Idem — Despite section 15, a later designation revokes an earlier designation, to the extent of any inconsistency.

(3) Idem — Revocation of a will revokes a designation in the will.

(4) Where will invalid — A designation or revocation contained in an instrument purporting to be a will is not invalid by reason only of the fact that the instrument is invalid as a will.

(5) Idem — A designation in an instrument that purports to be but is not a valid will is revoked by an event that would have the effect of revoking the instrument if it had been a valid will.

(6) Earlier designations not revived — Revocation of a designation does not revive an earlier designation.

(7) Effective date — Despite section 22, a designation or revocation in a will is effective from the time when the will is signed.

53. Payment and enforcement — Where a participant in a plan has designated a person to receive a benefit under the plan on the death of the participant,

    (a) the person administering the plan is discharged on paying the benefit to the person designated under the latest designation made in accordance with the terms of the plan, in the absence of actual notice of a subsequent designation or revocation made under section 51 but not in accordance with the terms of the plan; and

    (b) the person designated may enforce payment of the benefit payable to him under the plan but the person administering the plan may set up any defence that he could have set up against the participant or his or her personal representative.

53.1 Regulations — The Lieutenant Governor in Council may make regulations prescribing classes of funds, trusts, schemes, contracts or arrangements for the purposes of this Part.

1994, c. 27, s. 63(5)

54. (1) Application of Part to plan — Where this Part is inconsistent with a plan, this Part applies, unless the inconsistency relates to a designation made or proposed to be made after the making of a benefit payment where the benefit payment would have been different if the designation had been made before the benefit payment, in which case the plan applies.

(2) Exception — This Part does not apply to a contract or to a designation of a beneficiary to which the *Insurance Act* applies.

54.1 (1) Application to retirement income funds — This Part applies to the designation of a beneficiary of a retirement income fund, whether the designation was made before or after the effective date, and even if the participant who made the designation died before the effective date.

(2) Exception — Despite subsection (1), this Part as it read immediately before the effective date continues to apply in a particular case if applying the Part as it read after the effective date would,

(a) change the result in a proceeding in which a judgment or final order was made before the effective date, even if the judgment or order is subject to appeal; or

(b) make a person liable to repay or account for retirement income fund proceeds received or paid by the person before the effective date.

(3) Definition — In this section, **"effective date"** means the date on which the *Statute Law Amendment Act (Government Management and Services), 1994* received Royal Assent.

1994, c. 27, s. 63(5)

Part IV — Survivorship

55. (1) Survivorship as to succession — Where two or more persons die at the same time or in circumstances rendering it uncertain which of them survived the other or others, the property of each person, or any property of which he or she is competent to dispose, shall be disposed of as if he or she had survived the other or others.

(2) Simultaneous death of joint tenants — Unless a contrary intention appears, where two or more persons hold legal or equitable title to property as joint tenants, or with respect to a joint account, with each other, and all of them die at the same time or in circumstances rendering it uncertain which of them survived the other or others, each person shall be deemed, for the purposes of subsection (1), to have held as tenant in common with the other or with each of the others in that property.

(3) Provision in will for substitute representative — Where a will contains a provision for a substitute personal representative operative if an executor designated in the will,

(a) dies before the testator;

(b) dies at the same time as the testator; or

(c) dies in circumstances rendering it uncertain which of them survived the other,

and the designated executor dies at the same time as the testator or in circumstances rendering it uncertain which of them survived the other, then, for the purpose of probate, the case for which the will provides shall be deemed to have occurred.

(4) Proceeds of insurance — The proceeds of a policy of insurance shall be paid in accordance with sections 215 and 319 of the *Insurance Act* and thereafter this Part applies to their disposition.

56. Application of Part — This Part applies in respect of deaths occurring on or after the 31st of March, 1978.

PART V — SUPPORT OF DEPENDANTS

57. Definitions — In this Part,

"child" means a child as defined in subsection 1(1) and includes a grandchild and a person whom the deceased has demonstrated a settled intention to treat as a child of his or her family, except under an arrangement where the child is placed for valuable consideration in a foster home by a person having lawful custody;

"cohabit" means to live together in a conjugal relationship, whether within or outside marriage;

"court" means the Ontario Court (General Division);

"dependant" means,

    (a) the spouse or same-sex partner of the deceased,

    (b) a parent of the deceased,

    (c) a child of the deceased, or

    (d) a brother or sister of the deceased,

to whom the deceased was providing support or was under a legal obligation to provide support immediately before his or her death;

"letters probate" and **"letters of administration"** include letters probate, letters of administration or other legal documents purporting to be of the same legal nature granted by a court in another jurisdiction and resealed in this province;

"parent" includes a grandparent and a person who has demonstrated a settled intention to treat the deceased as a child of his or her family, except under an arrangement where the deceased was placed for valuable consideration in a foster home by a person having lawful custody;

"same-sex partner" means either of two persons of the same sex who have cohabited,

    (a) continuously for a period of not less than three years, or

    (b) in a relationship of some permanence, if they are the natural or adoptive parents of a child.

"spouse" means a spouse as defined in subsection 1(1) and in addition includes either of a man or woman who,

    (a) were married to each other by a marriage that was terminated or declared a nullity, or

    (b) are not married to each other and have cohabited,

        (i) continuously for a period of not less than three years, or

        (ii) in a relationship of some permanence, if they are the natural or adoptive parents of a child.

1999, c. 6, s. 61(1), (2)

58. (1) Order for support — Where a deceased, whether testate or intestate, has not made adequate provision for the proper support of his dependants or any of them, the court, on application, may order that such provision as it considers adequate be made out of the estate of the deceased for the proper support of the dependants or any of them.

(2) Applicants — An application for an order for the support of a dependant may be made by the dependant or the dependant's parent.

(3) Same — An application for an order for the support of a dependant may also be made by one of the following agencies,

(a) the Ministry of Community and Social Services in the name of the Minister;

(b) a municipality, excluding a lower-tier municipality in a regional municipality;

(c) a district social services administration board under the *District Social Services Administration Boards Act*;

(d) a band approved under section 15 of the *General Welfare Assistance Act*; or,

(e) a delivery agent under the *Ontario Works Act, 1997*,

if the agency is providing or has provided a benefit under the *Family Benefits Act*, assistance under the *Ontario Works Act, 1997* or income support under the *Ontario Disability Support Program Act, 1997* in respect of the dependant's support, or if an application for such a benefit, assistance or income support has been made to the agency by or on behalf of the dependant.

(4) Idem — The adequacy of provision for support under subsection (1) shall be determined as of the date of the hearing of the application.

1997, c. 25, Sched. E, s. 12; 2002, c. 17, Sched. F, s. 1

59. Suspensory order — On an application by or on behalf of the dependants or any of them, the court may make an order suspending in whole or in part the administration of the deceased's estate, for such time and to such extent as the court may decide.

60. (1) Application — An application under this Part may be made to the court by notice of application in accordance with the practice of the court.

(2) Idem — Where an application for an order under section 58 is made by or on behalf of any dependant,

(a) it may be dealt with by the court as; and

(b) in so far as the question of limitation is concerned, it shall be deemed to be,

an application on behalf of all persons who might apply.

61. (1) Limitation period — Subject to subsection (2), no application for an order under section 58 may be made after six months from the grant of letters probate of the will or of letters of administration.

(2) Exception — The court, if it considers it proper, may allow an application to be made at any time as to any portion of the estate remaining undistributed at the date of the application.

62. (1) Determination of amount — In determining the amount and duration, if any, of support, the court shall consider all the circumstances of the application, including,

(a) the dependant's current assets and means;

(b) the assets and means that the dependant is likely to have in the future;

(c) the dependant's capacity to contribute to his or her own support;

(d) the dependant's age and physical and mental health;

(e) the dependant's needs, in determining which the court shall have regard to the dependant's accustomed standard of living;

(f) the measures available for the dependant to become able to provide for his or her own support and the length of time and cost involved to enable the dependant to take those measures;

(g) the proximity and duration of the dependant's relationship with the deceased;

(h) the contributions made by the dependant to the deceased's welfare, including indirect and non-financial contributions;

(i) the contributions made by the dependant to the acquisition, maintenance and improvement of the deceased's property or business;

(j) a contribution by the dependant to the realization of the deceased's career potential;

(k) whether the dependant has a legal obligation to provide support for another person;

(l) the circumstances of the deceased at the time of death;

(m) any agreement between the deceased and the dependant;

(n) any previous distribution or division of property made by the deceased in favour of the dependant by gift or agreement or under court order;

(o) the claims that any other person may have as a dependant;

(p) if the dependant is a child,

    (i) the child's aptitude for and reasonable prospects of obtaining an education, and

    (ii) the child's need for a stable environment;

(q) if the dependant is a child of the age of sixteen years or more, whether the child has withdrawn from parental control;

(r) if the dependant is a spouse or same-sex partner,

    (i) a course of conduct by the spouse or same-sex partner during the deceased's lifetime that is so unconscionable as to constitute an obvious and gross repudiation of the relationship,

    (ii) the length of time the spouses or same-sex partners cohabited,

    (iii) the effect on the spouse's or same-sex partner's earning capacity of the responsibilities assumed during cohabitation,

    (iv) whether the spouse or same-sex partner has undertaken the care of a child who is of the age of eighteen years or over and unable by reason of illness, disability or other cause to withdraw from the charge of his or her parents,

    (v) whether the spouse or same-sex partner has undertaken to assist in the continuation of a program of education for a child eighteen years of age or over who is unable for that reason to withdraw from the charge of his or her parents,

    (vi) in the case of a spouse, any housekeeping, child care or other domestic service performed by the spouse for the family, as if the spouse had devoted the time spent in performing that service in remunerative employment and had contributed the earnings to the family's support,

    (vi.1) in the case of a same-sex partner, any housekeeping, child care or other domestic service performed by the same-sex partner for the deceased or the deceased's family, as if the same-sex partner had devoted the time spent in performing that service in remunerative employment and had contributed the earnings to the support of the deceased or the deceased's family.

(vii) the effect on the spouse's or same-sex partner's earnings and career development of the responsibility of caring for a child,

(viii) the desirability of the spouse or same-sex partner remaining at home to care for a child; and

(s) any other legal right of the dependant to support, other than out of public money.

(2) Evidence — In addition to the evidence presented by the parties, the court may direct other evidence to be given as the court considers necessary or proper.

(3) Idem — The court may accept such evidence as it considers proper of the deceased's reasons, so far as ascertainable, for making the dispositions in his or her will, or for not making adequate provision for a dependant, as the case may be, including any statement in writing signed by the deceased.

(4) Idem — In estimating the weight to be given to a statement referred to in subsection (3), the court shall have regard to all the circumstances from which an inference can reasonably be drawn as to the accuracy of the statement.

1999, c. 6, s. 61(3)-(5)

63. (1) Conditions and restrictions — In any order making provision for support of a dependant, the court may impose such conditions and restrictions as the court considers appropriate.

(2) Contents of order — Provision may be made out of income or capital or both and an order may provide for one or more of the following, as the court considers appropriate,

(a) an amount payable annually or otherwise whether for an indefinite or limited period or until the happening of a specified event;

(b) a lump sum to be paid or held in trust;

(c) any specified property to be transferred or assigned to or in trust for the benefit of the dependant, whether absolutely, for life or for a term of years;

(d) the possession or use of any specified property by the dependent for life or such period as the court considers appropriate;

(e) a lump sum payment to supplement or replace periodic payments;

(f) the securing of payment under an order by a charge on property or otherwise;

(g) the payment of a lump sum or of increased periodic payments to enable a dependant spouse, same-sex partner or child to meet debts reasonably incurred for his or her own support prior to an application under this Part;

(h) that all or any of the money payable under the order be paid to an appropriate person or agency for the benefit of the dependant;

(i) the payment to an agency referred to in subsection 58(3) of any amount in reimbursement for an allowance or benefit granted in respect of the support of the dependant, including an amount in reimbursement for an allowance paid or benefit provided before the date of the order.

(3) Idem — Where a transfer or assignment of property is ordered, the court may,

(a) give all necessary directions for the execution of the transfer or assignment by the executor or administrator or such other person as the court may direct; or

(b) grant a vesting order.

(4) Agreement or waiver — An order under this section may be made despite any agreement or waiver to the contrary.

(5) Notice to parties before order — The court shall not make any order under this section until it is satisfied upon oath that all persons who are or may be interested in or affected by the order have been served with notice of the application as provided by the rules of court, and every such person is entitled to be present and to be heard in person or by counsel at the hearing.

(6) Exception — Despite subsection (5), where, in the opinion of the court,

(a) every reasonable effort has been made to serve those entitled to notice; or

(b) after every reasonable effort has been made, it is not possible to identify one or more of the persons entitled to notice,

the court may dispense with the requirement of notice in respect of any person who has not been served.

1999, c. 6, s. 61(6)

64. Interim order — Where an application is made under this Part and the applicant is in need of and entitled to support but any or all of the matters referred to in section 62 or 63 have not been ascertained by the court, the court may make such interim order under section 63 as it considers appropriate.

65. Inquiries and further orders — Where an order has been made under this Part, the court at any subsequent date may,

(a) inquire whether the dependant benefitted by the order has become entitled to the benefit of any other provision for his or her support;

(b) inquire into the adequacy of the provision ordered; and

(c) discharge, vary or suspend the order, or make such other order as the court considers appropriate in the circumstances.

66. Further powers of court — The court may at any time,

(a) fix a periodic payment or lump sum to be paid by a legatee, devisee or beneficiary under an intestacy to represent, or in commutation of, such proportion of the sum ordered to be paid as falls upon the portion of the estate in which he or she is interested;

(b) relieve such portion of the estate from further liability; and

(c) direct,

(i) the manner in which such periodic payment is to be secured, or

(ii) to whom such lump sum is to be paid and the manner in which it is to be dealt with for the benefit of the person to whom the commuted payment is payable.

67. (1) Distribution stayed — Where an application is made and notice thereof is served on the personal representative of the deceased, he or she shall not, after service of the notice upon him or her, unless all persons entitled to apply consent or the court otherwise orders, proceed with the distribution of the estate until the court has disposed of the application.

(2) Exception — Nothing in this Part prevents a personal representative from making reasonable advances for support to dependants who are beneficiaries.

(3) Liability of personal representative — Where a personal representative distributes any portion of the estate in violation of subsection (1), if any provision for support is ordered by the court to be made out of the estate, the personal representative is personally liable to pay the amount of the distribution to the extent that such provision or any part thereof ought, pursuant to the order or this Part, to be made out of the portion of the estate distributed.

68. (1) Incidence of provision ordered — Subject to subsection (2), the incidence of any provision for support ordered shall fall rateably upon that part of the deceased's estate to which the jurisdiction of the court extends.

(2) Idem — The court may order that the provision for support be made out of and charged against the whole or any portion of the estate in such proportion and in such manner as to the court seems proper.

69. Further directions — The court may give such further directions as it considers necessary for the purpose of giving effect to an order.

70. (1) Certified copy of order filed with the local registrar of the court — A certified copy of every order made under this Part shall be filed with the local registrar of the court out of which the letters probate or letters of administration issued.

(2) Idem — A memorandum of the order shall be endorsed on or annexed to the copy, in the custody of the local registrar, of the letters probate or letters of administration, as the case may be.

71. Property devised — Where a deceased,

    (a) has, in his or her lifetime, in good faith and for valuable consideration, entered into a contract to devise or bequeath any property; and

    (b) has by his or her will devised or bequeathed that property in accordance with the provisions of the contract,

the property is not liable to the provisions of an order made under this Part except to the extent that the value of the property in the opinion of the court exceeds the consideration therefor.

72. (1) Value of certain transactions deemed part of estate — Subject to section 71, for the purpose of this Part, the capital value of the following transactions effected by a deceased before his or her death, whether benefitting his or her dependant or any other person, shall be included as testamentary dispositions as of the date of the death of the deceased and shall be deemed to be part of his or her net estate for purposes of ascertaining the value of his or her estate, and being available to be charged for payment by an order under clause 63(2)(f),

    (a) gifts *mortis causa*;

    (b) money deposited, together with interest thereon, in an account in the name of the deceased in trust for another or others with any bank, savings office, credit union or trust corporation, and remaining on deposit at the date of the death of the deceased;

(c) money deposited, together with interest thereon, in an account in the name of the deceased and another person or persons and payable on death under the terms of the deposit or by operation of law to the survivor or survivors of those persons with any bank, savings office, credit union or trust corporation, and remaining on deposit at the date of the death of the deceased;

(d) any disposition of property made by a deceased whereby property is held at the date of his or her death by the deceased and another as joint tenants;

(e) any disposition of property made by the deceased in trust or otherwise, to the extent that the deceased at the date of his or her death retained, either alone or in conjunction with another person or persons by the express provisions of the disposing instrument, a power to revoke such disposition, or a power to consume, invoke or dispose of the principal thereof, but the provisions of this clause do not affect the right of any income beneficiary to the income accrued and undistributed at the date of the death of the deceased;

(f) any amount payable under a policy of insurance effected on the life of the deceased and owned by him or her;

(f.1) any amount payable on the death of the deceased under a policy of group insurance; and

(g) any amount payable under a designation of beneficiary under Part III.

(2) Idem — The capital value of the transactions referred to in clauses (1)(b), (c) and (d) shall be deemed to be included in the net estate of the deceased to the extent that the funds on deposit were the property of the deceased immediately before the deposit or the consideration for the property held as joint tenants was furnished by the deceased.

(3) Burden of proof — Dependants claiming under this Part shall have the burden of establishing that the funds or property, or any portion thereof, belonged to the deceased.

(4) Idem — Where the other party to a transaction described in clause (1)(c) or (d) is a dependant, he or she shall have the burden of establishing the amount of his or her contribution, if any.

(5) Exception — This section does not prohibit any corporation or person from paying or transferring any funds or property, or any portion thereof, to any person otherwise entitled thereto unless there has been personally served on the corporation or person a certified copy of a suspensory order made under section 59 enjoining such payment or transfer.

(6) Suspensory order — Personal service upon the corporation or person holding any such fund or property of a certified copy of a suspensory order shall be a defence to any action or proceeding brought against the corporation or person with respect to the fund or property during the period the order is in force.

(7) Rights of creditor — This section does not affect the rights of creditors of the deceased in any transaction with respect to which a creditor has rights.

1999, c. 12, Sched. B, s. 17

73. Validity of mortgage, etc. — Where provision for the support of a dependant is ordered under this Part, a mortgage, charge or assignment of or with respect to such provision, made before the order of the court making such provision is entered, is invalid.

74. (1) Person in institutions — Where a person by whom, or on whose behalf, an application may be made under this Part is a patient in a psychiatric facility under the *Mental Health Act* or a resident in a facility under the *Developmental Services Act* at the time of the deceased's death or at any time before the application under this Part is heard and disposed of, notice of the application for letters probate or letters of administration shall be served upon the Public Trustee on behalf of that person, and the time within which the Public Trustee may make an application under this Part runs from the date of the service of the notice.

(2) Notice to Public Trustee — Where a person interested in the estate in respect of which an application is made under this Part is a patient in a psychiatric facility under the *Mental Health Act* or a resident in a facility under the *Developmental Services Act*, notice of the application shall in every case be served upon the Public Trustee, who has the right to appear and be heard upon the application.

75. Costs — The court may direct that the costs of the application be paid out of the estate or otherwise as it thinks proper, and may fix the amount of the costs payable by any party, exclusive of necessary disbursements, at a lump sum having regard to the value of the estate and the amount of any support applied for or directed by its order.

76. Appeal — An appeal lies to the Divisional Court from any order of the court made under this Part.

77. (1) Enforcement — An order or direction made under this Part may be enforced against the estate of the deceased in the same way and by the same means as any other judgment or order of the court against the estate may be enforced.

(2) Realization of security — Where a court orders security for the payment under an order under this Part or charges a property therewith, the court may, upon application and notice to all persons having an interest in the property, direct its sale for the purpose of realizing the security or charge.

78. Crown bound — This Part binds the Crown.

79. Application of Part — This Part does not apply where the deceased died before the 31st day of March, 1978, but an application may be made under section 65 regardless of the time of the deceased's death.

SLRA

PREFERENTIAL SHARE

made under the *Succession Law Reform Act*
O. Reg. 54/95

1. For the purpose of section 45 of the Act, $200,000 is prescribed as the amount of the preferential share.

2. This Regulation comes into force on April 1, 1995.

INDEX

References are to section/rule numbers of the Acts, Regulations and Rules included in this work. Bankruptcy and Insolvency Act, BIA; Canada Evidence Act, CEA; Change of Name Act, CNA; Child and Family Services Act, CFSA; Child Support Guidelines (Ontario), CSG; Children's Law Reform Act, CLRA; Children's Law Reform Act Forms Regulation, CLRAF; Cost of Living Adjustments Methods of Calculation Regulation, CLA; Creditors' Relief Act, CRA; Criminal Code, CC; Divorce Act, DA; Domestic Violence Protection Act, 2000, DVPA; Election of Surviving Spouse Regulation, ESSR; Evidence Act, EA; Family Case Management Rules for the Superior Court of Justice in Toronto, FCMRSCJT; Family Law Act, FLA; Family Law Rules, FLR; Family Orders and Agreements Enforcement Assistance Act, FOAEAA; Family Responsibility and Support Arrears Enforcement Act, FRSAEA; Federal Child Support Guidelines, FCSG; Fees Charged by Director Regulation, FDR; Garnishment, Attachment and Pension Diversion Act, GAPDA; Intercountry Adoption Act, 1998, IAA; Income Tax Act, ITA; Interjurisdictional Support Orders Act, ISO; Marriage (Prohibited Degrees) Act, MPDA; Marriage Act, MA; Marriage Act General Regulation, MAR; Parental Responsibility Act 2000, PRA; Partition Act, PA; Pension Benefits Act, PBA; Reciprocal Enforcement of Support Orders Act, RESOA; Release of Information for Family Orders and Agreements Enforcement Regulations, IFOAR; Rules of Civil Procedure, RCP; Succession Law Reform Act, SLRA.

Index

Index

Index

Index

Will *(cont'd)*
- change in circumstances, SLRA, s. 17
- defined, SLRA, s. 1
- election by surviving spouse
- • family law proceedings, FLA, s. 6
- no undue influence, SLRA, s. 12(3)
- revocation, SLRA, ss. 8(3), 15, 16
- signed for testator by another, SLRA, s. 12(2)

Witnesses, *see also* Evidence; Husbands and Wives
- bequests void, SLRA, s. 12(1)
- questioning a witness and disclosure, FLR, r. 20
- • confidentiality, FLR, r. 20(24)–(26)
- • child protection case, FLR, r. 20(3)
- • cross-examination, FLR, r. 20(2)
- • other cases, FLR, r. 20(4)
- • refusal to answer questions, FLR, r. 20(19)
- • scope of cases, FLR, r. 20(18)

Y

Young Offenders
- apprehension where absent from custody, CFSA, s. 98
- custody review board, CFSA, s. 97
- locking up, CFSA, ss. 89(5), 100
- maximum security, CFSA, ss. 88, 89(3)(a), 94(2)

- medium security, CFSA, ss. 88, 89(3)(b), 94(1)
- open custody, CFSA, ss. 89(4), 95
- open temporary detention, CFSA, ss. 88, 89(2)(b), 93(1)
- regulations, CFSA, s. 217
- secure temporary detention, CFSA, ss. 88, 89(2)(a), 93(2)
- services and programmes
- • defined, CFSA, s. 88
- • person over 16, to, CFSA, s. 91
- • provision of, CFSA, s. 89
- • reports and information, CFSA, s. 92
- transfer from maximum to medium security, CFSA, s. 94(3), (4)

Young Offenders Act
- ministerial appointments under, CFSA, s. 90

Young Person
- defined, CFSA, ss. 88, 91(2)